LOKMANYA BAL GANGADHAR TILAK'S

Śrīmad Bhagavadgītā Rahasya

OR

Karma-Yoga-Śāstra

BIRTH 23 JULY 1856. DEATH 1 AUG. 1920.

Bal Gangadhar Tilak

LOKMANYA BAL GANGADHAR TILAK'S

Śrīmad Bhagavadgītā Rahasya

OR

Karma-Yoga-Śāstra

CONTAINING THE ORIGINAL SANSKRIT STANZAS, THEIR ENGLISH TRANSLATION AND COMMENTARIES ON THE STANZAS

Translated into English by

BHALCHANDRA SITARAM SUKTHANKAR

MANOHAR
2024

First published 1936
Reprinted 2024

ISBN 978-81-19953-64-6 (hardbound)
ISBN 978-81-19953-11-0 (ebook)

Published by
Ajay Kumar Jain *for*
Manohar Publishers & Distributors
4753/23 Ansari Road, Daryaganj
New Delhi 110 002

Printed and bound in India

The Hindu Philosophy of Life, Ethics and Religion.

OM-TAT-SAT

S'RĪMAD BHAGAVADGĪTĀ RAHASYA

OR

KARMA-YOGA-S'ĀSTRA

Including an external examination of the Gītā, the Original Sanskrit stanzas, their English translation, and commentaries on the stanzas.

BY

BAL GANGADHAR TILAK, B.A., LL.B.,

LAW LECTURER, AND PLEADER, POONA; SOMETIME ADDITIONAL MEMBER OF THE COUNCIL OF H. E. THE GOVERNOR OF BOMBAY FOR MAKING LAWS, AUTHOR OF *Orion or Researches into the Antiquity of the Vedas*, *Arctic Home in the Vedas*, *Vedanga Jyotish* AND *Vedic Chronology*, FOUNDER OF THE '*Kesari*' AND THE *Maratha* NEWSPAPERS ETC. ETC.

TRANSLATED BY

BHALCHANDRA SITARAM SUKTHANKAR, M.A., LL.B.,

Solicitor, High Court, Bombay.

Gibbs Prizeman; Petit Prizeman (Cercle Littéraire); Dakshina Fellow; etc.

tasmād asaktaḥ satataṁ kāryaṁ karma samācara ।
asakto hy ācaran karma paramāpnoti pūruṣaḥ ॥ (Gītā, 3. 19).

ŚAKA YEAR 1857; 1936 A. D.

POONA.

PROMINENT PERSONALITIES ON THE GĪTĀ, MR. TILAK, AND THE 'GĪTĀ-RAHASYA'.

1. SWAMI VIVEKANAND.

The Gita is a bouquet composed of the beautiful flowers of spiritual truths collected from the Upanishads.

2. Dr. ANNIE BESANT.

Among the priceless teachings that may be found in the great Hindu poem of the *Mahabharata*, there is none so rare and precious as this, "The Lord's Song". Since it fell from the divine lips of Shri Krishna on the field of battle, and stilled the surging emotions of his disciple and friend, how many troubled hearts has it quieted and strengthened, how many weary souls has it led to Him! It is meant to lift the aspirant from the lower levels of renunciation, where objects are renounced, to the loftier heights, where desires are dead, and where the Yogi dwells in calm and ceaseless contemplation while his body and mind are actively employed in discharging the duties that fall to his lot in life. That the spiritual man need not be a recluse, that union with the divine Life may be achieved and maintained in the midst of worldly affairs, that the obstacles to that union lie, not outside us, but within us, such is the central lesson of the BHAGAVAD-GITA.

It is a scripture of Yoga: now Yoga is literally Union; and it means harmony with the Divine Law, the becoming one with the Divine Life, by the subdual of all outward-going energies. To reach this, balance must be gained, as also equilibrium, so that self, joined to the Self, shall not be affected by pleasure or pain, desire or aversion, or any of the "pairs of opposites", between which untrained selves swing backwards and forwards. Moderation is, therefore, the key-note of the Gita and the harmonising of all the constituents of man, till they vibrate in perfect attunement with the One, the Supreme Self. This is the aim the disciple is to set before him. He must learn not to be attracted by the attractive, nor repelled by the repellent, but must see both as manifestations of the one

Lord, so that they may be lessons for his guidance, not fetters for his bondage. In the midst of turmoil, he must rest in the Lord of Peace, discharging every duty to the fullest, not because he seeks the results of his actions, but because it is his duty to perform them. His heart is an altar; love to his Lord, the flame burning upon it; all his acts, physical and mental, are sacrifices offered on the altar, and once offered, he has with them no further concern.

As though to make the lesson more impressive, it was given on a field of battle. Arjuna, the warrior-prince, was to vindicate his brother's title, to destroy a usurper who was oppressing the land; it was his duty as prince, as warrior, to fight for the deliverance of his nation and to restore order and peace. To make the contest more bitter, loved comrades and friends stood on both sides, wringing his heart with personal anguish, and making the conflict of duties as well as physical strife. Could he slay those to whom he owed love and duty, and trample on ties of kindred? To break family ties was a sin; to leave the people in cruel bondage was a sin; where was the right way? Justice must be done, else law would be disregarded; but how slay without sin? The answer is the *burden* of the book: Have no personal interest in the event; carry out the duty imposed by the position in life, realise that Ishvara, at once Lord and Law, is the doer, working out the mighty evolution that ends in bliss and peace; be identified with Him by devotion, and then perform duty as duty, fighting without passion or desire, without anger or hatred; thus Activity forges no bonds, Yoga is accomplished, and the Soul is free.

Such is the obvious teaching of this sacred book. But as all the acts of an Avatara are symbolical, we may pass from the outer to the inner planes, and see in the fight of Kurukshetra the battle-field of the Soul, and in the sons of Dhritarashtra, enemies it meets in its progress; Arjuna becomes the type of the struggling Soul of the disciple, and Shri Krishna is the Logos of the Soul. Thus, the teaching of the ancient battle-field gives guidance in all later days, and trains the aspiring soul in treading the steep and thorny path that leads to peace.

To all such souls in the East and West come these divine lessons; for the path is one, though it has many names, and all Souls seek the same goal, though they may not realise their unity.

(From Mrs. Besant's Pocket Gita published by G. A. Natesan & Co. Madras.)

3. Pt. MADAN MOHAN MALAVIYA.

I believe that in the whole history of mankind, the greatest outstanding personality having the deepest and the most profound knowledge and possessing super-human powers is Shri Krishna. I further believe that in all the living languages of the world, there is no book so full of truth-knowledge, and yet so handy as the *Bhagavadgita.*

This wonderful book of eighteen small chapters contains the essence of the Vedas and the Upanishads, and is a sure guide of the way to perfect happiness, here as well as hereafter. It preaches the three-fold way of Knowledge, Action, and Devotion, leading to the highest good of mankind. It brings to men the highest knowledge, the purest love and the most luminous action. It teaches self-control, the threefold austerity, non-violence, truth, compassion, obedience to the call of duty for the sake of duty, and putting up a fight against unrighteousness *(Adharma).*

Full of knowledge and truth and moral teaching, it has the power to raise men from the lowest depths of ignorance and suffering to the highest glories of divine beings. To my knowledge, there is no book in the whole range of the world's literature so high above all as the *Bhagavadgita,* which is a treasure-house of *Dharma,* not only for Hindus but for all mankind. Several scholars of different countries have by study of this book acquired a pure and perfect knowledge of the Supreme Being Who is responsible for the creation, preservation and destruction of the universe, and have gained a stainless, desireless, supreme devotion to His feet. Those men and women are very fortunate who have got this little lamp of light full of an inexhaustible quantity of the oil of love, showing the way out of the darkness and ignorance of the world. It is incumbent on such people to use it for all mankind groping in the darkness.

4. SIR VALENTINE CHIROL.

There is no more beautiful book in the sacred literature of the Hindus ; there is none in which the more enlightened find greater spiritual comfort.

It was a Hindu gentleman and a Brahmin who told me that if I wanted to study the psychology of the Indian unrest, I should begin by studying Tilak's career. "Tilak's onslaught in Poona upon Ranade, his alliance with the bigots of orthodoxy, his appeals to popular superstition in the new Ganapati celebrations, to racial fanaticism in the 'Anti-Cow-Killing movement', to Mahratta sentiment in the cult which he introduced of Śhivaji, his active propaganda amongst schoolboys and students, his gymnastic societies, his preaching in favour of physical training, and last but not least his control of the Press, and the note of personal violence which he imparted to newspaper polemics, represent the progressive stages of a highly-organised campaign which has served as a model to the apostles of unrest all over India". This was a valuable piece of advice, for, if any one can claim to be truly the father of Indian unrest, it is Bal Gangadhar Tilak.

(From *Indian Unrest* by Sir Valentine Chirol.)

5. HON'BLE G. K. GOKHALE.

Tilak's natural endowments are first-rate. He has used them for the service of the country and although I did not approve of his methods, I never questioned his motives. There is no man who has suffered so much for the country, who has had in his life to contend against powerful opposition so much as Tilak ; and there is no man who has shown grit, patience and courage so rare, that several times he lost his fortune and by his indomitable will gathered it together again.

(From Dnyan-Prakash dated 2-2-1915).

6. MAHATMA M. K. GANDHI.

"Early in my childhood I had felt the need of a scripture that would serve me as an unfailing guide through the trials and temptations of life. The Vedas could not supply that need, if only because to learn them would require fifteen to sixteen years of hard study at a place like Kashi, for which

I was not ready then. But the Gita, I had read somewhere, gave within the compass of its 700 verses the quintessence of all the Shastras and the Upanishads. That decided me. I learnt Sanskrit to enable me to read the Gita. To-day the Gita is not only my Bible or my Koran; it is more than that—it is my mother. I lost my earthly mother who gave me birth long ago; but this eternal mother has completely filled her place by my side ever since. She has never changed, she has never failed me. When I am in difficulty or distress, I seek refuge in her bosom.

It is sometimes alleged against the Gita that it is too difficult a work for the man in the street. The criticism, I venture to submit, is ill-founded. If you find all the eighteen chapters too difficult to negotiate, make a careful study of the first three chapters only. They will give you in a nutshell what is propounded in greater detail and from different angles in the remaining fifteen chapters.

Even these three chapters can be further epitomised in a few verses that can be selected from these chapters. Add to this the fact that at three distinct places, the Gita goes even further and exhorts us to leave alone all 'isms' and take refuge in the Lord alone, and it will be seen how baseless is the charge that the message of the Gita is too subtle or complicated for lay minds to understand.

The Gita is the universal mother. She turns away nobody. Her door is wide open to any one who knocks. A true votary of the Gita does not know what disappointment is. He ever dwells in perennial joy and peace that passeth understanding. But that peace and joy come not to the sceptic or to him who is proud of his intellect or learning. It is reserved only for the humble in spirit who brings to her worship a fullness of faith and an undivided singleness of mind. There never was a man who worshipped her in that spirit and went back disappointed.

The Gita inculcates the duty of perseverance in the face of seeming failure. It teaches us that we have a right to actions only but not to the fruit thereof, and that success and failure are one and the same thing at bottom. It calls upon us to dedicate ourselves, body, mind and soul, to pure duty, and not to become mental voluptuaries at the mercy of all chance desires and undisciplined impulses. As a "Satyagrahi", I can declare that the Gita is ever presenting me with fresh lessons. If somebody tells me that this is my delusion, my reply to him would be that I shall hug this delusion as my richest treasure.

I would advise every one to begin the day with an early morning recitation of the Gita. Take up the study of the Gita not in a carping or critical spirit, but in a devout and reverent spirit. Thus approached, she will grant your every wish. Once you have tasted of its sweet nectar, your attachment to it will grow from day to day. The recitation of the Gita verses will support you in your trials and console you in your distress, even in the darkness of solitary confinement. And, if with these verses on your lips you receive the final summons and deliver up your spirit, you will attain 'Brahma-Nirvana,' the Final Liberation.

The Gita enabled the late Lokamanya Tilak out of his encyclopædic learning and study, to produce a monumental commentary. For him it was a store-house of profound truths to exercise his intellect upon. I believe his commentary on the Gita will be a more lasting monument to his memory. It will survive even the successful termination of the struggle for Swarajya. Even then his memory will remain as fresh as ever on account of his spotless purity of life and his great commentary on the Gita. No one in his life time, nor even now, could claim deeper and vaster knowledge of the Shastras than he possessed. His masterwork commentary on the Gita is unsurpassed and will remain so for a long time to come. Nobody has yet carried on more elaborate research in the questions arising from the Gita and the Vedas."

Paying a glowing tribute to the memory of the Late Lokmanya Tilak, Gandhiji said "his vast learning, his immense sacrifices and his life-long service have won for him a unique place in the hearts of the people"

(From Speeches of Mahatma Gandhi at Benares and at Cawnpore).

7. BABU AUROBINDO GHOSE.

What is the message of the Gita and what its working value, its spiritual utility to the human mind of the present day, after the long ages that have elapsed since it was written and the great subsequent transformations of thought and experience? The human mind moves always forward, alters its view-point and enlarges its thought-substance, and the effect of these changes is to render past systems of thinking obsolete or, when they are preserved, to extend, to modify and subtly or visibly to alter their value. The vitality of an ancient doctrine consists in the extent to which it naturally lends itself to such a treatment; for that means that whatever may have been the limitations or the obsolescences of the form of its thought, the truth of substance, the truth of living vision and experience on which its system was built, is still sound and retains a permanent validity and significance. The Gita is a book that has worn extraordinarily well, and it is almost as fresh and still in its real substance quite as new, because always renewable in experience, as when it first appeared in or was written into the frame of the 'Mahabharata'. It is still received in India as one of the great bodies of doctrine that most authoritatively govern religious thinking; and its teaching is acknowledged as of the highest value if not wholly accepted by almost all shades of religious belief and opinion. Its influence is not merely philosophic or academic but immediate and living, an influence both for thought and action, and its ideas are actually at work as a powerful shaping factor in the revival and renewal of a nation and a culture. It has even been said recently by a great voice that all we need of spiritual truth for the spiritual life is to be found in the Gita. It would be to encourage the superstition of the book to take too literally that utterance. The truth of the spirit is infinite and cannot be circumscribed in that manner. Still it may be said that most of the main clues are there and that after all the later developments of spiritual experience and discovery, we can still return to it for a large inspiration and guidance. Outside India too it is universally acknowledged as one of the world's great scriptures, although in Europe its thought is better understood than its secret of spiritual practice.

Neither Mr. Tilak nor his works really require any presentation of foreword.

His Orion and his Arctic Home have acquired at once a world-wide recognition and left as strong a mark as can at all be imprinted on the ever-shifting sands of oriental research. His work on the Gita, no mere commentary, but an original criticism and presentation of ethical truths, is a monumental work, THE FIRST PROSE WRITING OF THE FRONT RANK IN WEIGHT AND IMPORTANCE IN THE MARATHI LANGUAGE, AND LIKELY TO BECOME A CLASSIC. This one book sufficiently proves that had he devoted his energies in this direction, he might easily have filled a large place in the history of Marathi literature and in the history of ethical thought, so subtle and comprehensive in its thinking, so great the perfection and satisfying force of its style. But it was psychologically impossible for Mr. Tilak to devote his energies in any great degree to another action than the one life-mission for which the Master of his works had chosen him. His powerful literary gift has been given up to a journalistic work, ephemeral as even the best journalistic work must be, but consistently brilliant, vigorous, politically educative through decades, to an extent seldom matched and certainly never surpassed. His scholastic labour has been done almost by way of recreation. Nor can anything be more significant than the fact that the works which have brought him a fame other than that of the politician and patriot, were done in periods of compulsory cessation from his life work,—planned and partly, if not wholly, executed during the imprisonments which could alone enforce leisure upon this unresting worker for his country. Even these by-products of his genius have some reference to the one passion of his life, the renewal, if not the surpassing, of the past greatness of the nation by the greatness of its future. His Vedic researches seek to fix its pre-historic point of departure; the Gita-rahasya takes the scripture which is perhaps the strongest and most comprehensive production of Indian spirituality and justifies to that spirituality by its own authoritative ancient message the sense of the importance of life, of action, of human existence, of man's labour for mankind which is indispensable to the idealism of the modern spirit.

Mr. Tilak himself, his career, his place in Indian politics are also a self-evident proposition, a hard fact baffling and dismaying in the last degree to those to whom his name has been anathema, and his increasing pre-eminence figured as a portent of evil. Yet is Mr. Tilak a man of various and no ordinary gifts, and in several lines of life he might have achieved present distinction or a pre-eminent and enduring fame. Though he has never practised, he has a close knowledge of law and an acute legal mind which, had he cared in the least degree for wealth and worldy position, would have brought him to the front at the bar. He is a great Sanskrit scholar, a powerful writer and a strong, subtle and lucid thinker. He might have filled a large place in the field of contemporary Asiatic scholarship. He is the very type and incarnation of the Maratha character, the Maratha qualities, the Maratha spirit, but with the unified solidity in the character, the touch of genius in the qualities, the vital force in the spirit which make a great personality readily the representative man of his people. The Maratha race, as their soil and their history have made them, are a rugged, strong and sturdy people; democratic in their every fibre; keenly intelligent and practical to the very marrow; following in ideas, even in poetry, philosophy and religion, the drive towards life and action; capable of great fervour, feeling and enthusiasm, like all Indian people, but not emotional idealists; having in their thought and speech, always a turn for strength, sense, accuracy, lucidity and vigour; in learning and scholarship, patient, industrious, careful, thorough and penetrating; in life, simple, hardy and frugal; in their temperament, courageous, pugnacious, full of spirit, yet with a tact in dealing with hard facts and circumventing obstacles; shrewd yet aggressive diplomatists, born politicians, born fighters. All this Mr. Tilak is with a singular and eminent completeness, and all on a large scale, adding to it all a lucid simplicity and genius, a secret intensity, and inner strength of will, a single-mindedness in aim of quite extraordinary force, which remind one of the brightness, sharpness and perfect temper of a fine sword hidden in a sober scabbard.

The indomitable will and the unwavering devotion have been the whole meaning of Mr. Tilak's life; they are the reason of his immense hold on the people. For he does not owe his pre-eminent position to wealth and great social position, professional success, recognition by Government, a power of fervid oratory or of fluent and telling speech; for he had none of these things to help him. He owes it to himself alone and to the thing his life has meant and because he has meant it with his whole mind and his whole soul. He has kept back nothing for himself or for other aims, but has given all himself to his country. As he emerged on the political field, his people saw more and more clearly in him their representative man, themselves in large, the genius of their type. They felt him to be of one spirit and make, with the great men who had made their past history, almost believed him to be a reincarnation of one of them returned to carry out his old work in a new form and under new conditions. They beheld in him the spirit of Maharashtra once again embodied in a great individual. He occupies a position in his province which has no parallel in the rest of India.

The landmarks of Mr. Tilak's life are landmarks also in the history of his province and his country.

His first great step associated him in a pioneer work whose motive was to educate the people for a new life under the new conditions, on the one side, a purely educational movement of which the fruit was the Ferguson College, fitly founding the reawakening of the country by an effort of which co-operation in self-sacrifice was the moving spirit, on the other, the initiation of the Kesari newspaper, which figured increasingly as the characteristic and powerful expression of the political mind of Maharashtra. Mr. Tilak's career has counted three periods each of which had an imprisonment for its culminating point. His first imprisonment in the Kolhapur case belongs to this first stage of self-development and development of the Maratha country for new ideas and activities and for the national future.

The second period brought in a wider conception and a profounder effort. For now it was to reawaken not only the political mind but the soul of the people by linking its future to its past; it worked by a more strenuous and popular propaganda which reached its height in the organisation of the Shivaji and the Ganapati festivals. His separation from the Social reform leader, Agarkar, had opened the way for the peculiar role which he has played as a trusted and accredited leader of conservative and religious India in the paths of democratic politics. It was this position which enabled him to effect the union of the new political spirit with the tradition and sentiment of the historic past and of both with the ineradicable religious temperament of the people of which these festivals were the symbol. The congress movement was for a long time purely occidental in its mind, character and methods, confined to the English-educated few, founded on the political rights and interests of the people read in the light of English history and European ideals, but with no roots either in the past of the country or in the inner spirit of the nation. Mr. Tilak was the first political leader to break through the routine of its somewhat academical methods, to bridge the gulf between the present and the past, and to restore continuity to the political life of the nation. He developed a language and a spirit and he used methods which indianised the movement and brought into it the masses. To his work of this period we owe that really living, strong and readily organised movement in Maharashtra which has shown its energy and sincerity in more than one crisis and struggle. This divination of the mind and spirit of his people and its needs and this power to seize on the right way to call it forth prove strikingly the political genius of Mr. Tilak; they made him the one man predestined to lead them in this trying and difficult period when all has to be discovered and all has to be reconstructed. What was done then by Mr. Tilak in Maharashtra has been initiated for all India by the Swadeshi movement. To bring in the mass of the people to found the greatness of the future on the greatness of the past, to infuse Indian politics with Indian religious fervour and spirituality, are the indispensable conditions for a great and powerful political awakening in India. Others, writers thinkers, spiritual leaders, had seen this truth. Mr. Tilak was the first to bring it into the actual field of practical politics The second period of his labour for this country culminated in a longer and harsher imprisonment which was as it were the second seal of the divine hand upon his work; for there can be no diviner seal than suffering for a cause.

A third period, that the Swadeshi movement, brought Mr. Tilak forward prominently as an All-India leader: it gave him at last the wider field, the greater driving power, the larger leverage he needed to bring his life-work rapidly to a head, and not only in Maharashtra but throughout the country. From the inception of the Boycott Movement to the Surat catastrophe and his last and longest imprisonment, which was its equal, the name and work of Mr. Tilak are a part of Indian history.

These three imprisonments, each showing more clearly the moral stuff and quality of the man under the test and glare of suffering, have been the three seals of his career. The first found him one of a small knot of pioneer workers; it marked him out to be the strong and inflexible leader of a strong and sturdy people. The second found him already the inspiring power of a great awakening of the Maratha spirit; it left him an uncrowned king in the Deccan and gave him that high reputation throughout India, which was the foundation-stone of his commanding influence. The last found him the leader of an All-India party, the foremost exponent and head of a thorough-going Nationalism; it sent him back to be one of the two or three foremost men of India adored and followed by the whole nation. No prominent man in India has suffered more for his country; none has taken his sacrifices and sufferings more quietly and as a matter of course.

All the Indian provinces and communities have spoken with one voice, Mr. Tilak's principles of work have been accepted; the ideas which he had so much troubled to enforce have become the commonplaces and truisms of our political thought. The only question that remains is the rapidity of a new inevitable evolution. That is the hope for which Mr. Tilak still stands, a leader of all India.

Mr. Tilak's name stands already for history as a Nation-builder, one of the half-dozen greatest political personalities, memorable figures, representative men of the nation in this most critical period of India's destinies, a name to be remembered gratefully so long as the country has pride in its past and hope for its future.

(8) SHRIMANT BALASAHEB PANT PRATINIDHI, RAJA SAHEB OF AUNDH.

The Bhagvadgeeta has been regarded from time immemorial as one of the three *prasthanas* or the status books of Indian philosophy, and is commented on in their own way by eminent Acharyas like the great Shankara, Ramanuja, Nimbarka, Madhva, Vallabha, and others, each of whom, however, being the pioneer of an independent school of philosophy, twisted the import of this great book in such a way as to make it in conformity with his own system. The illustrious Dnyaneshwar wrote his first treatise on this book in Marathi and the Geeta-Rahasya of the late Lokmanya Tilak is its only befitting successor. The author of the Dnyaneshwari had prominently in his view its devotional aspect, which he naturally emphasised in his work; but, as the author of the Geeta-Rahasya rightly points out, the "Geeta" is neither a book of knowledge nor of devotion nor of action: but rather a harmonious combination of them all. Geeta-Rahasya can thus be said to be the most honest and impartial commentary on the book.

The work of translating such a book into English was by no means easy for Solicitor Sukthankar; and he too ought to have realised it at the time of undertaking this job. His responsibility was twofold: to make the translation intelligible, and at the same time not to cause any damage to the original; and judging from the translation that we have in hand, he can be very well said to have carried out his work most satisfactorily. We went through almost all the portion of the translation and found it to be quite interesting and intelligible without the help of the original. That the translation is most strictly faithful to the text only shows his self-control and unbiassed bent of mind, which a true translator ought to have. To make the translation worthy of the original, Solicitor Sukthankar seems to have spared no pains.

B. S. Sukthankar

Geeta-Rahasya, apart from being one of the greatest philosophical treatises in Marathi, is the crown-work of the late Lokamanya; and was badly in need of such a translation for becoming known to the world at large. The Geeta-Rahasya being an indicator to its writer's philosophy of life, the translation will not only help the world to judge the writer and realise the value of his original work, but will also help it to understand the real meaning of the Geeta itself and make it aware of him as a master-intellect that everybody can be proud of. We must all be very grateful to Solicitor Sukthankar for his commendable work of translation, and hope him every due and well deserved reward for his efforts.

---

(9) THE HON'BLE MR. JUSTICE FAIZ B. TYABJI,
High Court, Bombay.

It is a sincere pleasure to me to hear that Lokmanya Tilak's scholarly works are being rendered available in English. The Gita has been frequently translated into English though it is not surprising that scholars are not altogether satisfied with the renderings that have so far been published. A work giving a really spiritual interpretation of this inspiring work must supply an urgent need of the young men and women of to-day. The danger of being cut off from what is considered religion requires particular attention in these days. The danger is the more serious, as our young men are apt to fear that their spiritual needs cannot be met from texts that are the foundations of religion. The great religions, it is true, have had their foundations in the East. But, it is thought that their interpretation, so as to adopt them to the needs of to-day, must be sought from the West. To turn, therefore, to the most spiritual expressions of our own religious teachers, as interpreted by the modern teachers in the East, is an extremely necessary part of the educational experiences through which we should all pass. To men of ripe experience, it must be a peculiar satisfaction to have such a work available. I am looking forward with keen interest to this publication.

---

(10) SIR MOHAMMAD IQBAL.

I have always held the Bhagavad-Gītā in the highest admiration.

(11) SRI MEHER BABA.

The Bhagavad-Gita has exerted a tremendous spiritual influence on humanity at large. As the Blessed Lord Sri Krishna was born a Hindu, the Gita is more often than never regarded as a sacred book of the Hindus; but really speaking, it is a sacred book of not merely the Hindus but of the entire human race. The message that it contains was meant not merely for India, but for the whole world. Let mankind act in accordance with its message, and the universal brotherhood will surely be automatically brought about.

Those who cast doubts on the perfect sainthood of Shri Krishna, know not what they are doing. He was certainly a God-incarnate; and because He was a Sadguru, a Perfect Saint, He was successful in inundating the world with spirituality and lofty spiritual teachings.

(12) Rao Bahadur Vidvatkulaśekhara C. V. VAIDYA, M.A., LL.B.

THE AGE OF THE GITA AND GITA-JAYANTI.

I propose to place my views on the "Age of the Gītā" as succinctly as possible. When was this unique work composed, is the question which naturally arises in every mind.

The Gītā itself purports to state that it was taught by Lord Śrī Kṛṣṇa to Arjuna, hero of the Mahābhārata War, on the field of battle, before the fight commenced, but when the fighters were actually facing each other, ready to commence the fight. It follows, therefore, that the date of the Gītā is the date of the commencement of the Bhārata fight. This date is the subject of dispute between European scholars, followed by some Indian scholars, and myself. I hold that the date assigned to the fight by all ancient Indian writers, especially astronomers, is the correct one, viz. Mārgaśīrṣa Śuddha 13, Pre-Śaka 3180 (3102 B. C.). I will not enter into the details of the controversy here, but merely indicate my grounds.

The Bhārata heroes are referred to in the 'Śatapatha Brāhmana', and the date of this Brāhmaṇa has been fixed by Shankar Balkrishna Dikshit, a great modern Indian astronomical researcher, at about 3,000 B. C. from the astronomical statement in it that the Kṛttikās rise exactly in the East. Attempt has lately been made by Winternitz to dislodge this date by suggesting that the statement (एता वै कृत्तिकाः प्राच्यो दिशो नच्यवन्ते) in the 'Śatapatha' means only that the Kṛttikās come on the East line, and not that they rise in the East. But this rendering is negatived by the very next sentence 'all other stars deviate from the East' (सर्वाणि ह वा अन्यानि नक्षत्राणि च्यवन्ते) in the 'Śatapatha', as shown by me in detail in an article published in the Bhandarkar Research Institute Journal. If, then, Parikṣit and others, mentioned in the 'Śatapatha' of 3,000 B. C. as recent kings, are taken to be the grandson and great-grandsons of Arjuna, the date of the fight, viz. one year before the commencement of the Kali age, given by all Indian astronomers, or 3102 B. C., is perfectly borne out by the 'Śatapatha' statement. European scholars, and some Indian scholars, too, place the fight about 1400 B. C. on the strength ot the pedigrees of kings given in Purāṇas from the Nine Nandas to Bṛhadratha, son of Jarāsandha. The evidence of the Purāṇas, however, has no value when compared with the evidence of the 'Śatpatha'. Indeed, Purāṇa genealogies are not reliable, particularly for ancient dynasties, especially as they are contradicted by the evidence of Megasthenes, recorded about 320 B. C., as shown by me in detail in "Mahābhārata-Mīmāṁsā", a Hindi work. This short summary of the controversy will show to the reader that the year of the Bhārata fight must be taken to be 3102 B. C.

With regard to the exact day of the fight, there is also a controversy. But the difference is only of two days. The Gītā-Jayantī day is Mārgaśīrṣa śuddha 11, 'Ekādaśī' day; but the statement in the Mahābhārata and the course of the fight as described therein lead to no other day than *śuddha* 13, and this is the date accepted by old writers and commentators of the Mahābhārata. They have consented to hold the Jayanti for 3 days continually, viz., from Ekādaśi to Trayodaśi.

To speak in English dates, the Mahābhārata fight commenced in December 3102 B. C., and the 'Gītā' was preached on the morning of that day.

Having placed before the reader the day by date and year on which the doctrines of the 'Gītā' were preached by Śrī Kṛṣṇa, we go on to state that this cannot be the date of the 'Gītā' as it is before us. For the first chapter, etc., cannot have belonged to the teaching, as it was actually given. The whole story is told afterwards by some one, and that is Vyāsa undoubtedly. As the teaching of Christ is given in several books of the New Testament written by St. John and others, so Vyāsa may be taken to be the writer who first recorded this teaching in a work to be studied and recited. When this was written by Vyāsa cannot be definitely stated. He must, however, have done it within a few years of the fight, and we may roughly say that the date of the original 'Gītā' is somewhere about 3100 B. C.

But it is clear that the work as it is before us is not exactly that of Vyāsa. We know for certain that the original work of Vyāsa, called 'Jaya' or Victory (ततो जयमुदीरयेत्, जयो नामेतिहासोऽयम्) was twice recast or further expanded, once by Vaiśampāyana, who related 'Bhārata' to Janamejaya, and again by Sauti, who related it to Śaunaka and other Brahmins in Naimiṣāraṇya. This work has three names, viz. 'Jaya', 'Bhārata', and 'Mahābhārata', and the extent of the 'Bhārata', of Vaiśampāyana is also given as 24,000 ślokas, while that of the *Mahābhārata* is, as is well-known, one lakh of verses. The original of the 'Gītā', no doubt, belonged to the 'Jaya' (Victory) of Vyāsa; but the work as it is before us belongs, in our opinion, most certainly, to the 'Bhārata' of Vaiśampāyana, and not to the *Mahābhārata* of Sauti. The arguments for this view are given at length in the last chapter of Mahābhārata-Mīmāṁsā; but it may here be stated briefly that the greatness of this work is described even in the Mahābhārata itself, wherein it is related that Arjuna again asked Śri Kṛṣṇa to teach him what was taught on the battlefield. But Śri Kṛṣṇa answered: "What I told you then, being in the required Yogic mood (योगयुक्तेन चेतसा), I cannot tell you again. I will tell you, however, another episode". And thus the 'Anugītā' s introduced in the *Mahābhārata.* Then, again, the verses in the 'Gītā' are constantly repeated in the *Mahābhārata* throughout its length as of some authoritative work. It is hence certain that the 'Gītā' does not belong to the Mahābhārata of Sauti but it belongs to the 'Bhārata' of Vaiśampāyana. The date of the former is conceded to be about 250 B. C. as shown at length in "Mahābhārata-Mīmāṁsā" (Chapter I); but the date of Vaiśampāyana's 'Bhārata' cannot be indubitably fixed, and hence the date of the 'Gita', as it is to-day, is uncertain.

But, there are various arguments which point to 1400 B. C. speaking roughly in centuries, as the probable age of the 'Gītā'. In the first place the language of the 'Gītā' strikes one as a spoken language and not classical Sanskrit of the time when it was dead and spoken only by Pandits. We know that Buddha preached his new religion to the people in Pali, a Prakrit; and hence it is certain that in his time Sanskrit was dead as a spoken language of the common people. The 'Gītā', therefore, precedes Buddha of 500 B. C. Again, there is no reference to Buddhism in the 'Gītā', though there are many references to the doctrines of Buddhism in the 'Mahābhārata'. Some people think that in Chapter XVI there is a reference to Buddhist tenets in the description of the Āsurī character. But this is a description of Atheists. For Buddhism is in favour of Renunciation, and not the enjoyment of the world. On the other hand, there is not the least doubt that 'Gītā' is post-Upaniṣadic. The doctrine of Renunciation was first preached by the 'Bṛhadāraṇyaka', and it pervades the spirit of all the thirteen old Upaniṣads. It is clear the 'Gītā' is not for Renunciation. Indeed, Arjuna is actuated by that spirit when he asks the first and subsequent question in the Gītā and Śrī Kṛṣṇa sums His preaching in the pithy verse (संन्यासः कर्मयोगश्च निःश्रेयसकरावुभौ । तयोस्तु कर्मसंन्यासात्कर्मयोगो विशिष्यते ॥ Gī. 5. 2.). This is wrongly interpreted by those who believe that the object of the 'Gītā' is to preach 'Saṁnyāsa'. Lokamānya Tilak has pointed out its true import, which is also the natural one. As the "Maitrāyaṇīya Upanisad" must be dated 1900 B. C.

roughly, as shown by Tilak from an astronomical statement in it, the 'Gītā' must be placed between 1900 B. C. and 500 B. C. This is a wide range, no doubt; but it supplies one with limits, which are certain and unassailable.

There are a few arguments which will give us a more definite approximation to the probable date. It has been rightly shown by some scholars that the 'Gītā' is not only pre-Buddhistic but pre-Pāṇinīan. Many forms in it are against Pāṇinī's rules. More interesting still is (मासानां मार्गशीर्षोऽहम) as the month names are modern and not Vedic names, new names being introduced about 2,000 B. C. according to Shanker Balkrishna Dikshit. But, according to Vedāṅga Jyotiṣa, the first month is Māgha, and hence the 'Gītā' seems to be prior to the 'Vedāṅga Jyotiṣa' also, the date of which is about 1190 B. C. even according to the calculation of Archbishop Pratt, who worked the date out for Max Müller. Dikshit takes its date to be about 1400 B. C. It may thus be taken without much difficulty that 1400 B. C. is the probable date of the *Gītā.*

Another sentence furnishes a further argument in favour of this date. It may be accepted that Śrī Kṛṣṇa was already considered a divine being, indeed as an incarnation of the Highest Deity at the time of the Gītā; but not probably Arjuna. Yet, when Śrī Kṛṣṇa says ('वृष्णीनां वासुदेवोऽस्मि पाण्डवानां धनञ्जयः',), he lays the foundation of Arjuna-worship. From Pāṇinī's Sūtra ('वासुदेवार्जुनाभ्यांकम्'), we are sure that during Pāṇini's time both Vāsudeva and Arjuna were worshipped, though Arjuna lost his position later on. Gītā is therefore pre-Pāṇinīan undoubtedly. If we take the date of Pāṇinī to be about 800 B. C., as most Indians Scholars do, though Europeans scholars place him about 300 B. C., we may take, the Gītā to about 1200 B. C. or at least to 1,000 B. C. When we further remember that Śrī Kṛṣṇa identifies Himself with Mārgaśīrṣa as being the first of months, as in other things, we can take the Gītā still further back, i. e., about 1,400 B. C., before the latest possible date for Vedāṅga Jyotiṣa.

The exact age of the Gītā is, no doubt difficult to determine for want of detailed knowledge of the political, social and religious history of India, before Buddha. The doctrine of Ahiṁsā is preached no doubt in the Gītā. But it is not the doctrine of Buddha. It had already been preached by the Upaniṣads (अहिंसन् सर्वाणि भूतान्यत्र तीर्थेभ्यः Chāndogya), and the Gītā keeps to it. Hiṁsā in sacrifice is not Hiṁsā as Hindus then believed. Buddha prohibited it altogether. This religious question is not at the root of the teaching of the Gītā. The question which was agitating Arjuna was wholly a moral one; and related, not to the slaughter of animals in sacrifices to God but to the slaughter of men in battle, slaughter of even relatives even in a just war. The question was only a moral or a political one no doubt; but in India all questions are only a part of the great question: what is the duty of man in this life both from the worldly point of view and the view of the highest goal of human existence? It was hence necessary that the question should be discussed fully from these points of view and the Bhagavad-Gītā discusses it so thoroughly from all sides and in such a simple yet eloquent manner, in language so deep and meaningful, that the Gītā will always remain at the head of religious, philosophical and moral treatises. The answer of Srī Kṛṣṇa to the vital question which is at the root of the Gītā is remarakable. The view is summed up at the end in the verse:

यस्य नाहंकृतो भावो बुद्धिर्यस्य न लिप्यते ।
हत्वापि स इमाँल्लोकान्न हन्ति न निबध्यते ॥

(Extract from Mr. C. V. Vaidya's article in the
Kalyan Kalpataru, Gita Number, 1935.
Gītā Press, Gorakhpur, INDIA.)

---

(13) MRS. SOPHIA WADIA.

GITA-JAYANTI.

It is computed that Moksada Ekadasi—the eleventh day of Marga-Sirsa, which is auspicious to those seeking spiritual realization—was the day when Sri Krisna began to deliver on the field of duty His Sermon to the mentally confused Arjuna. Therefore that day is regarded as the birth-day of the Gita. Very many Hindus celebrate this day—Gita-Jayanti. The Bhagavad-gita is reverenced as the song of life, and its reciters and readers are said to attain fortune, victory, prosperity and righteousness. That its doctrines emancipate the human soul and enlighten it with Wisdom and Peace is a well-recognized fact.

The message of the Gītā has a universal appeal. Its teachings are fundamentally psychological and practical; they are addressed to man, the thinker, from whom no blind belief in them is demanded, but whose reason is kindled into conviction. The Gita is a drama; its characters are human passions and principles in Nature personified. Its historical back-ground and martial 'melange' have misled some, but more and more is it being recognized that the Gitā symbolizes the eternal struggle between the material and the spiritual in every human being. Any thinking individual is capable of recognizing that the story of the Gītā is the story of life. The more one listens to the Song of life, the more one realizes that it is the song of his own life. Thus the Gita is understood by each thinking soul in his own way, according to his own stage in evolution. To each the Gita offers the solution of his own problems. Thus any deluded mortal of any community using the lessons taught can become enlightened and immortal.

The Gītā has not only universal appeal; its influence is universalizing. It may be regarded as the book of democracy; it teaches that Spirit is the seed of all, and in the hearts of all beings It is rooted. The pure democratic doctrines of the Gita do not advocate any process of levelling down all human beings to an equality in material things; they advocate the realization of an existing unity in Spirit, Which manifests as harmony in diversities. The socialism of the Gita is founded on the maxim of *noblesse oblige* and the method of attaining it is by the unfoldment of nobility at every stage and in every station of life. The social philosophy of the Gita recognises the divisions and differences of the human kingdom, and it does not attempt the impossible task of doing away with or ignoring them; it teaches their meaning and purpose, and reveals that they are but the results of the natural processes of evolution. Thus, for example, the Gita does not say that castes and classes are useless and should be destroyed; it explains Varnas or castes from the point of view of the soul; they are expressions of varying qualities of the evolving human consciousness. By merit and merit alone a man is of high or low caste or class, and birth, family, religion or wealth do not determine the soul's station in life; its own qualities bespeak its stage of evolution. By self-control and self-effort any sinner can become pure.

The inspiration of the Gita produces a series of progressive awakenings, but all of them result in reliance on the Self within, which is perceived as the Inner Ruler. No prophet, no priest can save that Self; no king, no emperor can have power over it. It is its own saviour and holds sway over its own kingdom of the mind, its own empire of the heart. Thus the Gita destroys priest-made orthodoxy and sectarianism, but does not leave the man barren and lonely; for it brings to him the companionship of the Sage and the Prophet. It illuminates for the Muslims his Koran, for the Parsi his Avesta, for the Christian his Bible. These are no more regarded as infallible books, but as avenues leading to the understanding and appreciation of their great recorders. For example, the teaching about Sraddha will purify and deepen the faith of the Muslims; the austerities and mortifications of body, speech, and mind, will make the Zoroastrian more enlightened about the triad of good deeds, good words, and good thoughts, which he reveres; the Sikh's martial ardour, the Jain's gentleness, will become more elevated qualities; the Christian will learn why ordinarily he is not able to live up to the Sermon on the Mount, and by what stages he can reach the position where he will be able to do so; and so on. That which is the force of evil in every religion will weaken, and the unifying spirit of true religion will become more and more manifest.

The principle of democracy, in which each grade of intelligence has its duties to discharge, contributes substantially to the unfoldment of the quality of self-reliance. The philosophy of the Gita is the philosophy of responsibility to neighbour and stranger, to country and race, to the whole of nature, visible and invisible; its practice resolves itself into the Religion of Duty. The performance of duties requires a discernment of what are not our duties; otherwise like Arjuna, we shall want to run away from our real duty, thinking that it consists in giving way to the enemy within and making peace with the wrong-doer in the world. The Gita has a unifying force; that power can bind men and women of different religions into a single whole; for, he who practises self-control, who attempts purification of his own thoughts, words and deeds, who endeavours to live his days and years in an enlightened manner, comes in unison and harmony, unconsciously to himself, with all others who are engaged in the same task.

To make the celebration of "Gita-Jayanti" an institution, we must first restore the book to its original position, from which it has fallen to assume a sectarian character. It is not a religious code but a spiritual poem; its teachings, both metaphysical and ethical, have naught to do with religious rites, priests or temples; it is not other-worldly—it deals with the problems of life in this world. Its message is clear, its language is simple, and no man needs an intermediary to approach it or to appreciate it. It is not fragmentary and there are no lacunae to be filled up by some expounder or by some study of other texts. It itself is perfectly rounded off; in itself it is complete. It grades off gently to depth after depth in the mighty ocean of wisdom. It rises tier over tier like an awe-inspiring mountain. Any man, any woman, in the East as in the West, can find his or her own place in its scheme, the very next step to be taken by him, the way to take that step, and the way to keep on progressing.

The right approach to the Gita consists in having our mind fresh to penetrate its verses. The effect is magical.

(Extract from Mrs. Sofia Wadia's article in the Kalyan Kalpa-Taru, Gita Number 1935, Gita Press, Gorakhapur, INDIA).

A PAGE FROM THE AUTHOR'S NOTE-BOOK

A fac-simile copy of an important memorandum entered by Lokamanya Tilak in his own hand-writing in a note-book, while in the Mandalay Jail, where the Gita-Rahasya was written.

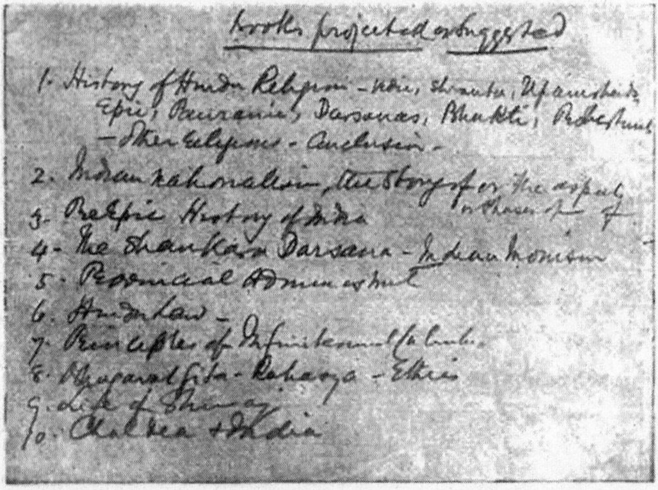
Works projected or suggested

1. History of Hindu Religion — Vedic, Shrauta, Upanishads, Epic, Pauranic, Darsanas, Bhakti, Protestant — Other religions — Conclusion —
2. Indian Nationalism, the story of or the aspects [illegible]
3. Pre-Epic History of India
4. The Shankara Darsana — Indian Monism
5. Provincial Administration
6. Hindu Law —
7. Principles of Infinitesimal Calculus
8. Bhagavad Gita-Rahasya — Ethics
9. Life of Shivaji
10. Chaldea & India

Out of the ten works mentioned in the above list, only the Gita-Rahasya was actually written, which incidentally shows the importance attached by the author to that subject. The other contemplated works have remained in the form of jotted notes.

Let me begin by telling you what induced me to take up the study of *Bhagvad Gita*. When I was quite a boy, I was often told by my elders that strictly religious and really philosophic life was incompatible with the hum-drum life of every day. If one was ambitious enough to try to attain Moksha, the highest goal a person could attain, then he must divest himself of all earthly desires and renounce this world. One could not serve two masters, the world and God. I understood this to mean that if one would lead a life which was the life worth living, according to the religion in which I was born, then the sooner the world was given up the better. This set me thinking. The question that I formulated for myself to be solved was: Does my religion want me to give up this world and renounce it before I attempt to, or in order to be able to, attain the perfection of manhood? In my boyhood I was also told that *Bhagvada Gita* was universally acknowledged to be a book containing all the principles and philosophy of the Hindu Religion, and I thought if this be so I should find an answer in this book to my query; and thus began my study of the *Bhagvad Gita*. I approached the book with a mind prepossessed by no previous ideas about any philosophy, and had no theory of my own for which I sought any support in the *Gita*. A person whose mind is prepossessed by certain ideas, reads the book with a prejudiced mind; for instance, when a Christian reads it, he does not want to know what the *Gita* says but wants to find out if there are any principles in the *Gita* which he has already met with in the Bible, and if so the conclusion he rushes to is that the *Gita* was copied from the Bible. I have dealt with this topic in my book *Gita Rahasya* and I need hardly say much about it here, but what I want to emphasise is this, that when you want to read and understand a book, especially a great work like the *Gita*—you must approach it with an unprejudiced and unprepossessed mind. To do this, I know, is one of the most difficult things. Those who profess to do it may have a lurking thought or prejudice in their minds which vitiates the reading of the book to some extent. However I am describing to you the frame of mind one must get into if one wants to get at the truth; and however difficult it be, it has to be done. The next thing one has to do is to take into consideration the time and the circumstances in which the book was written and the purpose for which the book was written. In short, the book must not be read devoid of its context. This is especially true about a book like *Bhagvad Gita.* Various commentators have put as many interpretations on the book, and surely the writer or composer could not have written or composed the book for so many interpretations being put on it. He must have put one meaning and one purpose running through the book, and that I have tried to find out. I believe I have succeeded in it, because having no theory of mine for which I sought any support from the book so universally respected, I had no reason to twist the text to suit my theory. There has not been a commentator of the *Gita* who did not advocate a pet theory of his own and has not tried to support the same by showing that the *Bhagvad Gita* lent him support. The conclusion I have come to is that the *Gita* advocates the performance of action in this world even after the actor has achieved the highest union with the Supreme Deity by Jnana (knowledge) or Bhakti (Devotion). This action must be done to keep the world going by the right path of evolution which the Creator has destined the world to follow. In order that the action may not bind the actor, it must be done with the aim of helping His purpose, and without any Attachment to the coming result. This I hold is a lesson of the *Gita.* Jnana-Yoga there is, yes. Bhakti-Yoga there is, yes. Who says not? But they are both subservient to the Karma-Yoga preached in the *Gita.* If the *Gita* was preached to desponding Arjuna to make him ready for the fight—for the Action—how can it be said that the ultimate lesson of the great book is Bhakti or Jnana alone? In fact, there is a blending of all these Yogas in the *Gita*; and as the air is not Oxygen or Hydrogen, or any other gas alone, but a composition of all these in a certain proportion, so in the *Gita* all these Yogas are blended into one.

I differ from almost all the commentators when I say that the *Gita* enjoins Action even after the perfection in Jnana and

Bhakti is attained and the Deity is reached through these mediums. Now, there is a fundamental unity underlying the Logos (Ishvara), man, and world. The world is in existence because the Logos has willed it so. It is His Will that holds it together. Man strives to gain union with God; and when this union is achieved, the individual will merges in the mighty Universal Will. When this is achieved, will the individual say: "I shall do no Action, and I shall not help the world"—the world which is, because the Will with Which he has sought union has willed it to be so? It does not stand to reason. It is not I who say so: the *Gita* says so. Shri Krishna himself says that there is nothing in all the three worlds that He need acquire, and *still* He acts. He acts because if He did not, the world will be ruined. If man seeks unity with the Deity, he must necessarily seek unity with the interests of the world also, and work for it. If he does not, then the unity is not perfect, because there is union between two elements out of the three (man and Deity) and the third (the world) is left out. I have thus solved the question for myself and I hold that serving the world, and thus serving His Will, is the surest way of Salvation; and this way can be followed by remaining *in* the world and not going away from it.

(A summary of the speech of Mr. Tilak, re: *Gita Rahasya*).

The Karma-Yoga which I preach is not a new theory; neither was the discovery of the Law of Karma made as recently as to-day. The knowledge of the Law is so ancient that not even Shri Krishna was the great Teacher who first propounded it. It must be remembered that Karma-Yoga has been our sacred heritage from times immemorial when we Indians were seated on the high pedestal of wealth and lore. Karma-Yoga or to put it in another way, the law of duty, is the combination of all that is best in spiritual science, in actual action and in an unselfish meditative life. Compliance with this universal law leads to the realisation of the most cherished ideas of man. Such was the doctrine taught by our forefathers, who never intended that the goal of life should be meditation alone. No one can expect Providence to protect one who sits with folded arms and throws his burden on others. God does not help the indolent. You must be doing all that you can to lift yourself up, and then only may you rely on the Almighty to help you. You should not, however, presume that you have to toil that you yourself might reap the fruit of your labour. That cannot always be the case. Let us then try our utmost and leave the generations to come to enjoy that fruit. Remember, it is not you who had planted the mango-trees the fruit whereof you have tasted. Let the advantage now go to our children and their descendants. It is only given to us to toil and work. And so, there ought to be no relaxation in our efforts, lest we incur the curse of those that come after us. Action alone must be our guiding principle, action disinterested and well thought out. It does not matter who the Sovereign is. It is enough if we have full liberty to elevate ourselves in the best possible manner. This is called immutable Dharma, and Karma-Yoga is nothing but the method which leads to the attainment of Dharma or material and spiritual glory. God has declared His will. HE has willed that self can be exalted only through its own efforts. Everything lies in your hands. Karma-Yoga does not look upon this world as nothing; it requires only that your motives should be untainted by selfish interest and passion. This is the true view of practical Vedanta, the key to which is apt to be lost in sophistry.

(Poona Sarvajanik Sabha Quarterly).

CONTENTS

(GENERAL)

LIST OF ILLUSTRATIONS.

Explanation of the Abbreviations used in the Gītā-Rahasya, and information about the treatises referred to by the Abbreviations.

—:0::0:—

NOTE :—These are not in the same order as in the original, as they have been re-arranged according to the English Alphabet, whereas in the original, they are arranged according to the Marathi Alphabet—Trans.).

Ai. Brā. *Aitareya Brāhmaṇa*; *pañcikā* and *khaṇḍa*, (Dr. Houda's Edition).

Ai. or Ai. U. } *Aitareyopaniṣad*; chapter, *khaṇḍa* and stanza (Anandasrama Edition).

Aṣṭā. *Aṣṭāvakragītā*; chapter and stanza, (*Gītā-Saṁgraha* published by Messrs Ashtekar & Co.)

Atharva. *Atharvaveda*; the figures after this show respectively, the *kāṇḍa*, the *sūkta*, and the *ṛcā*.

Bhāg. *Śrīmad Bhāgavatapurāṇa*, (Nirnaya-Sagara Edition).

Bhā. Jyo. *Bhāratīya Jyotiḥ Śāstra* (Written by the late Balkrishna Dikshit).

Bṛ. or Bṛha. } *Bṛhadāraṇyakopaniṣat*; *adhyāya*, *brāhmaṇa* and *mantra* (Ānandasrama Edition). The usual reference is to the Kaṇvapāṭha, but in one place, there is a reference to the Mādhyandina-śākhā.

Bra. Sū. See. Ve. Sū. below.

Chān. *Chāndogyopaniṣat*; chapter, *khaṇḍa* and *mantra*. (Anandasrama Edition).

Dā. or Dāsa. } The *Dāsabodha* of Śrī Samartha (Edition of the Satkaryottejaka Sabha, Dhulia).

Gā. Tukārāma's *Gāthā* (Damodar Savlarama's Edition, 1900).

Gī. *Bhagavadgītā*, chapter and stanza; Gī. Śāṁ. Bhā.; *Gītā Śāṁkarabhāṣya*. Gītā. Rā. Bhā., *Gītā Rāmānujabhāṣya*. The Anandasrama Edition of the Gītā and of the *Śāṁkarabhāṣya* contains at the end a glossary, which I have found very useful; and I am very grateful for it to the compiler. The *Rāmānujabhāṣya* is the one printed in the Venkatesvara Press; The *Madhvabhāṣya* is the one printed by Krishnacharya of Kumbhakonam; The *Ānandagiri* Commentary, and the *Paramārtha-prapā*, are those printed in the Jagadhitecchu Press; the *Madhusūdana* Commentary is the one printed in the Native Opinion Press; the *Śrīdharī* and *Vāmanī* (Marathi) Commentaries are those printed in the Nirnayasagara Press; the *Paiśācabhāṣya* is the one printed in the Anandasrama Press; the *Tatvadīpikā* of the Vallabha school is the one printed in the Guzarati Printing Press; the *Nīlakaṇṭhī* is from the Bombay Mahābhārata; and the *Brahmānandī* is the one printed in Madras; these are the commentaries of which I have made use. But, as the Guzarati Printing Press has recently published together in one volume all these commentaries except the *Paiśācabhāṣya* and the *Brahamānandī*, as also the commentary of the Nimbārka School and some other commentaries, in all fifteen, that one volume is now sufficient for all needs.

Gī. Ra. or Gītā Ra. *Gītā-Rahasya.* The first essay of this book.

Hari. *Harivaṁśa*; *parva*, chapter and stanza (Bombay Edition).

Īśā. *Īśāvāsyopaniṣat.* (Anandasrama Edition).

Jai. Sū. The *Mīmāṁsā-Sūtras* of Jaimini; chapter, *pāda*, and *sūtra.* (Calcutta Edition).

Jñā. *Jñāneśvarī* with translation; Indira Press Edition.

Ka. or Kaṭha. *Kaṭhopaniṣat*; *vallī* and *mantra* (Anandasrama Edition).

Kai. *Kaivalyovaniṣat*; *khaṇḍa* and *mantra*; Twenty-eight Upaniṣads (Nirnaya-Sagara Edition).

Kauṣī. *Kauṣītakyupaniṣat* or *Kauṣītaki Brāhmaṇopaniṣat*; chapter and *khaṇḍa*; sometimes the first chapter of this Upaniṣad is referred to as the third chapter according to the order of the Brāhmaṇas; (Anandasrama Edition).

Kena. *Kenopaniṣat* (= *Talavakāropaniṣat*), *khaṇḍa* and mantra (Anandasrama Edition).

Ma. Bhā. *Śriman Mahābhārata.* The following letter shows the various Parvas, and the numbers are of the chapters and the stanzas. I have everywhere used the Sanskrit Edition published at Calcutta by Babu Pratapchandra Roy. If the same stanzas have to be referred to in the Bombay edition, they will be found a little in advance or behind.

Maitryu. *Maitryupaniṣat* or *Maitrāyaṇyupaiṣat*; *prapāṭhaka* and *mantra* (Anandasrama Edition).

Manu. *Manu-Smṛti*, chapter and stanza. (Dr. Jolly's Edition; but in the Mandalik's or in any other edition, these stanzas will mostly be found in the same places; the commentaries on Manu are from the Mandalik edition).

Matsya. *Matsya-Purāṇa* (Anandasrama Edition).

Mi. Pra. *Milinda Praśna*, Pali text, English translation. (Sacred Books of the East Series).

Muṇ. or Muṇḍa. } *Muṇḍakopaniṣat*; *muṇḍaka*, *khaṇḍa* and *mantra* (Anandasrama Edition).

Nār. Pañ. *Nārada Pañcarātra.* (Calcutta edition).

Nā. Sū. *Nārada-Sūtras* (Bombay edition).

Nṛsiṁha. U. *Nṛsiṁhottara tāpanīyopaniṣat.*

Pañca. *Pañcadaśī* with commentary (Nirnaya-Sagara Edition).

Pātañjala-Sū. *Pātañjala-Yoga-Sūtras.* (Tukarama Tatya's Edition).

Praśna. *Praśnopaniṣat*; *praśṇa* and *mantra.* (Anandasrama Edition).

Ṛg. *Ṛg-veda*; *maṇḍala*, *sūkta*, and *ṛcā*.

Rāmapū. *Rāmapūrvatāpinyupaniṣat* (Anandasrama Edition).

S. B. E. *Sacred Books of the East Series.*

Sāṁ. Kā. *Sāṁkhya Kārikā* (Tukarama Tatya's Edition).

Śān. Sū. *Śāṇḍilya-Śūtras* (Bombay Edition).

Śiva. *Śiva-gītā*; chapter and stanza; *Gītā-Saṁgraha* of Messrs Ashtekar & Co.,

Sūrya. Gī. *Sūrya-Gītā*; chapter and stanza, (Madras Edition).

Śve. *Śvetāśvataropaniṣat*; chapter and *mantra* (Anandasrama Edition).

Tai. or Tai. U. } *Taittirīya Upaniṣat*; *vallī*, *anuvāka*, and *mantra* (Anandasrama Edition).

Tai. Brā. *Taittirīya Brāhmaṇa*; *kāṇḍa*, *prapāṭhaka*, *anuvāka* and *mantra* (Anandasrama Edition).

Tai. Saṁ. *Taittirīya Saṁhitā*; *kāṇḍa*, *prapāṭhaka*, *anuvāka* and *mantra.*

Tukā. Gā. Tukārāma's *Gāthā*; See Gā. above.

Vāja. Saṁ. *Vājasaneyi Saṁhitā*; chapter and *mantra* (Bebar Edition).

Vālmīki Rā. or Vā. Rā. *Vālmīki Rāmāyaṇa*; *kāṇda*, chapter and stanza (Bombay Edition).

Ve. Sū. *Vedānta-Sūtras* or *Brahma-Sūtras*; chapter, *pāda*, and *sūtra*.

Ve. Sū. Śāṁ. Bhā. *Śāṁkarabhāṣya* on the *Vedānta-Sūtras*; the Anandasrama Edition has been used everywhere.

Viṣṇu. *Viṣṇu-Purāṇa*; *aṁśa*, chapter, and stanza (Bombay Edition).

Yājña. *Yājñavalkya-Smṛti*; chapter and stanza (Bombay Edition); I have in one or two places referred to the *Aparārka* commentary (Bombay Edition) on this.

Yo. or Yoga. *Yoga-Vāsiṣṭha*; chapter, *sarga*, and stanza. There are two sub-divisions, Pū. (*pūrvārdha*) and U. (*uttarārdha*) of the sixth chapter (Commentated Nirnaya-Sagara Edition).

NOTE :—Besides these, there are many Sanskrit, English, Marathi, and Pali treatises, which have been mentioned in various places; but as a general rule, the names of those books have been given in full, wherever they occur, or they have been mentioned in such a way as to be easily intelligible; and they have, therefore, not been mentioned in the above list.

GENERAL RULES REGARDING THE TRANSLATION.

(i) Wherever a philosophical Sanskrit word used in the Marathi text (not being a technical philosophical term which has been Anglicised), has been rendered by me into English, I have, wherever necessary, placed immediately after such rendering the actual word used by the author in the original, in italics, and within brackets; e. g., bodily (*kāyika*), Self-Realised (*ātma-jñānin*), occasional (*naimittika*), etc. This has been done to enable such of my readers as are acquainted with Sanskrit to understand what the Author himself wanted to say, in case my rendering has not been correct.

(ii) If the word in the original text is a technical philosophical word, which has been Anglicised, I have used the word in Roman characters, beginning with a capital letter, e. g., Jīva, Parameśvara, Prakṛti, Paramātman, Ātman etc.

(iii) Diacritical signs have been used in order to ensure correct pronunciation by the reader, whose attention is drawn to the tabular statement at p. viii showing what diacritical sign has been used for indicating which sound.

(iv) Technical philosophical English words are used with an initial capital letter in order to distinguish them from when they are not so used, e. g., Real, Matter, Spirit, the Imperceptible, Knowledge, Mind, Consciousness, the Qualityless etc., unless the words have been used as adjectives, or in a non-technical sense, e. g., the qualityless Brahman etc.

(v) If in the text itself, there is a Sanskrit word in brackets after another Sanskrit word, (which latter one has been rendered by me into English), the Author's word in brackets, though in Sanskrit, *has not been put into italics*, in order to distinguish the case from where I have put such words in italic characters, in brackets, after the rendering, as mentioned in (i) above.

(vi) If the Sanskrit word in the original has been retained in the translated text, its rendering in English is placed after it in brackets; e. g., the *kārya* (product), *karma* (Action) etc. This has been done only where the retention has been necessary on account of the context.

(vii) I have not added anything of my own in the translated text except as follows :–In almost all places where the Author has given a Sanskrit quotation, he has immediately afterwards translated this quotation or given a summary of it in Marathi; and this, of course, has been translated into English. In some places, however, the Author has not translated a Sanskrit quotation into Marathi; and in these cases, I myself have translated it into English, for the convenience of the reader not acquainted with Sanskrit; but, wherever this has been done, I have added the word "—Trans." after the translation. Any inaccuracies in such translations, would, of course, be mine. Where, however, such a quotation has been from the Gītā itself, I have rendered into English, the translation of that quotation, as made by the Author himself, in his translation of the stanzas of the Gītā (as appearing in this Volume).

B. S. SUKTHANKAR.

SCHEME OF TRANSLITERATION OF SANSKRIT

अ ... ... *a*	क ... ... *k*	ठ ... ... *ṭh*	ब ... ... *b*
आ ... ... *ā*	ख ... ... *kh*	ड ... ... *ḍ*	भ ... ... *bh*
इ ... ... *i*	ग ... ... *g*	ढ ... ... *ḍh*	म ... ... *m*
ई ... ... *ī*	घ ... ... *gh*	ण ... ... *ṇ*	य ... ... *y*
उ ... ... *u*	ङ ... ... *ṅ*	त ... ... *t*	र ... ... *r*
ऊ ... ... *ū*	च ... ... *c*	थ ... ... *th*	ल ... ... *l*
ऋ ... ... *ṛ*	छ ... ... *ch*	द ... ... *d*	व ... ... *v*
ए ... ... *e*	ज ... ... *j*	ध ... ... *dh*	श ... ... *ś*
ऐ ... ... *ai*	झ ... ... *jh*	न ... ... *n*	ष ... ... *ṣ*
ओ ... ... *o*	ञ ... ... *ñ*	प ... ... *p*	स ... ... *s*
औ ... ... *au*	ट ... ... *ṭ*	फ ... ... *ph*	ह ... ... *h*

ं (*anusvāra*) *ṁ*, : (*visarga*) *aḥ*, क्ष............*kṣ*, ज्ञ............*jñ*

ऽ (*avagraha*) ... ... ’

THE NUMBER OF VERSES ATTRIBUTED TO THE VARIOUS CHARACTERS FIGURING IN THE GĪTĀ IN ORDER OF ĀDHYĀYAS.

Chapter.	Dhṛtarāṣṭra.	Sañjaya.	Ārjuna.	Lord Śrī Kṛṣṇa.	Total No.
I ...	1	25	21	...	47
II ...	...	3	6	63	72
III ...	...	...	3	40	43
IV ...	...	..	1	41	42
V ...	...	...	1	28	29
VI ...	...	...	5	42	47
VII ...	...	...	...	30	30
VIII ...	...	...	2	26	28
IX ...	...	...	...	34	34
X ...	...	...	7	35	42
XI ...	...	8	33	14	55
XII ...	...	...	1	19	20
XIII ...	...	...	...	34	34
XIV ...	...	...	1	26	27
XV ...	...	...	...	20	20
XVI ...	...	...	...	24	24
XVII ...	...	...	1	27	28
XVIII ...	...	5	2	71	78
	1	41	84	574	700

The Pictorial map of the Prominent Schools of Indian Philosophy

Designed by:— R. B. TILAK

(Copyright)

EXPLANATION OF THE PICTORIAL MAP OF THE PROMINENT SCHOOLS OF INDIAN PHILOSOPHY mentioned in the GĪTĀ-RAHASYA.

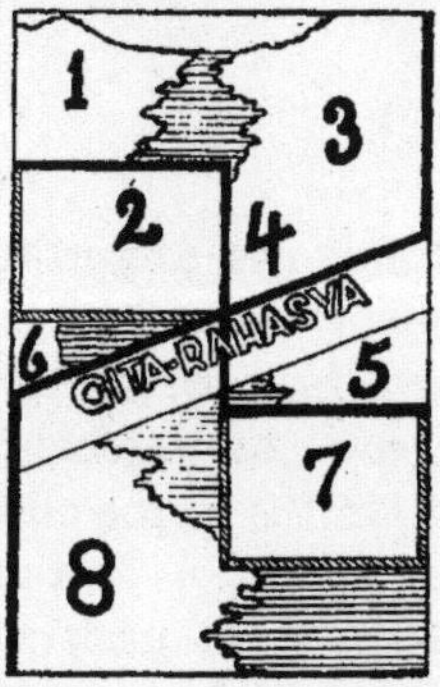

The river is the River of Time, on the banks which are the various Ages through which India has passed, namely, (1) the Vedic Age, (2) the Age of the Gita, (3) the Age of Buddha, (4) the Age of Shri Shankaracharya, (5) the Age Dnyaneshvara, Tukarama and others being the Age of Devotion, (6) the Age of Shri Samartha Ramadasa, showing the revival of Action, and (7) the deputation of Indian Leaders at the gates of the Houses of Parliament and (8) Mahatma Gandhi, in the Present Age.

Nos. 1, 2, 6, 7 and 8 are the Ages of Action, or of Karma-Yoga starting with the Vedic Karma age, and ending with the present days, and forming a big L, which means the Lucky Ages ; whereas Nos. 3, 4 and 5 are the Ages of Renunciation, which are only a small passing cloud on the Karma-Yoga tradition of India.

The narrow bed of the river in the Ages of Renunciation, spreads out as it flows down along the plains of the Ages of Action, suggesting the widening out of the view-point of Philosophy from the narrow Pass of Renunciation to the broad Fields of Action.

The two inset pictures in the form of the 'Svastika' show the five Pandavas on the Kuru field, and the five Indian leaders near the Houses of Parliament, in each case, on the Field of Action. The last picture is of Mahatma Gandhi, the latest Karma-Yogin of India.

R. B. TILAK.

AUTHOR'S DEDICATION.

(IN SANSKRIT VERSE)

How very profound is the importance of the Gītā, which was expounded in ancient times by wise men, and which was further explained in various ways by Ācārayas, and how limited is the scope of my intelligence? Still, I am impelled by my rashness to explain the same once more, keeping before my eyes the old Śāstras as well as notable modern ideas; and honourable people desiring to understand what is doable and what not-doable, deserve to hear this (new) explanation. Having made this request to revered persons in the sweet words of Kālidāsa, I, a Brahmin, (by name) Bāla, the son of Gangādhara, born in the family of Tilaka, belonging to the clan (*gotra*) of the Ṛṣi Śāṇḍilya, and a resident of the town of Poona, situate in the Mahārāṣṭra, following the path of the Good, and with the words of Hari * in my mind, do dedicate this work to the Lord of Lakṣmī, the Soul of the World, in the Śalivāhana Śaka 1837. May the Blessed Lord, the Highest Puruṣa, be pleased by this dedication.

---

* "Whatever you do, or eat, or offer by way of sacrifice, or give, or perform by way of austerity, dedicate all that to Me, O, son of Kunti".

(Gītā 9. 27).

।। श्री गणेशाय नमः ।।

GĪTĀ-RAHASYA OR KARMA-YOGA

॥ श्री गणेशाय नमः ॥

PART I.—THE GĪTĀ AND THE MAHĀBHĀRATA.

The statement made by me above that the Gītā, which supports Action, has been included in the Mahābhārata for sufficient reasons, and at a proper place, for morally justifying the lives of great persons like Śrī Kṛṣṇa, and that it must have been a part of the Mahābhārata, is fully confirmed if one considers the construction of these two books. But before entering into such a comparison, it is necessary to briefly consider the present form of these two books. Śrīmat Śaṁkarācārya has stated at the very outset in his commentary on the Gītā, that there are 700 stanzas in the Gītā; and we find the same number of stanzas in all the available editions of the book. Out of these 700 stanzas, there is one stanza of Dhṛtarāṣṭra, 40 of Sañjaya, 84 of Arjuna, and 575 of the Blessed Lord. But the Gītā-Mahātmya (Eminence of the

Gītā) of five and a half stanzas at the commencement of that chapter of the Bhīṣmaparva, which comes after the eighteen chapters of the Gītā are over, that is, of the 43rd chapter of the Bhīṣmaparva, in the edition of the Mahābhārata published at the Ganpat Krishnaji Press at Bombay, it is stated that :–

ṣaṭśatāni saviṁśāni ślokānāṁ prāha keśavaḥ ।
arjunaḥ saptapañcāśat saptaṣaṣṭiṁ tu sañjayaḥ ।
dhṛtarāṣṭraḥ ślokam ekaṁ gītāyā mānam ucyate ॥

that is : "In the Gītā, there are 620 stanzas of Keśava, 57 of Arjuna, 67 of Sañjaya, and 1 of Dhṛtarāṣṭra", in all 745 stanzas. These stanzas are to be found in the edition of the Mahābhārata printed by Mr. Krishnacarya, according to the reading adopted in the Madras Presidency ; but we do not find them in the edition of the Mahābhārata printed in Calcutta ; and Nilakantha, who has written a commentary on the Bhārata, has said with reference to these five and a half verses, that "*gauḍaiḥ na paṭhyante*" (i.e., "they are not to be found in the Gauda, that is, Bengali, reading"—Trans.). It would, therefore, appear that these five and a half stanzas have been interpolated into the Mahābhārata ; but even if these five and a half stanzas are considered an interpolation, yet, it is not possible to say how these 45 stanzas, which are in excess of the stanzas of the Gītā which are now available, were obtained by anybody. As the Mahābhārata is a very extensive treatise, it is possible to interpolate stanzas into it, or to take away existing stanzas ; but the same is not the case with the Gītā. The Gītā was a text in daily recital, and there were formerly many people and there are still some people, who can repeat the whole of the Gītā by heart in the same way as the Vedas. We do not come across many variant readings in the present Gītā, and that is why the few variant readings which exist are well-known to the commentators. Nay, it may even be said that the Gītā has been made to contain exactly 700 stanzas, in order that nobody should be in a position to add to or take away from that number ; then, how have 45 stanzas—and those too of the Blessed Lord—been included in the Gītā in the Bombay and the Madras editions of the Mahābhārata ? The total number of stanzas attributed to Sañjaya and Arjuna is the same according to this arrangement, as in the present available editions of the Gītā, namely, one hundred and twenty-four; and as there is a likelihood of ten other stanzas being attributed to Sañjaya, on account of difference of opinion, just as the seventeen stanzas "*paśyāmi devān*", etc., in the eleventh chapter (11. 15-31) have been so attributed, one can say that although the total of the stanzas attributed to Sañjaya and Arjuna may be the same, there might have been a difference in counting the respective stanzas attributed to Arjuna and Sañjaya. But, one cannot account for the 45 additional stanzas, that is, for 620, instead of the now available 575 stanzas attributed to the Blessed Lord. If it is said that a praise (*stotra*) or 'a description for purposes of meditation' (*dhyāna*) of the Gītā or some other similar subject has been included in this chapter, then, not only is such subject-matter not to be found in the Bombay edition of the Bhārata, but that edition has a Gītā of only 700 stanzas. Therefore, there is no alternative except to take as authoritative the present Gītā of 700 stanzas. This disposes of the Gītā. But if one considers the Mahābhārata, the difference in the matter of the Gītā is as nothing. There is a statement in the Mahābhārata itself that it contains a hundred thousand stanzas; but we do not come across that number of stanzas in the now available editions of the Mahābhārata, and the number of chapters in the various Parvas is also not according to the index given in the beginning of the Bhārata, as has been clearly proved by Rao Bahadur Chintamanrao Vaidya in his criticism on the Bhārata. In these circumstances, one has to take in hand only certain definite editions of these two treatises for purpose of comparison; and therefore, I have compared them by taking as authoritative the Gītā of 700 stanzas, which was accepted as authoritative by Śrīmat Śaṁkarācārya, and the edition of the Mahābhārata printed in Calcutta by Babu Pratapchandra Roy; and the references in this book to the stanzas quoted from the Mahābhārata are according to the above-mentioned edition of the Mahābhārata printed at Calcutta. If these verses have to be referred to in the editions printed by Krishnacharya according to the Bombay or Madras readings, they will be found either in advance of or subsequent to the place mentioned by me.

If one compares the Gītā of 700 stanzas and the edition of the Mahābhārata printed by Babu Pratapchandra Roy at Calcutta, it will firstly be seen that it is stated in many places in the Mahābhārata itself that the Bhagavadgītā is a part of the Mahābhārata. The first of these references is in the index given in the second chapter of the Ādiparva. There is first a statement, where the various Parvas have been described, that "*pūrvoktaṁ bhagavadgītāparva bhīṣmavadhas tataḥ*" (Ma. Bhā. Ā. 2. 69); and afterwards in enumerating the chapters and the stanzas in the 18 parvas, there is a clear reference to the Bhagavadgītā in the description of Bhīṣmaparva as :—

kaśmalaṁ yatra pārthasya vāsudevo mahāmatiḥ ।
mohajaṁ nāśayāmāsa hetubhir mokṣadarśibhiḥ ॥

that is, "in which treatise, Vāsudeva has removed the dejection of Arjuna, due to Ignorance, by showing him the Path which leads to Release". In the same way, in the first chapter of the Ādiparva, where Dhrtarāṣṭra is explaining his growing despair regarding the success of Duryodhana and others, starting each stanza with the words "*yadā śrauṣaṁ*", it is stated that "when Arjuna became confused, and Kṛṣṇa showed to him His Cosmic Form, I despaired of victory" (Ma. Bhā. Ā. 1. 179). After these three references in the Ādiparva, it again became necessary to refer to the Gītā in describing the Nārāyaṇīya religion at the end of the Śāntiparva. The four names Nārāyaṇīya, Sātvata, Ekāntika, and Bhāgavata are synonymous; and this chapter explains the devotional energistic path preached by Ṛṣi Nārāyaṇa or by the Blessed Lord to Nārada in the Śvetadvīpa. (Śān. 334. 351). The underlying principle of this Bhāgavata religion is, that by worshipping Vāsudeva in solitude, and by carrying on one's duties in the world according to one's religion, one attains Release; and I have already shown in previous chapters that it has also been maintained in the Bhagavadgītā, that the Karma-Yoga is superior to the Path of Renunciation. In describing the tradition of this Nārāyaṇīya doctrine, Vaiśaṁpāyana says to Janamejaya that this doctrine had been preached to Nārada by Nārāyaṇa Himself, and that the same doctrine has been "*kāthito* HARIGĪTĀSU *samāsavidhi kalpataḥ*" (Ma. Bhā. Śān. 346. 10), i. e., "mentioned in the Harigītā or the Bhagavadgītā". It is also stated later on in the eighth stanza of the 348th chapter, that:

samupoḍhe ṣvanīkeṣu kurupāṇḍavayor mṛdhe ।
arjune vimanske ca gītā bhagavatā svayaṁ ॥

that is, "these rites of the solitudinal (*ekāntika*) Nārāyāṇīya doctrine, were taught by the Blessed Lord to the dejected Arjuna on the occasion of the war between the Kauravas and the Pāṇḍavas"; and the tradition of the Nārāyaṇīya doctrine in that war has been given there; and it is again stated that this path, as also the path of ascetics, that is, the Path of Renunciation, have both been mentioned in the HARIGĪTĀ (Ma. Bhā. Śān. 348. 53). Besides these six references in the Ādiparva and the Śāntiparva, there is also one more reference to the Bhagavadgītā in the Anugītāparva included in the Aśvamedhaparva. Some days after the Bhāratī war was over, and Yudhiṣṭhira had been placed on the throne, when Śrī Kṛṣṇa and Arjuna were one day sitting together, and Śrī Kṛṣṇa had said to Arjuna: "It is no more necessary for me to stay here; I wish to go to Dvārakā", Arjuna said to Him, that he had forgotten what Śrī Kṛṣṇa had preached at the commencement of the war, and requested Him to preach the same thing again (Aśva. 16). Then, to satisfy this request, Śrī Kṛṣṇa preached the Anugītā to Arjuna before going to Dvārakā. In the beginning of this Anugītā, the Blessed Lord has Himself said that: "It is your misfortune that you have forgotten the advice which I gave to you in the commencement of the war. It is impossible for Me to repeat the same advice in the same way again, and therefore I will tell you instead something else" (Ma. Bhā. Aśva. Anugītā 16. 9-13); and some of the chapters of the Anugītā are similar to those of the Gītā. The Gītā has thus been referred to SEVEN times in the Mahābhārata, including this reference. Therefore, it follows from the intrinsic evidence in the Mahābhārata itself, that the Bhagavadgītā is a part of the present Mahābhārata.

But, as the course of doubts is uncontrolled, some persons are not satisfied even by these seven references, and they inquire why it may not be said that these references were themselves also interpolated into the Mahābhārata afterwards; and thus their doubt as to whether or not the Gītā was a part of the Mahābhārata still remains. This doubt has its origin in the idea that the Gītā deals only with the Knowledge of the Brahman. But, as I have already shown that this idea itself is incorrect, this doubt should, strictly speaking, not remain. Nevertheless, instead of depending solely on this evidence, I shall now show, by reference to other evidence also, that this doubt is unfounded. When there is a doubt whether or not two works were written by one and the same author, literary critics consider two matters in the first place, namely, SIMILARITY OF DICTION and SIMILARITY OF MEANING. Out of these, similarity of diction includes not only the words themselves, but also the composition. Considering the matter from this point of view, one must see to what extent the diction of the Gītā is similar to the diction of the Mahābhārata. But as the Mahābhārata is a very extensive work, the diction in it varies according to the occasion. For instance, if one refers to the description of the fight between Karṇa and Arjuna in the Karṇaparva, it will be seen that the diction in this *parva* is different from the diction of the other parts of the Mahābhārata. Therefore, it is difficult to definitely say whether or not the language of the Gītā is similar to the language of the Mahābhārata. But if one considers the matter in a general way, then, as Mr. Kashinath Trimbak Telang* says, the language and the metrical arrangement of the Gītā is archaic *(ārṣa)* or ancient. For instance, Kashinathpant has shown that the meanings in which the words '*anta*' (Gī. 2. 16), '*bhāṣā*' (Gī. 2. 54), 'Brahma' (=*prakṛti*. Gī. 14. 3), 'Yoga' (=Karma-Yoga), and the consonant '*ha*' used for completing the meter (Gī. 2.9) etc. have been used

* The translation of the Bhagavadgītā made by the late Mr. Kasinath Trimbak Telang, has been published in the Sacred Books of the East Series Vol. VIII, edited by Prof. Max Müller. To this translation, a critical dissertation has been added by him by way of introduction in the English language. The references made to the opinions of the late Mr. Telang in this Appendix are (with one exception) to this introduction.

in the Gītā, do not appear to have been used in the same sense in the poems of Kālidāsa etc.; and we come across the form "*namaskṛtvā*" in stanza 11. 35, and a compound like "*śakya ahaṁ*" in stanza 11. 45, though as variant readings, which are contrary to the grammar of Pāṇini. Also in the phrase "*senānīnām ahaṁ skandaḥ*" (Gī. 10. 24), the sixth case (possessive) form "*senānīnām*" is not correct according to Pāṇini. The late Mr. Telang has not given detailed illustrations of archaic metrical construction. But I think that he has called the metrical arrangement of the Gītā 'archaic' (*ārṣa*) with special reference to the 36 stanzas in the eleventh chapter, which contain the description of the Cosmic Form (Gī. 11. 15–50). In each stanza, out of these 36, there are eleven letters to a line. But there is no meter which is consistently followed, and we find that if one line is in the *indravajrā* meter, the second is in the *upendravajrā*, the third in the *śālinī*, and the fourth one in a different meter altogether; and there are thus eleven different meters to be found in these 36 verses, that is, 144 lines. Nevertheless, each line contains only eleven letters, and the rule seems to be followed that the first, fourth, eighth and the last two letters are long (*guru*) and the sixth one is usually short (*laghu*); and therefore, an inference may be drawn that these stanzas have been written in the *triṣṭupa* metre used in the Ṛg-Veda or in the Upaniṣads. We do not come across odd-numbered meters of eleven letters to a line like this in any poem of Kālidāsa. In the *Śākuntala*, the stanza: "*amī vediṁ paritaḥ kḷptadhiṣṇyāḥ*" is in this meter. But Kālidāsa himself has described this meter as 'Ṛk.-chanda' that is, a meter used in the Ṛg-Veda. From this it is clear that the Gītā was written when archaic meters were in vogue. We come across similar archaic words and Vedic metres in other places in the Mahābhārata. But another convincing proof of the similarity of diction of the two books is the similar stanzas to be found in the Mahābhārata and in the Gītā. Examining all these stanzas in the Mahābhārata and ascertaining correctly how many of them are to be found in the Gītā is a very difficult task. Yet, in reading the Mahābhārata, I found stanzas in it which are either word for word similar to the stanzas in the Gītā, or are similar but with slight verbal alterations, and these are not a few in number. This easily solves the question of the similarity of language or diction. We find the following stanzas or semi–stanzas either word for word the same or with only one or two words different in the Gītā and in the Mahābhārata (Calcutta edition):—

GĪTĀ.	MAHĀBHĀRATA.
1. 9, *nānā śāstra praharaṇā* etc. (semi-stanza).	Bhīṣma-parva 51. 4. As in the Gītā, Duryodhana is again describing his army to Droṇācārya.
1. 10, *aparyāptaṁ* etc. (whole stanza)	Bhīṣma. 51. 6.
1. 12-19, (Eight stanzas)	Bhīṣma. 51. 22-29. The stanzas are just the same as in the Gītā, with slight verbal alterations.
1. 45, *aho bata mahatpāpaṁ* etc. (whole stanza)	Droṇa. 197. 50. Same as in the Gītā, with slight verbal alterations.
2. 19, *ubhau tau na vijānītaḥ* etc. (semi-stanza)	Śānti. 224. 14. In the Balivāsava-saṁvāda, with verbal alterations ; and in the Kaṭhopaniṣad (2. 18).
2. 28, *avyaktādīni bhūtāni* etc. (whole stanza)	Strī. 2. 6 ; 9. 11. Instead of '*avyakta*', the word '*abhāva*' is used ; rest is the same.
2. 31, *dharmyāddhi yuddhāc chreyo* etc. (semi-stanza)	Bhīṣma. 124. 36. Bhīṣma says the same words to Karṇa.
2. 32, *yad dṛcchayā* etc. (whole stanza)	Karṇa. 57. 2. Instead of 'Pārtha', the word 'Karṇa' is used in the conversation between Duryodhana and Karṇa.

2. 46, *yāvān artha udapāne* etc. (whole stanza)	Udyoga. 45. 26. Has appeared with slight verbal alterations in the Sanatsujātīya chapter.
2. 59, *viṣayā vinivartante* etc. (whole stanza)	Śānti. 204. 16. Has appeared word for word in the conversation between Manu and Bṛhaspati.
2. 67, *indriyāṇāṁ hi caratāṁ* etc. (whole stanza)	Vana. 210. 26. Has appeared with slight verbal alterations in the conversation between the Brahmin and the Hunter; and there is also the '*rūpaka*' (simile) of the chariot in the earlier portion.
2. 70, *āpūryamāṇam acala pratiṣṭhāṁ* etc. (whole stanza)	Śānti. 250. 9. Has appeared word for word in the Śukānupraśna.
3. 42, *indriyāṇi paraṇyāhuḥ* etc. (whole stanza)	Śānti. 245. 3 and 247. 2. Has appeared with slight verbal alterations twice in the Śukānupraśna; but this stanza is originally from the Kaṭhopaniṣad (Kaṭha. 3. 10).
4. 7, *yadā yadā hi dharmasya* etc. (semi-stanza)	Vana. 189. 27. Has appeared word for word in the Mārkaṇḍeyapraśna.
4. 31, *nāyaṁ loko 'stya yajña-sya* etc. (semi-stanza)	Śānti. 267. 40. Has appeared in the Gokāpilīya chapter, and the whole chapter deals with the Yajña.
4. 40, *nāyaṁ loko 'sti na paro* etc. (semi-stanza)	Vana. 199. 110. Has appeared word for word in the Mārkaṇḍeya-samasyā-parva.

5. 5, *yat sāṁkhyaiḥ prāpyate sthānaṁ* etc. (whole stanza)	Śānti. 305. 19 and 316. 4. Has appeared in these two places with slight verbal alterations in the conversation between Vasiṣṭha and Karāla and between Yājñavalkya and Janaka, respectively.
5. 18, *vidyā vinaya saṁpanne* etc. (whole stanza)	Śānti. 238. 19. Has appeared word for word in the Śukānupraśna.
6. 5, *ātmaiva hy ātmano bandhuḥ* etc. (semi-stanza and half of the next stanza)	Udyoga. 33. 63, 64. Has appeared word for word in the Viduranīti.
6. 29, *sarvabhūtastham ātmānaṁ* etc. (semi-stanza)	Śānti. 238. 21. In the Śukānupraśna, and also in the Manu-Smṛti (Manu.12.91), Īśāvāsyopaniṣad (Īśa. 6) and literally in the Kaivalyopaniṣad (Kai. 1. 10).
6. 44, *jijñāsur api yogasya* etc. (semi-stanza)	Śānti. 235. 7. Has appeared with slight verbal alterations in the Śukānupraśna.
8. 17, *sahasra yuga paryantaṁ* etc. This stanza has been given in the Gītā without first explaining what '*yuga*' means.	Śānti. 231. 31. Has appeared literally in the Śukānupraśna; and the method of computation of a '*yuga*' has also been mentioned previously. This has appeared with slight verbal alterations also in the Manu-Smṛti (Manu. 1. 73).
8. 20, *yaḥ sa sarveṣu bhūteṣu* etc. (semi-stanza)	Śānti. 339. 23. Has appeared twice with slight verbal alterations in the Nārāyaṇīya-dharma.

9.	32, *striyo vaiśyās tathā* etc. (whole stanza and half of the next stanza)	Aśva. 19. 61 and 62. These verses have appeared with slight verbal alterations in the Anugītā.
13.	13, *sarvataḥ pāṇipādaṁ* (whole stanza)	Śānti. 238. 29. and Aśvā. 19. 49. This stanza has appeared word for word in the Śukānupraśna and in the Anugītā as also in other places. It is originally from the Śvetāśvataropanisad (Śve. 3. 16).
13.	30, *yada bhūta pṛthag bhāvaṁ* etc. (whole stanza)	Śānti. 17. 23. The same words have been addressed by Yudhiṣṭhira to Arjuna.
14.	18, *ūrdhvaṁ gacchanti satvasthā* etc. (whole stanza)	Aśva. 39. 10 This stanza has appeared word for word in the conversation between the disciple and the preceptor in the Anugītā.
16.	21, *trividhaṁ narakasy edaṁ* etc. (whole stanza)	Udyoga. 32. 70. Has appeared word for word in the Viduranīti.
17.	3, *śraddhāmayo yaṁ puruṣaḥ* etc.. (semi-stanza)	Śānti. 263. 17. Has appeared in the portion on Devotion in the conversation between Tulādhāra and Jājali.
18.	14, *adhisthānaṁ tathā kartā* etc. (whole stanza)	Śānti. 347. 87. Has appeared word for word in the Nārāyaṇīya-dharma.

In this way, it is seen that 27 whole stanzas and 12 semi-stanzas appear sometimes word for word the same, and sometimes with slight verbal differences both in the Mahābhārata and in the Gītā; and if a more thorough examination is made, there is a likelihood that one may come across many other stanzas and semi-stanzas which are common to both. If one wishes to see in how many places there are common combinations of two words or three words, or of quarter portions of a stanza, which are common to the Mahābhārata and to the Gītā, the above-mentioned list will have to be considerably increased*. But, if we leave aside the similarity of words, and consider merely the question of similarity of stanzas in the above list, we cannot but say that the Mahābhārata and the Gītā must have been written by the same hand. Considering the matter with reference to the different chapters, we see that out of the above-mentioned 33 stanzas, 1 comes in the Mārkaṇḍeya-praśna, ½ in the Mārkaṇḍeya-samasyā, 1 in the Brahmin-Hunter conversation, 2 in the Viduranīti, 1 in the Sanātsujātīya, 1 in the Manu-Bṛhaspati conversation, 6½ in the Śukānu-praśna, 1 the Tulādhāra-Jājali conversation, 1 in the Vasiṣṭha-Karāla and Yājñavalkya-Janaka conversation, 1½ in the Nārāyaṇīya-dharma, 2½ in the Anugītā, and the rest in the Bhīṣma, Droṇa, Karṇa, and Strī parvas; and in almost all these places, these stanzas have come at proper places with reference to the anterior and posterior contexts and are not interpolations. Nay, some of these stanzas seem to have been taken into the Gītā by way of summarising. For instance, in order to understand the stanza "*sahasra yuga paryantaṁ*" etc. (Gī. 8. 17), it would have been necessary to define the words '*varṣa*' and '*yuga*'; and in the Bhārata (Śān. 231) and the Manu-Smṛti, this stanza has been given after first defining these words. But in the Gītā, this stanza has been mentioned without defining '*yuga*'

* If one considers the whole of the Mahābhārata from this point of view, there will be at least a hundred similar portions of stanzas; but I will mention only a few out of them here: *kiṁ bhogair jīvitena vā* (Gī. 1. 32); *naitat vay upapadyate* (Gī. 2. 3); *trāyate mahato bhayāt* (2. 40); *aśāntasya kutaḥ sukhaṁ* (2. 66); *utsīdeyur ime lokāḥ* (3. 24); *mano durnigrahaṁ calaṁ* (6. 35); *mam ātmā bhūtabhāvanaḥ* (9. 5); *moghāśā mogha karmāṇaḥ* (9. 12); *samaḥ sarveṣu bhūteṣu* (9. 29); *dīptánalārkadyutiṁ* etc. (11. 17); *sarva bhūtahite ratāḥ* (12. 4); *tulya nindā stutiḥ* (12. 19); *saṁtuṣṭo yena kenacit* (12. 19); *samaloṣṭaśma kāṁcanaḥ* (14. 24); *trividhā karmacodanā* (18. 18); *nirmamaḥ śāntaḥ* (18. 53); *brahmabhūyāya kalpate* (18. 53); etc., etc.,

etc. Considering the matter from this point of view, it cannot be said that these stanzas could have been adopted from the Gītā into the various chapters of the Mahābhārata ; and it is improbable that all these stanzas have been taken into the Gītā from all those various chapters. Therefore, one is bound to come to the conclusion that the writer of the Gītā must have been the same as the person who wrote these chapters. I must also mention here that, just as, many stanzas from the Manu-Smṛti find their way into the Mahābhārata, * so also can we trace to the Manu-Smṛti, the whole of the stanza "*sahasra yuga paryantaṁ*" (8. 17) in the Gītā, with slight verbal alterations; and the semi-stanza "*śreyān svadharmo viguṇaḥ paradharmāt svanuṣṭhitāt*" (Gī. 3. 35 and Gī. 18. 47) with the alteration that instead of '*śreyān*', the word '*varaṁ*' has been used; and the semi-stanza "*sarva bhūtastham ātmānaṁ*" (Gī. 6. 29), with the variation "*sarva bhūteṣu cātmanaṁ*" (Manu. 1. 73; 10. 97; 12. 91). In the Anuśāsanaparva of the Mahābhārata, there is even a clear reference to the Manu-Smṛti in the words "*manunā bhihitaṁ śāstraṁ*" (Anu. 47. 35).

If instead of considering the similarity of words, one considers the similarity of meaning, the same conclusion is fortified. I have in previous chapters shown the similarity between the Karma-Yoga of the Gītā and the Energistic Bhāgvata or Nārāyaṇīya religion. It is true that the genesis of Saṁkarṣaṇa from Vāsudeva, Pradyumna from Saṁkarṣaṇa, Aniruddha from Pradyumna, and Brahmadeva from Aniruddha, being the genesis of the visible world mentioned in the Nārāyaṇīya-dharma (Śān. 339. 71, 72) has not been adopted into the Gītā. There are besides other differences between the religion of the Gītā and the Nārāyaṇīya religion. But, although the idea of the four-fold *(catur-vyūha)* Parameśvara is not accepted by the Gītā, yet, if one considers the propositions of the Gītā that, (i) the devotion to the singular (*eka-vyūha*), Vāsudeva is the 'king of paths'; that (ii) whatever other deities are worshipped, that amounts to the worship of Vāsudeva;

* Prof. Bühler has, in his translation of the Manu-Smṛti, published in the Sacred Books of the East Series (Vol. XXV, pp. 533, et *seq.*), included a list of the stanzas from the Manu-Smṛti which are to be found in the Mahābhārata.

that (iii) devotees are of four kinds; that (iv) devotees of the Blessed Lord must perform their duties according to their religion, and keep going the cycle of Yajñas; and that (v) it is not proper to take to Renunciation (*saṁnyāsa*) etc., one comes to the conclusion that the Gītā religion is the same as the Bhāgavata religion; and as I have stated before, the tradition of Vivasvān-Manu-Ikṣvāku is common to both. In the same way, the Vedānta or the Spiritual Knowledge expounded in the Gītā is consistent with the Knowledge of the Brahman as mentioned in the Sanatsujātīya, the Śukānu-praśna, the Yājñavalkya-Janaka conversation, or the Anugītā, as will be appreciated by any one who reads those chapters. Just as the Gītā, while accepting the 25 Fundamental Elements of Kāpila-Sāṁkhya philosophy, and the doctrine of the efflorescence of the constituents (*guṇotkarṣa*), yet accepts as Eternal, a further Element beyond Prakṛti (Matter) and Puruṣa (Spirit), so also has it been maintained in detail, in the Vasiṣṭha-Karāla-Janaka conversation, and in the Yājñavalkya-Janaka conversation in the Śāntiparva that there is a '26th' Element beyond the 25 Elements, and that one does not obtain Isolation (*kaivalya*) unless one has acquired the Knowledge of that '26th' Element. It is not that this similarity of thought appears only with reference to Karma-Yoga and Spiritual Knowledge; but there are many chapters to be found in the Mahābhārata which correspond with the other subsidiary subjects in the Gītā. For instance, in the beginning of the first chapter of the Gītā, Duryodhana has described both the armies to Droṇācārya, and he has again given the same description later on in the 51st chapter of the Bhīṣmaparva to Droṇācārya. There is in the beginning of the Śāntiparva, a dejection expressed by Yudhiṣṭhira, which is similar to the dejection experienced by Arjuna in the latter part of the first chapter of the Gītā; and when there was occasion to kill Bhīṣma and Droṇa by 'Yoga', Arjuna has again uttered similar words of dejection (Bhīṣma. 97. 4-7 and 108. 88-94). Arjuna has said in the beginning of the Gītā that it was no use obtaining victory if he were to kill those very persons for whom that happiness was to be acquired (Gī. 1. 32, 33); and later on, after all the Kauravas had been killed in the war, Duryodhana has given expression to the same sentiment (Salya. 31. 42–51). As in the beginning of the second chapter, two different paths, namely, the Sāṁkhya and the Karma-Yoga have been mentioned, so also have two paths been described not only in the Nārāyaṇīya-dharma, but also in the Jāpakopākhyāna, and the Janaka-Sulabhā conversation in the Śāntiparva (Śān. 196 and 320); and the ideas expressed in the third chapter that Karma (Action) is superior to *akarma* (Inaction), and that if one does not perform Action, he will not find even food to eat, are expressed in the beginning of the Vanaparva by Draupadī to Yudhiṣṭhira (Vana. 32); and the same ideas have been repeated again in the Anugītā. The idea that Brahmadeva created the Yajña and human beings at the same time etc., which appear in the Gītā, appear also in other places in the Śāntiparva, besides in the descriptions of the Nārāyaṇīya religion (Śān. 267), and also in the Manu-Smṛti; and the idea that there is no sin in performing Action according to one's own religious duties, has also appeared in the Tulādhāra-Jājali conversation, and in the Brahmin-Hunter conversation (Śān. 260–263 and Vana. 206–215). Besides this, the little information which the Gītā contains regarding the creation of the Cosmos, in the seventh and eighth chapters, is similar to the description of such creation given in the Śukānupraśna in the Śāntiparva (Śān. 231); and the information regarding the various physical postures (*āsana*) prescribed in the Pātañjala-Yoga, which appears in the sixth chapter of the Gītā is again repeated in detail in the Śukānupraśna (Śān. 239), and later on in the 300th chapter of the Śāntiparva and also in the Anugītā (Aśva. 19). The description of ordinary and best things given in the conversation between the preceptor and the disciple (Aśva. 43 and 44), and the description of the manifestations of the Blessed Lord given in the tenth chapter of the Gītā, may without the slightest doubt be said to be exactly the same in meaning. It is stated in the Mahābhārata that the Cosmic Form which was shown by the Blessed Lord to Arjuna, was also shown by Him to Duryodhana and others at the time of previous conciliatory efforts, and to Uttanka, after the war was over, when Śrī Kṛṣṇa was going back to Dvārakā; and also that it was shown by Nārāyaṇa to Nārada, and by Dāśarathī Rāma to Paraśurāma. (U. 130; Aśva. 55; Śān. 339; Vana. 99). It is true that the description of the Cosmic Form given in the Gītā, is more detailed and beautiful than the descriptions in all these four places; but considering the matter from the point of view of similarity of subject, there is nothing new in the description in the Gītā, as will be clearly seen by anybody who reads these various descriptions. There are to be found descriptions in the Anugītā (Aśva. 36-39), and also in other places in the Śāntiparva (Śān. 285; and 300–311) as to how diversity comes into being in the world as a result of the *sattva*, *rajas*, and *tamas* constituents, what the characteristic features of these constituents are, and how all the activity is of these constituents and not of the Ātman, which are similar to the descriptions in the 14th and 15th chapters of the Gītā. In short, although the description of certain things given in the Gītā may be more exhaustive, having regard to the occasion where it appears in the Gītā, and although the arrangement of those various subjects may also be different in the Gītā, yet, we come across ideas in the Mahābhārata which are more or less the same as those in the Gītā, but are spread out in some place or other; and I need not say that with this similarity of ideas, there is also to some extent a similarity of diction. The similarity in the matter of the month of Mārgaśīrsa is indeed astounding. As this month has been given primary importance in the Gītā, as is shown by the words "*māsānāṁ mārgaśīrṣo 'ham*" (Gī. 10. 35), so also, where there was twice occasion to mention the names of months with reference to fasting in the Anuśāsanaparva of the Mahābhārata, the counting of the months has been started with Mārgaśīrṣa (Anu. 106 and 109). The ideas of Self-Identification, or of universal good, as also the difference between the Materialistic, Intuitionist, and Metaphysical aspects, and the description of the Devayāna and the Pitṛyāṇa paths taken after death, which appear in the Gītā, have also appeared several times in the Mahābhārata; but as this has been dealt with in great detail in the previous chapters, I shall not repeat the same subject-matter here.

Whether one considers the similarity of diction, or the similarity of subject-matter, or the six or seven references to the Gītā, which we find in the Mahābhārata, one cannot but come to the conclusion that the Gītā is a part of the Mahābhārata, and that the same man who wrote the Mahābhārata as it now exists, must also have written the Gītā as it now exists. But, I have seen people attempting to disregard all those proofs, and to dispose of them with scant respect in some way or other, and to prove that the Gītā is an interpolation. But, in my opinion, the line of reasoning adopted by these critics, who treat external evidence as no evidence, and who yield to the domination of the demon of doubt in their hearts, is illogical, and therefore, unacceptable. If it could not be reasonably explained why the Gītā should be a part of the Mahābhārata, it would be a different matter. But, when it is proved, as has been stated in the beginning of this Appendix, that (i) the Gītā is not a purely devotional treatise, or one which deals purely with Vedānta; that (ii) it was necessary to preach the Activistic Gītā, in order to explain the principles of Morality, or the undercurrents which guided the lives of exemplary great men, as described in the Mahābhārata, and that (iii) there was no better place, even from the poetic view-point, for placing the Gītā, than the place in which it appears in the Mahābhārata, one comes to the necessary conclusion that the Gītā has been included for proper reasons and at the proper place in the Mahābhārata, and that it is not an interpolation. The Rāmāyaṇa is also an excellent and a universally respected archaic epic like the Mahābhārata; and in it also the principles of veracity, filial duty, maternal duty, regal duty etc., have been cleverly explained with reference to the various incidents in it. But, as it was not the original intention of Vālmīki to make that epic "replete with many incidents, full of numerous doctrines regarding Morality and Immorality, and capable of giving to everybody exemplary illustrations of properly moral lives", it goes without saying that the importance of the Mahābhārata is greater than that of the Rāmāyaṇa, from the point of view of the decisions contained in them respectively with reference to Morality and

Immorality, the Doable and the Not-Doable, and Ethics. The Mahābhārata is not merely an epic or merely a history, but it is a Saṁhitā (summary) dealing with delicate situations of Duty and Non-Duty; and if such a religious epitome does not contain the scientific and logical description of the Philosophy of Karma-Yoga, where else could it come? Such an exposition could certainly not have been included in a treatise which deals merely with Vedānta. An epitome of religion is certainly the most proper place for it; and if the writer of the Mahābhārata had not so included it, this immense book, which deals with religious and moral duties—which is in fact the fifth Veda—would to that extent have remained incomplete. The Bhagavadgītā has been included in the Mahābhārata in order to fill up this gap, and it is our great good fortune that India found an excellent Jñānin and a noble soul like the writer of the Mahābhārata, who was as proficient in worldly affairs as in Vedānta, for sponsoring the subject-matter of Karma-Yoga.

Though it has thus been proved that the present Bhagavadgītā is a part of the present Mahābhārata, yet, this matter must be dealt with in greater detail. We understand the words 'Bhārata' and 'Mahābhārata' as synonymous; but, as a matter of fact, those two works are different from each other. Considering the matter grammatically, any book which would contain a description of the illustrious deeds of the kings of the Bhārata clan could properly be called 'Bhārata'. The etymology of the words 'Rāmāyaṇa' and 'Bhāgavata' is the same; and on that account, any book which contains a description of the Bhāratī war would be sufficiently identified by being called 'Bhārata', however extensive it were. The Rāmāyaṇa is not a small work; then why is it not called 'Mahā-Rāmāyaṇa'?; and why should the Bhārata be called 'Mahā-Bhārata'? It is stated at the end of the Mahābhārata that the work has been given the name 'Mahābhārata' on account of its two features of (i) greatness (*mahatva*) and of (ii) dealing with the Bhārata clan (*bhāratatva*), (Svargā. 5. 44). But if we take the mere literal meaning of the word 'Mahābhārata', it means 'the big Bhārata'; and if this meaning is accepted, the question whether there was a 'small' Bhārata and whether such a small Bhārata did not contain the Gītā, naturally arises. There is a statement in the Ādiparva of the present Mahābhārata, that the Mahābhārata consists of 24000 stanzas, not taking into account the sub-chapters (*upākhyāna*), (Ā. 1. 101); and it is said later on that this was originally known as 'Jaya' (Ā. 62. 20). The word 'Jaya' seems to intend to convey the idea of the 'victory' *(jaya)* of the Pāṇḍavas in the Bhāratī war; and if that meaning is adopted, it will be seen that the book called 'Jaya' originally contained only a description of the Bhāratī war, and that several sub-chapters were added later on to this historical book, so as to make of it the large work known as the 'Mahābhārata', which dealt both with history and with Ethics. This conclusion is fortified by the specific reference to two different works named, 'Bhārata' and 'Mahābhārata', in the incantation relating to oblations to Ṛṣis to be found in the Āśvalāyana-gṛhya-sūtra, which runs as:—"*sumantu-jaimini-vaiśaṁpāyana — paila — sūtra — bhāṣya — bhārata — mahābhārata — dharmācāryāḥ*" (Ā. Gṛ. 3. 4. 4). When the 'little Bhārata' had thus been included in the 'Mahābhārata', the 'little Bhārata' ceased to exist as an independent work, and it was naturally believed that only one work, namely the 'Mahābhārata' was the Bhārata. Even in the present version of the Mahābhārata, there is a statement that the Bhārata was first recited by Vyāsa to his own son Śuka, and afterwards to his other disciples (Ā. 1. 103); and it is clearly stated that the five disciples Sumantu, Jaimini, Paila, Śuka, and Vaiśaṁpāyana wrote five distinct Bhārata-Saṁhitās or Mahābhāratas (Ā. 63. 90); and there is a story that out of these five Mahābhāratas, Vyāsa retained only the Mahābhārata of Vaiśaṁpāyana, and the Aśvamedhaparva out of the Mahābhārata of Jaimini. This explains why the names Sumantu etc., appear before the mention of the words 'Bhārata-Mahābhārata' in the incantation about oblations to Ṛṣis. But it is not necessary to enter so deep so into that subject-matter here. The conclusion which has been drawn by Rao Bahadur Chintamanrao Vaidya in his criticism on the Mahābhārata, after considering this subject-matter, is in my opinion correct; and therefore, it is quite enough if I say here that the present version of the Mahābhārata is not the original Mahābhārata, but that there were various editions of the Bhārata and the Mahābhārata; and that the present Mahābhārata is the form it ultimately acquired. It cannot be said that the first original Bhārata out of these did not contain the Gītā. It is quite clear that the writer of the Mahābhārata has written the present Gītā on the authority of former works, just as the Sanatsujātīya, the Viduranīti, the Śukānupraśna, the Yājñavalkya-Janaka conversation, the Viṣṇu-sahasranāma, the Anugītā, the Nārāyaṇīya-dharma and other chapters were so written, and that it was not written independently. At the same time, it cannot be definitely said that the writer of the Mahābhārata did not make any change in the original Gītā. From what has been stated above, anybody will come to the conclusion that the present Gītā of 700 stanzas is a part of the present Mahābhārata, that both have been compiled by the same hands, and that the present Gītā has not been subsequently interpolated by anybody into the present Mahābhārata. I will say later on what in my opinion is the date of the present Mahābhārata, as also what I have to say regarding the original Gītā.

PART II-THE GĪTĀ AND THE UPANIṢADS.

Let us now consider the inter-relation between the Gītā and the various Upaniṣads. Not only have the various Upaniṣads been generally referred to in the present Mahābhārata, but the description about the warfare between the Vital Organs (*prāṇendriya*) contained in the Bṛhadāraṇyaka and the Chāndogya (Bṛ. 1. 3; Chān. 1. 2) appears in the Anugītā (Aśva. 23); and the words "*na me steno janapade*" etc., uttered by the king Kaikeya Aśvapati (Chān. 5. 11. 15), appear in the Śāntiparva, where the story of that king is related (Śān. 77. 8). Similarly, the principles enunciated in the Bṛhadāraṇyaka, that "*na pretya saṁjñāsti*", i. e., "after death, the Knower (*jñātā*) does not any more possess any name (*saṁjñā*)", and that the Knower is merged in the Brahman (Bṛ. 4. 5. 13) appear in the Śāntiparva in the conversation between Janaka and Pañcaśikha; and in the same place, at the end, the illustration of the river and the sea, which appears in the Praśna and the Muṇḍaka Upaniṣads (Praśna. 6. 5; Muṇ. 3. 2. 8), has been used with reference to the man who has become free from Name and Form. Besides, the comparison of Reason with a charioteer, after comparing the organs with horses, which appears in the conversation between the Brahmin and the Hunter (Vana. 210), and in the Anugītā, has been taken from the Kaṭhopaniṣad (Ka. 1. 3. 3); and the stanzas "*eṣa sarveṣu bhūteṣu gūḍhātmā*" (Kaṭha. 3. 12), and "*anyatra dharmād anyatrādharmāt*" (Kaṭha. 2. 14) also appear with slight verbal alterations in the Śāntiparva (187. 29 and 331. 44). I have already stated above that the stanza "*sarvataḥ pāṇipādaṁ*" etc., from the Śvetāśvatara appears several times in the Mahābhārata, as also in the Gītā. But this similarity does not end here, and there are numerous other sentences from the Upaniṣads, which appear in various places in the Mahābhārata. Nay, we may safely assert that the Spiritual Knowledge in the Mahābhārata has been practically adopted from the Upaniṣads.

Not only is the Spiritual Knowledge contained in the Bhagavadgītā consistent with the Upaniṣads, like the Mahābhārata, but, as has been stated by me in the ninth and the thirteenth chapters above, the Path of Devotion described in the Gītā is also fully consistent with this Spiritual Knowledge. Without, therefore, repeating the same subject-matter, I will only say here in short, that the non-lamentability of the Ātman mentioned in the second chapter of the Gītā, the form of the Imperishable Brahman described in the eighth chapter, the consideration of the Body (*kṣetra*) and the Ātman (*kṣetrajña*) contained in the thirteenth chapter, and especially the form of the 'Knowable' (*jñeya*) Parabrahman described in that chapter, are all subjects which have been literally copied into the Gītā from the Upaniṣads. Some of the Upaniṣads are in prose, whereas others are in verse. Expressions from the prose Upaniṣads cannot, of course, come as they are in the Gītā, which is in verse form; yet, the ideas "whatever is, is; and whatever is not, is not" (Gī. 2. 16), "*yaṁ yaṁ vāpi smaran bhāvaṁ*" etc. (Gī. 8. 6), (i. e., "whatever ideas are entertained in the Mind" etc.—Trans.) etc., which appear in the Gītā, are from the Chāndogyopaniṣad; and the ideas and sentences, "*kṣīṇe puṇye*" etc. (Gī. 9. 21), "*jyotiṣāṁ jyotiḥ*" (Gī. 13. 17), or "*mātrāsparśāḥ*" (Gī. 2. 14) etc., are from the Bṛhadāraṇyakopaniṣad, as will be apparent to anyone who has read those Upaniṣads. But, if one does not consider the prose Upaniṣads, but considers only the Upaniṣads in verse form, this similarity becomes more explicit; because, some verses from these verse-formed Upaniṣads have been taken literally and word for word into the Gītā. For instance, six or seven stanzas from the Kaṭhopaniṣad have been taken as they are, or with slight verbal alterations into the Gītā. The stanza "*āścaryavat paśyati*" etc. (2. 29) in the Gītā is very similar to the stanza "*āścaryo vaktā*" etc., in the second *valli* of the Kaṭhopaniṣad (Kaṭha. 2. 7); and the stanza "*na jāyate mriyate vā kadācit*" etc. (Gī. 2. 20), and the semi-stanza "*yad icchanto brahmacaryaṁ caranti*" etc. (Gī. 8. 11), are word for word the same in the Gītā and in the Kaṭhopaniṣad (Kaṭha. 2. 19; 2. 15). I have already mentioned above that the stanza "*indriyāṇi parāṇyāhuḥ*" (Gī. 3. 42) in the Gītā has been taken from the Kaṭhopaniṣad (Kaṭha. 3. 10). Similarly, the simile of the pippala (*aśvattha*) tree in the fifteenth chapter of the Gītā, has been taken from the Kaṭhopaniṣad; and the stanza "*na tad bhāsayate sūryo*" etc. (Gī. 15. 6), has been adopted into the Gītā with slight verbal alterations from the Kaṭha and the Śvetāśvatara Upaniṣads. Many other ideas and stanzas from the Śvetāśvataropaniṣad find their way into the Gītā. I have shown above in the ninth chapter that the word 'Māyā' appears for the first time in the Śvetāśvataropaniṣad, and that it must have been taken from that place into the Gītā and the Mahābhārata. Besides this, the description of the place proper for the study of Yoga, given in the sixth chapter of the Gītā, namely, "*śucau deśe pratiṣṭhāpya*" etc. (Gī. 6. 11) seems to be taken from the incantation "*same śucau*" etc. (Śve. 2. 10), and the words "*samaṁ kāyaśirogrīvaṁ*" etc. (Gī. 6. 13) seem to have been taken from the incantation "*trir unnataṁ sthāpya samaṁ śarīram*" (Śve. 2. 8), if one considers the similarity of wording between the two. Similarly, the stanza "*sarvataḥ pāṇipādaṁ*" etc. and the following semi-stanza are also seen to be word for word the same both in the Gītā (13. 13) and in the Śvetāśvataropaniṣad (Śve. 3. 16); and the words "*aṇoraṇīyāṁsaṁ*" or "*ādityavarṇaṁ tamasaḥ parastāt*" are also to be found both in the Gītā (8. 9) and the Śvetāśvataropaniṣad (Śve. 3. 9, 20). Further similarity of wording between the Gītā and the Upaniṣads is apparent from the fact that the two semi-stanzas "*sarvabhūtastham ātmānaṁ* (Gī. 6. 29) and "*vedaiś ca sarvair aham eva vedyo*" (Gī. 15. 15) are to be found just as they are in the Kaivalyopaniṣad. But it is not necessary to further point out this similarity of wording. Nobody can entertain the slightest doubt that the Vedānta in the Gītā has been enunciated on the authority of the Upaniṣads. What has to be principally considered is whether there is a difference between the exposition of it in the Upaniṣads and the exposition in the Gītā; and if so, what that difference is. We will, therefore, now turn to that subject-matter.

The Upaniṣads are numerous, and the language of some of them is so modern, that one can clearly see that these Upaniṣads are not of the same date as the older Upaniṣads. Therefore, in considering the similarity of subject-matter between the Gītā and the Upaniṣads, I have principally referred in this chapter, for purposes of comparison, to those Upaniṣads, which are mentioned in the Brahma-Sūtras. If one tries to examine the similarity between the theories in these Upaniṣads and the Spiritual Knowledge in the Gītā, one will see, first of all, that though the characteristic features of the qualityless Parabrahman is the same in both, yet, in describing how the Qualityful came into existence out of the Qualityless, the Gītā uses the words '*māyā*' or '*ajñāna*' instead of the word '*avidyā*'. I have explained above in the ninth chapter that the word '*māyā*' has appeared in the Śvetāśvataropaniṣad, and that this word is synonymous with '*avidyā*' embodied in Names and Forms; and I have shown above that some of the stanzas from the Śvetāśvataropaniṣad appear word for word in the Gītā. The first conclusion to be drawn from this is, that although the doctrine "*sarvaṁ khalv idaṁ brahma*" (Chān. 3. 14. 1), or "*sarvam ātmānaṁ paśyati*" (Bṛ. 4. 4. 23), or "*sarvabhūteṣu cātmānaṁ*" etc. (Īśā. 6), or possibly even the whole of the Spiritual Knowledge in the Upaniṣads has been adopted into the Gītā, yet, it was only after the word '*māyā*' came to be used in the Upaniṣads with reference to Name-d and Form-ed '*avidyā*', that the Gītā has come to be written.

Now, if one considers what difference exists between the respective expositions of Vedānta in the Gītā and the Upaniṣads, one sees that greater importance has been given in the Gītā to the Kāpila-Sāṁkhya philosophy. In the Bṛhadāraṇyaka or the Chāndogya, which deal with Spiritual Knowledge, Sāṁkhya philosophy has not even once been mentioned; and although the words '*avyakta*', '*mahān*' etc. from Sāṁkhya philosophy are found in the Kaṭha and other Upaniṣads, yet, those words are clearly interpreted there according to Vedānta philosophy and not according to Sāṁkhya philosophy; and the same argument applies to the exposition in the Maitryupaniṣad. The idea of boycotting Sāṁkhya philosophy has been carried to such an extent, that the diversity of Names and Forms in the world has been explained in the Vedānta-Sūtras by the 'Trivṛt-karaṇa' (union of three Elements) consistently with the Chāndogya, instead of by reference to the 'Pañcīkaraṇa' (union of five Elements) of Sāṁkhya philosophy (Ve. Sū. 2. 4. 20). Although this method of explaining the Perishable and Imperishable in Metaphysics without the slightest reference to Sāṁkhya philosophy has not been adopted in the Gītā, yet, it must also be borne in mind that Sāṁkhya doctrines have not been taken as they are into the Gītā. The Sāṁkhya doctrine that the visible world came into existence from the three-constituented imperceptible Matter (*prakṛti*) by the process of the 'developing-out of the constituents' (*guṇotkarṣa*), and that the Spirit (*puruṣa*) is qualityless and is the See-er, is accepted by the Gītā. But the Sāṁkhya doctrine regarding the Perishable (*kṣara*) and Imperishable (*akṣara*) has always been mentioned in the Gītā with the rider of the Non-Dualistic Vedānta that Matter (*prakṛti*) and Spirit (*puruṣa*) are not independent Elements, but are the forms or manifestations (*vibhūti*) of one and the same Parabrahman in the shape of the Ātman. This tacking on of the order of creation of the universe according to the Dualistic Sāṁkhya philosophy with the Non-Dualistic doctrines of the Upaniṣads, which looks upon the Brahman and the Ātman as one and the same, is to be found in the exposition of Metaphysics in other places in the Mahābhārata, as in the Gītā; and thereby the inference made above, that the Gītā and the Mahābhārata must have been written by one and the same person, is intensified.

The Path of Devotion or the worship of the Perceptible contained in the exposition in the Gītā is an important matter which is not found in the Upaniṣads. It is true that mere ritualistic performances like Yajñas etc., are considered inferior, from the point of view of Spiritual Knowledge, in the Upaniṣads as also in the Bhagavadgītā; but we do not come across the worship of a perceptible human-formed Parameśvara in the older Upaniṣads. As the Realisation of the imperceptible and qualityless Parabrahman is difficult, the writers of the Upaniṣads admit the principle that one must worship the Mind, Ether, the Sun, Fire, Yajña, and other similar qualityful symbols. But the symbols, which have been mentioned in the ancient Upaniṣads for worship, do not include the human-formed Parameśvara. It is stated in the Maitryupaniṣad that Rudra, Śiva, Viṣṇu, Acyuta, Nārāyaṇa, etc., are all forms of the Paramātman (Mai. 7. 7); and the Śvetāśvataropaniṣad even contains the words 'Maheśvara' etc; and there are also in the Śvetāśvatara such expressions as "*jñātvā devaṁ mucyate sarvapāśaiḥ*" (Śve. 5. 13), (i. e., "by Realising God, all bonds are broken"—Trans.) or, "*yasya deve parā bhaktiḥ*" (Śve. 6. 23). But one cannot definitely say that human-formed incarnations of Nārāyaṇa, Viṣṇu etc; are intended by these expressions; because, the deities Rudra and Viṣṇu are both Vedic, that is, ancient; and it cannot be said that the above-mentioned Upaniṣads did not refer to the ancient sacrificial ritual, which was later on given the form of the worship of Viṣṇu, as shown, by the words "*yajño vai viṣṇuḥ*" (Tai. Saṁ. 1. 7. 4). Nevertheless, if some one says that the idea of human-formed incarnations was conceived in those days, that cannot be said to be improbable; because, the word '*bhakti*' (Devotion) which is to be found in the Śvetāśvataropaniṣad cannot at first sight be properly applied to worship in the shape of a Yajña. As the expressions used in the Mahānārāyaṇa

Nṛsiṁhatāpanī, Rāmatāpanī, or Gopālatāpanī Upaniṣads are clearer than those in the Śvetāśvataropaniṣad, such a doubt can really speaking not arise at all about them. But, as there are no means for definitely fixing the dates of these Upaniṣads, one cannot, with their help, satisfactorily solve the question as to when the worship of the human-formed Viṣṇu came into vogue. Nevertheless, the fact that the Vedic Path of Devotion is very ancient is satisfactorily proved in other ways. The grammarian Pāṇini, after first mentioning in a *sūtra* that the word '*bhaktiḥ*' is to be taken as meaning 'that, towards which Devotion exists' (Pā. 4. 3. 95), says in another *sūtra*, namely, "*vāsudevārjunābhyāṁ bun*" (Pā. 4. 3. 98), that the man who is devoted to Vāsudeva should be called 'Vāsudevaka', and the man who is a devotee of Arjuna should be called 'Arjunaka'; and Patañjali, in commenting on this in his Mahābhāṣya, has said that the word 'Vāsudeva' in this *sūtra* is the name of a Kṣatriya, or of the 'Bhagavanta'. Dr. Bhandarkar has proved that the commentary of Patañjali was written about 250 years before the Christian era; and there is no dispute about the fact that Pāṇini belonged to a much earlier period. Besides, even Buddhistic religious texts contain a reference to Devotion; and I have proved later on in detail that the Bhāgavata religion must have been the cause for principles of Devotion entering into the Buddhistic Mahāyāna cult. Therefore, it is proved beyond doubt that the Path of Devotion was well established in India long before the date of Buddha, that is to say necessarily more than 600 years before the Christian era. The Nārada-Pañcarātra, or the Bhakti-Sūtras written by Śāṇḍilya or Nārada, are later in point of time. But thereby, the ancientness of the Bhāgavata religion, or of the Path of Devotion, is in no way affected. It will be seen from the exposition made in the Gītā-Rahasya that (i) the present Path of Devotion has been gradually evolved out of the forms of worship of the Qualityful mentioned in the ancient Upaniṣads; that (ii) the Pātañjala Yoga has given further importance to the Path of Devotion, as in that Yoga some perceptible or visible object has to be placed before the eyes for fixing the mind; and that (iii) the Path of Devotion has not come into India from anywhere else, nor was there any necessity for it to come from anywhere else. Supporting, from the point of view of the Vedānta of the Upaniṣads, this Path of Devotion, and especially the worship of Vāsudeva, which had in this way come into existence in India, is an important part of the subject-matter of the Gītā.

But a still more important part of the Gītā is the harmonisation of the Karma-Yoga with Devotion and the Knowledge of the Brahman. Although the Upanisads have considered the duties fixed for the four castes, or the ritualistic performances mentioned by the Śrutis as inferior, yet, some of the Upaniṣads say that they have got to be performed for the purification of the Mind, and that it is not proper to give them up even after the Mind has been purified. Nevertheless, several of the Upanisads may be said to ordinarily incline towards Abandonment of Action. There are statements in some Upaniṣads, as in the Īśāvāsyopaniṣad, that Action must be performed so long as life lasts, such as, "*kurvann eveha karmāṇi*", (i. e., "Action must be performed in this world"—Trans.); but no other Upaniṣad has justified this Karma-Yoga, which had been in vogue from ancient times, by doing away with the conflict between Spiritual Knowledge and Worldly Action as has been done in the Gītā. Nay, one may safely say that the doctrines of the Gītā on this matter are different from the doctrines enunciated by many of the writers of the Upaniṣads. As I have fully discussed this question in the eleventh chapter of the Gītā-Rahasya, I do not propose to take up more space by dealing with it here.

The 'acquisition of Yoga' (*yoga-sādhana*), which has been referred to in the sixth chapter of the Gītā, has been fully and scientifically dealt with in the Pātañjala Yoga-Sūtras; and these Sūtras are now-a-days considered an authoritative text on this subject. These Sūtras are divided into four chapters. The word '*yoga*' has been defined in the commencement of the very first chapter as "*yogas cittavṛttinirodhaḥ*", (i. e., "Yoga means the control of the activities of the Mind" —Trans.); and it is stated that "*abhyāsavairāgyābhyāṁ tannirodhaḥ*", that is, "this control (*nirodhaḥ*) can be acquired by practice and by indifference to the world"; and afterwards the means of acquiring the Yoga such as, *yama*, *niyama*, *āsana*, *prāṇāyāma*, etc. have been described; and in the 3rd and 4th chapters, it is explained how perfection and the supernatural powers of '*aṇimālaghimā*' (i. e, 'self-contraction, levitation' etc.— Trans.) are acquired by the '*asamprajñāta*' or '*nirvikalpa samādhi* (non-differentiating mental absorption), and how by this kind of concentration, one ultimately reaches Release in the shape of 'Brahma-nirvāṇa'. In the Bhagavadgītā also, there is first mentioned the necessity of the control of the Mind (Gī. 6. 20); and after stating that the Mind must be controlled by the two means of practice (*abhyāsa*), and indifference to the world (*vairāgya*), (Gī. 6. 35), it is ultimately stated how one should acquire the non-differentiating mental absorption, and what happiness that gives. But on that account, one cannot say that the Bhagavadgītā accepts as correct the Pātañjala-Yoga, or that the Pātañjala-Sūtras are earlier in point of time than the Bhagavadgītā. The Blessed Lord has nowhere advised that one should spend one's life holding one's nose in the hand for controlling the breath, in order to acquire perfect concentration, as directed in the Pātañjala-Sūtras. Control of the Mind and mental absorption have been mentioned in the Gītā as means for acquiring that Equability of Mind, which is necessary for acquiring Karma-Yoga. Therefore, it must be said that in this matter, the Gītā comes nearer to the Śvetāśvatara or the Kaṭha Upaniṣads than the Pātañjala-Sūtras. The Dhyānabindu, Churikā, and Yoga-tattva Upaniṣads deal with Yoga. But, as Yoga is the principal subject-matter in them, and its praises are sung everywhere, it is not proper to attempt to fully harmonise these one-sided Upaniṣads with the Gītā, which considers the Karma-Yoga as the most superior path; and such a harmony cannot in fact be brought about. In the introduction to his English translation of the Bhagavadgītā, Mr. Thompson has said that the Karma-Yoga in the Gītā is a form of the Pātañjala-Yoga; but such a thing is absolutely impossible; and I say that this confusion has arisen in the mind of Mr. Thompson, because he has not understood the correct meaning of the word 'Yoga' in the Gītā. Because, whereas the Gītā Karma-Yoga is Energistic, the Pātañjala-Yoga is just the opposite, that is to say, renunciatory; and it is, therefore, not possible that the one should have come out of the other; and it is nowhere stated in the Gītā that such is the case. Nay, the original meaning of the word 'Yoga' was Karma-Yoga; and one may safely say that that word came to be commonly understood in the single meaning of 'Yoga' in the shape of 'Concentration of the Mind', after the days of the Pātañjala-Sūtras. Whatever may be the case, the Desireless Path of Action adopted in ancient times by Janaka and others was similar to the Yoga, that is, the Karma-Yoga of the Gītā; and it has clearly been adopted from the Bhāgavata religion traditionally handed down by Manu to Ikṣvāku etc., and was not derived from the Pātañjala-Yoga.

This will have clearly shown to my readers the similarity and the dissimilarity between the Gītā-doctrine and the Upaniṣads. Most of these matters have been dealt with by me in the Gītā-Rahasya. I shall, therefore, say here only this much that, although the Knowledge of the Brahman in the Gītā has been mentioned on the authority of the Upaniṣads, yet, the Gītā has not merely copied the Metaphysical Knowledge in the Upaniṣads, but by adding to it the worship of Vāsudeva, as also the Sāṁkhya Science of the Perishable and the Imperishable, that is to say, of the creation of the universe, it has principally expounded the Vedic religion of Karma-Yoga, which is easy to follow, and is beneficial in this life and the next; and in this way the Gītā is superior to the Upaniṣads. It is, therefore, not proper to stretch the meaning of the Gītā doctrinally, in order to establish a non-existing harmony between the Gītā and the renunciatory Upaniṣads, except in the matter of the Knowledge of the Brahman. It is true that the Metaphysical Knowledge in both is the same. Yet, although the head in the shape of the Spiritual Knowledge is the same, the Sāṁkhya path and the Karma-Yoga are the two equally important hands of the Vedic religion; and the Gītā has emphatically supported Action based on Knowledge, as has been done in the Īśāvāsyopaniṣad, as is clearly shown in the eleventh chapter of the Gītā-Rahasya.

PART III—THE GĪTĀ AND THE BRAHMA-SŪTRAS.

Having in this way considered the similarity and the dissimilarity between the Bhagavadgītā and the Upaniṣads, which chiefly deal either with Spiritual Knowledge, or with Devotion, or with Yoga, it is really speaking not necessary to compare the Gītā with the Brahma-Sūtras; because, as Bādarāyanācārya has written his Brahma-Sūtras in order to systematically consider the Metaphysical doctrines mentioned in the various Upanisads, these Sūtras cannot contain any thoughts which are not in the Upaniṣads. Still, there is a clear reference to the Brahma-Sūtras at the beginning of the 13th chapter of the Bhagavadgītā, where the subject-matter of the Body and the Ātman is being dealt with, in the words:

ṛṣibhir bahudhā gītaṁ chandobhir vividhaiḥ pṛthak ।
brahma-sūtrapadaiś caiva hetumadbhir viniścitaiḥ ॥
(Gī. 13. 4),

that is, the Body and the Ātman have been described "in various ways, in different metres, by different Ṛṣis, disconnectedly; and also definitely and logically in the Brahma-Sūtra-padas"; and, if one considers these Brahma-Sūtras to be the same as the present Vedānta-Sūtras, it follows that the present Gītā must have been written after the date of the present Vedānta-Sūtras. It is, therefore, very necessary to determine which these Brahma-Sūtras are, in order to fix the date of the Gītā.* Because, there is no work now available besides the Vedānta-Sūtras, which bears the name of Brahma-Sūtras, nor has such a work been referred to anywhere; and it is not proper to say that the Gītā was written after the date of the present Brahma-Sūtras; because, it is traditionally believed that the Gītā is more ancient than these Brahma-Sūtras. Possibly, the phrase "*brahma-sūtra-padaiḥ*" has been interpreted in the Śāṁkarabhāṣya to mean "the phrases in the Śrutis or the Upanisads, which refer to the Brahman", in order to get over this difficulty. But, on the other hand, Ānandagiri, who

* This subject-matter has been considered by the late Mr. Telang; and Prof. Tukaram Ramchandra Amalnerkar B. A. has also published an essay on this subject in 1895.

has written a commentary on the Śāṁkarabhāṣya, and Rāmānujācārya and Madhvācārya, who are other commentators on the Gītā, have said that the words "*brahma-sūtra-padaiś caiva*" mean the Sūtras "*athāto brahma jijñāsā*" etc. of Bādarāyaṇācārya; and Śrīdhara Svāmi interprets them in both ways. We have, therefore, to determine the true meaning of this stanza independently. This stanza mentions TWO DIFFERENT places, where the subject-matter of the Body and the Ātman have been described; for, it says that this subject-matter has been mentioned "in DIFFERENT ways, by different Ṛṣis, DISCONNECTEDLY," and also *(caiva)* "definitely and logically in the Brahma-Sūtra-padas"; and this is apparent from the word '*caiva*' (i. e., 'and also'). Not only are these two places different, but the first place, namely, the description given by Ṛṣis, is "in different metres, and disconnected, and in different ways"; and, as appears by the third case plural termination of the word '*ṛṣibhiḥ*', it has been made by VARIOUS Ṛṣis; whereas, the other description contained in the Brahma-Sūtra-padas is "definite and logical". This is the special difference between the two, which has been brought out in this stanza. The word '*hetumat*' appears in various places in the Mahābhārata, and means an 'exposition made according to the method of logicians, by showing reason and conclusion'. Take for instance, the conversation of Sulabhā with Janaka, or what Śrī Kṛṣṇa said in the Darbar of the Kauravas, when He went there as an ambassador. It is stated in the Mahābhārata itself that the first conversation was '*hetumat*' and '*arthavat*' (Śān. 320. 191); and that the other one was '*sahetuka*' (Udyo. 131. 2). From this, it follows that where pros and cons are discussed, and some unambiguous and definite conclusion has been drawn at the end, that method of dealing with the subject is called '*hetumadbhir viniścitaiḥ*'. These words cannot be applied to miscellaneous and inconsistent conclusions drawn in one way in one place and in another way in another place. Therefore, if we have to maintain the distinction and contrast between "*ṛṣibhiḥ bahudhā vividhaiḥ pṛthak*" (i. e., "by Ṛṣis, in different places, in different ways, and disconnectedly"—Trans.) and "*hetumādbhir viniścitaiḥ*" (i. e., "definitely and logically"—Trans.), it becomes necessary to say that the words "the description in various ways, by different Ṛṣis, disconnectedly, and in different metres" intend to mean the disconnected and miscellaneous sentences appearing in the different Upaniṣads; and that the words "definite and logically advanced Brahma-Sūtra-padas" signify the description in the Brahma-Sūtras, in which a definite and unambiguous conclusion has been drawn in the end by showing pros and cons. It must also be borne in mind that, as the ideas mentioned by the Ṛṣis in the Upanisads were related by them, as they occurred to them, that is to say, disconnectedly, the true import of the Upanisads cannot be understood unless the ideas contained in them are harmonised. And, therefore, it becomes necessary to mention the work in which the Upanisads have been harmonised with each other by the explanation of reasons and conclusions, at the same time when the Upanisads themselves are mentioned.

When this stanza in the Gītā has been interpreted in this way, it is quite clear that the Upaniṣads and the Brahma-Sūtras were earlier in point of time than the Gītā. There is, of course, no dispute about the most important ones of these Upaniṣads; because, the stanzas from these Upaniṣads are found to have been copied word for word into the Gītā. But, there is room for doubt where the Brahma-Sūtras are concerned; because, although the word 'Bhagavadgītā' has not appeared literally in the Brahma-Sūtras, yet, the Bhagavadgītā is believed by the writers of the Bhāṣyas to have been referred to by the word 'Smṛti' in some of the Sūtras at least. The Brahma-Sūtras, which, according to the Śāṁkarabhāṣya, refer to the Bhagavadgītā by the word '*smṛti*' are principally the following ones.—

BRAHMA-SŪTRAS chapter, *pada*, and *sūtra*	GĪTĀ Chapter and stanza.
1. 2. 6, *smṛteś ca* ǀ	Gī. 18. 61, *īśvaraḥ sarvabhūtānāṁ* etc., (whole stanza)
1. 3. 23, *api ca smaryate* ǀ	Gī. 15. 6, *na tad bhāsayate sūryaḥ* etc.
2. 1. 36, *upapadyate cāpy-upalabhyate ca* ǀ	Gī. 15. 3, *na rūpam asyeha tathopalabhyate* etc.

2.	3. 45, API CA SMARYATE I	Gī. 15. 7, *mamaivāṁśo jīvaloke jīvabhūtaḥ* etc.
3.	2. 17, *darśayati cātho api smaryate* I	Gī. 13. 12, *jñeyaṁ yat tat pravakṣyāmi* etc.
3.	3. 31, *aniyamaḥ sarvāsām-avirodhaḥ śabdānumānā-bhyām* I	Gī. 8. 26, *śuklakṛṣṇe gatī hyete* etc.
4.	1. 10, *smaranti ca* I	Gī. 6. 11, *śucau deśe* etc.
4.	2. 21, YOGINAḤ PRATI CA SMARYATE I	Gī. 8. 23, *yatra kāle tvanāvṛttim āvṛttiṁ caiva yoginaḥ* etc.

Even if some out of these 8 references are considered ambiguous, yet, in my opinion the fourth (Bra. Sū. 2. 3. 45) and the eighth (Bra. Sū. 4. 2. 21) are absolutely unambiguous; and it must be borne in mind that on this question the four commentators, Śaṁkarācārya, Rāmānujācārya, Madhvācārya, and Vallabhācārya, are of the same opinion. The *sūtra* "*api ca smaryate*" (2. 3. 45) i. e., "and the Smṛti says the same thing", appears in the Brahma-Sūtras, in the course of the consideration of the mutual inter-relation between the Personal Self (*jīvātman*) and the Absolute Self (*paramātman*), after it has first been definitely stated in the *sūtra*, "*nātmā 'śruter nityatvāc ca tābhyaḥ*" (Bra. Sū. 2. 3. 17), that the Individual Self is not created from the Highest Self like the other objects in the world; after stating in the *sūtra*, "*aṁśo nānāvyapadeśāt*" etc. (2. 3. 43), that the Jīvātman is a 'part' (*aṁśa*) of the Paramātman, and after giving the authority of the Śrutis by saying "*mantra varṇāc ca*" (2. 3. 44) This Smṛti is the sentence "*mamaivāṁśo jīvaloke jīvabhūtaḥ sanātanaḥ*" in the Gītā (Gī. 15. 7) according to all the commentators. But the last reference is even more unambiguous than this. I have stated above in the tenth chapter that the two periods of Devayāna and Pitṛyāṇa occupy the six months of the Uttarāyaṇa and the six months of the Dakṣiṇāyana respectively; and that instead of interpreting these phrases as indicating 'time', Bādarāyanācārya has interpreted them as meaning the respective deities presiding during those periods of time (Ve. Sū. 4. 3. 4). The *sūtra*, "*yoginaḥ prati ca smaryate*" (Bra. Sū. 4. 2. 21), that is, "these periods of time are proper in the case of Yogins according to the Smṛti", has been written in answer to the doubt whether the words '*dakṣiṇāyana*' and '*uttarāyaṇa*', are never to be understood as indicating 'time'; and it has been clearly stated in the Gītā in the following words, that these periods of time are proper for Yogins, namely, "*yatra kāle tvanāvṛttim āvṛttiṁ caiva yoginaḥ*". From these references, one has to say with the commentators that in these two places at least the word '*smṛti*' used in the Brahma-Sūtras has reference only to the Bhagavadgītā.

But if one believes that the Brahma-Sūtras have been specifically mentioned in the Gītā, and that the Gītā has been specifically referred to in the Brahma-Sūtras by the word '*śmṛti*', there arises an inconsistency between the two from the point of view of date of writing; because, as the Bhagavadgītā contains a clear reference to the Brahma-Sūtras, the Brahma-Sūtras must be looked upon as prior in point of time to the Gītā; and if one interprets the word '*smṛti*' in the Brahma-Sūtras as meaning the Gītā, the Gītā becomes earlier in point of time than the Brahma-Sūtras. The same Brahma-Sūtras cannot once be earlier in point of time and again later in point of time than the Gītā. Well; if, in order to escape from this difficulty, we interpret the words "*brahma-sūtra-padaiḥ*", as has been done in the Śāṁkarabhāṣya, then the words "*hetumadbhir viniścitaiḥ*" become meaningless; and if we say that the word '*smṛti*' used in the Brahma-Sūtras refers to some Smṛti other than the Gītā, then we have to say that all the commentators were wrong; and even if we say that they were all wrong, the fact still remains that we cannot say what work is referred to by the word '*smṛti*'. Then, how are we to get out of this difficult position? In my opinion, there is only one way in which we can escape this difficulty. If we say that the same man who wrote the Brahma-Sūtras also gave their present form to the Bhārata and to the Gītā, the difficulty is solved. It is usual to refer to the Brahma-Sūtras as 'Vyāsa-Sūtras', and Ānandagiri has stated in his commentary on the Śāṁkarabhāṣya on the *sūtra*, "*śeṣatvāt puruṣārtha-vādo yathānyeṣv iti jaiminiḥ*" (Ve. Sū. 3. 4. 2), that Jaimini was the disciple of Vyāsa, who wrote the Vedānta-Sūtras; and in the same way, he has described the Brahma-Sūtras in the opening stanzas of his work in the following terms, namely, "*śrīmadvyāsapayonidhir nidhirasau*". Vyāsa, the writer of the Mahābhārata, had five disciples named, Paila, Suka, Sumantu, Jaimini, and Vaiśaṁpāyana; and I have, on the authority of the present Mahābhārata, referred above to the story that Vyāsa taught the Mahābhārata to them. When one takes both these things together, and considers the matter, one can draw the inference that the work of giving their present form to the original Bhārata and to the Gītā included in it, as also that of writing the Brahma-Sūtras was done by one and the same Bādarāyaṇa Vyāsa. This does not mean that Bādarāyaṇācārya wrote something new in the shape of the present Mahābhārata. All that I mean to say is that as the Mahābhārata is a very extensive work, some portions of it may have been lost or become disintegrated at the time of Bādarāyaṇa; and that Bādarāyaṇācārya may, therefore, have critically examined different portions of the Mahābhārata which were then available, and either corrected or supplemented them wherever he found the book to be disconnected or incorrect or incomplete, or added indexes etc., and in that way either revived the book or given it its present form. It is well known that even in Marathi literature, Ekanātha has in this way revised the *Jñāneśvarī*; and there is even a story that as the Vyākaraṇa Mahābhāṣya in Sanskrit literature was once lost, Chandraśekharācārya had to revive it again. In this way, one can easily understand how the stanzas of the Gītā are to be found in the other chapters of the Mahābhārata; and the fact of the clear reference to the Brahma-Sūtras in the Gītā and of the reference to the Gītā in the Brahma-Sūtras by the word '*smṛti*', is easily explained. As the original Gītā, which is the foundation of the present Gītā, was available even before the time of Bādarāyaṇācārya, it was referred to in the Brahma-Sūtras by the word '*smṛti*'; and it is stated in the Gītā, while revising the Mahābhārata, that the subject-matter of the Body and the Ātman has been considered in detail in the Brahma-Sūtras *. There are other references in the present Mahābhārata to *sūtra*-works, similar to the reference to the Brahma-Sūtras in the present Gītā. For instance, in the Aṣṭāvakra-Dik conversation in the Anuśāsanaparva, we find the sentence, "*anṛtāḥ striya ity evaṁ sūtrakāro vyavasyati*" (Anu. 19. 6). Similarly, there are also clear references elsewhere in the Mahābhārata to the Śatapatha-brāhmaṇa (Śānti. 318. 16–23), the Pañcarātras (Śānti. 339. 107), the Nirukta of Yāska (Śānti. 342. 71), and Manu (Anu. 37. 16). But, as it was not usual for people to learn by heart all the parts of the Mahābhārata, a doubt naturally arises about the extent to which the reference to other books in the Mahābhārata in other places besides the Gītā, can be looked upon as reliable for the purpose of the determination of the date of either. Because, those parts which are not learnt by heart can easily be tampered with by the addition of interpolated stories or stanzas. Yet, in my opinion, there is no reason why we should not take advantage of these other references in order to prove that the reference to the Brahma-Sūtras in the Gītā is not a sole, or an unprecedented, and therefore, an unreliable reference.

---

* The Brahma-Sūtras are the most important book on Vedānta, and the Gītā is the most important book on Karma-Yoga, as has been shown by me in previous chapters. Therefore, if my inference that the Brahma-Sūtras and the Gītā were written by one and the same person, that is, by Vyāsa, is correct, Vyāsa becomes saddled with the authorship of both these books. I have proved this above by inferential argument. But in the new edition of the Mahābhārata according to the southern recension, which has been published by Mr. Krishnacarya of Kumbakonam, we find the following 34th stanza in the 212th chapter of the Śāntiparva (in the Vārṣṇeyādhyātma-prakaraṇa) in the description of how the various sciences and histories came into existence at the beginning of the Yuga, namely,

vedāntakarmayogaṁ ca vedavid brahmavid vibhuḥ |
dvaipāyano nijagrāha silpaśāstraṁ bhṛguḥ punaḥ ||

In this stanza, "*vedāntakarmayogaṁ*" is a compound word in the singular number. But that has to be interpreted as meaning 'Vedānta *and* Karma-Yoga'. Possibly the original reading was "*vedāntaṁ*

I have proved above by critically examining the meaning of the words in the stanza "*brahma-sūtra-padaiś caiva*" etc., that the Bhagavadgītā contains a reference to the present Brahma-Sūtras or Vedānta-Sūtras. But, I think there is another important and forcible reason for this reference to the Brahma-Sūtras having come into the Bhagavadgītā, and that too in the 13th chapter, that is, in the chapter which deals with the subject of the Body and the Ātman. I have already explained in the previous chapters that though the essential principle of the worship of Vāsudeva has been taken into the Bhagavadgītā from the Bhāgavata or the Pañcarātra religion, yet, the four-fold (*catur-vyūya*) theory of the Pañcarātra religion regarding the coming into existence of Saṁkarṣaṇa, that is Jīva (Personal Self) from Vāsudeva, of Pradyumna, that is, the Mind (*manas*) from Saṁkarṣaṇa, and of Aniruddha, that is, Individuation (*ahaṁkāra*) from Pradyumna, is not accepted by the Bhagavadgītā. The Brahma-Sūtras lay down the doctrine that the Personal Self (*jīvātman*) has not sprung from anything else (Ve. Sū. 2. 3. 17) and that it is an eternal 'part' (*aṁśa*) of the Highest Ātman

karmayogaṁ ca", and in writing or in printing, the diacritical nasal sign '*ṁ*' in '*ntaṁ*' may have been dropped. It is clearly stated in this stanza that Vyāsa obtained the two sciences of Vedānta and Karma-Yoga, and that Bhṛgu obtained the *śilpa-śāstra* (i. e., 'the fine or mechanical arts'—Trans.). But, this stanza is not to be found in the edition printed in the Ganpat Krishnaji Press in Bombay or in the Calcutta edition. The 212th chapter of the Śāntiparva in the Kumbakonam edition is the 210th chapter of the Bombay and Calcutta editions. I am very grateful to my friend Dr. Ganesh Krishna Garde for having drawn my attention to this stanza in the Kumbakonam recension. According to his opinion, the word '*karmayoga*' in this place refers to nothing else but the Gītā, and the authorship of both the Gītā and the Vedānta-Sūtras is by this stanza given to Vyāsa. Some doubt may arise on this point, because this reading is to be found in only one out of three editions of the Mahābhārata; but it at least proves that my inference about the author of Vedānta being the same as the author of Karma-Yoga, is neither new, nor without authority.

(*paramātman*), (Ve. Sū. 2. 3. 43). Therefore, Bādarāyaṇācārya has, in the second part of the second chapter, found fault with the Bhāgavata doctrine, by saying that the genesis of Saṁkarṣaṇa from Vāsudeva according to that religion is not possible (Ve. Sū. 2. 2. 42); and, by arguing that, since the Mind is an organ pertaining to the Personal Self, it is impossible for Pradyumna (Manas) to spring from Jīva (Ve. Sū. 2. 2. 43), because, we never see it happen in the world that the cause or the means spring from the doer, he has to that extent logically refuted the Bhāgavata doctrine. To this, the followers of the Bhāgavata doctrine are likely to reply that they consider Vāsudeva (Īśvara), Saṁkarṣaṇa (Jīva), Pradyumna (Manas), and Aniruddha (Ahaṁkāra) as four equal Jñānins, and look upon the *genesis* of the one from the other as merely symbolical or unimportant. But, from this point of view, instead of there being one Parameśvara, one gets four Paramesvaras; and the Brahma-Sūtras, therefore, say, that even this reply is not satisfactory; and Bādarāyaṇa has ultimately expressed his opinion that the idea that Jīva has sprung from the Parameśvara is not acceptable to the Vedas, that is, to the Upaniṣads. (Ve. Sū. 2. 2. 44, 45). It is true that the Bhagavadgītā has adopted the principle of of Action based on Devotion of the Bhāgavata religion. Nevertheless, the doctrine of the Gītā is that the Jīva has not sprung from the Parameśvara, and is not a 'son' of the Parameśvara, but a part *(aṁśa)* of the Paramātman (Gī. 15. 7). This doctrine about the Jīva does not form part of the original Bhāgavata doctrine; and it was, therefore, necessary to explain on what authority it had been based; because, if that had not been done, there was a likelihood of a misunderstanding arising that while accepting the Energistic Devotional principle of the Bhāgavata doctrine, the Bhagavadgītā was also accepting the arrangement of the 'four-folded genesis' *(caturvyūha)* in that doctrine. Therefore, when there was occasion to refer to the nature of the Individual Self (Jīvātman) in the chapter on the Body and the Ātman, that is to say, in the very beginning of the 13th chapter, it became necessary for the Blessed Lord to explain that "My opinion about the Ātman (*kṣetrajña*), that is, the Jīva, is not the same as in the Bhāgavata doctrine, but is consistent with the opinion of the Ṛsis, who have written the Upaniṣads". And thereafter, it became necessary for Him to say in the natural course, that, as different Ṛsis had given disconnected descriptions in the different Upaniṣads, He accepted the harmonisation of all those opinions in the Brahma-Sūtras (Ve. Sū. 2. 3. 43). Considering the matter from this point of view, it will be seen that the Path of Devotion in the Bhāgavata doctrine has been adopted in to the Gītā in such a way that the objections taken to that doctrine in the Brahma-Sūtras could be obviated. Rāmānujācārya has in his commentary on the Vedānta-Sūtras given a different meaning altogether to these Sūtras (Ve. Sū. Rā. Bhā. 2. 2. 42–45). But, in my opinion, these interpretations are stretched, and not acceptable. Thibaut seems to be inclined to accept the view of the Rāmānujabhāṣya; but from the writings of Thibaut, one does not get the idea that he has properly understood the true nature of this discussion. Even in the description of the Nārāyanīya doctrine, which is made at the end of the Śāntiparva of the Mahābhārata, it is first stated that "Vāsudeva IS ALSO (*sa eva*) Saṁkarṣana, that is, Jīva, or the Ātman" (See Śān. 339. 39 and 71 and 334. 28 and 29); and the further descent of Pradyumna from Saṁkarsana etc. has then been mentioned; and in one place, it is clearly stated that some consider the Bhāgavata doctrine as four-folded (*catur-vyūha*), others as three-folded (*tri-vyūha*), others as two-folded (*dvi-vyūha*), and others again as single-folded (*eka-vyūha*), (Ma. Bhā. Śān. 348. 57). But instead of accepting these various aspects of the Bhāgavata doctrine, the present Gītā has accepted only that aspect of it, which would be consistent with the opinions of the Upaniṣads and the Brahma-Sūtras on the question of the mutual inter-relation between the Body and the Ātman; and when this matter is taken into account, one clearly understands why it was necessary to refer to the Brahma-Sūtras in the Gītā. Nay, we may even go so far as to say that the present Gītā has made an improvement in this respect on the original Gītā.

PART IV—THE RISE OF THE BHĀGAVATA RELIGION AND THE GĪTĀ.

I have stated in several places in the Gītā-Rahasya, and also above in this Appendix, that the principal subject-matter of the Gītā is to harmonise-the Spiritual Knowledge of the Upaniṣads, and the Sāṁkhya theories about the Mutable and the Immutable, with Devotion, and principally with Desireless Action; and thereby to fully justify the Karma-Yoga scientifically. But, those who do not realise the skilfulness of the Gītā in harmonising these various subjects, or those who have a pre-conceived notion that it will be difficult to harmonise all these subjects, get the impression that many of the statements in the Gītā are mutually conflicting. For instance, these critics object that the statement in the thirteenth-chapter, that all whatsoever, which exists in this world, is nothing but the qualityless Brahman, is inconsistent with the statement in the seventh chapter that all this world is nothing but the qualityful Vāsudeva (7. 19); as also that the statement that "Friend and foe are alike to Me" (9. 29) is inconsistent with the other statement that "Jñānins and Devotees are much beloved of Me" (7. 17; 12. 19), both of which statements have been made by the Blessed Lord. But I have explained in many places in the Gītā-Rahasya, that there is no real conflict between these statements, and that although it was necessary to make these apprently conflicting statements in considering the same question, once from the Metaphysical point of view and again from the point of view of Devotion, yet, the Gītā has finally harmonised them from the comprehensive philosophical point of view. But, even to this explanation it is objected by some, that (i) although it is now possible to thus harmonise the Realisation of the imperceptible Brahman, with the Devotion to the perceptible Parameśvara, yet, it is impossible that there could have been any such harmonisation in the original Gītā; that (ii) the original Gītā was not full of conflicting statements like the present Gītā, and that (iii) Vedāntists or the protagonists of Sāṁkhya doctrines interpolated statements in favour of their respective doctrines into the original Gītā. For instance, Prof. Garbe says that the original Gītā contained a harmonisation of Devotion with only Sāṁkhya and Yoga; and the harmonisation of Devotion with Vedānta and with the Karma-mārga of the Mīmāṁsā School was brought about by somebody afterwards; and he has even appended to his German translation of the Gītā, a list of those stanzas, which according to him had been subsequently interpolated into the original Gītā! These theories are entirely wrong in my opinion. These people have conceived these wrong ideas as a result of their having failed to understand the historical tradition of the various aspects of the Vedic religion, and the real meanings of the words '*sāṁkhya*' and '*yoga*' used in the Gītā, and especially because these people had before their eyes the history of the unphilosophical, that is, purely devotional Christian religion. The Christian religion was originally purely devotional; and the attempt to harmonise it with the philosophical doctrines of the Greeks, or with other philosophies, was made afterwards. But that is not the case with us. The Ritualist path of the Mīmāṁsā school, the Knowledge preached by the writers of the Upaniṣads, and Sāṁkhya and Yoga, had all reached their highest development before the Path of Devotion arose in India. Therefore, it was impossible from the very beginning that our people should countenance an independent Path of Devotion, which would be independent of all these sciences, and especially independent of the Knowledge of the Brahman preached in the Upanisads; and when this impossibility is taken into account, one is forced to come to the conclusion, that the form of the preaching of the Gītā-religion must, from the very beginning, have been more or less similar to the exposition contained in the present Gītā. The exposition of the Gītā in the Gītā-Rahasya has been made by me on this basis; yet, as this is a very important question, I shall here briefly state what results are arrived at, according to me, regarding the original form and the tradition of the Gītā-religion, from the historical point of view.

I have shown in the tenth chapter of the Gītā-Rahasya that the most pristine form of the Vedic religion was not pre-eminently Devotional, or Realisational, or Yogic, but was ritualistic, that is, Actional; and that the Veda-Saṁhitās, and the Brāhmaṇas have principally enunciated this Activistic religion of sacrificial Yajñas. As this religion was later on systematically expounded in the Mīmāṅsā-Sūtras of Jaimini, it acquired the name 'Mīmāṁsaka-mārga'. But although the name 'Mīmāṁsā' was new, yet, the sacrificial religion was undoubtedly ancient, and was probably the first stage of the Vedic religion from the historical point of view. Before acquiring the name 'Mīmāṁsaka-mārga', it used to be known as 'Trayī-dharma', that is, 'the religion supported by the three Vedas'; and the same name is to be found in the Gītā (See Gī. 9. 20 and 21). When this ritualistic Trayī-dharma was being rigorously observed, how was it possible to Realise the Parameśvara by this Karma, that is, this external paraphernalia of Yajñas and sacrificial rites? There then gradually arose the doubts and objections, that as Realisation was a mental process, it would be impossible to acquire Realisation, unless one contemplated on the form of the Parameśvara etc.; and this Trayī-dharma gradually came to include the Knowledge contained in the Upaniṣads, as is evident from the introductory passages at the commencement of the Chāndogya and other Upaniṣads. This Knowledge of the Brahman contained in the Upaniṣads has subsequently acquired the name 'Vedānta'. But although this word 'Vedānta' has come into existence subsequently like the word 'Mīmāṁsā', yet, the Knowledge of the Brahman, or the Path of Knowledge, does not, on that account, become something new. It is true that the Jñāna-kāṇḍa came to be formulated after the Karma-kāṇḍa; yet, one must not forget that both of them were ancient. The Kāpila-Sāṁkhya philosophy is another and an independent branch of this Path of Knowledge. I have stated in the Gītā-Rahasya, that whereas Vedānta was Non-Dualistic, Sāṁkhya philosophy was Dualistic, and that the Sāṁkhya doctrines regarding the genesis of the Cosmos are fundamentally different. But although the Non-Dualistic Knowledge of the Brahman mentioned in the Upaniṣads is fundamentally different from the Dualistic Sāṁkhya philosophy, yet, from the point of view of Knowledge, both these paths were equally antagonistic to the prior ritualistic Path of Action (*karma-mārga*). This naturally gave rise to the problem of the harmonisation of Karma with Knowledge; and there had arisen two sects in this matter already in the times of the Upaniṣads. The Bṛhadāraṇyaka and other Upaniṣads and the Sāṁkhya philosophers began to say that on account of the perpetual conflict between Karma and Jñāna, it was not only proper but even necessary to give up Karma after the Acquisition of Knowledge; and on the other hand, the Īśāvāsya and other Upaniṣads began to say, that one cannot give up Karma even after the Acquisition of Knowledge, and that a Jñānin must continue performing Action for the purpose of carrying on the affairs of the world, after making his Reason desireless, by cultivating apathy towards the world. An attemrt has been made in the commentaries on these Upaniṣads to do away with this conflict. But, these doctrine-supporting interpretations in the Śāṁkarabhāṣya are stretched; and they cannot be accepted if one considers the Upaniṣads independently, as has been stated by me at the end of the eleventh chapter of the Gītā-Rahasya. It becomes clear from the exposition in the Maitryupaniṣad that this attempt was not restricted only to the harmonisation of Karma in the form of ritualistic performances with the Knowledge of the Brahman; but that about this time, attempts were also made to harmonise, as far as possible, the Science of the Mutable and the Immutable, which had arisen independently in the Sāṁkhya philosophy, with the Knowledge of the Brahman in the Upaniṣads. The Bṛhadāraṇyaka and other ancient Upaniṣads do not attach much importance to the Kāpila Sāṁkhya philosophy. But, the Maitryupaniṣad wholly adopts the Sāṁkhya terminology, and propounds the theory that the 24 Elementary Principles of the Sāṁkhyas have originally sprung from one Parabrahman. But even the Kāpila Sāṁkhya philosophy is in support of Renunciation, that is to say, contrary to Energism (*karma*). Therefore, it is seen that from very ancient times there were already three schools of Vedānta philosophy, namely, (1) the path of merely performing ritual in the shape of Sacrifice etc.; (2) the path of abandoning Action, by means of Knowledge and Apathy to the world, that is to say, the Path of Knowledge or the Sāṁkhya Path; and (3) the Knowledge-Action (*jñāna-karma-samuccaya*) path of continually performing Action, with Knowledge, and with an apathetic frame of mind. From the Path of Knowledge, out of these three paths, the two subsidiary branches of Yoga and Devotion have subsequently come into existence. It is stated in the Chāndogya and other ancient Upaniṣads, that it is necessary to meditate on the Brahman in order to acquire the Knowledge of the Parabrahman; and that it is necessary to concentrate the Mind, and for that purpose, to place before the eyes, in the first place, some qualityful symbol of the Parabrahman, in order to succeed in this thought, contemplation, or meditation. As the Concentration of the Mind acquired in worshipping the Brahman thus acquired a special importance later on, Yoga, in the shape of the 'Concentration of the Mind', became an independent path by itself; and, by a tangible human-formed Parameśvara being taken for worship, instead of a qualityful symbol, the Path of Devotion gradually came into existence. This idea of Devotion in the Path of Devotion has not come into existence independently, at some intermediate period of time, and inconsistently with the Spiritual Knowledge contained in the Upaniṣads; nor has it been imported into India from some other country. When one considers *seriatim* all the various Upanisads, one comes to the conclusion that, in the beginning, the various parts of the Yajña, or the OM-kāra, and later on, Vedic deities like Rudra, Viṣṇu, etc., or qualityful perceptible symbols of the Brahman like Ether etc., came to be worshipped for the purpose of the meditation on the Brahman; and that with the same end in view, that is, with the idea of reaching the Brahman, the Devotion to, that is, a kind of worship of, Rāma, Nṛsiṁha, Śrī Kṛṣṇa, Vāsudeva, etc., came to be started thereafter. Out of these, the Yoga-tattva and other Upaniṣads on the Yoga, or the Nṛsiṁha-tāpanī, Rāma-tāpanī, and other Upaniṣads, which are devotional, are clearly seen to be more ancient than the Chāndogya and other Upaniṣads, when one considers their language. Therefore, it becomes necessary to say from the historical point of view, that the Paths of Yoga and of Devotion, acquired importance only after the three paths of (i) Karma, (ii) Jñāna, or Saṁnyāsa, and (iii) Jñāna-Karma-samuccaya, described in the Chāndogya and other ancient

Upaniṣads had come into existence. But, although the paths of Yoga and of Devotion acquired importance later on, the importance of the previous Knowledge of the Brahman was not thereby diminished; and it was not possible that it should be so diminished; and therefore, even in those Upaniṣads, which support Yoga or Devotion, we find statements that the Knowledge of the Brahman is the ultimate ideal of Devotion and of Yoga; and that Rudra, Viṣṇu, Acyuta, Nārāyaṇa, or Vāsudeva and other objects of worship, are only forms of the Paramātman or of the Parabrahman (See Maitryu. 7. 7; Rāmapū. 16; Amṛtabindu. 22 etc.). In short, the various sub-divisions of religion, which have from time to time been promulgated by various Self-Realised (*ātma-jñānin*) sages into the Vedic religion, at different times, have arisen from the aspects of religion which were then already in vogue; and it has been the principal tendency of the growth of the Vedic religion, from the very beginning, to harmonise new aspects of religion with the older aspects; and the writers of the Smṛtis have later on expounded the arrangement of the various stages of life, by adhering to this tendency of harmonising various aspects of religion. When one considers this ancient Indian tendency of harmonising various aspects of religion, it is not proper to say that the Gītā-religion was the only exception to this previous and subsequent tendency.

I have mentioned above the general history of the growth of the principal aspects of the Vedic religion, namely, the ritualistic Karma mentioned in the Brāhmaṇas, the Spiritual Knowledge in the Upaniṣads, the Kāpila-Sāṁkhya philosophy, Yoga in the shape of Concentration of the Mind, and Devotion. Let us now consider the origin of the consideration of all these various aspects of religion which has been made in the Gītā—that is, whether it has been taken into the Gītā directly from various distinct Upaniṣads, or there is any intermediate stage. Where the Knowledge of the Brahman alone is being considered in the Gītā, stanzas from the Kaṭha and other Upaniṣads have been adopted word for word into the Gītā; and where the Jñāna-Karma (Knowledge-Action) combination path is being dealt with, illustrations have been taken from the Upanisads of persons like Janaka etc. From these facts, one would think that the Gītā must have been based on the Upaniṣads themselves. But, if we consider the genesis of the Gītā-religion, which has been given in the Gītā itself, we find that the Upaniṣads are nowhere mentioned in it. Just as Sacrifice included in Knowledge is considered superior in the Gītā to the sacrifice of wealth (Gī. 4. 33), so also does the Chāndogyopaniṣad say that human life is a kind of Yajña (sacrifice), (Chān. 3. 16, 17); and in describing the worth of such a sacrifice, it says that, "the Cult of this Yajña was taught by a Ṛṣi named Ghora Āngirasa to Devakīputra Kṛṣṇa" There is no authority for looking upon this Devakīputra Kṛṣṇa as the same as the Kṛṣṇa of the Gītā. But, even if it is assumed for a moment that both of them were one and the same, yet, it must still be borne in mind that Ghora Āngirasa has nowhere been mentioned in the Gītā as an authority for considering the Sacrifice included in Spiritual Knowledge as superior. Besides, although the path followed by Janaka was a combination of Jñāna and Karma, yet, Devotion had not been incorporated into that path in his times, as is quite clear from the Bṛhadāraṇyakopaniṣad; and, therefore, Janaka does not appear in the traditional history of the path, which combines Jñāna and Karma with Devotion; nor has the Gītā so included him. It is stated at the beginning of the fourth chapter of the Gītā (Gī. 4. 1-3) that the religion of the Gītā was first taught by the Blessed Lord to Vivasvān in the beginning of the Yuga, then by Vivasvān to Manu, and then by Manu to Ikṣvāku; but that, as it got lost in course of time, it had again to be preached to Arjuna. Although these stanzas are of utmost importance for understanding the growth of the Gītā-religion, commentators have not gone beyond giving their literary meaning, in order to elucidate them; and it would appear that doing so would even not have been in their interests. Because, if it were admitted that the Gītā-religion was originally of a particular cult, other religious cults could not but to that extent suffer in importance. But, I have shown with authorities in the commencement of the Gītā-Rahasya, as also in my commentary on the first and second stanzas of the fourth chapter of the Gītā, that the tradition of the Gītā is consistent with the tradition of the Bhāgavata religion in the Tretāyuga, that is, the last Yuga, which has been mentioned in the Nārāyaṇīya Upākhyāna of the Mahābhārata. Considering this similarity between the tradition of the Bhāgavata doctrine and of the Gītā-religion, one is forced to admit that the Gītā is a book which supports the Bhāgavata religion; and if there is any doubt about it, that is fully removed by the statement of Vaiśaṁpāyana in the Mahābhārata (Ma. Bhā. Śān. 346. 10), that: "in the Gītā, only the Bhāgavata religion has been mentioned". When it has been thus proved, that the Gītā is not an independent treatise dealing with Vedānta, that is to say, with the Spiritual Knowledge of the Upaniṣads, but that it supports the Bhāgavata religion, it need not be said that any criticism on the Gītā, which does not take into account the Bhāgavata religion, must be incomplete and confusing. I will, therefore, give here in short, all the available information regarding the date when the Bhāgavata religion was first promulgated, and as to what its original form was. I have stated above in the Gītā-Rahasya that this Bhāgavata religion was also known as the 'Nārāyaṇīya', the 'Sātvata', or the 'Pāñcarātra' religion.

As, many of the Vedic religious treatises written after the date of the Upaniṣads and before the date of Buddha, have been lost, the only available principal works relating to the Bhāgavata religion, in addition to the Gītā, are the Nārāyaṇīya Upākhyāna mentioned in the 18th chapter of the Śāntiparva of the Mahābhārata (Ma. Bhā. Śān. 334–351), the Śāṇḍilya-Sūtras, the Bhāgavata-Purāṇa, the Nārada-Pañcarātra, the Nārada-Sūtras, and the works of Rāmānujācārya and others. Out of these, the works of Rāmānujācārya have been avowedly written in about the twelfth century of the Śālivāhana era for supporting a doctrine, that is to say, in order to harmonise the Gītā with the Qualified-Monistic (*viśiṣṭādvaita*) Vedānta of the Bhāgavata religion. Therefore, one cannot rely on these books for determining the original form of the Bhāgavata religion; and the same is the case with the books written by Madhvācārya and other followers of the Vaiṣṇava doctrine. The Śrīmad Bhāgavata-Purāṇa is earlier in point of time than these. But, it is stated in the very beginning of this Purāṇa (Bhāg. Skan. 1. Ch. 4 and 5) that, because the exposition of the Renunciatory Bhāgavata religion contained in the Mahābhārata, and necessarily also in the Gītā, had not been made as it ought to have been made, and as Vyāsa on that account felt sorry, since "Desireless Action (*naiṣkarmya*) by itself was useless without Devotion", he, at the instance of Nārada, and in order to put an end to his mental anguish, wrote the Bhāgavata-Purāṇa, which maintained the worth of Devotion. If this story is considered from the historical point of view, it will be seen that when the doctrine of Desireless Action to which importance had been given in the original Bhāgavata religion of the Bhārata, lost its influence in course of time, and Devotion acquired importance instead, the Bhāgavata-Purāṇa came to be written in order to expound this second Bhāgavata religion (that is, in which Devotion was predominant). The Nārada-Pañcarātra is also of the same kind; that is, it deals purely with Devotion, and contains a specific reference by name to the Bhāgavata-Purāṇa of 12 *skandhas*, the Brahma-Vaivarta-Purāṇa,, the Viṣṇu-Purāṇa, the Gītā, and the Mahābhārata (see Nā. Pañ. 2. 7. 28-32; 3. 14. 73 and 4. 3. 154). It, therefore, follows that this work is less important than the Bhāgavata-Purāṇa for determining the original form of the Bhāgavata religion. It is possible that the Nārada-Sūtras and the Śāṇḍilya-Sūtras are earlier in date than the Nārada-Pañcarātra. Still, as the Nārada-Sūtras contain a reference to Vyāsa and to Śuka (Nā. Sū. 83), there is no doubt that they are later in point of time than the Bhārata and the Bhāgavata; and as the Śāṇḍilya-Sūtras contain stanzas taken from the Bhagavadgītā (Śāṇ. Sū. 9. 15 and 83), they must be later in point of time than the Gītā and the Mahābhārata, though earlier than the Nārada-Sūtras (Nā. Sū. 83). Therefore, in order to determine the original and the ancient form of the Bhāgavata religion, one has ultimately to rely on the Nārāyaṇīya Upākhyāna of the Mahābhārata. Both in the Bhāgavata-Purāṇa (1. 3. 24) and in the Nārada-Pañcarātra (4. 3. 156-159; 4. 8. 81), Buddha has been referred to as an incarnation of Viṣṇu. But the ten incarnations mentioned in the Nārāyaṇīyākhyāna do not include Buddha; and Haṁsa is stated to be the first incarnation, whereas the incarnation of Kalki is mentioned immediately after that of Kṛṣṇa (Ma. Bhā. Śān. 339. 100). This fact also proves that the Nārāyaṇīyākhyāna is earlier in point of time than the

Bhāgavata-Purāṇa and the Nārada-Pañcarātra. In the Nārāyaṇīyākhyāna, there is a statement that the Bhāgavata religion, that is, the Nārāyaṇīya religion, was originally founded by the two Ṛṣis Nara and Nārāyaṇa, who were the incarnations of the Parabrahman; and that when the Ṛṣi Nārada went at their direction to the Śvetadvīpa, the Blessed Lord Himself first preached this religion to him there; the statement in the Nārāyaṇīyākhyāna that the Śvetadvīpa, where the Blessed Lord resided, was in the Kṣīra-samudra, which was stated to be to the north of the Mountain Meru, is consistent with the ancient description of the Cosmos given in the Purāṇas; and no one on our side attaches much importance to it. But the Western Sanskritist Webber has perverted this very story, and started the argument that the Philosophy of Devotion mentioned in the Bhāgavata religion was imported into India from the Śvetadvīpa, that is to say, from some country outside India; and that in as much as this Philosophy of Devotion was in those days not in vogue in any religion except the Christian religion, the idea of Devotion was picked up by the followers of the Bhāgavata religion from Christian countries. But, there is proof that Pāṇini knew the doctrine of Devotion to Vāsudeva, and there are references to the Bhāgavata religion or to the Philosophy of Devotion both in the Buddhistic and Jain religious treatises; and there is no doubt that both Pāṇini and Buddha lived before Christ. Therefore, even Western philosophers have now pronounced this argument of Webber to be without foundation. I have stated above that Devotion, as a part of religion, came into existence in India after the date of the Upaniṣads which contain Spiritual Knowledge. It is, therefore, beyond doubt that the Bhāgavata religion, which consisted of Devotion to Vāsudeva, came into existence after the Upaniṣads, which preached Spiritual Knowledge, and before Buddha. The only question is how many centuries * before Buddha that religion

* The word *'bhaktimān'* (in Pali, *'bhattimā'*) appears in the Ther Gāthā (stanza 370); and one Jātaka even contains a reference to Devotion. Besides this, the well-known French Pali scholar Senart, delivered a lecture on the subject of 'The Origin of the Buddhistic religion' in 1909, in which he has clearly said that the Bhāgavata religion existed before the Buddhistic religion. *cf:*

came into existence; and although it is not possible to answer that question with absolute precision, yet, as will appear from what follows, it is not at all impossible to get a rough idea of its date.

It has been stated in the Gītā that the Bhāgavata religion preached by Śrī Kṛṣṇa to Vivasvān was lost before that date (Gī. 4. 2); and the philosophy of this religion gives the name 'Vāsudeva' to the Parameśvara, 'Saṁkarṣaṇa' to Jīva, 'Pradyumna' to Manas, and 'Aniruddha' to Ahaṁkāra. Out of these, Vāsudeva is the name of Śrī Kṛṣṇa himself; Saṁkarṣaṇa is the name of his elder brother Balarāma; and Pradyumna and Aniruddha are names of his son and grandson. Besides, the word 'Sātvata', which is another name for this religion, is also the name of the community, namely, the Yādava community, in which Śrī Kṛṣṇa was born. From this it is clear, that this religion was promulgated in the family and the community in which Śrī Kṛṣṇa was born, and that it was preached by Śrī Kṛṣṇa to his dear friend, Arjuna; and the story in the Purāṇas is the same. Besides, as there is also a tradition that the Sātvata community came to an end with the death of Śrī Kṛṣṇa, it was impossible that this religion could have been further promulgated even in the Sātvata community after the death of Śrī Kṛṣṇa. It is possible to historically explain the

---

"No one will claim to derive from Buddhism, Vishnuism or the Yoga. Assuredly Buddhism is the borrower"......"To sum up, if there had not previously existed a religion made up of the doctrines of Yoga, or Vishnuite legends, of devotion to Vishnu-Krishna, worshipped under the title of Bhagavata, Buddhism would not have come to birth at all". This essay of Senart has been published in the form of a translation in the issues of the *Indian Interpreter*, a Missionary quarterly published at Poona, for the months of October 1909 and Jan. 1910; the passages quoted above will be found at pages 177 & 178 of the January issue. Dr. Bühler also has said that "the ancient Bhāgavata, Sātvata or Pāñcarātra sect, devoted to the worship of Narayana and his deified teacher Krishna-Devakiputra, dated from a period long anterior to the rise of the Jainas in the 8th Century"—Indian Antiquary, Vol. XXXII (1894), p. 248. A further detailed exposition of this matter has been made in the sixth part of this Appendix below, to which the reader is referred.

various names of this religion, by saying that this religion, which was thus promulgated by Śrī Kṛṣṇa, may have been in existence before His time to some extent or other under the name of the 'Nārāyaṇīya' or 'Pāñcarātra' religion; and that it later on acquired the name of 'Sātvata', after it was spread in the Sātvata community; and that it came to be called the 'Bhāgavata' religion in the belief that the Blessed Lord Śrī Kṛṣṇa and Arjuna were respectively the incarnations of Nara and Nārāyaṇa. Thus, it is not necessary to imagine that there were three or four different Śrī Kṛṣṇas, and that each of them added a little to the religion; and there is in fact no evidence for coming to such a conclusion. This idea has gained ground on account of the good or bad changes which have taken place in the original religion. But if, though Buddha, Christ, or Mahomed were each one individual by themselves, there came about many good or bad changes in their religions, then there is no occasion in my opinion for believing that there must have been several Śrī Kṛṣṇas, on the ground that the original Bhāgavata religion later on acquired different forms, or that different ideas later on gained ground regarding Śrī Kṛṣṇa. Whichever religion is taken, it is quite easy and natural that it should change its form in the course of time; and it is not necessary on that account to believe that there were several Kṛṣṇas, or Buddhas, or Christs, or Mahomeds. * Some people—especially

* The life of Śrī Kṛṣṇa includes amorous passages with Gopis (cowherdesses) side by side with prowess, devotion and philosophy; and these things are mutually inconsistent. On this ground, many learned people maintain now-a-days that the Śrī Kṛṣṇa of the Mahābhārata was a different person from the Śrī Kṛṣṇa of the Gītā or of Gokul; and this opinion has been accepted by Dr. Bhandarkar in his book 'Vaiṣṇavism, Śaivism, and other sects". But, according to me, such an opinion is incorrect. It may be that the amorous descriptions which we read in the stories about Gopis may have been added afterwards; and it is not necessary on that account to believe that there were various persons bearing the name of Śrī Kṛṣṇa; and there is no authority except imagination for doing so. Besides, it is not that stories about Gopis came into vogue for the first time in the days of the Bhāgavata; for, Gopis are referred to in the *Buddha-carita* (4. 14) written by Aśvaghoṣa in the beginning of the

Western imaginative people—have raised a doubt that Śrī Kṛṣṇa, the Yādavas, the Pāṇḍavas, or the Bhāratī war, were not historical facts at all, but are mere imaginary personages or stories; and in the opinion of some other persons, the Mahābhārata is nothing but a tremendous metaphysical allegory dealing with the Absolute Self. But, any impartial man will have to come to the conclusion that all such doubts are without any basis, if he considers the evidence of ancient works. There is no doubt that there is historical authority at the root of these stories. In short, in my opinion, there were not four or five Śrī Kṛṣṇas, but there was only one historical personage of that name. Now, in considering the date of this Śrī Kṛṣṇa, Rao Bahadur Chintamanrao Vaïdya has expressed an opinion that Śrī Kṛṣṇa, the Yādavas, the Pāṇḍavas, and the Bhāratī war, were all synchronous, that is to say, they all existed at the commencement of the Kaliyuga; that according to the method of calculation of time mentioned in the Purāṇas, a period of five thousand years or more has elapsed since then; and that, this is the true date of Śrī Kṛṣṇa. * But if one considers the generations of various kings from the Pāṇḍavas upto the Śālivāhana era, which have been described in the Purāṇas, this date is inconsistent with that calculation. Therefore, on the authority of the statement in the Bhāgavata, or in the Viṣṇu-Purāṇa, that "there are 1115 (or 1015) years from the birth of the king Parikṣita upto the coronation of Nanda" (Bhāg. 12. 2. 26; and Viṣṇu. 4. 24. 32), historical scholars have now come to the conclusion that the Pāṇḍavas and the Bhāratī war must have been at least 1400 years before the Christian era. Necessarily, this will also be the date of Śrī Kṛṣṇa; and if this date is accepted, it follows that Śrī Kṛṣṇa promulgated the Bhāgavata religion at least 1400 years before Christ, and about 800 years before Buddha. Some persons have

Śaka era, as also in the *Bālacarita* (3. 2) written by Bhāsa. I, therefore, consider the opinion of Chintamanrao Vaidya more to the point than that of Dr. Bhandarkar.

* This opinion of Rao Bahadur Chinatamanrao Vaidya has been expressed in his English criticism on the Mahābhārata; and he also made the same statement in the lecture delivered by him on on the same subject in Poona in 1914 on the occasion of the anniversary of the Deccan College.

raised an objection to this argument, that although Śrī Kṛṣṇa and the Pāṇḍavas may be historical personages, yet, a considerable time must have elapsed between the death Śrī Kṛṣṇa and the time when Brahmins gave to a Kṣatriya warrior like Him the position, first of a superman, then of Viṣṇu, and ultimately of the Parabrahman; and that on that account the date of the rise of the Bhāgavata religion cannot be looked upon as the same as the date of the Bhāratī war. But, this opinion seems to be worthless. There is a world of difference between the ideas of the modern critics as to who should be deified and who not, and similar ideas of people living three or four thousand years ago (Gī. 10. 41); and there are statements in Upaniṣads, which existed prior to the date of Śrī Kṛṣṇa, that a Jñānin himself becomes merged in the Brahman (Bṛ. 4. 4. 6); and it is clearly stated in the Maitryupaniṣad that Rudra, Viṣṇu, Acyuta and Nārāyaṇa are all Brahman (Maitryu. 7. 7). Then, why should there have been delay in the matter of Śrī Kṛṣṇa acquiring the Parabrahman status? If we consider history, Buddha used to call himself '*brahmabhūta*' (See Selasutta, 14; Theragāthā, 831); and he was worshipped as a god in his life-time; and it appears from reliable Buddhistic works that shortly after his death, he had acquired the position of '*devādhideva*', or of the Parabrahman according to Vedic religion; and the same is the case with Christ. It is true that Śrī Kṛṣṇa was not an ascetic like Buddha or Christ, and that the Bhāgavata religion does not support Renunciation. But, there could have been no difficulty on that account in the promulgator of the Bhāgavata religion acquiring the form of a god or of the Brahman from the very beginning, as was acquired by the promulgators of the Buddhist and Christian religions.

Though the date of Śrī Kṛṣṇa has been defined in this way, and although it is proper and logical to look upon that date as the date of the rise of the Bhāgavata religion, Western scholars are, for quite a different reason, unwilling to do so. Many of these scholars are still of opinion that the Ṛg-Veda is not more ancient than 1500 or perhaps 2000 years before Christ, and therefore, they think it improbable that the devotional Bhāgavata religion could have come into existence about 1400 years before Christ; because the Vedic religious literature itself establishes the order that the Ṛg.-Veda was followed by the Yajurveda and the Brāhmaṇa treatises, and that the Upaniṣads dealing with Spiritual Knowledge and the Sāṁkhya philosophy came afterwards, and that the devotional philosophical books came into existence last of all; and if one considers the treatises on the Bhāgavata religion themselves, one also clearly sees that the Spiritual Knowledge of the Upaniṣads, the Sāṁkhya philosophy, Yoga in the form of 'Concentration of the Mind', and other aspects of religion were current long before the advent of the Bhāgavata religion. Even if we economise time considerably, we have to admit that a period of at least ten to twelve hundred years must have elapsed between the date of the Ṛg-Veda and the advent of the Bhāgavata religion, in order to give sufficient time for these various aspects of religion to have come into existence and fully developed themselves; and if it is believed that the Bhāgavata religion was promulgated by Śrī Kṛṣṇa in His own time, that is to say, about 1400 years before Christ, then a sufficient period of time is not allowed for the growth of these various aspects of religion according to the opinion of these scholars; because, these scholars place the Ṛg-Veda itself at 1500 to 2000 years before Christ; and on that computation, one has to say that the Bhāgavata religion came into existence about 100 years or at most 500 to 600 years after that date; and therefore, some Western scholars have even come forward to dissociate Śrī Kṛṣṇa from the Bhāgavata religion on this or on some other meaningless excuse, and to say that the Bhāgavata religion must have come into existence after the date of Buddha. But, the references to the Bhāgavata religion, which the Jain and Buddhistic treatises themselves contain, clearly show that that religion must have been in existence before the date of Buddha: and therefore, Dr. Bühler has said that instead of placing the date of the advent of the Bhāgavata religion after the date of Buddha, the date of the Ṛg-Veda itself must be pushed back, as has been stated by me in my book called *Orion.* * The dates fixed by Western scholars for our Vedic literature on

---

* See the Review made by Dr. Bühler of my book *Orion* in the issue of the *Indian Antiquary* for September 1894 (Vol. XXIII, pp. 238-249).

some insufficiently sound grounds, are wrong; and the date of the starting-point of the Vedic era cannot be taken at less than 4500 years before Christ, as has been proved in my book *Orion* on the strength of the phrases in the Vedas, which show the then existing Udagayana (i.e., period during which the Sun seems to travel towards the North—Trans.); and this conclusion has now been accepted by many Western scholars. When in this way, the date of the Ṛg-Veda has been taken back, a sufficient period of time can be allowed for the growth of all the various aspects of the Vedic religion, and there is no more any necessity for pushing forward the date of the rise of the Bhāgavata religion. As the Brāhmaṇa treatises written after the Ṛg-Veda contain the astronomical calculation of the year starting with the Sun in the Kṛttikā constellation, their date has to be fixed at about 2500 years before Christ, as has been shown by the late Shankara Balkrishna Dikshit in his History of the Indian Astronomical Science (*bhāratīya-jyotiḥ-śāstra*) written in the Marathi language. But, I do not see this method of fixing the dates of ancient books by considering how the Udagayana was then started being applied to the Upaniṣads. Some scholars have come to the conclusion that none of the Upaniṣads can be more than 400 to 500 years before Buddha, on the ground that the language and construction of devotional Upaniṣads like the Rāmatāpanī, or Yogic Upaniṣads like the Yogatattva, is not archaic. But, if one considers the matter according to the abovementioned method of calculation of time, it will be seen that such a conclusion is wrong. It is true that the dates of all the Upaniṣads cannot be fixed according to the astronomical method of calculation; yet, this method is very useful for fixing the date of the principal Upaniṣads. Prof. Max Müller* has said that, from the linguistic point of view, the Maitryupaniṣad is more ancient than Pāṇini, because, we find in this Upaniṣad, many compounds of words, used in a *chanda*, which had gone out of vogue at the date of Pāṇini, but which are to be found in the Maitrāyaṇi Saṁhitā. But the Maitrāyaṇyupaniṣad is not the very first nor a very ancient Upaniṣad. Not only has harmony been established between

* See Sacred Books of the East Series Vol. XV Intro pp. xlviii-lii.

Knowledge of the Brahman and Sāṁkhya philosophy in the Maitrāyaṇyupaniṣad, but in many places, phrases or even stanzas from the Chāndogya, Bṛhadāraṇyaka, Taittirīya, Kaṭha, and Īśāvāsya are seen being taken as authorities. The actual names of these Upanisads are not mentioned in the Maitryupaniṣad; but as, in quoting these phrases, words implying quotation such as '*evaṁ hyāha*' or '*uktaṁ ca*' (i. e., 'so it is said') are placed before the quotations, there is no doubt that these quotations are taken from some other book, and are not written by the writer of the Maitryupaniṣad; and one can easily determine which Upaniṣad has been quoted from, by a reference to these other Upaniṣads. Now, where the description of the Brahman in the shape of '*kāla*' (Time) or '*saṁvatsara*' (Year) is made in the Maitryupaniṣad (Maitryu. 6. 14), it is stated that: "the Dakṣiṇāyana (i. e., when the Sun seems to travel towards the South—Trans.) lasts from the day when the Sun enters to Maghā constellation until it reaches the centre-point of the Śraviṣṭhā, that is, the Dhaniṣṭhā constellation (cf. "*maghādyaṁ śraviṣṭhārdhaṁ*"); and that the Uttarāyaṇa (or Udagayana, during which the Sun seems to travel towards the North—Trans.) used to be from the beginning of the Sārpa, that is, the Āśleṣā constellation, in an inverse order upto the centre-point of the Dhaniṣṭhā constellation, that is, counting backwards as Āśleṣā, Puṣya, etc.". It is quite clear that these expressions, which show the method of calculation of the Udagayana, must have been used with reference to the period of the Udagayana which was then in vogue; and in this way, the date of that Upaniṣad can easily be mathematically calculated. But no one seems to have considered the matter from this point of view. This state of the Udagayana, referred to in the Maitryupaniṣad, is earlier than the state of the Udagayana referred to in the Vedāṅga-Jyotiṣa; because, it is clearly stated in the Vedāṅga-Jyotiṣa that the commencement of the Udagayana is from the beginning of the Dhaniṣṭhā constellation, whereas in the Maitryupaniṣad, the commencement is from the middle of the Dhaniṣṭhā. There is a difference of opinion as to whether the term '*ardhaṁ*' in the phrase '*śraviṣṭhārdhaṁ*' is to be interpreted as meaning 'exactly half' or 'somewhere between Dhaniṣṭhā and Śatatārakā'. Whatever may be the case, there is no doubt about the fact that the state of the Udagayana mentioned in the Maitryupaniṣad is earlier in point of time than that mentioned in the Vedāṅga-Jyotiṣa. Therefore, it must be said that the Udagayana at the date of the Vedāṅga-Jyotiṣa was about half a constellation behind the Udagayana at the date of the Maitryupaniṣad. It is proved by astronomical calculations that the state of the Udagayana mentioned in the Vedāṅga-Jyotiṣa existed about 1200 to 1400 years before Christ;* and in as much as the Udagayana takes about 480 years to recede by half a constellation, it follows by mathematical calculation that the Maitryupaniṣad must have been written somewhere between 1880 to 1680 years before Christ. At any rate, there is no doubt that this Upaniṣad was previous in point of time than the Vedāṅga-Jyotiṣa. It need not, therefore, be said that the Chāndogya and other Upaniṣads, from which quotations have been taken into the Maitryupaniṣad, are still earlier in point of time. The date of the Ṛg-Veda being in this way fixed at 4500 years before Christ, that of the Brāhmaṇas, dealing with sacrificial ritual, being fixed at about 2500 years before Christ, and that of the Chāndogya and other Upaniṣads dealing with Spiritual Knowledge being fixed at about 1600 years before Christ, the reason for which Western scholars bring forward the date of the Bhāgavata religion ceases to exist, and there is no more any difficulty in the way of Śrī Kṛṣṇa and the Bhāgavata religion being tied together by the cord of synchrony, like a cow and a calf; and then, this date also becomes consistent with the state of things mentioned in Buddhistic treatises, or established by other historical evidence. The Vedic age comes to an end, and the Sūtras and the Smṛtis begin, at about this time.

The above-mentioned calculation of time proves beyond doubt that the Bhāgavata religion came into existence about

* I have discussed the date of the Vedāṅga-Jyotiṣa in my work *Orion* in English; the late Shankara Balkrishna Diksit has also done so in his book called *'Historical Survey of the Bhāratīya-Jyotiḥ Śāstra* (pp. 87 to 94 and 127 to 139). The date of Vedic treatises according to the Udagayana, has been considered in the same place.

1400 years before Christ, that is to say, about 700 to 800 years before Buddha. This age is very ancient; yet, the Path of Action mentioned in the Brāhmaṇa-treatises is still more ancient, and, as has been stated above, the Spiritual Knowledge contained in the Upaniṣads and in Sāṁkhya philosophy was fully in vogue long before the promulgation of the Bhāgavata religion. It is, in my opinion, entirely wrong to imagine that a clever Jñānin like Śrī Kṛṣṇa would have promulgated His religion at such a time without reference to this Spiritual Knowledge or these aspects of Religion; and that, even if He had done so, it would have become acceptable to the Rājarṣis and Brahmarṣis of those days or found circulation among the people. As the Jews to whom Christ first preached His religion, were not acquainted with religious philosophy at the time, He had no need to harmonise His own religion with any religious philosophy. It was enough for Him to show that His Philosophy of Devotion was only a continuation of the Ritualistic religion described in the Old Testament of the Bible; and that was all He attempted to do. But, when one compares this history of the Christian religion with the Bhāgavata religion from the historical point of view, one must not forget that the people to whom the Bhāgavata religion was preached were, at the time at which it was preached, fully conversant, not only with the Path of Action, but also with the Vedāntic Knowledge of the Brahman and the Kāpila Sāṁkhya philosophy, and that they had by that time also learnt to harmonise those three religions. It would have been most unreasonable to ask such people to put on the shelf their Ritualistic religion, or the Spiritual Knowledge derived from the Upaniṣads, or Sāṁkhya philosophy, and to accept the Bhāgavata religion merely by faith. Unless the Bhāgavata religion satisfactorily answered such questions as, 'what is the result of the sacrificial ritual described in the Vedic treatises and in vogue at the time'?, 'whether the Spiritual Knowledge mentioned in the Upaniṣads or in Sāṁkhya philosophy is futile?', or, 'whether the Philosophy of Devotion can be harmonised with Yoga in the shape of Concentration of the Mind?', which questions would naturally arise, it would have been impossible for that religion to gain any ground at all. It, therefore, follows logically that, it was necessary to discuss all these matters, to start with, in dealing with the Bhāgavata religion; and the same conclusion is emphasised, if one considers the Nārāyaṇīyopākhyāna included in the Mahābharata. In this Ākhyāna, the Spiritual Knowledge of the Upaniṣads and the Sāṁkhya theory of the Perishable and the Imperishable have both been harmonised with the Bhāgavata religion; and it is clearly stated that: "it is called the 'Pāñcarātra' religion because the four Vedas and Sāṁkhya and Yoga are all included in it" (Ma. Bhā. Śān. 339. 107); and that "all these (philosophies) including the Vedas and the Araṇyakas (naturally also, including the Upaniṣads) are all parts of each other" (Śān. 348. 82). Although this explanation of the meaning of the word 'Pāñcarātra' may not be grammatically correct, yet, it clearly shows that the Bhāgavata religion had, already to start with, harmonised all kinds of philosophies. Still, harmonising the Philosophy of Devotion with other aspects of religion is also not any important part of the Bhāgavata religion. It is not that the religious principle of Devotion was first enunciated in the Bhāgavata religion. Worship of Rudra or of Viṣṇu in some form or other had been started before the advent of the Bhāgavata religion; and it becomes clear from the phrases quoted above from the Maitryupaniṣad (Maitryu. 7.7), that the idea that any object of worship whatsoever is a symbol, or some kind of form of the Brahman, had also previously come into existence. It is true that the Bhāgavata religion has taken Vāsudeva as an object of worship instead of Rudra etc.; but at the same time, it is admitted both in the Gītā and also in the Nārāyaṇīyopākhyāna, that whatever may be the object of worship, the worship reaches one and the same Bhagavanta, and that Rudra and Bhagavāna are not two. (Gī. 9. 23; Ma. Bhā. Śān. 341. 20-26). Therefore, one cannot consider the worship of Vāsudeva as the principal aspect of the Bhāgavata religion. The Sātvata community by which the Bhāgavata religion was observed, produced Sātyaki and other warriors, as also devotees of the Blessed Lord like Bhīṣma and Arjuna, and also Śrī Kṛṣṇa, who engaged and caused others to be engaged in numerous activities, involving personal prowess. Therefore, the most important teaching of the original Bhāgavata religion was, that the illustration of these persons should be copied by other devotees of the Blessed Lord, who should perform worldly activities like warfare, etc., which were then in vogue, according to the arrangement of the four castes. It is not that those times did not produce persons with a renounced frame of mind, who had adopted the principle of Devotion as a result of intense renunciation, and given up worldly life; but that was not the principal element of the Bhāgavata religion of the Sātvatas or of Śrī Kṛṣṇa. The sum and substance of the advice of Śrī Kṛṣṇa is, that after the Devotee of the Blessed Lord has acquired the Knowledge of the Parameśvara, by means of Devotion, he must, like the Parameśvara, exert himself for the maintenance and upkeep of the world. Already at the time of the Upaniṣads, Janaka and others had laid it down that even those people, who had Realised the Brahman, might without any difficulty take part in Desireless Action. But in those days, the Philosophy of Devotion had not entered their doctrine; and whether or not to perform worldly Action after the Acquisition of Knowledge was in those days considered a matter of personal volition only (Ve. Sū. 3. 4. 15). The Bhāgavata religion went beyond this and laid down that Desireless Energism (*naiṣkarmya*) was better than Total Renunciation; and it brought about a proper fusion of Energism, not only with Spiritual Knowledge, but also with Devotion. This is the most important achievement of the Bhāgavata religion in the history of the Vedic religion, and is something which is different from what was done by the Smārta religion. The original promulgators of this religion, namely the Nara and Nārāyaṇa Ṛṣis, also engaged in Desireless Energism in this way; and it is stated in one place in the Mahābhārata that every one must do what was done by them (Ma. Bhā. Udyo. 48. 21, 22); and in the Nārāyaṇīyākhyāna, the characteristic feature of this religion is clearly defined as "*pravṛtti lakṣaṇaś caiva dharmo nārāyaṇātmakaḥ*" (Ma. Bhā. Śān. 347. 81), i. e., "the Nārāyaṇa or Bhāgavata religion is Energistic or Activistic". This principle of Desireless Action of the Nārāyaṇīya or the Bhāgavata religion is known as '*naiṣkarmya*'; and this was the most important aspect of the original Bhāgavata religion. But later on in course of time, this principle lost importance, and Devotion to Vāsudeva combined with apathy towards the world came to be looked upon as the important part of this religion, as is apparent from the Bhāgavata; and in the Nārada-Pañcarātra, *mantras* and *tantras* are included in the Bhāgavata religion along with the Philosophy of Devotion. Yet, it is patent from the Bhāgavata itself, that these are not the fundamental aspects of this religion; because, wherever there has been occasion in the Bhāgavata to refer to the Sātvata or the Nārāyaṇīya religion, it is stated that the religion of the Sātvatas or of Nārāyaṇa Ṛṣi (that is, the Bhāgavata religion) is 'of the nature of *naiṣkarmya*' (Bhāg. 1. 3. 8 and 11. 4. 6); and it is stated that it had become necessary to preach the Devotional Bhāgavata-Purāṇa (Bhāg. 1. 5. 12), because due importance had not been given to Devotion in the '*naiṣkarmya*' religion. This proves beyond any doubt that the original Bhāgavata religion was based on *naiṣkarmya* or Desireless Action, and that later on its form was changed in the course of time, and Devotion became the principal factor in it. I have already dealt above in the Gītā-Rahasya with the other various historical questions, namely, (i) what was the difference between the original Bhāgavata religion, which maintained a permanent fusion between Spiritual Knowledge, Devotion, and Prowess, and the path prescribed by the Smṛtis in the shape of the arrangement of the various stages of life; (ii) how, as a result of the growth of the purely ascetic Jain and Buddhist religions, the Karma-Yoga in the Energistic Bhāgavata religion lost ground, and it (the Bhāgavata religion) acquired its new form of Renunciation with Devotion; and (iii) how the Vedic sects which came into existence after the fall of Buddhism gave to the Bhagavadgītā itself either a renunciatory, or a purely Devotional, or a Qualified-Monistic (*viśiṣṭādvaita*) form. I shall, therefore, not repeat the same subject-matter here.

From the short dissertation made above, my readers will have seen (i) when, the Bhāgavata religion first came into prominence in the ancient course of the Vedic religion, (ii) how, although it was Energistic in the beginning, it later on became devotional; and (iii) how, still later on, in the time of Rāmānujācārya, it acquired the form of Qualified-Monism. The most ancient of these various forms of the Bhāgavata religion, that is to say, the Desireless Activistic form, is the form of the Gītā-religion. I shall now briefly explain what inferences can be drawn about the date of this original Gītā. Although the time of Śrī Kṛṣṇa and of the Bhāratī war may be the same, that is to say, about 1400 years before the Christian era, yet, it cannot be said that the original Gītā and the original Bhārata, which are the two principal treatises dealing with the Bhāgavata religion, were also written at the same time. Whatever religious sect may come into existence, literature on it does not come into existence immediately; and the same argument applies to the Bhārata and to the Gītā. There is a story recited at the commencement of the present Mahābhārata, that after the Bhāratī war was over, Janamejaya, the great-grandson of the Pāṇḍavas made a sacrifice of serpents; that, Vaiśaṁpāyana recited to him for the first time the whole of the Bhārata including the Gītā; and that, when it had been recited by Sauti to Śaunaka, the Bhārata was thereafter promulgated. It is quite clear that some period of time must have elapsed between the date when the Bhārata came to be preached by Sauti and other preachers, and the date when it acquired its present tangible literary form; but there is now no means by which to definitely decide what that period of time was. Still, if one draws the conclusion that the archaic original epic-formed Bhārata came to be written within 500 years after the Bhāratī war, that will not be too daring a surmise; because, Buddhistic treatises were written in even a shorter period of time after the death of Buddha. In writing an archaic epic, it is not enough to merely describe in it the feats of the principal hero; but it is necessary to say whether or not what was done by the hero was right. Nay, that this is possibly one of the most important parts of an archaic epic, appears from other such epics, in literatures other than the Sanskrit literature. From the modern point of view, this justification of the deeds of the heroes must be made on the pure basis of Ethics. But, in ancient times, there was no difference between Religion and Ethics; and, therefore, there was no way in which to make this justification other than from the point of view of Religion; and then, as need not be said, it was necessary to justify their deeds on the basis of that very Bhāgavata religion, which had been promulgated by the heroes in the Bhārata, or which was acceptable to them.

But another reason for doing so was that, it was not possible to fully justify the deeds or prowess of the heroes of the Mahābhārata on the basis of the religious principles of other religious paths, as all the other Vedic religious paths, besides the Bhāgavata religion, which were then in vogue, were more or less renunciatory. Therefore, it became necessary to expound the Energistic Bhāgavata religion in the original epic Bhārata. This was done in the original Gītā; and although it might not have been the first treatise to categorically expound the original form of the Bhāgavata religion, yet, it is one of the principal books on that religion; and there seems to be no reason why its date should not be roughly fixed at about 900 years before Christ. Since the Gītā is, at any rate, the most important, if not the first treatise on the Bhāgavata religion, it was necessary to show that the Desireless Karma-Yoga promulgated by it was not inconsistent with the other religious paths then in vogue, namely, the Karma-kāṇḍa, the Spiritual Knowledge in the Upaniṣads, the Sāṁkhya philosophy, the Yoga philosophy dealing with 'Concentration of the Mind', and the Philosophy of Devotion; and I may even say that that was the principal object of this book. Some persons raise the doubt that, the systematic sciences of Vedānta and Mīmāṁsā could not have been dealt with in the original Gītā, as they came into existence only at a later date; and that, therefore, Vedānta must have been subsequently interpolated into the Gītā. But, although the systematic sciences of Vedānta and Mīmāṁsā may have come into existence later on, yet, as has been stated above, the subject-matter dealt with by them was very ancient. Therefore, there is no difficulty, from the point of view of time, in the way of these subjects having appeared in the original Gītā. Nevertheless, I do not say that no change was made in the original Gītā, when the original Bhārata became the Mahābhārata. History shows us that whatever religion is taken, sub-sects come into existence in it in course of time, as a result of differences of opinion; and the same law applies to the Bhāgavata religion. It is clearly stated in the Nārāyaṇīyopākhyāna itself, that the Bhāgavata religion was considered by some as four-folded *(catur-vyūha)*, that is, made up of the four aspects of Vāsudeva, Saṁkarṣaṇa, Pradyumna, and Aniruddha; and that it was considered by others as three-folded, and by others as two-folded, and by others again as single-folded (Ma. Bhā. Śān. 348. 57); and some such other differences may also have arisen later on. At the same time, the Spiritual Knowledge contained in the Upaniṣads and the Sāṁkhya philosophy were being further developed. Therefore, if there was any dis-arrangement in the original Gītā, it would not have been unnatural, or inconsistent with the purpose of the original Gītā, for the writer of the new Bhārata to see that that defect was removed, and that the Bhāgavata religion was made consistent with the growing knowledge of the Piṇḍa and the Brahmāṇḍa; and I have, therefore, shown in the Part of this Appendix headed 'the Gītā and the Brahma-Sūtras' above, that the present Gītā contains, on that account, a reference to the Brahma-Sūtras. There might also have been other similar differences in the original Gītā. Still, it was not possible that many such changes should be made in the original Gītā. It does not appear that the authority of the Gīts was acquired by it after the date of the Mahābhārata. I have stated above that the Brahma-Sūtras themselves have taken the Gītā as authoritative by using the word 'Smṛti'. If a material change had been made in the original Gītā, when the original Bhārata was changed into the Mahābhārata, this authoritativeness of the Gītā would certainly have suffered. But instead of that, its authority has, on the other hand, increased. We have, therefore, to draw the inference that whatever changes were made in the original Gītā, they were not material, and that the changes which were made, were made in such a way as to promote and carry out its original import. It is clear from the various Gītās which have been mentioned in the different Purāṇas on the basis of the present Bhagavadgītā, that the form which it then acquired was a permanent form, and that there were no further changes in it. Because, if the Gītā had not become fully authoritative, that is to say, invariable, at least some centuries before the date of the most ancient of these Purāṇas, it would not have been possible to conceive the idea of including other Gītās on the basis of this Gītā in those Purāṇas. And the attempts made by various doctrine-supporting commentators to stretch the meanings of the words in one and the same Gītā in order to show that the purport of the Gītā was consistent with their own doctrines, would also in that case not have become necessary. A doubt is raised by some scholars that many changes must have been made from time to time in the Gītā in the present Mahābhārata, on the ground that the present Gītā contains many mutually contradictory doctrines. But, I have shown above that these inconsistencies are not substantial, and that this mental confusion is due to people not having properly understood the previous and subsequent Vedic methods of expounding religion. In short, it will be seen from the above exposition that (i) the original Bhārata and the original Gītā, which propounded the original Bhāgavata religion, were written about 500 years after the rise of the Bhāgavata religion, which harmonised the various ancient Vedic aspects of religion, and specially supported the Path of Energism, that is to say, about 900 years before Christ; that (ii) though, when the Bhārata was changed into the Mahābhārata, there might have been some minor improvements in the original Gītā, which would be promotive of its purport, yet, the form of the original Gītā was not then substantially changed; and that (iii) after the present Gītā had been included in the present Mahābhārata, there was no subsequent change in it, nor was it possible that any such change should take place. The fixing of the form and the date of the original Gītā and the original Bhārata have been made by me approximately and in a liberal way, because that amount of information which would be necessary for fixing those matters definitely is not now available. But, the same is not the case with the present Mahābhārata and the present Gītā; and there are ways available for fixing their respective dates. I have, therefore, discussed that matter separately in the next part of this Appendix. My readers must, however, bear it in mind that the present Gītā and the present Mahābhārata, that is to say, the forms in which the Gītā and the Mahābhārata are now found by us, after changes have taken place in their respective forms in course of time, are not the original forms of those respective books.

PART V—THE DATE OF THE PRESENT GĪTĀ.

I have proved above in a general way that the Bhagavadgītā is the most important work dealing with the Bhāgavata religion; that this Bhāgavata religion came into existence about 1400 years before Christ; and that the original Gītā must have come into existence some centuries after that; and I have also said that though the original Bhāgavata religion favoured Desireless Action, it gradually assumed a Devotional form, and ultimately came to include the principles of Qualified-Monism (*viśiṣṭādvaita*). More information about the original Gītā or the original Bhāgavata religion is not available, at least at the present day; and the same was the case with the present Mahābhārata and the present Gītā about 50 years ago. But, as a result of the efforts of Dr. Bhandarkar, the late Mr. Kashinathpant Telang, the late Mr. Shankar Balkrishna Dikshit, and Rao Bahadur Chintamanrao Vaidya, many proofs have now become available for fixing the date of the present Bhārata and the present Gītā; and very recently, the late Mr. Tryambak Gurunath Kale has also adduced some more proofs. This part of the Appendix has been briefly made up by me by putting together all these matters and adding to them whatever addition was necessary in my opinion. In the beginning of this Appendix I have shown with proofs that the present Mahābhārata and the present Gītā must have been written by one and the same hand. When these two treatises are accepted as being written by the same hand, and therefore necessarily contemporaneous, one can easily fix the date of the Gītā by fixing the date of the Mahābhārata. I have, therefore, in this part of the Appendix mentioned first the various important proofs which are now available for fixing the date of the present Mahābhārata, and then shown independently those proofs, which are useful for fixing the date of the present Gītā. I have followed this course in order that the fixing of the date of the Gītā should not suffer, if some one finds the proofs adduced by me for fixing the date of the Mahābhārata not sufficiently definite.

THE FIXING OF THE DATE OF THE MAHABHARATA—The Mahābhārata is an extremely extensive work; and it is stated in that book itself, that it consists of one hundred thousand stanzas. But Rao Bahadur Vaidya has shown in the first Appendix to his criticism in English on the Mahābhārata, that the present edition of the Mahābhārata consists of less than that number of stanzas, and that we do not arrive at that total, even by adding the Harivaṁśa to it. * Nevertheless, there is no reason for not accepting the poāition that the larger book, which came into existence when the Bhārata became the Mahābhārata, must have been more or less the same as the present edition of the Mahābhārata. I have stated above that this Mahābhārata makes a mention of the Nirukta of Yāska and of Manu-Saṃhitā, and that the Gītā even mentions the Brahma-Sūtras. The other proofs which are available for fixing the date of the Mahābhārata are as follows:–

(1) This book of eighteen *parvas* and the Harivaṁśa, found their way into the Java and Bali Islands before Śaka 400 to 500; and it has been translated into the ancient language of those places known as 'Kavi'; and the following eight *parvas* of that translation, namely, the Ādi, Virāṭa, Udyoga, Bhīṣma, Āśramavāsi, Musala, Prāsthānika, and Svargārohaṇa *parvas* are now available; and some of them have been printed. But, although the translation has been made into the Kavi language, the original Sanskrit stanzas from the Mahābhārata have been retained in many places. I have considered some of the stanzas from the Udyogaparva. All these stanzas can be found here and there in the chapters of the Udyogaparva of the Calcutta edition of the present Mahābhārata. This proves that the Mahābhārata of a hundred thousand stanzas had become authoritative in India at least 200 years before Śaka 400; because, it would otherwise not have been necessary at all to take it into the Java and Bali Islands. The Mahābhārata has also been translated into the Tibetan language, but, that is later in point of time than this. †

* "*The Mahābhārata, a Criticism*" p. 185. Wherever this criticism of Rao Bahadur Vaidya on the Mahābhārata has been referred to, this book is meant.

† See the reference to the Mahābhārata of the Java Island at pp. 32–38 of the issue of the *Modern Review* for July 1914. A reference to the Mahābhārata in the Tibetan language has been made in Rockhill's *Life of the Buddha*, p. 228, Note I.

(2) There is now available a stone inscription of the Gupta kings made in Cedi Saṁvat 197, that is to say, the 367th year of the Śaka era, which contains a clear reference that the Mahābhārata was a book of a hundred thousand verses; and this reference clearly proves that the Mahābhārata must have been in existence at least 100 to 200 years before Śaka 367. *

(3) Many of the dramas of Bhāsa, which have now been published, have been written on the basis of certain chapters of the Mahābhārata. It, therefore, follows that the Mahābhārata was then available and was looked upon as authoritative. The drama, *Bālacarita* of Bhāsa contains a reference to the incidents of the youth of Śrī Kṛṣṇa and to Gopis. Therefore, we have to say that the Harivaṁśa must also then have been in existence. There is no doubt that Bhāsa lived before Kālidāsa. Tanjore Ganapati Shastri, who has edited the dramas of Bhāsa, has stated in his preface to the drama *Svapnavāsavadattā* that Bhāsa lived even before Cāṇakya; because, a stanza found in the dramas of Bhāsa, is to be found in the Artha-Śāstra of Cāṇakya; and it is clearly stated in that place that that stanza is a quotation. But although this period of time is not definite, yet, Bhāsa can certainly not be placed in my opinion later than the second or third century A. D.

(4) It is established from Buddhistic treatises, that a Buddhist poet named Aśvaghoṣa lived at the beginning of the Śālivāhana era. This Aśvaghoṣa wrote two epics in Sanskrit on the Buddhistic religion, called *Buddhacarita* and *Saundarānanda*. In both these epics, stories from the Bhārata have been referred to. There is besides a book in the shape of a lecture on the Vajrasūcikopaniṣad which is attributed to Aśvaghoṣa; or it may even be said that this Vajrasūci Upaniṣad was written by him. Prof. Webber published this book in Germany in 1860, and it contains the stanzas "*saptavyādhā daśārṇeṣu*" etc. from the Śrāddha-Māhātmya, in the Harivaṁśa (Hari. 24. 20 and 21); and some other stanzas from the Mahābhārata itself (such as, Ma.

* This stone inscription has been fully reproduced at page 134 of the third part of the book called *Inscriptionum Indicarum*, and it has been referred to by the late Mr. Shanker Balkrishna Dikshit in his *Bhāratīya Jyotiḥ-Śāstra* at page 108.

Bhā. Śān. 261. 17). This clearly proves that the present Mahābhārata of a hundred thousand stanzas including the Harivaṁśa was in existence before the commencement of the Śaka era.

(5) The Bhārata and the Mahābhārata have been independently referred to in the Āśvalāyana-Gṛhya-Sūtra (3. 4. 4), and a stanza from the Yayāti Upākhyāna of the Mahābhārata (Ma. Bhā. Ā. 78. 10) appears in one place in the Baudhāyana-Dharma-Sūtra (2. 2. 26). Bühler says that this one stanza is not sufficient proof for saying that the Mahābhārata existed before Baudhāyana *; but this objection is groundless, because the Gṛhyaśeṣa-Sūtra of Baudhāyana contains a reference to the Viṣṇu-Sahasranāma (Bau. Gṛ. Śe. 1. 22. 8); and further on, in the same Sūtra (2. 22. 9), the stanza "*patraṁ puṣpaṁ phalaṁ toyaṁ*" etc. from the Gītā (Gī. 9. 26) has been mentioned. These references in the Baudhāyana-Sūtra were first pointed out by the late Mr. Tryambak Gurunath Kale †; and they prove that the objection raised by Prof. Bühler is groundless, and that both Āśvalāyana and Baudhāyana were conversant with the Mahābhārata. Bühler has established on other evidence that Baudhāyana must have lived about 400 years before Christ.

(6) Where the incarnations of Viṣṇu have been mentioned in the Mahābhārata itself, there is no reference to Buddha; and where the ten incarnations are mentioned in the Nārāyaṇīyopākhyāna (Ma. Bhā. Śān. 339. 100), the Haṁsa is taken as the first incarnation, and Kalki is placed immediately after Kṛṣṇa to make up the total of ten. Yet, where the future state of the Kali-Yuga is referred to in the Vanaparva, it is stated that:— "*eḍūkacinhā pṛthivī na devagṛha-bhūṣitā*", i. e., "on the earth, there will be '*eḍūka*' instead of temples of gods" (Ma. Bhā. Vana. 190. 68). An *eḍūka* is a pillar, tower, and other edifice, erected as a memorial over some buried hair, tooth etc. of Buddha; and it is now-a-days known as '*ḍāgobā*'. '*ḍāgobā*' is a corruption from the Sanskrit word '*dhātu-garbha*' (in Pali, *ḍāgaba*),

* Sacred Books of the East. Vol. XIV. Intro. p. xli.

† The whole of the essay of the late Mr. Tryambak Gurunath Kale has been published in *The Vedic Magazine and Gurukul Samachar* Vol. VII Nos. 6, 7, pp. 528–532. There the name of the writer is wrongly mentioned as 'Prof. Kale'.

and '*dhātu*' means the 'memento which is buried'. In Ceylon and in Burma there is many a *ḍāgobā*, in numerous places. This shows that the Mahābhārata must have been written after the date of Buddha, but before he was looked upon as an incarnation. The words 'Buddha' and 'Prati-Buddha' occur in various places in the Mahābhārata (Śān. 194. 58; 307. 47; 343. 52). But there the words only mean a Jñānin, a Knower, or a Sthitaprajña. That word does not seem to have been taken from the Buddhist religion; nay, there is good reason for believing that the Buddhists themselves have taken these words from the Vedic religion.

(7) In the Mahābhārata, the enumeration of constellations does not start with Aśvinī, but with Kṛttikā. (Ma. Bhā. Anu. 64 and 89); and the zodiacal signs Meṣa, Vṛṣabha, etc. are nowhere mentioned. This is a matter of very great importance from the point of view of the date of the Mahābhārata; because, one can easily draw the inference from this fact that the Mahābhārata must have been written before the zodiacal signs Meṣa, Vṛṣabha etc. were known in India as a result of contact with the Greeks, that is to say, before the date of Alexander. But a still more important fact is the enumeration of the constellations starting with Śravaṇa. It is stated in the Anugītā that Viśvāmitra started the enumeration of the constellations with Śravaṇa (Ma. Bhā. Aśva. 44. 2, and Ādi 71. 34). That has been interpreted by commentators as showing that the Uttarāyaṇa then started with the Śravaṇa constellation, and no other interpretation is proper. At the date of the Vedāṅga-Jyotiṣa, the Uttarāyaṇa used to start with the Sun in the Dhaniṣṭhā constellation. According to astronomical calculations, the date when the Uttarāyaṇa should start with the Sun in the Dhaniṣṭhā constellation comes to about 1500 years before the Śaka era; and according to astronomical calculations, it takes about a thousand years for the Uttarāyaṇa to start one constellation earlier. According to this calculation, the date when the Uttarāyaṇa ought to start with the Sun in the Śravaṇa constellation comes to about 500 years before the Śaka era. Therefore, it can be proved mathematically that the present Mahābhārata must have been written about 500 years before the Śaka era. The late Mr. Shankar Balkrishna Dikshit has drawn the same conclusion in his Bhāratīya Jyotiḥ-Śāstra.

(Bhā. Jyo. pp. 87–90, 111 and 147). The important feature of this evidence is that the date of the present Mahābhārata cannot be taken to much more than 500 years before the Śaka era.

(8) Rao Bahadur Vaidya has in his criticism in English on the Mahābhārata shown that the Greek ambassador named Megasthenes, at the Court of Chandragupta (320 B. C.), knew some of the stories in the Mahābhārata. The works of Megasthenes are not now available in their entirety. But extracts made from them by other persons have been collected together, and were first published in German; and they have been translated into English by M'Crindle. It is stated in this book, (pp. 200–205), that the Heracles mentioned by Megasthenes was none but Śrī Kṛṣṇa; and that at the date of Megasthenes, this Śrī Kṛṣṇa, used to be worshipped by the Śauraseni people, and that these Śauraseni people used to live in Muttra. * It is also stated there that Heracles was the fifteenth in line of descent from Dionisus; and there is a statement even in the Mahābhārata (Ma. Bhā. Anu. 147. 25–33) that Śrī Kṛṣṇa was fifteenth in line of descent from Dakṣa Prajāpati. Also the descriptions given by Megasthenes (p. 94) of the *karṇa-prāvaraṇa, ekapāda* (one-footed—Trans.), *lalāṭākṣa* (cyclops, with one eye

* See M'Crindle's *Ancient India—Megasthenes and Arrian* pp. 200-205. This statement of Megasthenes has been fortified in a very curious way by a recent discovery. The Progress Report of the Archaeological Department of the Bombay Government for the year 1914 has been recently published. It reproduces the inscription on a *garuḍadhvaja* (eagle monolith) known as 'Khāmbabābā' at Besanagar near Bhilsā in the Gwalior State In that inscription, it is stated that a Greek or *yavana* named Heliodorus who had been converted to Hinduism, had constructed a temple to Vāsudeva in front of that monolith; and that this Heliodorus was the ambassador sent by the Greek king Antiocledes who ruled at Takṣaśilā, to the Court of the king Bhagabhadra ruling at Bhilsā. It has now been established from the coins of the king Antiocledes, that he was ruling in 140 B. C. This, therefore, clearly establishes not only that the worship of Vāsudeva was already in vogue at this time, but also that *yavanas* had started building temples to Vāsudeva. I have stated above that not only Megasthenes, but also Pāṇini knew of the worship of Vāsudeva.

only in the forehead—Trans.) and other strange people, and of ants (*pipīlikā*) who bring up gold are also to be found in the Mahābhārata (Ma. Bhā. Sabhā. 51 and 52). These and other facts clearly prove that not only the Mahābhārata but also the history of Śrī Kṛṣṇa and the worship of Śrī Kṛṣṇa were in vogue already at the date of Megasthenes.

When it is remembered that all the proofs mentioned above are not mutually inter-dependent but are independent, it becomes clear beyond doubt that the present Mahābhārata was in vogue at least about 500 years before the Śaka era. It is quite likely that some stanzas have been interpolated into or deleted from the Mahābhārata after that date. But we are now dealing with the question not of any particular stanzas but of the principal book itself; and it is quite clear that this book must have been written at least 500 years before the Śaka era. I have shown at the commencement of this Appendix that the Gītā is a part of the Mahābhārata, and has not been interpolated into it subsequently; therefore, the Gītā must be considered to be of the same date. The original Gītā may have been earlier than this; because, as has been shown in the fourth part of this Appendix, the tradition of the original Gītā has to be taken much further back. But, whatever may be said, it is absolutely clear that its date cannot be placed after the date of the Mahābhārata. This fact is established not merely by the evidence mentioned above; for, there is also independent evidence about it, which I shall now place before my readers.

THE FIXING OF THE DATE OF THE GĪTĀ—The evidence mentioned above does not contain a clear reference by name to the Gītā. Its date has been fixed there by reference to the Mahābhārata. I shall now set out the evidence which contains a clear reference to the Gītā. But before I do so, it must be mentioned that the late Mr. Telang has fixed the date of the Gītā as being before Āpastaṁba, that is to say, at least 300 years before Christ; and Dr. Bhandarkar has in his book in English named *Vaiṣṇavism, Śaivism, and other sects* accepted the same opinion. * Prof. Garbe is of the opinion that the date

* See Telang's *Bhagavadgītā*, S. B. E. Vol. VIII Intro pp. 21 and 34; Dr. Bhandarkar's *Vaiṣṇavism, Śaivism, and other sects*, p. 13; Dr. Garbe's *Die Bhagavadgītā* p. 64.

fixed by Mr. Telang is not correct, and that the original Gītā must have been written about 200 years before Christ, and that it was revised in the second century after Christ. But it will be seen that the opinion of Dr. Garbe is incorrect for the following reasons:–

(1) The Śāṁkarabhāṣya is the most ancient among the criticisms and commentaries on the Gītā which are now available. Śrī Śaṁkarācārya has also written a commentary on the Sanatsujātīya chapter of the Mahābhārata; and he has in many places in his works taken the statements from the Anugītā, the Manu-Bṛhaspati conversation, and the Śukānupraśna in the Mahābhārata as authoritative. It is, therefore, clear that in his times, the Mahābhārata and the Gītā used to be looked upon as authoritative. The birth of Śrī Śaṁkarācārya is fixed at Śaka 710 on the authority of a sectarian stanza, as has been proved by Prof. Kashinath Bapu Phatak. But in my opinion this date must be taken back by another hundred years; because, it is stated in the book named *Darśana-Prakāśa,* which belongs to the Mahānubhāva sect, that Śrī Śaṁkarācārya entered the cave in the year "*yugma payodhi rasanvita śāke*", that is, in Śaka 642 *; and at that time, the Ācārya was only 32 years old. Therefore, the date of his birth is proved to be Śaka 610. In my opinion, this date is more correct than the date fixed by Prof. Phatak. But I cannot deal with that question in detail here. In the Śāṁkarabhāṣya on the Gītā, many previous commentators are referred to; and Śaṁkarācārya has in the very beginning of that commentary stated that he has refuted the opinions of all the previous commentators and written a new commentary on the Gītā. Therefore, whether one takes the date of the birth of the Ācārya as Śaka 610 or Śaka 710, the Gītā must undoubtedly have been in vogue at least 200 to 300 years before that time. Let us now see in what way and to what extent we can go further back than that date, for fixing the date of the Gītā.

---

* This is a peculiar Sanskrit way of describing dates; *yugma* means *two*; *payodhi* means 'ocean', of which there were believed to be *four*; and *rasa* means 'taste', of which there are *six* kinds; and these digits are to be read from right to left; thus we get the Śaka year 642—Trans.

(2) The late Mr. Telang has shown that Kālidāsa and Bāṇabhatta both knew of the Gītā. The stanza "*anavāptam avāptavyaṁ na te kiṁcana vidyate*" in the Viṣṇu-Stuti in the Raghuvaṁśa (10. 31) of Kālidāṣa, is similar to the stanza "*nān avāptam avāptavyaṁ*" etc., in the Gītā (Gī. 3. 22); and in the paranomastic (*śleṣa-pradhāna*) sentence "*mahābhāratam ivānanta gītā karṇan ānanditataraṁ*" in the Kādambarī of Bāṇabhatta, there is a clear reference to the Gītā. Kālidāsa and Bhāravi are clearly referred to in a stone inscription dated Śaka 556; and it is now definitely proved, as shown by the late Mr. Pandurang Govind Shastri Parakhi, in his essay in Marathi on Bāṇabhatta, that Bāṇabhatta was in the service of the king Śrī Harṣa, in about Śaka 528.

(3) In the Bhīṣma-parva of the Mahābhārata, which has found its way into Java, there is a chapter called the 'Gītā'; and in it, we find word for word 100 to 125 stanzas from various chapters in the Gītā. But there are no stanzas in it from the 12th, 15th, 16th, and 17th chapters. Yet, there is no objection, on that account, to saying that the Gītā was then as in its present form; because, the Gītā has been translated there into the Kavi language, and the Sanskrit stanzas found in it are taken by way of extracts or illustrations here and there. Therefore, it would not be proper to draw the conclusion that the Gītā then contained only as many stanzas as are found in this translation. Dr. Narhar Gopal Sardesai got this information in Java when he went there; and he has published it in the issue of the *Modern Review* for July 1914 as also in the Magazine called *Chitramaya Jagat.* It is clear from this, that the Bhīṣmaparva of the Mahābhārata contained the Gītā at least 200 years before Śaka 400 to 500, and that the stanzas in it were in the same sequence as in the present Gītā.

(4) In the first chapter of this book, I have given some information about the references to the Gītā or the other Gītās written on the basis of the Bhagavadgītā, which are found in the Viṣṇu-Purāṇa, the Padma-Purāṇa etc. In order that the Gītā should have been adopted in this way, it must have become authoritative and an object of respect even in those days. It is clear that nobody would otherwise think of imitating it. It is, therefore, also clear that

the Gītā must be at least 100 to 200 years earlier in point of time than the earliest of these Purāṇas. One cannot take the commencement of the age of the Purāṇas at later than the second century A. D.; and therefore, the date of the Gītā is taken back at any rate to somewhere about the beginning of the Śaka era.

(5) It has been stated above that both Kālidāsa and Bāṇa knew about the Gītā. The dramas of Bhāsa, who lived before Kālidāsa, have been recently published. In the drama called *Karṇabhāra*, out of these dramas, we find the following as the twelfth stanza :–

> *hato 'pi labhate svargaṁ jitvā tu labhate yaśaḥ* ।
> *ubhe bahumate loke nāsti niṣphalatā raṇe* ॥

This stanza is exactly the same as the stanza: "*hato va prāpsyasi svargaṁ*" etc. (Gī. 2. 37); and, as it is proved from the other dramas of Bhāsa that he was fully acquainted with the Mahābhārata, one can safely draw the conclusion that in writing the stanza mentioned above, he had in mind the stanza in the Gītā referred to above. It, therefore, follows that the Mahābhārata and the Gītā existed before the date of Bhāsa. Pandit Ganapati Shastri has proved that Bhāsa must have lived 200 to 300 years before the Śaka era. But, some are of the opinion that he lived 100 to 200 years after the Śaka era. Even if this latter opinion is correct, the Mahābhārata and the Gītā must have become commonly accepted books at least 100 to 200 years before the date of Bhāsa, that is to say, about the beginning of the Śaka era.

(6) But, the late Mr. Tryambak Gurunath Kale has published in the English magazine issued by the Gurukul and called the *Vedic Magazine*, a forcible proof about old writers having adopted stanzas from the Gītā (Vol. 7, Nos. 6 and 7 pp. 528–532, Mārgaśīrṣa and Pauṣa Saṁvat 1970). Before this publication, Western Sanskritists were of opinion that the Gītā was not found referred to in any books more ancient than the Sanskrit dramas or the Purāṇas, e. g., in the Sūtra treatises etc.; and that therefore, the Gītā must have been written shortly after the age of the Sūtras, that is to say, in about the second century of the Christian era. But the late Mr. Kale

has shown that this surmise is wrong. In the Baudhāyana-Gṛhyaśeṣa-Sūtra (2. 22. 9), the stanza, "*patraṁ puṣpaṁ*" etc. (Gī. 9. 26) has been taken *verbatim* with the opening remark "*tadāha bhagavān*" in the following words:—

> *deśābhāve dravyābhāve sādhāraṇe kuryān manasā vārcayed iti* । *tadāha bhagavān*—
> *patraṁ puṣpaṁ phalaṁ toyaṁ yo me bhaktyā prayacchati* ।
> *tad aham bhakty upahṛtam aśnāmi prayatātmanaḥ* ॥ *iti* ;

and it is stated further on, that one should become meek-minded by Devotion and then recite these incantations, cf. "*bhaktinamraḥ etān mantrān adhīyīta*"; and it is stated at the end of the third *praśna* of this Gṛhyaśesa-Sūtra, that by reciting the twelve-lettered incantation "*oṁ namo bhagavate vāsudevāya*", one acquired the same merit as that of performing an Aśvamedha-Yajña. From this it is clear that the Gītā, as also the worship of Vāsudeva, was fully in vogue before the date of Baudhāyana. Besides this, there is the following sentence in the Pitṛmedha-Sūtra of Baudhāyana, in the beginning of the third *praśna*, namely,

> *jātasya vai manuṣyasya dhruvaṁ maraṇam iti vijāniyāt*
> *tasmāj jāte na prahṛṣyen mṛte ca na viṣīdet* ।,

which can clearly be seen to have been inspired by the following stanza in the Gītā :—

> *jātasya hi dhruvo mṛtyuḥ dhruvaṁ janma mṛtasya ca* ।
> *tasmādaparihārye 'rthe na tvaṁ śocitum arhasi* ॥
> (Gī. 2. 27);

and when, in addition to this, you take the stanza "*patraṁ puṣpaṁ*" etc., there remains no doubt whatsoever about the matter. It has been stated above that we find in the Baudhāyana-Sūtra, one stanza from the Mahābhārata itself. The date of Baudhāyana is about 100 to 200 years before Āpastaṁba; and Prof. Bühler has come to the conclusion that the date of Āpastaṁba cannot be more than 300 years before Christ. * But, in my oninion, that date must be taken

* See Sacred Books of the East Series, Vol. II. Intro. p. xliii ; and also the same Series Vol. XIV. Intro. p. xliii.

slightly forward; because, there is no mention in the Mahābhārata of the zodiacal signs Meṣa, Vṛṣabha etc.; and the sentence "*mīnameṣayor meṣavṛṣabhayor va vasantaḥ*" of Baudhāyana has been quoted in the *Kāla-Mādhava*, and has also been taken in the *Bhāratīya-Jyotiḥ-Śāstra* (p. 102) written by the late Shankar Balkrishna Dikshit. From this also, one can draw the definite inferences, that the Mahābhārata is earlier in point of time than Baudhāyana; that Baudhāyana lived at least 400 years before the Śaka era; and that the Mahābhārata and the Gītā were written at least 500 years before the Śaka era. The late Mr. Kale has placed the date of Baudhāyana at 700 to 800 years before Christ, but that is not correct. He has evidently lost sight of the statement of Baudhāyana regarding the zodiacal signs.

(7) It will be clearly seen by anybody from the above evidence that the present Gītā was in existence at least 500 years before the Śaka era; that it was known both to Baudhāyana and Āśvalāyana; and that one can trace the gradual history of it uninterruptedly right down to the date of Śrī Śaṁkarācārya. But all this evidence is from Vedic religious treatises; the evidence which I am now going to mention is from literature other than Vedic literature, that is to say, from Buddhistic literature; and the above-mentioned ancientness of the Gītā is more forcibly and independently established, in an unambiguous way, by that evidence. I have stated above the opinions of Bühler and of the celebrated French scholar Sénart that the Bhāgavata religion had come into existence before Buddhism; and I have dealt with the question of the growth of Buddhism and of its relation to the Hindu religion etc., independently, in the next part of this Appendix. I am giving here in short only such references as are necessary for fixing the date of the Gītā. From the sole fact that the Bhāgavata religion was previous to Buddhism, one cannot draw the definite conclusion that the Gītā was also prior in point of time to Buddha; because, there is no definite evidence for saying that the Bhāgavata religion came into existence simultaneously with the Gītā. It is, therefore, necessary to see whether or not Buddhist writers refer anywhere specifically to the Gītā. It is clearly stated even in the ancient Buddhistic treatises, that the four

Vedas, the Vedāṅgas, the Vyākarana, Astronomy, Itihāsa, Nighaṇṭu and other books relating to the Vedic religion existed at the time of Buddha. There is, therefore, no doubt that the Vedic religion had reached its perfection before the date of Buddha. Although the new religious sect which was formed after that date by Buddha, was, from the Metaphysical point of view, un-Ātmic (denying the existence of the Ātman—Trans.), yet, from the point of view of conduct in life, it followed the Path of Renunciation preached in the Upaniṣads, as will be shown in the next part. But at the date of Aśoka, this state of Buddhism had changed and Buddhist mendicants had given up living in the woods, and are seen to have gone as far as China towards the East, and as far as Alexandria and Greece towards the West, for the propagation of religion, and on other philanthropic missions. Why Buddhist mendicants gave up living in the woods and started doing philanthropic works is a question of immense importance in the history of Buddhism. If one considers the ancient Buddhistic treatises, it is stated in the Khaggavisāṇa-Sutta in the Sutta-nipāta that the '*bhikṣu*' (mendicant), who reached the state of an *arhata* (Perfect) should live in the woods like a rhinoceros, without doing anything; and it is stated in the Mahāvagga (5. 1. 27) in the story of Sonakolīvisa, the personal disciple of Buddha that: "for the mendicant who has reached the state of *nirvāṇa* (Annihilation)—" *katassa paṭicayo natthi karaṇīyaṁ na vijjati* "—" nothing remains to be done, and nothing of what has been done remains to be suffered for". This is Pure Renunciation, similar to the Path of Renunciation of our Upaniṣads. Not only is the sentence "*karaṇīyaṁ na vijjati*" similar in meaning to the words "*tasya kāryaṁ na vidyate*" in the Gītā, but it is word for word the same. But when this original renunciatory mode of life of Buddhist mendicants changed, and they began to perform philanthropic works, there arose a conflict between the old thought and the new thought, and those who belonged to the former began to call themselves '*theravāda*' (older sect), and the new school of thought called their sect '*mahāyāna*' (superior path) and began to refer to the older sect as '*hīnayāna*' (inferior path). Aśvaghoṣa belonged to the Mahāyāna sect and was of the opinion that

Buddhist *yatins* should take part in philanthropic works Therefore, in the advice which Buddha is shown to have given to Nanda, at the end of the poem *Saundarānanda*, when Nanda had reached the state of an *arhata*, he first says:—

avāptakāryo 'si parāṁ gatiṁ gataḥ
na te 'sti kiṁcit karaṇīyam aṇvapi ı

(Sau. 18. 54)

that is, "your duty in life is over, you have acquired the highest state; now there does not remain for you even the least duty (of your own)". And then, he goes on to say:—

vihāya tasmād iha kāryam ātmanaḥ
kuru sthirātman parakāryam apy atho ı

(Sau. 18. 57.)

that is, "therefore, give up Action for yourself, but become perfectly equable in Reason, and perform Action for others"; There is a world of difference between the preaching of Buddha in the ancient books, which advocated Abandonment of Action, and the words put by Aśvaghoṣa into the mouth of Buddha in the *Saundarānanda-kāvya;* and it will be seen that this argument of Aśvaghoṣa, is similar not only in meaning but also literally and word for word to what is stated in the third chapter of the Gītā, namely, "*tasya kāryaṁ na vidyate*" (i. e., "for him no duty (for his own benefit) has remained"—Trans.)... and "*tasmād asaktaḥ satataṁ kāryaṁ karma samācara*", i. e., "therefore, perform desirelessly that duty which has befallen you" (Gī. 3. 17, 19). From this, one can draw the inference that this argument has been borrowed by Aśvaghoṣa from the Gītā; because, as has been shown above, the Mahābhārata existed before Aśvaghoṣa. But this fact does not remain only in inference. It is stated in the book called *Tārānātha*, which is a history of Buddhism written in the Tibetan language, that the "Jñānin Śrī Kṛṣṇa and Gaṇeśa" were responsible for Rāhulabhadra, the preceptor of Nāgārjuna, who was the principal protagonist of the Māhāyāna sect, getting the idea of this Activistic improvement in the original renunciatory path of the Buddhists. This book (*Tārānātha*) was translated into German from the Russian, but not into English. I have taken an extract from it (*Tārānātha*) from the book written by Dr. Kern in 1896 on the Buddhist religion. * Even Dr. Kern is of opinion that there is a reference to the Bhagavadgītā, by the word 'Śrī Kṛṣṇa'. There are some stanzas in the book named *Saddharma-Puṇḍarīka* out of the Buddhist religious treatises of the Mahāyāna sect, which are quite similar to the stanzas in the Bhagavadgītā. But, this and all other matters will be considered by me in the next part of this Appendix. All that I have to say at present is that Buddhist writers themselves admit that though the original Buddhistic religion advocated Asceticism, the Bhagavadgītā was responsible for the coming into existence of the Mahāyāna sect, which advocated Action and Devotion; and the similarity shown above between the writings of Aśvaghoṣa and the Gītā only strengthens this conclusion. Western scholars have come to the conclusion that Nāgārjuna, the first promulgator of the Mahāyāna sect, lived 100 to 150 years before the Śaka era; and it is quite clear that the Mahāyāna doctrine must have been initiated during the reign of the king Aśoka. Therefore, it is proved independently from Buddhistic books and from the histories of Buddhism written by Buddhist writers themselves, that the Bhagavadgītā was in existence before the rise of the Mahāyāna sect, and possibly even before the date of Aśoka—that is, at least 300 years before the Christian era.

When one considers all the proofs mentioned above, there does not remain the slightest doubt that the present Bhagavadgītā was in existence at least 500 years before the Śaka era. The opinions of Dr. Bhandarkar, the late Mr. Telang, Rao Bahadur Chintamanrao Vaidya, and the late Mr. Dikshit were more or less the same, and they must be taken as correct on this point. The opinion of Prof. Garbe is different; and he has taken the words "*yogo naṣṭaḥ*"—i. e., "in whom Yoga has been destroyed", from the stanzas relating to the tradition of the Gītā doctrine in the fourth chapter of the Gītā, as an authority for his opinion; and he has interpreted the word '*yogo*' there to mean 'Pātañjala-Yoga'. But I have shown above with authorities

* See Dr. Kern's *Manual of Indian Buddhism*, *Grundriss* III. 8, p. 122. The principal book of the Mahāyāna sect called *Amitāyu-Sutta* was translated into Chinese about 148 A. D.

that the word '*yogo*' in this place does not mean 'Pātañjala-Yoga but means Karma-Yoga. Therefore, the opinion of Prof. Garbe is wrong and unacceptable. It, therefore, follows beyond doubt that the date of the present Gītā must be taken as not later than 500 years before the Śaka era. I have shown in Part IV above that the original Gītā must have been some centuries older.

PART VI—THE GĪTĀ AND BUDDHISTIC LITERATURE.

In order to fully realise the importance of the evidence of Buddhistic works adduced by me above for fixing the date of the present Gītā, it is necessary to consider here shortly the general similarities and dissimilarities between the Gītā on the one hand and the Buddhistic treatises or Buddhistic religion on the other hand. I have mentioned above in any number of places that the Sthitaprajña of the Gītā belongs to Path of Energism; and that that is the most important feature of the Gītā-doctrine. But, if one keeps aside for a moment this special feature of the Sthitaprajña, and considers only his mental and moral qualities, one sees a very strange similarity between the characterictics of the Sthitaprajña (Gī. 2. 55–72), the Brahma-niṣṭha (4. 19–23; 5. 18–28), and the Bhakti-yogin (12. 13–19), mentioned in the Gītā, and the characteristics mentioned in various Buddhistic works of an *arhata* who has become fit for Nirvāṇa, that is to say, of a Buddhist *yatin*, who has reached the state of perfection (Dhammapada stanzas 360–423 and Muni-Sutta and Dhammika-Sutta out of the Sutta-nipāta). In these descriptions, we also find similarity of words where, like the Sthitaprajñā, or the '*bhaktimān*', the true mendicant (*bhikṣu*) is described as being 'peaceful' (*śānta*), 'desireless' (*niṣkāma*), 'mine-less' (*nirmama*), 'desireless' (*nirāśī*), or (*nirissita*), 'equal in pain or happiness' (*sama-duḥkha-sukha*), 'non-commencing' (*nirārambha*), 'homeless' (*aniketana* or *aniveśana*), 'equal towards praise or disparagement' (*sama-nindāstuti*), and 'one who considers respect or disrespect, profit or loss, as the same' (See Dhammapada 40, 41 and 91; Sutta-nipāta, Muni-sutta 1. 7 and 14, Dvayatānupassana-sutta 21–23; and Vinaya-piṭaka, Culla-vagga 7. 4. 7). The idea that what is light to the Jñānin is darkness to the Ajñānin (Ignorant) conveyed by the words "*yā niśā sarvabhutānāṁ tasyāṁ jāgarti saṁyamī*" (Gī. 2. 69) is to be seen in the 40th stanza of the Dvayatānupassana-sutta and the words "*arosaneyyo na roseti*"—i. e., "one who is himself not worried, and who does not worry others", in the 10th stanza of the Muni-sutta, is similar to the description in the Gītā in the words "*yasmān no'dvijate loko lokān nodvijate ca yaḥ*" (Gī. 12.15). Similarly, we find in the Salla-sutta, with slight verbal differences, the following ideas of the Gītā, namely, 'that which has come to birth, is sure to die', or, 'in as much as the beginning or the end of created things is imperceptible (*avyakta*), it is futile to lament over them' (See Salla-sutta, 1 and 9; and Gī. 2. 27 and 28); and the description to be found in the tenth chapter of the Gītā and in the Anugītā (Ma. Bhā. Aśva. 43, 44) in the words "the Sun out of the luminaries, the Moon out of the constellations, Gāyatri out of the Vedic incantations" etc. is repeated just as it is in the Sela-sutta (21, 22) and Mahāvagga (6. 35. 8). There are besides numerous other similarities of ideas which have been shown in the notes appended by the late Mr. Telang to his English translation of the Gītā. But, on account of the insufficiency of the means then available for determining how these similarities came to be, or whether these ideas were originally from the Buddhistic literature or from the Vedic religious literature, and what inferences can be drawn from these facts, the late Mr. Telang has not written anything in this matter beyond merely showing this strange similarity of words and meaning. But much more information about the Buddhistic religion has now become available; and as these questions are solved by that information, I will now briefly mention that information about the Buddhistic religion here. The English translation of the Gītā, made by the late Mr. Telang, has been published in the Sacred Books of the East Series. English translations of Buddhistic religious treatises have been published further on in the same Series. This information has been principally taken from those translations; and the references to these Buddhistic treatises, as authorities, are to the translations in this Series; and the Pali words or sentences quoted in some places have been taken from the original Pali books.

The Buddhistic religion is, like the Jain religion, somewhat like a son who has separated from his father after taking from him as much of his wealth as he wanted. Therefore, it is not a stranger religion, but is only a branch, which has come into existence in India, out of the previous Brahmin religion. This position has now been established beyond doubt. In the old Pali treatises to be found in Ceylon, such as, the Mahāvaṁsa or the Dīpavaṁsa, there is a description about the kings who ruled after Buddha, as also the historical tradition of the various Buddhistic preceptors. Calculating time by reference to these books, one comes to the conclusion that Gautama Buddha reached the age of 80 years and died 543 years before Christ. But some of the stories in these books are inconsistent with each other. Therefore, Prof. Max Müller has made a critical examination of this calculation of time, and laid down the proposition that the true date of the death of Buddha must have been 473 years before the Christian era; and Dr. Bühler has shown that the same date is arrived at from the stone inscriptions of Aśoka. But some critics like Prof. Rhys-Davids or Dr. Kern say, that this date must be pushed forward by between 65 to 100 years; and Prof. Geiger has very recently examined all these opinions, and drawn the conclusion that the true date of death of the Buddha must have been 483 years before the Christian era.* Whichever date is accepted, this much at least is beyond doubt, that the Vedic religion had reached its fullest expansion before the birth of Buddha; and that, not only the Upaniṣads but also other religious works like the Dharma-Sūtras, were in existence before that date; because, there are statements in the ancient Buddhistic religious treatises in the Pali language, that Gautama Buddha had personal discussions and conversations with some highly moral Brahmins, and bearded ascetics, who were well-versed in "the four Vedas, the Vedāngas, Vyākaraṇa,

---

* Some information about the date of the death of Gautama Buddha will be found in the Introduction to the English translation of the Dhammapada made by Prof. Max Müller (S. B. E. Vol. X, Intro. pp. xxxv–xlv); and that matter has been examined by Dr. Geiger in his Introduction to the translation of the Mahāvaṁṣa, published in 1912 (The *Mahāvaṁṣa* by Dr. Geiger, Pali Text Society, Intro. p. xxii *et seq.*).

Astronomy, Itihāsa (history), Nighaṇṭu (medicine) etc., and had converted them to his own religion. (See the description of Sela in the Sela-sutta out of the Sutta-nipāta and Vaththu-gāthā 30-45). And just as ritualistic *śrauta* sacrifices have been deprecated in the Kaṭha and other Upaniṣads (Kaṭha. 1. 18; Muṇḍa. 1. 2. 10), or in the Gītā, consistently with those Upaniṣads (2. 40-45; 9. 20 and 21), so also, and to a certain extent in the same words, has Buddha proved in the Tevijja-sutta (Traividya-Sūtra), that "*yajñas, yāgas,* etc. are useless and discardable"; and he has explained how that state, which is described by Brahmins as '*brahmasahavyatāya*' (*brahma-sahavyatyaya=brahma-sāyujyatā*) can, according to him, be attained. From this it is clear, that the Buddhistic religion has come into existence by bringing about an improvement in the two branches of the Brahmin religion, namely, the Karma-kāṇḍa and Jñāna-kāṇḍa—that is, the state of a householder and the state of an ascetic, or in other words, Activism (*pravṛtti*) and Renunciation (*nivṛtti*)—after those two branches had become fully established. The ordinary rule of every reform is that some of the former matters remain and others change; and let us now consider, according to this rule, which things out of the Vedic religion remain in Buddhism and which have been given up. This question must be considered from the point of view of the state of the householder and of Asceticism. But as Buddhism was originally renunciatory or purely Inactivistic, we will first consider the aspect of Renunciation in both the religions, and then consider the state of the householder in both.

If one considers the Vedic Path of Renunciation, the principal element in it, will be seen to be the belief that all the activities in the world of Action are productive of Desire, that is to say, full of unhappiness; and that, in order to enable the Ātman to permanently escape from it, that is, from the cycle of births and deaths, (i) the Mind has to be made desireless and renounced, and must be fixed on the eternal Parabrahman in the form of the Ātman, which forms the foundation of the entire visible universe, and (ii) one has to totally abandon the duties of family life and remain perpetually steeped in this Ātmified state. Out of these, the visible world is defined by Name and

Form, and is perishable; and its unobstructed activity continues as a result of Causality (*karma-vipāka*).

kammanā vattatī loko kammanā vattatī pajā (*prajā*) ।
kammanibandhanā sattā (*satvāni*) *rathassā 'ṇīva yāyato* ॥

(Suttani. Vāseṭhasutta, 61).

that is; "the world, as also its inhabitants, continue in life as a result of Karma; just as the course of the moving chariot is regulated by its axis, so also is every created being bound by Karma". This principle of the Jñāna-kāṇḍa of the Vedic religion, or perhaps even the idea of the cycle of birth and death, as also the Vedic deities, Brahmā, Indra, Maheśvara, Īśvara, Yama etc., and their various spheres, such as, *svarga*, (heaven) *pātāla* (antipodes) etc., described in the Brahmin religion, were accepted by Buddha; and on that account, such technical words of Vedānta and Sāṁkhya philosophy, as '*nāma-rūpa*' '*karma-vipāka*', '*avidyā*', '*upādāna*', '*prakṛti*' etc., as also the traditions about Brahmā and other Vedic deities (maintaining always the superiority of Buddha) are always to be found with some difference or other in Buddhistic literature. But, although the doctrines of the Vedic religion, regarding the world of Action, that the visible world is perishable and non-permanent, and that its activities are going on as a result of Causality, were accepted by Buddha, yet, the doctrine of the Vedic religion or of the Upaniṣads, that there is some eternal, all-pervasive, element like Parabrahman, which is uniform with the Ātman, and is undefined by Name and Form, and which is the foundation of the perishable universe defined by Name and Form, was not accepted by Buddha. This is the crucial difference between the two religions. Gautama Buddha has clearly said (Sabbāsava-sutta 9–13), that the Ātman or the Brahman does not exist in reality, but is a mere illusion; and that, therefore, no one should waste his time in thinking about the Ātman and the Non-Ātman, or on the meditation of the Brahman. That Buddha did not admit any theory about the Ātman, is patent from the Brahmajāla-sutta out of the Digghanikāyā.*

* The Brahmajāla sutta has not been translated into English; but a summary of it has been given by Prof. Rhys-Davids in the Sacred Books of the East Series Vol. XXVI. Intro. pp. xxiii-xxv, to which the reader is referred.

In this *sutta* after mentioning 62 different ideas about the Ātman, as to whether the Ātman and the Brahman are one cr two, it is stated that they are all illusory 'visions' (*dṛṣṭi*); and even in the Milinda-praśna, it is clearly stated by Nāgasena to the Greek Milinda (Minander), that according to Buddhism, "the Ātman is not something which really exists" (Mi. Pra. 2. 3. 6 and 2. 7. 15). When one accepts the position that both the Ātman and the Brahman are illusions, and not real, the very foundation of religion is really speaking destroyed; because, in that case, all that remains is non-permanent things; and permanent happiness, as also some one who can realise that permanent happiness, ceases to exist; and it is on this account that Śrīmad Śaṁkarācārya has condemned that opinion as unacceptable even on logical grounds. But, as we have now to consider only what the original Buddhistic religion was, we will not enter into that discussion here, but will see how Buddha has further justified his own religion. Although Buddha did not accept the existence of the Ātman, yet, he has fully accepted the two positions that (1) as a result of Causality, the Body which is defined by Name and Form (and not the Ātman) has to take birth over and over again in this perishable world; and that (2) this cycle of re-incarnation or worldly life itself, is full of unhappiness, and it is necessary to acquire permanent peace or happiness by escaping from it. When in this way, the unhappiness of worldly life, and the necessity of overcoming such unhappiness have been admitted, the Vedic question about the way in which that unphappiness can be removed, and how the highest happiness can be reached, still remains; and it becomes necessary to give some satisfactory answer to that question. The writers of the Upaniṣads themselves have said that one cannot escape the Cycle of Worldly Life (*bhava-cakra*) by performing sacrificial ritual: and Buddha has gone even further than that, and said that all these sacrificial Actions involved destruction of life, and were on that account totally prohibited and unacceptable. Also, if the Brahman itself is considered to be a stupendous 'Illusion', then the Knowledge of the Brahman also becomes an illusory and impossible path for destroying unhappiness. Then, in what way can one escape from this unhappy Cycle of

Worldly Life? The reply of Buddha to this question is that a good doctor first determines the root cause of any disease, and then removes that cause in order to cure the disease. In the same way, in order to cure the disease of worldly unhappiness, a wise man must (3) understand what the cause of that unhappiness is, and (4) follow that path by which that cause can be totally destroyed. Now, when one considers the question of the cause of this unhappiness, one sees that Thirst or Desire is the root of all the unhappiness in the world; and that when once the Name-d and Form-ed Body has been destroyed, other Name-d and Form-ed Bodies come into existence one after the other from this seed of Desire, which survives the destruction of the Name-d and Form-ed body. And Buddha has come to the conclusion that (i) in order to escape the painful cycle of birth and death, the path of becoming a Saṁnyāsin or a *bhikṣu*, after having destroyed Desire by control of the organs, by meditation, and by asceticism, becomes the only true path; and that (ii) eternal peace and happiness can be reached only by this Renunciation based on indifference to worldly life. In short, Buddhism does not attach any importance to sacrificial ritual etc., nor to the meditation on the Ātman and the Non-Ātman; but rests on the four visible factors, (i) the fact of the existence of worldly unhappiness, (ii) the cause of such unhappiness, (iii) the necessity of controlling or removing it, and (iv) the means in the shape of Renunciation, for totally doing away with it; or, in Buddhistic terminology, on 'unhappiness' (*duḥkha*), 'origin of unhappiness' (*samudaya*), 'control of unhappiness' (*nirodha*), and 'the path of destroying it' (*mārga*); and Buddha has called these four fundamental elements of his religion, the 'Sublime Verities' (*ārya-satya*). Although the Buddhistic religion is in this way founded on the visible foundation of the four 'Sublime Verities', instead of on the Upaniṣadic Knowledge of the Ātman, yet, as the Path (the fourth Verity) preached by Buddha for acquiring eternal peace or happiness, namely, the path of making the Mind desireless by destroying Thirst or Desire, is the same as the path mentioned in the Upaniṣads for obtaining Release, it becomes quite clear that Desirelessness of the Mind is the ultimate visible ideal according to both these religions. But the writers of the Upaniṣads, who look upon the Brahman as identical with the Ātman, refer to this Desirelessness of the Mind as '*ātmaniṣṭhā*', '*brahma-saṁsthā*', '*brahma-bhūtatā*', or '*brahma-nirvāṇa*' (Gī. 5. 17–25; Chān. 2. 23. 1), that is to say, the merging the Ātman into the Brahman, all which words are denotative of the Ultimate Root; whereas, Buddha refers to that state as merely '*nirvāṇa*', which means 'obtaining Rest', or 'the destruction of Desire in the same way as a lamp goes out', which definition merely denotes some Action. This is the difference between the two religions. Because, when you say that the Brahman or the Ātman is an illusion, the questions 'who acquires the rest?', and, 'in what does he rest?', do not any more remain. (*cf.*- Ratana-sutta, 14, and Vaṅgīsa-sutta 12 and 13, out of the Sutta-nipāta); and Buddha has clearly said, that a wise man should not waste time in thinking about these moot questions (Sabbāsava-sutta 9–13, and Milinda Praśna 4. 2.4 and 5). As there is no re-birth after this state has been reached, the word 'death', which is applied to the ordinary phenomenon of one body being destroyed and another body being acquired, cannot be applied to '*nirvāṇa*', even according to Buddhism. '*nirvāṇa*' is the 'death of death', or, as is stated in the Upaniṣads, it is 'the path of overcoming death', and not merely 'death'. When any man has reached this state, he does not any more care for his body, just as the serpent does not care for the slough which it has thrown away. This illustration which has been given in the Bṛhadāraṇyakopaniṣad (4. 4. 7) has been given in each stanza in the Uraga-sutta in the Sutta-nipāta in describing the true Buddhist mendicant (*bhikṣu*). And, as the Ātman is always free from sin as also from merit (Bṛ. 4. 4. 23), he the *bhikṣu* does not suffer from such sins as matricide, patricide etc. This principle of the Vedic religion (Kauṣi. 3. 1) has also been adopted just as it is in the Dhammapada (Dhamma. 294 and 295, and Milinda-Praśna, 4. 5. 7). In short, although Buddha did not accept the existence of the Brahman and of the Ātman, yet, as that very path which has been mentioned in the Upaniṣads as leading to Release, namely, the path of making the Mind peaceful, apathetic, and desireless, is also the path for the acquisition of Nirvāṇa according to Buddhism, the descriptions of the Buddhist monk and of the

Vedic Saṁnyāsin are exactly similar to each other from the point of view of their mental condition. And, therefore, the doctrines regarding the responsibility for sinful or meritorious actions, or regarding the escape from the cycle of birth and death, are the same in the Vedic Paths of Renunciation as in Buddhism. But, as the Vedic religion was prior in point of time to Gautama Buddha, there is not the slightest doubt that these ideas were originally from the Vedic religion.

I have so far pointed out the differences and the similarities between the Vedic and the Buddhistic Paths of Renunciation. Let us now see what Buddha had to say regarding the state of a householder. Although Buddhism is based on four visible foundations, namely, the existence of unhappiness in worldly life, etc., and does not attach any importance to the Philosophy of the Ātman and the Non-Ātman, yet, it must be borne in mind that Buddhism was not fundamentally Energistic, like the purely Materialistic religion of modern philosophers like Comte, or even like the Gītā-religion. It is true that Buddha does not accept the philosophical 'vision' (*dṛṣṭi*) of the Knowledge of the Ātman described in the Upaniṣads. But, as Buddhism has adopted *in toto* the doctrine enunciated by Yājñavalkya in the Bṛhadāraṇyakopaniṣad (Bṛ. 4. 4. 6), that it is the highest duty of every man in this world to give up worldly life altogether, and to make the Mind desireless and free from slavery to the objects of pleasure, that religion has fundamentally become a religion of Renunciation purely. The sum and substance of the whole advice of Buddha is, that it is impossible to acquire the highest happiness, or the position of an *arhata*, if one remains in the state of a householder. Still, it is not that Buddhism does not at all deal with the state of a householder. Buddhistic treatises have given the name *'upāsaka'* to those persons who, without becoming monks, put faith in BUDDHA, in his RELIGION, and in the SOCIETIES of MONKS, and who surrender themselves to these three, by reciting the incantation *'buddhaṁ śaraṇaṁ gacchāmi'*, *'dharmaṁ śaraṇaṁ gacchāmi'*, *'saṅghaṁ śaraṇaṁ gacchāmi'*, i. e., 'I surrender myself to Buddha, to his religion, and to the religious societies'. These Upāsakas may be taken to be the householders of Buddhism; and Buddha himself has in some places preached how these Upāsakas should live in the state of householders, when he had occasion to give this advice (Mahāparinibbāṇa-sutta, 1. 24). Buddha did not accept either the Śrauta religious sacrifices pertaining to the state of a householder, which involved the slaughter of animals, or the division of society into the four castes. When these things are eliminated, all that remain out of the duties of a householder, are the five Mahāyajñas of the Smṛtis, philanthrophy and other charitable duties, and leading a moral life; and in describing the state of a householder, these are the only things which are referred to in Buddhistic religious treatises. Buddha has said that every householder, or Upāsaka, must perform the five Mahāyajñas; and he has also clearly laid down that the Buddhist Upāsaka must observe such rules of Morality as, Non-Violence (*ahiṁsā*), Veracity (*satyaṁ*), Not-Stealing (*asteyaṁ*), Sympathy towards all created things (*sarvabhūtānukaṁpā*), Self-Identification (although he did not accept the existence of the Ātman), Purity, or mental chastity, and especially, making charitable gifts of food, raiment etc. to Buddhist monks or Buddhist monastaries. This is technically known in Buddhism as '*śīla*' (Morality); and these rules of Morality have, like the five Mahāyajñas, been adopted by Buddha from the Dharma-Sūtras or the ancient Smṛti treatises (Manu. 6. 92 and 10. 63) of the Brahmin religion, as becomes quite clear when one compares both *. Nay, Buddha himself has praised the old Brahmin race with reference to this mode of life in the Brāhmaṇa-Dhammika-sutta; and some of the stanzas from the Manu-Smṛti have been adopted word for word into the Dhammapada (See Manu 2. 121, and 5. 45; and Dhammapada, 109 and 131). But, it is not that Buddhism has adopted only the five Mahāyajñas and the principles of Morality from our Vedic treatises. Buddha had also accepted the opinion expressed in some of the earlier Upaniṣads, that Release is never attained according to the Vedic religion by remaining in the state of a householder. For instance, while comparing the Upāsaka with a Bhikṣu in the Dhammika-sutta in the Suttanipāta, Buddha has clearly stated that a householder may by living a pure life, at most reach the sphere of the 'self-illumined' (*svayaṁprakāśa*) gods; but that in order to escape

* See Dr. Kern's *Manual of Buddhism* (Grundriss, III. 8) p. 68.

the cycle of births and deaths, he must give up his wife and children, and ultimately take up the life of a monk. (See Dhammika-sutta, 17. 29; and Bṛ. 4. 4. 6; Ma. Bhā. Vana. 2. 63). There is a statement in the Tevijjasutta that in arguing with ritualising Vedic Brahmins, Buddha used to adopt the following argument in order to justify his advocacy of Renunciation, namely, "if your Brahman does not have any wife or children or any mental emotions, how will you reach that Brahman by remaining with your wife and children and performing ritualistic sacrifices (Te. Su. 1. 35; 3.5); and it is well known that Buddha himself acquired the state of Release after having given up his wife and son in the bloom of youth, and lived the life of a monk for six years. The same is the teaching of the Jain saint Mahāvīra, who lived at the same time as Buddha, but who entombed himself (became *samādhistha*) before Buddha. But the important difference between these two religions is that Mahāvīra did not deny the existence of the Ātman like Buddha, and that Jain monks followed—and even to this day follow—the rules of abandoning clothes and other worldly pleasures, and the creed of Non-Violence (*ahiṁsā*), even more rigorously than Buddhist monks. Buddha himself used to eat the flesh known as '*pavatta*' (in Sanskrit, *pravṛtta*), i. e., 'flesh which is already there', of animals which had not been killed for eating, except the flesh of elephants, lions, and some other animals; and he had also permitted Buddhist monks to eat '*pavatta*' flesh and fish; and according to Buddhism, going about naked without clothes, is a crime (Mahāvagga. 6. 31. 14; and 8. 28. 1). In short, although the definite advice of Buddha to his disciples was that one should become a monk, denying the existence of the Ātman, yet, he was not in favour of severe religious austerities entailing bodily pain (Mahāvagga. 5. 1. 16, and Gī. 6. 16); and the normal arrangement in the monasteries (*vihāra*) built for the residence of Buddhist monks was such. that they could perform the Yogic practices of *prāṇāyāma* etc., without suffering bodily pain. Nevertheless, as it is a fixed principle of Buddhism that the state of a householder must be given up in order to acquire the bliss of Nirvāṇa, or the state of an *arhata* (Perfect), that mode of life does not contravene the statement that Buddhism supports Renunciation (*saṁnyāsa*)

Although Buddha was firmly of opinion that the Knowledge of the Brahman, or the meditation on the Ātman and the Non-Ātman, was a great net of confusion, yet, he had accepted the Upaniṣadic procedure of making the Mind 'free from the slavery to objects of pleasure' (*nirviṣaya*) by cultivating indifference towards worldly life, which (procedure) pertained to the Path of Renunciation, in order to achieve the visible object of escaping from the painful cycle of birth and death, and obtaining perpetual Peace (*śānti*); and when it has once been proved that Buddhism accepts all the Vedic moral precepts relating to the state of a householder, with only slight modifications here and there, except those relating to the division of society into four castes and to the slaughter of animals for ritualistic sacrifice into the fire, there is no wonder that the descriptions of Vedic Saṁnyāsins given in the Upaniṣads or in the Manu-Smṛti etc., and the descriptions of Buddhist monks or of an *arhata*, or such rules of Morality as Non-Violence etc., should be the same—nay, sometimes word for word the same—in both the religions. All these things are originally from the Vedic religion; but, these are not the only things which have been taken by Buddhists from the Vedic religion. Buddhistic Jātaka-treatises like the Daśaratha-Jātaka, are in the same way only transformations of ancient Vedic stories from the Purāṇas, which have been made consistent with Buddhism. Not only Buddhists, but even Jains, have in this way transformed Vedic stories in their Abhinava-Purāṇa; and the Mahomedan religion, which came into existence after the death of Christ, has similarly perverted one story from the life of Christ, as has been stated by Prof. Sale*; and it has been established by recent researches, that Jews in the same way transformed the religious stories of the ancient Chaldeans, for describing the creation of the Universe, the Deluge, or the Arc of Noah, in their Old Testament. If we see that the Buddhistic religious treatises have thus adopted—and that too, sometimes absolutely literally—the descriptions, stories, or ideas to be found in the Upaniṣads, the ancient Dharma-Sūtras,

* See Sale's *Koran* "To the Reader", (Preface), p. X; and the Preliminary Discourse, Sec. IV, p. 58, (Chandos Classics Edition).

or in the Manu-Smṛti, then, one can naturally draw the inference that the stanzas 'enmity is increased by victory', and 'enmity does not destroy enmity', from the Udyogaparva (Ma. Bhā. Udyo. 71. 59 and 63), or the stanza, 'the anger of another should be conquered by peacefulness' from the Viduranīti (Ma. Bhā. Udyo. 38. 63), or the statement of Janaka that, "if you annoint one of my hands with sandalwood-paste and cut off the other hand, it will be all the same to me" (Ma. Bhā. Śān. 320. 36), as also the several other stanzas from the Mahābhārata, which are seen to be word for word the same in Buddhistic treatises (Dhammapada 5 and 223, and Milinda-Praśna 7. 3. 5), must have been originally in the Mahābhārata, from where they were adopted by Buddhists. But, though one can, without fear of contradiction, say that the stanzas or ideas from the Vedic Upaniṣads, Brahma-Sūtras, or the Manu-Smṛti, which one comes across in the Buddhistic treatises, were copied by them from those Vedic treatises, since those treatises were undoubtedly more ancient than Buddha, one cannot say the same thing about the Mahābhārata. As the Mahābhārata contains a reference to Buddhistic Ḍāgobās, it is quite clear that the last edition of that work must have been made after the date of Buddha; but one cannot merely on the ground of similarity of stanzas, draw the conclusion that the present Mahābhārata must have been prior in point of time to the Buddhistic treatises; and as the Gītā is a part of the Mahābhārata, the same argument may be applied to the Gītā. Besides, as has been stated above, the Gītā contains a reference to the Brahma-Sūtras and the Brahma-Sūtras contain a refutation of Buddhistic opinions. Therefore, we will now consider whether or not we can find some other evidence in Buddhistic treatises, in addition to the similarity between the descriptions of the Sthitaprajña etc., in the Gītā and the Buddhistic treatises, which will remove such a doubt, and establish beyond question the fact that the Gītā was earlier in point of time than the Buddhistic treatises.

I have stated above that the original form of Buddhism totally denied the existence of the Ātman, and was in favour of Renunciation; but it did not retain this its form for long. Not only did several sub-sects come into existence after the death of Buddha, as a result of differences of opinion about the rules of conduct to be followed by monks, but such differences of opinion came into existence also as regards the philosophy of Buddhism. And now-a-days there are even people, who assert that Buddha, by saying that there was no Ātman, intended only to say that, "instead of wasting your time in dry discussions about the Knowledge of the unimaginable Ātman, make the Mind desireless by practising indifference to worldly life; let there be an Ātman, or no Ātman; concentration of the Mind is of primary importance, and you must first make an effort to acquire that concentration". And these critics say that Buddha did not intend to deny the existence of the Brahman or of the Ātman, because, in the Tevijja-Sutta, Buddha himself has described the state of '*brahma-sahavyatāya*'; and in the Sela-sutta and the Theragāthā, he has described his own state by saying: "I am Brahmabhūta" (Sela. Su. 14; Ther. Gā. 831). But, whatever the original intention of Buddha may have been, yet, there is no doubt that various philosophical opinions, arguments, or doctrinal sects, saying "neither the Ātman nor the Brahman, nor any other Eternal Substance is the fundament of the universe; all that we see is transient and non-existent", or, "whatever can be seen is only Knowledge", came into existence later on out of his doctrines (Ve. Sū. Śāṁ. Bhā. 2. 2. 18–26). This atheistic or un-Ātmic Buddhistic doctrine is also known as '*kṣaṇikavāda*' (Theory of Transience), '*śūnyavāda*' (Theory of Non-Existence), or '*vijñāna-vāda*' (Theory of Knowledge). But it is not necessary for us to deal with all these various sects here. We have to deal with the historical aspect of the matter; and I shall, therefore, mention here only as much as is necessary for solving that historical question, namely, the history of only the Mahāyāna sect. As the existence of the Ātman or the Brahman (and necessarily also of the Paramātman, or the Parameśvara), had been denied or considered of minor importance in the religion originally preached by Buddha, it was hardly possible that he could have personally preached in his lifetime the path of reaching the Parameśvara by means of Devotion; and so long as his imposing figure and his course of life were before the eyes of the people, there was no necessity for that religious path. But the path of devotion gradually came into favour with ordinary people, and it became necessary to show them some easier and more practical course than the atheistic renunciatory path of giving up worldly life, becoming a monk, and (without knowing in what to become annihilated) attaining Annihilation (*nirvāṇa*), where one was. Nay, it is even possible that the ordinary devotees of Buddha, followed the Vedic Path of Devotion, which was then in vogue, and started the worship of Buddha of their own accord. Therefore, shortly after the Annihilation (*nirvāṇa*) of Buddha, some Buddhist philosophers gave to Buddha himself the form of a "self-created (*svayaṁbhu*), and eternal (*anādyanta*), Highest Spirit (*puruṣottama*)"; and preached that attaining 'Annihilation' (*nirvāṇa*) was only his pastime, and that "the true Buddha can never be destroyed and is always eternal". And it also came to be preached in Buddhistic treatises, that as "the true Buddha is the father of the world and the people are his children", he is "equable towards everybody, and loves none and hates none"; and that, "when the state of religion gets disrupted, he takes incarnations from time to time, for 'propagating religion' in the shape of Buddha"; and that "by worshipping this *devātideva* (god of gods) Buddha, by worshipping his religious books, and by preaching before his Ḍāgobā", nay, "by devoutly offering to him a few lotus-buds or even a single flower", man attains the highest of states (See Saddharma-Puṇḍarīka 2. 77-98; 5. 22; 15. 5-22; and Milinda-Praśna 3. 7. 7). * It is even stated in the Milinda-Praśna that "although the whole of the life of a man may have been spent in evil actions, yet, if he surrenders himself to Buddha at the moment of death, he will without doubt reach heaven" (Mi. Pra. 3. 7. 2); and it is stated in detail in the second and third chapters of the Saddharma-Puṇḍarīka, that "as the spiritual status, inherent nature, and spiritual knowledge of all persons is not the same, Buddha, out of kindness and by his skill (*upāyakauśalya*), created this path (*yāna*) of Devotion, in addition to the Renunciatory un-Ātmic

* The work *Saddharma-Puṇḍarīka* has been translated in Volume XXI of the Sacred Books of the East Series. This book is originally in the Sanskrit language; and the original Sanskrit text has also now been published.

path". It was not possible at any time to entirely discard the doctrine preached by Buddha himself that one must take up the state of a monk in order to reach 'Annihilation' (*nirvāṇa*); because, doing so would have amounted to cutting at the very foundation of the original preaching of Buddha. But there was no objection to saying that it was the duty of Buddhist monks to perform philanthrophical and charitable acts like the propagation of religion with a desireless (*nirissita*) frame of mind, instead of living alone and in dejection in the forest like a 'rhinoceros', though they might be monks. * This opinion has been advocated in the Saddharma-Puṇḍarīka and other treatises of the Mahāyāna sect, and Nāgasena has told Milinda (Mi. Pra. 6. 2. 4), that, "it is not impossible to attain Annihilation (*nirvāṇa*) by remaining in the state of a householder, and that many such cases are to be seen". Anybody will easily realise that these ideas are not from the original un-Ātmic and renunciatory Buddhistic religion, and that they cannot be supported on the basis of the Theory of Non-Existence (*śūnya-vāda*), or the Theory of Knowledge (*vijñāna-vāda*); and many Buddhists at first thought that these ideas were inconsistent with the original preaching of Buddha. But this new opinion naturally became more and more popular later on, and the Path followed by those who adhered to the original preaching of Buddha acquired the name of 'Hīnayāna' (inferior path), and the new path came to be known as 'Mahāyāna' (superior path) †. The

* The refrain (*dhruva-pada*) of the 41 stanzas of the Khaggavisāṇa-sutta out of the Sutta-nipāta is "*eko care khaggavisāṇa kappo*". '*khaggavisāṇa*' means 'rhinoceros', and the refrain means that the Buddhist monk should live alone in the woods like a rhinoceros.

† In describing the difference between the Hīnayāna and the Mahāyāna sects, Dr. Kern says as follows:—"Not the Arhat, who has shaken off all human feeling, but the generous, self-sacrificing, active Bodhisattva is the ideal of the Mahayanists, and this attractive side of the creed has, more perhaps than anything else, contributed to their wide conquests, whereas Southern Buddhism has not been able to make converts, expect where the soil has been prepared by Hinduism and Mahayanism"—*Manual of*

Buddhistic religion now in vogue in China, Japan, Tibet etc., is of the Mahāyāna sect; and the societies of monks belonging to the Mahāyāna sect were principally responsible for the vigorous expansion of Buddhism after the Annihilation (*nirvāṇa*) of Buddha. Dr. Kern has come to the conclusion that this reform in Buddhism must have taken place about 300 years before the Śālivāhana Śaka,* because, there was a big conference of Buddhist monks in the reign of the Śaka king Kaniska. We find statements in Buddhistic works that monks of the Mahāyāna sect were present at that conference; and the Chinese translation of the most important *sūtra*-book of this Mahāyāna sect called Amitāyu-sutta, made in about 148 A. D., is now available. But in my opinion, this date must be taken still further back; because, the stone inscriptions made by Aśoka about 230 B. C. do not contain any reference to the atheistic Buddhistic religion, but to the humanitarian and Activistic Buddhistic religion. It is, therefore, clear that the Mahāyāna doctrine of Buddhism had begun to acquire the Activistic form before that date. The Buddhist monk Nāgārjuna was the principal protagonist and not the originator of this sect.

As it was not possible that the original atheistic Buddhistic religion, which denied the existence of the Brahman and the Ātman, and accepted only the Renunciatory path of the Upaniṣads which (path) aimed at freeing the mind from the slavery to objects of pleasure, should gradually and naturally

---

Indian Buddhism, p. 69. 'Southern Buddhism' means Hīnayāna; the Philosophy of Devotion has found a place in the Mahāyāna creed. "Mahayanism lays great stress on devotion, in this respect as in many others, harmonising with the current of feeling in India which led to the growing importance of *Bhakti*" (Ibid. p. 124).

* See Dr. Kern's *Manual of Indian Buddhism* pp. 6, 69 and 119. Milinda (the Greek king named Minander) ruled in the country called Bactria, in the north-west of India about 140 or 150 B. C.; and it is stated in the Milinda-Praśna that Nāgasena then converted him to Buddhism. As this work of proselytising, was carried on only by the Buddhists belonging to the Mahāyāna path, it is quite clear that the Mahāyāna path was in existence at that time.

give rise to the Activistic path of Devotion, it is quite clear that there must have been some other contemporary cause outside the Buddhist religion which was responsible for giving to the Buddhist religion this Activistic devotional form, which it acquired soon after the death of Buddha; and when one considers what that cause must have been, one cannot but think of the Bhagavadgītā. Because, out of the other religions which were then in force in India, the Jain and the Upaniṣadic religions were wholly renunciatory; and although the Pāśupata or Śaiva or other sects of the Vedic religion advocated Devotion, yet, as has been clearly shown by me in the eleventh chapter of the Gītā-Rahasya, Activism has not been harmonised with Devotion, anywhere except in the Bhagavadgītā. In the Gītā, the Blessed Lord has called Himself 'the Most excellent Spirit' (*puruṣottama*); and there are such statements in the Gītā as "I am the Puruṣottama, Who is the 'father' and 'grand-father (9. 17) of all"; or, "I am 'equable' towards all, for, to Me none is dear, nor inimical" (9. 29); or, "though I am unborn and inexhaustible, yet, I have to take incarnations from time to time for the protection of the religion" (4. 6-8); or, "however sinful a man may be, he becomes a saint by beginning to worship Me" (9. 30); or, "if any flower, leaf, or even a little water, is offered to me with Devotion, I accept it with pleasure" (9. 26); or, "Devotion is a very easy path for persons who have not acquired Knowledge" etc.; and the doctrine that the Brahman-devoted (*brahmaniṣṭha*) must accept the Path of Activism has not been expounded in detail anywhere except in the Gītā. Therefore, one is forced to draw the conclusion that, just as the purely renunciatory path of the Destruction of Desire has been taken into the original Buddhistic religion from the Upaniṣads, so also has the principle of Activistic Devotion been adopted into the Mahāyāna sect from the Bhagavadgītā. But, this fact does not rest only in inference; for, it is clearly stated in the book written by the Buddhist Tārānātha in the Tibetan language, which deals with the history of the Buddhistic religion, that "Rāhulabhadra, the preceptor of Nāgārjuna, was a Brahmin converted to Buddhism; and the Jñānin Śrī Kṛṣṇa and Gaṇeśa were responsible for this Rāhulabhadra getting these ideas (of the Mahāyāna sect)"; and there is a similar statement in another Tibetan book.* It is true that this book of Tārānātha is not very ancient; but, I need not say that the statements in it have not been made without the authority of ancient works; because, it is not likely that any Buddhist writer will, without any reason, make a reference in this way to saints from another religion in explaining the principles of his own religion. Therefore, the fact that a Buddhist writer has himself, clearly and by name, referred to Śrī Kṛṣṇa, is a matter of very great importance; because, as there is no other book in Vedic religion dealing with the path of Activistic Devotion except the Bhagavadgītā written by Śrī Kṛsna, this reference clearly shows that not only the Bhāgavata religion but also the Bhagavadgītā written by Śrī Kṛṣṇa for expounding the Bhāgavata religion, were already is existence before the Mahāyāna sect; and Dr. Kern is of the same opinion. When it is proved that the Gītā existed before the date of the Mahāyāna sect, one can immediately draw the inference that the Mahābhārata must also have then been in existence. It is true that it is stated in Buddhistic treatises that the doctrines expounded by Buddha were collected together immediately after his death. But from that it does not follow that the very ancient Buddhistic treatises which are now available had also been written at that date. The Mahāparinibbāṇa-sutta is considered to be a very ancient treatise out of the now available Buddhistic treatises. But Prof. Rhys-Davids has shown that this book could not have been written for at least a 100 years after the death of Buddha, having regard to

* See Dr. Kern's *Manual of Indian Buddhism* p. 122 "He (Nāgārjuna) was a pupil of the Brahmana Rahulabhadra, who himself was a Mahayanist. This Brahmana was much indebted to the sage Krishna and still more to Ganesha. This quasi-historical notice, reduced to its less allegorical expression, means that Mahayanism is much indebted to the Bhagavadgita, and more even to Shaivism". It would seem that Dr. Kern understands the word '*gaṇeśa*' as indicating Śaivism. Dr. Kern has translated the book Saddharma-Puṇḍarīka in the Sacred Books of the East Series; and this opinion has been advocated by him in the Introduction to that book (S. B. E. Vol. XXI. Intro. pp. xxv-xxviii).

the reference made in it to the city of Pāṭaliputra; and it is stated in the Vinayapiṭaka, at the end of the Cullavagga, that there had been a second conference of Buddhistic monks a 100 years after the death of Buddha. From this it follows, that the Vinayapiṭaka and other Buddhistic Pali works found in Ceylon, had been written after the date of this conference. * It is stated by Buddhist writers themselves that these works were taken there by Mahendra, the son of Aśoka, when he started the preaching of the Buddhistic religion in the Siṁhaladvīpa (Ceylon) about 241 B. C.; and that they must first have appeared in book-form about 100 to 150 years after that date. It was usual in those times to learn these books by heart, and therefore, even if one assumes that there was no change in them on that account after the date of Mahendra, yet, one cannot say that nothing was added to these treatises from the then available Vedic treatises when they were first prepared, after the death of Buddha, or after that, upto the date of Mahendra or Aśoka. Therefore, as it is proved by other evidence also, that the Mahābhārata was certainly in existence at any rate before King Alexander, that is to say, 325 B. C., though it may have been written after the date of Buddha, it is not impossible to find some stanzas from the Mahābhārata in the books taken into Ceylon by Mahendra, as other stanzas are found taken into them from the Manu-Smṛti. It is seen, in short, that seeing that the Buddhistic religion was being propagated after the death of Buddha, ancient Vedic Gāthās and traditions came to be collected together in the Mahābhārata; that the stanzas from that work which appear in Buddhistic treatises have been taken by the Buddhist writers from the Mahābhārata; and that the writer of the Mahābhārata did not take those stanzas from Buddhistic works. But even if one assumes for the sake of argument that (*a*) these stanzas were not taken by the Buddhist writers from the Mahābhārata, but were taken from some other Vedic treatises, which were the basis of the Mahābhārata, but which are not now to be found, and that, (*b*) on that account, the date of the Mahābhārata cannot be fixed from this similarity of stanzas, yet, the following four facts, namely, (1) principles of Activism and Devotion

* See S. B. E. Vol. XI. Intro. pp. xv-xx, and p. 58.

cannot gradually and naturally be evolved from the un-Ātmic and renunciatory original Buddhistic religion, (2) the specific reference by name to Śrī Kṛṣṇa made by Buddhist writers themselves in connection with the origin of the Mahāyāna sect, (3) the similarity in meaning and terminology between the Activistic and Devotional doctrines in the Gītā and the doctrines of the Mahāyāna sect, and (4) the absence of Activistic devotional principles in the other Jain or Vedic schools of thought, which were then in existence, prove beyond the slightest doubt that (i) the Bhāgavata religion was in vogue before the growth of the Mahāyāna sect of Buddhism; that, (ii) the Bhagavadgītā had then become an accepted work on all hands; that, (iii) the Mahāyāna sect has been formed on the authority of this Gītā; and that (iv) the doctrines enunciated by Śrī Kṛṣṇa in the Gītā were not borrowed by Him from Buddhism. The date of the present Gītā which has been fixed by me by reference to the other pieces of evidence mentioned above is fully consistent with this.

PART VII—THE GĪTĀ AND THE CHRISTIAN BIBLE.

When it has in this way been definitely established, as mentioned above, that the devotional Bhāgavata religion came into existence in India about 1400 years before Christ, and that the Gītā written by Śrī Kṛṣṇa was, according to the opinion of Buddhist writers themselves, responsible for Activistic Devotional doctrines entering the original renunciatory Buddhistic religion promulgated before the date of Christ, the the argument advanced in certain Christian Missionary treatises, that, because many of the doctrines of the Gītā are to be found in the Christian Bible, that is, in the New Testament, these doctrines must have been taken into the Gītā from the Christian religion, and especially the statements made by Dr. Laurincer in his German translation of the Gītā, published in 1869, will necessarily be seen to be absolutely false. Dr. Laurincer has shown at the end of his book (that is, of his German translation of the Gītā) more than a hundred cases of similarity of words between the Bhagavadgītā and the Bible, and principally the New Testament. For instance, the sentence "At that day, ye shall know that I am in my Father, and ye in me, and I in you" (John. 14. 20), is not only similar in meaning but also almost word for word the same as the following sentences from the Gītā, namely, "*yena bhūtāny aśeṣena drakṣyasy ātmany atho mayi*" (i. e.. "by this Knowledge, you will realise that all beings are in you, and also in Me"—Trans.), (Gī. 4. 35), and "*yo māṁ paśyati sarvatra sarvaṁ ca mayi paśyati*", (i. e., "he who sees that I, the Parameśvara Paramātman am everywhere, and sees all beings in Me"—Trans.). Similarly, the sentence "he that loveth me, shall be loved of my Father and will love him" (John 14. 21) is in every way similar to the sentence "*priyo hi jñānino 'tyarthaṁ ahaṁ sa ca mama priyaḥ*" (i. e., "I am much beloved of the Jñānin, and I too love (much) the Jñānin"—Trans.), (Gī. 7. 87). From this and many other similar sentences, Dr. Laurincer has drawn the conclusion that the writer of the Gītā knew about the Bible; and he has said that the Gītā must have been written about 500 years after the Bible. An English translation of this portion of the work of Dr. Laurincer had been published in Vol. II. of the *Indian Antiquary*; and the late Mr. Telang has, in the introduction to his versified translation of the Bhagavadgītā, fully refuted that argument *. Dr. Laurincer is not looked upon as a Western Sanskritist, and his knowledge and pride of the Christian religion was more than his knowledge of the Gītā. Therefore, his opinions have not been accepted not only by the late Mr. Telang, but also by important Western Sanskritists like Max Müller and others. That all the statements made by him, showing hundreds of similarities of ideas and words between the Gītā and the Bible, would turn round on him like ghosts, when once it was proved that the Gītā was earlier than Christ. had possibly never entered the head of poor Laurincer! But the saying that, things which one does not see even in one's dreams, sometimes actually happen, is true; and, really speaking, it is not even necessary now to give any reply to the arguments of Dr. Laurincer. Yet, as these false opinions of Dr. Laurincer are seen being repeated in authoritative English works, it is necessary to mention here in short what has now been found, after modern researches in this matter. It must first be borne in mind that from the mere fact

* See *Bhagavadgītā* translated into English blank verse, with notes etc. by K. T. Telang 1875 (Bombay). This book is different from the translation in the Sacred Books of the East Series by the same author.

that there are similar doctrines in two different books, one cannot definitely determine which book was written first and which afterwards. Because, there arise the two possibilities that (1) the ideas in the first book may have been taken from the second book, or (2) the ideas in the second book may have been taken from the first book. Therefore, after one has first independently determined the dates of two books, one has to subsequently decide who has taken from whom. Besides, as it is not impossible that similar thoughts should strike two writers in two different countries independently of each other, whether at the same time or at different times, one has, in considering the similarity between the two books also to consider whether or not that similarity could have arisen in an independent way; and whether or not there was any mutual intercourse between the two countries in which these two books were written, and, on that account, a chance of these ideas having gone from one country to the other. When once the matter has been considered from all points of view, it is not only impossible that anything should have been taken into the Gītā from the Bible, but on the other hand, it will be seen to be perfectly possible that such of the doctrines enunciated in the Christian Bible as are similar to those in the Gītā, must have been taken into the Bible from Buddhism—that is, ultimately from the Gītā, or from the Vedic religion—by Christ or by His disciples; and some Western scholars have now begun even to openly say so. When in this way, orthodox Christians saw that the scales were turned against them, it is no wonder that they were greatly surprised about the matter, and felt inclined to flatly deny this fact. But all that I have to say to such persons is that, as this question is not religious, but historical, the only logical and honest thing which every one—and especially those who have themselves raised the question of the similarity of ideas—can do, is to joyfully and impartially accept all the inferences which can be drawn according to ordinary historical methods from the material which has now become available to us.

The New Testament has been written as an improvement on the Jewish religion propounded in the Jewish Bible, that is to say, in the Old Testament of the Bible. God is known in the Jewish language as 'Iloha' (Ilāha, in Arabic); but according to the rules made by Moses, the principal deity of worship in the Jewish religion has been given the special name of 'Jehovah'. Western scholars themselves have now proved that the word 'Jehovah' is not an original Jewish word, but has come from the Chaldean word '*yavhe*' (in Sanskrit, *yavha*). Jews are not idolators. The principal observance of their religion consists in pleasing the Jehovah by sacrificing animals or other things into the fire, and following the code of religion and morality laid down by God, and thereby obtaining the happiness of themselves and of their community in this world. To mention the matter in short, the Jewish religion is Activistic and ritualistic like the Vedic Karma-kāṇḍa. Christ has, on the other hand, preached in numerous places that, "I will have mercy, and not sacrifice" (Matthew 9. 13); "Ye cannot serve God and Mammon" (Matthew 6. 24); "If thou wilt be perfect, go and sell that thou hast.........and come and follow me" (Matthew 19. 21); and when He sent His disciples to different countries for propagating His religion, He told them: "Provide neither gold, nor silver, nor brass in your purses, nor scrip for your journey, neither two coats, neither shoes, nor yet staves" etc., (Matthew 10. 9–13), and asked them to follow other similar rules of Renunciation. It is true that the modern Christian countries have coolly shelved this preaching of Christ. But, just as the cult of Śaṁkarācārya does not become a cult of royal pleasure, because, the present Śaṁkarācārya owns elephants and horses, so also can we not, on account of this behaviour of the Western Christian countries, say that the original Christian religion supported Activism. Just as, though the original Vedic religion was based on ritualistic performances (Karma-kāṇḍa), the Path of Knowledge (Jñāna-kāṇḍa) later on sprang out of it, so also are the Jewish and the Christian religions mutually inter-related. But, the Christian religion did not gradually come out of the Jewish religion, as the Jñāna-kāṇḍa, and later on, the Devotional Bhāgavata religion, came out of the original ritualistic Karma-kāṇḍa in hundreds of years. History tells us that a sect of ascetics called ESI or ESIN suddenly came from somewhere into the Jewish countries about 200 years at most before Christ. Although these Esis belonged to the Jewish religion, yet, they had given up sacrifical ritual, and used to spend their lives in a peaceful place in contemplation of the Almighty, and they used at most to take part in harmless occupations like agriculture etc. for maintaining themselves. The most prominent principles of this sect were to remain celibates, to eschew meat and liquor, not to kill animals, not to take oaths, and to live together socially in monasteries; and, if any one of them acquired any property, to look upon that property as the common property of the society; and if any one had a desire to enter their sect, it was necessary for him to serve as an apprentice for at least three years, and after that to consent to observe certain rules. Their monastery was at Endgi on the western coast of the Dead Sea, and they used to live there peacefully and as ascetics. The respectful references made by Christ Himself and His disciples in the New Testament to the opinions of the Esi sect (Matthew 5. 34; 19. 12; James 5. 12; The Acts 4. 32-35), clearly show that Jesus Christ was a follower of this sect, and He has to a great extent furthered the renunciatory religion of this sect. But though the renunciatory devotional path of Christ is in this way traced to the Esi sect, still it is necessary to give some satisfactory explanation from the historical point of view, as to how the renunciatory Esi path suddenly came into existence out of the original Activistic Jewish religion. Some answer this question by saying that Christ did not belong to the Esi sect. But though this statement is taken as correct, one cannot in that way escape the questions, (i) what was the origin of the renunciatory religion preached in the New Testament of the Bible, and (ii) how such a religion suddenly entered the Activistic Jewish religion; for, the only difference is, that instead of having to explain the origin of the Esi sect, one has to answer these two questions; because, nothing comes into existence anywhere suddenly. It grows gradually, and the growth starts from a much earlier period; and it is a well-established rule of Sociology, that where such a growth is not noticed, the matter is usually found to have been adopted from a foreign country or from a foreign people. It is not that the former Christian writers had not realised this difficulty; but before Europeans had come to know about Buddhism, that is to say, upto the 18th century of the Christian era, Christian research scholars were of the opinion that the renunciatory doctrines of the Esi sect must have entered the Activistic Jewish religion, as a result of the philosophy of the Greeks, and especially of Pythagoras, after an intimate relationship had been established between the Greeks and the Jews. Recent researches prove this inference to be false. Yet, this shows that the idea, that it was not naturally possible for the Esi or Christian renunciatory religion to have come out of the ritualistic Jewish religion, and that there must have been some reason for it which was outside the Jewish religion, is not a new idea; and that this idea had been accepted as correct by Christian scholars before the 18th century.

Colebrooke has said that there is a great deal of similarity between the philosophy of Pythagoras and that of Buddhism *; and therefore, if the above theory is accepted, the parentage of the Esi sect naturally comes to be traced to India; but it is also not now necessary to mince matters about this question. It will be seen by a comparison of the Buddhistic religious works with the New Testament of the Bible that the similarity between not only the Esi religion but also the life of Christ and the preachings of Christ on the one hand and the Buddhism on the other hand, is a hundred times greater than the similarity between the Esi or the Christian religion and Pythagorian philosophers. Just as the Devil tried to tempt Christ, and just as Christ fasted for forty days when He acquired the state of a Siddha (perfect man), so also did Māra tempt Buddha, and Buddha on that occasion fasted for forty-nine days (seven weeks) as has been stated in the biography of Buddha. In the same way, performing by the force of Faith alone such things as walking on water, making one's face or body suddenly appear brilliant like the Sun, or redeeming even thieves or prostitutes, who had surrendered themselves, are similar in the case of Buddha and of Christ; and the principal moral precepts of Christ, such as, "Love thy neighbour", or "Love thy enemies" etc. will sometimes be found to have been given word for word, before the date of Christ, in the Buddhistic religion. The philosophy of Devotion did not originally form part of Buddhism. But, as has been stated above, that principle had

* See Colebrooke's *Miscellaneous Essays,* Vol. I. pp. 399, 400.

been adopted by the Mahāyāna Buddhist sect at least 200 to 300 years before Christ, from the Bhagavadgītā. But Mr. Arthur Lilly has authoritatively shown in his books that this similarity does not exist only as regards these things, but that there are hundreds of other small and big incidents, in which there is a similar similarity between the Christian and the Buddhist religions. Nay, the symbol of the Cross, which has become sacred to Christians on account of the fact that Christ was crucified on a Cross, had also become a holy symbol in the Vedic and Buddhistic religions in the shape of a '*svastika*', hundreds of years before Christ; and modern research scholars have proved that not only in Egypt and other countries in the ancient continents of the earth, but even in Peru and Mexico in America, the *svastika* was looked upon as an auspicious sign many centuries before Columbus*. From this one has to draw the conclusion, that the *svastika* sign, which had become a matter of regard and reverence long before the date of Christ, was made use of in one particular way by the devotees of Christ. There is also a great deal of similarity between the Buddhist monks and the old Christian missionaries (specially the earliest preachers) so far as their dress and religious observances are concerned. For instance, the ceremony of initiation after a bath, that is to say 'baptism', was in vogue long before the date of Christ; and it has now been proved that Buddhist monks had wholly adopted the procedure of sending religious preachers to different countries and thus propagating their religion, long before the date of Christian missionaries.

It is quite natural for a thinking person to ask himself why there should be such a strange and comprehensive similarity between the lives and the moral preachings of Buddha and Christ, and also between the religious observances of both these religions†.

* See *The Secret of the Pacific* by C. Reginald Enoch, 1912, pp. 248-252.

† Mr. Arthur Lily has written a separate book on this subject called *Buddhism in Christendom*; and he has also briefly expressed his opinion in the last four chapters of his book, *Buddha and Buddhism*. The exposition made by me in this part of the Appendix has been made principally on the authority of this book. The

When this similarity first came to the notice of Western scholars by the study of Buddhistic treatises, some Christian scholars began to say that Buddhists must have adopted these principles from the Asiatic Christian sect known as the 'Nestorian' sect. But such a thing is absolutely impossible; because, the founder of the Nestorian sect himself came into existence about 425 years after Christ, whereas Buddha was born about 500 years before Christ, that is to say, nearly 900 years before Nestor; and it has now been established beyond doubt from the stone inscriptions of Aśoka that in his times, that is to say, at least 250 years before the Christian era, Buddism was followed to a very large extent in India and in the surrounding countries, and works containing the life of Buddha etc. had also been written. The ancientness of of the Buddhistic religion being in this way undoubtable, there remain only two possible conclusions regarding the similarity to be seen between the Christian and the Buddhistic religions, namely, that (1) this similarity must have arisen in the two places independently of each other, or that (2) these principles must have been taken by Christ or His disciples from Buddhism. Prof. Rhys-Davids says that this similarity has arisen as a result of the similarity between the circumstances of both Christ and Buddha, and that it has arisen in both the places naturally and independently *. But any one will realise after a little consideration that this solution is not satisfactory; because, when anything comes into existence anywhere independently, it grows very gradually, and we can also see the course of the growth. For instance, we can logically show the gradual growth of the Jñāna-kāṇḍa out of the Karma-kāṇḍa, and also how the philosophy of Devotion, the Pātañjala-Yoga, and ultimately the Buddhistic religion grew gradually out of the Jñāna-kāṇḍa, that is, from the Upaniṣads. But the renunciatory Esi or Christian religions have not grown in the same way from the Activistic Jewish

book *Buddha and Buddhism* was published in 1900 in The World's Epoch Makers Series; and in the tenth part of that book, about 50 similarities between the Buddhist and the Christian religions have been shown.

* See *Buddhist Suttas,* S. B. E. Series, Vol. XI, p. 163.

religion. And I have stated above that modern Christian scholars have now admitted the position that the Christian religion came into existence suddenly, and that there was some cause outside the Jewish religion which was responsible for its having done so. Besides, the similarity between the Christian and the Buddhistic religions is so strange and so complete, that it is impossible for such a similarity to arise in an independent way. It would be different if it could be proved that it was totally impossible for Jewish people to have come to know anything about Buddhism. But history clearly proves that after the date of Alexander—and certainly at the date of Aśoka (that is, at least 250 years before Christ)—Buddhist monks had found their way to Alexandria in Egypt, and Greece, in the east of Europe. It is stated in one Aśokan stone inscription itself that Aśoka had entered into a treaty with Antiochus, who was a Greek king ruling over the Jewish and the surrounding countries. In the same way, there is a statement in the Bible itself, that learned persons had travelled into Jerusalem from the East when Christ was born (Matthew 2. 1). Christians say that these sages were Magis, belonging to the Iranian religion, and not from India. But whatever is said, the meaning is the same. Because, history clearly tells us that long before this date, Buddhism had spread to Kashmir and Kabul, and that it had travelled to the East of Europe as far as Iran and Turkey. Besides, Plutarch himself has clearly recorded * that a monk from India used to come every

* See Plutarch's *Morals—Theosophical Essays*, translated by C. N. King (George Bell & Sons), pp. 96 and 97. There is a reference in the Mahāvaṁśa written in the Pali language (29. 39) to a Greek, that is, *yavana* town named Alasandā (*yona-nagarā 'lasandā*); and it is stated there that some years before the Christian era, while the work of building a temple was going on in Ceylon, many Buddhist monks had gone from that place to Ceylon for the celebration. The English translator of the Mahāvaṁśa says that a town named Alasandā established by Alexander in Kabul is meant in this place, and not Alexandria in Egypt. But this is not correct; because, this small place would not have been referred to by anybody as a city of *yavanas*. Besides, the stone inscription of Aśoka mentioned above, itself contains a clear reference to Buddhist monks having been sent to the kingdom of the *yavanas*.

year to the shore of the Red Sea, that is to say, somewhere near Alexandria during the life of Christ. In short, there is now no doubt whatsoever that Buddhist monks had started entering Jewish countries two or three hundred years before Christ; and once the fact of this intercourse is admitted, it naturally follows that Buddhism was principally responsible for the renunciatory Esi religion, and later on, for the renunciatory and devotional Christian religion finding entry into the Jewish countries. The English writer Lilly has drawn this very inference; and he has mentioned in his book the similar opinions of the French scholars E'mile Bournouff and Rosni in support of his opinion * ; and Prof. Sedan, who was the Professor of Philosophy at Leipzig University in Germany, has also expressed the same opinion in his books on this subject. The German Professor Schroeder has said in one of his Essays that the Christian religion is not exactly similar to Buddhism; that, though there may be a similarity between the two in some matters, there is a great deal of dissimilarity in other matters; and that, therefore, the opinion that the Christian religion was derived from the Buddhistic religion cannot be accepted. But, as this statement is irrelevant, it does not carry any weight whatsoever. It is nobody's case that the Christian and Buddhistic religions are similar to each other in all respects; because, if such were the case, nobody would have said that these two religions are different from each other. The principal question is, what was the reason for the renunciatory devotional Christian religion being promulgated as an improvement on the fundamentally purely Activistic Jewish religion; and when one thinks of the history of the Buddhist religion, which was undoubtedly more ancient than the Christian religion, it does not appear historically logical to say that the renunciatory principles of Ethics and Devotion in Christianity were discovered by Christ independently. There is no information to be found in the Bible as to what Christ was doing from the 12th to the 30th year of His life, or where He was during that period. And it is quite clear that He must have spent this time in the acquisition of knowledge, in religious meditation, and in travel. Therefore, it is impossible to say definitely

* See Lilly's *Buddha and Buddhism* pp. 158 ff.

that He could not have come into contact, directly or indirectly, with Buddhist monks during this period of His life; because, the activities of Buddhist monks had at that date gone as far as Greece. There is a clear statement in a book to be found in a Buddhist monastary in Nepal that Jesus Christ had at that time come to India, and that He there acquired the knowledge of Buddhism. This book was found by a Russian named Nicholas Notovisch, and he published a translation of it into the French language in 1894. Many Christian scholars say, that though the translation of Notovisch may be correct, the original book itself is a fraud written by some one; and I too am not very emphatic on the position that these scholars should accept that book as authentic. Whether the book found by Notovisch was reliable or not, it will be quite clear from the dissertation made by me above that, from the purely historical point of view, it was not impossible, at least for the disciples of Christ who wrote His life in the New Testament, if not for Christ Himself, to have become acquainted with Buddhism; and if this position is not improbable, it does not appear logical to say that the strange similarity to be found between the lives or the preachings of Christ and Buddha, was something which came into existence independently*. In short, the purely ritualistic path of the Mīmāṁsakas, the Knowledge-Action (*naiṣkarmya*) path of Janaka and others, the Path of Knowledge and Renunciation of the writers of the Upaniṣads and the Sāṁkhya philosophers, the Pātañjala Yoga in the shape of 'Concentration of the Mind', and the Pāñcarātra or the Bhāgavata religion, that is, the Philosophy of Devotion, are all religious paths which grew originally from the ancient Vedic religion. Leaving aside, out of these, the Path of the Knowledge of the Brahman, the Path of Energism, and the Path of Devotion, Buddha has preached his renunciatory religion to the four castes on the basis of the philosophy of (i) Yoga in the form of 'Concentration of the Mind', and (ii) Karma-Sāṁnyāsa

* The same is the opinion of Mr. Rameshchandra Dutt, and he has expressed it in detail in his book. See Rameshchandra Dutt's *History of Civilisation in Ancient India* Vol. II, Chapter XX pp. 328–340.

(Abandonment of Action); but the supporters and followers of Buddha, later on added to his religion the principles of Devotion and of Desireless Action, and spread this reformed Buddhistic religion on all sides. After the Buddhistic religion had in this way spread everywhere at the date of Aśoka, the principles of Renunciation began to find a way into the purely Activistic Jewish religion; and Christ ultimately added to it the Philosophy of Devotion, and established His own religion. When one gives proper weight to this gradual growth, which is established by historical facts, one comes to the definite conclusion that far from the Gītā having taken something from the Christian religion, as suggested by Dr. Laurincer, there is a very strong probability, and almost a certainty, that the principles of Self-Identification, Renunciation, Non-Enmity, and Devotion, to be found in the New Testament of the Bible, must have been taken into the Christian religion from Buddhism, and therefore, indirectly from the Vedic religion; and that, Indians had no need to look to other people for finding these religious principles.

I have in this way considered the seven questions mentioned by me at the beginning of this Appendix. Other important questions such as, what was the effect of the Bhagavadgītā on the Path of Devotion now followed in India etc., arise in the train of these questions. But, instead of saying that these questions have a bearing on the Gītā, one must say that they deal with the ancient history of the Hindu religion. For this reason, and principally because this Appendix has been lengthened out beyond my expectations, although I have attempted to make it as short as possible, I shall now finish this External Examination of the Gītā.

THE ORIGINAL STANZAS

OF THE

GITA

WITH

TRANSLATION AND COMMENTARY.

AUTHOR'S PREFACE.

I have explained in detail in the various chapters of the Gītā-Rahasya, that (i) the highest benefit of every human being in this world and in the next, lies in first acquiring as much Equability of Reason (*buddhi*) as possible by Knowledge and Faith, but withal and principally, by the easy and royal road of Devotion, and thereafter doing his duties till death, desirelessly, according to his own religion, in the interests of universal welfare; that (ii) it is not necessary, to give up Action or to practise any religious austerities for attaining Release; and that (iii) this is the sum and substance of the Gītā-Religion. In the same way, I have shown in the fourteenth chapter of this book the clear continuity of the eighteen chapters of the Gītā from this point of view, as also which parts of the other methods of attaining Release have been included in the Activistic religion of the Gītā, and how. When the whole matter has been thrashed out in this way, there remains really nothing to be done beyond giving the plain translation of the stanzas in the Gītā, according to my rendering of them, in their proper order, in the Marathi vernacular. But, it was not possible for me to show in the general Exposition in the Gītā-Rahasya how the subject-matter of each chapter of the Gītā has been divided, or how commentators have stretched the meanings of certain words in the stanzas for supporting their particular doctrine. Therefore, taking both these matters into consideration, I have thought it necessary to give some notes, in the shape of a commentary, immediately after the translation of each stanza, in order that the prior and subsequent context should be understood on the spot. Nevertheless, in these commentaries, I have only touched in passing on those matters, which have been fully dealt with in the Gītā-Rahasya, and I have given the reference to the particular chapter of the Gītā-Rahasya in which that particular subject-matter has been dealt with. In order to enable the reader to distinguish these commentaries from the original matter, I have enclosed them within square brackets, thus, [ ], and put a dotted line by the side. * I have translated the stanzas as far as possible literally, and in several places I have retained the original word in the translation, and given after it its meaning in Marathi, saying 'that is, so and so'; † and I have thus included in the translation itself, what would otherwise have to be given as small foot-notes. Even though this has been done, it has also become necessary to add some words here and there in the translation, in order to give the complete meaning of the original Sanskrit stanza in Marathi, on account of the difference between the Sanskrit and the Marathi idiom; and very often, the word used in the original has also to be given in the translation by way of reference. In order to distinguish these additional words, I have placed them within round brackets, thus, ( ). In Sanskrit books, the number of the stanza is always given at the end. But, in the translation I have given it in the beginning. So that, if some one wants to find out the translation of a particular stanza, he must refer to what follows the figure showing the number of the stanza. I have arranged the translation in such a way that, if one reads only the translation, omitting the commentaries, there is no break in the sense. Similarily, where a sentence has been finished in the original in more than one stanza, I have completed its purport in the translation of the same number of stanzas. Therefore, the translation of some of the stanzas has to be read in continuity. Where such stanzas occur, I have not placed a full stop at the end of the translation of the stanza. Still, it must not be forgotten that a translation will be a translation in any case. It is true that I have attempted to bring out the plain, broad, and principal meaning of the Gītā in the translation; yet, it is impossible to transport into the translation, by means of other words, and just as it is, the power of metaphorically creating numerous figurative meanings, which exists in Sanskrit words, and especially in the loving, sweet, and

*** Instead of using a dotted margin for distinguishing the commentary, as was done by the author, I have made the distinction by putting the commentary within square brackets, and using a different type—Translator.**

† This, too, hns been placed by me within round brackets, thus, ( ), though in the original author's text, it is not within brackets—Trans.

exhaustive speech of the Blessed Lord, "giving new pleasures at every step". Evidently, one who merely reads the Marathi translation cannot make a metaphorical use of the stanzas in the Gītā on various occasions, as can be done by a person who understands the Sanskrit language. Nay, there is very often a chance of such a person making mistakes. It is, therefore, my earnest entreaty to everybody that, whoever can do so, should not fail to study the original Gītā in Sanskrit; and that is one of the reasons why I have given the original stanza side by side with the translation In order that it should be convenient to grasp the subject-matter of each chapter of the Gītā, I have given separately, in the beginning, the contents showing all these subjects, according to stanzas, and in the order of the chapters, on the basis of the groups of sections adopted in the Vedānta-Sūtras. If one does not read each stanza separately, but reads the groups of stanzas as a whole by reference to this index, the present misunderstanding about the import of the Gītā will to a considerable extent be reduced; because, the different meanings of some stanzas which have been given by doctrine-supporting commentators, who have stretched the meaning of the stanzas for proving their doctrines, have been usually given, disregarding this previous and subsequent context. (For example, see my commentary on Gī. 3. 19; 6. 3; and 18. 2). Considering the matter from this point of view, it may well be said that this translation of the Gītā and the Gītā-Rahasya are mutually complementary. And he who wishes to fully understand what I want to say, must read both these parts. As it is usual to learn by heart the whole of the Gītā, one does not come across important variant readings in it. Nevertheless, I must state here that I have accepted as genuine the text of the Gītā as given in the Śāṁkarabhāṣya, which is the most ancient of Bhāṣyas on the Gītā now available.

Detailed contents showing the subjects mentioned in the various chapters of the Gītā, according to the stanzas.

Note :—The divisions of the various subjects in the different chapters of the Gītā, which have been made in these contents according to the stanzas, have been shown in the original stanzas printed further on by the sign §§ printed at the beginning of the stanza ; and, in the translation, a separate paragraph has been started from that stanza.

CHAPTER I—ARJUNA-VIṢĀDA YOGA.

(The Yoga of the Dejection of Arjuna).

1. The question of Dhṛtarāṣṭra to Sañjaya. 2-11. The description given by Duryodhana to Droṇācārya of the armies on either side. 12—19. The blowing of conches by way of greetings to each other in the beginning of the war. 20-27. The survey of the army after the chariot of Arjuna has been brought forward. 28-37. The dejection of Arjuna at seeing his own relatives in both the armies, and realising that the generation will become extinct by their being killed. 38-44. The results of sins like extinction of the *kula* (family). 45-47. The decision of Arjuna not to fight, and his throwing away his bow and arrows.

CHAPTER II—SĀṀKHYA YOGA.

(The Yoga according to the Sāṁkhya system).

1-3. The encouragement given by Śrī Kṛṣna. 4-10. The reply of Arjuna, his doubt as to his own duty, and his surrendering himself to Śrī Kṛṣṇa for an elucidation of what his *dharma* (duty) was. 11-13. The non-lamentability of the Ātman. 14-15. The inconstancy of the Body ; and, of pain and happiness. 16-25. The discernment between the Real (*sat*) and the Unreal (*asat*), and the justification of the non-lamentability of the Ātman by the description of the immortality, and other features, of the Ātman. 26, 27. The reply, on the basis of the immortality of the Ātman. 28. The inconstancy and non-lamentability of the perceptible creation according to the Sāṁkhya system. 29, 30. It is true that the Ātman is difficult to Realise, but you should acquire true Knowledge, and give up lamentation. 31–38. The necessity of warfare according to the religion of the Kṣatriyas. 39. The conclusion of the argument on the basis of the Sāṁkhya system, and the beginning of the argument on the basis of Karma-Yoga. 40. Even a little observance of Karma-Yoga is beneficial. 41. The steadying of the Discerning (*vyavasāyātmikā*) Reason. 42–44. A description of the unsteadiness of Mind of the followers of the Mīmāṁsā school, who are engrossed in the Karma-kāṇḍa (ritual). 45, 46. The advice to perform Action with a steady and concentrated (*yogastha*) Reason. 47. The four canons (*catuḥ-sūtrī*) of the Karma-Yoga. 48–50. The nature of Karma-Yoga, and the superiority of the Reason of the Doer (*kartā*) over the Action (*karma*). 51–53. Release, by following the Karma-Yoga. 54–70. A description of the qualities of the Sthitaprajña in reply to the question of Arjuna, including, as occasion arises, a description of the growth of Desire (*kāma*), Anger (*krodha*), and other emotjons, as a result of Attachment (*āsakti*) to the objects of pleasure. 71, 72. The Brāhmī state.

CHAPTER III—KARMA-YOGA.

(The Yoga of Right Action).

1, 2. "Should Action (ritual) be abandoned or performed; what is the truth?", being the question asked by Arjuna. 3–8. The definite advice to Arjuna that, although there are the two paths (*niṣṭhā*), (i) Sāṁkhya (*karma-saṁnyāsa* or Abandonment of Action) and (ii) Karma-Yoga, yet, as nobody can escape Karma (Action), Karma-Yoga is superior, and the path to be followed. 9–16. The advice to perform even the sacrificial ritual of the Mīmāṁsā school after abandoning Attachment; the antiquity of the Yajña-cakra (cycle of sacrificial ritual), and the necessity of it, for the continuance and maintenance of the world. 17–19. In as much as the Jñānin (one who has acquired Knowledge) has no more any self-interest left, he must perform all Action, which befalls him, with a disinterested, that is, desireless frame of mind; because, no one can escape Karma (action or ritual). 20–24. The illustration of Janaka and others; the importance of universal welfare (*lokasaṁgraha*), and the illustration of the Blessed Lord Himself. 25–29. The difference between the

Actions of the Jñānin and the Ajñānin (one who is ignorant); and, the necessity for one, who has acquired Knowledge, to give an illustration of righteous action, to the one who has not acquired Knowledge, by his own conduct in performing Action desirelessly. 30. The advice to Arjuna to perform warfare like a Jñānin, that is, with the intention of dedicating it to the Parameśvara. 31, 32. The result of performing Action, by Faith, according to this advice of the Blessed Lord, and of not doing so. 33, 34. The overpowering influence of Prakṛti, and the control of the organs. 35. The Desireless Action to be performed, should be according to the duty prescribed for the doer, even if one meets his death in the performance of such Action. 36–41. Desire (*kāma*) compels a man to commit sin in spite of his Will; and, the destruction of that Desire by the control of the organs. 42, 43. The order of superiority among the organs; and, the control of the organs by means of the Knowledge of the Ātman.

CHAPTER IV—JÑĀNA-KARMA-SAṀNYĀSA YOGA.

(The Yoga of Jñāna, and Abandonment of Action).

1–3. The doctrinal tradition of Karma-Yoga. 4–8. An explanation of why, when, and how the Parameśvara, Who is free from birth, takes transcendental births or incarnations by Māyā. 9, 10. Reincarnation is escaped from, and the Blessed Lord is reached, by understanding the principle underlying these transcendental births and Karma. 11, 12. If the worship is performed in some other way, the Fruit obtained, is relative to the worship; e. g. worship of deities for obtaining Fruit relating to this life. 13–15. The unbinding (*nirlepa*) Action of the Blessed Lord relating to the four castes; the destruction of the bond of Action by understanding the underlying principle; and the advice to perform Action (*karma*) accordingly. 16–23. The difference between '*karma*' (Action), '*akarma*' (Non-Action), and '*vikarma*' (Wrong Action); *akarma* means unattached-Action; that, is the correct Karma; and, the bond of Karma is destroyed only by such Action. 24–33. Description of various kinds of Metaphorical Yajñas (sacrifices); and the superiority of the Sacrifice performed with the '*brahma-buddhi*'; that is, of the Jñāna-Yajña'. 34–37. Advice about Knowledge from one who has acquired Knowledge; Self-Identification; and, the annihilation of sin or merit by Knowledge. 38–40. The means of acquiring Knowledge; *buddhi* (–Yoga) and *śraddhā* (Faith); ruin, in the absence of these. 41, 42. A description of the individual uses of (Karma–) Yoga and Jñāna (Knowledge), and the advice to engage in warfare with the help of both.

CHAPTER V—SAṀNYĀSA-YOGA.

(The Yoga of Renunciation).

The direct question of Arjuna whether Saṁnyāsa (Renunciation) or Karma-Yoga is superior. The definite answer of the Blessed Lord, that though both lead to Release, Karma-Yoga is superior. 3–6. By giving up Desire, the Karma-Yogin becomes a *nitya-saṁnyāsin* (a perpetual ascetic); and Saṁnyāsa (renunciation) itself is not successful without Karma (Action); therefore, both are the same in principle. 7–13. As the mind of the Karma-Yogin is always in a state of Renunciation and his Actions are only the actions of the organs, he is always unattached, peaceful, and Released. 14, 15. The real Activity, and Enjoyment is of Matter (*prakṛti*), but as a result of ignorance, it is supposed to be that of the Ātman or of the Parameśvara. 16, 17. Release from re-birth as a result of the annihilation of this ignorance. 18–23. A description of the Equability of vision, the steadiness of the Reason, and the indifference towards pain or happiness, resulting from *brahmajñāna* (Knowledge of the Brahman). 24–28. The Karma-Yogin is always *brahma-bhūta* (merged in the Brahman), *samādhistha* (mentally absorbed) and *mukta* (Released) in this very life, though he may be performing Action for the benefit of the entire creation. 29. The result of Realising that the Parameśvara is the recipient of all Yajña (sacrificial ritual) and *tapa* (austerities), (though He does not take on Himself the Doership), and that He is the friend of the whole creation.

CHAPTER VI—DHYĀNA-YOGA.

(The Yoga of Meditation).

1, 2. The one who performs Action without entertaining any Hope of Fruit (*phalāśā*) is the true Saṁnyāsin or Yogin;

'Saṁnyāsin' does not mean one who is *niragni* (one who does not perform Fire-Worship, or other ritualistic Action), and *akriya* (one who performs no Action at all). 3, 4. The mutual interchange of of *kārya* (Result), and *kāraṇa* (Cause) of *śama* (Abandonment) and *karma* (Action) in the '*siddhāvasthā*' (perfect state), and the *sadhanāvasthā* (preparatory stage) of the Karma-Yogin; and the characteristic feature of the Yogārūḍha (one who is installed in Yoga). 5, 6. The freedom of the Ātman to successfully acquire Yoga. 7–9. Even among the *jitātman-yogayukta* (those who have conquered Self and are steeped in Yoga), the one who has attained Equability of Reason is the best. 10–17. A description of the bodily postures (*āsana*), and food, and recreation, necessary for *yoga-sādhana* (the successful practice of Yoga). 18–23. A description of the Yogin, and of the beatific happiness of the *yoga-samādhi* (mental absorption resulting from Yoga). 24–26. How to gradually make the Mind, Absorbed (*samādhistha*), Peaceful (*śānta*), and Self-devoted (*ātmaniṣṭha*). 27, 28. The Yogin alone is 'Merged in the Brahman' (*brahmabhūta*) and intensely happy. 29–32. The Self-Identification of the Yogin with the entire creation. 33–36. The control of the restless Mind by Practice (*abhyāsa*), and by Indifference to worldly affairs (*vairāgya*). 37–45. A description of how the *yoga-bhraṣṭa* (one who has abandoned the practice of Karma-Yoga), or the *jijñāsu* (one who has got the desire to understand what the Karma-Yoga is) acquires growing merit, birth after birth, and ultimately complete Release, given in reply to the question of Arjuna. 46, 47. The Karma-Yogins, and among them those who are Devout, are better than the *tapasvins* (those who perform religious austerities), the Jñānins (the scients), and mere Karmins (those who merely perform Action or Ritual); and, the advice to Arjuna to become a (Karma-) Yogin.

CHAPTER VII—JÑĀNA-VIJÑĀNA YOGA.

(The Yoga of Spiritual and Worldly Knowledge).

1—3. The beginning of the disquisition on Jñāna (Spiritual Knowledge) and Vijñāna (worldly knowledge), for the attainment of Karma-Yoga; the rarity of persons who make an effort to attain Karma-Yoga. 4–7. Consideration of the *kṣara* (perishable) and the *akṣara* (imperishable); the eight-fold *aparā-prakṛti* (inferior material manifestation), and the (*parā-prakṛti* (superior material manifestation), in the shape of Jīva, of the Blessed Lord; and the further development of everything out of it. 8–12. A brief survey of the form of the Parameśvara, which pervades the *sāttvika* (equable) and other divisions of that development. 13–15. This is the qualityful (*guṇamayī*) and insuperable (*dustara*) Māyā (Illusion) of the Parameśvara; and the overcoming of that Māyā by surrendering oneself to the Parameśvara. 16–19. Devotees are of four kinds; and the Jñānin is the most superior among them. The completion of Jñāna (Knowledge) after innumerable births, and the permanent fruit in the shape of assimilation with the Blessed Lord. 20–23. The worship of deities in the hope of obtaining non-permanent objects of Desire; but even there, the Blessed Lord wields the power to give fruit or benefit according to one's Faith in the Blessed Lord. 24–28. The real form of the Blessed Lord is imperceptible (*avyakta*); but that form becomes difficult of Realisation on account of 'Māyā' (Illusion); the mental confusion about the couples of opposites (*dvaṁdva*); and the Realisation of the true form of the Parameśvara by the destruction of the confusion created by Māyā. 29, 30. Ultimate Acquisition of Knowledge by Realising that the Brahman, the *adhyātma* (Absolute Self), *karma* (Action), the *adhi-bhūta* (absolute Matter), *adhi-daiva* (the highest Deity), and *adhi-yajña* (the highest sacrifice) are all Parameśvara.

CHAPTER VIII—AKṢARA-BRAHMA YOGA.

(The Yoga of the Imperishable Brahman)

1–4. The definitions of the terms '*brahma*', '*adhyātma*', '*adhi-bhūta*', '*adhi-daiva*', '*adhi-yajña*', and '*adhi-deha*', in reply to the question of Arjuna; all of these contain the same Īśvara. 5–8. Release by thinking of the Blessed Lord at the moment of death; but, that which is always in the mind, is also in the mind at the moment of death; therefore, the advice to always think of the Blessed Lord; and, to fight. 9–13. The concentrated meditation on the Om-kāra, that is, on the Parameśvara at the moment of death; and the result of it. 14–16. The annihilation of re-birth as a result of constant thinking of the Blessed Lord, the states of Brahma-loka etc., are not permanent. 17–19. The day and night of Brahmadeva, the creation of the Cosmos from the Imperceptible in the beginning of his day, and the merging of it, in that same Imperceptible, in the beginning of his night. 20–22. The Imperceptible (*avyakta*) and Imperishable (*akṣara*) Spirit (*puruṣa*) is even beyond that Imperceptible; the possibility of attaining the Ultimate Imperceptible, by means of Devotion; and, the end of re-birth as a result of such attainment. 23–26. The paths of Devayāna and Pitṛyāṇa; the first puts an end to re-birth, the second is just the opposite. 27–28. The result which is obtained by the Yogin who understands the principle underlying these two paths is the highest, and therefore, the advice to act accordingly.

CHAPTER IX—RĀJAVIDYĀ-RĀJAGUHYA YOGA.

(The Yoga of the 'King of Cults' and the 'King of Mysticisms'),

1–3. The Path of Devotion, which includes Spiritual Knowledge (*jñāna*) and Worldly Knowledge (*vijñāna*), is productive of Release and is nevertheless easy and realisable; therefore, it is the King of Paths (*rāja-mārga*). 4–6. The unintelligible Yogic activity of the Parameśvara; being in the entire creation, He is nevertheless, not in it; and the entire creation being in Him, is yet not in Him. 7–10. He makes use of the illusory Prakṛti for the construction and destruction of the Cosmos, and the creation and destruction of created beings (*bhūta*); and in spite of all this, He is untouched by Desire, that is to say, Unattached (*alipta*). 11, 12. Those who do not realise this, and defy the Parameśvara, Who has taken a human form, are fools, and *āsuri* (ungodly). 13–15. On the other hand, those who go in for various other devotional practices by means of the Jñāna-yajña are *daivi* (godly). 16–19. The Īśvara is All-pervading, and He is the parent, the owner, and the maintainer of the universe, and the doer of whatever is good or bad. 20–22. Although the paraphernalia of Yajñas and Yāgas according to the Śrutis may be productive of heaven, yet, that fruit is non-permanent; if it is said that the same is necessary for '*yoga-kṣema*' (maintenance and protection), then, that can be obtained even by Devotion. 23–25. Devotion to other deities is indirectly Devotion to the Parameśvara, but the fruit is consistent with the deity and the mental belief. 26. If there is Devotion, the Parameśvara is satisfied even by the offering of a petal of a flower. 27, 28. The advice to dedicate all acts to the Īśvara; escape from the bonds of Karma, and Release by doing so. 29–33. The Parameśvara is equal to all; whether one is a sinner, or born in a low caste, or a woman, a Vaiśya, or a Śūdra, all attain the same end, if they become unlimited Devotees. 34. The advice to Arjuna to adopt this path.

CHAPTER X. VIBHŪTI-YOGA.

(The Yoga of Manifestations)

1–3. The destruction of sin by realising that the unborn Parameśvara is prior to the gods and the Ṛṣis. 4–6. Manifestations of the Īśvara, and Yoga; the origin of Reason (*buddhi*), and other qualities (*bhāva*), the origin of the seven Ṛṣis and of Manu, and of everything in order of succession from the Īśvara. 7–11. The Acquisition of Knowledge by the Devotees of the Blessed Lord, who have Realised this; but to these too, '*buddhi-siddhi*' (the success of *buddhi*) is given by the Blessed Lord. 12–18. The request of Arjuna to the Blessed Lord to describe to him, His manifestations and Yoga. 19–40. A description of the most important out of the innumerable manifestations of the Blessed Lord. 41, 42. All that which is '*vibhūtimat*' (manifested), '*śrī-mat*' (illustrious) and '*urjita*' (elevated) is the effulgence of the Parameśvara, but only in part.

CHAPTER XI—VIŚVA-RŪPA-DARSANA YOGA.

(The Yoga of the Showing of the Cosmic Form)

1–4. The request of Arjuna to the Blessed Lord to show to him His Īśvaric form, as described in the previous chapter. 5–8. The giving to Arjuna of transcendental vision to enable him to see this wonderful and transcendental form. 9–14. The description of the Cosmic Form (*viśva-rūpa*) by Sañjaya. 15–31. The praise of the Cosmic Form by Arjuna, who had become humble as a result of surprise and terror; and, his request to the Cosmic Form-ed Lord to become propitious and explain who He was. 32–34. The reply that: "I am 'Time' or 'Death' (*kāla*)"; and the encouraging advice to Arjuna to become the instrument for killing those warriors, who had already become engulfed in that 'Time' or 'Death'. The praise, the beseeching for forgiveness, and the request to resume the former form made by Arjuna to the Cosmic Form-ed Lord. 47-51. Impossibility of visualising the Cosmic Form otherwise than by exclusive worship; resuming by the Blessed Lord of His former form. 52-54. A vision of the Cosmic Form impossible even to gods in the absence of Devotion. 55. Therefore, the final advice, in the form of a general summary, to Arjuna to perform Action after becoming '*niḥsaṅga*' (unattached) and '*nirvaira*' (non-inimical), with the intention of dedicating everything to the Parameśvara.

CHAPTER XII—BHAKTI-YOGA.

(The Yoga of Devotion)

1. The question of Arjuna, with reference to the summarising advice given at the end of the last chapter, as to whether the 'worship of the Perceptible' (*vyaktopāsanā*), or, the 'worship of the Imperceptible' (*avyaktopāsanā*) was superior. 2-8. The end of both is the same; but, the worship of the Imperceptible is arduous, whereas, the worship of the Perceptible is easy and speedily successful; the advice, therefore, to worship the Perceptible with a desireless frame of mind. 9-12. The various devices, such as, Practice (*abhyāsa*), Knowledge (*jñāna*), Meditation (*dhyāna*) etc., for concentrating one's attention on the Blessed Lord; and the best path, in any case, is the 'Abandonment of the Fruit of Action' (*karma-phala-tyāga*). 13-19. A description of the mental condition of the Devotee and the love of the Blessed Lord for him. 20. Those believing Devotees, who live according to this religion, are most beloved of the Blessed Lord.

CHAPTER XIII—KṢETRA-KṢETRAJÑA-VIBHĀGA YOGA.

(The Yoga of the Division of the Cosmos into the Body and the Ātman)

1, 2. Definitions of the terms '*kṣetra*' and '*kṣetrajña*' acquaintance with them, means acquaintance with the Parameśvara. 3, 4. The consideration of the Body (*kṣetra*) and the Ātman (*kṣetrajña*) according to the Upaniṣads, and according to the Brahma-Sūtras. 5, 6. The nature of the form of the Body. 7-11. The nature of the form of Knowledge (*jñāna*); the opposite of it, that is, Ignorance (*ajñāna*). 12–17. The nature of the form of the Knowable (*jñeya*). 18. The result of Realising all this. 19–21. The consideration of Matter (*prakṛti*) and Spirit (*puruṣa*). Prakṛti is the active agent, and Purusa is inactive, but is the one who derives the benefit, sees, etc. 22, 23. The Puruṣa is the Paramātman within the Body; the end of re-birth as a result of the Realisation of this Prakṛti and Puruṣa. 24, 25. The ways of acquiring the Knowledge of the Ātman, namely, meditation (*dhyāna*), the Sāṁkhya-Yoga, the Karma-Yoga, and Devotion by hearing sermons with a believing frame of mind. 26–28. The birth of the moveable and immoveable creation from the union between the Body and the Ātman; that which is imperishable in it, is the Parameśvara; reaching the Parameśvara by one's own efforts. 29, 30. Prakṛti is the active agent, the Ātman is inactive; all created things are contained in One, and they all spring from One; attainment of the Brahman by Realising this. 31–33. The Ātman is eternal and qualityless, that is to say, though it enlightens the Body, it is unattached (*nirlepa*). 34. The highest Perfection as a result of Realising this difference between the Body and the Ātman.

CHAPTER XIV—GUṆATRAYA-VIBHĀGA YOGA.

(The Yoga of the division of Matter into three constituents.)

1, 2. A consideration of the diversity of created beings included in Spiritual Knowledge and Worldly Knowledge, having regard to the different constituents; this too is productive of Release. 3, 4. The Parameśvara is the father of all created beings; and, Prakṛti, which is dependent on the Parameśvara, is their mother. 5–9. The influence of the *sattva*, *rajas*, and *tamas* constituents on the created universe. 10–13. Impossibility of there being only one constituent; the growth of the third constituent by the defeat of the other two; and, the nature of the growth of each. 14–18. The result of Action, according to the predominance of any particular constituent, and the state which is obtained after death. 19–20. The attainment of Release by going beyond the three constituents. 21–25. A description of the nature and the mode of living of the Triguṇātīta (one who has gone beyond the three constituents) given in answer to the question of Arjuna. 26, 27. The acquiring of the Triguṇātīta state by solitudinal (*ekāntika*) Devotion, and the attainment thereafter of the Parameśvara, Who is the ultimate resolution of all Release, all religion, and all happiness.

CHAPTER XV—PURUṢOTTAMA-YOGA.

(The Yoga of the most Excellent Spirit).

1, 2. The similarity between the Vedic and the Sāṁkhya descriptions of the Cosmic Tree (*brahma-vṛkṣa*) in the form of the '*aśvattha*' (pippala) tree. 3–6. The cutting of that tree by '*asaṅga*' (unattachment) is the only way for the attainment of the Immutable State (*avyaya-pada*), which is beyond it; a description of this Immutable State. 7–11. The forms of the '*jīva*' and the '*linga-śarīra*' (Subtle Body), and their mutual relationship, which can be realised by scients. 12–15. The all-pervasiveness of the Parameśvara. 16–18. The nature of the *kṣara* (perishable) and the *akṣara* (imperishable); the Purusottama is beyond both. 19, 20. By the Relisation of this mystic Puruṣottama, one acquires All-Knowledge (*sarvajñatā*) and Accomplishment (*kṛtakṛtyatā*).

CHAPTER XVI—DAIVĀSURA-SAMPAT-VIBHĀGA YOGA.

(The Yoga of the division into godly and ungodly endowment).

1–3. The 26 qualities of godly (*daivi*) endowment. 4. The nature of ungodly (*āsuri*) endowment. 5. Godly endowment is productive of Release, and ungodly endowment is productive of bondage. 6–20. A detailed description of the ungodly; they are destined to perdition, birth after birth. 21, 22. The three-folded door of Hell—Desire (*kāma*), Anger (*krodha*), and Avarice (*lobha*)—bliss, as a result of giving these up. 23, 24. The advice to Arjuna to decide about the Doable and the Not-Doable consistently with the Śāstras, and to act accordingly.

CHAPTER XVII—ŚRADDHĀ-TRAYA-VIBHĀGA YOGA

(The Yoga of the Division into three kinds of Faith)

1–4. A description of three kinds of Faith, such as, the *sāttvika* etc., according to the inherent nature of Prakṛti, in reply to the question of Arjuna; as the Faith, so the man. 5, 6

The *āsura* is different from this. 7–10. The *sāttvika*, *rājasa*, and *tāmasa* kinds of food. 11–13. The three kinds of Yajña. 14–16. The three divisions of Austerity (*tapa*) namely, *śārīra* (bodily), *vācika* (vocal) and *mānasa* (mental). 17–19. Each of these is again of three kinds, by a division according as it is *sāttvika* etc. 20–22. The three kinds of gifts, namely, *sāttvika* etc. 23. The '*brahma-nirdeśa*' (symbol of the Brahman) 'OM-TAT-SAT' 24–27. Out of these, the word OM is indicative of the beginning of Action, the word TAT refers to Desireless Action, and the word SAT refers to Proper Action. 28. That which remains, namely, the Unreal (*asat*), is fruitless, whether in this life or in the next.

CHAPTER XVIII—MOKṢA-SAṀNYĀSA YOGA.

(The Yoga of Release by Renunciation).

1, 2. The definitions of Saṁnyāsa (Renunciation) and Tyāga (Abandonment) according to the doctrine of Karma-Yoga in reply to the question of Arjuna. 3–6. The explanation about the eligibility and non-eligibility of Action; even actions (or ritual) like Yajñas and Yāgas must be performed, with a Desireless frame of mind, just like other Actions. 7–9. The *sāttvika*, *rājasa*, and *tāmasa* varieties of Abandonment of Action; out of these, performing one's duty, abandoning the Hope of Fruit (*phalāśā*) is the only *sāttvika-tyāga* (equable Abandonment). 10, 11. The one who abandons the Fruit of Action is the '*sāttvika-tyāgin*'; because, no one escapes mere Action. 12. The three-fold Fruit of Action does not become a source of bondage to the '*sāttvika tyāgin*'. 13–15. There are five reasons for any Action taking place; man is not the only reason. 16, 17. Therefore, when a man has got rid of the egotistical feeling (*ahaṁkāra-buddhi*) that 'I am the doer', he remains unattached, though he performs Action. 18–19. The three-fold nature of, and the Sāṁkhya form of '*karma-codanā*' (the inspiration to perform Action), and '*karma-saṁgraha*' (the performance of Action). 20–22. The three kinds of Jñāna according to the three qualities *sāttvika* etc.; the Realisation that '*avibhaktaṁ vibhakteṣu*' is *sāttvika*. 23–25. The three kinds of Karma (Action); of these, that in which the Hope for Fruit is absent is *sāttvika*. 26–28. The three kinds of Doers (*kartā*); the Unattached (*niḥsaṅga*) Doer is *sāttvika*. 29–32. The three kinds of Reason (*buddhi*). 33–35. The three kinds of Perseverance (*dhṛti*). 36–39. The three kinds of Happiness; that which arises out of Self-Identification is *sāttvika*. 40. The three divisions of the entire universe according to different constituents. 41–44. The justification of the four castes on the basis of the three different constituents; the inherent Actions of Kṣatriyas, Vaiśyas, and Śūdras. 45, 46. Ultimate Perfection by doing one's own duties, as prescribed for the four castes. 47–49. Living according to another's religion is fraught with danger; Action according to one's own religion, though faulty, ought not to be abandoned; and when all Actions are done according to one's own religion (*dharma*), with a desireless frame of mind, one attains the '*naiṣkarmya-siddhi*' (The Perfection of Desireless Action). 50–56. An explanation of how this Perfection (*siddhi*) is obtained, even after performing all Actions. 57, 58. The advice to Arjuna to follow this Path. 59–63. Individuation (*ahaṁkāra*) is helpless before the inherent nature of Prakṛti; one must surrender oneself to the Īśvara; the advice to Arjuna that he should realise this mystic secret, and then do whatever he wants. 64–66. The final promise of the Blessed Lord that if Arjuna surrendered himself to Him, giving up all other Paths of Religion, He would redeem him from all sins. 67–69. The benefit to be derived by maintaining the tradition of the Path of Karma-Yoga. 70, 71. A description of the results thereof. 72, 73. Arjuna becomes ready to fight, after the clearing of his doubts as to what he ought to do. 74–78. The summing up by Sañjaya after he had told this story to Dhṛtarāṣṭra.

SRĪMAD BHAGAVADGĪTĀ

प्रथमोऽध्यायः

धृतराष्ट्र उवाच ।

धर्मक्षेत्रे कुरुक्षेत्रे समवेता युयुत्सवः ।
मामकाः पाण्डवाश्चैव किमकुर्वत संजय ॥ १ ॥

CHAPTER I.

[In the present Mahābhārata, the tradition as to how the Gītā preached to Arjuna by Śrī Kṛṣṇa in the beginning of the Bhāratī war, was subsequently promulgated, has been described as follows: In the beginning of the war, Vyāsa went to Dhṛtarāṣṭra and said to him, "If you desire to see the war, I will give you your eye-sight". * But, Dhṛtarāṣṭra said that he did not wish to see the destruction of his own clan (*kula*). Thereupon, Vyāsa gave to a bard (*sūta*) named Sañjaya such spiritual eye-sight as would enable him to actually see everything that was taking place on the battle-field, while sitting where he as, and made arrangements that he should relate to Dhṛtarāṣṭra what was happening in the war, and then went away. (Ma. Bhā. Bhīṣma. 2). When, according to this arrangement, Sañjaya first went to give to Dhṛtarāṣṭra the news of the fall of Bhīṣma in the war, Dhṛtarāṣṭra lamented the death of Bhīṣma and commanded Sañjaya to relate to him the entire history of the war. Sañjaya has first described the armies on both sides, and then started to recite the Gītā in answer to the question of Dhṛtarāṣṭra. The same history was later on related by Vyāsa to his disciples, and thereafter, by Vaiśampāyana, one of those disciples, to Janamejaya, and finally by Sauti to Śaunaka; and the Gītā is comprised in all the printed editions of the Mahābhārata, from the 25th to the 42nd chapters of the Bhīsmaparva. According to this tradition—]

Dhṛtarāṣṭra said: (1) O Sañjaya, what did my sons

* Dhṛtarāṣṭra was totally blind, having lost both his eyes—Trans.

संजय उवाच ।

§§ दृष्ट्वा तु पाण्डवानीकं व्यूढं दुर्योधनस्तदा ।
आचार्यमुपसंगम्य राजा वचनमब्रवीत् ॥ २ ॥
पश्यैतां पाण्डुपुत्राणामाचार्य महतीं चमूम् ।
व्यूढां द्रुपदपुत्रेण तव शिष्येण धीमता ॥ ३ ॥

and the sons of Pāṇḍu, desirous of war, do, when they assembled together, on the sacred field, the Kurukṣetra ?

[The Kurukṣetra is an open space of ground surrounding the city of Hastināpura. The present city of Delhi stands on this field. Kuru, the common ancestor of the Kauravas and the Pāṇḍavas, was ploughing this field laboriously by his own hands. That is why it is called '*kṣetra*' (or, field). It is said in the Bhārata, that, when Indra thereafter gave to Kuru the blessing that all those who would die on that field in war or while performing religious austerities, would obtain Heaven, Kuru stopped ploughing the field. (Ma. Bhā. Śalya. 53). As a result of this blessing, this field came to be called '*dharmakṣetra*' or 'sacred ground'. There is also a story that Paraśurāma killed all the Kṣatriyas on twenty-one successive occasions on this field, and in that way offered a pious oblation to the manes of his deceased ancestors (made a *pitṛ-tarpaṇa*); and there have been big wars, even in modern times, on this field.]

Sañjaya said: *(2) Thereupon, seeing that the army of the Pāṇḍavas was (standing) drawn up in battle-array, the prince Duryodhana went to the Preceptor (Droṇa), and said—

[It is stated in the chapters of the Mahābhārata before the Gītā that when Bhīṣma had first arranged the array of the Kaurava army, the Pāṇḍavas, in accordance with the rules of war, arranged their army in an array (*vyūha*) called the 'Vajra'. (Ma. Bhā. Bhī. 19. 4-7; Manu. 7.191). During the course of the war, these military arrays used to be changed every day.]

(3) O Ācārya! behold this mighty host of the sons of Pāṇḍu, of which the array has been arranged by your

* The words 'Dhṛtarāṣṭra said', 'Sañjaya said' etc. have been underlined by me, for distinction, though in the author's text they have not been so underlined—Trans.

अत्र शूरा महेष्वासा भीमार्जुनसमा युधि।
युयुधानो विराटश्च द्रुपदश्च महारथः ॥ ४ ॥
धृष्टकेतुश्चेकितानः काशिराजश्च वीर्यवान्।
पुरुजित्कुंतिभोजश्च शैब्यश्च नरपुंगवः ॥ ५ ॥
युधामन्युश्च विक्रान्त उत्तमौजाश्च वीर्यवान्।
सौभद्रो द्रौपदेयाश्च सर्व एव महारथाः ॥ ६ ॥
अस्माकं तु विशिष्टा ये तान्निबोध द्विजोत्तम।
नायका मम सैन्यस्य संज्ञार्थं तान्ब्रवीमि ते ॥ ७ ॥

talented pupil, the son of Drupada (Dhṛṣṭadyumna). (4) In it there are heroes, mighty bowmen, the equals of Bhīma and Arjuna in battle, (namely) Yuyudhāna (Sātyaki) Virāṭa, and the *maharathī* Drupada, (5) and Dhṛṣṭaketu, Cekitāna, and the valiant king of Kāśi, Purujit Kuntibhoja, and that eminent man named Śaibya, (6) as also the heroic Yudhāmanyu, and the valiant Uttamaujā, and the son of Subhadrā (Abhimanyu), and the (five) sons of Draupadī all of whom are holders of great chariots.

[That warrior who could fight single-handed with ten thousand archers was known as '*mahārathī*', that is, 'holder of a great chariot'. A description has been given in the 8 chapters (164th to 171st) of the Udyoga-parva, stating which warrior in both the armies was a '*rathī*', or a '*mahārathī*', or an '*atirathī*'. There it is stated that Dhṛṣṭaketu was the son of Śiśupāla; similarly, Purujit Kuntibhoja are not the names of two persons. It is stated there that Purujit was the legitimate son of the king Kuntibhoja, to whom Kunti had been given in adoption; that, Kuntibhoja was his family-name; and that, he was the maternal uncle of Dharma, Bhīma, and Arjuna (Ma. Bhā. U. 171. 2). Yudhāmanyu and Uttamaujā were both from the Pāncāla country, and Cekitāna was a Yādava. Yudhāmanyu and Uttamaujā were the protectors of the wheels of Arjuna's chariot. Śaibya was the king of the Śibi country.]

(7) O best of the twice-born! I shall now mention to you the names of the most distinguished on our side,

भवान् भीष्मश्च कर्णश्च कृपश्च समितिंजयः ।
अश्वत्थामा विकर्णश्च सौमदत्तिस्तथैव च ॥ ८ ॥

अन्ये च बहवः शूरा मदर्थे त्यक्तजीविताः ।
नानाशस्त्रप्रहरणाः सर्वे युद्धविशारदाः ॥ ९ ॥

अपर्याप्तं तदस्माकं बलं भीष्माभिरक्षितम् ।
पर्याप्तं त्विदमेतेषां बलं भीमाभिरक्षितम् ॥ १० ॥

who are the leaders of my army, for your information; learn, who they are. (8) They are yourself and Bhīṣma, and Karṇa, and Kṛpa, the victorious in battle, Aśvatthāmā, and Vikarṇa (one of the hundred brothers of Duryodhana), as also the son of Somadatta (Bhūriśravā); (9) and there are besides several other valiant men, who are ready to to sacrifice their lives for me, and all of them can fight with various weapons, and are proficient in the art of war. (10) This our army, which is protected by Bhīṣma is *aparyāpta*,* (that is, unlimited or boundless), whereas that their army, protected by Bhīma, is *paryāpta*, (that is, *parimita*, or limited).

[There is a difference of opinion as to how the words '*paryāpta*' and '*aparyāpta*' are to be understood. '*paryāpta*' ordinarily means 'sufficient'. Therefore, some interpret this stanza as meaning, "the army of the Pāṇḍavas is sufficient, and our army is insufficient *(aparyāpta)*". But, this interpretation is not correct. In the foregoing chapters of the Udyogaparva, Duryodhana, while describing their army to Dhṛtarāṣṭra has given the names of the above-mentioned commanders of his army, and has said: "As my army is very large and well-trained, I am bound to win the war" (U. 54. 60–70); similarly, when Duryodhana again describes his army to Droṇācārya, further on in the Bhīṣmaparva, he has uttered the words of the above stanzas

* Dr. Annie Besant translates '*aparyāpta*' as 'insufficient' (See The *Bhagavadgītā* translated by Annie Besant and Bhagvandas. Theo. Pub. House, 1926 p. 5). But Telang translates it as 'unlimited' (See. S. B. E. Series Vol. VIII p. 38)—Trans.

of the Gītā (Bhīṣma. 51. 4–6); and as this description has been given in a joyful frame of mind, in order to encourage the whole army, the word '*aparyāpta*', cannot possibly be interpreted otherwise than as meaning 'unlimited', 'boundless', or 'innumerable'. The root meaning of the word '*paryāpta*' is 'that which is capable of being surrounded, (*āpa*=to occupy), on all sides (*pari*)'. But, when the word '*paryāpta*', is used after some word in the fourth (dative) case, as in 'for a particular purpose, *paryāpta*', or 'to some person (or thing), *paryāpta*', then the word '*paryāpta*', means 'that which is sufficient for, or capable of performing that particular purpose'; and if there is no word before the word '*paryāpta*', it, by itself, means 'sufficient', 'limited', or 'countable'. For instance, take the words '*grāsūn ṭākaṇyā sārakheṁ*' (that which is capable of over-whelming) in the Marathi language, which are synonymous with the Sanskrit word '*paryāpta*'. When you say '*amakyālā grāsūn takaṇyā sārakheṁ*', (that which is capable of overwhelming some thing or some one), it means that it is 'sufficient for him or it', and remains over; but, if you simply say '*grāsūn ṭākaṇyā sārakheṁ*', it means that 'some one else can overwhelm it'. In the present stanza, as there is no word before the word '*paryāpta*', this latter meaning is the correct meaning; and the Brahmānandagirī commentary gives illustrations of the word being used in that sense in books other than the Bhārata. The explanation given by some, that Duryodhana, getting frightened, says that his army is '*aparyāpta*', that is, 'insufficient', is not correct; because, there is no description anywhere of Duryodhana having got frightened; on the other hand, it is stated that the Pāṇḍavas arranged their army in the military array known as Vajravyūha, because the army of Duryodhana was large; and that, Yudhiṣṭhira was dejected at seeing the huge army of the Kauravas (Ma. Bhā. Bhīsma. 19. 5 and 21). The reason for saying that the Pāṇḍava army was 'protected by Bhīma', although Dhṛṣṭadyumna was the *generalissimo*, is that Bhīma had been posted in the front of of the Vajravyūha, in which the Pāṇḍavas had arranged their army on the first day of the war, for protecting it;

अयनेषु च सर्वेषु यथाभागमवस्थिताः ।
भीष्ममेवाभिरक्षन्तु भवन्तः सर्व एव हि ॥ ११ ॥
§§ तस्य संजनयन् हर्षं कुरुवृद्धः पितामहः ।
सिंहनादं विनद्योच्चैः शङ्खं दध्मौ प्रतापवान् ॥ १२ ॥

and because he was the only person whom Duryodhana could see in the forefront as the protector of the army. (Ma. Bhā. Bhīṣma. 19. 4–11, 33 and 34); and that is why these two armies have been respectively described as '*bhīmanetra*' (of which, Bhīma is the eye) and '*bhīṣmanetra*' (of which, Bhīṣma is the eye) in the chapters of the Mahābhārata prior to the Gītā (Ma. Bhā. Bhīṣma. 20. 1).]

(11) (And therefore) Do you all respectively stand in all the various '*ayanas*', (that is, 'openings in the army'), as you have been directed to do, and do you all protect Bhīṣma on all sides.

[Duryodhana has elsewhere (Ma. Bhā. Bhī. 15. 1–20 ; 99. 40, 41) given his reasons for directing that Bhīṣma, who was himself a powerful warrior, and who could not be defeated by anybody, should be protected on all sides, by saying that it was necessary for all to be careful, because Bhīṣma had resolved not to fight with Śikhaṇḍi, and was liable to be killed by him.
cf.

arakṣyamāṇaṁ hi vṛko hanyāt siṁhaṁ mahābalam ।
mā siṁhaṁ jaṁbukeneva ghātayethāḥ śikhaṇḍinā ॥

that is, "If the extremely powerful Lion is not protected, even a wolf will kill him; therefore, do not allow the Lion to be destroyed by a fox like Śikhaṇḍi". Bhīṣma was capable of dealing single-handed with any person whosoever except Śikhaṇḍi; and, he did not look for help from anybody else.]

(12) (At this moment), The oldest of the Kauravas, the (powerful) grand-sire (the *generalissmo* Bhīṣma) roared aloud like a lion in order to engladden him (Duryodhana), and blew his conch (as a sign of readiness for battle).

ततः शङ्खाश्च भेर्यश्च पणवानकगोमुखाः ।
सहसैवाभ्यहन्यन्त स शब्दस्तुमुलोऽभवत् ॥ १३ ॥

ततः श्वेतैर्हयैर्युक्ते महति स्यन्दने स्थितौ ।
माधवः पाण्डवश्चैव दिव्यौ शङ्खौ प्रदध्मतुः ॥ १४ ॥

पाञ्चजन्यं हृषीकेशो देवदत्तं धनंजयः ।
पौण्ड्रं दध्मौ महाशङ्खं भीमकर्मा वृकोदरः ॥ १५ ॥

अनन्तविजयं राजा कुन्तीपुत्रो युधिष्ठिरः ।
नकुलः सहदेवश्च सुघोषमणिपुष्पकौ ॥ १६ ॥

काश्यश्च परमेष्वासः शिखण्डी च महारथः ।
धृष्टद्युम्नो विराटश्च सात्यकिश्चापराजितः ॥ १७ ॥

द्रुपदो द्रौपदेयाश्च सर्वशः पृथिवीपते ।
सौभद्रश्च महाबाहुः शङ्खान् दध्मुः पृथक् पृथक् ॥ १८ ॥

(13) Thereupon, conches, kettle-drums, tabors, drums, cowhorns, these (martial musical instruments) suddenly blared forth; and that sound was tumultuous, (that is to say, saturating all the four sides). (14) Thereupon, Mādhava (Śrī Kṛṣṇa), and the son of Pāṇḍu (Arjuna), who were seated in a large chariot, to which pure white horses were yoked, also blew their divine conches (in order to say by way of reply that their side was also ready). (15) Hṛṣīkeśa, (that is, Śrī Kṛṣṇa), (blew) the (conch called) Pāñcajanya; Arjuna (blew) the Devadatta; Vṛkodara, the doer of terrible deeds (that is, Bhīmasena) blew the mighty conch named Pauṇḍra; (16) king Yudhiṣṭhira, the son of Kunti, blew the Anantavijaya; and Nakula and Sahadeva blew the Sughoṣa and the Maṇipuṣpaka. (17) Similarly, Kāśirāja, holder of an excellent bow, Śikhaṇḍi, the mighty car-warrior, and Dhṛṣṭadyumna, Virāṭa, and Sātyaki, the unconquered, (18) Drupada, and the (five) sons of Draupadī, and the mighty-armed Saubhadra (Abhimanyu), all these, O King (Dhṛtarāṣṭra) ! blew severally their respective conches on all sides.

स घोषो धार्तराष्ट्राणां हृदयानि व्यदारयत् ।
नभश्च पृथिवीं चैव तुमुलो व्यनुनादयन् ॥ १९ ॥

§§ अथ व्यवस्थितान् दृष्ट्वा धार्तराष्ट्रान् कपिध्वजः ।
प्रवृत्ते शस्त्रसंपाते धनुरुद्यम्य पाण्डवः ॥ २० ॥

हृषीकेशं तदा वाक्यमिदमाह महीपते ।

अर्जुन उवाच ।

सेनयोरुभयोर्मध्ये रथं स्थापय मेऽच्युत ॥ २१ ॥

यावदेतान्निरीक्षेऽहं योद्धुकामानवस्थितान् ।
कैर्मया सह योद्धव्यमस्मिन् रणसमुद्यमे ॥ २२ ॥

योत्स्यमानानवेक्षेऽहं य एतेऽत्र समागताः ।
धार्तराष्ट्रस्य दुर्बुद्धेर्युद्धे प्रियचिकीर्षवः ॥ २३ ॥

संजय उवाच ।

एवमुक्तो हृषीकेशो गुडाकेशेन भारत ।
सेनयोरुभयोर्मध्ये स्थापयित्वा रथोत्तमम् ॥ २४ ॥

(19) That tumultuous din, which shook the earth and the firmament, rent the hearts of Kauravas.

(20) Then, seeing that the Kauravas were properly arrayed, and when the attack by weapons was about to start, the Pāṇḍava, on whose standard is depicted Māruti, (that is to say, Arjuna), took up his bow, and spoke thus, (21) O king Dhṛtarāṣṭra, to Śrī Kṛṣṇa,—Arjuna said :—(Please) station my chariot between the two armies, (22) so that I will, in the meantime, observe these people who stand here desirous to engage in battle; and I shall also see those persons with whom I have to fight in this war, and (23) gaze on those fighters who have collected here with the intention of helping the cause of the evil-minded Duryodhana. Sañjaya said :—(24) O Dhṛtarāṣṭra! when Guḍākeśa, (that is, the conqueror of idleness, namely, Arjuna), had spoken thus to Him, Hṛṣīkeśa, (that is, the Conqueror of the organs, namely, Śrī Kṛṣṇa), drove and

placed the splendid chariot (of Arjuna) between the two armies; and—

[The meanings given by me above to the two words '*hṛṣīkeśa*' and '*guḍākeśa*' are consistent with the interpretations of the commentators. In the Nārada-Pañcarātra, the etymology of 'Hṛṣīkeśa' has been given as: '*hṛṣīka*' means 'the organs', and their '*īśa*', that is, 'the Lord', is the '*hṛṣīkeśa*'. (Nā. Pañca. 5. 8. 17). And it is stated in Kshirasvami's commentary on the *Amarakośa* that the word '*hṛṣīka*', that is, 'the organs', is derived from the root '*hṛṣ*'—'to give pleasure'; and that the organs are called '*hṛṣīka*', because they give pleasure to the human being. Nevertheless, there is a doubt whether the meanings of the words '*hṛṣīkeśa*' and '*guḍākeśa*' given above are correct; because, the word '*hṛṣīka*' as meaning 'the organs', and the word '*guḍākā*', as meaning 'idleness' or 'sleep' are not in common use; and the words '*hṛṣīkeśa*' and '*guḍākeśa*' can be etymologically derived in another way. Instead of breaking up the word '*hṛṣīkeśa*' into '*hṛṣīka*' + '*īśa*', and the word '*guḍākeśa*' into '*guḍākā*' + '*īśa*', they can respectively be broken up as, *hṛṣī* + *keśa*, and, *guḍā* + *keśa*; and then '*hṛṣīkeśa*' will mean "one whose hair (*keśa*) are standing up 'as a result of joy' (*hṛṣī*)", and are flowing, that is to say, Śrī Kṛṣṇa; and '*guḍākeśa*' will mean "one whose hair (*keśa*) are *guḍā* or *gūḍha*, that is, closely growing or matted", that is to say, Arjuna. Nilakaṇṭha, who has written a commentary on the Bhārata, has suggested this alternative meaning of the word '*guḍākeśa*' in his commentary on Gītā 10. 20; and having regard to the name Romaharṣaṇa, of the father of Sūta, this second interpretation of the word '*hṛṣīkeśa*' can also not be said to be improbable. Nay, in the Nārāyaṇopākhyāna in the Śāntiparva of the Mahābhārata, in giving the etymological meanings of the principal names of Viṣṇu, '*hṛṣī*' has been interpreted as meaning 'joy-giving' and '*keśa*' has been interpreted as meaning 'rays'; and the word '*hṛṣīkeśa*' has been interpreted as meaning "One who fills the world with joy by means of the rays of His incarnations, the Sun and the Moon"; and

भीष्मद्रोणप्रमुखतः सर्वेषां च महीक्षिताम् ।
उवाच पार्थ पश्यैतान् समवेतान्कुरूनिति ॥ २५ ॥
तत्रापश्यत् स्थितान् पार्थः पितॄनथ पितामहान् ।
आचार्यान्मातुलान्भ्रातॄन् पुत्रान्पौत्रान्सखींस्तथा ॥ २६ ॥
श्वशुरान् सुहृदश्चैव सेनयोरुभयोरपि ।
तान्समीक्ष्य स कौन्तेयः सर्वान्बन्धूनवस्थितान् ॥ २७ ॥
कृपया परयाविष्टो विषीदन्निदमब्रवीत् ।

अर्जुन उवाच ।

§§ दृष्ट्वेमं स्वजनं कृष्ण युयुत्सुं समुपस्थितम् ॥ २८ ॥
सीदन्ति मम गात्राणि मुखं च परिशुष्यति ।
वेपथुश्च शरीरे मे रोमहर्षश्च जायते ॥ २९ ॥

it is stated that He is on that account called '*hṛṣīkeśa*' (Śān. 345. 47 and 342. 64, 65; Udyo. 69. 9). And it is similarly stated in the previous stanzas that the word '*keśava*' is derived from '*keśa*', i. e., 'rays' (Śān. 341. 47). Whichever of these meanings is taken, it is impossible to give a fully satisfactory reason as to why Śrī Kṛṣṇa and Arjuna got these names. But this is not the fault of the etymologists. When it comes to defining proper names which have become very common, these kinds of difficulties or differences of opinion are quite likely to arise.]

(25) HE said, in the presence of Bhīṣma and Droṇa, and all other kings: "O Arjuna! look at these Kauravas assembled (here)". (26) Then Arjuna noticed that all who were assembled there, were (his own) elders, ancestors, preceptors, maternal-uncles, brothers, sons, grand-sons, and friends, (27) and fathers-in-law, and dear ones in both the armies; (and, in this way) when he had seen that all who had assembled there were his kinsmem, Arjuna, the son of Kunti, (28) being filled with intense pity and despair, began to say as follows:

Arjuna said: "O Kṛṣṇa! seeing these my kinsmen, assembled (here) desirous of engaging in battle, (29) my limbs droop down, my mouth is parched up, my body

गाण्डीवं स्रंसते हस्तात् त्वक्चैव परिदह्यते ।
न च शक्नोम्यवस्थातुं भ्रमतीव च मे मनः ॥ ३० ॥

निमित्तानि च पश्यामि विपरीतानि केशव ।
न च श्रेयोऽनुपश्यामि हत्वा स्वजनमाहवे ॥ ३१ ॥

न काङ्क्षे विजयं कृष्ण न च राज्यं सुखानि च ।
किं नो राज्येन गोविंद किं भोगैर्जीवितेन वा ॥ ३२ ॥

येषामर्थे काङ्क्षितं नो राज्यं भोगाः सुखानि च ।
त इमेऽवस्थिता युद्धे प्राणांस्त्यक्त्वा धनानि च ॥ ३३ ॥

आचार्याः पितरः पुत्रास्तथैव च पितामहाः ।
मातुलाः श्वशुराः पौत्राः श्यालाः संबन्धिनस्तथा ॥ ३४ ॥

एतान्न हन्तुमिच्छामि घ्नतोऽपि मधुसूदन ।
अपि त्रैलोक्यराज्यस्य हेतोः किं नु महीकृते ॥ ३५ ॥

निहत्य धार्तराष्ट्रान्नः का प्रीतिः स्याज्जनार्दन ।
पापमेवाश्रयेदस्मान् हत्वैतानाततायिनः ॥ ३६ ॥

shivers, and my hairs stand on end, (30) the Gāṇḍiva (bow) slips from my hand, and the whole of my body is hot; I cannot also stand, and my mind is awhirl; (31) similarly, O Keśava! all omens appear adverse (to me), and I do not perceive (that) any good will come from killing my own kinsmen in war. (32) O Kṛṣṇa! I have no desire for victory, nor for sovereignty, nor for pleasures. O Govinda! of what use is having sovereignty or enjoyment or life itself to us? (33) (Even) those for whose sake we desire kingdom, or enjoyments and pleasures, are standing here for battle, having given up (the hope of) life or wealth; (34) though preceptors, fathers, sons, as well as grand-fathers, maternal-uncles, fathers-in-law, grand-sons, brothers-in-law, as also relatives (35) have all uprisen to kill (us), yet, I do not wish to kill (them), O Madhusūdana, even for obtaining the kingdom of the three worlds; then, why (talk) of the earth? (36) O Janārdana! what pleasure may be ours by killing these Kauravas? Although they are felons, yet, by killing them, sin will but attach (itself) to us.

तस्मान्नार्हा वयं हन्तुं धार्तराष्ट्रान् स्वबान्धवान् ।
स्वजनं हि कथं हत्वा सुखिन : स्याम माधव ॥ ३७ ॥
§§ यद्यप्येते न पश्यन्ति लोभोपहतचेतस : ।
कुलक्षयकृतं दोषं मित्रद्रोहे च पातकम् ॥ ३८ ॥
कथं न ज्ञेयमस्माभि : पापादस्मान्निवर्तितुम् ।
कुलक्षयकृतं दोषं प्रपश्यद्भिर्जनार्दन ॥ ३९ ॥

[*agnido garadaś caiva śastrapāṇir dhanāpahaḥ* ।
kṣetradārāharaś caiva ṣad ete ātatāyinaḥ ॥
(Vasiṣṭha-Smṛ. 3. 16),

that is, "he who has come to burn one's house, he who administers poison, he who comes to kill with a weapon in his hand, he who robs one of one's money, or of one's wife, or of one's field, these six are 'felons' *(ātatāyinaḥ)*". Even Manu has said that such felons should be killed without any qualm of conscience, and that there is no sin in doing so (Manu. 8. 350, 351).]

(37) Therefore, it is not proper that we ourselves should kill the Kauravas, who are our kinsmen; for how, O Mādhava! can we become happy by killing our own kinsmen?

(38) Although these, whose minds have been overpowered by greed, do not see the guilt resulting from the extinction of a family, and the sin of treachery towards a friend, (39) yet, O Janārdana! when we clearly see the guilt of the extinction of a family, how can it not enter our minds to turn away from this sin?

[See my disquisition in the first, and again in the fourteenth chapters of the Gītā-Rahasya, on the questions: (i) what is the import of the fact that Arjuna became doubtful regarding his own duty to fight, when he saw in advance with his own eyes that the war would entail the killing of elders, the death of relatives, and the extinction of families; (ii) what is the relation between that fact and the subsequent argument in the Gītā, and (iii) what is the importance of the first chapter of the Gītā from this point of view, etc. To what extent the argument that, those who are wise should follow the doctrine "*na pāpe pratipāpaḥ syāt*" (i. e., 'Do not commit a sin in retaliation of

कुलक्षये प्रणश्यन्ति कुलधर्माः सनातनाः
धर्मे नष्टे कुलं कृत्स्नमधर्मोऽभिभवत्युत ॥ ४० ॥

अधर्माभिभवात् कृष्ण प्रदुष्यन्ति कुलस्त्रियः ।
स्त्रीषु दुष्टासु वार्ष्णेय जायते वर्णसंकरः ॥ ४१ ॥

संकरो नरकायैव कुलघ्नानां कुलस्य च ।
पतन्ति पितरो ह्येषां लुप्तपिण्डोदकक्रियाः ॥ ४२ ॥

another's sin'—Trans.), and should remain inactive, but should not become wicked for punishing the evil-minded, though the latter might not realise their own wickedness as a result of their minds having been over-powered by avarice, and the other common arguments mentioned in this place, are applicable or should be made applicable to the present circumstances, is a question as important as the ones mentioned above; and I have explained in the Chapter XII of the Gītā-Rahasya at pages 544 to 554 what, in my opinion, is the answer of the Gītā to these questions. If one bears in mind the fact that the exposition to be found in the subsequent chapters of the Gītā has been made in order to solve the doubt which had arisen in the mind of Arjuna as shown in the first chapter, one can no more have any doubt about the import of the Gītā. These doubts arose in the mind of Arjuna, because the Bhāratī war was a civil war, due to a split between persons belonging to the same kingdom and the same religion, who had come forward to kill each other. Whenever similar circumstances have arisen in modern history, similar doubts have also arisen. Arjuna now clearly specifies the evils which flow from the extinction of a family.]

(40) On the extinction of a family, the eternal rites of families are destroyed; and when these rites (of the family) have perished, lawlessness predominates over the whole family. (41) When lawlessness prevails, O Kṛṣṇa, the women of the family become corrupt; and when they have become corrupt, then, O Vārṣṇeya! ('descendant of Vṛṣṇi'—Trans.), there follows caste-confusion. (42) And when there is caste-confusion,

दोषैरेतै : कुलघ्नानां वर्णसंकरकारकै : ।
उत्साद्यन्ते जातिधर्मा : कुलधर्माश्च शाश्वता : ॥ ४३ ॥
उत्सन्नकुलधर्माणां मनुष्याणां जनार्दन ।
नरके नियतं वासो भवतीत्यनुशुश्रुम ॥ ४४ ॥
§§ अहो बत महत्पापं कर्तुं व्यवसिता वयम् ।
यद्राज्यसुखलोभेन हन्तुं स्वजनमुद्यताः ॥ ४५ ॥
यदि मामप्रतीकारमशस्त्रं शस्त्रपाणयः ।
धार्तराष्ट्रा रणे हन्युस्तन्मे क्षेमतरं भवेत् ॥ ४६ ॥

संजय उवाच ।

एवमुक्त्वार्जुनः संख्ये रथोपस्थ उपाविशत् ।
विसृज्य सशरं चापं शोकसंविग्नमानसः ॥ ४७ ॥

it (necessarily) leads the destroyer of the family and the (entire) family to hell ; and as a result of the cessation of the ritual of offering rice-balls and water, their ancestors also fall down (to hell—Trans.). (43) By these sins of the destroyers of families, which result in caste-confusion, the eternal caste-rites and family-rites are abolished ; (44) and O Janārdana ! we have heard that persons whose family rites are abolished, must necessarily undergo residence in hell.

(45) Alas ! we are engaged in committing a heinous sin in that we have uprisen to kill our own kinsmen out of greed of the pleasures of sovereignty. (46) If, rather than this, (these) Kauravas, bearing arms slay me in the battle, I having become unarmed and having given up retaliation in return, that would be happier for me. Sañjaya said : (47) Having spoken thus on the battle-field, Arjuna, whose mind was agitated by grief, casting aside the bow and arrows (in his hands), sat down (quiet) on his seat in the chariot.

[As it was customary to fight standing in the chariot, the words "sat down on his seat in the chariot" more clearly bring out the idea that he had no desire to fight, as a result of his dejection. It would appear from the descriptions of

इति श्रीमद्भगवद्गीतासु उपनिषत्सु ब्रह्मविद्यायां योगशास्त्रे श्रीकृष्णार्जुनसंवादे अर्जुनविषादयोगो नाम प्रथमोऽध्यायः ॥ १ ॥

chariots given in some places in the Mahābhārata that in the times of the Mahābhārata these chariots were ordinarily two-wheeled, and that larger chariots were sometimes drawn by four horses, and that both the master of the chariot (the *rathī*) and the charioteer (*sārathī*) used to sit in the anterior part of the chariot, side by side. In order that it should be possible to find out whose the chariot was, they used to erect a particular ensign (*dhvaja*) on the chariot. It is a well-known tradition that Māruti himself used to sit on the ensign of Arjuna.]

Thus ends the first chapter entitled The DEJECTION OF ARJUNA in the dialogue between Śrī Kṛṣṇa and Arjuna on the Yoga included in the Science of the Brahman that is, on the Karma-Yoga, in the Upaniṣad sung, (that is, told) by the Blessed Lord.

[I have interpreted these concluding lines as showing that the Gītā does not deal only with the Science of the Brahman (*brahma-vidyā*), but contains an exposition of the Karma-Yoga consistently with the Science of the Brahman. See Chap. I (page 4), Chapt. III (page 82) and Chap. XI (page 489) of the Gītā-Rahasya. Although these concluding lines are not to be found in the Mahābhārata, yet, they must have come into existence before the date of the commentaries in support of Renunciation (*saṁnyāsa*); because, no scholar, who is a follower of the doctrine of Renunciation, will give the concluding lines as above. This clearly shows that the Gītā does not support the doctrine of Renunciation, but contains an exposition of Karma-Yoga, as a science, in the form of a conversation. I have shown the difference between the scientific method and the catechismal method in the beginning of Chap. XIV of the Gītā-Rahasya.]

द्वितीयोऽध्यायः

संजय उवाच ।

तं तथा कृपयाविष्टमश्रुपूर्णाकुलेक्षणम् ।
विषीदन्तमिदं वाक्यमुवाच मधुसूदनः ॥ १ ॥

श्रीभगवानुवाच ।

कुतस्त्वा कश्मलमिदं विषमे समुपस्थितम् ।
अनार्यजुष्टमस्वर्ग्यमकीर्तिकरमर्जुन ॥ २ ॥
क्लैब्यं मा स्म गमः पार्थ नैतत्त्वय्युपपद्यते ।
क्षुद्रं हृदयदौर्बल्यं त्यक्त्वोत्तिष्ठ परंतप ॥ ३ ॥

CHAPTER II.

Sañjaya said: (1) To him, (Arjuna, who was) thus filled with pity, and whose eyes were filled with tears and turbid, and who was dejected, Madhusūdana (Śrī Kṛṣṇa) spoke these words: The Blessed Lord said: (2) O Arjuna! how has this infamous conduct *(kaśmalaṁ)* not practised (at any time) by the Āryas, (that is, by good men), which leads to hell, and which brings one into disrepute, entered your mind, in this time of peril? (3) O Pārtha! be not effeminate (like this): this is not worthy of you. O, (thou) harasser of foes, casting off this base weakness of heart, stand up (to fight).

[It is true that I have in this place given the literal meaning of the word '*parantapa*' as 'harasser of foes'. But I do not consider logical, the theory of most of the commentators, that these oft-recurring adjectival epithets, or names of Kṛṣṇa and Arjuna, have been used in the Gītā in a hidden meaning, or with a particular intention. In my opinion, these names have been used as was convenient for prosody, and do not convey any intentional meaning; and, therefore, I have on many occasions not reproduced in the translation, the name used in the stanza, but have generally translated them as 'Arjuna' or 'Śrī Kṛṣṇa'.]

अर्जुन उवाच ।

§§ कथं भीष्ममहं संख्ये द्रोणं च मधुसूदन ।
इषुभिः प्रतियोत्स्यामि पूजार्हावरिसूदन ॥ ४ ॥
गुरूनहत्वा हि महानुभावान् श्रेयो भोक्तुं भैक्ष्यमपीह लोके ।
हत्वार्थकामांस्तु गुरूनिहैव भुञ्जीय भोगान् रुधिरप्रदिग्धान् ॥ ५ ॥
न चैतद्विद्मः कतरन्नो गरीयो यद्वा जयेम यदि वा नो जयेयुः ।
यानेव हत्वा न जिजीविषामस्तेऽवस्थिताः प्रमुखे धार्तराष्ट्राः ॥ ६ ॥

Arjuna said: (4) O Madhusūdana! how shall I counter-attack in battle with arrows, Bhīṣma and Droṇa, who, O Destroyer of enemies, are entitled to (high) reverence? (5) It is meritorious to live in this world even by begging, without killing one's reverend elders; for by killing such elders, (though they might be) abashed by monetary considerations* I shall have to enjoy in this world blood-tainted enjoyments.

[The plural word '*gurūn*' must be taken here as meaning 'elders' and not as 'preceptors'; for there was no preceptor in the army other than Droṇācārya, who taught the martial arts. When, before the commencement of the war, Yudhiṣṭhira took off his shield on the battle-field, and went in all humility to such 'elders', that is, to Bhīṣma, Droṇa, and Śalya in order to place his head on their feet, and to beseech their blessings, they gave due praise to him, who had followed the course of conduct laid down by propriety, and they all explained to him their reason for fighting on the side of Duryodhana as follows:—

arthasya puruṣo dāso dāsastv artho na kasyacit I
iti satyaṁ mahārāja baddho 'smy arthena kauravaiḥ II

that is, "Man is the slave of wealth, wealth is the slave of nobody; this being the true state of things, O Mahārāja Yudhiṣṭhira, the Kauravas have tied me by the bonds of wealth" (Ma. Bhā. Bhī. 43. 35, 50 and 76). The words 'abashed by monetary considerations' used above signify the meaning conveyed in this stanza.]

(6) Nor do we know which of the two is more meritorious

* Dr. Besant & Bhagvandas translate '*arthakāmān*' as 'well-wishers' (see footnote on p. 24, *The Bhagvadgītā*, 1926)—Trans.

कार्पण्यदोषोपहतस्वभावः पृच्छामि त्वां धर्मसंमूढचेताः ।
यच्छ्रेयः स्यान्निश्चितं ब्रूहि तन्मे शिष्यस्तेऽहं शाधि मां त्वां प्रपन्नम् ॥७॥

न हि प्रपश्यामि ममापनुद्याद्यच्छोकमुच्छोषणमिन्द्रियाणाम् ।
अवाप्य भूमावसपत्नमृद्धं राज्यं सुराणामपि चाधिपत्यं ॥ ८ ॥

संजय उवाच ।

एवमुक्त्वा हृषीकेशं गुडाकेशः परंतप ।
न योत्स्य इति गोविन्दमुक्त्वा तूष्णीं बभूव ह ॥ ९ ॥

तमुवाच हृषीकेशः प्रहसन्निव भारत ।
सेनयोरुभयोर्मध्ये विषीदन्तमिदं वचः ॥ १० ॥

for us, whether we should vanquish, or that we should be vanquished (by them). To live by killing whom, we have no desire, those very Kauravas are standing here in front (to fight).

[This stanza refers to a test of the respective merits of Action or Inaction, which is similar to the theory of 'the greatest good of the greatest number'; and its net import is that it is impossible to decide by that test whose victory is better (See Gītā-Rahasya, p. 115 and 116).

(7) As, on account of my natural temperament having been destroyed by adverse circumstances, my mind is in doubt as to (my) '*dharma*' (that is, my duty), I am asking You. Tell me that which is assuredly meritorious. I am your disciple, instruct me, who have surrendered myself to You. (8) For, though I might win a prosperous kingdom on the earth free from foes, or even the sovereignty of the gods (of heaven), yet, I do not see aught (any means) which will remove this my grief, which is drying up my organs. Sañjaya said: (9) After Guḍākeśa, the harasser of enemies, (that is, Arjuna), had spoken thus to Hṛṣīkeśa (Śrī Kṛṣṇa), he became quiet after saying to Govinda: "I shall not fight". (10) (Thereafter) O Bhārata (Dhṛtarāṣṭra)!, Śrī Kṛṣṇa, smiling as it were, spoke thus to Arjuna, who was sitting dejected between the two armies.

[The Blessed Lord is now going to give advice on the question of one's duty in this world, to Arjuna, who was pulled on one side by the inherent duty of the Kṣatriyas, and on the other side by the fear of the sin of killing one's elders, and causing the extinction of families; and who was engulfed in the doubt whether he should 'kill or be killed', and was prepared to give up the fight and live the life of a mendicant. Arjuna's objection was that his Ātman would not be benefited by a terrible act like war. Therefore, the advice in the Gītā starts by showing how those great men, who have attained the fullest bliss of their Ātmans by Realising the Parabrahman, live in this world. The Blessed Lord says that if one scrutinises the affairs of the world, one sees that from times immemorial there are two ways in which persons, who have acquired the Knowledge of the Brahman, have been leading their lives. (See Gītā, 3. 3; and Gītā-Rahasya, Chap. XI). After acquiring the Knowledge of the Self, men like Śuka, gave up worldly life and led the lives of mendicants, whereas, other men like Janaka, who had also acquired the Knowledge of the Self, spent their time in numerous worldly activities according to their own *dharma*, even after the Acquisition of Knowledge, for the universal good. The first mode of life is known as the 'Sāṁkhya', or the Sāṁkhya-niṣṭhā, and the other is known as 'Karma-Yoga' or 'Yoga' (*cf.* stanza 39). But the Gītā has laid down the doctrine that though both these modes of life were in vogue, the Karma-Yoga was the superior mode, as will be shown later on (Gī. 5. 2). Out of these two Niṣṭhās, the mind of Arjuna was inclined towards the Saṁnyāsa (Renunciation) -Niṣṭhā. Therefore, the Blessed Lord has first brought home to him his mistake, on the basis of the philosophy relating to that path of life; and then, from the 39th stanza onwards, He has started the exposition of Karma-Yoga. Though the followers of the Sāṁkhya path do not take part in Action after the Acquisition of Knowledge, yet, there is no difference between the Knowledge of the Brahman according to the Sāṁkhya path and according to Karma-Yoga. Therefore, the Blessed Lord has first explained to Arjuna in a

श्रीभगवानुवाच ।

§§ अशोच्यानन्वशोचस्त्वं प्रज्ञावादांश्च भाषसे ।
गतासूनगतासूंश्च नानुशोचन्ति पण्डिताः ॥ ११ ॥
न त्वेवाहं जातु नासं न त्वं नेमे जनाधिपाः ।
न चैव न भविष्यामः सर्वे वयमतः परम् ॥ १२ ॥

ridiculing way that if the Ātman is indestructible and permanent, even according to the Saṁkhya system, then his question, "How shall I kill so and so" was mere worthless talk.]

The Blessed Lord said :- (11) You are lamenting for those, for whom you should not lament, and yet talk about Knowledge ! Knowers do not lament (whether) the dead or the not-dead.

[In this stanza it is stated that one should not lament whether life continues or has become extinct. Out of these, lamenting over one who is dead, is only natural; and it is proper to give advice not to do so. But a doubt having arisen as to why and in what manner it is possible to lament the fact of some one not being dead, commentators have indulged in a considerable amount of discussion on this point; and many have said that it is a matter of lamentation that the lives of fools and ignorant people should be spared. But, instead of hair-splitting in this way, we should interpret the word 'lament' in a broad way, as meaning 'to feel happy or unhappy', or 'to mind'. All that is intended here is, that the Jñānin looks upon both these matters as one and the same.]

(12) Just realise that not only is it not that I was not (in the past), but it is not that you and these kings were not (in the past); nor is it that all of us will not be again in the future.

[In commenting on this stanza, it is stated in the Ramānujabhāṣya that, if both 'I', that is, the Supreme Being, and 'you and these kings', that is, the other Ātmans, existed in the past and will be born again in the future, then, according to this stanza, the Supreme Being, and the

देहिनोऽस्मिन् यथा देहे कौमारं यौवनं जरा ।
तथा देहान्तरप्राप्तिर्धीरस्तत्र न मुह्यति ॥ १३ ॥

Ātman both become separate, independent, and permanent entities. But, this argument is not correct. It is a partisan argument in support of a particular doctrine; because, this stanza is intended to explain only that both are permanent; and their mutual inter-relation is not stated here, nor was there any occasion for doing so. When that occasion arose later on, we find stated in clear terms in the Gītā itself, the Non-Dualistic (*advaita*) doctrine that the Parameśvara, that is, the Blessed Lord, is the embodied Ātman in the bodies of all created beings (Gī. 8. 4; 13. 31).]

(13) Just as, for the One Which assumes a corporeal form, there is (acquired) infancy, youth, and old age, in this Body, so also, is another Body (later on) acquired; (therefore) those who have acquired Knowledge, do not suffer from any ignorance in this matter.

[The great ignorance or fear in the mind of Arjuna was "How shall I kill a particular person?" Therefore, in order to dispel that ignorance, the Blessed Lord first philosophically examines the questions 'what is death', and 'what is killing' (Stanzas 11 to 30). Man is not merely something encased in a body, but an aggregate of the Body and the Ātman. Out of these, the Ātman, which becomes perceptible as 'I', as a result of Individuation (*ahaṁkāra*), is permanent and immortal. It is to-day, it was yesterday, and it will also be to-morrow. Therefore, the words 'to kill' or 'to die' cannot be properly applied to the Ātman, and there is no room for lamentation in that matter. Then remains the Body. That, of course, is admittedly non-permanent and destructible, and will come to an end, if not to-day or to-morrow, at least after a 100 years. *Cf.* "*adya vā 'bdaśatānte vā mṛtrur vai prāṇināṁ dhruvaḥ* (that is, "Death is certain for living beings, whether to day, or after a hundred years"— Trans.), (Bhāg. 10. 1. 38); and as the Ātman definitely acquires later on another body in accordance with the previous Action (*karma*), though it gets out of one body, it is also not proper to lament over the loss of that body. In short,

§§ मात्रास्पर्शास्तु कौन्तेय शीतोष्णसुखदुःखदाः ।
आगमापायिनोऽनित्यास्तांस्तितिक्षस्व भारत ॥ १४ ॥
यं हि न व्यथयन्त्येते पुरुषं पुरुषर्षभ ।
समदुःखसुखं धीरं सोऽमृतत्वाय कल्पते ॥ १५ ॥

it is definitely proved, that whether one looks at the matter from the point of view of the Body or of the Ātman, lamentation on account of death is foolish. But, though this fact is thus proved, yet, it is necessary to explain why one should not lament, on account of the suffering which one goes through while the existing life is being destroyed. Therefore, the Blessed Lord now deals with the form of this bodily happiness and unhappiness, and shows that it is not proper to lament on account of that suffering.]

(14) O Son of Kunti ! these contacts (with bodily organs) of *'mātrā'*, (that is, of things in the external world), which produce cold and heat, or happiness and unhappiness, come into existence and die out ; (therefore) they are non-permanent (that is, destructible). O Bhārata ! do you bear these (without lamentation) ; (15) because, O, pre-eminent among men ! it is the Jñānin alone, (who is) equal towards happiness and unhappiness, who (on that account) is not affected by them, that becomes capable of attaining immortality, (that is to say, the state of the Immortal Brahman).

[The man who has not Realised that the Name-d and Form-ed Cosmos is illusory, by Realising the identity of the Brahman and the Ātman, looks upon as real, the happiness and unhappiness or the cold and heat arising from the contact of the physical organs with the external world, and wrongly attributes those properties to the Ātman; and, on that account, suffers grief. But the man who has realised that all the emotions are of the Prakṛti, and that the Ātman (Self) is a Non-doer and Unattached, looks upon happinesss and unhappiness as alike; and the Blessed Lord is now telling Arjuna, that he (Arjuna) should bear unhappiness and happiness with such an equable frame of Mind; and the same import has been explained in a more

§§ नासतो विद्यते भावो नाभावो विद्यते सतः ।
उभयोरपि दृष्टोऽन्तस्त्वनयोस्तत्त्वदर्शिभिः ॥ १६ ॥

exhaustive manner in the subsequent chapters. The word '*mātrā*' has been interpreted in the Śāṁkarabhāṣya as meaning 'the organs, by which external things can be measured or known', *Cf.*, '*mīyate ebhiriti mātrā*'. But, some commentators interpret '*mātrā*' as meaning 'the external objects, such as, sound, touch, etc., which can be measured by means of the physical organs'; and they interpret '*mātrāsparśa*' as meaning 'the contact of those external objects with the physical organs'; and that is the interpretation which has been accepted by me; because, where the ideas appearing in this stanza, appear again later on in the Gītā (Gī. 5. 21, 23), the word '*bāhya-sparśa*' has been used; and if the word '*mātrā-sparśa*' is interpreted in the way in which I have interpreted it, both these words become consistent with each other. But, though these two words can be made consistent with each other in this way, the word '*mātrā-sparśa*' seems to be the more ancient of the two; because, the word '*mātrā-saṅga*' has been used in the Manu-smṛti in the same sense (6. 57); and it is stated in the Bṛhadāraṇyakopaniṣad, that the Ātman of a Jñānin becomes '*asaṁsarga*' (*Cf. mātrā 'saṁsargaḥ*), that is, detached from the Mātrās, that is to say, that he becomes free; and there is no connotation (*saṁjñā*) for him after his death (Bṛ. Mādhyan. 4. 5. 14; Ve. Sū. Śāṁ. Bhā. 1. 4. 22). The words 'heat and cold', or, 'happiness and unhappiness' are synecdochial, and include the opposite couples (*dvaṁdva*) of 'love and hostility', 'real and unreal', 'death and immortality' etc. As these opposite couples belong to the Māyā-world and the true Parabrahman is, as described in the Nāsadīya-Sūkta, beyond this duality, one cannot attain the Brahman, otherwise than by peacefully bearing these opposite couples and releasing the Reason from the grip of these couples (Gī. 2. 45; 7. 28 and Gī. Ra. Ch. IX p. 314 and 351). The same meaning is now made clear from the point of view of the Philosophy of the Absolute Self—].

(16) That which is not (*asat*), cannot be as if it is; and

that which is (*sat*), cannot be as if it is not; in this way, the see-ers of the Essence of things have perceived the truth about 'is' and 'is not' (*sat* and *asat*), (that is to say, they have defined their connotation, after having perceived the truth).

[The word '*anta*' in this stanza has the same meaning as in the compounds '*rāddhānta*', '*siddhānta*', or '*kṛtānta*', (Gī. 18, 13); and the Śāsvatakośa defines the various meanings of the word '*anta*' as "*svarūpaprāntayor antam antike 'pi prayujyate*" (Śā. 381) (that is, "the border of a form (body), or of a region, as also Death—Trans.).According to this stanza '*sat*' means the 'Brahman', and, '*asat*' means the Name-d and Form-ed visible world (See Gī. Ra. Ch. IX, p. 307 and pp. 335 to 339). Although the doctrine "that which is, cannot cease to be", looks like the Satkāryavāda theory, (See Gītā-Rahasya Ch. VII, p. 210 and Ch. IX. pp. 325 and 335—Trans.), one must bear in mind that its meaning is slightly different. Where one thing is produced out of another thing, e. g., the tree from the seed, the only principle which can be applied is that of the Satkāryavāda. That is not the idea to be conveyed in the present stanza; and, all that is being said is that, the existence (*astitva* or *bhāva*) of '*sat*', that is, of 'that which exists', and the 'non-existence' (*abhāva*) of '*asat*', that is, of 'that which does not exist', are both permanent, that is, ever-lasting. When we thus look upon the respective existence and non-existence of these two as permanent, it follows as a matter of course that '*asat*' is not the result of the destruction of that which was '*sat*'. But this doctrine is not the same as the Satkāryavāda doctrine, which initially takes for granted the coming into existence of one thing from another thing, as an effect from a cause (Gī. Ra. Ch. VII, p. 211). The Mādhva-bhāṣya reads the words "*vidyate bhāvaḥ*" out of "*nāsato vidyate bhāvaḥ*", which is the first quarter of this stanza, as '*vidyate+abhāvaḥ*'; and it has interpreted these words as meaning that "there is no '*abhāva*' that is, 'destruction' of the '*asat*' (unreal), that is, '*avyakta*' (imperceptible) Prakṛti;

and, as it has been stated in the second quarter of the stanza that the '*sat*' too is not destroyed, Madhvācārya has, according to his Dualistic doctrine, interpreted the entire stanza as meaning that both the '*asat*' and the '*sat*' are permanent. But, this meaning is not the straight-forward meaning of the stanza. It is a stretched meaning; for, it can be seen that the two mutually opposite words '*abhāva*' and '*bhāva*' have been used in this place in the same way as the mutually opposite words, '*asat*' and '*sat*'; and if the word '*abhāva*' has beed used in the second line of the stanza, namely, in the phrase, "*nābhāvo vidyate sataḥ*", it is quite clear that the word intended to be used in the first line of the stanza must have been '*bhāva*' and not '*abhāva*'; besides, it was not necessary at all to use the words '*abhāva*' and '*vidyate*' twice, in order to say that both '*asat*' and '*sat*' are permanent. But, even if this repetition is looked upon as a respectful repetition, as suggested by Madhvācārya, it has been clearly stated later on in the 18th stanza, that the human body to be seen in the perceptible or visible world is destructible, that is to say, non-permanent. It, therefore, clearly follows that according to the Bhagavadgītā, the Body cannot be looked upon as permanent, in the same way as the Ātman. Whereas the latter is permanent, the former is non-permanent. Nevertheless, I have given here the meaning of this stanza according to Madhvācārya, by way of example, in order to show my readers how the meanings of words are stretched by doctrine-supporting commentators with the intention of supporting their own doctrine. However, as that which is '*sat*' can never cease to exist, it is no use lamenting over the *sat*-formed (*satsvarūpa*) Ātman; and as the Name-d and Form-ed Body etc., as also the emotions of pleasure or displeasure, are essentially destructible from the philosophical point of view, it is also not proper to lament their loss. This justifies the words "you are lamenting that over which you should not lament" used in speaking to Arjuna. The Blessed Lord now further explains the meanings of the words '*sat*' and '*asat*', in the next two stanzas—]

अविनाशि तु तद्विद्धि येन सर्वमिदं ततम् ।
विनाशमव्ययस्यास्य न कश्चित् कर्तुमर्हति ॥ १७ ॥
अन्तवन्त इमे देहा नित्यस्योक्ताः शरीरिणः ।
अनाशिनोऽप्रमेयस्य तस्माद्युध्यस्व भारत ॥ १८ ॥
य एनं वेत्ति हन्तारं यश्चैनं मन्यते हतम् ।
उभौ तौ न विजानीतो नायं हन्ति न हन्यते ॥ १९ ॥

(17) Know that That (fundamental Ātman-formed Brahman) Which has pervaded or occupied this whole (world) is indestructible. The destruction of this Inexhaustible (Principle), none can bring about.

[This is the description of what has been referred to as '*sat*' in the last stanza. Now, the Blessed Lord says, that the Ātman, which is the Owner of the Body, falls into this category of the Permanent, and He goes on to explain what is to be called 'Non-permanent' or '*asat*'—]

(18) These bodies acquired by the eternal, indestructible, and unimaginable Owner of the Body (Ātman) are said to be perishable, (that is non-eternal). Therefore, fight! O Bhārata!

[In short, if one thus discriminates between what is eternal and what non-eternal, the idea that 'I am killing a particular person' is proved to be false; and the reason given by Arjuna for not fighting falls to the ground. This conclusion is now made more clear—]

(19) He who thinks that It (the Owner of the Body or the Ātman) is the killer, or, who thinks that It is slain, both these do not possess true Knowledge; (because) this (Ātman) does not kill, and is not killed.

[Because, the Ātman is permanent and itself a Non-Doer, and the whole activity is of Prakṛti. This and the next stanza appear in the Kaṭhopaniṣad (Kaṭha. 2. 18, 19). It is also stated in several places in the Mahābhārata that everything is swallowed up by '*kāla*' (Time, or Death); and that 'kills' or 'is killed' are worldly names for this pastime of Death (Śān. 25. 15). The Blessed Lord has again explained to Arjuna later on (11. 33) this very

न जायते म्रियते वा कदाचिन्नायं भूत्वा भविता वा न भूयः।
अजो नित्यः शाश्वतोऽयं पुराणो न हन्यते हन्यमाने शरीरे ॥ २० ॥

वेदाविनाशिनं नित्यं य एनमजमव्ययम्।
कथं स पुरुषः पार्थ कं घातयति हन्ति कम् ॥ २१ ॥

वासांसि जीर्णानि यथा विहाय नवानि गृह्णाति नरोऽपराणि।
तथा शरीराणि विहाय जीर्णान्यन्यानि संयाति नवानि देही ॥ २२ ॥

नैनं छिन्दन्ति शस्त्राणि नैनं दहति पावकः।
न चैनं क्लेदयन्त्यापो न शोषयति मारुतः ॥ २३ ॥

principle in terms of the Philosophy of Devotion when He says that He himself has already killed Bhīṣma, Droṇa, and the others in His form of Death, and that Arjuna should now become only the nominal implement (*nimitta*).]

(20) This (Ātman) is never born nor does It ever die; nor is it that It, having (once) existed, will not be again; It is unborn, ever-lasting, immutable, and primeval; and it is not killed, though the Body is killed. (21) O Pārtha! that man who has Realised that It is indestructible, ever-lasting, unborn, and inexhaustible, how and whom can he cause to be killed, and how and whom can he kill? (22) Just as a man, casting off old clothes puts on others and new ones, so the *dehi*, (that is to say, the Ātman, which owns the Body), casting off old bodies, becomes united with others and new bodies.

[This simile of clothes is in ordinary use. In another place in the Mahābhārata, the illustration has been given of leaving one house (*śālā*), and going to another house (Śān. 15. 56); and one American writer has expressed the same idea by giving the illustration of putting on a new cover on a book. The same argument is here applied to the Body, which was applied above in the 13th stanza to the states of infancy, youth, and old age.]

(23) Weapons do not cut It (that is, the Ātman); fire does not burn It; so also does water not moisten It; the wind

अच्छेद्योऽयमदाह्योऽयमक्लेद्योऽशोष्य एव च ।
नित्यः सर्वगतः स्थाणुरचलोऽयं सनातनः ॥ २४ ॥

अव्यक्तोऽयमचिन्त्योऽयमविकार्योऽयमुच्यते ।
तस्मादेवं विदित्वैनं नानुशोचितुमर्हसि ॥ २५ ॥

§§ अथ चैनं नित्यजातं नित्यं वा मन्यसे मृतम् ।
तथापि त्वं महाबाहो नैनं शोचितुमर्हसि ॥ २६ ॥

जातस्य हि ध्रुवो मृत्युर्ध्रुवं जन्म मृतस्य च ।
तस्मादपरिहार्येऽर्थे न त्वं शोचितुमर्हसि ॥ २७ ॥

does not dry It up. (24) This (Ātman), which is uncleaveable, uncombustible, not-to-be-moistened, and not-to-be-dried up, is permanent, all-pervading, stable, immoveable, and, eternal (that is, everlasting). (25) This (Ātman) is said to be imperceptible (that is, not perceptible by the organs), unthinkable (that is, impossible of being understood even by the Mind), and immutable (that is, such as is not subject to the attribute of any modification). Therefore, knowing this (Ātman) to be such, it is not proper that you should grieve over It.

[This description has been taken from the Upaniṣads, and is of the qualityless Ātman, and not of a qualityful Ātman; because, the adjectives '*avikārya*' (immutable), or '*acintya*' (unthinkable) cannot be applied to the Qualityful. This reason for not grieving has been given on the authority of that description. Now, some one may advance the argument that, as he does not accept the Ātman as eternal, this argument is not acceptable to him. Therefore, the Blessed Lord first mentions this assumptive proposition (*pūrva-pakṣa*) and replies to it as follows—]

(26) Or, even if you believe that this Ātman, (is not permanent, but with the Body) is constantly born, and constantly dies, even then, O Mahābāho! (mighty-armed—Trans.), it is not proper that you should grieve over It; (27) because, to one that is born, death is certain, and to one that dies, birth is certain; therefore, about an (this)

§§ अव्यक्तादीनि भूतानि व्यक्तमध्यानि भारत ।
अव्यक्तनिधनान्येव तत्र का परिदेवना ॥ २८ ॥

unavoidable (according to your abovementioned opinion) matter, you ought not to grieve.

[The argument, mentioned in the two above stanzas 26 and 27, is not for supporting the doctrine of the Gītā. It must be remembered that this is a reply to the assumptive proposition, raised by the words '*atha ca*' = 'or'. The only thing to be shown is: whether one looks upon the Ātman as permanent, or as non-permanent, there is no room for lamentation in either case. I have already mentioned above that the doctrine advanced by the Gītā is, that the Ātman is existent (*sat*), unborn, immutable, and un-imaginable, or qualityless. The Blessed Lord now gives another argument, on the basis of the Sāṁkhya system, in support of the theory that there should be no lamentation over the Body, as it is non-permanent—].

(28) All created beings are imperceptible in the beginning, perceptible in the middle, and imperceptible again in death; (if this is the case with every being) then, O Bhārata! where is (there room for) lamentation?

[The word '*avyakta*' means 'that which is not perceivable by the organs'; the argument advanced in this stanza is based on the Sāṁkhya doctrine that the entire perceptible universe has come out of One original imperceptible Substance by gradual degrees, and that in the end, that is, at the time of the final Dissolution (*pralaya*), the entire perceptible universe is again dissolved into the same Imperceptible (Gī. 8. 18). See the explanation of this Sāṁkhya doctrine in the seventh and the eighth chapters of the Gītā-Rahasya. If the perceptible form of anything soever is, in this way, going to be destroyed sometime or other, there remains no cause at all for lamenting over something, which, by its very nature, is liable to destruction. This same stanza appears in the Strīparva of the Mahābhārata (Ma. Bhā. Strī. 2. 6), where the word '*abhāva*' (non-existent) has been used instead of '*avyakta*'. Also, later on, the word '*adarśana*', i.e., 'to go out of sight', has been

§§ आश्चर्यवत् पश्यति कश्चिदेनमाश्चर्यवद्वदति तथैव चान्यः ।
आश्चर्यवच्चैनमन्यः शृणोति श्रुत्वाप्येनं वेद न चैव कश्चित् ॥ २९ ॥
देही नित्यमवध्योऽयं देहे सर्वस्य भारत ।
तस्मात् सर्वाणि भूतानि न त्वं शोचितुमर्हसि ॥ ३० ॥

used with reference to death in the stanza: "*adarśanād āpatitaḥ punaś cādarśanaṁ gatāḥ । na te tava na teṣāṁ tvaṁ tatra kā paridevanā* ॥" (Strī. 2. 13), (that is, "emerged from the Invisible, and returning into the (same) Invisible, these are not thine, nor art thou theirs; wherefore, then (any) lamentation (for them)?"—Trans.). If lamentation is futile both according to the Sāṁkhya and the Vedānta philosophies, and if the same conclusion is reached, even looking upon the Ātman as non-permanent, why do people lament over death? The reply is: this is due to ignorance of the nature of the Ātman, because—]

(29) Some look at this (Ātman—Trans.) as a wonder (wonderful thing), others speak of It as a wonder, and some others (than them) hear (of It—Trans.) as a wonder; but even after (seeing and describing in this way, and) hearing, no one (out of these) Knows It (really).

[Though learned people enter into discussions about the Ātman, as a wonder, yet, as very few persons ever realise the true nature of It, many people lament over death. Do not you do likewise, but Realise the true nature of the Ātman after mature deliberation, and cease to lament; that is what this stanza means. The Ātman has been described in the same way in the Kaṭhopaniṣad (Kaṭha. 2. 7).]

(30) The Owner of the Body, (that is, the Ātman), (which is) in every Body, is always unkillable, (that is, never liable to destruction); therefore, O Bhārata (Arjuna)! it is not proper that you should lament about all (i. e., any) created things.

[It has thus far been proved that there is no reason to 'lament' if some one kills or is killed, because according to the Sāṁkhya philosophy, or the philosophy of the Path of Renunciation, the Ātman is immortal, and the Body

§§ स्वधर्ममपि चावेक्ष्य न विकम्पितुमर्हसि ।
धर्म्याद्धि युद्धाच्छ्रेयोऽन्यत् क्षत्रियस्य न विद्यते ॥ ३१ ॥

is inherently mortal. But if, on that account, some one draws the conclusion that there is no 'sin' in somebody killing someone else, that will be a very serious mistake. Only the meaning of the words 'dying' and 'killing' has been analysed here, and this explanation has been given only for the purpose of first removing the fear attendant on death or on killing. Man is a combination of the Body and the Ātman. As the Ātman, out of these, is immortal, the words 'dying' or 'killing' do not apply to It. Then remains the Body; but as the Body is naturally mortal, there is no reason for lamentation if it is destroyed. But, even accepting the position that one should not lament over death, or become happy or unhappy if some one dies or is killed accidentally or in course of time, one does not thereby solve the question, why a person should enter upon such a terrible act as war and destroy the bodies of others. Because, although the Body is mortal, yet, as the Body is the only means by which one can attain the permanent benefit of the Ātman or obtain Release, both suicide and the unjustified killing of another person are looked upon as grave sins by religion. Therefore, though it is not proper to lament over death, yet, it is necessary to give some other satisfactory reason why one person should kill another. This is known as the discrimination between '*dharma*' (Right) and '*adharma*' (Wrong); and this is the subject-matter really propounded in the Gītā. The Blessed Lord, therefore, first tells Arjuna that as fighting is the duty of all Kṣatriyas according to the arrangement of four castes accepted even in the Sāṁkhya philosophy, not only should he not lament over the fact of death or of killing, but that both dying or being killed in war were things which were his lot according to the religion of Kṣatriyas—]

(31) Besides, even if you consider your own duty, you ought not to falter (on this occasion); because, there is

यदृच्छया चोपपन्नं स्वर्गद्वारमपावृतम् ।
सुखिनः क्षत्रियाः पार्थ लभन्ते युद्धमीदृशम् ॥ ३२ ॥
अथ चेत्त्वमिमं धर्म्यं संग्रामं न करिष्यसि ।
ततः स्वधर्मं कीर्तिं च हित्वा पापमवाप्स्यसि ॥ ३३ ॥
अकीर्तिं चापि भूतानि कथयिष्यन्ति तेऽव्ययाम् ।
संभावितस्य चाकीर्तिर्मरणादतिरिच्यते ॥ ३४ ॥

nothing more meritorious to a Kṣatriya than warfare enjoined by duty.

[This argument about "one's own duty" *(svadharma)* appears twice later on (Gī. 3. 35 and 18. 47). This and the subsequent stanza say, that although the fourth stage *(āśrama)* in the shape of Renunciation of Action (*karma-saṁnyāsa*), is the last step according to the Path of Renunciation or the Sāṁkhya philosophy, yet, as it had been enjoined by Manu and other writers of the Smṛtis that before reaching that stage, Brahmins had to follow the duties of Brahmins, and Ksatriyas, the duties of Kṣatriyas, and in that way to complete the state of a householder (*gṛhasthāśrama*), it was the duty of Arjuna, who was in the state of a householder, to fight.]

(32) And O Pārtha! this war, which is indeed a door of Heaven, found open without effort, falls to the lot of only those Kṣatriyas, who are fortunate. (33) But, if you will not carry on this (for you) righteous warfare, then you will have abandoned your duty and lost your honour, and incurred sin; (34) (not only that, but) also (all) men will tell of your everlasting infamy! And to one who has been honoured, infamy is (a) greater (death) than death.

[This same principle has been explained by Śrī Kṛṣṇa to Yudhiṣṭhira in the Udyogaparva (Ma. Bhā. U. 72. 24). The stanza there is as follows: "*kulīnasya ca yā nindā vadho vā 'mitrakarṣaṇa* । *mahāguṇo vadho rājan na tu nindā kujīvikā*" (that is, 'ill-fame of a well born (person) is (his) murder; it is not only an ill-fame which spoils life, but indeed the highest form of murder'—Trans.). But, as this idea has been conveyed in the Gītā in a shorter form, and

भयाद्रणादुपरतं मंस्यन्ते त्वां महारथाः ।
येषां च त्वं बहुमतो भूत्वा यास्यसि लाघवम् ॥ ३५ ॥
अवाच्यवादांश्च बहून् वदिष्यन्ति तवाहिताः ।
निन्दन्तस्तव सामर्थ्यं ततो दुःखतरं नु किम् ॥ ३६ ॥
हतो वा प्राप्स्यसि स्वर्गं जित्वा वा भोक्ष्यसे महीम् ।
तस्मादुत्तिष्ठ कौन्तेय युद्धाय कृतनिश्चयः ॥ ३७ ॥
सुखदुःखे समे कृत्वा लाभालाभौ जयाजयौ ।
ततो युद्धाय युज्यस्व नैवं पापमवाप्स्यसि ॥ ३८ ॥

also as the Gītā is more in vogue, the line, "*saṁbhāvitasya*" etc., from the Gītā gets easily fixed in the memory, and people use it as a proverb. Many other stanzas from the Gītā are similarly to be heard quoted everywhere. The Blessed Lord now explains what the form of the infamy is, on the present occasion—]

(35) (All Masters of great chariots will think that you withdrew from the battle on account of fear; and those by whom you are highly thought of (to-day), will hold you in less esteem. (36) Also, your enemies, decrying your power, will speak much (about you) that should not be spoken; and what indeed more painful than that? (37) Killed, you will go to heaven; victorious, you will enjoy the earth; therefore, arise, O Arjuna! determined on battle.

[Though the above exposition has shown that, according to the Sāṁkhya philosophy, not only should one not lament the fact of death or of killing, but that fighting according to the rules laid down for one's own caste is a duty, yet, the Blessed Lord now answers the doubt whether the killer is responsible for the 'sin' of the deaths caused in warfare. Strictly speaking, the argument in reply to this question pertains to the Path of Karma-Yoga, and the introduction to that doctrine starts here.]

(38) Looking upon happiness and unhappiness, gain and loss, victory and defeat, as alike, then start the battle; acting thus you will not incur (any) sin.

[There are two paths of leading one's life in the world; the one is the Sāṁkhya, and the other is the Yoga. Out of

§§ एषा तेऽभिहिता सांख्ये बुद्धिर्योगे त्विमां शृणु ।
बुद्ध्या युक्तो यया पार्थ कर्मबन्धं प्रहास्यसि ॥ ३९ ॥

these two, it is not proper to lament over the Ātman or the Body according to the philosophy of that very Sāṁkhya Path, or the Path of Renunciation, by considering the doctrines of which, Arjuna had come to the point of giving up warfare and starting begging. The Blessed Lord has proved to Arjuna, that happiness and pain have to be borne with an equable frame of mind; that, warfare was the only proper thing to do for Kṣatriyas having regard to the rules of conduct applying to them; and that, if warfare was carried on with an equable frame of mind, a man incurs no sin whatsoever. But as Sāṁkhya philosophy is of the opinion that it is the highest duty of everyone in this world, under any circumstances, to give up worldly life and take up Saṁnyāsa (Renunciation), that philosophy does not solve the questions: (i) why Arjuna should not take up Saṁnyāsa at that very moment, giving up warfare; or, (ii) why he should follow the rules of conduct laid down for his own caste; and then, the original objection of Arjuna may be said to remain unanswered. Therefore, the Blessed Lord now says as follows—]

(39) This *buddhi* (that is, Knowlege, or argument) stated to you is according to the Sāṁkhya (that is, the Sāṁnyāsa)-Niṣṭhā. Now hear that *buddhi* (that is, Knowledge) according to the (Karma-) Yoga, (which I am describing to you), being possessed of which, O Pārtha, you will (even without giving up Action) cast off the bonds of Action.

[This stanza is of very great importance in order to understand the import of the Bhagavadgītā. The word 'Sāṁkhya' is not to be understood here as meaning 'Kāpila-Sāṁkhya', or only 'Vedānta', nor is the word 'Yoga' to be understood as meaning 'Pātañjala-Yoga'; but, 'Sāṁkhya' must be taken here as meaning the 'Saṁnyāsa-mārga' (Path of Renunciation) and 'Yoga' as meaning the 'Karma-Yoga' (Path of Proper Action), as is clear from Gītā 3. 3. These two paths are independent of

§§ नेहाभिक्रमनाशोऽस्ति प्रत्यवायो न विद्यते ।
स्वल्पमप्यस्य धर्मस्य त्रायते महतो भयात् ॥ ४० ॥

each other, and the followers of these paths are known respectively as 'Sāṁkhya'='Saṁnyāsa-mārgin' and 'Yoga'= 'Karma-Yoga-mārgin' (Gī. 5. 5). As the followers of the Sāṁkhya-niṣṭhā out of these consider it more meritorious to give up Action in the end completely some time or other, the philosophy of this path does not completely answer Arjuna's question: "Why should I fight?". Therefore, the Blessed Lord now starts to impart the Knowledge pertaining to the Niṣṭhā of Karma-Yoga, or shortly Yoga, according to which true manhood consists in continuing to perform Action lifelong, with a disinterested frame of mind, and without adopting Saṁnyāsa, even after the acquisition of true Knowledge; and this Path of Action has been emphasised from now on right to the last chapter of the Gītā, by showing many reasons for following that path and by giving satisfactory explanations of many doubts. When one bears in mind this explanation of the exposition of the subject-matter of the Gītā, given by the Blessed Lord Himself, there remains no doubt any more that the Gītā supports the path of Karma-Yoga. The Blessed Lord first states the most important propositions of Karma-Yoga-]

(40) Here, (that is, in this path of Karma-Yoga), Action (once) commenced is not destroyed, (and afterwards) obstacles do not arise; even a little (practice) of this religion protects (one) from great danger.

[The importance of this doctrine has been shown in Chapter X of the Gītā-Rahasya (p. 392, bottom); and a fuller explanation is also given later on in the Gītā (Gī. 6. 40-46). This stanza means that according to the path of Karma-Yoga, even if perfection is not reached in one life, the Action performed is not wasted, but comes in useful in the subsequent births, and the merit being thus accumulated from birth to birth, true Release is reached ultimately, sometime or other. The Blessed Lord now propounds the second important doctrine of Karma-Yoga—]

§§ व्यवसायात्मिका बुद्धिरेकेह कुरुनन्दन ।
बहुशाखा ह्यनन्ताश्च बुद्धयोऽव्यवसायिनाम् ॥ ४१ ॥

(41) O Kurunandana, (that is, descendant of Kuru, or Arjuna—Trans.), in this (path) the (mental organ in the shape of) Reason, which performs the *vyavasāya*, (that is, the discernment between the Doable and the Not-Doable), has got to be one, (that is, concentrated); but, the *buddhayaḥ* (that is, the Desires) of those whose Reason is not (in this way) concentrated, are many-branched and (of) endless (kinds).

[The word '*buddhi*' has many meanings in Sanskrit. Of these, it has been used in the meaning of 'Knowledge' in the 39th stanza; and later on in the 49th stanza, '*buddhi*' is to be interpreted as meaning 'understanding', 'desire', 'wish', or 'motive'. But as the adjective '*vyavasāyātmikā*' precedes the word '*buddhi*' in the first line of this stanza, it there means the "organ of Reason which performs '*vyavasāya*', that is, which discerns between the Doable and the Not-Doable" (Gītā-Raha. Ch. VI, pp. 179 to 187). When this organ of Reason has first decided whether any matter is good or evil, the Mind conceives the desire or wish to act accordingly; therefore, this Desire or wish is also called '*buddhi*'. But the adjective '*vyavasāyātmikā*' does not in the latter case precede that word. If it becomes necessary to show the difference, the phrase '*vāsanātmaka*' *buddhi* is used. In the second line of this stanza, the word '*buddhi*' has been used by itself. It is not preceded by the adjective '*vyavasāyātmikā*'. Therefore, the word '*buddhayaḥ*' in the plural form means 'desires' or 'flights of imagination'; and the second line of this stanza means: "Those whose '*vyavasāyātmikā buddhi*', that is to say, the discerning mental organ of Reason, is not steady, (that is, the *avyavasāyinaḥ*—Trans.) conceive ever new waves of imagination or desires every moment". Unless one keeps in mind these two meanings of the word '*buddhi*', namely, (i) the discerning and deciding mental organ, and (ii) Desire, it will not be possible to clearly understand the true import of the exposition of the word '*buddhi*' in the

§§ यामिमां पुष्पितां वाचं प्रवदन्त्यविपश्चितः ।
वेदवादरताः पार्थ नान्यदस्तीति वादिनः ॥ ४२ ॥

कामात्मानः स्वर्गपरा जन्मकर्मफलप्रदाम् ।
क्रियाविशेषबहुलां भोगैश्वर्यगतिं प्रति ॥ ४३ ॥

भोगैश्वर्यप्रसक्तानां तयापहृतचेतसाम् ।
व्यवसायात्मिका बुद्धिः समाधौ न विधीयते ॥ ४४ ॥

doctrine of Karma-Yoga. The Blessed Lord now shows how when the Discerning Reason is not steady or concentrated, the Mind is continually disintegrated by different desires, and the man runs after different pursuits, wishing to-day to do something for getting a son, and to-morrow something else for attaining heaven, etc.—]

(42) O Pārtha! (those) fools who rejoice in the words (showing the gain to be made) appearing in the Vedas (Karma-kāṇḍa), and who say that nothing else is of importance, say in a flowery way that: (43) "By means of many Actions (such as, Yajñas, Yāgas, etc.), one obtains the fruit of (re–)birth, and (birth after birth) pleasures and prosperity are obtained"; and these (people) with a desire-filled Mind, who run after heaven, (44) are attracted by those words, and become immersed in pleasures and prosperity, and thereby their *vyavasāyātmikā buddhi* (that is, their Reason which decides between the Doable and the Not-Doable) cannot (ever) be concentrated (that is, fixed on one point).

[The above three stanzas make up only one sentence, and contain a description of Jñāna-less ritualists following the Mīmāṁsā path, who are continually engrossed in the performance of sacrificial rites in the shape of Yajñas or Yāgas solely for the selfish purposes of attaining one object to-day and another object to-morrow according to the Karma-kāṇḍa prescribed by the Śrutis and the Smṛtis; and this description has been made on the basis of the

§§ त्रैगुण्यविषया वेदा निस्त्रैगुण्यो भवार्जुन।
निर्द्वन्द्वो नित्यसत्त्वस्थो निर्योगक्षेम आत्मवान्॥ ४५॥

Upaniṣads. For instance, it is stated in the Muṇḍakopaniṣad that:

iṣṭāpūrtaṁ manyamānā variṣṭhaṁ nānyac chreyo vedayante pramūḍhāḥ ।
nākasya pṛṣṭhe te sukṛte 'nubhūtvemaṁ lokaṁ hīnataraṁ vā viśanti ॥
(Muṇ. 1. 2. 10).

that is, "these fools, who believe that only the 'performance of sacrificial ritual' (*iṣṭāpūrtaṁ*) is meritorious and that nothing else is meritorious, come back to this mortal world after having enjoyed happiness in heaven"; and similar statements, derogative of Jñāna-less Karma (ritual) are also to be found in the Īśāvāsya and Kaṭha Upaniṣads (Kaṭha. 2. 5; Īśā. 9. 12). It is true that these people, who, without acquiring the Knowledge of the Parameśvara, are steeped in the performance of Karma (ritual), obtain the fruits of their respective ritual in the shape of heaven etc. But, as their Desire is entangled to-day in this ritual and the next day in some other ritual, and is straying about in all directions, they never attain Release, how many soever times they may have gone to heaven. In order to obtain Release, the organ of Reason must be steady or concentrated on a single point. For the present, the Blessed Lord says only as follows—]

(45) O Arjuna! as the Vedas (consisting of the Karmakāṇḍa) deal (in this way) only with the subject-matter of the three constituents, do you become *'nistraiguṇya'* (that is, *triguṇātīta*), (that is, 'beyond the reach of the three constituents'—Trans.), *'nitya-sattvastha'* (that is, abiding in eternal Truth—Trans.*), and free from the Opposites (of happiness and unhappiness etc.); and without being steeped in the selfish interests of *'yogakṣema'* etc., become Self-devoted (*ātmavān*).

* The author has retained in his Marathi translation, the word *'nityasattvastha'* from the original, and in the commentary he has explained it as being synonymous with *'nistraiguṇya'* or *'triguṇātīta'*;

['*traiguṇya*' means the 'worldly life (*saṁsāra*) of Prakṛti made up of the three constituents *sattva*, *rajas*, and *tamas*'; and it has been clearly shown in the Gītā-Rahasya (p. 314 and 353) that the true Brāhmaṇa is beyond that, and that worldly life is made up of the perishable Opposites of happiness and unhappiness, life and death etc. It has been stated in the 43rd stanza of this very chapter, that people, who follow the Mīmāṁsā doctrine, perform the Yajñas etc. prescribed by the Śrutis, in order to obtain the happiness pertaining to this worldly life of Prakṛti or Māyā, and that they are entirely steeped in these practices; some perform a sacrificial ritual in order to obtain a son, whereas others perform some other sacrificial rite in order that rain should fall. All this ritual is necessary for 'the maintenance of worldly life', that is, for '*yogakṣema*'. It is, therefore, clear that one who wishes to attain Release, must go beyond these ritualistic practices, which are the result of the *sattva*, *rajas* and *tamas* constituents, and which bring about only *yogakṣema*, and must concentrate his attention on the Parabrahman, Which is beyond all this. And the words '*nirdvaṁdva*' (beyond the Opposites—Trans.) and '*niryogakṣema*' (beyond the anxiety for new acquisitions and the protection of old acquisitions—Trans.) have been used above to convey this idea. In this place, a doubt is likely to arise as to how *yogakṣema* will be carried on, if these desire-prompted (*kāmya*)

---

but this is difficult to understand, as there seems no reason for repeating the idea. The late Mr. Telang, therefore, translates '*sattva*' here as 'courage'; and Dr. Besant as 'purity'. As '*sattva*' is one of the three constituents, and as the Blessed Lord has just asked Arjuna to be 'beyond the three constituents', '*nityasattvastha*' cannot be understood as referring to the '*sattva*' constituent. Therefore, Prof W. D. P. Hill (*Bhagavadgītā* Ox. Univ. Press, 1928, p. 120) has translated the word '*sattva*' in its more general sense of 'Truth', which has been adopted by me. Sadashiva Shastri Bhide has got over the difficulty by explaining '*nistraiguṇya*' as 'free from the *desires* to enjoy pleasures arising from the three constituents', and by then explaining '*nityasattvastha*' as meaning 'possessing the *sāttvika* qualities of equability, perseverance, enthusiasm' etc.—Translator.

ritualistic performances prescribed in the Karma-kāṇḍa are not carried on (Gī. Ra. pages 405 and 535). The reply to that question is not given here; but when this subject comes again later on in Chapter IX, it is stated that the Blessed Lord looks after this *yogakṣema* (i. e., 'bestows the things wanted and preserves the security of the things possessed'—Trans.); and it is only in these two places that the word *'yogakṣema'* appears in the Gītā (See Gī. 9. 22, and my commentary thereon). The word *'nityasattvastha'* means the same as *'triguṇātīta'* (beyond the three constituents); because, it is stated later on that by the continual growth of the *sattva* constituent, one acquires the *'triguṇātītāvasthā'* (the state of being beyond the three constituents—Trans.), and that that is the true *'siddhāvasthā'* (the state of Perfection—Trans.), (Gī. 14. 14 and 20, Gī. Ra. pp. 226 and 227). In short, the advice given here is that one should give up the desire-prompted ritual prescribed by the Mīmāṁsā school for obtaining. *yogakṣema*, which is based on the three constituents, and go beyond the Opposites of happiness and unhappiness etc., and become *brahma-niṣṭha* (devoted to the Brahman) or *ātma-niṣṭha* (devoted to the Ātman). But, it must be borne in mind at the same time that the injunction to become *ātma-niṣṭha* does not mean that all this ritual should totally and for all intents and purposes be given up. The adverse criticism made in the above stanza of the desire-prompted ritual prescribed by the Vedas, or the inferiority which is shown of that ritual, is not the inferiority of the ritual itself, but of the desire-prompted Reason behind it. If this desire-prompted Reason does not govern the Mind, mere sacrificial ritual does not in any way close the door to Release (Gī. Ra. pp. 404 to 408). That is why the Blessed Lord has given it as His definite and most valuable opinion later on in the beginning of the 18th chapter (Gī. 18. 6), that these very ritualistic performances prescribed by the Mīmāṁsā writers should certainly be performed, for the purification of the Mind (*cittaśuddhi*), and for public welfare (*lokasaṁgraha*), giving up the Hope for Fruit (*phalāśā*) and Attachment (*saṅga*). When you take together these two statements made in two different places

यावानर्थ उदपाने सर्वतः संप्लुतोदके ।
तावान्सर्वेषु वेदेषु ब्राह्मणस्य विजानतः ॥ ४६ ॥

in the Gītā, it becomes quite clear that the inferiority of the Mīmāṁsaka Karma-kāṇḍa shown in the stanzas in this chapter has reference to the desire-prompted Reason, and not only to the ritual. With this object in mind, it has been stated in the Bhāgavata that:

vedoktam eva kurvāṇo niḥsaṅgo 'rpitam īśvare ।
naiṣkarmyāṁ labhate siddhiṁ rocanārthā phalaśrutiḥ ॥
(Bhāg. 11. 3. 46),

that is, "the 'recital of fruits (*phalaśruti*)' to be obtained by the performance of Vedic ritual, which has been given in the Vedas, has been given '*rocanārtha*', that is, only in order that the person who performs the ritual should find it agreeable; and therefore, that man who, instead of performing such ritual for obtaining the promised fruit, performs it unattachedly (with a *niḥsaṅga* Reason), that is to say, after giving up the Hope for Fruit and with the sole intention of dedicating it to the Īśvara, attains the '*naiṣkarmya-siddhi*' (the Perfection of Desireless Action)". In short, the summary of the advice in the Gītā is, that although it has been stated in the Vedas that a particular sacrificial ritual should be performed for a particular purpose, yet, one should not be taken in by that Desire, but should perform the ritual because it is '*yaṣṭavya*', that is, because the performance of the ritual is a duty; that, one should give up the desire-promptedness of one's Reason, but not the ritualistic sacrifices (Gī. 17. 11); and that the other rites should also be performed in the same way. And the same meaning has been expressed in the subsequent stanzas.]

(46) To that extent to which there is a use (that is, necessity) for a well when there is a flood of water everywhere (clearly, there is no necessity whatsoever), to the same extent is there any necessity of the Vedas (containing the ritualistic Karma-kāṇḍa) for the enlightened Brāhmaṇa (that is to say, for him, there is no more any necessity of the Vedic Karma-kāṇḍa which describes desire-fulfilling ritual).

[There is no difference of opinion as to the broad meaning (*phalitārtha*) of this stanza; but, commentators have entered into a useless hair-splitting discussion about the terms used in it. "*sarvataḥsaṁplutodake*" is a compound phrase in the seventh case (locative case); but if it is looked upon not merely as the locative case, nor as an adjectival phrase qualifying the word '*udapāna*', but as the '*sati saptamī*' (locative absolute), one can syntactically work out the sentence in a simple way as: "*sarvataḥsaṁptutodake sati udapāne yāvān arthaḥ (na svalpam api prayojanaṁ vidyate) tāvān vijānataḥ brāhmaṇasya sarveṣu vedeṣu arthaḥ*", without taking any outside words as implied; and this also gives the following clear and simple meaning:—"Just as no one cares for wells when there is water everywhere, (because drinking-water can be had anywhere without difficulty and sumptuously), so has the man, who has attained Knowledge, no more any use for mere 'Vedic' ritual like sacrificial Yajñas etc". The Vedic ritual has to be performed for obtaining the final Release-giving Knowledge, and not merely for obtaining heaven; and that man who has already obtained this Knowledge, has nothing new to learn by performing Vedic ritual. That is why it is stated later on in the 3rd chapter of the Gītā (3. 17) that "to him who has acquired Knowledge, there is no more any duty left in the world". When one can without difficulty obtain as much pure water as desired from a large lake or from a river, who will even look at a well? In such circumstances, no one attaches the slightest importance to a well. In the last chapter of the Sanatsujātīya (Ma. Bhā. Udyo. 45. 26), this very stanza occurs again with a slight verbal difference; and the meaning of it has been given in the commentary on it by Madhvācārya in the same way as above; and in the Śukānupraśna, where the relative worth of Jñāna (Knowledge) and Karma is being described, it is clearly stated that "*na te* (*jñāninaḥ*) *karma praśaṁsaṁti kūpaṁ nadyāṁ pibann iva*", that is, "just as one who gets water from the river, does not attach any importance to a well, so do 'they', that is, the Jñānins, not attach the slightest importance to Karma" (Ma. Bhā. Śān. 240. 10).

In the same way, in the 17th stanza of the Pāṇḍavagītā, the simile of a well is used for saying that the man who, ignoring Vāsudeva, worships other gods, is like a fool who, "*tṛṣito jāhnavītīre kūpaṁ vāñcchati durmatiḥ*", that is, "being thirsty, and being able to get drinking-water on the banks of the Bhāgīrathī (Ganges), still craves for a well". It is not that this simile appears only in the Vedic Sanskrit texts; but it has been adopted even in the Pali Buddhistic books. The dictum that the man who has destroyed Thirst does not have anything further to acquire, is acceptable also to Buddhism; and in referring to it, it is called a '*dṛṣṭānta*', and appears in the Pali text called *Udāna* (U. 7. 9) in the form of the stanza "*kim kayirā udapādena āpā ce sabbadā siyum*", which means, 'what is the use of a well after water can be had in all places'. We experience it even now-a-days in big towns, that when a person has taken a water-pipe in the house, he does not any more care for a well. From these facts, and especially from the exposition in the Śukānupraśna, the reader will realise the appropriateness of the simile used in the Gītā, and see that the meaning of this stanza as given by me above is straightforward and correct. But commentators on the Gītā analyse the sentence in this stanza in a slightly different way, whether because by accepting this interpretation some inferiority becomes attached to the Vedas, or because they wish to keep intact the doctrinal proposition, that 'a Jñānin need no more perform Action, because Knowledge includes the performance of Action'. They take the word '*tāvān*' as implied in the first, and the word '*yāvān*' as implied in the second part of the stanza, and analyse the stanza as follows: "*udapāne yāvān arthaḥ tāvān eva sarvataḥ-saṁplutodake yathā saṁpadyate tathā yāvān sarveṣu vedeṣu arthaḥ tāvān vijānataḥ brāhmaṇasya saṁpadyate*", that is to say, "to that extent to which wells can be put to use for the purpose of bathing and of drinking water, to the same extent can use be made of large lakes (*sarvataḥsaṁpluto-dake*) for the same purpose; in the same way, Jñānins can, by means of their Knowledge, obtain from the Vedas as much benefit as it is possible to obtain". But as, according to this interpretation, the word '*tāvān*' has to be taken as implied in the first part of the stanza, and the word '*yāvān*' in the second part of the stanza, I have not accepted it. The interpretation and working out (*anvaya*) of the stanza adopted by me is arrived at without taking any words as implied; and, as is quite clear from the previous stanzas, this stanza is intended to give expression to the inferiority of the pure (that is, Jñāna-less) Karmakāṇḍa in the Vedas. But, the inference that because a person who has attained Knowledge has no use for the ritual of Yajñas or Yāgas, he need not perform them, and may give them up altogether, is not borne out by the Gītā; because, although a Jñānin does not care for the fruit to be obtained by this ritual, yet, he must go on performing the ritual, if not for the fruit, at least because the performance of Yajñas and Yāgas is his duty as laid down in the Śāstras; and, therefore, he can never give up the ritual. The Blessed Lord has given it as His definite opinion in unmistakeable terms in the 18th chapter, that though a Jñānin may have no Hope for Fruit, yet,he must desirelessly perform Yajñas and Yāgas in the same way as he desirelessly performs other acts (See my commentary on the previous stanza and on Gī. 6. 19); and the Blessed Lord now further clearly states this version about Desireless Action in the next stanza—]*

* Annie Besant and Bhagvandas (*Bhagavadgītā*, Theo. Pub. House, 1926, p 42) translate this stanza as: "All the Vedas are as useful to an enlightened Brāhmaṇa as is a tank in a place covered all over with water", which is similar to the interpretation of the author. Telang translates it as: "To the instructed Brāhmaṇa, there is in all the Vedas as much utility as in a reservoir of water into which waters flow from all sides" (S. B. E. Series, Vol VIII, p. 48); and W. D. P. Hill's translation is practically the same (the *Bhagavadgītā*, Oxf. Univ. Press, 1928, p. 121). Both these latter authors have attached explanatory notes, to which the reader is referred. The divergence is based on the interpretation of '*sarvataḥ saṁplute*', which is translated by some as "filled *from* all sides", and by others as, "when there is a flood *on* all sides"—Trans.

§§ कर्मण्येवाधिकारस्ते मा फलेषु कदाचन ।
मा कर्मफलहेतुर्भूर्मा ते संगोऽस्त्वकर्मणि ॥ ४७ ॥

(47) Your authority extends only to the performance of Action; (obtaining or not obtaining) the Fruit, is never within your authority (that is, never within your control); (therefore,) do not be one who performs Action with the (avaricious) motive (in the mind) that a particular fruit should be obtained (of his Action); nor do you also insist on not-performing Action.

[The four quarters of this stanza are mutually complementary; and, therefore, without their overlapping each other, the entire import of the Karma-Yoga is given in a short and beautiful form; nay, one may even safely say that these four parts of the stanza are the *catuḥ-sūtrī* of the Karma-Yoga. It is stated to begin with, that "your authority extends only to the performance of Action". But as the Fruit of an Action is inseparable from the Action, there is room for the doubt that, 'he who has the authority to perform the Action, has also the authority to take the fruit, since he who owns the tree, also owns the fruit'; therefore, in order to solve that difficulty, the Blessed Lord has pronounced in a clear way in the 2nd quarter of the stanza that, "your authority does not extend to the Fruit"; and then He has pronounced the 3rd proposition, which arises from that dictum, namely, "do not be one who performs Action having in mind the Hope for Fruit". (*karmaphala-hetuḥ*', is a Bahuvrīhi-samāsa, thus, '*karmaphale hetur yasya sa karmaphalahetuḥ*'), (that is, 'he is a *karmaphala-hetuḥ*, whose motive is in the Fruit of the Action'—Trans.). But someone may advance the argument that because an Action and the fruit of it are mutually interlinked, one must give up the fruit (Action ?—Trans.) at the same time as giving up the Hope for Fruit. In order to make it clear that such an inference would not be correct, the clear advice has been given, that one should give up the Hope for Fruit but, at the same time, "one should not insist on not doing Action, that is, on giving up Action". In short, saying that one should perform Action, does not amount to saying

§§ योगस्थः कुरु कर्माणि संगं त्यक्त्वा धनंजय।
सिद्ध्यसिद्ध्योः समो भूत्वा समत्वं योग उच्यते ॥ ४८ ॥
दूरेण ह्यवरं कर्म बुद्धियोगाद्धनंजय।
बुद्धौ शरणमन्विच्छ कृपणाः फलहेतवः ॥ ४९ ॥
बुद्धियुक्तो जहातीह उभे सुकृतदुष्कृते।
तस्माद्योगाय युज्यस्व योगः कर्मसु कौशलम् ॥ ५० ॥

that one should entertain the Hope for Fruit; and conversely, saying that one should give up the Hope for Fruit, does not amount to saying that one should eschew Action. The meaning of this stanza is, that one should necessarily perform one's duty, having given up the 'Hope for Fruit'; and that, one should not be attached to the Action, and at the same time should not give up the Action—"*tyāgo na yukta iha karmasu nāpi rāgaḥ*" (Yoga. 5. 5. 54); and the meaning has been emphasised again in the 18th chapter, where it is stated that the obtaining of Fruit is not a matter within one's own control, and that it is necessary to have the co-operation of many other things for that purpose (Gī. 18. 14–16 and Rahasya, Chapter V. p. 154 and Ch. XII). The Blessed Lord now clearly defines the characteristics of Karma-Yoga by saying that, such Action means 'Yoga' or 'Karma-Yoga'—]

(48) O Dhananjaya! casting off Attachment and looking upon as alike the being fruitful and unfruitful (of Action), perform Action being '*yogastha*' (that is, 'steadfast in the path of Karma-Yoga'—Trans.); the (mental) state of being Equable (towards the Action being fruitful or unfruitful) is known as (Karma-) Yoga. (49) For, (external) Karma is by far inferior to the Yoga (of the Equability) of Reason; (therefore) surrender yourself to (this equable) Reason; the '*phalahetavaḥ*' (that is, those, who perform Action only with an eye to the Fruit) are '*kṛpaṇa*' (that is, low, or on a lower level). (50) He, who is steeped in the (equable) Reason remains untouched both by sin or merit in this (world); therefore, take shelter in Yoga. The cleverness (skilfulness or trick) of performing

Action (without acquiring merit or sin) is known as (Karma-) Yoga.

[The description of the nature of Karma-Yoga given in these stanzas is very important, and I have to refer the reader to the discussion of that subject in Chapter III of the Gītā-Rahasya (pp. 76 to 87). But, the proposition of Karma-Yoga mentioned in the 49th stanza, namely that, 'the Reason is superior to the Action', is of utmost importance. As the word '*buddhi*' (Reason) in these stanzas is not preceded by the adjective '*vyavasāyātmikā*', it must be understood in this stanza as mĕaning 'desire' or 'understanding'. Some persons try to interpret the word '*buddhi*' here as meaning 'Jñāna', and to interpret the stanza as meaning that 'Karma is of less importance than Jñāna'; but this interpretation is not correct. Because, as the description of Equability given in the 48th stanza is continued in the 49th and the subsequent stanzas, the word '*buddhi*' must be interpreted as meaning an 'equabilising *buddhi*'. The goodness or badness of an act does not depend on the act itself, and though the act may be one and the same, it becomes good or bad according to the good or evil intention of the doer; therefore, the Reason is superior to the Action. As this and other principles of morality have been dealt with in Chapters IV, XII, and XV of the Gītā-Rahasya (p. 119; p. 530; and pp. 668 to 675), I do not propose to deal with them here in a more exhaustive way. It has been stated above in the 41st stanza that in order that the Desiring Reason (*vāsanātmaka buddhi*) should remain equable and pure, the Discerning Reason (*vyavasāyātmaka buddhi*), which decides about the Doable and the Not-Doable must in the first instance become steady. This has been already stated above in the 41st stanza. Therefore, the word '*sāmyabuddhi*' (Equable Reason) means and includes both the steady Discerning Reason (*vyavasāyātmaka buddhi*) and PureDesire (*vāsanātmaka buddhi*); as this Equable Reason is the basic structure on which whether Pure Conduct or Karma-Yoga is based, the Blessed Lord has, with reference to His statement in the 39th stanza (that He would explain to Arjuna the 'device' or 'Yoga' by

§§ कर्मजं बुद्धियुक्ता हि फलं त्यक्त्वा मनीषिणः।
जन्मबन्धविनिर्मुक्ताः पदं गच्छन्त्यनामयम् ॥ ५१ ॥
यदा ते मोहकलिलं बुद्धिर्व्यतितरिष्यति।
तदा गन्तासि निर्वेदं श्रोतव्यस्य श्रुतस्य च ॥ ५२ ॥

means of which Arjuna would not be affected by Action, though he might perform it), explained to Arjuna in this stanza that, that 'device' or 'skill' consists in 'keeping one's Reason, steady, holy, equable, and untainted', and that it is known as 'Yoga'; and He has in this way defined the word 'Yoga' twice over. Although the words "*yogaḥ karmasu kauśalam*" appearing in the 50th stanza are thus capable of being interpreted in a straightforward way, some commentators have attempted to stretch the words, and to interpret them to mean that, '*karmasu yogaḥ kauśalam*', that is to say, "*kauśala* or skill, means the Yoga in the performance of Action". But, as there was no occasion here to give a definition of the word '*kauśala*', and the matter in point was to show the meaning of the word 'Yoga', this interpretation cannot be looked upon as correct. Besides, when it is possible to inter-relate the words in a simple and straightforward way as '*karmasu kauśalam*', it is not proper to transpose the words so as to inter-relate them as '*karmasu yogaḥ*'. The Blessed Lord now says that when a man performs Action in this way with an equable Reason, there is no neglect of worldly activities, and at the same time, one cannot but achieve complete Perfection or Release—]

(51) The Jñānins, when acting in union with (Equable) Reason, having abandoned the Fruit of Action, and becoming free from the shackles of births, reach the state (of the Parameśvara) where there is no unhappiness. (52) When your Reason shall have crossed the turgid enclosure of Ignorance, you will become indifferent towards whatever you may have heard or have to hear.

[That is to say, yon will not desire to hear anything more; because, you will have already obtained the Fruit which can be obtained by hearing these things. The word '*nirveda*' is primarily used to signify 'being tired of worldly life', or,

श्रुतिविप्रतिपन्ना ते यदा स्थास्यति निश्चला ।
समाधावचला बुद्धिस्तदा योगमवाप्स्यसि ॥ ५३ ॥

अर्जुन उवाच ।

§§ स्थितप्रज्ञस्य का भाषा समाधिस्थस्य केशव ।
स्थितधीः किं प्रभाषेत किमासीत व्रजेत किम् ॥ ५४ ॥

'Renunciation'. In this stanza, it ordinarily means 'tiredness' or 'not wanting'. It will be seen from the subsequent stanzas that this 'tiredness' is only with reference to the ritual prescribed in the Śrutis, which relates to the objects of the three constituents.]

(53) When your Reason, confused by (all kinds of) sentences from the Vedas, will become fixed and immoveale in the state of mental absorption, then will you attain this Yoga (in the shape of an Equable Reason).

[In short, as has been stated above in 2. 44, when a person, being taken in by the description of obtainable fruits given in Vedic hymns, falls into the turmoil of performing a particular act for obtaining a particular fruit, his Reason gets all the more confused instead of becoming steady. Therefore, Arjuna is advised to give up paying attention to such statements of advice, and to attain a fixed concentration of the Mind, so that he would attain the Karma-Yoga consisting of Equability of Reason, and be able to perform Action without incurring any sin, and without being in need of any further advice. It is stated that the Karma-yogin, whose Reason or *prajñā* has become steady (i. e., *sthita*) in this way, is called a 'Sthitaprajña'; and Arjuna now asks how such a person acts or behaves.]

Arjuna said: (54) O Keśava! who should be called a *samādhistha sthitaprajña*' (that is, the Steady-in-Reason, steeped in Mental Absorption—Trans.)? How does such a Sthitaprajña, speak, sit or walk? (tell me that).

[In this stanza, the word '*bhāṣā*' has been used in the meaning of '*lakṣaṇa*' (characteristics); and I have translated it as meaning 'who should be called', having regard to the root, '*bhāṣ*', of the word '*bhāṣā*'. It has been made

श्रीभगवानुवाच ।

प्रजहाति यदा कामान् सर्वान् पार्थ मनोगतान् ।
आत्मन्येवात्मना तुष्टः स्थितप्रज्ञस्तदोच्यते ॥ ५५ ॥
दुःखेष्वनुद्विग्नमनाः सुखेषु विगतस्पृहः ।
वीतरागभयक्रोधः स्थितधीर्मुनिरुच्यते ॥ ५६ ॥
यः सर्वत्रानभिस्नेहस्तत्तत्प्राप्य शुभाशुभम् ।
नाभिनन्दति न द्वेष्टि तस्य प्रज्ञा प्रतिष्ठिता ॥ ५७ ॥
यदा संहरते चायं कूर्मोऽङ्गानीव सर्वशः ।
इन्द्रियाणीन्द्रियार्थेभ्यस्तस्य प्रज्ञा प्रतिष्ठिता ॥ ५८ ॥
विषया विनिवर्तन्ते निराहारस्य देहिनः ।
रसवर्जं रसोऽप्यस्य परं दृष्ट्वा निवर्तते ॥ ५९ ॥

clear in Chapter XII of the Gītā-Rahasya (p. 510 to 527) that the mode of life of the Sthitaprajña is the basis of the doctrine of Karma-Yoga, and from this fact the importance of the description which follows will become apparent.]

The Blessed Lord said: (55) O Pārtha! when (a person) abandons all desires (that is, *vāsanā*) of his heart, and is pleased by himself in his own self, then he is called a Sthitaprajña. (56) He, whose heart is not agitated in the midst of calamities, who is void of longing in pleasures, and from whom affection, fear, and wrath have departed, is called a Steady-in-Reason sage (*sthitaprajña muni*—Trans.) (57) His Reason is (said to be) steady whose Mind is without Attachment in all things, and who feels no exultation or aversion about the agreeable or disagreeable which befalls him. (58) When a person draws in (his) senses from the objects (such as, sound, touch etc.) of the senses, as the tortoise draws in its limbs (such as, hands, feet, etc.) from all sides, then his Reason is (said to be) steady. (59) The objects of sense leave the foodless person, yet, the relish (that is, the sweetness) in them, does not leave him; but after he has experienced the Parabrahman, (all the objects together with) the relish also (in them), (that is, the objects of sense as also the relish in them) leaves him.

[The senses are fed by food. Therefore, when a person does not take food, or fasts, the senses become weak, and incapable of enjoying their respective objects. But getting rid in this way of the enjoyment of objects of sense, is the external action of enforced weakness. The desire (relish) for the objects of sense is not thereby reduced; therefore, one should acquire that Knowledge of the Brahman, by which such Desire will be destroyed; when a person has thus experienced the Brahman, his Mind, and at the same time, his senses also come automatically under control; and it is not necessary to fast or do anything else in order to obtain control over the senses. That is what this stanza means. And the same meaning is clearly conveyed later on in the stanzas in Chapter VI (See Gī. 6. 16, 17; as also 3. 6, 7), where it is stated that the Yogin should eat moderately, and that he should not give up food or pastime altogether. In short, it must be borne in mind that the Gītā looks upon fasting and other practices, which weaken the body, as one-sided, and therefore, eschewable; and lays down the doctrine that, moderate food and pastime, and the Knowledge of the Brahman, are the best means of controlling the senses. Some commentators interpret the word '*rasa*' in the stanza as meaning 'the sweet, bitter, and other tastes experienced by the tongue', and interpret the stanza to mean that though one can overcome the objects of the other senses by fasting, the relish of the tongue, that is, the desire for food and drink, is intensified, instead of being destroyed, by fasting for many days; and, there is also a stanza to the same effect in the Bhāgavata (Bhāg. 11. 8. 20). But in my opinion, it is not correct to interpret this stanza in the Gītā in that way; because, that meaning becomes inconsistent with the second part of the stanza. Besides, the word used in the Bhāgavata is not '*rasa*' but '*rasanaṁ*'; and we also do not find there the second part of the stanza in the Gītā. It is, therefore, not proper to consider the stanza in the Gītā, as meaning the same thing as the stanza in the Bhāgavata. The Blessed Lord now says in more explicit terms, in the two following stanzas, that it is not possible to obtain complete control

यततो ह्यपि कौन्तेय पुरुषस्य विपश्चितः।
इन्द्रियाणि प्रमाथीनि हरन्ति प्रसभं मनः ॥ ६० ॥
तानि सर्वाणि संयम्य युक्त आसीत मत्परः।
वशे हि यस्येन्द्रियाणि तस्य प्रज्ञा प्रतिष्ठिता ॥ ६१ ॥

over the senses, except by the Realisation of the Brahman—]

(60) Because, O son of Kuntī, these boisterous senses forcibly carry away in an improper direction, the Mind of even the intelligent person, who makes efforts merely (for controlling the senses). (61) (Therefore), one should control all these senses and become '*yukta*' (that is, *yoga-yukta*) and solely devoted to Me. His Reason is (said to have become) steady, whose senses are thus subject to his control.

[In this stanza, it is stated that one should obtain control over the senses by moderate eating, and should at the same time, become '*matparāyaṇa*', that is, should fix his mind on the Īśvara, in order to obtain the Knowledge of the Brahman; and the reason for that will be clear from my interpretation of the 59th stanza. Even Manu has given a warning to the man who merely controls his senses, when he says: "*balavān indriyagrāmo vidvāṁsam api karṣati*" (Manu. 2. 2-15), (that is, "the powerful group of the senses drags about even the wise man"—Trans.); and the same meaning is conveyed by the 60th stanza above. In short, the implied import of these three stanzas (that is, 59, 60, and 61—Trans.) is as follows; namely that, one who has to become a 'Sthitaprajña' must moderate his food and pastimes, and acquire the Knowledge of the Brahman; that, the Mind becomes free from the slavery of the senses only when one acquires the Knowledge of the Brahman; and that, the device of mortifying the body is only external and not efficacious; and the words '*matparāyaṇa*' also give the first indication of the Path of Devotion (See Gī. 9. 34). The word '*yukta*', which has been used in the above stanza, means 'one who has been perfected by means of Yoga'. In Gītā 6. 17, the word '*yukta*' means 'moderate'. But this word is used in the Gītā mostly to

ध्यायतो विषयान्पुंसः सङ्गस्तेषूपजायते ।
सङ्गात्संजायते कामः कामात्क्रोधोऽभिजायते ॥ ६२ ॥
क्रोधाद्भवति संमोहः संमोहात्स्मृतिविभ्रमः ।
स्मृतिभ्रंशाद्बुद्धिनाशो बुद्धिनाशात्प्रणश्यति ॥ ६३ ॥
रागद्वेषवियुक्तैस्तु विषयानिन्द्रियैश्चरन् ।
आत्मवश्यैर्विधेयात्मा प्रसादमधिगच्छति ॥ ६४ ॥

mean 'the person who has become an adept in bearing both pain and pleasure with a placid mind, by practising the Yoga of Equable Reason, which has been prescribed in the Gītā'. (See Gī. 5. 23). A person who has become an adept in this way is known as a '*sthitaprajña*', and his state is known as the '*siddhāvasthā*' (the state of Perfection); that state has been described at the end of this chapter, and also again at the end of Chapter V and of Chapter XII. The Blessed Lord has so far explained what is necessary for becoming a Sthitaprajña, after having lost pleasure in the objects of the senses. HE now first explains in the following stanza how pleasure arises in the objects of the senses, how this pleasure gives rise to the emotions of *kāma* (Desire), *krodha* (Anger), etc., how man is thereby ultimately ruined, as also how it is possible to overcome them.]

(62) The *saṅga* (that is, intimacy) of the man, who contemplates on the objects of the senses, with these objects of sense, continually grows. From this intimacy, there grows later on *kāma* (that is, the Desire to possess those objects of the senses); (and when there is an obstruction in the matter of the satisfaction of this Desire) from this Desire, there arises Anger; (63) from Anger, there arises *saṁmoha* (that is, Indiscrimination); from Indiscrimination, confused memory; from confusion of memory, destruction of Reason; and from destruction of Reason, there arises the total destruction (of the man). (64) But he (the man), whose Ātman (that is, whose internal sense) is within his control, is satisfied (in his Mind), though he moves about among the objects of the senses, with senses which have escaped from love and hate, and which are perfectly within

प्रसादे सर्वदुःखानां हानिरस्योपजायते ।
प्रसन्नचेतसो ह्याशु बुद्धिः पर्यवतिष्ठते ॥ ६५ ॥

नास्ति बुद्धिरयुक्तस्य न चायुक्तस्य भावना ।
न चाभावयतः शान्तिरशान्तस्य कुतः सुखम् ॥ ६६ ॥

his control. (65) When the Mind is satisfied, all his unhappiness is destroyed, because the Reason of the man, whose Mind is satisfied, is also immediately steadied.

[It must be borne in mind that these two stanzas (that is, 64 and 65—Trans.) clearly lay down the following propositions, namely, (i) the Sthitaprajña does not give up either Action or the objects of sense, but merely the '*saṅga*' (intimacy), and moves about among the objects of the senses with an unattached frame of mind; and that (ii) the peace of mind which he obtains is not the result of giving up Action, but of giving up the Desire for Fruit of Action; because, except for this, there is no difference between this Sthitaprajña and the Sthitaprajña who follows the Path of Renunciation. Both of them need the qualities of absence of Desire and peace of Mind; but the Sthitaprajña of the Gītā does not renounce Action, but desirelessly performs every kind of Action for universal good, and the other Sthitaprajña does not do so: this is the important difference between the two (See Gī. 3. 25). But the commentators on the Gītā, who favour the Path of Renunciation, look upon this difference as a minor difference, and for supporting their own doctrine, insist that the description of a Sthitaprajña given here is of the Sthitaprajña according to the Path of Renunciation. The Blessed Lord now describes those whose mind is not at peace, thereby more fully describing the nature of the Sthitaprajña—]

(66) The man, who is not '*yukta*', (that is, who has not become *yoga-yukta* as mentioned above), possesses neither (steady) Reason, nor *bhāvanā* (that is, Niṣṭhā, or fixedness, in the shape of a firm Reason); who has not fixedness, can have no tranquility; and how can he who is not tranquil,

इंन्द्रियाणां हि चरतां यन्मनोऽनुविधीयते ।
तदस्य हरति प्रज्ञां वायुर्नावमिवाम्भसि ॥ ६७ ॥

तस्माद्यस्य महाबाहो निगृहीतानि सर्वशः ।
इन्द्रियाणीन्द्रियार्थेभ्यस्तस्य प्रज्ञा प्रतिष्ठिता ॥ ६८ ॥

या निशा सर्वभूतानां तस्यां जागर्ति संयमी ।
यस्यां जाग्रति भूतानि सा निशा पश्यतो मुनेः ॥ ६९ ॥

acquire happiness? (67) The Mind which follows in the wake of the senses, which roam about (that is, move), (among the objects of sense), enslaves the Reason of a man, just as the wind (enslaves) a boat in the water. (68) Therefore, O Arjuna! his Reason is (said to have become) steady, whose senses (are) controlled on all sides from the objects of sense.

[In short, control of the senses by means of the control of the Mind is at the root of all means of reaching Perfection. When the senses have become disintegrated on account of the objects of sense and run in all directions, it is not possible for a man even to get the desire of obtaining Self-knowledge. As the desire is wanting, there is no resolute endeavour in that direction, and then there is neither tranquility nor happiness. Though this is what is meant, control of the senses does not mean totally destroying the senses and giving up all Action altogether; and, as is stated in the 64th stanza, the message of the Gītā is that one should perform all Action desirelessly, as has been shown in Chapter IV of the Gītā-Rahasya.]

(69) The Sthitaprajña is awake in that which is night for everyone else; and such a Jñānin looks upon that as night in which every other living being is awake.

[This paradoxical description is metaphorical. Ingnorance means 'darkness' and Knowledge means 'light' (Gī. 14. 11). That which the Ignorant dislike, that is, what to them is darkness, is desired by the Jñānin; and that in which the Ignorant are engrossed—that is, what for them is light—is 'darkness' for the Jñānin, that is to say, he does not want it. This is what is meant. For instance,

आपूर्यमाणमचलप्रतिष्ठं समुद्रमापः प्रविशन्ति यद्वत् ।
तद्वत्कामा यं प्रविशन्ति सर्वे स शान्तिमाप्नोति न कामकामी ॥ ७० ॥

§§ विहाय कामान् यः सर्वान् पुमांश्चरति निस्पृहः ।
निर्ममो निरहंकारः स शान्तिमधिगच्छति ॥ ७१ ॥

a Jñānin looks upon desire-prompted Action as contemptible, whereas ordinary people are steeped in such Action; and that Desireless Action, which the Jñānin likes, is disliked by others.]

(70) Just as all water enters, from all sides, the sea, of which the shores are not transgressed, though it is being filled on all sides, so is (true) tranquility obtained only by that person who is entered by all objects of sense (without disturbing his tranquility); not by one, who desires the objects of sense (is it possible that this tranquility is acquired.)

[This stanza does not mean that one should abandon Action in order to attain tranquility; what is meant is that the minds of ordinary people are confused by the Hope of Fruit, or by Desire, and their peace of mind is destroyed by the Action they perform; but the Mind of the man who has reached the Siddhāvasthā (the state of Perfection) is not distressed by Hope of Fruit. Whatever the number of Actions he has to perform, his peace of Mind is not disturbed, and he performs them remaining as peaceful as the sea; and he does not, therefore, suffer from pain or happiness. (See stanza 64 above and Gī. 4. 19). The Blessed Lord now summarises this subject, and tells Arjuna what this state of the Sthitaprajña is called—]

(71) He alone acquires tranquility, who performs Action having given up all Desire (that is, all Attachment) and become desireless, and who has not got mine-ness and egoism.

[The word '*carati*' (performs Action) has been interpreted by commentators who support the doctrine of Renunciation as meaning 'goes about begging'; but, that interpretation is wrong. The meaning which has been given to the words '*caran*' and '*caratām*' in the 64th and the 67th stanzas

एषा ब्राह्मी स्थितिः पार्थ नैनां प्राप्य विमुह्यति ।
स्थित्वा स्यामन्तकालेऽपि ब्रह्मनिर्वाणमृच्छति ॥ ७२ ॥

above must also be taken here. The Gītā has nowhere preached that the Sthitaprajña should become a mendicant. On the other hand, it has been clearly stated in the 64th stanza, that he should freely 'move about among the objects of sense', keeping his senses under control. Therefore, the word '*carati*' must be interpreted here as 'performs Action' or 'takes part in worldly affairs'. Śrī Samartha (Rāmadāsa) has given, in the latter half of the Dāsabodha, an excellent description of how the 'desireless scient' (Sthitaprajña) takes part in worldly affairs; and the same is the subject-matter of Chapter XIV of the Gītā-Rahasya.]

(72) O Pārtha! this is (called) that Brāhmic state; having attained this, the man does not remain in ignorance; and remaining in this state even at the end (that is, at the moment of death), he attains Release in the shape of '*brahmanirvāṇa*' (that is, of merger in the Brahman).

[The Brāhmic state is the ultimate and the best state in Karma-yoga (See Gī. Ra. Ch. IX pp. 319 and 344); and the important point about it is, that when this state has been reached, there is no more any Ignorance. This important point is particularly mentioned here, because, even if a man on any particular day experiences the Brāhmic state for a short time, he does not thereby get any permanent benefit. Because, if that man is not in that state of mind at the moment of death, he cannot escape re-birth according to the desire which may be in his mind at the moment of death (See Gī. Ra. p. 398). Therefore, in describing the Brāhmic state in this stanza, it is particularly mentioned that the Sthitaprajña maintains this state of mind even at the moment of death (cf. "*antakāle 'pi*", that is, 'even at the moment of death'). The importance of the Mind being pure at the moment of death has been described in the Upanisads (Chān. 3. 14. 1; Praśna. 3. 10.), and later on in the Gītā itself (Gī. 8. 5-10). As desire-prompted Action is the reason for being re-born several times, it is clear

इति श्रीमद्भगवद्गीतासूपनिषत्सु ब्रह्मविद्यायां योगशास्त्रे श्रीकृष्णार्जुन-
संवादे साङ्ख्ययोगो नाम द्वितीयोऽध्यायः ।

that Desire should be annihilated at least at the moment of death. And it naturally follows that in order that Desire should be annihilated at the moment of death, one must have practised the annihilation of Desire before one reaches the point of death ; because, the act of destroying Desire is extremely difficult, and it is not only difficult but absolutely impossible for any one to be easily able to annihilate Desire, except by 'special divine blessing'. (*viśeṣānugraha*). The doctrine that Desire should be pure at the moment of death has been accepted not only in the Vedic religion but also in other religions (See Gītā Ra. p. 614.]

Thus ends, the Second Chapter entitled SAṀKHYA-YOGA in the dialogue between Śrī Kṛṣṇa and Arjuna on the Yoga included in the Science of the Brahman, (that is, on the Karma-Yoga) in the Upaniṣad sung, (that is, told) by the Blessed Lord.

[As there is a description of the Sāṁkhya or the Saṁnyāsa doctrine in the beginning of this Chapter, it is called 'Sāṁkhya-Yoga'. But one must not, on that account, think that the whole of the chapter contains no other subject. There are usually many subjects in one and the same chapter ; but the chapter is named by reference to the subject which is in the beginning, or is the most important one in the chapter (See Gītā-Rahasya Ch. XIV, p. 625.]

तृतीयोऽध्यायः

अर्जुन उवाच ।

§§ ज्यायसी चेत्कर्मणस्ते मता बुद्धिर्जनार्दन ।
तत्किं कर्मणि घोरे मां नियोजयसि केशव ॥ १ ॥
व्यामिश्रेणेव वाक्येन बुद्धिं मोहयसीव मे ।
तदेकं वद निश्चित्य येन श्रेयोऽहमाप्नुयाम् ॥ २ ॥

CHAPTER III.

[After the Blessed Lord had proved to Arjuna that the dread which he had felt about killing Bhīṣma, Droṇa, and others was foolish, having regard to the immortality and the non-lamentability of the Ātman according to Sāṁkhya philosophy, and made to Arjuna a short exposition of his own duty, the principal subject-matter of the Gītā, namely, the exposition of the Karma-Yoga, was started in the Second Chapter; and, after stating that the only skilful way, or Yoga, by which it was possible to perform Action without incurring either merit or sin, was to perform it with a disinterested frame of mind, there is given a description, at the end, of the Karma-Yogin Sthitaprajña, whose Reason has thus become Equable. But, that does not exhaust the exposition of the Karma-Yoga. It is true that if any act is performed with an equable frame of mind, one does not incur sin. But, if it cannot be disputed that Equability of Reason is superior to Action (Gī. 2. 49), then it would be quite enough if one makes one's Reason equable like that of a Sthitaprajña; and it does not follow that it is necessary to perform Action. Therefore, when this doubt has been raised by Arjuna in the shape of a question, the Blessed Lord lays down in this and in the next chapter, that 'Action must be performed'.]

Arjuna said:—(1) O Janārdana! if it is Your opinion that the (Equable–) Reason is superior to Action, then, O Keśava! why are You engaging me in a terrible Action (of war)? (2) By this seemingly mixed (that is, double-meaninged) advice, You are, so to say, confusing my understanding;

श्रीभगवानुवाच ।

§§ लोकेऽस्मिन् द्विविधा निष्ठा पुरा प्रोक्ता मयाऽनघ ।
ज्ञानयोगेन साङ्ख्यानां कर्मयोगेन योगिनाम् ॥ ३ ॥

therefore, tell me definitely only that thing by which I shall attain *śreya* (that is, bliss).

The Blessed Lord said :—(3) O sinless Arjuna! I have said before (that is, in the Second Chapter) that in this world, the path is of two kinds: that of the Sāṁkhyas, by the Jñāna-Yoga, and that of the Yogins, by the Karma-Yoga.

[I have translated the word '*purā*'='before', as meaning, 'in the Second Chapter', and that is the straightforward meaning; because, the Blessed Lord has, in the Second Chapter, first described the Sāṁkhya philosophy, and then the Karma-Yoga philosophy. But, the word '*purā*' can also be interpreted to mean 'from the beginning of the world'; because, where the Narāyaṇīya or Bhāgavata religion has been described in the Mahābhārata, it is stated that the Blessed Lord created the two independent paths of Sāṁkhya and Yoga [*nivṛtti* (Renunciation) and *pravṛtti* (Action)], in the beginning of the world (See Śān. 340 and 347). As I have shown in great detail in Chapter XI of the Gītā-Rahasya (pp. 420 to 437) that (i) the word '*mokṣa*' (Release) is to be taken as understood behind the word '*niṣṭhā*', that (ii) '*niṣṭhā*' means 'that path by following which one ultimately attains Release', and that (iii) there are only two such paths, according to the Gītā, which are independent of each other, and are not parts of each other, I shall not repeat the same subject-matter here. The difference between these two paths has also been shown by me in the form of a tabular statement at the end of Chapter XI of the Gītā-Rahasya (p. 491). The Blessed Lord has thus mentioned the two paths of attaining Release. Now He clearly defines the nature of that *naiṣkarmya-siddhi* (Perfection by Desireless Action) which is incidental to them—]

न कर्मणामनारम्भान्नैष्कर्म्यं पुरुषोऽश्नुते ।
न च संन्यसनादेव सिद्धिं समधिगच्छति ॥ ४ ॥
न हि कश्चित्क्षणमपि जातु तिष्ठत्यकर्मकृत् ।
कार्यते ह्यवशः कर्म सर्वः प्रकृतिजैर्गुणैः ॥ ५ ॥

(4) (But) It is not that a man attains *naiṣkarmya* (that is, performing Action after destroying its binding force—Trans.) by not commencing Action; nor does one attain Perfection by merely making a Renunciation (tyāga) of Action; (5) because, whoever he may be, he does not remain even for a moment without performing (some or other) Action. The constituents of Prakṛti compel every being, that has become dependent, to (always) perform (some or other) Action.

[Commentators, who support the Path of Renunciation, have interpreted the word '*naiṣkarmya*' occurring in the first part of this stanza, as meaning 'Jñāna'; and in order to support their own doctrine, they have interpreted the stanza as meaning, "Knowledge is not acquired by not starting Action, that is to say, Knowledge can be acquired only by performing Action, in as much as Action is the instrument by means of which Knowledge can be acquired". But this interpretation is neither straightforward nor correct. The word '*naiṣkarmya*' occurs any number of times both in the Vedānta and the Mīmāṁsā philosophies, and Sureśvarācārya has even written a book entitled *Naiṣkarmya-siddhi.* But these principles of Naiṣkarmya are not new, but have been in vogue from before the time not only of Sureśvarācārya but even of the Sūtras on the Mīmāṁsā and the Vedānta. It need not be said that Karma (Action) is necessarily binding. Therefore, it is necessary to devise some means whereby the binding-force or faults of Karma or Action can be destroyed, in the same way as Doctors purify mercury by 'killing' it before it is used; and the state of performing Action by this device is known as 'Naiṣkarmya'. As Action, thus crippled. does not become an obstruction to Release, how to acquire this state is an important question in the science of Release. The Mīmāṁsā school answers this question by saying that if one performs the 'Daily' (*nitya*) ritual, daily, and the 'Occasional' (*naimittika*) ritual, when there is occasion for it, and eschews the 'Desire-prompted' (*kāmya*) and 'Prohibited' (*niṣiddha*) acts, one will escape the bond of Action, and can without difficulty obtain the '*naiṣkarmyāvasthā*' (the state of Abstention from Action). But Vedānta science has proved that this device of the Mīmāṁsā school is wrong; and this matter has been discussed in Chapter X of the Gītā-Rahasya (pp. 378, 379). There are others who maintain, that Action ('Karma') will not bind a person, if he does not perform it, and that therefore, one should abandon all Action, is order to attain the state of Inaction (*naiṣkarmyāvasthā*). In their opinion '*naiṣkarmya*' means 'Absence of Action' (*karma-śūnyatā*). But it has been stated in the fourth stanza that this is not correct, and that Perfection (*siddhi*), that is, Release (*mokṣa*) cannot be attained in that way; and the reason for saying so has been given in the fifth stanza. Even if one contemplates giving up of Action, yet, in as much as Action, like sitting, sleeping etc., does not stop so long as the Body exists (Gī. 5. 9 and 18. 11), no man whosoever can at any time totally abstain from Action. Therefore, Naiṣkarmya in the shape of total Abstention from Action is impossible. In short, the scorpion of 'Karma' never dies. Therefore, one must devise some means whereby that scorpion will become poisonless. The doctrine of the Gītā is that this device consists in destroying the Attachment which ties a person to the Action, and this device has been later on described several times in an exhaustive manner. But even to this position an objection may be raised that: though Naiṣkarmya may not mean 'total Abstention from Action', yet, in as much as, those who follow the Path of Renunciation, obtain Release by giving up all Action, the giving up of all Action is necessary for obtaining Release. But to this line of reasoning the reply of the Gītā is that, though the followers of the Path of Renunciation attain Release, that is not because they have given up Action; for, their attaining Release is the result of their Jñāna (Knowledge). If Release were to be obtained merely by

कर्मेन्द्रियाणि संयम्य य आस्ते मनसा स्मरन् ।
इन्द्रियार्थान् विमूढात्मा मिथ्याचारः स उच्यते ॥ ६ ॥
यस्त्विन्द्रियाणि मनसा नियम्यारभतेऽर्जुन ।
कर्मेन्द्रियैः कर्मयोगमसक्तः स विशिष्यते ॥ ७ ॥

abstaining from Action, even a stone ought to obtain it. Therefore, the following three facts stand proved, namely, (1) Naiṣkarmya does not mean total Abstention from Action; (2) no one can possibly give up Action even if he says that he will do so; and (3) giving up Action is not a means for obtaining Siddhi (Perfection); and this is what has been stated in the above stanza. When these three conclusions have been arrived at, the only way in which Naiṣkarmya-siddhi (Perfection by Desireless Action) can be attained is, by not giving up Action, but continually performing Action after destroying the '*āsakti*' (Attachment) by means of Jñāna (Knowledge). Because, though Jñāna alone does not give Release, yet, in as much as it is impossible to totally abstain from Action, it is necessary to perform Action, after having destroyed one's Attachment (*āsakti*) to Action, in order to get rid of the Bond of Action. This is what is known as 'KARMA-YOGA'; and the Blessed Lord now says that this method, which combines Jñāna (Knowledge) with Karma (Action) is of higher importance, that is, superior—]

(6) That fool, who merely controls the Action (of the hands and feet etc.), but continually thinks by his Mind of the objects of the senses, is called *mithyācāra* (that is, a hypocrite). (7) But the worth of that man, who controls his senses by means of his Mind, and starts the Karma-Yoga by means (solely) of the organs of Action, with an unattached Reason is, O Arjuna! very great.

[These two stanzas amplify the statement in the previous chapter that: 'in the Karma-Yoga, the Reason is superior to Action' (Gī. 2. 49). This stanza clearly says that the man, whose Mind is not pure, but who restrains the activities of his organs of Action only out of fear of others, or in order that other persons should call him good,

नियतं कुरु कर्म त्वं कर्म ज्यायो ह्यकर्मणः ।
शरीरयात्राऽपि च ते न प्रसिद्ध्येदकर्मणः ॥ ८ ॥

is not really a virtuous man, but a hypocrite. Those who point to the dictum: "*kalau kartā ca lipyate*", that is, "in the Kaliyuga, fault is found not with Reason, but with the Action", and who say that, whatever the state of one's Reason, one's Action should not be bad, should carefully note the principle laid down in the above stanza of the Gītā. It becomes clear from the 7th stanza, that the name 'Karma-Yoga' has been given in the Gītā only the 'Yoga of performing Action desirelessly'. Some supporters of the Path of Renunciation interpret this stanza as meaning that though this Karma-Yoga may be superior to the Path of Hypocrisy described in the 6th stanza, yet, it is not superior to the Path of Renunciation. But this argument is only a doctrine-supporting argument; because, the doctrine that Karma-Yoga is more worthy than, or superior to, the Path of Renunciation has been laid down not only in this stanza, but again in the beginning of Chapter V, as also in several other places (Gītā-Ra. p. 425 and 426). As the Karma-Yoga is, in this way, proved to be superior, the Blessed Lord now advises Arjuna to follow that Path only—]

(8) Perform the Action which has been *niyata* (that is, prescribed), (according to your *dharma*); because, it is better to perform Action than not to perform Action; (see) besides, (that), if you do not perform Action, (you will not get even food to eat and) even the Body will not be maintained.

[By the words 'besides' and 'even' (cf.: "*api ca*") it has been shown that 'keeping alive the body (*śarīra-yātrā*) is a very secondary object. Now the Blessed Lord starts the subject of Sacrificial Ritual (*yajña-karma*) in order to show what Action is '*niyata*' that is, 'prescribed', and for what other important reasons that Action has to be performed. As the Śruti religion of sacrificial ritual has now become extinct, readers do not now-a-days attach much importance to this subject. But, as these Yajñas and Yāgas (that is,

§§ यज्ञार्थात्कर्मणोऽन्यत्र लोकोऽयं कर्मबन्धनः।
तदर्थं कर्म कौन्तेय मुक्तसङ्गः समाचर ॥ ९ ॥

sacrificial ritual) were in full swing in the days of the Gītā, those were the things which were principally understood by the word 'Karma'; and it was, therefore, necessary to expound in the Gītā whether this religious ritual should be performed or not, and, if so, in what way. Besides, it must be borne in mind, that the word 'Yajña' does not mean only 'the Jyotiṣṭoma and other Yajñas prescribed by the Śrutis' or, 'sacrificing something or other into the Fire (*agni*)', (Gī. 4. 32). The word 'Yajña' embraces all Action, which was enjoined by Brahmadeva on all created beings, in accordance with the four different castes, after he had created the Cosmos, in order to achieve the smooth running of the Cosmos, that is to say, for '*lokasaṁgraha*' (universal welfare), (Ma. Bhā. Anu. 48, 3; and Gī. Ra. pp. 400–408); and these very rites have been described in our religious texts (*dharma-śāstra*), and are what are here meant by the word '*niyata*' (prescribed rites). Therefore, though the sacrificial ritual of the Śrutis is now extinct, this exposition of the cycle of Yajñas cannot be said to be meaningless in these days. From the point of view of religion, all this ritual has been prescribed because, it is '*kāmya*', that is, in order that man should thereby derive benefit and become happy. But in the second chapter above (Gī. 2. 41–44) is stated the doctrine that these purposeful or desire-prompted rites of the Mīmāṁsakas obstruct Release, that is to say, are inferior in worth. And here it is shown that it is necessary to perform that very ritual. Therefore, the Blessed Lord has explained in an exhaustive manner in the following stanzas how the good or evil contact or binding effect of these Actions can be made to disappear, and how the Naiskarmyāvasthā (state of Desireless Activity) is reached while performing Action; and all this is consistent with the Nārāyaṇiya or Bhāgavata religion described in the Bhārata.]

(9) This world is bound by Action other than that which is performed for the Yajña; perform (even) the Action (to be

performed) for it, (that is, for the Yajña), abandoning the Attachment or Hope of Fruit.

[In the first half of this stanza is given the doctrine of the Mīmāṁsā school, and in the other half, the doctrine of the Gītā. The Mīmāṁsā school says that in as much as the ritual of Yajñas and Yāgas has been placed on everybody's shoulders by the Vedas themselves, and in as much as this cycle of Yajñas is necessary in order that the affairs of the world created by the Īśvara should go on smoothly, nobody can give up Action (ritual); and that if he does so, he is to be looked upon as lost to the religion of the Śrutis. But it is a doctrine of the Law of Causality (*karmavipāka-prakriyā*) that, man has to suffer the consequences of each one of his acts; and according to this doctrine, it follows that man has to suffer the good or bad consequences of even the Action performed by him for the Yajña. To this the reply of the Mīmāṁsā school is that, in as much as the Vedas themselves have enjoined the performance of the 'Yajñas', and in as much as all Action which has to be done for the purpose of the Yajña must consequently be deemed to be acceptable to the Īśvara, such Action cannot be a source of bondage to the doer; but any other Action, performed for any purpose except for a Yajña, e. g., for one's own living, is an act not for the purpose of a Yajña, but merely for the benefit of oneself. Therefore, the Mīmāṁsā school refers to such Action as '*puruṣārtha-karma*' (Action performed for oneself); and it has laid down that every person must suffer the consequences, good or evil, of all such Action, that is, of Action other than that performed for the purposes of a Yajña, or in other words, of Puruṣārtha-karma; and this is the proposition referred to in the first line of the above stanza (Gī. Ra. Ch. III, pp. 72 to 75). The meaning, which some commentators arrive at, by taking 'Yajña' to mean 'Viṣṇu' (which is a secondary interpretation) so as to explain 'Yajñārtha' as meaning 'for the sake of Viṣṇu', or 'in order to dedicate it to the Parameśvara', is, according to me, a stretched and uncouth meaning. But here a question arises, namely: if a man does no other Action except what is necessary for the performance of a Yajña, does he escape the bondage of Action? For, Yajña is also an Action, and one cannot escape the fruit of it in the shape of obtaining heaven, mentioned in the Śāstras. And it has been clearly stated in Chapter II of the Gītā (Gī. 2. 40-44 and 9. 20, 21), that this Fruit in the shape of obtaining Heaven is obstructive to Release. Therefore, in the second part of the above stanza, it has been again emphasised that even the prescribed (*niyata*) ritual, which a man has to perform for the purposes of a Yajña, should be performed by him without entertaining the Hope of Fruit, that is to say, merely as a duty; and the same doctrine has been propounded later on when the '*sāttvika* sacrifice' has been defined (Gī. 17. 11 and 18. 6). When in this way all Actions are performed for the purposes of a Yajña, and that too without entertaining the Hope of Fruit, (1) they cannot affect a person adversely in any other way, according to the Mīmāṁsā doctrine, because they have been performed for the purpose of a Yajña, and (2) one does not thereby obtain the Śāstric, yet non-permanent, Fruit in the shape of heaven, as they have been performed 'without entertaining the Hope of Fruit', but attains Release. Such is the import of this stanza; and the same meaning has been again emphasised later on in the 19th stanza, as also in the 23rd stanza of Chapter IV. In short, the doctrine of the Mīmāṁsā school that "one should perform Action for the purposes of the Yajña, as it has not a binding effect", has been amended and amplified by the Bhagavadgītā as: "even the Action to be performed for the purposes of the Yajña, should be performed without entertaining the Hope of Fruit". But even to this position an objection is raised, by asking whether it is not better, for obtaining Release by escaping the bond of Karma, that one should take Saṁnyāsa (renounce the world) and give up all ritual, rather than go through the useless effort of amending this doctrine of the Mīmāṁsā school, and keeping alive the duty of a householder to perform Yajñas and Yāgas. The clear answer of the Bhagavadgītā to this is in the negative;

सहयज्ञाः प्रजाः सृष्ट्वा पुरोवाच प्रजापतिः ।
अनेन प्रसविष्यध्वमेष वोऽस्त्विष्टकामधुक् ॥ १० ॥
देवान् भावयतानेन ते देवा भावयन्तु वः ।
परस्परं भावयन्तः श्रेयः परमवाप्स्यथ ॥ ११ ॥
इष्टान्भोगान् हि वो देवा दास्यन्ते यज्ञभाविताः ।
तैर्दत्तानप्रदायैभ्यो यो भुङ्क्ते स्तेन एव सः ॥ १२ ॥

because, but for the cycle of Yajñas, the affairs of the world will not go on. Nay; this cycle has been created by Brahmadeva in the beginning of the world in order to maintain the world; and in as much as the well-being or the welfare of the world is what is desired by the Blessed Lord, no one can escape the performance of this Yajña-ritual. And this very import is embodied in the next stanza. In reading this chapter, my readers must bear in mind that the word 'Yajña' has not been used in the narrow meaning of the Yajña prescribed by the Śrutis, but that it includes the Yajñas prescribed by the Smṛtis as also all worldly Action prescribed for the four castes, according to their respective authority.]

(10) In ancient days, Brahmadeva created living beings (*prajā*) together with the Yajña and said (to them): 'By means of this (Yajña), may you grow; may this be to you a *kāma-dhenu* (that is, something which fulfils all desires). (11) By this Yajña, do you give pleasure (that is, prosperity) to the gods; (and) may those gods (in return) give you pleasure (that is, prosperity); pleasing each other (in this ay), may you (both) attain the highest *śreya* (that is, benefit); (12) because, the gods, being satisfied by the Yajña, will give you (all) desired enjoyments. He who enjoys (by himself alone) what has been given by them, not giving it (back) to them, is indeed a thief'.

[After Brahmadeva created this Universe that is, the world of the gods and all the other worlds, he was filled with anxiety as to how all these worlds would be maintained. He, therefore, performed austere religious practices for a thousand years; and having thereby pleased the Blessed Lord, He (the Blessed Lord) created the Activistic cycle

यज्ञशिष्टाशिनः सन्तो मुच्यन्ते सर्वकिल्बिषैः ।
भुञ्जते ते त्वघं पापा ये पचन्त्यात्मकारणात् ॥ १३ ॥

of Yajñas for the maintenance of all these worlds, and directed both the gods and the men to follow that arrangement and thereby protect each other: such is the description given in the Nārāyaṇīya doctrine mentioned in the Mahābhārata (Ma. Bhā. Śān. 340. 38 to 62); and the same has been repeated in the above stanza, slightly differently and with minor verbal alterations. This fortifies the proposition that the doctrine enunciated in the Activistic Bhāgavata religion is propounded in the Gītā. But, as the Bhāgavata religion considered the slaughter of animals included in the Yajñas as objectionable (Ma Bhā. Śān. 336 and 337), Yajñas by sacrifice of wealth took the place of the sacrifice of animals; and ultimately, the opinion that the Yajña by means of prayer *(japayajña)*, or by means of Knowledge (*jñāna-yajña*) was the most superior Yajña, came into vogue (Gī. 4. 23–33). It is clear that the word 'Yajña' means, all the Action (duties) prescribed for the four castes; and that this Yajña-ritual or Yajña-*cakra* (cycle of Yajñas) has to be kept going without a hitch in the interests of the maintenance of society (Manu. 1. 87). Nay, the 'Yajña-*cakra*' (cycle of Yajñas) mentioned later on in the 28th stanza is a kind of universal service (*lokasaṁgraha*), (See Gī. Ra. Ch. XI). It is, therefore, stated even in the Smṛtis that the Action productive of universal welfare, which the Blessed Lord thus created in the beginning of the world for the welfare both of the world of men and of the world of gods, should necessarily be kept going; and the same meaning has been made perfectly clear in the next stanza.]

(13) Those good men, who partake of what remains after the performance of the Yajña, are redeemed from all sin. But those, who (without performing the Yajña) cook (food) for themselves (only), such sinful persons eat only sin.

[In the Ṛg-Veda hymn 10. 117. 6, the same meaning is conveyed; and it is stated that: "*nārymaṇaṁ puṣyati no sakhāyaṁ kevalāgho bhavati kevalādi*", that is, "he who does

अन्नाद्भवन्ति भूतानि पर्जन्यादन्नसंभवः ।
यज्ञाद्भवति पर्जन्यो यज्ञः कर्मसमुद्भवः ॥ १४ ॥

not feed the '*aryamā*', that is, the friend, but eats alone, should be looked upon as a sinner". Similarly, there are to be found such stanzas in the Manu-Smṛti, as: "*agham sa kevalam bhunkte yaḥ pacatyātmakāraṇāt* । *yajñaśiṣṭāśanam hy etat satām annam vidhīyate*" ॥ (3.118), that is, "He who cooks (food) only for himself, eats only sin; what remains over after the performance of the Yajña is called *amṛt* and what remains over after everybody else has eaten (*bhukta-śeṣa*) is called *vidhas*" (Manu. 3. 285); and that food alone is the proper food for respectable people (see, Gī. 4. 31). The Blessed Lord now gives a more detailed explanation of how the Yajña is necessary for the maintenance of the world, or how the world depends on the performance of Yajñas, instead of the Yajña and other ritual being merely for the purpose of burning rice and sesamum into the fire, or merely for the purpose of obtaining heaven—]

(14) Living beings come into existence from food; food results from rain; rain results from the Yajña; and the Yajña results from Karma (that is, ritual—Trans.).

[Even the Manu-Smṛti describes the origin of man, and of the food necessary for his sustenance, in the same way. The stanza in the Manu-Smṛti is: "the oblation made into the Fire in a Yajña reaches the Sun, and then rain results from the Sun, that is, ultimately from the Yajña; food results from the rain, and life, from food" (Manu. 3. 76); and the same stanza appears in the Mahābhārata (Ma. Bhā. Śān. 262. 11). In the Taittirīya Upaniṣad (2. 1), this evolution is taken even further back, and the order of evolution is given as: "from the Paramātman was first born ether; and afterwards, air, fire, water, and earth came into existence, one after the other; and from the earth spring the vegetables, and from the vegetables, man". Therefore, the Blessed Lord, consistently with that order of creation, takes the evolution of created beings, which, in the last stanza has been brought as far as Karma, still further back to

कर्म ब्रह्मोद्भवं विद्धि ब्रह्माक्षरसमुद्भवम् ।
तस्मात्सर्वगतं ब्रह्म नित्यं यज्ञे प्रतिष्ठितम् ॥ १५ ॥

Prakṛti (Nature or Matter), and behind Prakṛti, right upto the Imperishable (*akṣara*) Brahman——]

(15) Know (that) the origin of Action (is) from the Brahman (that is, from Prakṛti), and this Brahman has sprung out of the *akṣara* * (that is to say, from the Parameśvara); therefore, (know that) the All-pervading Brahman is always 'primarily worshipped' (*adhiṣṭhita*—Trans.) in the Yajña.

[Some commentators interpret the word 'Brahman' in this stanza, not as Prakṛti, but as Veda. Although this interpretation would be correct in the meaning that "the Brahman, that is, the Vedas, originate from the Parameśvara", yet, the words "the All-pervading Brahman is in the Yajña", do not become intelligible according to that interpretation. Therefore, the meaning of the word 'Brahman', given in the Rāmānujabhāṣya, consistently with its meaning in the stanza, "*mama yonir mahat brahma*" Gī. 14. 3), (where it means Prakṛti), namely, 'Prakṛti, which is the Fundamental Substance of the world' appeals to me as better. Besides, the description, "*anuyajñaṁ jagat sarvaṁ yajñaś cānujagat sadā*", that is, "the Yajña is followed by the world, and the world is followed by the Yajña", which appears in the Śāntiparva of the Mahābhārata, where the chapter of Yajñas is going on (Śān. 267. 34), also becomes consistent with the present stanza, if the word is taken to mean Prakṛti. For, I have explained at considerable length in Chapters VII and VIII of the Gītā-Rahasya, that the world is nothing but Prakṛti, as also how Prakṛti springs from the Parameśvara, and how the entire activity of the world springs from the three-constituented Prakṛti. Besides, there is a description even in the Puruṣasūkta that the Gods created the world by first performing a Yajña.]

* '*akṣara*', means 'the Imperishable'—Trans.

एवं प्रवर्तितं चक्रं नानुवर्तयतीह यः ।
अघायुरिन्द्रियारामो मोघं पार्थ स जीवति ॥१६ ॥
§§ यस्त्वात्मरतिरेव स्यादात्मतृप्तश्च मानवः ।
आत्मन्येव च संतुष्टस्तस्य कार्यं न विद्यते ॥ १७ ॥
नैव तस्य कृतेनार्थो नाकृतेनेह कश्चन ।
न चास्य सर्वभूतेषु कश्चिदर्थव्यपाश्रयः ॥ १८ ॥

(16) The life of that man who does not move the cycle (that is, the cycle (*cakra*), whether of Action, or of sacrificial ritual), which has thus been started (for the maintenance of the world), is sinful; and the existence, O Pārtha ! of this slave of the senses (that is, of the person, who enjoys all by himself, without giving anything to the gods) is worthless.

[It has thus been proved that sacrificial Action, or the respective duties of the four castes, have been created by Brahmadeva—and not by man—and that these duties are necessary both for keeping the world going on (stanza 14), as also for maintaining oneself (stanza 8); and that, therefore, the Cycle of Sacrifice (*yajña-cakra*) has got to be continually kept going on in this world, unattachedly. That is to say, I have shown how the Karma-kāṇḍa in the Mīmāṁsā philosophy, or in the '*trayī dharma*' has been left untouched in the Gītā-religion by the device of the Unattached Reason (See Gītā-Rahasya, Ch. XI, pp. 478 to 482). But some commentators belonging to the School of Renunciation take exception to this by saying that, as the Self-Knower (*ātma-jñānin*) obtains Release in this world, and as he has already acquired here all that is to be acquired, it is not necessary for him to perform any Action whatsoever in the world, nor should he perform Action. Therefore, the Blessed Lord now gives in the three following stanzas the answer of the Gītā to that objection—]

(17) But, for the man who is merged only in the Ātman, content in the Ātman, and pleased with the Ātman, nothing (as of his own) remains (in balance). (18) Similarly, here (that is, in this world) he has nothing to gain whether by doing or by not doing (any particular thing) ; and there is

तस्मादसक्तः सततं कार्यं कर्म समाचर ।
असक्तो ह्याचरन् कर्म परमाप्नोति पूरुषः ॥ १९ ॥

no purpose (as of his own) which is mixed up with all created beings; (19) *tasmāt,* (that is, because the Jñānin does not in this way set store by anything in this world), you too do not have any Attachment (to the Fruit), but perform (your) duty; because, the man who performs Action, having given up Attachment, attains the highest (state).

[As commentators have very much distorted the meaning of these three stanzas (17 to 19), I will first explain their plain meaning. These three stanzas form really speaking only one sentence, in the shape of a reason and an inference. Out of these, the 17th and 18th stanzas first show the reasons generally given for the Jñānin not performing Action; and the inference drawn by the Gītā is stated in the 19th stanza, which starts with the word '*tasmāt*' (that is, 'therefore'), which shows the inference. It has been clearly stated in the 4th and 5th stanzas in the beginning of this chapter, that the Actions of sleeping, sitting, getting up, nay, of existing itself etc., cannot be given up in this world, even if one wants to do so; and that, therefore, '*naiṣkarmya*' is not achieved by giving up Action, nor is such Renunciation of Action any means for attaining Perfection (*siddhi*). But the argument advanced against this point of view by the School of Renunciation is: "It is not that we give up Action in order to obtain Perfection. Whatever anybody does in this world, he does it either for his own gain or for the gain of another. But the highest ideal of every man, namely, the Siddhāvasthā (State of Perfection), or Mokṣa (Release), is attained by a Jñānin as a result of Knowledge; and therefore, as there does not remain any more anything else which he has to acquire (stanza 17), it is all the same to him whether he performs a particular Action or does not perform it. Very well, if it is said that he must perform such Action for the benefit of other people, then he has nothing to do with other people (stanza 18). Then, why should he perform

Action at all?" To this the answer of the Gītā is: "If it is just the same whether one performs Action or not, then why should one insist on not performing Action? Perform whatever befalls you according to the Śāstras with a frame of mind free of insistence and thus become free. In this world, nobody has escaped Action, be he a Jñānin (sage) or an Ajñānin (ignorant person)". One cannot escape Action, and at the same time, the Jñānin does not need it for himself! Apparently, this seems to be a very great difficulty; but, the Gītā does not consider this problem as difficult, and says: "In as much as you cannot escape Action, therefore, it must be performed. But as there is now left no selfish instinct any more in you, perform it selflessly, that is, desirelessly; that is all". This very advice has been given to Arjuna in the 19th stanza by using the word '*tasmāt*' and, in order to further strengthen the argument, the illustration is given later on in the 22nd stanza, that the Blessed Lord, Who is the most Supreme Jñānin, continues to perform Action, notwithstanding that there is left nothing for Him to do. In short, the Gītā says that: "even taking as correct the state of a Jñānin as described by the School of Renunciation, that state, instead of proving the necessity of Renunciation of Action, strengthens, on the other hand, the position of continuing to perform Action desirelessly". But as this line of argument and this proposition of the Karma-Yoga science is not acceptable to the commentators of the School of Renunciation, they have not paid the slightest heed to the above mentioned logical arrangement of 'reason and inference' or to the general trend of argument, or even to the illustration given later on of the Blessed Lord Himself (See stanzas 7, 8, 9, 22, 25, and 30); and, breaking up these three stanzas, they have considered them as independent of each other; and, imagining the final doctrine of the Gītā to be contained in the statement, "for the Jñānin, no duty of his own remains" etc., which appears in the first two stanzas, they have maintained that the Blessed Lord advises the Jñānin to give up Action! But thereby, the advice given to Arjuna immediately afterwards in the third, that is to say, in the 19th stanza to "perform Action unattachedly" loses its bearing and cannot be accounted for. In order to get over this difficulty, these commentators have explained the advice to Arjuna to perform Action, as having been given because he was an Ajñānin (ignorant person); and they have thus satisfied themselves. But, even doing so, the word '*tasmāt*' in the 19th stanza becomes meaningless, and the interpretation advanced by these commentators becomes inconsistent with the previous and subsequent context, as also with the various statements in several places in the Gītā that a Jñānin should perform Action desirelessly, as also with His own illustration given later on by the Blessed Lord (See Gī. 2. 47; 3. 7, 25; 4. 23; 6.1; 18. 6-9; and Gī. Ra. Ch. XI. pp. 445 to 450). Besides, seeing that this chapter contains an exposition of the Karma-Yoga, no sane person will bring forward a totally out-of-place proposition like 'Renunciation of Action is the best' in the middle of the exposition of the Yoga of Action. Then, how could the Blessed Lord have done such a foolish thing? Therefore, these interpretations, which are stretched and purely doctrine-supporting, cannot be taken as acceptable. It has been stated in the Yoga-Vāsiṣṭha that even a Jñānin, who is a '*jīvan-mukta*' (Released in this life) must perform Action; and to the question of Śrī Rāma as to why the Emancipated should do so, Vasiṣṭha has given the following reply, namely,

jñasya nārthaḥ karmatyāgaiḥ nārthaḥ karmasamāśrayaiḥ ।
tena sthitaṁ yathā yad yat tat tathaiva karotyasau ॥

(Yoga. 6 U. 199. 4),

that is, "the 'Jña', that is, the Jñānin (Knower) has nothing to gain whether by performing or by abandoning Action; therefore, (*tena*), he performs it, as it arises". Similarly, in the concluding *upasaṁhāra* of this book, appears the stanza:

mama nāsti kṛtenārtho nākṛteneha kaś ca na ।
yathāprāptena tiṣṭhāmi hy akarmaṇi ka āgrahaḥ ॥

(Yoga. 6 U. 216. 14),

of which the first line shows the reason, by saying "to me, it is just the same whether something is done or not",

§§ कर्मणैव हि संसिद्धिमास्थिता जनकादयः ।
लोकसंग्रहमेवापि संपश्यन्कर्तुमर्हसि ॥ २० ॥

in the same words as the Gītā; and it is stated in the second line that, "why should I insist on not performing Action? I am performing whatever befalls me according to the Śāstras". Also, a little higher up, the Yoga-Vāsiṣṭha has borrowed *verbatim* from the Gītā the stanza: "*naiva tasya kṛtenārtho*" etc., and in the next stanza, it says: *yad yathā nāma saṁpannaṁ tat tathāstv itareṇa kim* ", that is, "therefore, (the *jīvan-mukta*) performs whatever befalls him, and does not pay attention to anything else". (Yo. 6 U. 125. 49, 50). Not only in the Yoga-Vāsiṣṭha, but also in the Ganeśagītā, where the same meaning is to be conveyed, the stanza is:

kiṁcid asya na sādhyaṁ syāt sarvajantuṣu sarvadā ।
ato 'saktatayā bhūpa kartavyaṁ karma jantubhiḥ ॥
(Ganeśagītā 2. 18),

that is, "there is nothing left for him to earn from other living beings; for this reason *(ataḥ)*, O Raja! everybody has to perform his duties with an unattached Reason". From this it will be clear that the mutual relation between the three stanzas as showing respectively the reason and the inference, as stated by me, is correct. As the Yoga-Vāsiṣṭha gives in one stanza what is shown in three stanzas in the Gītā, there remains no room for doubting the relation of reason and inference in that stanza. This line of reasoning of the Gītā has been later on adopted by the Buddhist writers of the Mahāyāna sect (Gī. Ra. pp. 798 and 816). The Blessed Lord now gives an illustration for emphasising the statement made above that, there no more remains any self-interest for the person who has attained Knowledge; that, he must perform his duties with a desireless Reason; and that, Desireless Action of this kind ends in Release, instead of obstructing it—]

(20) Janaka and others thus attained Release by performing Action. In the same way, it is proper that you should perform Action, keeping an eye to universal welfare.

यद्यदाचरति श्रेष्ठस्तत्तदेवेतरो जनः।
स यत्प्रमाणं कुरुते लोकस्तदनुवर्तते ॥ २१ ॥

[The first part of this stanza contains an illustration of how Release is attained by means of Desireless Action; and a different subject-matter has been started from the second part of this stanza. It has been proved that although a Jñānin has nothing to do with other people, yet, as such a person cannot escape the performance of Action, he must perform Action desirelessly. Although the argument that, 'since one cannot escape the performance of Action, one must perform it', may be perfectly logical, yet, it does not satisfy ordinary persons as much as it should. They are afraid in their minds that Action is to be performed merely because it is unavoidable, and that nothing else is to be gained thereby. Therefore, the Blessed Lord starts the second part of the stanza in order to show that securing universal welfare by one's Action is a real ideal to be reached in this world by the Jñānin. This is the reason for the words '*evāpi*' in the phrase '*lokasaṁgraham evāpi*'; and these words clearly show that a different subject has now been commenced. The word '*loka*' in the phrase '*lokasaṁgraha*' has a comprehensive meaning, and includes the putting, not only mankind, but the entire world, on a proper path, and making a '*saṁgraha*' of it, that is, maintaining, feeding, protecting, and defending it in a proper way, without allowing it to be destroyed. As these and other matters have been dealt with by me in an exhaustive manner, in Chapter XI of the Gītā-Rahasya (pp. 455 to 467), I shall not deal with them again here. The Blessed Lord now first explains why this duty or right of achieving '*lokasaṁgraha*' (universal welfare) falls to the lot of the Jñānin—]

(21) Ordinary people do what is done by the Exalted (that is, by the Self-Realised Karma-Yogin). That thing which is accepted by him as correct is followed by people.

[The Taittirīya Upaniṣad, after first giving the advice, '*satyaṁ vada*' (speak the truth), '*dharmaṁ cara*' (act righteously) says: "if you are in doubt how to act in any

न मे पार्थास्ति कर्तव्यं त्रिषु लोकेषु किंचन।
नानवाप्तमवाप्तव्यं वर्त एव च कर्मणि ॥ २२ ॥
यदि ह्यहं न वर्तेयं जातु कर्मण्यतन्द्रितः।
मम वर्त्मानुवर्तन्ते मनुष्याः पार्थ सर्वशः ॥ २३ ॥
उत्सीदेयुरिमे लोका न कुर्यां कर्म चेदहम्।
सङ्करस्य च कर्ता स्यामुपहन्यामिमाः प्रजाः ॥ २४ ॥

particular contingency of life, act as the knowing, Yoga-practising, religious Brahmin acts in that matter" (Tai. 1. 11. 4); and a stanza to the same effect also appears in the Nārāyaṇīya-dharma (Ma. Bhā. Śān. 341. 25). The Marathi stanza of Śrī Samartha, '*jasā vartato lokakalyāṇa-kārī* । *jagīṁ vartatī sarvahī tyā prakārīṁ*", (that is, "as the public benefactor acts, so also do all act in the world"—Trans.), is nothing but a translation of this stanza. This '*lokakalyāṇakārī*' person (i. e., 'public benefactor'—Trans.) of Śrī Samartha is the '*śreṣṭha*' Karma-Yogin of the Gītā. The word '*śreṣṭha*' does not mean a Self-Realised Ascetic (*ātma-jñānin saṁnyāsin*), (See Gī. 5. 2). The Blessed Lord now points to Himself as an illustration, for further emphasising the proposition that although a Self-Realised person may have got over his selfishness, he does not escape the performance of Actions for public welfare—]

(22) O Pārtha! (see this that,) there is left no duty (of mine) in the three worlds for Me; nor is there any not-acquired (thing left) to acquire; yet, I am performing Action; (23) because, if I, giving up idleness, do not take part in Action, then, O Pārtha! all men will follow in all respects the path followed by Me. (24) If I do not perform Action, these worlds will become *utsanna* (that is, extinct); I shall be the cause of *saṁkara* (that is, caste-confusion—Trans.); and these created beings will be destroyed by my hands.

[The Blessed Lord has made clear in this stanza in a very nice way that '*lokasaṁgraha*' (universal welfare) is not some humbug. So also does the illustration of Himself given by the Blessed Lord fully bear out the interpretation put by me on stanzas 17 to 19 above, namely, that,

§§ सक्ताः कर्मण्यविद्वांसो यथा कुर्वन्ति भारत ।
कुर्याद्विद्वांस्तथासक्तश्चिकीर्षुर्लोकसंग्रहम् ॥ २५ ॥
न बुद्धिभेदं जनयेदज्ञानां कर्मसंगिनाम् ।
जोषयेत्सर्वकर्माणि विद्वान्युक्तः समाचरन् ॥ २६ ॥

though no duty remains to be performed for the Jñānin (for himself), after he has acquired Knowledge, yet, he must perform all Action desirelessly. Nay, otherwise this illustration will be out of place and meaningless (See Gī. Ra. pp. 446–7). The important difference between the Sāṁkhya path and the Karma-Yoga path is that the Jñānins following the Sāṁkhya path do not attach the slightest importance to what will become of the world if the cycle of Yajñas come to an end, and they give up all Action, whereas the Jñānins following the Karma-Yoga path keep performing all their various Actions, according to their respective religion (*dharma*), for the purpose of universal welfare (*lokasaṁgraha*), looking upon it as an objective of the utmost importance and necessity, and though they may not need to perform such Actions for their own benefit. (See Gītā Rahasya, Chapter XI, p. 491). The Blessed Lord has thus told Arjuna what He Himself does. HE now shows in the following stanzas the difference between the Actions of the Jñānin (scient) and the Ajñānin (ignorant), and explains what a Jñānin has to do in order to reform the Ajñānin—]

(25) O Arjuna! (therefore) the Jñānin who desires to achieve universal welfare must behave in the same way as Ajñānins, who are attached to (worldly) Action, but having given up Attachment. (26) The Jñānin should not unsettle the *buddhi* (that is, Faith—Trans.) of Ajñānins attached to Action, but should (himself) become *yukta* (that is, *yoga-yukta*), and a performer of all Actions, and make others perform them willingly.

[This stanza means that one should not unsettle the faith, or conviction of the Ajñānins (ignorant), and the same direction is again given in the 29th stanza. But, this does not mean that people are to be kept in ignorance. In the

25th stanza, it has been stated that the Jñānin must achieve universal welfare (*lokasaṁgraha*); and 'universal welfare' means enlightening people. But to this an objection may be raised that though '*lokasaṁgraha*' may be a duty, yet, it is not necessary on that account that a Jñānin should personally perform Action; and it will be quite enough if he imparts wisdom to people. To this objection, the Blessed Lord replies that: 'if knowledge is merely orally imparted to those persons, who have not got into the firm habit of righteous Action, (and ordinary people belong to this category), we see that they make use of that Knowledge of the Brahman for supporting their own misdeeds; and they talk nonsense, saying, "such and such a Jñānin says so"'. Besides, if a Jñānin absolutely gives up all Action, that becomes an illustration for the Ajñānin to become idle. When people thus become wicked in thought, or mischievous, or idlers, a '*buddhi-bheda*' is said to have taken place; and it is not proper that a Jñānin should in this way unsettle (make a *bheda* of) the conviction (*buddhi*) of other people. Therefore, the Gītā has laid down the important doctrine that, it is an important duty of a man who has become a Jñānin, to remain himself in worldly life, for the purpose of '*lokasaṁgraha*', that is, in order to make people wise, and put them on the righteous path, and thus to give a living example to others of performing righteous, that is, Desireless Action, and make them act righteously. (See Gītā-Rahasya pp. 561–2). But some commentators disregard this import of the Gītā, and put a perverse interpretation on this stanza to mean: "the Jñānin should hypocritically perform the same acts which are performed by the Ajñānins, in order that the Ajñānins should remain Ajñānins, and perform Actions"! As if the Gītā has been written in order to teach people hypocrisy, and in order to keep people in ignorance and make them perform Actions like beasts! Those persons, who firmly believe that Jñānins should not perform Action will naturally look upon '*lokasaṁgraha*' as hypocritical. But, that is not the true message of the Gītā. The Blessed Lord says that '*lokasaṁgraha*' is one of the important duties of a Jñānin, and that a Jñānin must perform Action

प्रकृतेः क्रियमाणानि गुणैः कर्माणि सर्वशः ।
अहंकारविमूढात्मा कर्ताहमिति मन्यते ॥ २७ ॥
तत्त्ववित्तु महाबाहो गुणकर्मविभागयोः ।
गुणा गुणेषु वर्तन्त इति मत्वा न सज्जते ॥ २८ ॥
प्रकृतेर्गुणसंमूढः सज्जन्ते गुणकर्मसु ।
तानकृत्स्नविदो मन्दान् कृत्स्नविन्न विचालयेत् ॥ २९ ॥

not for keeping people in ignorance, but in order to place before them an excellent example, and to thereby improve them, (See Gītā-Rahasya, Chapters XI and XII). To proceed further; there is the likelihood of a doubt that if a Self-Realised Jñānin begins to do all worldly Actions in this way for universal welfare, he too will become an Ajñānin. Therefore, the Blessed Lord now shows the difference between the conduct of a Jñānin and an Ajñānin, though both may take part in worldly life, as also what the Ajñānin has to learn from the Jñānin—]

(27) Though all Actions take place as a result of the constituents (*sattva, rajas,* and *tamas*) of Prakṛti, the (Ajñānin person) befooled by egoism looks upon himself as the doer. (28) But, O mighty-armed Arjuna ! he (the Jñānin), who realises the principle that the constituents, as also Actions, are both different from himself, and that all this is nothing but the mutual inter-play of the constituents, does not become attached to it. (29) People befooled by the constituents of Prakṛti become attached to the constituents and to Actions; such non-scient and dull-minded people should not be spoiled by the Jñānins (by putting them on a wrong path by abandoning Action themselves).

[This stanza repeats the exposition made in the 26th stanza. The propositions laid down in the above stanzas, namely: Prakṛti and the Ātman are different from each other; Prakṛti or Māyā does everything, the Ātman does nothing; and he, who has Realised this, is the true '*buddha*' or '*jñānin*' etc., form part of the Kāpila-Sāṁkhya philosophy; and the reader is referred to the exhaustive exposition of this subject made in the seventh chapter of the Gītā-Rahasya (pp. 222 to 226). Many persons interpret the 28th stanza as

§§ मयि सर्वाणि कर्माणि संन्यस्याध्यात्मचेतसा ।
निराशीर्निर्ममो भूत्वा युद्ध्यस्व विगतज्वरः ॥ ३० ॥
§§ ये मे मतमिदं नित्यमनुतिष्ठन्ति मानवाः ।
श्रद्धावन्तोऽनसूयन्तो मुच्यन्ते तेऽपि कर्मभिः ॥ ३१ ॥
ये त्वेतदभ्यसूयन्तो नानुतिष्ठन्ति मे मतम् ।
सर्वज्ञानविमूढांस्तान्विद्धि नष्टानचेतसः ॥ ३२ ॥

meaning that the '*guṇaḥ*', that is, the 'senses', rove about in the '*guṇaḥ*', that is, the 'objects of the senses'. This interpretation is not incorrect; because, the eleven organs of sense and the five 'objects of the senses' (that is, *viṣaya*), such as, '*śabda*' (sound), '*sparśa*' (touch) etc. form part of the 23 qualities of the original Prakṛti according to Sāṁkhya philosophy; but I think that, the statement, "*guṇā guṇeṣu vartante*", has been made with reference to all the twenty-four qualities (Gī. 13. 19–22; and 14. 23). I have translated those words literally and in an exhaustive way. And saying that, although the Jñānin and the Ajñānin may both perform the same act, yet, there is a great difference between them from the point of view of Reason (See Gītā-Rahasya, pp. 430 and 450), the Blessed Lord now advises as follows, by way of summarising all this exposition—]

(30) (For this reason, O Arjuna!) making a '*saṁnyāsa*' (that is, dedication) of all Actions to Me 'with a mind fixed on the Highest Self' (that is, with an *adhyātmabuddhi*—Trans.), and giving up Hope (for the Fruit) as also Mine-ness, fight, without any mental perturbation.

[The Blessed Lord now explains the result of acting according to this advice and of not so acting—]

(31) Those devout (persons), who always act according to this advice of Mine, without finding fault with it, they too become free from Karma, (that is, from the bonds of Karma). (32) But, know that those, who do not act according to this My teaching, finding fault with it with a fault-finding vision, such '*sarvajñāna-vimūḍha*' (that is, utter fools), thoughtless persons, are utterly ruined.

[The description of the consequences of following or not following Karma-Yoga, given above to prove that the

§§ सदृशं चेष्टते स्वस्याः प्रकृतेर्ज्ञानवानपि ।
प्रकृतिं यान्ति भूतानि निग्रहः किं करिष्यति ॥ ३३ ॥
इन्द्रियस्येन्द्रियस्यार्थे रागद्वेषौ व्यवस्थितौ ।
तयोर्न वशमागच्छेत्तौ ह्यस्य परिपन्थिनौ ॥ ३४ ॥

Karma-Yoga, which prescribes Desireless Action, is the best, clearly shows what the doctrine propounded by the Gītā is. In order to supplement this disquisition on the Karma-Yoga, the Blessed Lord now describes the strength of Prakṛti (inherent nature), and the control of the senses necessary for resisting that power—]

(33) Even the Jñānin acts according to the natural tendency of his Prakṛti; all created beings act according to the inclination of (their respective) Prakṛtis; (in these circumstances) what can restraint (that is, pressure) do? (34) The liking and repulsion between the senses and the objects of sense (such as, sound, touch, etc.) are both *vyavasthita* (that is, fundamentally fixed). One should not become subject to this affection and repulsion, because, they are the (highway-robbing) enemies of men.

[The word '*nigraha*' in the 33rd stanza does not mean mere 'control', but means 'coercion', or 'insistence'. The Gītā favours the proper control of the senses. What is meant here is that it is not possible to totally destroy the natural tendencies of the senses by self-coercion or persistence. For instance, so long as the body exists, a man leaves his home to go and beg when he is hungry, however much he may be a Jñānin or wise, because hunger, thirst, etc. are natural tendencies. Therefore, this stanza means that the duty of a wise man lies, not in uselessly determining to totally kill the senses by force, but in keeping them within his control by '*saṁyamana*' (concentration), and turning his natural tendencies to universal welfare. Similarly, it is quite clear from the word '*vyavasthita*' in the 34th stanza that pain and happiness are two independent emotions, and that the one is not the absence of the other (Gī. Ra. Ch. IV pp. 136 and 182). In the incessant activity of Prakṛti, that is, of the

§§ श्रेयान्स्वधर्मो विगुणः परधर्मात्स्वनुष्ठितात् ।
स्वधर्मे निधनं श्रेयः परधर्मो भयावहः ॥ ३५ ॥

creation, it very often happens that we have to do things, which we do not want to do (Gī. 18. 59). It is impossible for us to refuse to perform them. On these occasions, the Jñānin performs these acts with a desireless frame of mind and purely as a matter of duty, and remains untouched by the sin or the merit of the Action, whereas, the Ajñānin becomes Attached to these things and thereby suffers pain. This is the great difference between the two from the point of Reason, as has been stated by the poet Bhāsa. But now the following difficulty arises: even taking it for granted that one should not forcibly kill the senses, nor give up Action, but should perform all Actions with an unattached Reason, yet, is it not more proper for the Jñānin to take to agriculture, commerce, mendicancy, or other similar mild and harmless Action, rather than to terrible and destructive acts like warfare? To this the Blessed Lord replies as follows—]

(35) Even if it may be easier to follow the religion of another, yet, one's own religion (that is, according to the religion of the four castes) is more meritorious, though it might be '*viguṇa*' (that is, full of faults); though death results (while acting) according to one's own religion, there is bliss in that; (but) the religion of another is risky!

['One's own religion' means the 'code of duties prescribed for every one by the Śāstras according to the arrangement of the four castes laid down by the writers of the Smṛtis'; it does not mean the science of Release (*mokṣa-dharma*). As the arrangement of the four castes, made by the writers of the Śāstras by allocating activities consistently with the special qualities of each, is for the benefit of everybody (Gī. 18. 41), the welfare of Brahmins and Kṣatriyas and the welfare of the entire society, lies in their respectively performing their own duties, notwithstanding that they become Jñānins (sages); and it is not proper for them to meddle with that arrangement every now and then. This is what the Blessed Lord says (Gī. Ra. pp. 464 and 697).

अर्जुन उवाच ।

§§ अथ केन प्रयुक्तोऽयं पापं चरति पूरुषः ।
अनिच्छन्नपि वार्ष्णेय बलादिव नियोजितः ॥ ३६ ॥

There is a Gujarati proverb in vogue which has the same meaning namely, "*jenūṁ kāma tenāthī thāya* । *bijo kare to gothāṁ khāya*". Anybody will admit that, even where the four-caste arrangement is not in vogue, it is in the best interests of everybody, that the man who has spent the whole of his life in the army should, when the occasion arises, do the business of a fighting-soldier, rather than that of a tailor; and the same argument applies to the four-caste arrangement. The question whether the four-caste arrangement is good or bad, is a different question altogether, and does not arise here. It is an unquestionable fact that other forms of activity are as necessary for the proper maintenance and protection of society as agriculture or other similarly harmless and gentle occupations. This stanza means that whatever occupation one may have once adopted, whether according to the four-caste arrangement, or of one's own free will, it becomes one's 'religion', and it is not proper to find fault with it when occasion arises and to forsake one's duty; and if necessary, one must die in the performance of one's own duty in life. Whatever occupation is considered, some fault or other can certainly be found with it (Gī. 18. 48). But it is not proper that one should, on that account, give up one's prescribed (*niyata*) duty. This very principle has been enunciated in the Brāhmaṇa-Hunter dialogue and Tulādhāra-Jājali dialogue in the Mahābhārata; and the first half of the 35th stanza is to be found in the Manu-Smṛti (Manu. 10. 97), and also later on again in the Gītā (18. 47). With reference to the statement, "one cannot carry out one's determination to kill the senses" in the 33rd stanza, Arjuna now asks why that should be so, and why a man is pulled towards evil deeds, against his will.]

Arjuna said: (36) O Vārṣṇeya! (that is, O Śrī Kṛṣṇa) now tell me by what inspiration does a man commit sin, not

श्रीभगवानुवाच ।

काम एष क्रोध एष रजोगुणसमुद्भवः ।
महाशनो महापाप्मा विद्ध्येनमिह वैरिणम् ॥ ३७ ॥
धूमेनाव्रियते वह्निर्यथादर्शो मलेन च ।
यथोल्बेनावृतो गर्भस्तथा तेनेदमावृतम् ॥ ३८ ॥
आवृतं ज्ञानमेतेन ज्ञानिनो नित्यवैरिणा ।
कामरूपेण कौन्तेय दुष्पूरेणानलेन च ॥ ३९ ॥
इन्द्रियाणि मनो बुद्धिरस्याधिष्ठानमुच्यते ।
एतैर्विमोहयत्येष ज्ञानमावृत्य देहिनम् ॥ ४० ॥
तस्मात्त्वमिन्द्रियाण्यादौ नियम्य भरतर्षभ ।
पाप्मानं प्रजहि ह्येनं ज्ञानविज्ञाननाशनम् ॥ ४१ ॥

himself desiring it, as though coerced ? The Blessed Lord said: (37) Know that in this matter, the enemy is that Desire, which is most greedy and most sinful, born out of the *rajas* constituent, and that Anger; (38) just as fire is covered by smoke, or a mirror by dust, or as the embryo is enveloped by the amnion, so has everything been enveloped by it; (39) O Kaunteya! that which is an insatiable fire, that constant enemy of Jñānins in the shape of Desire, has enveloped all Knowledge.

[This is a repetition of the statement of Manu that:

na jātu kāmaḥ kāmānām upabhogena śāmyati ।
haviṣā kṛṣṇavartmeva bhūya evābhivardhate ॥

(Manu. 2. 94);

that is, "Desire is never satisfied by the enjoyment of the objects of Desire; it grows more and more as does the fire to which fuel is added" (See Gī. Ra. Ch. V, p. 143)].

(40) The Senses, the Mind and the Reason are said to be the *adhiṣṭhāna* (that is, the house, or fortress) of it; by the support of these, it puts aside Knowledge and throws the man into confusion. (41) Therefore, O most excellent Bhārata! first control the senses and destroy this sinner, who is the destroyer of Jñāna (Spiritual Knowledge) and Vijñāna (specified Knowledge).

§§ इन्द्रियाणि पराण्याहुरिन्द्रियेभ्यः परं मनः ।
मनसस्तु परा बुद्धिर्यो बुद्धेः परतस्तु सः ॥ ४२ ॥
एवं बुद्धेः परं बुद्ध्वा संस्तभ्यात्मानमात्मना ।
जहि शत्रुं महाबाहो कामरूपं दुरासदम् ॥ ४३ ॥

(42) It is said that the senses (which know material external objects as they experience them) are '*para*' (that is, beyond); the Mind is beyond the senses, the *vyavasāyātmikā* (that is, discerning—Trans.) Reason is beyond the Mind; and It (the Ātman) is beyond the Reason. (43) O Mighty-armed Arjuna! thus Realising that, which is beyond the Reason, and controlling yourself by yourself, destroy this enemy, which is difficult to conquer, in the shape of Desire.

[In order that a person should be able to perform all Actions according to his own religion, and for universal welfare, having got rid of Attachment (*āsakti*) in the shape of Desire, one must have perfect control over his senses; and that is the only control over the senses, which is meant here. The Gītā does not say that one should forcibly kill the senses, and give up all Action (see Gī. Ra. Ch. V, p. 153). The stanza "*indriyāṇi parāṇyāhuḥ* etc." above (3.42) is from the Kaṭhopaniṣad, and I have shown in the Gītā-Rahasya that four or five other stanzas have been taken into the Gītā (see Appendix p. 741) from the Kaṭhopaniṣad. The purpose of the senses is to collect the impressions of the external world; and after the Mind has co-ordinated them, the Reason distinguishes between them; and the Ātman (Self) is beyond all these, and different from all these. This is, in short, the summary of the Science of the Body and the Ātman. (See the exhaustive consideration of this subject-matter at the end of Chapter VI of the Gītā-Rahasya pp. 179 to 201). As I have exhaustively considered in the tenth chapter of the Gītā-Rahasya (pp. 383 to 395) the moot questions relating to the doctrine of Causality (*karma-vipāka*), such as, how a man is incited to a particular act as a result of the emotions of Desire, Anger etc., notwithstanding that he may not wish to perform it, or how a man finds out a way even out of this

इति श्रीमद्भगवद्गीतासु उपनिषत्सु ब्रह्मविद्यायां योगशास्त्रे
श्रीकृष्णार्जुनसंवादे कर्मयोगो नाम तृतीयोऽध्यायः ॥ ३ ॥

situation by means of sense-control, as he has Freedom of Will, I shall not take up space by repeating the same subject-matter here. The question of the control of the senses has been considered later in Chapter VI of the Gītā.]

Thus ends the third chapter, entitled KARMA-YOGA in the dialogue between Śrī Kṛṣṇa and Arjuna on the Yoga included in the Science of the Brahman (that is, on the Karma-Yoga) in the Upaniṣad sung (that is told) by the Blessed Lord.

चतुर्थोऽध्यायः

श्रीभगवानुवाच ।

§§ इमं विवस्वते योगं प्रोक्तवानहमव्ययम् ।
विवस्वान्मनवे प्राह मनुरिक्ष्वाकवेऽब्रवीत् ॥ १ ॥
एवं परंपराप्राप्तमिमं राजर्षयो विदुः ।
स कालेनेह महता योगो नष्टः परंतप ॥ २ ॥
स एवायं मया तेऽद्य योगः प्रोक्तः पुरातनः ।
भक्तोऽसि मे सखा चेति रहस्यं ह्येतदुत्तमम् ॥ ३ ॥

CHAPTER IV.

[This chapter further emphasises the principles of Karma-Yoga which have been explained so far, namely, (i) as nobody can escape Karma (Action), Action must be performed, though the Reason may have become desireless ; (ii) 'Karma' means, such *karma* as Yajñas and Yāgas etc.; (iii) but, as this Karma (ritual) of the Mīmāṁsā school is productive of heaven, and consequently to a certain extent binding, it must be performed having given up Attachment (*āsakti*) ; (iv) even though selfishness disappears as a result of Knowledge, Action does not cease to be necessary ; and, therefore, even a Jñānin must perform Desireless Action, as such Action is essential in the interests of universal welfare. In order that Arjuna should not suspect that this course of conduct, or Niṣṭhā was something new, which had been prescribed for him, the Blessed Lord now first explains the ancient tradition of this teaching which has been handed down from preceptor to disciple.]

(1) I expounded this *avyaya* (that is, inexhaustible, or which is not touched by past, present, or future, and is permanent) (Karma-) Yoga to Vivasvat (that is, the Sun); Vivasvat expounded it to (his son) Manu ; and Manu expounded it to (his son) Ikṣvāku. (2) This Yoga, come into existence by this tradition, came to be known to the Royal Sages ; but, O Śatrutāpana ! (Arjuna), after the lapse of considerable time, it ceased to exist on this world. (3) That same ancient Yoga (Karma-Yoga-mārga) has been

expounded by Me to you to-day, as being the most supreme mystery (of all mysteries), because you are My disciple, and and are beloved of Me.

[I have proved in Chapter III of the Gītā-Rahasya (pp. 76–88) that the single word 'Yoga' used in these three stanzas has been used in the meaning of 'Karma-Yoga', that is, 'the method of performing Action with an Equable Reason', out of the two paths of life, namely, the Sāṁkhya and the Yoga. Although the tradition of this path of life which has been stated in these stanzas is of the utmost importance for understanding its origin, commentators do not seem to have paid much attention to the matter. In the description of the Bhāgavata religion given in the Nārāyaṇīya Upākhyāna of the Mahābhārata, Vaiśaṁpāyana says to Janamejaya that in the Śvetadvīpa, this religion was, from the Blessed Lord,

nāradena tu saṁprāptaḥ sarahasyaḥ sasaṁgrahaḥ |
eṣa dharmo jagannāthāt sākṣān nārāyaṇān nṛpa ||
evameṣa mahān dharmaḥ sa te pūrvaṁ nṛpottama |
kathito harigītāsu samāsavidhikalpitaḥ ||

(Ma. Bhā. Śān. 346. 9, 10)

that is, "acquired by Nārada; and O Rājā! the same illustrious religion has been imparted to you in the Harigītā, that is, in the Bhagavadgītā, together with the briefly stated ritual (*samāsavidhikalpitaḥ*)". Later on, it is again stated (Ma. Bhā. Śān. 348. 8) that, "this religion was expounded to Arjuna, who had become despondent in the war". This clearly shows that the Karma-Yoga in the Gītā has arisen out of the Bhāgavata doctrine (Gī. Ra. pp. 12 to 16). The tradition of this doctrine from the beginning of the universe has not been given in the Gītā out of fear of its taking up too much space; and reference has been made only to Vivasvān, Manu, and Ikṣvāku; but the real meaning of this statement becomes clear when one considers the entire tradition of the Nārāyaṇīya doctrine. Brahmadeva had seven lives. After the description of the tradition of the Nārāyaṇīya religion given in the first six of these lives is over, Vaiśaṁpāyana has again said to Janamejaya in the course of the further description of the Nārāyaṇīya doctrine as follows:—When the Kṛta-Yuga of the seventh, that is to say, the present life of Brahmadeva was over,

tretāyugādau ca tato vivasvān manave dadau ।
manuś ca lokabhṛtyartham sūtāyekṣvākave dadau ॥
ikṣvākuṇā ca kathito vyāpya lokān avasthitaḥ ।
gamiṣyati kṣayānte ca punar nārāyaṇam nṛpa ।
yatīnām cāpi yo dharmaḥ sa te pūrvam nṛpottama ।
kathito harigītāsu samāsavidhikalpitaḥ ॥

that is, "this doctrine was propounded by Vivasvān to Manu in the beginning of the Tretā-yuga; Manu gave it to his son Ikṣvāku for universal welfare, and Ikṣvāku then propounded it to the world; O Rājā! when the world has been destroyed, (this doctrine) will go back to Nārāyaṇa. This doctrine, and side by side with it, "*yatīnām cāpi*", that is, 'the Saṁnyāsa doctrine also', has been explained to you before in the Bhagavadgītā" (Ma. Bhā. Śan. 348. 51-53). From this, it becomes clear, that the tradition of the Bhāgavata doctrine given here relates only to the Tretāyuga, which came before the Dvāpāra-yuga at the end of which the Bhāratīya war took place; and that more has not been described out of fear for the amount of space which the description would take up. This Bhāgavata doctrine is nothing else but 'Yoga' or 'Karma-Yoga'; and this tradition of the Karma-Yoga having been propounded to Manu, appears not only in the Gītā, but has also been referred to in the Bhāgavata-purāṇa (Bhāg. 8. 24. 55); and the importance of the Karma-Yoga propounded to Manu has also been described in the 52nd chapter of the Matsyapurāṇa. But the subject-matter stated in any of these places is not as exhaustive and complete as in the Nārāyaṇīya Upākhyāna. When one realises that the tradition of 'Vivasvān to Manu to Iksvaku' does not at all apply to the Sāṁkhya doctrine; and that no third Niṣṭhā in addition to the Sāṁkhya and the Yoga doctrines has been propounded in the Gītā, the fact that this tradition is of the Karma-Yoga comes to be proved in a second way (Gī. 2. 39). But, although the tradition of the Sāṁkhya and the Yoga doctrines may not

अर्जुन उवाच।

§§ अपरं भवतो जन्मं परं जन्म विवस्वतः।
कथमेतद्विजानीयां त्वमादौ प्रोक्तवानिति ॥ ४ ॥

श्रीभगवानुवाच।

बहूनि मे व्यतीतानि जन्मानि तव चार्जुन।
तान्यहं वेद सर्वाणि न त्वं वेत्थ परंतप ॥ ५ ॥

be the same, yet, as the exposition of the Sāṁkhya or Saṁnyāsa doctrine is incidentally included in the exposition of Karma-Yoga (Gī. Ra. Ch. XIV, p. 660), Vaiśaṁpāyana has said that the *yati-dharma*, or the Saṁnyāsa doctrine, has been described in the Bhagavadgītā. In the description of the duties applicable to the four stages of life, given in the Manu-Smṛti, there is at the end of the sixth chapter a description of the Yati-dharma (religion of Ascetics), which is followed by a description, as of an alternative path, of the Karma-Yoga described in the Gītā or in the Bhāgavata doctrine, under the name of the 'Karma-Yoga of Vedic Saṁnyāsins'; and it is clearly stated there, that "the highest Release is ultimately obtained by continually doing one's duties desirelessly" (Manu. 6. 96); and this clearly shows that the Karma-Yoga was acceptable to Manu. And I have quoted authorities at the end of Chapter XI of the Gītā-Rahasya (pp. 505 to 509) to show that it was also acceptable to the other Smṛti-writers. Arjuna now raises the following doubt as to this tradition—].

Arjuna said: (4) Your birth is subsequent, and that of Vivasvat was beyond (that is, earlier); (that being so) how can I realise that You expounded (this Yoga) '*ādau*' (that is, before—Trans.)?

[In replying to this question of Arjuna, the Blessed Lord describes the work done by Him in His various incarnations and again emphasises the Attachment-less Karma-Yoga or the Bhāgavata doctrine, saying "I too have been performing Actions in this fashion"—].

The Blessed Lord said: (5) O Arjuna! both yourself and

अजोऽपि सन्नव्ययात्मा भूतानामीश्वरोऽपि सन्।
प्रकृतिं स्वामधिष्ठाय संभवाम्यात्ममायया ॥ ६ ॥

यदा यदा हि धर्मस्य ग्लानिर्भवति भारत।
अभ्युत्थानमधर्मस्य तदाऽत्मानं सृजाम्यहम् ॥ ७ ॥

Myself have lived through many lives. I know all this; (and) O Parantapa! you do not (this is the difference). (6) Being the Lord of (all) created beings, and free from births, (and) though the form of My Ātman never suffers '*vyaya*' (that is, modification), yet, governing My own Prakṛti, I come to birth by My own Māyā.

[In the Spiritual Knowledge contained in this stanza, a fusion has been made of the Kāpila-Sāṁkhya with the Vedānta philosophy. The Sāṁkhya doctrine is that the Prakṛti creates the world of its own accord; but the Vedāntins look upon Prakṛti as a form of the Parameśvara, and believe that the world is created as a result of the Parameśvara governing (becoming *adhiṣṭhita* in) His own Prakṛti. This unimaginable power of the Parameśvara to create the entire cosmos from His Imperceptible form is called 'Māyā' in the Gītā; and there are similarly such statements in the Śvetāśvataropaniṣad as "*māyāṁ tu prakṛtiṁ vidyān māyinaṁ tu maheśvaram*" (Śve. 4. 10), that is, "Prakṛti is nothing else but Māyā, and the Parameśvara is the Lord of that Māyā", and "*asmān māyī sṛjate viśvam etat*" (Śve. 4. 9), that is, "from it, the Lord of Māyā, creates this world". See the exhaustive discussion made by me in Chapter IX of the Gītā-Rahasya on the questions, (i) why is Prakṛti called 'Māyā'? (ii) what is the form of this Māyā? (iii) what is meant by saying that the world is created as a result of Māyā? etc. Having thus explained how the Imperceptible (*avyakta*) Parameśvara becomes Perceptible (*vyakta*), that is to say, how Karma is seen to have come into existence, the Blessed Lord now explains when and why He does so—].

(7) O Bhārata! whenever Righteousness declines and Unrighteousness becomes powerful, then I Myself come to

परित्राणाय साधूनां विनाशाय च दुष्कृताम् ।
धर्मसंस्थापनार्थाय संभवामि युगे युगे ॥ ८ ॥

§§ जन्म कर्म च मे दिव्यमेवं यो वेत्ति तत्त्वतः ।
त्यक्त्वा देहं पुनर्जन्म नैति मामेति सोऽर्जुन ॥ ९ ॥

वीतरागभयक्रोधा मन्मया मामुपाश्रिताः ।
बहवो ज्ञानतपसा पूता मद्भावमागताः ॥ १० ॥

birth. (8) I take birth in different Yugas for protecting the Righteous and destroying the Unrighteous, and for establishing Righteousness.

[In both these stanzas, the word 'Dharma' does not mean 'the Vedic religion relating to life in the other world'. The word principally means and includes the duties of the four castes, justice, morality, and other similar things. The import of this stanza is that when injustice, immorality, cruelty, and tyranny begin to rule in the world and the righteous are harassed and the unrighteous predominate, the Blessed Lord becomes incarnated in the shape of a brilliant and powerful human being, in order that proper order should rule in the world which He created, and that the world should derive happiness (Gī. 10. 41); and He thus re-establishes the disorganised condition of the world. It has been stated in the previous chapter that '*lokasaṁgraha*' (Universal welfare) is only another name for the work which the Blessed Lord does by becoming incarnated in this manner; and that the Self-Realised (*ātma-jñānins*) must do the same work as far as their power or authority extends. (Gī. 3. 20). It has thus been stated when and for what reason the Parameśvara becomes incarnated. The Blessed Lord now explains what state is attained by those persons who realise this principle and act according to it—]

(9) He, who understands the principle underlying these transcendental births and Actions, he, O Arjuna !, after shedding the Body, comes and joins Me, without being re-born. (10) Many people, whose love, anger, and fear have gone, who are devoted to Me, and seek shelter in Me,

§§ ये यथा मां प्रपद्यन्ते तांस्तथैव भजाम्यहम् ।
मम वर्त्मानुवर्तन्ते मनुष्याः पार्थ सर्वशः ॥ ११ ॥

becoming (thus) pure by the austerity in the shape of Knowledge, have come and become merged in My Form.

[In order to understand the transcendental births of the Blessed Lord, it is necessary to understand how the Paramesvara becomes qualityful as a result of Māyā; and when one understands that, one acquires Spiritual Knowledge; and when one fully understands the transcendental Karma or Action of the Blessed Lord, one becomes acquainted with the principle of remaining unattached to Karma even after performing it. In short, when one has fully understood the transcendental births and the transcendental Karma of the Paramesvara, one becomes fully acquainted with both Spiritual Knowledge and Karma-Yoga; and, as that is all which is necessary for obtaining Release, such a person cannot but ultimately obtain union with the Blessed Lord. Therefore, when a man has Realised the transcendental births and the transcendental Karma of the Blessed Lord, that is all he need Realise; and it is not necessary to separately study Spiritual Knowledge or the Desireless Karma-Yoga. Therefore, the Blessed Lord asks you to contemplate on His births and deeds, and understand the principle underlying them, and act accordingly; and says that, having done this, nothing else is required to be done for obtaining union with the Blessed Lord. This is indeed the true worship of the Blessed Lord. The Blessed Lord now mentions the fruit and the usefulness of inferior kinds of worship—]

(11) In that way in which they worship Me, I give them Fruit accordingly. O Pārtha! whichever path is followed, a man ultimately comes and joins into My path.

[The latter portion of this stanza, namely, "*mama vartmānuvartante*" etc., has come above (3. 23) in a somewhat different meaning; and that will show how the meaning of words differs in the Gītā according to anterior and posterior contexts. The Blessed Lord now explains why

काङ्क्षन्तः कर्मणां सिद्धिं यजन्त इह देवताः ।
क्षिप्रं हि मानुषे लोके सिद्धिर्भवति कर्मजा ॥ १२ ॥
§§ चातुर्वर्ण्यं मया सृष्टं गुणकर्मविभागशः ।
तस्य कर्तारमपि मां विद्ध्यकर्तारमव्ययम् ॥ १३ ॥

different persons reach Him by different paths, if it is true that by whichever way one goes, one ultimately reaches the Parameśvara—]

(12) People, who desire (only) the Fruit of Action (and not the destruction of the bonds of Karma), worship deities in this world, because, (that) Fruit of Action is soon obtained in this world of human beings.

[These very ideas have appeared again later on in Chapter VII (See Gī. 7. 21, 22). The true fruit of the worship of the Parameśvara is Release, and it is obtained only after the bond of Action has been fully destroyed, after a considerable length of time and by deep and solitary worship; but, very few persons are so far-sighted or industrious. This stanza means that almost all people want to have something or other in this world, as the Fruit of their Action; and that such people run after deities (Gī. Ra. Ch. XIII p. 589). But the Gītā says that this is in the end a kind of worship of the Parameśvara, and that when this Yoga grows, it ultimately culminates in Desireless Worship, and eventually Release is obtained (Gī. 7. 19). The Blessed Lord has explained before that the Parameśvara becomes incarnated for the re-establishment of Righteousness. HE now explains in short what is necessary to be done for the re-establishment of Righteousness.—]

(13) I Myself have created the arrangement of the four castes (into Brahmins, Kṣatriyas, Vaiśyas, and Śūdras), consistently with the differences in their qualities and Actions. It is I, Who am the Maker of it, and (I am) also an *akartā* (that is, One Who has not made that arrangement), and *avyaya* (that is, inexhaustible—Trans.).

[This stanza means that although the Parameśvara is the Doer (*kartā*), yet, as He is always unattached (*niḥsaṅga*) as

न मां कर्माणि लिम्पन्ति न मे कर्मफले स्पृहा ।
इति मां योऽभिजानाति कर्मभिर्न स बद्ध्यते ॥ १४ ॥
एवं ज्ञात्वा कृतं कर्म पूर्वैरपि मुमुक्षुभिः ।
कुरु कर्मैव तस्मात्त्वं पूर्वैः पूर्वतरं कृतम् ॥ १५ ॥

described in the next stanza, He is necessarily a Non-Doer (*akartā*), (See Gītā. 5. 14). There are also other apparently inconsistent descriptions later on of the form of the Parameśvara, e.g., "*sarvendriyaguṇābhāsaṁ sarvendriyavivarjitaṁ*" (Gī. 13. 14). See the description of the difference between the qualities of the four different castes later on in Chapter XVIII (18. 41-49). The Blessed Lord now explains the hidden meaning of the words, 'One Who does, and at the same time, does not do', which the Blessed Lord has used with reference to Himself—]

(14) I am not touched by the *lepa*, (that is, the adverse effect) of Karma, because, My Desire is not in the Fruit of Action. He who Knows Me in that way, is not affected by Karma.

[It has been stated above in the 9th stanza that "he who understands My birth and My Action attains Release". This stanza contains an elucidation of the principle of 'Action' mentioned in that stanza. The word 'understands' means and includes 'understands and acts accordingly'. This stanza means that the Blessed Lord is not affected by the Action which He performs, because He does not perform the Action, entertaining the Hope of Fruit; and he who understands this principle and acts accordingly cannot be affected by Action. The Blessed Lord now fortifies the proposition laid down in this stanza by an actual example—]

(15) Knowing this, those who strove after Emancipation in ancient times, also performed Action; therefore, do you also perform the Action (Karma) performed by the ancients in the past.

[A definite advice has been given to Arjuna to perform Action, as there is no antagonism between Action and Release. But this gives rise to a doubt as to what is essentially

§§ किं कर्म किमकर्मेति कवयोऽप्यत्र मोहिताः ।
तत्ते कर्म प्रवक्ष्यामि यज्ज्ञात्वा मोक्ष्यसेऽशुभात् ॥ १६ ॥

कर्मणो ह्यपि बोद्धव्यं बोद्धव्यं च विकर्मणः ।
अकर्मणश्च बोद्धव्यं गहना कर्मणो गतिः ॥ १७ ॥

meant by the opinion of the School of Renunciation that 'Release is attained by Abandonment of Action, that is, by Inaction (*akarma*)'. Therefore, the Blessed Lord now starts a disquisition on what Action is; and He ultimately lays down in the 23rd stanza the proposition that Non-Action (*akarma*) does not consist in giving up Action; and that, Desireless Action is to be called Non-Action (*akarma*).]

(16) Even the Wise are confused as to what is *karma* (Action—Trans.), and what is *akarma* (Abandonment of Action—Trans.); (therefore,) I shall explain to you that kind of Karma, by knowing which, you will be free from sin.

['*akarma*' is a '*nañ-samāsa*'; and the '*a*'='*nañ*', in it, grammatically means both 'absence of' (*abhāva*), or 'impropriety of' (*aprāśastya*); and it cannot be said that both these meanings may not be meant here. Nevertheless, as a third division of Action called '*vikarma*' has been mentioned in the next stanza, the word '*akarma*' in this stanza must be taken to mean particularly, that 'Abandonment of Action' which the School of Renunciation called 'the literal abandonment of Action'. Nay, it will be seen from my commentary on the 18th stanza, that it is not necessary to totally abandon Action, as prescribed by the School of Renunciation; that, such Abandonment of Action is not true '*akarma*'; and that, the true meaning of the word '*akarma*' is quite different.]

(17) The path (*gatiḥ*—Trans.) of Karma is moot; (therefore,) it is necessary to understand what is *karma*, (that is, Action—Trans.) and it is necessary to understand what is *vikarma (viparīta karma)*, (that is, Wrong Action—Trans.); and it is also necessary to understand what is

कर्मण्यकर्म यः पश्येदकर्माणि च कर्म यः ।
स बुद्धिमान् मनुष्येषु स युक्तः कृत्स्नकर्मकृत् ॥ १८ ॥

akarma (not performing Action). (18) That man, who sees Inaction in Action, and Action in Inaction, is the Jñānin (sage—Trans.) among men; he is *'yukta'*, (that is, *'yoga-yukta'*), (that is, steeped in the Karma-Yoga—Trans.), and one who performs all Actions.

[This and the following five stanzas contain a description of '*karma*', and '*akarma*' and '*vikarma*'; and whatever has been left over here has been made up later on in Chapter XVIII, where the three kinds of Abandonment of Action (*karma-tyāga*), the three kinds of Action (*karma*) and the three kinds of Doers (*kartā*) have been explained (Gī. 18. 4–9 ; 23–25 ; and 26–28). It is necessary to explain here in short and clearly what the doctrines of the Gītā are about *karma*, *akarma*, and *vikarma*, having regard to the disquisitions on Karma in these two places; because, the commentators have created a considerable amount of confusion about these things. The followers of the School of Renunciation favour the 'literal' abandonment of Action; and, therefore, they try to stretch the meaning of the term '*akarma*' here in support of their own doctrine; and the followers of the Mīmāṁsā school favour desire-prompted Action like Yajñas and Yāgas; and look upon everything else as '*vikarma*'. There are besides, the differences of the Mīmāṁsā school between the Daily (*nitya*) and the Occasional (*naimittika*) Action; and the supporters of the Śāstras try at the same time to push forward their own doctrine. In short, as a result of this stretching in all directions, it ultimately becomes very difficult to understand what the Gītā understands as '*akarma*' and what as '*vikarma*'. Therefore, it must be borne in mind in the first instance, that the scientific basis on which this point has been considered in the Gītā is the path of the Karma-Yogin, who performs Action desirelessly; and not of the Mīmāṁsakas, who perform Desire-prompted Action, nor of the followers of the School of Renunciation, who abandon Action. When one accepts this basis of the Gītā, it follows first of all that '*akarma*' cannot possibly mean '*karmaśūnyatā*' (total absence of Action); and that no man can under any circumstances be Inactive (Gī. 2. 5; 18. 11); because, nobody can escape sleeping, sitting, or at any rate, being alive; and if it is impossible to be totally Inactive (*karma-śūnya*), one has to decide what is meant by '*akarma*'. To this the reply of the Gītā is: Do not look upon 'Karma' as 'the mere performing of Action'; but decide as to whether an Action is '*karma*' or '*akarma*' by considering the good or bad results which flow from it. If the Cosmos itself is *karma*, man cannot escape *karma*, so long as he exists in the Cosmos. Therefore, the consideration of what a man should do or not do, must be from the point of view of to what extent such Action will prejudicially affect him. That Action, which being performed, does not prejudicially affect the Doer, must be deemed to have lost its nature of being a '*karma*' (that is, its '*karmatva*'), or its binding force (*bandhakatva*); and if in this way, any Karma loses its '*karmatva*' or '*bandhakatva*', then necessarily that '*karma*' becomes an '*akarma*'. It is true that the ordinary meaning of the word '*akarma*' is 'total absence of Action' (*karma-śūnyatā*); but considering the matter scientifically, that meaning is not appropriate here, because even 'sitting quiet', that is, 'not doing anything', is very often an Action in itself. For instance, if one sits quiet, when someone is hammering one's parents, and does not do anything to protect them, that is 'Inaction' (*akarma*), that is, 'total absence of Action' (*karmaśūnyatva*), according to the ordinary meaning of the word. It is nevertheless an 'Action' (*karma*), nay, even a Wrong Action (*vikarma*); and, according to the doctrine of Causality, one cannot escape the evil results of this kind of Action. Therefore, the Gītā says paradoxically and very skilfully in this stanza that he who understands that even '*akarma*' amounts to '*karma*' (sometimes, even very terrible *karma*); and also that even in performing Action, such Action is 'dead action' or '*akarma*' from the point of view of Causality, is the real Jñānin; and this meaning has been explained in different ways in the subsequent stanzas.

According to the Gītā science, the only true means by which one escapes the bondage of Action is by performing Action unattachedly, that is, 'giving up the Hope of Fruit' (See Gī. Ra. Ch. V. pp. 148 to 156 and Ch. X. p. 394). Therefore, that Action alone, which is performed in this way, that is, unattachedly, is the proper, that is, the *sāttvika* Action, according to the Gītā (Gī. 18. 9). That is the true 'Non-Action' (*akarma*) according to the Gītā; because, its '*karmatva*' (that is, its nature of being a '*karma*'), or its binding force (*bandhakatva*) according to the law of Causality (*karma-vipāka-prakriyā*) is lost. When, from all that men do, (and even sitting idle is included in the word 'do'), Action of the above kind, that is, *śāttvika* Action, or, '*akarma*' according to the Gītā, is deducted, all that remains can be divided into two parts, namely, (i) *rājasa* Action and (ii) *tāmasa* Action. Out of this, *tāmasa* Action is the result of Ignorance (*moha*), and therefore, it falls into the category of Wrong Action (*vikarma*). Thus, if Action is abandoned as a result of Ignorance, it is still a '*vikarma*', not an '*akarma*' (Gī. 18. 7). Then remains the *rājasa* Action. This Action is not of the first class, that is, *sāttvika*; nor is it what the Gītā describes as true '*akarma*'. The Gītā calls this '*rājasa* Action'; but if any one wants to do so, he may use the single word '*karma*' to mean this kind of *rājasa* Action. In short, whether a particular Action is a '*karma*' or an '*akarma*' is to be decided according to the binding force of the Action, and not from its nature of being an act, nor also according to what may be laid down in barren religious treatises. The Aṣṭāvakra-Gītā supports the Path of Renunciation. Yet, even in it, it is said that:

nivṛttir api mūḍhasya pravṛttir upajāyate ।
pravṛttir api dhīrasya nivṛttiphalabhāginī ॥

(Aṣṭā. 18. 61);

that is: "the '*nivṛtti*' of fools, that is, their turning away from Action, as a result of perversity or of Ignorance, in itself amounts to '*pravṛtti*' or 'Karma'; and the '*pravṛtti*' of the wise, that is to say, their Desireless Action, gives the same benefit as *nivṛtti* (*i.e.*, Renunciation) or *karmatyāga*

यस्य सर्वे समारम्भाः कामसङ्कल्पवर्जिताः ।
ज्ञानाग्निदग्धकर्माणं तमाहुः पण्डितं बुधाः ॥ १९ ॥
त्यक्त्वा कर्मफलासङ्गं नित्यतृप्तो निराश्रयः ।
कर्मण्यभिप्रवृत्तोऽपि नैव किंचित् करोति सः ॥ २० ॥
निराशीर्यतचित्तात्मा त्यक्तसर्वपरिग्रहः ।
शारीरं केवलं कर्म कुर्वन्नाप्नोति किल्बिषम् ॥ २१ ॥

(that is, Abandonment of Action)". This very meaning has been very skilfully, paradoxically, and metaphorically set out in the above stanza; and unless one carefully bears in mind this definition of '*akarma*', he cannot fully understand the argument about '*karma*' and '*akarma*' in the Gītā. The Blessed Lord now explains this very meaning more explicitly in the following stanzas—]

(19) He, whose *samārambhāḥ* (that is, Actions) are devoid of the Desire for Fruit, is referred to by Jñānins, as the learned man, whose Actions are reduced to ashes in the Fire of Knowledge.

[This clearly shows that, "*karma* (Action) is reduced to ashes by *jñāna*", is not to be understood as directing Abandonment of Action, but the performance of Action, having abandoned the Desire for Fruit. (Gī. Ra. Ch. X. pp. 394-400). Similarly, the meaning of the words '*sarvārambha-parityāgī*',—that is, 'one who gives up all *ārambha* or activity',—which appear later on in the description of the devotee of the Blessed Lord (Gī. 12. 16; 14. 25), is also made clear by this. Now the Blessed Lord makes the same meaning more explicit as follows—]

(20) (The man) Who, having given up the Attachment for the Fruit of Action, is always happy and *nirāśraya* [that is, one who does not possess a Reason, which has taken 'shelter' (*āśraya*—Trans.) in the means of obtaining the Fruit of Action, by wishing to do a particular Action, for a particular result] is (said to be) doing nothing whatsoever, though he may be engrossed in performing Actions. (21) When a person, who gives up the *āśīḥ* (that is, the Desire for Fruit), who regulates his Mind, and who has become free

यदृच्छालाभसंतुष्टो द्वन्द्वातीतो विमत्सरः ।
समः सिद्धावसिद्धौ च कृत्वापि न निबद्धयते ॥ २२ ॥
गतसङ्गस्य मुक्तस्य ज्ञानावस्थितचेतसः ।
यज्ञायाचरतः कर्म समग्रं प्रविलीयते ॥ २३॥

from all Attachments, performs Actions, which are merely *śārīra* (that is, performed by the Body, or only by the organs of Action), he does not incur sin.

[Some commentators interpret the word '*nirāśraya*' in the 20th stanza as 'one who has no home', that is, a Saṁnyāsin; but that is not correct. The word '*āśraya*' may be interpreted to mean 'house' or 'home'; but what is meant in the present place is not the 'home' of the person who does the act, but the 'home' in the shape of 'a motive for the act which he performs'; and what is meant is, that there should be no such 'home'; and the same meaning has been made clear in the words '*anāśritaḥ karmaphalaṁ*' (Gī. 6. 1); and the same meaning has also been adopted by Waman Pandit in his Marathi commentary on the Gītā known as the *Yathārthadīpikā*. Similarly, the word '*śārīra*' in the 21st stanza does not mean the Action of begging alms sufficient for the maintenance of the body, etc. The true meaning of the words '*kevalaṁ śārīraṁ karma*' is consistent with the description contained later on in Chapter V (5. 11) that, "Yogins, that is, Karma-Yogins perform all Actions merely by their organs of Action, without entertaining any Attachment or Desire in their minds". It is true that the organs of Action perform the Action, but as the Mind is equable, the person who performs the Action, does not incur either sin or merit.]

(22) The man, who is satisfied with whatever falls to his lot according to fortuitous circumstance, who is free from the pairs of Opposites (such as, happiness and unhappiness etc.), who is devoid of jealousy, and who considers it the same, whether there is success for the Action or not, is not bound by the merit or the sin of Actions, even though he performs (Actions). (23) (He) Who is without Attachment, free (from love and hate), whose Mind is concentrated on Knowledge

(in the shape of an Equable Reason), and who performs Actions (merely) for the purpose of a Yajña, his entire Karma is destroyed.

[The doctrine explained in Chapter III above (3. 9), that Action or ritual performed for the sake of a Yajña does not become binding according to the Mīmāṁsā school, and that when the same Action is performed with Attachment, it becomes productive of Release instead of leading to heaven, is again referred to in this stanza. The word '*samagraṁ*' in the phrase '*samagraṁ pravilīyate*' is very important. The Mīmāṁsā school looks upon the happiness of heaven as the highest ideal, or the *summum bonum*; and in their opinion, Action which leads to heaven is not binding; but the Gītā aims beyond heaven, that is, at Release; and from this point of view, even that Action which leads to heaven, is binding. Therefore, it is said that if Action is performed, even for the purpose of a Yajña, but with an unattached Reason, it is 'totally' (*samagra*) destroyed, that is to say, it does not become productive even of heaven but leads to Release. But, nevertheless, there is an important distinction to be borne in mind in the portion of this Chapter which deals with the Yajñas. In Chapter III, it has been stated that these same Yajñas, that is, the immemorial Yajña-*cakra* or the paraphernalia of ritualistic performances, prescribed by the Śrutis and the Smṛtis, must be kept going; but the Blessed Lord now says that the word 'Yajña' is not to be taken in the limited meaning of 'offering *til* (sesamum) or rice or animals into the fire', as offerings to deities, or as meaning the performance of the duties relative to the four castes, in accordance with their respective religion, though desirefully. The words '*idaṁ na mama*' uttered at the end of the hymn, while throwing the offering into the fire, which mean 'this is not mine', contain a selfless, non-egotistical principle, which is the most important part of the Yajña; and, performing in this way all the Actions of one's life, saying '*na mama*' (that is, 'this is not mine'), that is, giving up mine-ness and performing them merely with the idea of dedicating them to the Brahman, is in itself a

§§ ब्रह्मार्पणं ब्रह्म हविर्ब्रह्माग्नौ ब्रह्मणा हुतम् ।
ब्रह्मैव तेन गन्तव्यं ब्रह्मकर्मसमाधिना ॥ २४ ॥
दैवमेवापरे यज्ञं योगिनः पर्युपासते ।
ब्रह्माग्नावपरे यज्ञं यज्ञेनैवोपजुह्वति ॥ २५ ॥

stupendous Yajña, or '*homa*'; and by means of this Yajña, an offering of oblation (*yajana*) is made to the deity of all deities, that is, to the Parameśvara, or the Brahman. Needless to say, the doctrines of the Mīmāṁsā school relating to the sacrifice of wealth apply equally well to this stupendous sacrifice; and the person who performs every Action in the world unattachedly, and for the sake of Universal Welfare (*lokasaṁgraha*) becomes liberated from the 'entire' (*samagra*) consequence of the Action, and ultimately attains Release (Gī. Ra. Ch. XI, pp. 478 to 483). This stupendous Yajña in the form of dedicating everything to the Brahman is described in the beginning of the next stanza; and the Blessed Lord after describing thereafter the form of other specific Yajñas of lesser importance, sums up the whole thing in the 33rd stanza by saying that, "such a 'Jñāna-yajña' (sacrifice of Knowledge) is the best of all".]

(24) He, whose belief is that the *arpaṇa* (that is, the act of offering) is Brahman; that, the *havi* (that is, the oblation which is to be offered) is Brahman; that, the Brahman offered a sacrifice into the Brahman-fire; and that, (all) Karma is (in this way) Brahman, attains the Brahman.

[In the Śāṁkara-bhāṣya, the word '*arpaṇa*' has been interpreted as "the means by which the 'offering' (*arpaṇa*) is made, such as a ladle etc."; but that interpretation is rather far-fetched. It is more to the point to take the word '*arpaṇa*', as meaning the 'act of offering' or 'the act of offering into the fire'. Thus far, there has been a description of persons who perform the Yajña desirelessly, that is, in order to dedicate it to the Brahman (that is, make a '*brahmārpaṇa*' of it). The Blessed Lord now describes the desire-prompted Yajña addressed to particular deities—]

(25) Some (Karma-) Yogins perform sacrifice addressed to deities (instead of for dedicating it to the Brahman); and

श्रोत्रादीनीन्द्रियाण्यन्ये संयमाग्निषु जुह्वति ।
शब्दादीन्विषयानन्य इन्द्रियाग्निषु जुह्वति ॥ २६ ॥
सर्वाणीन्द्रियकर्माणि प्राणकर्माणि चापरे ।
आत्मसंयमयोगाग्नौ जुह्वति ज्ञानदीपिते ॥ २७ ॥

others make a sacrifice of a Yajña, by a Yajña, into the Brahman-fire.

[The latter portion of this stanza refers to the description in the *Puruṣa-Sūkta* that the gods offered a sacrifice to the Virāṭa-formed Yajña-*puruṣa*, *cf.*, "*yajñena yajñam ayajanta devāḥ*" (Ṛg. 10. 90. 16); and the words, "*yajñaṁ yajñenaiv-opajuhvati*" in this stanza are synonymous with the words "*yajñena yajñam ayajanta*" in the Ṛg-Veda, and seem to be used accordingly. It is evident that the Virāṭa-formed animal, which was sacrificed into the Yajña performed in the beginning of the world, and the god, for propitiating whom the sacrifice was made, must both have been of the form of the Brahman. In short, as the Brahman continually pervades all things in the world, the statement in the 24th stanza that, in performing all Actions desirelessly, the Brahman is always sacrificed by the Brahman, is scientifically correct; all that is wanted is that one's Mind has been formed accordingly. This is not the only stanza in the Gītā which refers to the *Puruṣa-Sūkta*, but later on, the description in Chapter X, is also consistent with that *Sūkta*. The Blessed Lord has now described the Yajñas performed for propitiating particular deities. HE now explains how the Yogic performance of Breath Control (*prāṇāyāma*) etc., prescribed in the Pātañjala-Yoga, or even the performance of religious austerities, is a kind of Yajña, if the words '*agni*' (fire), '*havi*' (sacrificial offering) etc., are taken in their symbolical meanings—]

(26) Others sacrifice the *śrotrādi* (that is, ears, eyes, etc.) organs into the Fire (*agni*) in the shape of a Limit (*saṁyamana*); and others again, sacrifice the objects of sense, such as, sound etc. into the Fire in the shape of the senses. (27) Others still, sacrifice all the Actions (that is, functions) of the various organs, and vital forces (*prāṇa*) into the Fire of

Yoga in the shape of Mental control, which has been lit by Knowledge (*jñāna*).

[In the above stanza, are described two or three different kinds of symbolical Yajñas e. g., (1) controlling the senses, that is, allowing them to perform their respective functions within proper limits; (2) totally destroying the senses, by wholly giving up the objects of sense, which go to feed the senses; (3) putting an end to the Actions, not only of the senses, but even of the vital forces (*prāṇa*) themselves, by entering into a complete mental absorption (*samādhi*), and remaining steeped in the joy of the Ātman. Now, if these are compared with a Yajña, then, in the first kind of Yajña, the limit (*saṁyamana*) which is placed on the senses becomes the Fire (*agni*); because, by working out the simile, all that enters the limit may be said to have been offered into the Fire. Similarly, in the second kind of Yajña, the organs themselves, and in the third kind of Yajña, both the organs and the *prāṇa* (vital forces) are compared with the material offered up as a sacrifice-offering, and the Control of the Ātman (*ātmasaṁyamana*) becomes the Fire. There are, besides, others, who only perform the Prāṇāyāma (i. e., control of the Prāṇa (life) in the shape of the breath—Trans.); and these are described further on in the 29th stanza. This idea of symbolically extending the original meaning of the word '*yajña*', namely, 'a sacrifice of various materials', and making it include religious austerities (*tapa*), Renunciation (*saṁnyāsa*), Mental absorption (*samādhi*), control of the *prāṇa* or breath (*prāṇāyāma*), and other means of getting merged into the Blessed Lord, has not been mentioned for the first time in the Gītā. In the 4th chapter of the Manu-Smṛti, where the state of the house-holder is being described, after stating that no house-holder should give up the five principal sacrifices (*mahā-yajña*) prescribed by the Smṛtis, namely, the Ṛsi-yajña, the Deva-yajña, the Bhūta-yajña, the Manuṣya-yajña, and the Pitṛ-yajña, it is stated that many persons "sacrifice the speech into the organs, or the Prāna (life) into the speech, or ultimately even propitiate

द्रव्ययज्ञास्तपोयज्ञा योगयज्ञास्तथापरे ।
स्वाध्यायज्ञानयज्ञाश्च यतयः संशितव्रताः ॥ २८ ॥
अपाने जुह्वति प्राणं प्राणेऽपानं तथाऽपरे ।
प्राणापानगती रुद्ध्वा प्राणायामपरायणाः ॥ २९ ॥

the Parameśvara by a Jñāna-yajña (that is, the sacrifice by Knowledge, or sacrificing everything into the sacrificial fire of Knowledge—Trans.)", (Manu. 4. 21-24). Considering the matter from the historical point of view, it can be seen that when the sacrifice of wealth of various kinds prescribed in the Śruti-texts for propitiating Indra, Varuṇa, and other deities fell into disuse, and the devices of attaining the state of the Parameśvara by Pātañjala-yoga, Saṁnyāsa, or Metaphysical Knowledge came more and more into vogue, the meaning of the word 'Yajña' was widened, and it was made to symbolically include all the various devices of obtaining Release. The principle at the root of this is the tendency to indicate subsequent religious methods by the same technical terms as had come to be formerly accepted in the religion. Whatever may be the case, it is clear from this exposition in the Manu-Smṛti, that this idea had acquired general acceptance before, or at any rate at the same time as, the Gītā.]

(28) In this way, some Yatins observing severe vows (that is, persons who have acquired mental control) perform the sacrifice of wealth; others perform the sacrifice by austerity, others by Yogic practices, others by *svādhyāya* (that is, by observing the ritual prescribed for one's own caste), and others by Jñāna (*i.e.*, Knowledge—Trans.). (29) Others taking to *prāṇāyāma*, and controlling the movements of the *prāṇa* (outgoing breath—Trans.) and the *apāna* (incoming breath—Trans.) breaths, sacrifice the *prāṇa*-breath into the *apāna*-breath, while others sacrifice the *apāna*-breath into the *prāṇa*-breath.

[The idea conveyed by this stanza is that performing the Prāṇāyāma (breath-control) according to the Pātañjala Yoga is a kind of Yajña. As this Yajña in the form of the Pātañjala-Yoga has been mentioned in the 29th stanza, the words 'sacrifice by Yogic practices' ('*yoga-yajña*') in the 28th stanza must be taken to mean the Yajña according to Karma-Yoga. The word '*prāṇa*' in the term '*prāṇāyāma*' usually indicates both the *śvāsa* (inhaling) and the *ucchvāsa* (exhaling) of the breath; but when a distinction is made between '*prāṇa*' and '*apāna*', the word '*prāṇa*' means the 'out-going' breath, that is to say, the '*ucchvāsa*' breath; and the word '*apāna*' means the 'incoming' breath (Ve. Sū. Śāṁ. Bhā. 2. 4. 12; and Chāndogya Śāṁ. Bhā. 1. 3. 3). It must be borne in mind that these meanings of the words '*prāṇa*' and '*apāna*' are different from their ordinary meanings. Taking these meanings, when the *prāṇa*, that is, the exhaled breath or the '*ucchvāsa*' has been sacrificed into the *apāna*, that is, the intaken breath, the *prāṇāyāma* which is performed, is known as the '*pūraka*'; and conversely, when the *apāna* has been sacrificed into the *prāṇa*, the *prāṇāyāma* which is performed is named '*recaka*'. When both the *prāṇa* and the *apāna* are controlled or stopped, the *prāṇāyāma* which is performed is named '*kumbhaka*'; now there remain besides these, the three breaths named *vyāna*, *udāna*, and *samāna*. Out of these, the breath '*vyāna*' is located at the meeting point between the *prāṇa* and the *apāna*, and comes to be used when one has to perform actions requiring force, when one partially controls the breath, such as, in drawing a bow or lifting up weights etc. (Chān. 1. 3. 5), The *udāna* breath is the one which leaves the body at the moment of death (Praśna. 3. 7) and the *samāna* breath is the breath which continually takes food-juices to every part of the body (Praśna. 3. 7). These are the ordinary meanings of these various kinds of breath according to the Vedānta-Śāstra; but in some places even quite different meanings are intended; for example, in the 212th Chapter of the Vana-parva of the Mahābhārata, quite different characteristics are mentioned of the *prāṇa* and other breaths; and '*prāṇa*' is explained as meaning the breath in the head, and the *apāna* is described as meaning the breath which escapes downwards from the body

अपरे नियताहारा : प्राणान्प्राणेषु जुह्वति ।
सर्वेऽप्येते यज्ञविदो यज्ञक्षपितकल्मषा : ॥ ३० ॥

यज्ञशिष्टामृतभुजो यान्ति ब्रह्म सनातनम् ।
नायं लोकोऽस्त्ययज्ञस्य कुतोऽन्य : कुरुसत्तम ॥ ३१ ॥

(Praśna. 3-5 and Maitryu. 2-6). According to the above stanza, the breath which is controlled is said to be 'sacrificed' into the other kinds of breath.]

(30) Others still moderating their food, sacrifice the *prāṇa* (vital airs) into *prāṇa* itself. All these being sin-diminished as a result of sacrifice, and (being) well-versed in sacrifice, (31) and partaking of the *amṛta* (food), which remains over after the sacrifice, attain the eternal Brahman. The non-performers of sacrifice have not (success even in) this world; how then, O Kuruśreṣṭha, (can they obtain) the next world?

[In short, although the performance of Yajñas is the duty of every human being, according to the directions of the Vedas, yet, it is not that this Yajña is only of one kind. Whether one performs Prāṇāyāma, or religious austerities, or the reading of the Vedas, or the Agniṣṭoma-yajña, or the Paśu-yajña (sacrificing animals), or throws *til*, rice, or clarified butter into the fire, or performs worship, or performs the five domestic sacrifices (*gṛha-yajña*), such as, *naivedya* (food offered to household gods), *vaiśvadeva* (food offered into the fire), etc., if one has destroyed the Attachment for the Fruit of Action, all these become Yajñas in the wider meaning of the word; and then, all the doctrines of the Mīmāṁsā school relating to the partaking of what remains after the performance of the Yajña, become applicable to each of them. The first of these rules is that 'no Action performed for the purpose of a Yajña has a binding effect'; and that rule has been mentioned above in the 23rd stanza (See commentary on Gī. 3. 9). The second rule is, that every householder should partake of food in the company of his wife, after he has performed the five principal sacrifices, and given food to guests, beggars etc., and that when a person lives in this manner, the householder-state becomes profitable, and leads to a happy state after death. It has been stated in the Manu-Smṛti, and in other Smṛtis, that every house-holder should always become a *vighasāśī*' (i. e., one who eats the *vighasa*—Trans.), and '*amṛtāśī*' (i. e., one who eats the *amṛta*—Trans.), after the word '*vighasa*' has been defined as meaning 'whatever remains over after the guests have eaten', and the word '*amṛta*' has been defined as meaning 'that which remains over after the performance of the Yajña'; *cf.*, *vighasaṁ bhuktaśeṣaṁ tu yajñaśeṣam athāmṛtam*"—Manu, 2. 285 (See Gī. 3. 13 and Gītā. Ra. p. 403). The Blessed Lord now says that this rule which applies to the ordinary domestic sacrifices also applies to all the various Yajñas mentioned above. Not only is any act performed for the purpose of a Yajña not binding, but if any portion of these acts, which remains over after the performance of the Yajña, is utilised by one for his own use, even that is not prejudicial. (See Gītā Ra. Chapter XII p. 535 bottom). The last sentence in this stanza, namely, "the non-performers of sacrifice have not (success even in) this world", is fraught with deep meaning and is important. It does not mean only that in the absence of the Yajñas there is no rain, and that in the absence of rain, the course of life on this world cannot go on; but, taking the word 'Yajña' in its wider meaning, the social principle, that unless every one sacrifices something or other dear to him, the ordinary course of the world cannot go on, by all getting equal opportunities, is necessarily included in it. For instance, the Western socialistic doctrine that unless every one controls his own freedom of action, all others cannot enjoy equal freedom of action, is an example of this principle; and if the same meaning is to be conveyed in the terminology of the Gītā, one will have to speak here in terms of a Yajña, by saying that 'unless every one to some extent performs a Yajña of his Freedom of Action, the course of life on this world cannot go on'. When the Yajña has thus been made the foundation of the entire social structure by thus giving it an extended and wide meaning, it need not be said in so many words that the social arrangement will not continue

एवं बहुविधा यज्ञा वितता ब्रह्मणो मुखे ।
कर्मजान्विद्धि तान्सर्वानेवं ज्ञात्वा विमोक्ष्यसे ॥ ३२ ॥
श्रेयान्द्रव्यमयाद्यज्ञाज्ज्ञानयज्ञः परंतप ।
सर्वं कर्माखिलं पार्थ ज्ञाने परिसमाप्यते ॥ ३३ ॥

properly, unless every human being learns to perform these Yajñas as pure duties.]

(32) In this way, various kinds of Yajñas, are always taking place in the mouth of the Brahman; know that all these arise from Karma; when you have acquired this Knowledge, you will obtain Release.

[The Yajñas of physical materials prescribed by the Śrutis, such as, the '*jyotiṣṭoma*' etc., are performed by throwing oblations into the Fire; and as the sacrificial fire is supposed to be the mouth of the gods, these sacrifices are stated by the Śāstras to reach the various deities. But, some one may raise the doubt that since the symbolical Yajñas mentioned above are not performed in Fire, which is the mouth of the gods, how can merit be acquired by performing them? Therefore, in order to remove this doubt, the Blessed Lord now says that these Yajñas are performed into the mouth of the Brahman itself. The purport of the second part of the stanza is that he who understands this extended meaning of the performance of a Yajña, and does not understand that word in the narrow meaning given to it by the Mīmāṁsā school, does not remain narrow-minded, but is enabled to understand the form of the Brahman. The Blessed Lord now explains which is the most superior of all these kinds of Yajñas—]

(33) O Parantapa! the *jñāna-maya yajña* (that is, the Yajña peformed by sacrificing everything into the Fire of Realisation—Trans.) is better than the *dravya-maya yajña* (that is, the Yajña, performed by sacrificing materials—Trans.); because, O Pārtha! all Actions of all kinds are ultimately merged in Jñāna.

[The word 'Jñāna-yajña' has occurred twice later on in the Gītā (Gī. 9. 15 and 18. 70). The Yajña of materials

§§ तद्विद्धि प्रणिपातेन परिप्रश्नेन सेवया ।
उपदेक्ष्यन्ति ते ज्ञानं ज्ञानिनस्तत्त्वदर्शिनः ॥ ३४ ॥
यज्ज्ञात्वा न पुनर्मोहमेवं यास्यसि पाण्डव ।
येन भूतान्यशेषेण द्रक्ष्यस्यात्मन्यथो मयि ॥ ३५ ॥

performed by men, is performed by them for attaining the Parameśvara. But one cannot attain the Parameśvara, unless one is acquainted with His form. Therefore, the method of acquiring the Knowledge of the form of the Parameśvara and of attaining the Parameśvara by leading a course of life which is consistent with that Knowledge, is known as the 'Jñāna-yajña'. This Yajña is mental, and is performed with the help of the Reason, and it is naturally considered more worthy than the Yajña of wealth. This Jñāna included in the Jñāna-yajña is of supreme importance in the Science of Release; and it is the firm doctrine of the Gītā that (i) all Karma is destroyed by means of this Jñāna; that, (ii) in any case the Jñāna of the Parameśvara must ultimately be obtained; and that, (iii) there is no Release except by the Acquisition of Jñāna. Nevertheless, I have proved in detail in Chapters X and XI of the Gītā-Rahasya that the words "all Actions of all kinds are ultimately merged in Jñāna" in this stanza are not to be understood as meaning that 'after a man has acquired Jñāna, he may give up Karma'. The Gītā preaches to everybody that (i) all Actions must be performed as a matter of duty for universal welfare, though they may not be needed for one's own self; that, (ii) as all these Actions are performed with Jñāna, that is, with an equable Reason, the person, who performs them, is not affected by the merit or sin of that Action (see, stanza 37 later); and that (iii) as this Jñāna-yajña leads to Release, one must perform the Yajña, but with Jñāna, and with a desireless frame of mind.]

(34) Remember that, philosopher-Jñānins will, by your offering obeisance (to them—Trans.), and questioning and service, teach you that Jñāna, (35) by having acquired which, O Pāṇḍava ! you will not again be overcome by mental

अपि चेदसि पापेभ्यः सर्वेभ्यः पापकृत्तमः ।
सर्वं ज्ञानप्लवेनैव वृजिनं संतरिष्यसि ॥ ३६ ॥
यथैधांसि समिद्धोऽग्निर्भस्मसात्कुरुतेऽर्जुन ।
ज्ञानाग्निः सर्वकर्माणि भस्मसात्कुरुते तथा ॥ ३७ ॥
§§ न हि ज्ञानेन सदृशं पवित्रमिह विद्यते ।
तत्स्वयं योगसंसिद्धः कालेनात्मनि विन्दति ॥ ३८ ॥

confusion in this fashion, and by means of which Knowledge, you will come to see everything created as located in yourself and ultimately in Me.

[There is a reference here to the Knowledge of the identity of the Ātman with all created beings, that is, to seeing the entire creation embodied in oneself, and seeing oneself embodied in the entire creation, which has been dealt with later on (Gī. 6. 29). As the Ātman (Self) and the Bhagavān (Blessed Lord) are fundamentally uniform, the entire creation is comprehended in the Ātman, that is, ultimately, also naturally in the Bhagavān, or the Blessed Lord; and the three-fold distinction between the Ātman (one's Self), the rest of the creation, and the Blessed Lord, naturally disappears. It is, therefore, said in the Bhāgavata-purāṇa, in describing the Bhagavad-bhakta (the devotee of the Blessed Lord) that " that man is the best Bhāgavata or devotee of the Blessed Lord, who sees the entire creation in the Blessed Lord and in himself (Bhāg. 11. 2. 45). See the further explanation of this important principle of the Gītā in Chapter XII of the Gītā-Rahasya (pp. 543 to 555); and also in Chapter XIII, from the point of view of Devotion (pp. 600–601).]

(36) Even if you are a sinner, greater than any other sinner, you will sail over the whole sin by (this) ship of Jñāna. (37) Just as the kindled fire reduces to ashes (all) fuel, in the same way, O Arjuna! (this) Jñāna-formed Fire reduces to ashes (the prejudicial or unprejudicial binding force of) all Action.

[The Blessed Lord has described the worth of Jñāna. HE now explains how this Jñāna can be acquired——]

(38) There is nothing indeed in this world so holy as

श्रद्धावाँल्लभते ज्ञानं तत्परः संयतेन्द्रियः ।
ज्ञानं लब्ध्वा परां शान्तिमचिरेणाधिगच्छति ॥ ३९ ॥

अज्ञश्चाश्रद्दधानश्च संशयात्मा विनश्यति ।
नायं लोकोऽस्ति न परो न सुखं संशयात्मनः ॥ ४० ॥

§§ योगसंन्यस्तकर्माणं ज्ञानसंछिन्नसंशयम् ।
आत्मवन्तं न कर्माणि निबध्नन्ति धनंजय ॥ ४१ ॥

Jñāna. That Jñāna is automatically acquired in course of time by the person who has mastered the Yoga (that is, the Karma-Yoga).

[The word 'Action' in the 37th stanza means 'the binding force or effect of Karma or Action' (Gī. 4. 19). Acquiring Knowledge by means of desireless Actions, which one has started by one's Reason, is the principal means of acquiring Knowledge, or the means accessible to Reason (*buddhi*); but, for those who cannot acquire Knowledge in this way by their own Reason, the Blessed Lord now prescribes the other path, namely, the Path of Faith—]

(39) That person having Faith, who, having acquired control over the senses, pursues this Knowledge, (also) acquires it; and when he has acquired Knowledge, he immediately afterwards experiences the highest peace.

[In short, that Knowledge (Jñāna), and the tranquility (*śānti*) which is acquired by means of the Reason (*buddhi*), is also acquired by Faith (*śraddhā*). But he who has neither Reason nor Faith—]

(40) But (he) who has himself neither Knowledge nor Faith, such a doubter is utterly destroyed. For the doubter, there is neither this world, nor the next, nor any happiness whatsoever.

[The Blessed Lord has shown two ways of acquiring Knowledge, namely, (i) one's own Reason and (ii) Faith. HE now explains the respective uses of the Jñāna-Yoga and the Karma-Yoga, and summarises the whole subject-matter—]

(41) O Dhanañjaya! Actions cannot bind the *ātma-jñānin* (Self-Realiser—Trans.) who has cast off Karma (that is, the

तस्मादज्ञानसंभूतं हृत्स्थं ज्ञानासिनात्मनः ।
छित्त्वैनं संशयं योगमातिष्ठोत्तिष्ठ भारत ॥ ४२ ॥

इति श्रीमद्भगवद्गीतासु उपनिषत्सु ब्रह्मविद्यायां योगशास्त्रे श्रीकृष्णार्जुनसंवादे ज्ञानकर्मसंन्यासयोगो नाम चतुर्थोऽध्यायः ॥ ४ ॥

bondage of Karma) by taking shelter in the (Karma–) Yoga, and whose doubts have been annulled by means of Jñāna. (42) Therefore, cutting off with the sword of Knowledge, this doubt, which has arisen in your heart as a result of Ignorance, take shelter, in the (Karma–) Yoga, (and) O Bhārata! stand up (and fight).

[Just as in the Īśāvāsyopaniṣad (Īśā. 11; Gī. Ra. Ch. VI, p. 501), after shortly showing the respective uses of *vidyā* and *avidyā*, a direction has been given to act without giving up either *vidyā* or *avidyā*, so in the Gītā, in these two stanzas, after shortly showing the respective uses of Jñāna and (Karma-) Yoga, the advice has been given to Arjuna to perform Action with the joint help of Jñāna and Yoga. The respective uses of these two are that when a man performs Action by the Desireless Jñāna-Yoga, the binding effect of Karma (Action) is destroyed, and it does not obstruct Release; and as a result of Jñāna, all doubt or mental confusion is annihilated and one attains Release. Therefore, the ultimate and final advice to Arjuna is, that he should not seek the protection of either Karma alone, or of Jñāna alone, but should make use of both, and fight. It has been shown in the Gītā-Rahasya (Ch. III, p. 80) that because Arjuna has to stand up and fight here by taking shelter or protection from Yoga, the word 'Yoga' must here be interpreted as meaning the Karma-Yoga. This fusion of Jñāna and Yoga, is also again referred to later on in the Gītā (Gī. 16. 1), in describing the characteristics of 'godly endowment' (*daivī saṁpatti*), by the words "*jñāna-yogavyavasthitiḥ*".]

Thus ends the fourth chapter entitled the JNANA-KARMA-SAṀNYASA YOGA in the dialogue between Śrī Kṛṣṇa and

Arjuna on the Yoga included in the Science of the Brahman (that is, on the Karma-Yoga), in the Upaniṣad sung (that is, told) by the Blessed Lord.

[It must be borne in mind that the word '*saṁnyāsa*' in the phrase '*jñāna-karma-saṁnyāsa*' is not literal *karma-tyāga* (Abandonment of Action), but is the Desireless '*saṁnyāsa*' or the 'Dedication' of all Action to the Parameśvara; and the same explanation has been given later on in the beginning of Chapter XVIII.]

पञ्चमोऽध्यायः

अर्जुन उवाच ।

§§ संन्यासं कर्मणां कृष्ण पुनर्योगं च शंससि ।
तच्छ्रेय एतयोरेकं तन्मे ब्रूहि सुनिश्चितम् ॥ १ ॥

CHAPTER V.

[In this chapter, has been given the clear answer of the Blessed Lord to the doubts likely to be raised by the followers of the Path of Renunciation to the doctrines laid down in Chapter IV, after expressing those doubts through the mouth of Arjuna. If Jñāna is the ultimate resolution of all Action (4. 33); if all Action is destroyed by Knowledge (4. 37); and if the sacrifice into Knowledge is superior to the sacrifice of wealth (4. 43), then, why has the Blessed Lord, after saying in the second chapter that "it is most meritorious for a Kṣatriya to fight the battle prescribed by his religion" (2. 31), summarised the fourth chapter by saying "therefore, stand up to fight, taking shelter in the Karma-Yoga" (4. 42)? To this the reply of the Gītā is that what is needed is the fusion of (i) Knowledge, which is necessary for Release, by removing all mental confusion and of (ii) Karma, which cannot be escaped from, and which though not necessary for Release, is yet necessary for Universal Welfare (4. 41). But, even to this an objection may be raised to the effect that, if both the Karma-Yoga and the Sāṁkhya-Yoga are proper according to the Śāstras, why should not a person adopt the Sāṁkhya-Yoga and abandon Action, if that pleases one better? Needless to say, there must be made a clear decision as to which of these two paths is the better one; and as Arjuna was seized with the same doubt, he now raises the following question, in the same way as he had raised the question in the beginning of the third chapter—]

(1) Arjuna said:—O Kṛṣṇa! once you say that the Path of Renunciation is superior, and again that Karma-Yoga (that is, the path of continuing to perform Action) is superior; therefore, tell me definitely that one, of these

श्रीभगवानुवाच ।

संन्यासः कर्मयोगश्च निःश्रेयसकरावुभौ ।
तयोस्तु कर्मसंन्यासात्कर्मयोगो विशिष्यते ॥ २ ॥

two, which is really *śreya,* (that is, more praiseworthy).

(2) The Blessed Lord said :—Karma-saṁnyāsa and Karma-Yoga, both these (paths or Niṣṭhās) are *niḥśreyasakara* (that is, producing Release) ; but, (that is, though both may be of the same value from the point of view of Release), the worth (that is, the efficacy) of Karma-Yoga, out of these two, is greater than that of Karma-Saṁnyāsa.

[This question and answer are both unambiguous and clear. The word '*śreya*' in the first stanza means 'more praise-worthy', or, better ; and, to the question of Arjuna about the relative value of the two courses, the reply of the Blessed Lord is, "*karma-yogo viśiṣyate*", that is "the Karma-Yoga is the better (path)". Nevertheless, as this doctrine is not consistent with the Sāṁkhya theory, that a man must abandon or make a literal Saṁnyāsa (Renunciation) of Action, after he has acquired Knowledge, some commentators, have taken hold of the word '*viśiṣyate*', and contented themselves with saying that that was a mere hollow praise of the Karma-Yoga by way of an *arthavāda,* after they had ineffectually struggled to twist this plain-meaninged question and answer; and saying, that the true intention of the Blessed Lord was not to praise the Karma-Yoga ! If it was the opinion of the Blessed Lord that there should be no Action after the acquisition of Knowledge, could He not have replied to Arjuna that: "out of these two paths, the Path of Renunciation is the better one"? But, as instead of doing so, the Blessed Lord, after saying in the first part of the second stanza that, "the paths of performing Action and abandoning Action, are both equally productive of Release", uses the word '*tu*', that is, 'but', in the second part of the stanza and unambiguously lays down the doctrine that, '*tayoḥ*', that is, 'out of these two paths', "the path of Performing

Action is more praise-worthy (*śreya*) than the path Abandoning Action", it is clearly proved that He was of the opinion that in the *siddhavasthā* (state of Perfection), the Jñānin must still go on performing desirelessly, till death, as a duty, and for Universal Welfare, the same selfless Action, which he was performing in the '*sādhanāvasthā*' (the state of Perfecting) for acquiring Knowledge. The same meaning has been made clear in Gītā 3. 7, and the term '*viśiṣyate*' has also been used there; and in the next stanza, that is, in Gītā 3. 8, the words "Action is superior to Inaction" were again clearly repeated. Now, it is true, that there are descriptions in several places in the Upaniṣads (Bṛ. 4. 4. 22) to the effect that Jñānins (those, who have acquired Knowledge) roam about begging, without having any '*lokaiṣaṇā*' (desire for society), or '*putraiṣaṇā*' (desire for children). But, it has not been stated in the Upaniṣads that this is the only path, which can be followed after a man has acquired Knowledge, and that there is no other path. Therefore, it is not proper to attempt to harmonise the Gītā with the above-mentioned sentences from the Upaniṣads. The Gītā does not say that this Path of Renunciation described in the Upaniṣads is not productive of Release. But, the firm doctrine of the Gītā is, that though the Karma-Yoga and Renunciation are both equally productive of Release, that is to say, though, from the point of view of Release, the effect of both is the same, yet, considering the course of life in the world, the better or more praise-worthy path is to continue to desirelessly perform Action even after one has acquired Knowledge. This interpretation of mine is not the one which has been accepted by the majority of commentators; and, they have treated the Karma-Yoga as secondary; but, in my opinion, these interpretations of the commentators are not plain and straight-forward; and, as I have given a detailed statement of my reasons for my interpretation in Chapter XI of the Gītā-Rahasya (pp. 420 to 431), I shall not take up space here by saying more about it. After the Blessed Lord had thus given His clear decision as to which of the two paths is more praise-worthy,

§§ ज्ञेयः स नित्यसंन्यासी यो न द्वेष्टि न काङ्क्षति ।
निर्द्वन्द्वो हि महाबाहो सुखं बन्धात्प्रमुच्यते ॥ ३ ॥
सांख्ययोगौ पृथग्बालाः प्रवदन्ति न पण्डिताः ।
एकमप्यास्थितः सम्यगुभयोर्विन्दते फलम् ॥ ४ ॥
यत् सांख्यैः प्राप्यते स्थानं तद्योगैरपि गम्यते ।
एकं सांख्यं च योगं च यः पश्यति स पश्यति ॥ ५ ॥
संन्यासस्तु महाबाहो दुःखमाप्तुमयोगतः ।
योगयुक्तो मुनिर्ब्रह्म न चिरेणाधिगच्छति ॥ ६ ॥

HE now proves that though these two paths might appear different to people in ordinary life, yet, they are not essentially different—]

(3) He, who does not hate (anything) and who does not desire (anything), that man should be looked upon as a 'permanent ascetic' (though he might be performing Action); because, O Mighty-armed Arjuna! he, who has been liberated from the pairs of Opposites (such as, pain and happiness, etc.), is, without effort, liberated from (all) the bonds (of Karma). (4) Fools say that Sāṁkhya (Karma-Saṁnyāsa) and Yoga (Karma-Yoga) are different; the learned do not say so; if any one path is properly followed, the result of both is achieved. (5) That (Released-) state, which is reached by the (followers of the) Sāṁkhya (Path), there too do the Yogins (that is, the Karma-Yogins) go; he who sees that the (two paths of) Sāṁkhya and Yoga are (in this way) the same, may be said to have seen (the true principle). (6) Even Renunciation, O Mahābāho! is difficult to achieve, in the absence of Yoga, (that is, in the absence of Karma). That sage who has become steeped in the Karma-Yoga, is not long in attaining the Brahman.

[A clear and exhaustive explanation has been given later on from the seventh to the seventeenth chapter of the Gītā as to how the same Release can be obtained by Karma-Yoga, that is, by not abandoning Action, as can be obtained by the Sāṁkhya-Yoga. All that is intended to be sald for

§§ योगयुक्तो विशुद्धात्मा विजितात्मा जितेन्द्रियः ।
सर्वभूतात्मभूतात्मा कुर्वन्नपि न लिप्यते ॥ ७ ॥
नैव किंचित् करोमीति युक्तो मन्येत तत्त्ववित् ।
पश्यञ्शृण्वन्स्पृशञ्जिघ्रन्नश्नन्गच्छन्स्वपञ्श्वसन् ॥ ८ ॥
प्रलपन्विसृजन्गृह्णन्नुन्मिषन्निमिषन्नपि ।
इन्द्रियाणीन्द्रियार्थेषु वर्तन्त इति धारयन् ॥ ९ ॥

the present is, that as there is no difference between the two paths from the point of view of Release, it is not proper to magnify the difference between these two paths, which have been in vogue from times immemorial, and to quarrel about it; and the same logical argument has been repeated over and over again later on (See Gī. 6. 2 and 18. 1, 2; and my commentary on it). The stanza "*ekaṁ sāṁkhyaṁ ca yogaṁ ca yaḥ paśyati sa paśyati*" has appeared twice with slight alterations in the Mahābhārata (Śān. 305. 19; 316. 4). Though Jñāna is considered of supreme importance in the Path of Renunciation, that Jñāna is not perfected unless Action is performed; and though in the Karma-Yoga, Action is performed, yet, one does not fail to reach the Brahman by it, since such Action is performed with the help of Jñāna (Gī. 6. 2); then, where is the sense of raising a cry that these two paths are different? If it is said that the performance of Action has in itself a binding-effect, the Blessed Lord says that such objection does not apply to Action performed desirelessly—]

(7) (He,) Who has become steeped in the (Karma-) Yoga, whose conscience is pure, who has conquered his Mind and his senses, and whose Ātman has become the Ātman of all created beings, remains untouched (by the merit or sin of Action), though he performs (all Actions). (8) (He,) Who has understood the basic principles, and is steeped in the Yoga, should realise that: "I do not do anything"; (and) in seeing, hearing, touching, smelling, eating, walking, sleeping, breathing, (9) speaking, excreting, taking, opening the eye-lids, and closing them, (should act) believing that (merely)

ब्रह्मण्याधाय कर्माणि सङ्गं त्यक्त्वा करोति यः ।
लिप्यते न स पापेन पद्मपत्रमिवाम्भसा ॥ १० ॥
कायेन मनसा बुद्ध्या केवलैरिन्द्रियैरपि ।
योगिनः कर्म कुर्वन्ति सङ्गं त्यक्त्वात्मशुद्धये ॥ ११ ॥

the senses are acting with reference to their respective objects.

[The last two stanzas form one sentence; and the various Actions described in them are the Actions of the different organs of the body; for instance, excretion is the action of the anus; taking, that of the hand; moving the eye-lids, that of the Vital Airs; seeing, that of the eyes, etc. "I do not do anything" does not mean that one should allow one's senses to do what they want. What is meant is that when once one has lost the egotistical sense of 'I', the unprompted senses are not capable of performing any evil action of their own accord, and remain under the control of the Ātman. In short, even if a man becomes a Jñānin, the organs of breathing etc., will continue to perform their respective functions. Nay, even remaining alive for a fraction of a second is in itself an Action; then, where remains the difference that the Jñānin, who follows the Path of Renunciation, gives up Action, and that the Karma-Yogin performs Action? Both are bound to perform Action. But, as the same acts cease to have a binding effect when the Attachment based on Egoism has been discarded, giving up the Attachment remains the only basic principle; and the Blessed Lord now further amplifies the same idea—]

(10) He, who performs Actions, dedicating them to the Brahman and unattachedly, to him sin does not adhere (touch), just as water does not adhere to the leaves of a lotus-plant. (11) Therefore, the Karma-Yogin performs all Actions (without entertaining the egotistical notion that he is performing them) for Self-purification, unattachedly, by the body (merely), or by the Mind (merely), or by the Reason (merely), and even by the senses merely

युक्तः कर्मफलं त्यक्त्वा शान्तिमाप्नोति नैष्ठिकीम् ।
अयुक्तः कामकारेण फले सक्तो निबध्यते ॥ १२ ॥
सर्वकर्माणि मनसा संन्यस्यास्ते सुखं वशी ।
नवद्वारे पुरे देही नैव कुर्वन्न कारयन् ॥ १३ ॥

[The words 'Body', 'Mind', and 'Reason' in this stanza have been used with reference to the bodily (*kāyika*), vocal (*vācika*) and mental (*mānasika*) divisions of Action. Although the adjective '*kevalaiḥ*' (merely) is placed, in the original, behind the word '*indriyaiḥ*' alone, it also applies to the words 'Body', 'Mind', and 'Reason' (Gī. 4. 21). Therefore, in my translation, I have placed it behind all the other words, as behind the word 'Body'. The meaning is, as explained in the 8th stanza above, that if a man performs any act, which is merely bodily (*kāyika*), or merely vocal (*vācika*), or merely mental (*mānasika*), giving up egoism, and without any Attachment to the Fruit of Action, he does not incur any sin (See Gītā 3. 27 ; 13. 29 ; and 18. 16). When there is no egoism, all the Action which is performed is merely the Action of the organs ; and as the Mind and the other organs are only the evolutes (*vikāra*) of Prakṛti, the doer does not incur the binding effect of such Action. The Blessed Lord now proves this doctrine according to the Śāstras—]

(12) He, who has become '*yukta*' (that is, Yoga-*yukta*), (that is, steeped in Yoga—Trans.) gives up the Fruit of Action and attains the final complete tranquility ; and the '*ayukta*' (that is, one who is not Yoga-*yukta*), becoming attached to the Fruit, as a result of *kāma* (that is, of desire), becomes bound (by the merit or the sin). (13) The embodied (man), who has controlled the senses, renouncing all Actions mentally (not literally), inhabits happily this (body-) city with its nine entrances, doing nothing and causing nothing to be done.

[That is to say, he realises that the Ātman is a non-doer, and that the entire activity is of Prakṛti ; and therefore, he lives quietly, or in a state of indifference (See Gītā 13. 20 and 18. 59). The two eyes, the two ears, the two nostrils,

§§ न कर्तृत्वं न कर्माणि लोकस्य सृजति प्रभुः ।
न कर्मफलसंयोगं स्वभावस्तु प्रवर्तते ॥ १४ ॥
नादत्ते कस्यचित्पापं न चैव सुकृतं विभुः ।
अज्ञानेनावृतं ज्ञानं तेन मुह्यन्ति जन्तवः ॥ १५ ॥

the mouth, the opening for urinating, and the anus are looked upon as nine openings or doors of the body. The Blessed Lord now gives a metaphysical explanation of the fact that the Karma-Yogin remains '*yukta*', though he is performing Actions—]

(14) The *prabhu* (that is, the Ātman or the Parameśvara) does not create either the capacity of men for Action, nor their Actions, nor the attendant Fruit of Action (accruing to the doers). Inherent nature, (that is, Prakṛti) performs (everything). (15) The *vibhu* (that is, the all-pervading Ātman or Parameśvara) does not acquire either the merit or the sin of anybody. As Knowledge is covered by the covering of Ignorance (that is to say, as a result of Māyā), all created beings are confused.

[The principle involved in both these stanzas is originally from the Sāṁkhya philosophy (See Gītā-Rahasya pp. 222 to 224). But, as according to Vedantists, the Ātman = the Parameśvara, they extend the principle that 'the Ātman is a non-doer' to the Parameśvara. The Sāṁkhyas look upon Prakṛti (Matter) and Puruṣa (Spirit) as the two fundamental principles, and look upon the Prakṛti as the active agent and the Ātman as inactive; but the Vedantists go even beyond that, and say that the root of both Puruṣa and Prakṛti is a quality-less Parameśvara, who is a Non-Doer (*udāsin*) like the Ātman of the Sāṁkhyas; and that the entire activity is of Māyā or of Prakṛti (Gī. Ra. p. 369). The Blessed Lord now explains that the ordinary man does not understand these things on account of Ignorance; and that, as the Karma-Yogin understands the difference between the Doer and the Non-Doer, he remains unscathed, notwithstanding that he performs Action —]

§§ ज्ञानेन तु तदज्ञानं येषां नाशितमात्मनः ।
तेषामादित्यवज्ज्ञानं प्रकाशयति तत्परम् ॥ १६ ॥
तद्बुद्धयस्तदात्मानस्तन्निष्ठास्तत्परायणाः ।
गच्छन्त्यपुनरावृत्तिं ज्ञाननिर्धूतकल्मषाः ॥ १७ ॥
§§ विद्याविनयसंपन्ने ब्राह्मणे गवि हस्तिनि ।
शुनि चैव श्वपाके च पण्डिताः समदर्शिनः ॥ १८ ॥
इहैव तैर्जितः सर्गो येषां साम्ये स्थितं मनः ।
निर्दोषं हि समं ब्रह्म तस्माद्ब्रह्मणि ते स्थिताः ॥ १९ ॥

(16) But those, whose own such Ignorance has been destroyed by Knowledge, their Knowledge throws light on the Highest Principle like the Sun; (17) and those, whose Reason has become engrossed in this Highest Principle, whose Internal Sense (*antahkaraṇa*) has found happiness in It, and become fixed on It, and devoted to It, their sin is entirely washed away by Knowledge; and they do not come to birth again.

[The Blessed Lord now gives a further description of the state of the '*brahma-bhūta*' (merged in the Brahman) or '*jīvanmukta* (Released in this life) state of these Karma-Yogins (not Saṁnyāsins), whose Ignorance has thus been destroyed—]

(18) Those who have become Pandits (that is, Jñānins), their vision is the same towards the Brahmin endowed with Knowledge and humility, as towards a cow, or an elephant, or a dog, or a *cāṇḍāla*. (19) Those, whose Mind, has thus become steady in a state of Equability, conquer the mortal world, wherever they are (that is, without having to wait for death); because, the Brahman is faultless and equable; therefore, these persons (with an equable Reason) are (always) merged in the Brahman (that is, they have become *brahma-bhūta* already in this world).

[This is a repetition of the statement in the Upaniṣads that he, who has Realised that the Ātman-formed Parameśvara is a Non-Doer, and that the entire activity is

न प्रहृष्येत्प्रियं प्राप्य नोद्विजेत् प्राप्य चाप्रियम् ।
स्थिरबुद्धिरसंमूढो ब्रह्मविद्ब्रह्मणि स्थितः ॥ २० ॥
बाह्यस्पर्शेष्वसक्तात्मा विन्दत्यात्मनि यत्सुखम् ।
स ब्रह्मयोगयुक्तात्मा सुखमक्षय्यमश्नुते ॥ २१ ॥

of Prakṛti, has 'become steeped in the Brahman' (*brahma-saṁstha*); and he attains Release, *cf.* "*brahma-saṁstho 'mṛtatvam eti*" (Chān. 2. 23. 1). Yet, it is clear from stanzas 1 to 12 above that, according to the Gītā, a man does not escape Action even though he has reached this state. This sentence from the Chāndogyopaniṣad has been interpreted by Śaṁkarācārya so as to support the Path of Renunciation; but, if one considers the anterior and posterior context in the original Upaniṣad, it will be seen that the greater possibility is of this statement having been made with reference to the person who performs Actions appropriate to the three stages of life, even after having become *brahma-saṁstha*; and this same import has been very clearly set out at the end of the Upaniṣad (See Chān. 8. 15. 1). As this state is reached during life after a man has attained the Knowledge of the Brahma (*brahma-jñāna*), it is called the '*jīvan-muktāvasthā*' (state of being Released in life), (See Gī. Ra. Ch. X, pp. 413 to 415). This is the highest pinnacle of Metaphysics, and the Yoga devices, such as, the control of the mental tendencies (*citta-vṛtti-nirodha*) etc., by which this state can be reached, are explained at length in the next chapter. This chapter contains only a further description of this state.]

(20) One should not become glad because one has got the *priya* (that is, the desired thing); nor should one become dejected, if something undesirable happens. One whose mind has (thus) become steady, and who does not suffer from mental confusion, such a Knower of the Brahman is (said to have become) 'steady in the Brahman'. (21) He (alone), whose mind is not attached to the contacts (with the senses) of external objects, (that is, to the enjoyment of objects of sense), obtains (whatever) the happiness, which pertains to the Ātman; and such a person, who has become *yukta* as a

ये हि संस्पर्शजा भोगा दुःखयोनय एव ते ।
आद्यन्तवन्तः कौन्तेय न तेषु रमते बुधः ॥ २२ ॥
शक्नोतीहैव यः सोढुं प्राक्शरीरविमोक्षणात् ।
कामक्रोधोद्भवं वेगं स युक्तः स सुखी नरः ॥ २३ ॥
§§ योऽन्तःसुखोऽन्तरारामस्तथान्तर्ज्योतिरेव यः ।
स योगी ब्रह्मनिर्वाणं ब्रह्मभूतोऽधिगच्छति ॥ २४ ॥
लभन्ते ब्रह्मनिर्वाणमृषयः क्षीणकल्मषाः ।
छिन्नद्वैधा यतात्मानः सर्वभूतहिते रताः ॥ २५ ॥

result of union with the Brahman, enjoys inexhaustible happiness. (22) As enjoyments, born of contacts (with external objects), have a beginning and an end, they become the cause of unhappiness. The wise man, O Kaunteya! does not find happiness in them. (23) He, who has become capable (by control of the senses) of bearing in this world, before leaving this body (that is, till death), such pain as is born of Desire and Anger, is the liberated and the (truly) happy man.

[This is an expansion and elucidation of the advice of the Blessed Lord to Arjuna in the second chapter that he must bear pain as well as happiness (Gī. 2. 14). In Gītā 2. 14, the adjective "*āgamāpāyinaḥ*" (i. e., 'coming and going') has been applied to pain and happiness; whereas, here in the 22nd stanza, the word used is "*ādyantavantaḥ*" (i. e., 'with a beginning and an end'); and here the word '*bāhya*' has been used instead of the word '*mātrā*' used there; this stanza (i. e., stanza 21) also defines who is to be called '*yukta*'. Bearing pain and happiness equably, and not avoiding them, is the true characteristic of *yukta*-ness. See my commentary on Gītā 2. 61.]

(24) He who has thus become internally (that is, in his conscience) happy (without laying any store by external happiness or unhappiness), who has found tranquility within himself, and similarly, who has acquired (this) internal light, such a (Karma-) Yogin has become Brahman-formed, and attains the *brahma-nirvāṇa* Release (that is, the Release of being merged in and unified with the Brahman). (25) Those

कामक्रोधवियुक्तानां यतीनां यतचेतसाम् ।
अभितो ब्रह्मनिर्वाणं वर्तते विदितात्मनाम् ॥ २६ ॥
स्पर्शान्कृत्वा बहिर्बाह्यांश्चक्षुश्चैवान्तरे भ्रुवोः ।
प्राणापानौ समौ कृत्वा नासाभ्यन्तरचारिणौ ॥ २७ ॥
यतेन्द्रियमनोबुद्धिर्मुनिर्मोक्षपरायणः ।
विगतेच्छाभयक्रोधो यः सदा मुक्त एव सः ॥ २८ ॥

Ṛṣis, who have lost the sense of duality (that is, who have realised the principle that there is only one Parameśvara in all places), whose sins have been dissolved, and who have become engrossed in achieving the welfare of the entire creation by means of Self-control, attain Release in the shape of *brahma-nirvāṇa.* (26) The *yatin*s who are free from Desire and Anger, who are self-controlled and possessed of Self-Knowledge, attain the *brahma-nirvāṇa* Release '*abhitaḥ*' (that is, as if it is placed all round them, or in front of them; that is to say, wherever they are). (27) That Release-desiring Muni, who keeps outside the (painful or pleasing) contacts (of the organs) with external objects; who, having fixed his gaze between the two eye-brows, and equalised the *prāṇa* and the *apāna* breaths passing through his nostrils, (28) has obtained control over the senses, the Mind, and the Reason; and, who has become free from Desire, Fear, and Anger, may be said to be 'perpetually Released'.

[It will be seen from Chapter IX (pp. 320 and 344) and Chapter X (p. 414) of the Gītā-Rahasya, that this description is of the Jīvan-muktāvasthā (state of being Released, while alive). But, the assertion of some commentators that it is a description of a man who follows the Path of Renunciation is not correct in my opinion. Whether in the Path of Renunciation, or in the Path of Karma-Yoga, 'tranquility' (*śānti*) is one and the same; and to that extent, this description might apply to the Path of Renunciation; this cannot be denied; but, as in the beginning of this chapter, the Karma-Yoga has been mentioned as the superior path, and again in the 25th stanza, it is stated that Jñānins (sages) are engrossed in

§§ भोक्तारं यज्ञतपसां सर्वलोकमहेश्वरम् ।
सुहृदं सर्वभूतानां ज्ञात्वा मां शान्तिमृच्छति ॥ २९ ॥

इति श्रीमद्भगवद्गीतासु उपनिषत्सु ब्रह्मविद्यायां योगशास्त्रे श्रीकृष्णार्जुनसंवादे कर्मसंन्यासयोगो नाम पञ्चमोऽध्यायः ॥ ५ ॥

achieving Universal Welfare, it is clear that this description is of the Karma-Yogin Jīvan-mukta (Released-in-life) and not of the Saṁnyāsin (See Gī. Ra. p. 520). To proceed; since, Realising the Parameśvara, Who pervades the entire creation, is the highest ideal even according to the Path of Action (*karma-mārga*), the Blessed Lord finally says that—]

(29) Realising, (in this way), Me, Who am the Recipient of (all) sacrifice and austerities, the Overlord of all spheres (such as heaven, etc.) and the Friend of the entire creation, he attains tranquility.

Thus ends the fifth chapter entitled SAṀNYASA-YOGA in the dialogue between Śrī Kṛṣṇa and Arjuna on the Yoga included in the science of the Brahman (that is, on the Karma-Yoga) in the Upaniṣad sung (that is, told) by the Blessed Lord.

षष्ठोऽध्यायः

CHAPTER VI.

[Thus far it has been proved that, (i) though nothing except Knowledge is necessary for attaining Release, the Jñānin must continue to perform Actions even after the Acquisition of Jñāna, for universal welfare; but that, (ii) he must perform these with an Equable Reason, and having given up the Desire for Fruit, so that they may not have any binding effect; that, (iii) this is known as the Karma-Yoga; and that, (iv) this path of life is more praise-worthy than the path of Renunciation of Action (*karma-saṁnyāsa*). Nevertheless, the justification of Karma-Yoga is not thereby finished. Already in Chapter III, in describing Desire, Anger, etc., the Blessed Lord has explained to Arjuna, that these enemies make their home in the organs, the Mind, and the Reason of humans, and destroy their Spiritual Knowledge (*jñāna*) as also their Specified Knowledge (*vijñāna*), (3. 40); and advised him that he should, therefore, first conquer these enemies by controlling his senses. In order that this advice should be complete, it was necessary to explain (1) how to acquire control over the senses, and (2) what is Spiritual Knowledge and what Specified Knowledge; but, in the meantime, the Blessed Lord, in reply to the question of Arjuna, (i) explained to him which path of life, out of the paths of Karma-Yoga and Karma-Saṁnyāsa, was the better one; (ii) harmonised these two paths of life as far as possible; and (iii) showed how the Brahma-nirvāṇa Release could be obtained without giving up Action, and by performing Action with an unattached Reason. The Blessed Lord now starts in this chapter a description of the means by which it is possible to acquire this unattached (*niḥsaṅga*), or Brahman-devoted (*brahma-niṣṭha*) state, which is necessary even in Karma-Yoga. Nevertheless, in order that it should be clear that this explanation has not been given for preaching the Pātañjala-Yoga independently, the Blessed Lord, to start with, repeats here what has been expounded

श्रीभगवानुवाच ।

§§ अनाश्रितः कर्मफलं कार्यं कर्म करोति यः ।
स संन्यासी च योगी च न निरग्निर्न चाक्रियः ॥ १ ॥
यं संन्यासमिति प्राहुर्योगं तं विद्धि पाण्डव ।
न ह्यसंन्यस्तसंकल्पो योगी भवति कश्चन ॥ २ ॥

in the previous chapters, namely that, the true Saṁnyāsin is the person, who performs Actions, having given up the Hope for Fruit of Action, and not the one, who abandons Action (5. 3)—]

The Blessed Lord said :—

(1) That man is to be called a Saṁnyāsin and a Karma-Yogin, who performs (his Śāstra-enjoined) duties, without taking shelter in the Fruit of Action (that is, not having in his Mind a 'home' in the shape of Hope of Fruit). The *niragni* (that is, one who has given up Fire-ritual, such as, *agnihotra* etc.), or the *akriya* (that is, one who sits absolutely quiet, without performing any Action whatsoever), such a man is not (the true Saṁnyāsin, or the true Yogin). (2) O Pāṇḍava, understand that what is known as Saṁnyāsa is (Karma-) Yoga, because no one can become a (Karma-) Yogin unless he makes a Saṁnyāsa (i. e., Renunciation—Trans.) of the *saṁkalpa* (that is, of the Hope of Fruit in the shape of a Desireful Reason).

[This is only a repetition of the statements made in the previous chapters, such as, "*ekaṁ sāṁkhyaṁ ca yogaṁ ca*" (5. 5); or, "there is no Saṁnyāsa except by Yoga" (5. 6); or, "*jñeyaḥ sa nitya-saṁnyāsī*" (5. 3); and later on, where the whole subject-matter has been summarised in Chapter XVIII, the very same import is again repeated. In the state of a house-holder, one has to maintain an *agnihotra* (a perpetual sacrificial fire), and perform Yajñas, Yāgas etc. But, as it was not necessary for a person, who had become an ascetic, to thus maintain a perpetual fire, it is stated in the Manu-Smṛti, that he should become *niragni* (i. e., free from Fire-ritual), and live in the forest, and maintain himself by begging, and not take part in worldly affairs

§§ आरुरुक्षोर्मुनेर्योगं कर्म कारणमुच्यते ।
योगारूढस्य तस्यैव शमः कारणमुच्यते ॥ ३ ॥

(Manu. 6. 25 etc.). This dictum of Manu has been referred to in the first stanza above, and with reference to it, the Blessed Lord says that, "becoming '*niragni*' or '*niṣkriya*' is not a feature of true Saṁnyāsa". True Saṁnyāsa consists in giving up a Desireful Reason, or the Hope of Fruit. Saṁnyāsa consists in the frame of the Mind, and not in the external act of giving up the maintenance of the sacrificial fire, or ritual. Therefore, that man alone, who gives up the Hope of Fruit, or the *saṁkalpa*, and thus performs his duties, can be called the true Saṁnyāsin. This doctrine of the Gītā is different from the doctrine of the Smṛti-writers; and I have to refer the reader to Chapter XI of the Gītā-Rahasya (pp. 480–496), where I have clearly shown how the Gītā harmonises it with the doctrine of the Smṛtis. Having in this way explained what true Saṁnyāsa is, the Blessed Lord now explains the difference between the Actions to be performed in the *sādhanāvasthā*, that is, in the state before Knowledge has been acquired, and those to be performed in the *siddhāvasthā* that is, after the Acquisition of Knowledge, giving up the Hope of Fruit—]

(3) To the Muni who desires to become (Karma-) *yogārūḍha* (that is, enthroned on the Karma-Yoga—Trans.), Karma is said to be the *kāraṇa*, (that is the means); and when that same man has become *yogārūḍha* (that is, has become a complete Yogin), the *śama* (that is serenity—Trans.) is said to become later on the *kāraṇa* (for the Karma).

[Commentators have utterly misinterpreted the meaning of this stanza. The word '*yoga*' used in the first part of the stanza means Karma-Yoga ; and it is accepted by everybody that, for acquiring that Yoga, Karma is the *kāraṇa*, or the means; but commentators have interpreted the words, "after having become '*yogārūḍha*', *śama* becomes the *kāraṇa* for him", as supporting the Path of Renunciation. What they say is : '*śama*' means '*upaśama*' (that is, 'cessation'—Trans.) of Karma; and he who has acquired Yoga must, therefore, give up Karma! Because, according to them, the Karma-Yoga is a part (*aṅga*), that is, a preliminary accomplishment, of Saṁnyāsa. But, this interpretation is only a doctrine-supporting interpretation, and not the correct interpretation. For, (1) if the Blessed Lord has stated already in the first stanza of this chapter, that that man alone is a true Yogin, or *yogārūḍha*, who "performs his duty" without taking shelter in the Fruit of Action, and that the person who does not perform Action (who is an *akriya*) is not a true Yogin, it would be totally illogical to imagine, that the Blessed Lord could have in the third stanza advised the Yogin, or the *yogārūḍha*, to make the *śama* of Karma, that is, to give up Karma. Although it may be the opinion of the Saṁnyāsa school, that the *yogārūḍha* should not perform Action, after having attained tranquility, yet, that opinion is not acceptable to the Gītā; and there is clear advice in several places in the Gītā to the effect that the Karma-Yogin should, even in the State of Perfection (*siddhāvasthā*) continue to perform all Actions, desirelessly, and merely as duties, and so long as he is alive, in the same manner as the Blessed Lord. (*Cf.* Gī. 2. 71; 3. 7 and 19; 4. 19-21; 5. 7-12; 12. 12; 18. 56 and 57; and Gī. Ra. Ch. XI and XII). (2) The second reason is: How is it possible to interprete '*śama*' as meaning the '*śama*' of Karma? The word '*śama*' appears three or four times in the Bhagavadgītā (Gī. 10.4; 18.42); and in those places, as also in common parlance, it means 'peace of Mind'. Then, why should it be interpreted to mean the 'peace or the ending of Karma'? In order to get over this difficulty, commentators have, in the Paiśācya-bhāṣya on the Gītā, treated '*tasya*' as being the sixth (possessive) case of the neuter gender, and read the line as: '*tasyaiva karmaṇaḥ śamaḥ*', (that is, 'the *śama*, which is *tasya*, namely, of the Karma, referred to in the first half of the stanza), instead of referring the demonstrative pronoun '*tasyaiva*' in the phrase '*yogārūḍhasya tasyaiva*' to the word '*yogārūḍhasya*'! But, this syntax of the sentence is also not plain; because, undoubtedly, the second part of the stanza has been started in order to show the state reached afterwards, that is, after he has completed his training, by the man studying the Yoga, who has been described in the first part of the stanza; therefore, the word '*tasyaiva*' cannot be interpreted as meaning '*karmaṇaḥ eva*'; and even if that interpretation is taken, then, that word should be joined to the words '*kāraṇam ucyate*', instead of to the word '*śama*'. Then, the syntax of the sentence will run as follows, namely, '*śamaḥ yogārūḍhasya tasyaiva karmaṇaḥ kāraṇam ucyate*', which means, "the '*śama*' now becomes the *kāraṇa* for the Karma of the *yogārūḍha*'. (3) The third reason for rejecting the interpretation of the commentators is as follows: according to the Path of Saṁnyāsa, nothing remains to be done for the *yogārūḍha*, and all his Karma ends in '*śama*'; and if this is true, the word '*kāraṇa*' in the sentence, "the '*śama*' becomes the '*kāraṇa*' for the *yogārūḍha*", becomes totally meaningless. The word '*kāraṇa*' is always a relative (*sāpekṣa*) term. As soon as you say '*kāraṇa*' (means), there must be some '*kārya*' (effect) of it. But, according to the Saṁnyāsa doctrine, there is no more any *kārya* left for the *yogārūḍha*. If '*śama*' is taken as the '*kāraṇa*', or the means for Release, even that interpretation is not proper. Well; if it is said that '*śama*' is the '*kāraṇa*', that is, the means, for the Acquisition of Knowledge, then, this being a description of the *yogārūḍha*, that is, of one, who has already reached the state of complete perfection, he has already acquired Knowledge by means of Karma. Then, of what is this '*śama*', the '*kāraṇa*'? The commentators of the Saṁnyāsa school cannot give any satisfactory solution of this question. But, if one considers the matter, disregarding the interpretation of the commentators, then, in interpreting the second part of the stanza, the word '*karma*' in the first part of the stanza comes before the mind by reason of its proximity; and then, one gets the interpretation that: as the *yogārūḍha* cannot escape Action for Universal Welfare (*lokasaṁgraha*), though he has no self-interest left (Gī. 3. 17–19), '*śama*' now becomes the '*kāraṇa*' or the means, for him to perform that Action.

The same interpretation is arrived at, if one considers the statement in the previous chapter that, "*yuktaḥ karma-phalaṁ tyaktvā śāntim āpnoti naiṣṭhikīm*" (Gī. 5. 12), that is, "the Yogin attains complete tranquility by abandoning the Fruit of Action"; because, in that stanza, 'tranquility' is related not to the 'Abandonment of Action', but to the 'Abandonment of the Hope of Fruit'; and it has been clearly stated in that place, that the *karma-saṁnyāsa*, which the Yogin has to perform, has to be performed '*manasā*', that is, by the Mind (Gī. 5. 13); and that, by the Body, that is, by the organs of Action, such a Yogin must perform all the various Actions. In my opinion, the present stanza is an example of what is known in the *alaṁkāra-śāstra* (science of Figures of Speech) as the '*anyonyā-laṁkāra*', as it embodies some strangeness of meaning, or sweetness of sentiment as is produced by that *alaṁkāra*; for, after stating, in the first part of the stanza, when Karma becomes the '*kāraṇa*' of '*śama*', the latter part of the stanza states conversely, when '*śama*' becomes the '*kāraṇa*' of the Karma. The Blessed Lord says that in the beginning, that is, in the preparatory stage (*sādhanāvasthā*), Action (Karma) becomes the means (*kāraṇa*) of tranquility (*śama*), that is, of Yoga-siddhi; that is to say, when a person goes on performing, as far as possible, all Actions with a Desireless Mind, his Mind becomes peaceful, and he thereby ultimately attains complete perfection of Yoga (*yoga-siddhi*). But, when the Yogin has become *yogārūḍha* (steeped in Yoga), that is to say, when he has reached the state of perfection, (*siddhāvasthā*), this relation of cause and effect between Karma and '*śama*' is reversed; and instead of Karma being the means of obtaining '*śama*', or its '*kāraṇa*', the '*śama*' itself becomes the means for the Karma; that is to say, the *yogārūḍha*, thereafter performs all his Actions merely as duties, and without entertaining any Hope of Fruit, and with a peaceful Mind. In short, this stanza does not mean that a man becomes free from Karma in the state of Perfection; and all that the Gītā says is that, the relation of cause and effect between Karma and '*śama*'

यदा हि नेन्द्रियार्थेषु न कर्मस्वनुषज्जते ।
सर्वसंकल्पसंन्यासी योगारूढस्तदोच्यते ॥ ४ ॥

in the preparatory stage (*sādhanāvasthā*) becomes changed or inverted in the State of Perfection (*siddhāvasthā*), (Gī. Ra. Ch. XI, pp. 449 to 451). It is nowhere stated in the Gītā that the Karma-Yogin must ultimately give up Action; nor is it intended to say so. It is, therefore, not proper to take some stanza or other from the Gītā, wherever there is a chance of doing so, and by some stratagem or other to give it a renunciatory meaning, That is why the Gītā has become so difficult to understand for many in these days. The proposition, that the *yogārūḍha* must continue to perform Actions, is also borne out by the definition given in the next stanza. That stanza is as follows—]

(4) Because, when a man does not become attached to these objects of sense (such as, speech, touch etc.), nor to Karma, and when he makes a Renunciation of all *saṁkalpa* (that is, of the Hope of Fruit in the shape of a Desireful Reason, and not of Action, literally), he is called a '*yogārūḍha*'.

[This stanza may be said to be a continuation of the last stanza or perhaps even of the last three stanzas. This clearly shows that the Gītā advises the Yogārūḍha to give up not Action, but the Hope of Fruit, or the Desireful Reason, and to perform Action desirelessly, and with a peaceful frame of mind. The words '*saṁnyāsa* of *saṁkalpa*' appear in the second stanza above; and they must be given the same meaning here, as in that stanza. Karma-Yoga includes Saṁnyāsa in the shape of the Abandonment of the Hope of Fruit, and that man alone is the true Saṁnyāsin, or Yogin, or the true Yogārūḍha who performs all Actions, having abandoned the Hope of Fruit. The Blessed Lord now says that succeeding in such a Desireless Karma-Yoga, or Renunciation of Hope of Fruit, is a matter within the control of every man; and if he

§§ उद्धरेदात्मनात्मानं नात्मानमवसादयेत् ।
आत्मैव ह्यात्मनो बन्धुरात्मैव रिपुरात्मनः ॥ ५ ॥
बन्धुरात्मात्मनस्तस्य येनात्मैवात्मना जितः ।
अनात्मनस्तु शत्रुत्वे वर्तेतात्मैव शत्रुवत् ॥ ६ ॥
§§ जितात्मनः प्रशान्तस्य परमात्मा समाहितः ।
शीतोष्णसुखदुःखेषु तथा मानापमानयोः ॥ ७ ॥

himself makes the effort, it is not impossible for him to achieve it—]

(5) (Man) should himself bring about his own emancipation; one should not (at any time) discourage oneself; because, (every man) himself is (said to be) his own *bandhu* (that is, helper), or his own enemy. (6) Who has himself conquered himself, becomes his own helper; but who does not understand himself, acts towards himself as his own enemy.

[These two stanzas contain a description of the doctrine of Free Will (*ātma-svātaṁtrya*), and propound the principle that every one must bring about his own emancipation; and that, however powerful Prakṛti (Nature) may be, it is within one's own hands to conquer it and to bring about one's own betterment (Gī. Ra. Ch. X, pp. 383 to 391). In order that this principle should be firmly impressed on the mind, it has been stated (i) positively, that is, by showing, when the Ātman becomes one's friend; and again (ii) negatively, by showing when the Ātman may be said to be one's enemy; and this very principle is again referred to in 13. 28. As the word '*ātmā*' has three meanings in Sanskrit, namely, (1) the '*antarātman*', (2) one's self, and (3) the Internal Sense or the Mind, this word, '*ātmā*' appears several times in this and the following stanzas. The Blessed Lord now explains what result is obtained by bringing the Ātman under control—]

(7) Who has conquered the Ātman (that is, his Internal Sense), and who has attained tranquility, his '*paramātman*' becomes *samāhita* (that is, equal and steady) towards heat and cold, pain and happiness, honour and dishonour.

ज्ञानविज्ञानतृप्तात्मा कूटस्थो विजितेन्द्रियः ।
युक्त इत्युच्यते योगी समलोष्टाश्मकाञ्चनः ॥ ८ ॥

[In this stanza, the word '*paramātman*' has been used with reference to the Ātman itself. The Ātman within the body is ordinarily engrossed in the turmoil of pain and happiness; but, when this turmoil has been conquered by means of control of the senses, the same Ātman acquires the form of a '*paramātman*', or of the '*parameśvara*'. It is stated further on in the Gītā itself (Gī. 13. 22 and 31) that the Paramātman is not some substance, different in nature from the Ātman, but that the Ātman within the body of a man is essentially the Paramātman; and even in the Mahābhārata, there is a statement that—

ātmā kṣetrajña ıty uktaḥ saṁyuktaḥ prākṛtair guṇaiḥ ।
tair eva tu vinirmuktaḥ paramātmety udāhṛtaḥ ॥
(Ma. Bhā. Śān. 187. 24),

that is, "when the Ātman is *prākṛta*, that is, bound by the constituents of Prakṛti (by emotions, such as, happiness, pain etc.), it is called the '*kṣetrajña*' or the '*jīvātman*', within the body; and when it has become free from these constituents, the same Ātman is called the Paramātman". It will be seen from Chapter IX of the Gītā-Rahasya, that the same is the doctrine of the Non-Dualistic Vedānta. Those who are of opinion that the Gītā does not support Non-Dualism, but supports Qualified Monism (*viśiṣṭādvaita*), or pure Dualism, do not take the word '*paramātmā*' here as a single word, but break it up into '*paraṁ*' and '*ātmā*', and look upon the word '*paraṁ*' as an adverb qualifying the verb '*samāhitaḥ*'. This interpretation is far-fetched; but it will show how commentators, who want to establish a particular doctrine, stretch the meaning of the Gītā to support their own point of view.]

(8) He, whose Ātman has become satisfied by *jñāna* (that is, Spiritual Knowledge—Trans.) and by *vijñāna*, [that is, by specified (*vividha*) Jñāna], who has conquered his senses, who has become '*kūṭastha*' (that is, who has reached the origin), and has begun to look upon the earth, stone, and gold as one and the same, such a (Karma-) Yogin (alone)

सुहृन्मित्रार्युदासीनमध्यस्थद्वेष्यबन्धुषु ।
साधुष्वपि च पापेषु समबुद्धिर्विशिष्यते ॥ ९ ॥
§§ योगी युञ्जीत सततमात्मानं रहसि स्थितः ।
एकाकी यतचित्तात्मा निराशीरपरिग्रहः ॥ १० ॥

is said to be '*yukta*' (that is, to have reached the *siddhāvasthā*). (9) That man, whose Reason has become equal towards dear persons, friends, enemies, *udāsīnas*, *madhyasthas*, persons fit to be hated, and brethren, as also towards saints, and evil-minded persons, may be said to be of special worth.

['*suhṛd*' means a friend, who helps without expecting a return; '*udāsīna*' is a person, who, where there are two factions, does not desire the good or the evil of either party; '*madhyastha*' is a person, who wishes well by both sides; and '*bandhu*' is a relation. Such are the meanings given by commentators to these words. But it will do, if slightly different meanings are taken instead of taking these meanings; because, these words have not been used with the intention of showing a different meaning in each case; and several words are sometimes used in this way in order that an exhaustive meaning may be conveyed by the combination, and that nothing should be left over. In this way, after having briefly explained who may be called a '*yogī*', or a '*yukta*', or a '*yogārūḍha*' (Gī. 2. 61; 4. 18; and 5. 23), the Blessed Lord has also said that every man is free to achieve this Karma-Yoga for himself; and that it is not necessary for him to depend for assistance on anybody else for that purpose. The Blessed Lord now explains the means for achieving this Karma-Yoga—]

(10) He, who is a Yogin (that is, a Karma-Yogin) should, remaining alone in solitude; controlling his Mind, and his Ātman; not entertaining any desire whatsoever; and giving up *parigraha* (that is, bonds), take constantly to his Yoga-practice.

[It becomes clear from the next stanza that the word '*yuñjīta*' refers to the Yoga described in the Pātañjala-

शुचौ देशे प्रतिष्ठाप्य स्थिरमासनमात्मनः ।
नात्युच्छ्रितं नातिनीचं चैलाजिनकुशोत्तरम् ॥ ११ ॥

तत्रैकाग्रं मनः कृत्वा यतचित्तेन्द्रियक्रियः ।
उपविश्यासने युञ्ज्याद्योगमात्मविशुद्धये ॥ १२ ॥

समं कायशिरोग्रीवं धारयन्नचलं स्थिरः ।
संप्रेक्ष्य नासिकाग्रं स्वं दिशश्चानवलोकयन् ॥ १३ ॥

sūtras. But, this does not mean that the man, who wishes to achieve the Karma-Yoga must spend his entire life in the practice of the Pātañjala-Yoga. The Pātañjala-Yoga has been described in this chapter as a means for acquiring that Equable Reason, which is necessary in the Karma-Yoga; and solitude is necessary only to that extent. As a result of Prakṛti, many persons are not able to acquire in one life the Mental Absorption (*samādhi*) described in the Pātañjala-Yoga; and the Blessed Lord has said at the end of this very chapter, that such persons should practise the Karma-Yoga by steadying their Reason, as far as possible, instead of wasting their whole life in the practice of Pātañjala-Yoga; and that by doing so, they will ultimately attain Perfection (*siddhi*) after many births (Gī. Ra. Ch. X, pp. 389 to 390)—]

(11) Having unchangeably fixed one's '*āsana*' (that is, place of sitting—Trans.) on dried grass, covered by a deer-skin, over which too has been placed a piece of cloth, neither too high nor too low, in a pure place, (12) and controlling in that place the activities of the * Mental Vision (i. e., *citta*—Trans.) and of the senses, and concentrating the Mind, one should practice Yoga, sitting on that seat, for self-purification. (13) Becoming steady, holding the *kāya* (that is, the back), the head, and the neck fixedly in a vertical straight line, not looking towards the cardinal directions (that is, around oneself), and fixing the, gaze on the tip of

* See, Apte, *Practical Sanskrit-English Dictionary*, 1924, p. 435—Trans.

प्रशान्तात्मा विगतभीर्ब्रह्मचारिव्रते स्थितः ।
मनः संयम्य मच्चित्तो युक्त आसीत मत्परः ॥ १४ ॥
युञ्जन्नेवं सदात्मानं योगी नियतमानसः ।
शान्तिं निर्वाणपरमां मत्संस्थामधिगच्छति ॥ १५ ॥

one's nose, (14) not entertaining any fear, keeping a peaceful frame of mind, observing *brahmacarya* (that is, celibacy—Trans.), controlling the Mind, fixing one's Mental Vision on Me, becoming devoted to Me, one should become *yukta* (i. e., 'steeped in Yoga'—Trans.)

[The words "in a pure place" and "holding the back, neck, and the head fixedly in a vertical straight line" are from the Śvetāśvataropaniṣad (see Śve. 2. 8 and 10); and the whole of the description given above is not from the Haṭha-Yoga, but is more consistent with the description of Yoga given in the ancient Upaniṣads. In the Haṭha-Yoga, there is a coercive control of the senses; but it is stated later on in the 24th stanza of this very chapter, that "the senses should be controlled by the Mind" *Cf.* "*manasaiva indriyagrāmaṁ viniyamya*". This clearly shows that the Gītā does not countenance the Haṭha-Yoga. Similarly, it has been stated at the end of this chapter, that this description is not to be understood as directing a person to spend his whole life in the practice of Yoga. The Blessed Lord now further expounds the concrete results of this Yoga-practice—]

(15) By thus continually practising the Yoga, the Mind comes under control; and the (Karma-) Yogin attains the tranquility, to be found in Me, and which is ultimately productive of '*nirvāṇa*' (that is, which causes assimilation into Me).

[The word 'continually' in this stanza is not to be taken as meaning for twenty-four hours a day. All that is meant is, that one should perform this practice, for a few hours every day (see commentary on stanza 10). The reason for saying: "become '*maccitta*' and '*matparāyaṇa*' while thus practising Yoga", is that the Pātañjala-Yoga is

नात्यश्नतस्तु योगोऽस्ति न चैकान्तमनश्नतः ।
न चातिस्वप्नशीलस्य जाग्रतो नैव चार्जुन ॥ १६ ॥
युक्ताहारविहारस्य युक्तचेष्टस्य कर्मसु ।
युक्तस्वप्नावबोधस्य योगो भवति दुःखहा ॥ १७ ॥

only one of the devices or processes for controlling the Mind. When the Mind has been controlled by this practice, it is possible to fix it on other things instead of on the Blessed Lord. Therefore, the Gītā says that, (i) one should not thus misapply the concentrated Mind, but should utilise this concentration or '*samādhi*' of the Mind, for acquiring the Knowledge of the form of the Parameśvara; that, (ii) it is only when this is done that Yoga becomes beneficial; and that, (iii) otherwise, the practice is only productive of useless trouble; and the same meaning is conveyed later on in the 29th and 30th stanzas, and again in the 47th stanza at the end of the chapter. Those, who have only practised the physical control of, or acquired the Yoga of, the organs, without being devoted to the Parameśvara, only become adept in such practices, as '*jāraṇa*' (incantations to produce impotency, diseases, or infirmities), '*māraṇa*' (incantations to destroy or kill), '*vaśīkaraṇa*' (incantations for fascinating or enchanting and subduing), which are harmful to others. This state of things is not desirable either for the Gītā or for any other path of Release. The Blessed Lord now gives again a further elucidation of this Yoga-practice—]

(16) O Arjuna! he who eats too much, or who eats nothing at all, and he who sleeps too much, or who keeps awake too much cannot succeed in (this) Yoga. (17) Whose food and pastime are moderate, whose Action is just sufficient, and whose sleep and keeping awake are measured, to him, (this) Yoga becomes a destroyer of pain (that is, a producer of happiness).

[In this stanza, the word '*yoga*' means the practice of the Pātañjala-Yoga; and the word '*yukta*' means, moderate, enough, or measured; and further on also, in one or two places the word '*yoga*' has been used to mean the

§§ यदा विनियतं चित्तमात्मन्येवावतिष्ठते ।
निःस्पृहः सर्वकामेभ्यो युक्त इत्युच्यते तदा ॥ १८ ॥
यथा दीपो निवातस्थो नेङ्गते सोपमा स्मृता ।
योगिनो यतचित्तस्य युञ्जतो योगमात्मनः ॥ १९ ॥

Pātañjala-Yoga. Nevertheless, it does not, on that account, follow that this chapter deals independently with the Pātañjala-Yoga. It has been clearly stated in the foregoing lines that one's most important duty in life is to successfully practise the Karma-Yoga; and that this description of the Pātañjala-Yoga has been given as being a means for attaining that Karma-Yoga, and for that purpose only; and it becomes clear from the words "whose Action is just sufficient", that this Yoga-practice has to be carried on, without giving up other Action. The Blessed Lord now first gives a short description of a Yogin, and describes the nature of the happiness of mental absorption (*samādhi*)—]

(18) When the controlled Mind becomes fixed on the Ātman, and when there does not remain the desire for any enjoyment, the man is said to have become '*yukta*'. (19) Just as a lamp (that is, the flame of a lamp) kept in a breezeless place, remains unflickering, that same simile is applied to the Yogin, who practices Yoga, having controlled the Mind.

[Besides this simile, there are other similes in the Mahābhārata, such as, "the mind of a Yogin becomes '*yukta*', just as a man becomes '*yukta*' (concentrated) when taking a utensil filled with oil down a stair-case, or when protecting a boat in a storm (Śānti. 300. 31, 34). The simile in the Kaṭhopaniṣad of the charioteer and the horses of the chariot, is well-known; and although that simile has not been clearly used in the Gītā, yet, the 67th and 68th stanzas of the second chapter, and the 25th stanza of this chapter, have clearly been written with that simile in mind. Although the word '*yoga*' has the technical meaning of 'Karma-Yoga' in the Gītā, yet, that word has been used in various other meanings in the Gītā; for instance, in 9. 5 and 10. 7, the word '*yoga*' has been used to mean "the

यत्रोपरमते चित्तं निरुद्धं योगसेवया ।
यत्र चैवात्मनात्मानं पश्यन्नात्मनि तुष्यति ॥ २० ॥
सुखमात्यन्तिकं यत्तद्बुद्धिग्राह्यमतीन्द्रियम् ।
वेत्ति यत्र न चैवायं स्थितश्चलति तत्त्वतः ॥ २१ ॥
यं लब्ध्वा चापरं लाभं मन्यते नाधिकं ततः ।
यस्मिन् स्थितो न दुःखेन गुरुणापि विचाल्यते ॥ २२ ॥
तं विद्याद्दुःखसंयोगवियोगं योगसंज्ञितम् ।
स निश्चयेन योक्तव्यो योगोऽनिर्विण्णचेतसा ॥ २३ ॥

power to do something supernatural, or whatever is desired". Nay, as the word '*yoga*' has several meanings, the supporters of the Pātañjala-Yoga, or of the Sāṁkhya-Yoga, have found an opportunity of making use of that fact-for saying that the Gītā supports their respective doctrines. The Blessed Lord now describes in a more exhaustive manner the '*samādhi*' in the shape of 'total control of the Mental Vision' prescribed by the Pātañjala-Yoga—]

(20) That state in which the Mind remains entranced after it has become controlled by Yoga-practice, and seeing one's Ātman in which, one remains contented in the Ātman itself; (21) in which It experiences that summit of happiness, which is only Mind-Realised (*buddhigamya*) and imperceptible to the senses; and, having (once) become steady in which, It does not swerve from the '*tattva*' (that is, principle—Trans.); (22) similarly, having acquired which state, It does not consider any other attainment as greater, and having become steady in which, no pain, however big can move (It) therefrom; (23) that state is known as the "*viyoga* (i.e., disunion—Trans.) from the contact of pain", that is, as '*yoga*'; and this 'Yoga' must be practised determinedly, without allowing the Mind to get tired.

[These four stanzas make one sentence. The demonstrative pronoun "to him" ('*taṁ*'), used at the beginning of the 23rd stanza, refers to the description given in the first three stanzas; and the four stanzas complete the

§§ संकल्पप्रभवान्कामांस्त्यक्त्वा सर्वानशेषतः ।
मनसैवेन्द्रियग्रामं विनियम्य समन्ततः ॥ २४ ॥
शनैः शनैरुपरमेद्बुद्ध्या धृतिगृहीतया ।
आत्मसंस्थं मनःकृत्वा न किंचिदपि चिन्तयेत् ॥ २५ ॥

description of the '*samādhi*'. The words used in the beginning of the 20th stanza are similar to the description of 'Yoga' as, "*yogaś cittavṛttinirodhaḥ*", that is, "Yoga means the control of the activities of the Mental Vision (*citta*)" given in the Pātañjala-Yoga-Sūtras. The '*samādhi*' is the culmination of this control of the activities of the Mental vision; and that is called 'Yoga': this is the new definition of the word '*yoga*', which has now been intentionally given. It has been stated in the Upaniṣads and in the Mahābhārata, that a determined and industrious man can accomplish this Yoga in six months (Maitryu. 6. 28; Amṛtanāda. 29; Ma. Bhā. Aśva. Anugītā, 19. 66). Nevertheless, it has been stated above in the 20th stanza, and later on also in the 28th stanza, that this happiness, arising out of the *samādhi* of the Pātañjala-Yoga, is not the result merely of the control of the activities of the Mind, but arises after one has become acquainted with the nature of the Ātman, after having controlled the activities of the Mind. This painless condition is known as '*brahmānanda*' (the Brāhmic bliss), or, '*ātmaprasādaja* happiness' (the happiness resulting from the Realisation of the Ātman), or, '*ātmānanda*' (the Ātmic bliss), (Gī. 18. 37, and Gī. Ra. Ch. IX, p. 320). It is not that this Equability of the Mind, necessary for acquiring the Knowledge of the Ātman, can be acquired only by the Pātañjala-Yoga; and it is stated in the following chapters that the same result, namely, the purification of the Mind, can also be achieved by means of Knowledge (*jñāna*) and Devotion (*bhakti*); and, that course is usually considered more proper and easier. The Blessed Lord has thus given a description of the *samādhi*; He now explains how that *samādhi* is to be brought about—]

(24) Abandoning all the *kāma* (that is, wishes) arising out of *saṁkalpa* (that is, imagination—Trans.), and controlling the senses on all sides by the Mind, (25) you should gradually

यतो यतो निश्चरति मनश्चञ्चलमस्थिरम् ।
ततस्ततो नियम्यैतदात्मन्येव वशं नयेत् ॥ २६ ॥
§§ प्रशान्तमनसं ह्येनं योगिनं सुखमुत्तमम् ।
उपैति शान्तरजसं ब्रह्मभूतमकल्मषम् ॥ २७ ॥
युञ्जन्नेवं सदात्मानं योगी विगतकल्मषः ।
सुखेन ब्रह्मसंस्पर्शमत्यन्तं सुखमश्नुते ॥ २८ ॥

become tranquil, with a courageful Mind; and steadying the Mind on the Ātman, you should allow no thought to enter the Mind. (26) (while you are concentrating the Mental Vision in this fashion) Controlling the volatile and unsteady Mind in every direction, from which it may seek to escape, you should bring it within the control of the Ātman.

[The description of this process of attaining the *samādhi* (absorption) of the Mind is well-exemplified by the illustration of a chariot given in the Kaṭhopaniṣad (Kaṭha. 1. 3. 3). Just as the skilful charioteer takes the horses along a straight road, without allowing them to rush in this direction or that, the same kind of effort has a man to make in order to attain *samādhi*. He, who is accustomed to concentrate his mind on any particular subject, will easily understand the meaning underlying this stanza. When the Mind is controlled in one direction, it breaks out in another direction; and unless this is stopped, it is not possible to attain *samādhi*. The Blessed Lord now describes the result which can be obtained by controlling the Mind in this way—]

(27) The (Karma-)Yogin, who is thus peaceful-minded, devoid of the *rajas* quality, sinless, and *brahma-bhūta*, attains the highest kind of bliss. (28) The (Karma-) Yogin, who continually practises Yoga in this fashion, becomes liberated from all sins, and happily enjoys the beatific happiness arising from *brahma-saṁyoga* (i. e., union with the Brahman—Trans.).

[I have interpreted the word '*yogī*', in these two stanzas, as meaning 'Karma-Yogin'; because, as the Pātañjala-Yoga has been mentioned as one of the means for attaining

§§ सर्वभूतस्थमात्मानं सर्वभूतानि चात्मनि ।
ईक्षते योगयुक्तात्मा सर्वत्र समदर्शनः ॥ २९ ॥
यो मां पश्यति सर्वत्र सर्वं च मयि पश्यति ।
तस्याहं न प्रणश्यामि स च मे न प्रणश्यति ॥ ३० ॥

the Karma-Yoga, such a man who practises the Pātañjala-Yoga must be a Karma-Yogin. Nevertheless, it will do if the word '*yogī*' is taken to mean a person, who is in *samādhi.* It must not, however, be forgotten that the course of conduct advocated by the Gītā is beyond this. The same argument is advanced in the next two or three stanzas. The Blessed Lord now describes the Self-Identifying (*ātmaupamya*) vision towards the entire creation, acquired after a man has in this way experienced the happiness of the *nirvāṇa* (Absolute) Brahman—]

(29) Whose Ātman has (thus) become *yoga-yukta* (i. e., steeped in Yoga—Trans.), his vision becomes equalised in all directions, and he sees himself in all things, and sees (that) all created things (are) within himself. (30) Who: sees Me (the Parameśvara, Paramātman), (to be) everywhere, and who sees everything, within Me, him, I never abandon ; nor does he ever abandon Me.

[The description in the first out of these two stanzas, where the word '*ātman*' has been used, is from the imperceptible, that is, the metaphysical point of view; and the second description, where the first personal pronoun 'I' has been used, is from the perceptible, that is, the devotional point of view. But both these things mean the same (Gī. Ra. Ch. XIII, pp. 598 to 605). This vision of the identification of the Brahman with the Ātman, is the foundation both of Release and of Karma-Yoga. The first part of the 29th stanza has appeared with a slight difference in the Manu-Smṛti (Manu. 12. 91), in the Mahābhārata (Śān. 238. 21 and 268. 22), and also in the Upaniṣads (Kaiva. 1. 10; and Īśa. 6). Nay, the realisation of the identity of the entire creation with the Ātman is the origin of all Metaphysics and of Karma-Yoga, as has been shown by me at great

सर्वभूतस्थितं यो मां भजत्येकत्वमास्थितः ।
सर्वथा वर्तमानोऽपि स योगी मयि वर्तते ॥ ३१ ॥

आत्मौपम्येन सर्वत्र समं पश्यति योऽर्जुन ।
सुखं वा यदि वा दुःखं स योगी परमो मतः ॥ ३२ ॥

length in Chapter XII of the Gītā-Rahasya (see p. 537 etc.). Although a man may have obtained control over the senses, such control is useless in the absence of this Jñāna; and therefore, the Blessed Lord starts from the next chapter to speak about the Knowledge of the Parameśvara.]

(31) He, who worships Me (the Parameśvara), Who pervade every created thing, keeping in mind the idea of Unity, (that is, of the Identity of the Ātman with all created things), that Karma-Yogin, though he may be acting in all manner, is in Me. (32) O Arjuna! that (Karma-) Yogin, who has begun to look everywhere with a (Self-Identifying-) Vision according to which, others are the same as himself, such a man is considered *parama* (that is, most superior).

[The idea, that there is only one Ātman in the entire creation, is common to the Sāṁkhya-mārga as also to the Yoga-mārga; in the same way, even according to the Pātañjala-Yoga, this Equability is attained after a man has Realised the Parameśvara. But as both the Sāṁkhya-Yogins and the Pātañjala-Yogins support the Abandonment of Action, they never make occasion for utilising in actual life this feeling of Equability; and the Karma-Yogin of the Gītā, on the contrary, continually utilises in every day life this Equability of Reason, acquired by Metaphysical Realisation, and goes on performing all the different affairs of the world for Universal Welfare: this is the great difference between the two; and, that is why it is stated at the end of this chapter, that the Karma-Yogin is superior to the '*tapasvin*', (that is, the Pātañjala-Yogin) on the one hand, and the '*jñānin*' (that is, the Sāṁkhya-Yogin) on the other hand (stanza 46). Having heard this description of the Yoga of Equability, Arjuna now raises the following doubt—]

अर्जुन उवाच ।

§§ योऽयं योगस्त्वया प्रोक्तः साम्येन मधुसूदन ।
एतस्याहं न पश्यामि चञ्चलत्वात्स्थितिं स्थिराम् ॥ ३३ ॥
चञ्चलं हि मनः कृष्ण प्रमाथि बलवद् दृढम् ।
तस्याहं निग्रहं मन्ये वायोरिव सुदुष्करम् ॥ ३४ ॥

श्रीभगवानुवाच ।

असंशयं महाबाहो मनो दुर्निग्रहं चलम् ।
अभ्यासेन तु कौन्तेय वैराग्येण च गृह्यते ॥ ३५ ॥
असंयतात्मना योगो दुष्प्राप इति मे मतिः ।
वश्यात्मना तु यतता शक्योऽवाप्तुमुपायतः ॥ ३६ ॥

Arjuna said :—(33) O Madhusūdana, I do not think that this Yoga (that is, Karma-Yoga), acquired by *sāmya* (that is, by Equability of Reason), which You have preached will last permanently, having regard to the inconstancy (of the Mind); (34) because, O Kṛṣṇa ! the Mind is volatile, rebellious, powerful, and *dṛḍha* (that is, difficult to mould); I think that the control of it is as difficult as of the wind, (that is, as trying to bind the wind in an envelope).

[The word '*yoga*' in the 33rd stanza must be taken as meaning 'Karma-Yoga'; because, it is qualified by the adjective 'by means of *sāmya*', that is, 'by means of Equability of Reason'. Although the *samādhi* according to the Pātañjala-Yoga has been described in the foregoing lines, yet, the Pātañjala-Yoga is not meant by the word '*yoga*' in these stanzas; because, in Chapter II, the Blessed Lord has Himself defined Karma-Yoga as: "*samatvam yoga uccyate*" (2.48), that is, "Equalness of Reason, or Equability, is known as 'Yoga'". The Blessed Lord admits the correctness of the doubt of Arjuna and says—]

The Blessed Lord said :—(35) O Mighty-armed Arjuna, there is not the slightest doubt that the Mind is volatile, and that controlling it, is difficult; but, O Kaunteya, it can be kept under control by *abhyāsa* (that is, by practice—Trans.), and by *vairāgya* (that is, absence of Desire—Trans.). (36) That man whose Inner Sense (*antaḥkaraṇa*) is not within control,

अर्जुन उवाच ।

§§ अयतिः श्रद्धयोपेतो योगाच्चलितमानसः ।
अप्राप्य योगसंसिद्धिं कां गतिं कृष्ण गच्छति ॥ ३७ ॥

for him, it will be difficult in My opinion to achieve this Yoga (of Equable Reason); but, if one makes the effort, after controlling the Inner Sense, it is possible to acquire this Yoga.

[In short, that which appears difficult in the beginning can ultimately be achieved by practice and by industry. '*abhyāsa*' means 'doing any particular thing over and over again'; and '*vairāgya*' means "absence of '*rāga*' or of 'love'", that is to say, "absence of desire". In the Pātañjala-Yoga-Sūtras, after first describing the nature of Yoga, as "*yogaś cittavṛttinirodhaḥ*", that is, "controlling the activities of the Mental Vision is Yoga", (see the 20th stanza of this Chapter), it is stated in the next *sūtra* that "*abhyāsa vairāgyābhyāṁ tan nirodhaḥ*", that is, "Mental Vision is controlled by practice and by indifference to the world". The same words have been used in the Gītā, and the meaning is the same; but it cannot be stated, on that account, that, these words have been taken from the Pātañjala-Sūtras (See Gī. Ra. pp. 746–747). Although it is thus possible to attain *samādhi* (mental absorption) in this way, by controlling the Mind, and although it might be possible for some determined persons to acquire it by practice in six months, yet, another difficulty now arises, to the following effect, namely, this highest stage of the Karma-Yoga cannot be acquired by many people even after several births, as a result of their inherent nature. How are such people to attain this Perfection? Because, even if such a person begins to practise Karma-Yoga, in one life, after having practised the control of the senses as far as possible, yet, that practice is bound to remain incomplete at the moment of his death; and if in the next birth, he is to start over again from the beginning, the same thing will be repeated in his next birth. Therefore, the next question of Arjuna is as to what such persons should do—]

Arjuna said :—(37) O Kṛṣṇa, what state is attained by

कच्चिन्नोभयविभ्रष्टश्छिन्नाभ्रमिव नश्यति ।
अप्रतिष्ठो महाबाहो विमूढो ब्रह्मणः पथि ॥ ३८ ॥

एतन्मे संशयं कृष्ण छेत्तुमर्हस्यशेषतः ।
त्वदन्यः संशयस्यास्य छेत्ता न ह्युपपद्यते ॥ ३९ ॥

a man, instead of acquiring success in Yoga, who has Faith, but whose Mind, on account of his being *ayati* (that is, wanting in sufficient effort, or sufficient control, as a result of his natural proclivities), has moved from the (Karma-) Yoga, (consisting of an Equable Reason)? (38) O Mighty-armed Kṛṣṇa! is such a man, who, being encompassed by Ignorance, and not having become steady in the path of attaining the Brahman, has become *bhraṣṭa* (that is, alienated) from both sides, ruined (in the middle) like a broken cloud? (39) O Kṛṣṇa! You it is, Who must remove this doubt in my mind; because, no one other than You will be got for removing this doubt.

[Though in the *nañ-samāsa*, the prefixed *nañ* (i.e., *a*) is commonly taken to mean 'absence of', yet, as it is very often also used to denote dimunity, the word '*ayati*' in the 37th stanza has to be interpreted as meaning, 'one who makes little, that is, insufficient effort or control'. The words "alienated from both sides" that is, "*ito bhraṣṭas tato bhraṣṭaḥ*" used in the 38th stanza must be taken to refer to the Karma-Yoga. If Action is performed according to the directions of the Śāstras, though desirefully, one obtains heaven; and if it is performed with a Desireless Reason, one obtains Release, without being bound by the Action; these are the two results of Karma; but, this man, who is neither here nor there, does not get the Desire-born Fruit in the shape of heaven, etc., because, that has not been his motive; and cannot also attain Release, as he has not acquired Equability of Reason. Arjuna's question is whether, in this way, heaven is lost and Release is also lost to him; whether, *ghee* is lost to him, as also the oil, and

श्रीभगवानुवाच ।
पार्थ नैवेह नामुत्र विनाशस्तस्य विद्यते ।
न हि कल्याणकृत्कश्चिद्दुर्गतिं तात गच्छति ॥ ४० ॥
प्राप्य पुण्यकृताँल्लोकानुषित्वा शाश्वतीः समाः ।
शुचीनां श्रीमतां गेहे योगभ्रष्टोऽभिजायते ॥ ४१ ॥
अथवा योगिनामेव कुले भवति धीमताम् ।
एतद्धि दुर्लभतरं लोके जन्म यदीदृशम् ॥ ४२ ॥

there remains in his hands the empty vessel*, like a person abandoned by both sides. It is not that this question applies only to the means for the acquisition of the Karma-Yoga in the shape of the practice of Pātañjala-Yoga. It has been stated in the following chapters, that the Equability of Reason necessary for Karma-Yoga can be acquired either by the Pātañjala-Yoga, or by Devotion, or by Knowledge; and just as the means in the shape of Pātañjala-Yoga are likely to remain incomplete in one life, so also are the means in the shape of Devotion, or of Knowledge,—if those paths are followed,—also likely to remain incomplete in one life. Therefore, the reply given by the Blessed Lord to this question of Arjuna may be said to apply equally to all the various means in the path of Karma-Yoga.]

The Blessed Lord said:—(40) O Pārtha! such a man does not come to grief, whether in this world or in the next; because, my friend, no man, who performs beneficial Actions, ever reaches an unhappy end. (41) This Yoga-*bhraṣṭa* (that is, this man, who has fallen from the Path of Karma-Yoga), takes (re-) birth in the family of pure-minded rich people, after reaching the spheres (like heaven, etc.), which are attained by people, who perform good Actions, and (after) having remained there for many years; (42) or, he is

* This is a reference to the story of a fool, who went to buy clarified butter, as also oil, with a vessel (usually used for burning incense), which has openings on both sides and a partition in the middle; and who, putting the clarified butter on one side, inverted the vessel to put the oil in on the other side, and thus lost the clarified butter; and then lost the oil also, in inverting the vessel again, to see what had become of the clarified butter.—Trans.

तत्र तं बुद्धिसंयोगं लभते पौर्वदेहिकम् ।
यतते च ततो भूयः संसिद्धौ कुरुनन्दन ॥ ४३ ॥
पूर्वाभ्यासेन तेनैव ह्रियते ह्यवशोऽपि सः ।
जिज्ञासुरपि योगस्य शब्दब्रह्मातिवर्तते ॥ ४४ ॥
प्रयत्नाद्यतमानस्तु योगी संशुद्धकिल्बिषः ।
अनेकजन्मसंसिद्धस्ततो याति परां गतिम् ॥ ४५ ॥

born in the family of intelligent (Karma-) Yogins ; such (re-) births are very rare in (this) world. (43) The spiritual impressions acquired in the previous births, come to him again here (that is, in the birth which he has thus acquired) ; and, O Kurunandana! he attempts to acquire success (in Yoga), which is '*bhūyaḥ*' (that is, even higher). (44) As a result of that practice, made by him in the previous births, he is necessarily (that is, though he may not wish it) drawn (towards complete *siddhi*). He, who has experienced the *jijñāsā* (that is, the desire to possess the knowledge) of (Karma-)Yoga, such a man also goes beyond the *śabda-brahma* (that is, the desire-prompted ritual, such as, Yajñas, Yāgas, etc., prescribed by the Vedas—Trans.). (45) Becoming absolved of sin, while (thus) practising industriously, the (Karma-) Yogin, acquires success, after many births, and reaches a most superior state.

[The words '*yoga*', '*yoga-bhraṣṭa*' and '*yogī*' in these stanzas have been used as meaning 'Karma-Yoga', 'one who has fallen from the Karma-Yoga' and 'Karma-Yogin', respectively ; because, being born in a rich family cannot be proper for anyone else. The Blessed Lord says that one should start the practice of the Karma-Yoga with as much pure-mindedness as possible in the beginning. Whatever Action is performed in this way, however little it be, that will gradually bring more and more of success ; and in the next life, if not in this life, it will ultimately lead to Release. The stanzas, "if this 'course of conduct' ('*dharma*') is observed even to a small extent, it saves a person from the great danger" (Gī. 2. 40), and "one reaches Vāsudeva after many births" (Gī. 7. 19) further support this proposition. For further discussion on this subject, see pp. 389–395 of Chapter X of the Gītā-Rahasya. The word '*śabda-brahma*' used in the 44th stanza means 'desire-prompted ritual, such as, Yajñas and Yāgas, prescribed by the Vedas'; because, that ritual is enjoined by the Vedas; and it is performed, keeping faith in the Vedas; and the 'Veda' is the '*śabda*' (word), that is, the '*śabda-brahma*', which was in existence before the entire creation came into existence. Any person whosoever performs all Actions with some desire in the first instance; but, as the Mind is gradually purified by the performance of such Action, he gradually acquires the inspiration of performing Action desirelessly. That is why it is stated in the Upaniṣads, as also in the Mahābhārata that:

dve brahmaṇī veditavye śabda-brahma paraṁ ca yat ।
śabda-brahmaṇi niṣṇātaḥ paraṁ brahmādhigacchati ॥

that is, "it must be understood that the Brahman is of two kinds, namely, the *śabda-brahma*, and the other (that is, *nirguṇa-brahma*) beyond it; when a person has become well-versed in the *śabda-brahma*, he reaches the *nirguṇa-brahma*, which is beyond it" (Maitryu. 6. 22; Amṛtabindu, 17; Ma. Bhā. Śān. 231. 63; 269. 1). Getting tired of the desire-prompted ritual prescribed by the *śabda-brahma* (that is, the Vedas), the man gets the desire to practise the Karma-Yoga, which prescribes the same Actions, but for Universal Welfare; and in this way, this Desireless Karma-Yoga is for the first time practised to a certain extent. Later on, according to the rule "*svalpārambhaḥ kṣemakaraḥ*", this little practice slowly drags the man more and more forward by gradual degrees; and, ultimately gives him complete Release. This is the meaning of the words, "who has experienced the desire to possess the knowledge of Karma-Yoga, such a man also goes beyond the *śabda-brahma*", which appear in the 44th stanza; because, such a desire, or '*jijñāsa*', is the mouth of the grinding-mill in the shape of Karma-Yoga; and once one gets into this mill, then, either in this life or in the next, and sometime or other, one cannot but get complete success, and reach the (*nirguṇa*) Brahman, which is beyond the *śabda-brahma*. It would

§§ तपस्विभ्योऽधिको योगी ज्ञानिभ्योऽपि मतोऽधिकः ।
कर्मिभ्यश्चाधिको योगी तस्माद्योगी भवार्जुन ॥ ४६ ॥

appear at first sight that Janaka and others acquired this success in one life; but, considering the matter scientifically, those persons also must have acquired that fruit as a result of the spiritual training acquired in many previous births. In as much as practising Karma-Yoga, even to a small extent, nay, even the desire for doing so, is in this way always beneficial; and, also as one undoubtedly acquires Release by means of it, the Blessed Lord now says to Arjuna as follows—]

(46) The (Karma-) Yogin is superior to the *tapasvin*; he is also superior to the *jñānin*, and also superior to the *karmin*; *tasmāt*, (that is, therefore,—Trans.), O Arjuna, do you become a Yogin, (that is, a Karma-Yogin).

[The meaning of the word '*tapasvin*' in this stanza is, 'one, who, going into the forest, performs fasts and other body-tiring practices, or other devices of the Haṭha-Yoga, and obtains Release'; and, that is also the meaning of that word in common parlance. '*jñānin*' means naturally that '*sāṁkhya-niṣṭha*' person, who is described by the words "*jñānayogena sāṁkhyānāṁ* etc." (Gī. 3. 3); and who, by means of '*jñāna*', that is, by the Sāṁkhya path, abandons Action, and obtains Release. In the same way, '*karmin*' means the orthodox ritual-practiser of the Mīmāṁsā school, who aspires to heaven, and performs only desire-prompted ritual, and who is described in Gī. 2. 42–44, and 9. 20, 21. Persons in each of these three paths of life say that Release is obtained only by the path of life followed by them respectively; but, the Gītā says that the Karma-Yogin, and necessarily the path of life known as 'Karma-Yoga', is superior whether to the *tapasvin*, or the Mīmāṁsaka, or the Jñānin; and the same proposition has been enunciated before in the words "Action is better than Inaction" (Gī. 3. 8); and "Karma-Yoga is better than Karma-Saṁnyāsa" etc. (Gī. 5. 2); and in other stanzas

योगिनामपि सर्वेषां मद्गतेनान्तरात्मना ।
श्रद्धावान्भजते यो मां स मे युक्ततमो मतः ॥ ४७ ॥

(see Gītā-Rahasya, Ch. XI, pp. 424–426). Nay; the Karma-Yogin is superior even to the *tapasvin*, or the Mīmāṁsaka, or the Jñānin; and, that is why the Blessed Lord has, in stanza 46, again clearly advised Arjuna that: "do you become a (Karma-)Yogin", in the same way as He had advised Arjuna above to: "perform Action, being *yogastha*" (Gī. 2. 48; Gī. Ra. pp. 78–79); or, "arise, taking shelter in Yoga" (Gī. 4. 42). Again, if one does not thus consider the Karma-Yoga as the superior path, the word '*tasmāt*'='therefore', in the sentence, "therefore, do you become a Yogin", will become meaningless; but, how will this proposition be palatable to the commentators of the Saṁnyāsa school? Therefore, they have twisted the meaning of the word '*jñānin*', and interpreted it to mean "one who has acquired mere '*śabda-jñāna*' or 'bookish knowledge'"; but, this interpretation is purely doctrine-supporting. These commentators do not want to interpret the Gītā as saying that it considers the Jñāna-mārga, which gives up Karma, as inferior; because, thereby a slur is cast on the doctrines of their school. And, it is for this very reason, that they have perverted the meaning of the phrase "*karmayogo viśiṣyate*" (Gī. 5. 2); but, as this matter has been fully considered by me in Chapter XI of the Gītā-Rahasya (p. 424 *et seq.*), I shall not further discuss here the interpretation of this stanza given by me. In my opinion, it is unquestionable that the Karma-Yoga is absolutely the best path of life according to the Gītā. The Blessed Lord now explains in the next stanza the various degrees of superiority among Karma-Yogins—]

(47) Nevertheless, he, among all (Karma-Yogins), who, fixing his mind on Me, worships Me devotedly, is considered by Me as the most superior *yukta* (that is, the most completely perfect Karma-Yogin).

[The purport of this stanza is that, when to Karma-Yoga is added the affection included in Devotion, that Yogin becomes the most beloved of the Blessed Lord, as when sugar is added to milk. It does not mean that Devotion is better than the Desireless Karma-Yoga; because, later on in Chapter XII, the Blessed Lord has Himself clearly stated that Renunciation of the Fruit of Action is better than Meditation (*dhyāna*), (Gī. 12. 22). It is one thing to say that the mixture of Devotion and of Desireless Action is valuable, and it is quite another thing to say that the Desireless Karma-Yoga is useless, and that Devotion is superior to it. The doctrine laid down by the Gītā is of the first kind; and that laid down by the Bhāgavata-purāṇa is of the second kind. It has been stated in the first, and again in the last chapter of the Bhāgavata, after declaring that all kinds of *kriyāyoga* (ritual) are destructive of Spiritual Knowledge (see Bhāg. 1. 5. 34), that,

naiṣkarmyam apy acyuta bhāvavarjitaṁ
na śobhate jñānamalaṁ niranjanam ।

(Bhāg. 1. 5. 12 and 12. 12. 52),

that is, "even *naiṣkarmya*, i. e., 'Desireless Action' (Bhāg. 11. 3. 46), does not seem good, is useless, without devotion to the Blessed Lord". This will show that as the entire bias of the writer of the Bhāgavata is on Devotion, he even goes beyond the Bhagavadgītā, when occasion arises. This Purāṇa came to be written in the belief that due stress was not laid on Devotion in the Mahābhārata, and necessarily, in the Gītā. Therefore, it is not a matter of surprise, if one finds in it statements similar to those above. But, what we have to see is the summary or the import of the Gītā, and not what the Bhāgavata says. The occasion for writing, as also the time of writing, was different in each case; and, therefore, it is not possible to fully harmonise them with each other. This chapter has described the devices from the Pātañjala-Yoga, which are part of the devices necessary for cultivating the Equability of Reason required in Karma-Yoga. Knowledge, and Devotion, are other such devices; and their description starts from the next chapter.]

इति श्रीमद्भगवद्गीतासु उपनिषत्सु ब्रह्मविद्यायां योगशास्त्रे
श्रीकृष्णार्जुनसंवादे ध्यानयोगो नाम षष्ठोऽध्यायः ॥ ६ ॥

Thus ends, the sixth chapter entitled DHYANA-YOGA in the dialogue between Śrī Kṛṣṇa and Arjuna on the Yoga included in the Science of the Brahman (that is, on the Karma-Yoga), in the Upaniṣad sung (that is, told) by the Blessed Lord.

सप्तमोऽध्यायः

CHAPTER VII.

[After having proved that the Karma-Yoga is as much productive of Release as the Sāṁkhya-mārga, and yet, independent and superior to it; and that even a little practice of this Yoga is not useless, the Blessed Lord has explained how to acquire the control of the senses necessary in that path of life. But, the control of the senses is a purely external Action, and the purpose for which this exercise of the senses is necessary, has not yet been considered. The Blessed Lord had already explained to Arjuna in the third chapter that, enemies like Desire, Anger etc. fix their abode in the senses, and destroy both Spiritual Knowledge (*jñāna*) and Specified Knowledge (*vijñāna*), and that he should, therefore, first control the senses and destroy these enemies; and He had thus shown the necessity for the control of the senses; and He has also described the Yoga-*yukta* person in the last chapter as one who, after having controlled the senses, "has become satisfied by Jñāna and Vijñāna" (6. 8), and "sees the Parameśvara in all created beings, and all created beings in the Parameśvara" (6. 29). Therefore, as He has explained to Arjuna what is meant by the control of the senses, it has become necessary for Him, as a matter of course, to also explain to him what is 'Jñāna' and what is 'Vijñāna', as also the methods (*vidhi*) of the Karma-Yoga, by which one can acquire the complete Knowledge of the Parameśvara, without abandoning Action, and ultimately attain Release with certainty; and this same subject has been explained in the eleven chapters of the Gītā from the seventh chapter to the end of the seventeenth chapter; and in the last, that is, in the 18th chapter of the Gītā, a summary of the Karma-Yoga has been made. Realising that there is only One Indestructible Parameśvara, Who pervades all the various perishable things which fill the world, is known as 'Jñāna'; and understanding in what way the various perishable things come into existence out of one permanent

Parameśvara, is known as 'Vijñana' (Gī. 13. 30); and this is also known as '*kṣarākṣara-vicāra*' (the Consideration of the Mutable and the Immutable). But, in addition to this, one can also acquire the Knowledge of the form of the Parameśvara by understanding what is the nature of the Ātman or Self, to be found within the body or '*kṣetra*' of every person. This method of consideration is called '*kṣetra-kṣetrajña-vicāra*' that is, the, Consideration of the Body (*kṣetra*) and the Ātman (*kṣetrajña*). Out of these, the Blessed Lord has first started the Consideration of the Mutable and the Immutable; and taken in hand the Consideration of the Body and the Ātman in Chapter XIII. But, although the Parameśvara may be One, He has two aspects from the point of view of Worship, namely, the Imperceptible (*avyakta*) one, which is realisable only by the Reason; and the Perceptible (*vyakta*) one, which is empirical, that is, which can be actually experienced. It is, therefore, necessary to explain, as a part of this subject-matter, how one can Realise the Parameśvara by means of Reason, as also how it is possible to Realise the Imperceptible, by worshipping the perceptible form, in the first instance, with Faith or Devotion. One should not, therefore, be surprised if this subject-matter has taken up eleven chapters. Besides, as both these paths of life automatically produce the control of the senses, simultaneously with the Knowledge of Parameśvara, the Path of Knowledge and the Path of Devotion are both considered to be of greater value in the science of Release, than the Pātañjala-Yoga path. Nevertheless, it must be borne in mind that all this exposition is a part of the justification of the Path of Karma-Yoga, and is not something independent. Therefore, the division of the Gītā into three parts, according to which the first six chapters deal with Karma, the next six chapters deal with Devotion and last six chapters deal with Knowledge, is not a scientifically correct division. Broadly speaking, all these three subjects have been dealt with in the Gītā; but they are not independent, and have been dealt with as being parts of the Karma-Yoga, as has been explained by me in chapter

श्रीभगवानुवाच ।

§§ मय्यासक्तमनाः पार्थ योगं युञ्जन्मदाश्रयः ।
असंशयं समग्रं मां यथा ज्ञास्यसि तच्छृणु ॥ १ ॥
ज्ञानं तेऽहं सविज्ञानमिदं वक्ष्याम्यशेषतः ।
यज्ज्ञात्वा नेह भूयोऽन्यज्ज्ञातव्यमवशिष्यते ॥ २ ॥

XIV of the Gītā-Rahasya (pp. 638 to 644). Therefore, instead of repeating the same subject-matter here, let us see how the Blessed Lord starts the 7th chapter—]

The Blessed Lord said:—(1) O Pārtha! hear *yathā* (that is, in which manner or by what method) you will acquire complete and unquestionable knowledge of Me, while you are practising the Karma-Yoga, keeping your mind on Me, and taking shelter in Me. (2) Leaving nothing in balance, I am explaining to you this 'Jñāna' together with 'Vijñāna', by knowing which, there remains no other thing in this world to know.

[From the words "taking shelter in Me" and specially the word 'Yoga' used in the first stanza, it becomes quite clear that the 'Jñāna' and 'Vijñāna' explained further on, has been explained, not independently, but as a means for perfecting the Karma-Yoga, which has been described in the previous chapters (Gī. Ra. Ch. XIV, p. 641). Not only in this stanza, but also in other places in the Gītā, the words "*mad yogam āśritaḥ*" (Gī. 12. 11) "*mat paraḥ*" (Gī. 18. 57 and 11. 55) have been used with reference to the Karma-Yoga; and therefore, there remains no doubt that the Yoga which the Gītā ordains for practice, after one has taken shelter in the Parameśvara, is the Karma-Yoga, which has been dealt with in the last six chapters. Some persons interpret the word '*vijñāna*' as meaning the '*brahmajñāna* (Knowledge of the Brahman), which is acquired by experience', or the '*brahmasākṣātkāra*'. But, as the knowledge of the Parameśvara is divided into synthetic (*samaṣṭirūpa*) Knowledge, (that is, Jñāna), and analytical (*vyaṣṭirūpa*) Knowledge, (that is, Vijñāna), I think those are the two meanings, which are here conveyed

मनुष्याणां सहस्रेषु कश्चिद्यतति सिद्धये ।
यततामपि सिद्धानां कश्चिन्मां वेत्ति तत्त्वतः ॥ ३ ॥

by the words '*jñāna*' and '*vijñāna*' (See Gī. 13. 30 and 18. 20). The words "there remains no other thing in this world to know" in the second stanza, have been stated on the authority of the Upaniṣads. In the Chāndogyopaniṣad, the father of Śvetaketu, after asking him: "*yena......... avijñātaṁ vijñātaṁ bhavati*", that is, "what is That, by knowing Which, one can know everything", has explained to him that problem by saying: "*yathā somyaikena mṛt-piṇḍena sarvaṁ mṛnmayaṁ vijñātaṁ syād vācāraṁbhaṇaṁ vikāro nāmadheyaṁ mṛttikety eva satyaṁ*" (Chān. 6. 1. 4), that is, "just as, after once knowing what is contained in a ball of clay, one knows that all earthenware articles are only different evolutes of clay, bearing different Names and Forms, and nothing else, so also after knowing the Brahman, nothing else remains to be known"; and even in the Muṇḍakopaniṣad (Muṇ. 1. 1. 3), the first question is: "*kasmin nu bhagavo vijñate sarvam idaṁ vijñātaṁ bhavati*", that is, "by knowing what, is knowledge of all other things acquired ? ". From this, it is clear that what is meant here is the Non-Dualistic Vedānta doctrine that, (i) when one has acquired the Jñāna and the Vijñāna of the Parameśvara, nothing else remains to be learnt in this world; because, the Fundamental Element of this world is only one; that, (ii) this Fundamental Element pervades everything in different Names and Forms; and that, (iii) there is no other thing besides it in the world. Otherwise, the statement made in the second stanza does not become intelligible.]

(3) Only some persons out of thousands make an attempt to attain Perfection; and out of these (numerous) Perfect Beings, who make the attempt, only some gain true Knowledge of Me.

[Though the persons who are making the attempt, are referred to as '*siddha-puruṣa*' (Perfect Beings) in this place, yet, it must be borne in mind that they attain '*siddhi*' (Perfection) only after having acquired the Knowledge of

§§ भूमिरापोऽनलो वायुः खं मनो बुद्धिरेव च।
अहंकार इतीयं मे भिन्ना प्रकृतिरष्टधा ॥ ४ ॥
अपरेयमितस्त्वन्यां प्रकृतिं विद्धि मे पराम्।
जीवभूतां महाबाहो ययेदं धार्यते जगत् ॥ ५ ॥
एतद्योनीनि भूतानि सर्वाणीत्युपधारय।
अहं कृत्स्नस्य जगतः प्रभवः प्रलयस्तथा ॥ ६ ॥
मत्तः परतरं नान्यत्किंचिदस्ति धनंजय।
मयि सर्वमिदं प्रोतं सूत्रे मणिगणा इव ॥ ७ ॥

the Parameśvara. The Blessed Lord now starts the Consideration of the Mutable and the Immutable, being one of the two sub-divisions of this Knowledge of the Parameśvara, namely, (i) the Consideration of the Mutable and the Immutable and (ii) the Consideration of the Body and the Ātman—]

(4) The earth, water, fire, air, and ether (these five subtle elements), the Mind, the Reason, and Individuation, this is My Prakṛti divided into eight-divisions. (5) This Prakṛti is '*aparā*' (that is, of an inferior order). O Mahābāho, Arjuna, know that there is besides this, yet another Prakṛti of Mine, in the form of Jīva, which is *parā* (that is superior), by which this world is maintained. (6) Bear in mind that from both these, all created beings are created. I am the '*prabhava*' (that is, the origin) and the '*pralaya*' (that is, the end) of the entire Cosmos. (7) Beyond Me, O Dhananjaya, there is nothing else. Just as several beads are strung on a string, so is all this strung on Me.

[These four stanzas contain a summary of the science of the Mutable and the Immutable; and the same has been dealt with *in extenso* in the subsequent stanzas. The Sāṁkhya system says that (i) there are two independent Elements of the universe, namely, (a) the *acetana* (inanimate) or *jaḍa* (gross) Prakṛti (Matter) and (b) the '*sacetana*' (conscious) Puruṣa (Spirit); and that, (ii) everything is created out of these two Elements. But, as the Gītā does not admit this Duality, it looks upon Prakṛti and Purusa, as two manifestations (*vibhūti*) of one and the same

Parameśvara, of which Gross Matter (*jaḍa prakṛti*) is an inferior manifestation, and the 'Jīva' or 'Puruṣa' (that is, Spirit) is the superior one (See the 4th and 5th stanzas); and it further states that all moveable and immoveable creation is created out of these two (Gī. 13. 26). Out of these, the superior Prakṛti in the form of Jīva, considered as the Ātman (*kṣetrajña*), has been fully considered later on in the Chapter XIII. Then remains Gross Matter (*jaḍa prakṛti*). The Gītā does not look upon this as independent, but considers that the entire creation is created out of this Gross Matter, under the supervision of the Parameśvara (Gī. 9. 10). Nevertheless, though the Gītā does not look upon Prakṛti as independent, yet, the divisions of Prakṛti according to the Sāṁkhya system have been accepted with minor differences by the Gītā (Gī. Ra. Chapter VIII, p. 244–250); and the Gītā also accepts the Sāṁkhya theory of *guṇotkarṣa* regarding the subsequent creation of all things out of Prakṛti (Gī. Ra. Ch. IX, p. 334–335), after Gross Matter has come into existence out of the Parameśvara (Gī. 7. 14) as a result of Māyā. According to the Sāṁkhyas, Prakṛti and Puruṣa make up 25 Elements; out of these, Prakṛti gives rise to 23 Elements. Out of these twenty-three, the five Gross Elements, the ten senses, and the Mind, these 16, arise out of the remaining seven, that is, are Evolutes (*vikāra*) of those seven. Therefore, in considering the Fundamental Elements, these sixteen elements are left out of account; and when that is done, there remain only seven Elements as Fundamental Elements, namely, the Reason (*mahān*), Individuation (*ahaṁkāra*) and the five Fine Elements (*tanmātra*). These seven have been named '*prakṛti-vikṛti*' in the Sāṁkhya system, and these seven *prakṛti-vikṛti* and the Fundamental Prakṛti, now make up what is known as the 'Eight-fold Prakṛti'; and this known as the '*aṣṭadhā prakṛti*' (that is, Eight-fold Prakṛti) in the Mahābhārata (Śān. 310. 10-15). But the Gītā has not considered it proper to place the original Prakṛti in the same grade as the seven *prakṛti-vikṛti*; because, if that is done, the distinction that there is one Fundamental Prakṛti and that the remaining seven are its

§§ रसोऽहमप्सु कौन्तेय प्रभास्मि शशिसूर्ययोः ।
प्रणवः सर्ववेदेषु शब्दः खे पौरुषं नृषु ॥ ८ ॥
पुण्यो गन्धः पृथिव्यां च तेजश्चास्मि विभावसौ ।
जीवनं सर्वभूतेषु तपश्चास्मि तपस्विषु ॥ ९ ॥
बीजं मां सर्वभूतानां विद्धि पार्थ सनातनम् ।
बुद्धिर्बुद्धिमतामस्मि तेजस्तेजस्विनामहम् ॥ १० ॥

Evolutes (*vikāra*) is not shown. Therefore, there is a difference between the classification in the Mahābhārata and the classification in the Gītā, according to which latter, the seven *prakṛti-vikṛti* and the Mind make up the Fundamental eight-fold Prakṛti (Gī. Ra. p. 249). In short, it must be borne in mind that although the Gītā does not accept the independent Prakṛti of Sāṁkhya philosophy, the description of the further growth of Prakṛti is essentially the same in both places. As in the Gītā, so also in the Upaniṣads, there is a statement that,

etasmāj jāyate prāṇo manaḥ sarvendriyāṇi ca ।
khaṁ vāyur jyotir āpaḥ pṛthivī viśvasya dhāriṇī ॥

that is, "from this (*para-puruṣa*), Prāṇa (Vitality), the Mind, all the senses, ether, air, fire, water, and the earth, which supports the Universe, these (all) are created" (Muṇḍa. 2.1.3; Kai. 1. 15; Praśna. 6. 4). For further details, see Chapter VIII of the Gītā-Rahasya. It has been stated by the Blessed Lord in the 4th stanza that He Himself is the five Elements, namely, the Earth, Water, etc. Now, saying that He is also the qualities which are to be found in these Elements, the Blessed Lord makes clear what is meant by the statement made above, that all these things are strung on a string like beads—]

(8) I am the Liquidity, of water, O Kaunteya; I am the Effulgence, of the Sun and the Moon; I am the '*praṇava*' (that is, the Om-kāra), in all the Vedas; I am the Sound, of Ether; and I am also the Manhood, in all men. (9) And I am the *puṇyagandha* (that is, the smell), of the earth; and also, the Lustre, of fire; I am the Life-Force, in all created beings; and I am the Austerity, in those who perform austere practices. (10) O Pārtha! know that I am the

बलं बलवतामस्मि कामरागविवर्जितम् ।
धर्माविरुद्धो भूतेषु कामोऽस्मि भरतर्षभ ॥ ११ ॥
ये चैव सात्त्विका भावा राजसास्तामसाश्च ये ।
मत्त एवेति तान्विद्धि न त्वहं तेषु ते मयि ॥ १२ ॥

Eternal Seed, of all created beings; I am the Intelligence, of all intelligent people; and the Brilliance, of those who are bright. (11) I am the Strength, of all the strong, but not their *kāma* (that is, Desire) or *rāga* (that is, Attachment to objects of sense); and O Bharataśreṣṭha! I am also the *kāma*, which dwells in all created beings, which is not antagonistical to Morality. (12) And know also that the *sāttvika*, *rājasa*, and *tāmasa* 'Bhāva' (that is, objects) are all sprung out of Me; but they are in Me, and I am not in them.

[The meaning of the words "they are in Me and I am not in them" is very deep. The first, that is, the broad meaning, is that, all things have sprung from the Parameśvara, and that though the Parameśvara is the substratum in the shape of the qualities in all things, like the string round which the beads are strung, yet, the pervasiveness of the Parameśvara does not end there; and that, the Parameśvara pervades all these things and is also beyond; and the same meaning is brought out later on in the words, "I have occupied the whole of this universe by only a part of Myself" in Gī. 10. 42; but, there is another meaning, which is always implied, namely, "though the diversity in the three-constituented universe seems to have sprung from Me, yet, that diversity does not exist in My qualityless (*nirguṇa*) form"; and there are descriptions of the supernatural powers of the Parameśvara later on (Gī. 13. 14-16), which have been made on the basis of this second meaning; such as, "*bhūtabhṛt na ca bhūtasthaḥ*" (Gī. 9. 4 and 5) etc. If the pervasiveness of the Parameśvara is thus more than that of the universe itself, then it is clear that one must go beyond the Māyic universe in order to fully understand the true form of the

§§ त्रिभिर्गुणमयैर्भावैरेभिः सर्वमिदं जगत् ।
मोहितं नाभिजानाति मामेभ्यः परमव्ययम् ॥ १३ ॥
दैवी ह्येषा गुणमयी मम माया दुरत्यया ।
मामेव ये प्रपद्यन्ते मायामेतां तरन्ति ते ॥ १४ ॥

Parameśvara; and this meaning is now plainly brought out by the Blessed Lord—]

(13) This entire universe, being confused by the three '*bhāva*' (that is, objects), which are the embodiment of the three (*sattva, rajas* and *tamas*) constituents, does not realise Me, the Inexhaustible (Parameśvara), Who Am beyond them (that is, necessarily qualityless).

[Māyā, or ignorance is the inherent quality of the senses and of the Body, in which the three-constituents are embodied; it is not the quality of the Ātman; the Ātman is Jñāna-formed, and is permanent; and It is thrown into confusion, by the senses: this Non-Dualistic proposition, which has been mentioned in Chapter IX of the Gītā-Rahasya with reference to Māyā, has been stated in the above stanza. (See Gī. 7. 24 and Gī. Ra. Ch. IX, pp. 325–341.]

(14) This My divine Māyā, which is the embodiment of the constituents, is difficult to understand; and therefore, they alone, who surrender themselves to Me, can swim through this Māyā.

[This clearly shows that the Blessed Lord refers to the three-constituented Prakṛti of the Sāṁkhya system as His Māyā. It has been stated in the Nārāyaṇīyopākhyāna of the Mahābhārata that, the Blessed Lord, after showing His Cosmic Form to Nārada, said in the end :—

māyā hyeṣā mayā sṛṣṭā yan māṁ paśyasi nārada ।
sarvabhūtaguṇairyuktaṁ naiva tvaṁ jñātum arhasi ॥
(Śān. 339. 44)

that is, "O Nārada, that which you see, is the Māyā, which has been created by Me. Do not think that I possess the qualities, which are to be found in the created world". The same proposition has now been stated here. For a description of the nature of Māyā, please refer to Gī. Ra Ch. IX and X.]

न मां दुष्कृतिनो मूढाः प्रपद्यन्ते नराधमाः ।
माययापहृतज्ञाना आसुरं भावमाश्रिताः ॥ १५ ॥

§§ चतुर्विधा भजन्ते मां जनाः सुकृतिनोऽर्जुन ।
आर्तो जिज्ञासुरर्थार्थी ज्ञानी च भरतर्षभ ॥ १६ ॥

तेषां ज्ञानी नित्ययुक्त एकभक्तिर्विशिष्यते ।
प्रियो हि ज्ञानिनोऽत्यर्थमहं स च मम प्रियः ॥ १७ ॥

उदाराः सर्व एवैते ज्ञानी त्वात्मैव मे मतम् ।
आस्थितः स हि युक्तात्मा मामेवानुत्तमां गतिम् ॥ १८ ॥

(15) Those fools and evil-doers, whose Jñāna has been annihilated by Māyā, they, being inspired by an ungodly Reason, do not surrender themselves to Me.

[The Blessed Lord has explained that those, who are engulfed in Māyā, forget the Parameśvara and are destroyed. HE now describes what happens to those, who do not do so, but surrender themselves to the Parameśvara, and worship Him—]

(16) O Bharata-śreṣṭha Arjuna! four kinds of virtuous people worship Me, namely, the '*ārta*' (that is, those who are affected by disease), the '*jijñāsu*'-s (that is, those who desire to acquire Knowledge), the '*arthārthī*'-s (that is, those who entertain the desire for money or other desirable things), and the '*jñānin*'-s (that is, those who, although they are Accomplished (*kṛtākṛtya*), as they have acquired the Knowledge of the Parameśvara, and have nothing more to gain, yet, worship Me desirelessly). (17) Out of these, that Jñānin, who is an '*ekabhakti*' (that is, one, who, believing that there is no other, worships Me alone), and who always behaves like a '*yukta*' (that is, with a desireless frame of mind), is the highest in worth. I am most beloved of the Jñānin, and the Jñānin is (most) beloved of Me. (18) All these Devotees are '*udāra*' (that is, good); but, (among all of them) I hold the Jñānin as equal to Myself; because, having become *yukta-citta* (that is, having his Mind united (to Me)—Trans.) he has become steady in Me, Who Am the

बहूनां जन्मनामन्ते ज्ञानवान्मां प्रपद्यते ।
वासुदेवः सर्वमिति स महात्मा सुदुर्लभः ॥ १९ ॥

highest Goal (of every one). (19) After many births, the Jñānin, having come to the empirical conclusion that 'whatever is, is Vāsudeva', comes and reaches Me. Such a '*mahātmā*' (that is, noble soul—Trans.) is rare.

[One must thoroughly understand the import of the statement, made by the Blessed Lord, that by worshipping His form, a man acquires the Knowledge of the Parameśvara, after He had described that form, from the point of view of the Mutable and the Immutable, by saying that, (i) both Matter and Spirit are His forms, and that, (ii) He pervades everything on all sides homogeneously. Every one needs to perform worship, whether it is of the Perceptible, or of the Imperceptible; but, as, out of these two, the worship of the Perceptible is easier, that kind of worship has been described here; and that is known as '*bhakti*' (Devotion). Nevertheless, that kind of Devotion, in which a man entertains some kind of desire in his heart, and worships the Parameśvara for some particular object, is inferior; and, even those 'Knowledge-seekers' (*jijñāsus*), who are devoted with the intention of acquiring the Knowledge of the Parameśvara, must be considered as imperfect; because, their knowledge is not yet complete, as is apparent from their state of being 'Knowledge-seekers'. But, as all these are worshippers, they have all been referred to as '*udāra*' (that is, 'going by a good path'), (stanza 18). But, the import of the first three stanzas is that, the worship desirelessly offered (Bhāg. 1. 7. 10) by those Jñānins, who have gone further, that is, who have become Accomplished as a result of the Acquisition of Knowledge and for whom, there is nothing more left in this world to do or to acquire (Gī. 3. 17-19), is the highest kind of Devotion, The Devotion of devotees like Prahlāda and Nārada falls into this excellent category; and that is why the 'Yoga of Devotion' (*bhakti-yoga*) has been defined in the Bhāgavata as the 'desireless and endless worship of the Parameśvara' (Bhāg. 3. 29. 12; and Gī. Ra. Ch. XIII, p. 572). It may

§§ कामैस्तैस्तैर्हृतज्ञानाः प्रपद्यन्तेऽन्यदेवताः ।
तं तं नियममास्थाय प्रकृत्या नियताः स्वया ॥ २० ॥

यो यो यां यां तनुं भक्तः श्रद्धयार्चितुमिच्छति ।
तस्य तस्याचलां श्रद्धां तामेव विदधाम्यहम् ॥ २१ ॥

safely be said that the words *'ekabhakti'*, and *'vāsudeva'* in the 17th and 19th stanzas are from the Bhāgavata religion; nay, even that the above description of devotees is from the Bhāgavata religion. Because, in the Mahābhārata, while the description of this religion is being given, and after the four kinds of devotees have been first described, we find it stated that:

caturvidhā mama janā bhaktā evaṁ hi me śrutam ।
teṣām ekāntinaḥ śreṣṭhā ye caivānanyadevatāḥ ॥
aham eva gatis teṣām nirāśīḥ karmakāriṇām ॥
ye ca śiṣṭās trayo bhaktāḥ phalakāmā hi te matāḥ ।
sarve cyavana-dharmās te pratibuddhas tu śreṣṭhabhāk ॥

(Ma. Bhā. Śān. 341. 33–35).

that is, " the other three kinds of devotees do not perform Actions like the *'ananyadaivata'* ('no-other-deity') and the *'ekāntin'* (solitudinal) devotee, but perform Action with some desire or other; and therefore, they are *'cyavanśila'*, whereas, the *'ekāntin'*-s are *'pratibuddha'* (that is, scients), and superior. And later on the word 'Vāsudeva' has been given a metaphysical etymology by saying "*sarvabhūtādhivāsaś ca vāsudevas tato hy aham*", that is, " I am called 'Vāsudeva', because I reside (have my *vāsa*) in everything which is created" (Śān. 341. 40). The Blessed Lord now explains why different people worship different deities, though there is only one Parameśvara everywhere—]

(20) Various persons, being befooled by their respective desires, (such as, fruit in the shape of heaven etc.), according to their respective natures, follow those respective rules (of worship), and take to the worship of other (various) deities. (21) Whatever form or deity any devotee may desire to worship with Faith, I steady such his Faith therein.

स तया श्रद्धया युक्तस्तस्या राधनमीहते ।
लभते च ततः कामान्मयैव विहितान् हि तान् ॥ २२ ॥
अन्तवत्तु फलं तेषां तद्भवत्यल्पमेधसाम् ।
देवान्देवयजो यान्ति मद्भक्ता यान्ति मामपि ॥ २३ ॥

(22) Then, being full of that Faith, he becomes engaged in the '*rādhana*' (that is, the worship) of that deity; and then he obtains those very desired fruits, which have been created by Me Myself. (23) But, this fruit, which (these) short-sighted people obtain, is perishable (and not permanent like Release); those, who worship deities, reach the deities; and those who worship Me, come to Me.

[It is the common belief that though the Parameśvara is the One, Who gives Release, yet, the power to give the various things, which are necessary for the ordinary worldly life, can be given only by deities; and that, it is necessary to worship the deities for that purpose. How various people run after various deities (Gī. 17. 1–6.), after it has thus become necessary, according to them, to worship deities, some running after Mhasobā, others observing Saturday, after the deity Saturn, etc., has been very nicely described in the above stanzas. But, what must be borne in mind here is that, though the fruit to be obtained by worshipping various deities, may be looked upon as having been given by those respective deities, yet, ultimately that worship amounts to a worship of the Parameśvara (Gī. 9. 23); and, that fruit also is essentially given by the Parameśvara (stanza 22). Not only is this so, but even this idea of worshipping the various deities is given by the Parameśvara, according to the previous destiny of a particular person (stanza 21); because, in this world, there is nothing else but the Parameśvara. The same doctrine has been laid down in the Vedānta-Sūtras (3. 2. 38-41), and in the Upaniṣads (Kauṣī. 3. 8). The utility of these diverse kinds of worship is, that after worshipping various deities, the Mind becomes steady and pure, and one ultimately acquires the Knowledge of the One, and Permanent, Parameśvara. But, fruit obtained before the acquisition of that Knowledge is

§§ अव्यक्तं व्यक्तिमापन्नं मन्यन्ते मामबुद्धयः ।
परं भावमजानन्तो ममाव्ययमनुत्तमम् ॥ २४ ॥
नाहं प्रकाशः सर्वस्य योगमायासमावृतः ।
मूढोऽयं नाभिजानाति लोको मामजमव्ययम् ॥ २५ ॥

non-permanent. Therefore, the advice of the Blessed Lord to every one is, that he should not be enmeshed in this Hope of Fruit, but should aspire to become a 'Jñānin' devotee. As the Blessed Lord gives reward to every one according to his own Actions, (Gī. 4. 11), although He does everything, and gives all kinds of rewards, it is also said, that He essentially does nothing whatsoever Himself (Gī. 5. 14). The reader is referred to the further elucidation of this matter at page 369 in Chapter X and at pages 595-6 in Chapter XIII of the Gītā-Rahasya. The Blessed Lord now further explains what is meant above by saying that people run after deities according to their own natural inclinations, forgetting that the fruit of the worship of the deities is given by the Parameśvara Himself—]

(24) The '*abuddhi*' (that is, fools), not recognising my '*para*' (that is, superior), best of all, and imperceptible form, look upon Me, Who am imperceptible, as having become perceptible. (25) As I am enveloped in My Yoga-formed Illusion (that is, Māyā—Trans.), I do not (clearly) appear to all (in My own Form). Fools do not Realise, that I am Unborn, and Inexhaustible.

[The device of giving up the Yoga-form, that is, imperceptible form, and taking up the perceptible form (Gī. 4. 6 ; 7. 15 ; 9. 7), is called "Māyā", by Vedāntists ; and when the Parameśvara becomes enveloped in this Yoga-Māyā, He begins to possess a perceptible appearance. In short, the import of this stanza is, that the perceptible universe is Māyic, or non-permanent ; and that, the Parameśvara is Real, and Permanent. But the word '*māyā*' in this place, and also in other places, is taken by some as meaning 'a super-natural or wonderful power'; and these say that this Māyā is not Unreal, but is as permanent as the Parameśvara Himself. As the form of Māyā has been

वेदाहं समतीतानि वर्तमानानि चार्जुन ।
भविष्याणि च भूतानि मां तु वेद न कश्चन ॥ २६ ॥

considered by me at great length in Chapter IX of the Gītā-Rahasya, I will here only say that the proposition that Māyā is some wonderful and eternal pastime of the Parameśvara is acceptable even to the Non-Dualistic Vedānta, because, although Māyā is an 'Appearance', created by the senses, yet, as this is done by the senses at the direction of the Parameśvara, Māyā must be ultimately said to be the pastime of the Parameśvara. The only point at issue is, whether this Māyā is essentially Real, or Unreal; and on this point the doctrine of the Gītā clearly appears from the above stanzas to be the same as that of the Non-Dualistic Vedānta, namely that, that Māyā expressed by Name and Form, by which the Imperceptible Parameśvara is considered to have become perceptible—whether it is called a super-natural power or anything else—is merely an 'Appearance', or '*moha*', created by '*ajñāna*' or Ignorance; and that the true essential Parameśvara is different from it. Otherwise, there seems to be no reason for using the words '*abuddhi*' or '*mūḍha*' in this place. In short, Māyā is not Real, and the Parameśvara alone is Real, and the Gītā says that, being confused by this Māyā, people run after various deities. In the Bṛhadāraṇyakopaniṣad (Bṛ. 1. 4. 10), there is a similar statement; and it is stated there that those persons who, not recognising that the Ātman and the Brahman are one and the same thing, run after various deities, with a distinguishing mind are the 'animals of the gods', that is to say, just as men benefit from cows and other animals, so do these deities benefit from these ignorant devotees, and that these devotees do not obtain Release. So far, the Blessed Lord has given a description of those, who being fooled by Māyā, worship diverse deities, with a distinguishing mind. HE now explains how one escapes from this Māyā—]

(26) I know all *bhūta*-s (that is, created beings), (who existed, or exist, or will be) in the past, present, and future;

इच्छाद्वेषसमुत्थेन द्वन्द्वमोहेन भारत ।
सर्वभूतानि संमोहं सर्गे यान्ति परंतप ॥ २७ ॥
येषां त्वन्तगतं पापं जनानां पुण्यकर्मणाम् ।
ते द्वन्द्वमोहनिर्मुक्ता भजन्ते मां दृढव्रताः ॥ २८ ॥
§§ जरामरणमोक्षाय मामाश्रित्य यतन्ति ये ।
ते ब्रह्म तद्विदुः कृत्स्नमध्यात्मं कर्म चाखिलम् ॥ २९ ॥
साधिभूताधिदैवं मां साधियज्ञं च ये विदुः ।
प्रयाणकालेऽपि च मां ते विदुर्युक्तचेतसः ॥ ३० ॥

but, O Arjuna, none know Me; (27) because, O Bhārata, all created beings are steeped in ignorance in this world, as a result of the confusion created by the pairs of Opposites (such as, pain and happiness etc.) arising, O Parantapa, from Desire and Hate. (28) But, the virtuous people, whose sin is exhausted, become fixed in purpose, escaping from the ignorance created by the pairs of Opposites (of pain and happiness etc.), and worship Me.

[The Blessed Lord now describes the state of these people after they have thus become free from Māyā—]

(29) All those, who (thus) taking shelter in Me, attempt to escape from *jarāmaraṇa* (that is from the cycle of re-births) Realise what (all) Brahman, (all) Absolute Self, and all Karma (is). (30) Those, who know Me, along with the *adhibhūta*, the *adhidaiva*, and the *adhiyajña* (that is, who know that I am all that), such (being) *yukta-citta* (that is, Mind-united with Me—Trans.), Know Me, even at the time of death.

[See the explanation given in the next chapter of the words *adhyātma*, *adhibhūta*, *adhidaiva*, and *adhiyajña*. The words "even at the time of death" in the last stanza have reference to the doctrine of the Dharma-Śāstra and of the Upaniṣads that a man has his next birth according to the desire which is most prominent in his mind at the moment of his death. Nevertheless, the word "even" clearly shows that, unless a man has acquired complete Knowledge of the Parameśvara in his lifetime, he cannot acquire that

इति श्रीमद्भगवद्गीतासु उपनिषत्सु ब्रह्मविद्यायां योगशास्त्रे
श्रीकृष्णार्जुनसंवादे ज्ञानविज्ञानयोगो नाम
सप्तमोऽध्यायः ॥ ७ ॥

Knowledge right at the moment of death (See Gī. 2. 72). A further explanation has been given in the next chapter. It may be said that the next chapter has been introduced by the words '*adhibhūta*', etc., in this stanza.]

Thus ends the seventh chapter entitled JNANA-VIJNANA YOGA in the dialogue between Śrī Kṛṣṇa and Arjuna on the Yoga included in the Science of the Brahman (that is, the Karma-Yoga) in the Upaniṣad sung (that is, told) by the Blessed Lord.

अष्टमोऽध्यायः

CHAPTER VIII.

[The explanation of the Jñāna and Vijñāna included in the Karma-Yoga is continued in this chapter, and after first explaining the meaning of the various forms of the Parameśvara, such as, Brahman, *adhyātma*, *karma*, *adhibhūta*, *adhidaiva*, and *adhiyajña*, mentioned at the end of the last chapter, the inner import thereof is explained. But, as this explanation has been given merely by defining those several worlds, that is to say, in an extremely concise way, it is necessary to give a somewhat exhaustive explanation of this subject in this annotation. Different people form different ideas in different ways about the creator of the universe, on looking at the external universe. Some say that all things, which exist in the world, are only evolutes of the five primordial Elements *(mahābhūta)*, and that there is no other Original Principle, except these five primordial Elements. There are others, who maintain that all this world has been created from a Yajña as stated in the fourth chapter of the Gītā; and that, therefore, the Parameśvara is of the form of a *yajña-nārāyaṇa*; and that He can be worshipped only by a Yajña. A third class say that the various activities of the world are not carried out by the material objects by themselves; but that, in each of them, there is some active (*sacetana*) deity (or *puruṣa*), and that these deities carry on all these activities; and that, therefore, we must worship these deities. For example, the act of giving light is performed by the '*puruṣa*' called Sun, embodied in the globe, made up of the five primordial Elements, which is known as 'the Sun'; and this *puruṣa* is the subject-matter of worship. A fourth class says, that it is not proper to imagine that there exists in everything, some deity, other than the thing itself. Just as the Ātman exists in the body of a man, so does there also exist in everything, some subtle form of that very thing, that is to say, some subtle force, like the Ātman; and that thing is the original and true form of it. For instance, they say that the five gross primordial Elements have, at their core, the five Fine Elements (*tanmātra*-s); and that in the material organs, such as, the hand or the foot, there are similar fundamental subtle organs. The Sāṁkhya doctrine that each person has a different Ātman, and that there are innumerable such Ātmans, is based on this fourth theory. But in this stanza, the Sāṁkhya doctrine seems to be included in the *adhideha* class. These four schools of thought are respectively called the *adhibhūta*, the *adhiyajña*, the *adhidaivata*, and the *adhyātmaka*. Whenever the prefix '*adhi*' is placed behind any word, it conveys the meaning of '*tamadhikṛtya*', '*tadviṣayaka*', that is, 'in that matter', or, 'embodied in it'. According to this interpretation, '*adhidaivata*' means 'the Principle existing in many deities'. '*adhyātma*' ordinarily means 'the science which maintains that there is only one Ātman pervading everything'; but this is the interpretation by way of 'conclusion drawn' (*siddhānta-pakṣa*); that is to say, this is the conclusion (*siddhānta*) arrived at by the Vedānta-śāstra, after considering the pros and cons of the theory that there are numerous Ātmans in numerous human beings or things, which is the hypothetical position (*pūrvapakṣa*). So, when the hypothetical position has to be considered, it is assumed that the subtle form of the Ātman in everything is different, and this is the meaning conveyed by the word '*adhyātma*' in the present stanza. How one and the same exposition becomes diversified into different classes from the *adhyātma*, the *adhidaivata* and the *adhibbūta* points of view, has been made clear in the Mahābhārata, by giving an example of the organs of a man (See Ma. Bhā. Śān. 313 and Aśva. 41). The writer of the Mahābhārata says, that the question of the organs of human beings can be considered from three points of view, namely, the '*adhibhūta*', the '*adhyātmaka*' and the '*adhidaivata*'. All those things, which are perceivable by these organs, namely, that which has to be taken by the hands, that which has to be heard by the ears, that which has to be seen by the eyes, or that which has to be contemplated by the Mind, all this is the '*adhibhūta*'; and the subtle capacities of these organs, namely, the hands, feet, etc., (according to the Śāṁkhya system), that is to say, the subtle senses are the '*adhyātma*'-s of those organs; but when one keeps aside both these points of view, and considers the matter from the '*adhidaivata*' point of view, Indra is said to be the deity of the hands, Viṣṇu, of the feet; Mitra, of the anus; Prajāpati, of the organ of generation; Agni, of the speech; Sūrya (Sun), of the eyes; the eight cardinal points or Ether, of the ears; water, of the tongue; the earth, of the nose; the wind, of the skin; the Moon, of the mind; *buddhi* (Reason), of Individuation, and *puruṣa* (Spirit), of the Reason; and these various deities are said to be performing the various functions of these organs. Among the symbols of the form of the Brahman, which have been described in the Upaniṣads for purposes of worship, the Mind is described as the *adhyātma* symbol, and the Sun or the firmament as the '*adhidaivata*' symbol (Chān. 3. 18. 1). It is not that the distinction between the '*adhyātma*' and the '*adhidaivata*' has been made only for the purpose of worship. But, in considering the respective superiority of the organs of speech, or of seeing, or of hearing, etc., and of Vitality (*prāṇa*), the matter is considered once from the Metaphysical *(adhyātma)* point of view by taking the subtle form of the organs of the voice, the eyes, and the ears, and again from the Intuitionist (*adhidaivata*) point of view, taking the Agni, the Sun, and Ether, as the deities of those organs (Bṛ. 1. 5. 21-23; Chān. 1. 2, 3; Kauṣī. 4. 12, 13). In short, the distinction between '*adhidaivata*', '*adhibhūta*', '*adhyātma*' etc. has been in vogue since very old times; and the question as to which of these various ideas regarding the form of the Parameśvara is the correct idea, or as to the inner import of such ideas, having arisen in those times, Yājñavalkya has told Uddālaka Āruṇī in the Bṛhadāraṇyakopaniṣad (Bṛ. 3. 4), that there is only one Paramātman, Which subsists at the core of all created things, all deities, all *adhyātma*, all spheres, all Yajñas, and all bodies whatsoever, and Which makes them unwittingly perform their respective functions. This doctrine of the Upaniṣads has been accepted in the Antaryāmyadhikaraṇa of the Vedānta-Sūtras (Ve. Sū. 1. 2. 18-20), where it has been proved that

अर्जुन उवाच ।

§§ किं तद्ब्रह्म किमध्यात्मं किं कर्म पुरुषोत्तम ।
अधिभूतं च किं प्रोक्तमधिदैवं किमुच्यते ॥ १ ॥
अधियज्ञः कथं कोऽत्र देहेऽस्मिन्मधुसूदन ।
प्रयाणकाले च कथं ज्ञेयोऽसि नियतात्मभिः ॥ २ ॥

श्रीभगवानुवाच ।

अक्षरं ब्रह्म परमं स्वभावोऽध्यात्ममुच्यते ।
भूतभावोद्भवकरो विसर्गः कर्मसंज्ञितः ॥ ३ ॥

this Principle, which exists at the inner core of everything, is not the Prakṛti or the Jīvātman of the Sāṁkhya system, but the Paramātman. The Blessed Lord now tells Arjuna, with reference to this proposition, that there is only one Parameśvara, Who pervades every human body, all created beings (as *adhibhūta*), all Yajñas (as *adhiyajña*), all deities (as *adhidaivata*), all Karma, and all the subtle (that is, Metaphysical) forms of everything ; and that the diversity, or the various kinds of Knowledge of deities, Yajñas etc. is not true Knowledge. The words '*adhibhūta*' etc., used by the Blessed Lord at the end of the seventh chapter, create in Arjuna a desire to learn their meaning, and he first asks as follows—]

Arjuna said :—(1) O Puruṣottama, what is that Brahman ?; what is *adhyātma* ? ; what is *karma* ? ; what is to be called *adhibhūta* ?; and what is called *adhidaivata* ? ; (2) of what kind is the *adhiyajña* ? and O Madhusūdana, Who is (the *adhideha*) in this Body (that is, *deha*—Trans.) ? ; and how do those, who control their senses, Realise You, at the moment of their death ? (Tell me this).

[The words '*brahma*', '*adhyātma*', '*karma*', '*adhibhūta*', and '*adhiyajña*' are to be found in the last chapter; but, in addition to these, Arjuna has asked something new, namely, "who is the '*adhideha*' ?". If this is borne in mind, it will not be difficult to understand the meaning of the following answer.]

The Blessed Lord said :—(3) That Element, which is

अधिभूतं क्षरो भावः पुरुषश्चाधिदैवतम् ।
अधियज्ञोऽहमेवात्र देहे देहभृतां वर ॥ ४ ॥

parama (that is, higher—Trans.), (than anything else), and *akṣara* (this is, immutable), is BRAHMAN; (and) the fundamental quality of each and every object itself (that is, its SVA-*bhāva*) is called 'ADHYATMA'. That '*visarga*' or 'creative activity' which creates (the moveable and immoveable) created things (from the immutable Brahman) is called KARMA. (4) The *kṣara* (that is, 'conditioned by Name and Form', or 'perishable') state (of all things which have come into existence) is the 'ADHIBHUTA'; and the *puruṣa* (that is, the conscious (*sacetana*) Overlord (*adhiṣṭhātā*), Who exists in all things) is the 'ADHIDAIVATA'. HE, who is called the ADHIYAJNA [that is, the Lord (*adhipati*) of all Yajñas] is Myself, Who am (ADHIDEHA), (that is, am the Installed—Trans.), in this Body, O Most Superior among all embodied beings!

[The word '*parama*' in the third stanza is not an adjective of Brahma, but of '*akṣara*'. In Sāṁkhya philosophy, the imperceptible Prakṛti is also called '*akṣara*' (immutable), (Gī. 15. 16). But, the Brahman of the Vedāntists is beyond this imperceptible and immutable Prakṛti (see stanzas 20 and 31 of this chapter); and therefore, although the word '*akṣara*' alone is used, it may mean either the Sāṁkhya Prakṛti, or the Brahman. In order that such a doubt should not arise, the adjective '*parama*' has been placed before the word '*akṣara*' in defining the word Brahman (Gī. Ra. Chap. IX, pp. 274-277). I have explained the word '*svabhāva*' as "'the subtle form' (*sūkṣma-svarūpa*) of any and every object", following the example given above from the Mahābhārata. In the Nāsadīyasūkta, the visible world is called the '*visṛṣṭi*' (*visarga*), that is, 'growth' of the Parabrahman (Gī. Ra. p. 351); and the word '*visarga*' must be understood here in the same meaning. It is not necessary to interpret the word '*visarga*' as meaning the '*havirutsarga* of the Yajñas'. Why this visible world is itself called 'Karma' has been explained at p. 362 of Chapter X of the Gītā-Rahasya. '*kṣara*' is the mutable Name-d and Form-ed 'Appearance' of everything created; and, the Immutable Principle beyond it, is to be understood as the Brahman. The word '*puruṣa*' includes the '*puruṣa*' in the Sun, the Varuṇa-puruṣa or the deity in water, and other conscious (*sacetana*) subtle-formed deities, as also the Golden Embryo (*hiraṇya-garbha*). The word '*adhiyajña*' has not been defined here by the Blessed Lord; because a detailed description of the Yajña has been given above in the 3rd and 4th chapters, and the Blessed Lord has again later on stated (Gī. 9. 24; 5. 29; and Ma. Bhā. Śān. 340), that "I am the Lord and the recipient of all Yajñas". After having in this way described the characteristic features of the '*adhyātma*' etc., the Blessed Lord has ultimately said shortly that "(that which is called) the '*adhiyajña*' is Myself, Who Am in this *deha*", that is to say, that He is the *adhideha* as also the *adhiyajña* in the human body. The Sāṁkhyas believe that every body has a different Ātman (*puruṣa*), and these Ātmans are innumerable; but this doctrine is not acceptable to Vedānta Philosophy, which holds that although there may be innumerable bodies, there is only one Ātman in all of them (Gī. Ra. Ch. VII, p. 225). This very proposition is borne out by the sentence "I am the *adhideha*". Nevertheless, the words "I am" in this sentence have not been said only with reference to the '*adhiyajña*' or the '*adhideha*'; and their reference to the previous words *adhyātma*, etc., is patent. Therefore, the sum and substance of the whole seems to be :—take the various Yajñas, take the various deities in various things, take the five perishable elemental principles, take the subtle forms of substance, take the diversity of Ātmans, take Brahman, take Karma, or take the various bodies of different human beings, I am everywhere, that is, there is only one Parameśvara-principle in all things. According to some, there is no independent description here of the '*adhideha*' form; and the '*adhideha*' has been mentioned by implication in giving a definition of the '*adhiyajña*'; but, I do not consider this interpretation as correct. Wherever this

§§ अन्तकाले च मामेव स्मरन्मुक्त्वा कलेवरम् ।
यः प्रयाति स मद्भावं याति नास्त्यत्र संशयः ॥ ५ ॥
यं यं वापि स्मरन्भावं त्यजत्यन्ते कलेवरम् ।
तं तमेवैति कौन्तेय सदा तद्भावभावितः ॥ ६ ॥

subject-matter has been referred to, not only in the Gītā, but also in the Upaniṣads and in the Vedānta-Sūtras, (Bṛ. 3. 7; Ve Sū. 1. 2. 20), the embodied Ātman has been considered side by side with the *adhibhūta* and the other forms of the Parameśvara; and the doctrine has been laid down, that everywhere there is only one Paramātman. Besides, as there has been previously asked a question about the *adhideha*, it is logical to conclude that that aspect has been mentioned here distinctly and not by implication. One is likely to think at first sight that if all that which is, is the Parabrahman, then, in describing the various forms of the Parabrahman, such as, the *adhibhūta* etc., it was not necessary to consider the Parabrahman also. But, as this description of diversity has been addressed to people, who are engrossed in the different kinds of worship on the basis that the Brahman, the Ātman, the deities, the Yajñanārāyaṇa, etc., are all different from each other, the declaration that "I am all this", has been made after explaining the characteristics of the differences arising on account of the different beliefs of different people. When one looks at it from this point of view, no such doubt can arise. The Blessed Lord has thus explained this diversity by saying that although various distinctions may be made for purposes of worship, such as, the *adhibhūta*, the *adhidaivata*, the *adhyātma*, the *adhiyajña*, the *adhideha*, etc., yet, this diversity is not real; and that, as a matter of fact, there is only one Parameśvara, Who pervades everything. HE now gives His reply to the last question of Arjuna, namely, how the All-pervading Parameśvara is Realised at the moment of death—]

(5) And there is no doubt that he who leaves his body, thinking of Me at the moment of death, is merged in My form. (6) O, Kaunteya, thinking of whatever form (*bhāva*—Trans.) a man ultimately leaves his body, because, he has

तस्मात्सर्वेषु कालेषु मामनुस्मर युध्य च ।
मय्यर्पितमनोबुद्धिर्मामेवैष्यस्यसंशयम् ॥ ७ ॥

sadā, (that is, for the whole of his life) been engrossed in thinking of that form, that is the form (*bhāva*) in which he is (later on) merged.

[In the fifth stanza, the Blessed Lord has explained the necessity and the result of thinking of the Parameśvara at the moment of death; but, that is likely to give rise to the misunderstanding, that it will be enough if a person thinks of the Parameśvara only at the moment of death. Therefore, it is stated in the sixth stanza, that whatever is in the mind throughout life, does not leave the mind at the moment of death; and, the necessity of remembering and worshipping the Parameśvara throughout life, and not only at the moment of death, is made clear (Gī. Ra. Ch. X, p. 398). When one accepts this proposition, it naturally follows that those, who worship the Parameśvara at the moment of death are merged in the Parameśvara; and that those, who worship other deities at that moment, are merged in the other deities (Gī. 7. 23; 8. 13; and 9. 25); because, as has been stated in the Chāndogyopaniṣad, "*yathā kratur asmiṁl loke puruṣo bhavati tathetaḥ pretya bhavati*" (Chān. 3. 14. 1), that is, "a man gets a state after death, which is consistent with his '*kratu*' or *saṁkalpa*, that is, his resolution". There are similar sentences in other Upaniṣads as in the Chāndogya (Praśna. 3. 10; Maitryu. 4. 6). But the Gītā now says that unless the Mind is steeped in one particular aspiration throughout life, it is not possible to have that aspiration during the throes of the passing away of life. Therefore, consistently with the doctrine that it is necessary to meditate on the Parameśvara '*āmaraṇānta*' that is, throughout life (Ve. Sū. 4. 1. 12), the Blessed Lord now tells Arjuna that—]

(7) Therefore, think of Me at all times (that is, always), and fight; when you have dedicated your Mind and your Reason to Me, you will, (notwithstanding that you have fought), undoubtedly come and be merged in Me.

अभ्यासयोगयुक्तेन चेतसा नान्यगामिना ।
परमं पुरुषं दिव्यं याति पार्थानुचिन्तयन् ॥ ८ ॥
§§ कविं पुराणमनुशासितारमणोरणीयांसमनुस्मरेद्यः ।
सर्वस्य धातारमचिन्त्यरूपमादित्यवर्णं तमसः परस्तात् ॥ ९ ॥
प्रयाणकाले मनसाऽचलेन भक्त्या युक्तो योगबलेन चैव ।
भ्रुवोर्मध्ये प्राणमावेश्य सम्यक् स तं परं पुरुषमुपैति दिव्यम् ॥१०॥

(8) O Pārtha! when a man, with the help of practice, steadies his Mind, without letting it stray elsewhere, and meditates on the Highest Spirit, he goes and is merged in that Spirit.

[Those, who maintain that according the Bhagavadgītā, one must give up worldly life and take to Devotion, should pay attention to the proposition laid down in the seventh stanza. It is unquestionable that Release is obtained by Devotion combined with the Knowledge of the Parameśvara; and that, in order to possess that frame of mind at the moment of death, it is necessary to have that practice throughout life. But, it is not necessary, according to the Gītā, for this purpose, to give up Action. On the other hand, it is the proposition of the Gītā-science, that even the Devotee of the Blessed Lord must desirelessly perform all Actions, which fall to his lot, according to the duties allocated to him; and the same meaning has been conveyed by the words "continually meditate on Me, and fight". The Blessed Lord now describes how the Karma-Yogin, who desirelessly performs Action throughout life, with the idea of dedicating it to the Parameśvara, meditates on the effulgent Highest Spirit at the moment of death—]

(9) That (man), who meditates on the Puruṣa, Who is the *kavi* (that is, omniscient), Who is the Ancient, the All-ruler, the Minuter-than-the-atom, the *dhātā* (that is, the supporter, or the doer) of everything, Whose form is unimaginable, and Who is as brilliant as the Sun beyond the darkness, (10) after steadying his Mind by force of Yoga (in the shape of control of the senses), and being imbued with Devotion, and properly keeping the *prāṇa* (that is, the Vital breath—

यदक्षरं वेदविदो वदन्ति विशन्ति यद्यतयो वीतरागाः ।
यदिच्छन्तो ब्रह्मचर्यं चरन्ति तत्ते पदं संग्रहेण प्रवक्ष्ये ॥ ११ ॥
सर्वद्वाराणि संयम्य मनो हृदि निरुध्य च ।
मूर्ध्न्याधायाऽऽत्मनः प्राणमास्थितो योगधारणाम् ॥ १२ ॥
ॐइत्येकाक्षरं ब्रह्म व्याहरन्मामनुस्मरन् ।
यः प्रयाति त्यजन्देहं स याति परमां गतिम् ॥ १३ ॥

Trans.) between the two eye-brows at the moment of death, such (a man) goes and is merged in that effulgent Highest Spirit. (11) I shall briefly describe to you that *pada*, (that is, the OM-formed Brahman), which is called '*akṣara*' by the *vedavit*-s (that is, by those, who know the Vedas—Trans.); which, Yatins enter after having become *vītarāga* (that is, free from love—Trans.), and desiring which, they observe the rules laid down for *brahmacārin*-s. (12) Controlling all the openings (in the shape of the organs), and taking the life-breath into the head, after having controlled the Mind in the heart, and becoming steady in the Yoga of Mental Absorption, (13) and meditating on 'OM', the one-worded form of the Brahman, and thinking of Me, who gives up his body, he reaches a superlative state.

[The description of the form of the Parameśvara in stanzas 9 to 11, has been borrowed from the Upaniṣads. The words '*aṇoraṇīyān*' in the 9th stanza, as also the last quarter of that stanza is from the Śvetāśvatara Upaniṣad (Śve. 3. 8 and 9); and the first quarter of stanza 11, according to its implication, and the second quarter of it, literally, are from the Kaṭhopaniṣad (Kaṭha. 2. 15). In the Kaṭhopanisad, the words '*om ityetat*' have been clearly expressed after the words "*tat te padaṁ saṁgraheṇa bravīmi*". According to this, the words '*akṣara*' and '*pada*', in the eleventh stanza, must be taken to mean "the Brahman in the shape of the word 'OM'", or "the word 'OM'"; and it is absolutely clear from stanza 13, that the worship of the OM-kāra is meant there (see, Praśna. 5). Nevertheless, it cannot be said that the Blessed Lord did not mean "the imperishable Brahman" by the word 'OM', and "the highest

§§ अनन्यचेताः सततं यो मां स्मरति नित्यशः ।
तस्याहं सुलभः पार्थ नित्ययुक्तस्य योगिनः ॥ १४ ॥
मामुपेत्य पुनर्जन्म दुःखालयमशाश्वतम् ।
नाप्नुवन्ति महात्मानः संसिद्धिं परमां गताः ॥ १५ ॥
आब्रह्मभुवनाल्लोकाः पुनरावर्तिनोऽर्जुन ।
मामुपेत्य तु कौन्तेय पुनर्जन्म न विद्यते ॥ १६ ॥

state", by the word '*pada*'; because, it can be said that the letter '*om*' is a letter from the alphabet; and also that it is imperishable, as being the symbol of the Brahman (see, stanza 21 later on); that is why, I have retained the double-meaninged words '*akṣara*' and '*pada*' from the original Sanskrit in my translation of stanza 11. The Blessed Lord now further describes the superlative state, which is reached by this worship—]

(14) O Pārtha! whoever, with a feeling that there is none other than Me, ever and continually thinks of Me, to that *nitya-yukta* (that is, perpetually steeped-in-Yoga), (Karma-) Yogin, becoming merged in Me, si easy. (15) After having come and become merged in Me, that *mahātmā* (that is, noble soul—Trans.), who has attained the highest perfection, does not get re-birth, which is the home of unhappiness and non-permanent. (16) O Arjuna! there is bound to be a *punarāvartana* (that is, a return) from even the sphere of the Brahman and other spheres (such as, heaven etc.), (to this world sometime or other); but, O son of Kuntī! after having become merged in Me, there is no re-birth.

[The word '*punarāvartana*' in the 16th stanza means 'coming back to the earth after one's merit is over' (See Gī. 9. 21; Ma. Bhā. Vana. 260). Even if a man reaches the spheres of Indra, Sūrya, nay, even of the Brahman, by such ritual as Yajña, or the worship of the deities, or the recital of the Vedas, yet, as soon as the merit which he had acquired (before death) is exhausted, he has to return to this world (Bṛ. 4. 4. 6); or at any rate, it becomes necessary for him to fall into the cycle of re-births, after the sphere

§§ सहस्रयुगपर्यन्तमहर्यद्ब्रह्मणो विदुः ।
रात्रिं युगसहस्रान्तां तेऽहोरात्रविदो जनाः ॥ १७ ॥
अव्यक्ताद्व्यक्तयः सर्वाः प्रभवन्त्यहरागमे ।
रात्र्यागमे प्रलीयन्ते तत्रैवाव्यक्तसंज्ञके ॥ १८ ॥

of the Brahman has ceased to exist; therefore, all these states are of a lower order; and as there is no re-birth after the Realisation of the Parameśvara, that state is the highest: such is the import of the 16th stanza (See Gī. 9. 20, 21). In support of the statement that even the sphere of the Brahman is non-permanent, the Blessed Lord now explains how the entire cosmos, including the sphere of the Brahman, is created and destroyed over and over again—]

(17) Those persons, who (essentially) understand what is meant by 'day' and 'night', realise that the day of Brahmadeva is made up of a thousand (*mahā*-) Yugas (each *mahāyuga* being made up of the four Yuga periods called Kṛta, Tretā, Dvāpara, and Kali respectively), and that one thousand (similar) Yugas make one night (of his).

[This stanza has appeared in the Gītā without there being a previous explanation of the calculation of a Yuga; and it has to be understood by reference to such a table, which is to be found elsewhere. This table, as also this stanza from the Gītā, are to be found in the Bhārata (Śān. 231. 31), and in the Manu-Smṛti (Manu. 1. 73); and the same description has been given in the Nirukta of Yāska (Nirukta, 14. 9). The day of Brahmadeva is also known as a '*kalpa*'. The word '*avyakta*', used in the next stanza, means the *avyakta* (that is, imperceptible) Prakṛti of Sāṁkhya philosophy, and not the Parabrahman; because, it is clearly stated later on in the 20th stanza, that the Imperceptible in the form of the Brahman, is something beyond the '*avyakta*' described in this stanza. How the Perceptible (*vyakta*) universe springs from the Imperceptible, as also the method showing how the '*kalpa*' has to be computed, has been given at p. 264 in Chapter VIII of the Gītā-Rahasya, to which the reader is referred.]

(18) When this day (of Brahmadeva) starts, all perceptible

भूतग्रामः स एवायं भूत्वा भूत्वा प्रलीयते ।
रात्र्यागमेऽवशः पार्थ प्रभवत्यहरागमे ॥ १९ ॥
§§ परस्तस्मात्तु भावोऽन्योऽव्यक्तोऽव्यक्तात्सनातनः ।
यः स सर्वेषु भूतेषु नश्यत्सु न विनश्यति ॥ २० ॥
अव्यक्तोऽक्षर इत्युक्तस्तमाहुः परमां गतिम् ।
यं प्राप्य न निवर्तन्ते तद्धाम परमं मम ॥ २१ ॥
पुरुषः स परः पार्थ भक्त्या लभ्यस्त्वनन्यया ।
यस्यान्तःस्थानि भूतानि येन सर्वमिदं ततम् ॥ २२ ॥

(objects) are created out of the Imperceptible; and when (his) night starts, (they) become dissolved into the above-mentioned Imperceptible. (19) This collection of beings, coming (thus) to birth again and again, is dissolved when the night starts (as though put into a machine), being *'avaśa'* (that is, whether they personally wish it or not); and O Pārtha! (it) comes to birth (again) when the day starts.

[That is to say, although a man may have acquired a permanent residence in the sphere of the Brahman, as a result of his meritorious Actions, yet, as even the Brahmaloka is destroyed when Destruction (*pralaya*) starts, created beings cannot escape coming to birth again at the beginning of a new Kalpa. The Blessed Lord now explains the only way in which this can be avoided—]

(20) But, the other eternal Imperceptible, which is beyond the Imperceptible mentioned above, which does not come to an end even if all created things come to an end, (21) that Imperceptible, which is (also) called '*akṣara*' which is said to be the *parama* (that is, the most excellent or the ultimate) state, (and) having reached which, there is no return (to birth), that, indeed is My super-excellent sphere. (22) O Pārtha! that *para* (that is, highest) Spirit, within Which all created beings are contained, and by Which all this has been enclosed or pervaded, can be reached only by Devotion, which is *ananya* (that is, to-none-other—Trans.).

[The 20th and 21st stanzas make together only one sentence. The word '*avyakta*' in the 20th stanza, has first been applied to the Sāṁkhya Prakṛti, that is, to the

§§ यत्र काले त्वनावृत्तिमावृत्तिं चैव योगिनः।
प्रयाता यान्ति तं कालं वक्ष्यामि भरतर्षभ ॥ २३ ॥

Imperceptible mentioned in the 18th stanza; and later on, the same word has been applied to the Parabrahman, Which is beyond the Sāṁkhya Prakṛti; and it has been stated in the 21st stanza that this second Imperceptible is also called '*akṣara*' (that is, the Immutable); similarly, in the beginning of this chapter, there is the phrase "*aksaraṁ brahma paramaṁ*", (that is, "the immutable highest Brahman"; *cf.*, 8. 3—Trans.). In short, the word '*akṣara*' (Immutable) like the word '*avyakta*' (Imperceptible) has been used in two meanings in the Gītā; it is not that the Sāṁkhya Prakṛti alone is imperceptible and immutable, but the Parameśvara or the Brahman, Which "is not destroyed, even when all created things are destroyed" is also immutable and imperceptible. This clearly shows that the word '*akṣara*', used in giving the characteristics of the "Puruṣottama" in Chapter XV, where it is stated that He, is beyond the *kṣara* (mutable) and the *akṣara* (immutable), has been used with reference to the Sāṁkhya Prakṛti (see, Gī. 15. 16-18). In short, it must be borne in mind that, both the adjectives '*avyakta*' and '*akṣara*' have been used in the Gītā, sometimes with reference to the Sāṁkhya Prakṛti, and sometimes with reference to the Parabrahman beyond this Prakṛti (Gī. Ra. pp. 275-277). The form of the Parabrahman, which is beyond the Perceptible and the Imperceptible has been referred to in the ninth chapter of the Gītā-Rahasya, to which the reader is referred. So far, there has been a description of the '*akṣara brahma*' (Immutable Brahman), that is, of the goal, having reached which, a man escapes from the necessity of re-birth. The Blessed Lord now describes the difference, from the point of view of time of death and goal reached, between those for whom there is no '*anāvṛtti*', that is, no coming back after death, and those for whom there is '*āvṛtti*', that is, those who have to come back from heaven and take birth again—]

(23) I shall now mention to you, O Bharataśreṣṭha! the

अग्निर्ज्योतिरहः शुक्लः षण्मासा उत्तरायणम् ।
तत्र प्रयाता गच्छन्ति ब्रह्म ब्रह्मविदो जनाः ॥ २४ ॥
धूमो रात्रिस्तथा कृष्णः षण्मासा दक्षिणायनम् ।
तत्र चान्द्रमसं ज्योतिर्योगी प्राप्य निवर्तते ॥ २५ ॥
शुक्लकृष्णे गती ह्येते जगतः शाश्वते मते ।
एकया यात्यनावृत्तिमन्ययाऽऽवर्तते पुनः ॥ २६ ॥

time of death, having died when, the (Karma-) Yogins do not come back (to birth in this world); and (the time of death having died) when, they come again. (24) The Fire, *jyotiḥ* (that is, flames), daytime, the bright half (of the month), and the six months of the *uttarāyaṇa* (that is, northern solstice—Trans.), those men, knowers of Brahman, who die in these, attain the Brahman after death (and do not come back). (25) (Fire), smoke, night, the dark half (of the month), and the six months of the *dakṣiṇāyana* (that is, the southern solstice—Trans.), the (Karma-) Yogin (who dies) in these, going to the light of the Moon, (that is, the sphere of the Moon), returns (after his acquired merit is over). (26) In this way, the white and the black (that is, the light and the dark) have been considered the two '*śasvate gatī*' (that is, the eternal paths) of the world ; going by one path, one does not return ; and by the other path, one returns.

[These two paths are known in the Upaniṣads by the names '*devayāna*' (bright half) and '*pitṛyāṇa*' (dark half), or the '*arcirādi-mārga*' and the '*dhūmrādi-mārga*' ; and these paths have been described even in the Ṛg-Veda. When fire is set to the dead body of a man, that is, from fire itself, both these paths commence ; therefore, the word 'Fire' must be taken as implied from the previous stanza into the 25th stanza. As the only object of the 25th stanza is to show the difference between the path described in the previous stanza and the second path, the word 'Fire' has not been repeated in it. A further explanation about this matter has been given towards the end of Chapter X of the

§§ नैते सृती पार्थ जानन् योगी मुह्यति कश्चन ।
तस्मात्सर्वेषु कालेषु योगयुक्तो भवार्जुन ॥ २७ ॥
वेदेषु यज्ञेषु तपःसु चैव दानेषु यत्पुण्यफलं प्रतिष्टम् ।
अत्येति तत्सर्वमिदं विदित्वा योगी परं स्थानमुपैति चाद्यम् ॥ २८ ॥

Gītā-Rahasya (pp. 408 to 412), to which the reader is referred, and which will clearly explain the import of this stanza. The Blessed Lord now explains the benefit of realising the principle underlying these two paths—]

(27) O Pārtha! no (Karma-) Yogin, who (essentially) understands these two *sṛtī*-s (that is, paths) is overcome by Ignorance; therefore, O Arjuna! become (Karma-) Yoga-*yukta* at all times. (28) Understanding this (principle, which has been explained above), the (Karma-) Yogin transcends the fruit in the shape of merit mentioned in the Vedas, in the Yajñas, for austerity, and for charity, and reaches the highest state, which lies beyond.

[It is clear that the man, who has understood the principle underlying these two paths, namely, the *devayāna* and the *pitṛyāṇa*, that is, who has understood that, by going by the *devayāna* path, he does not incur re-birth, and that the *pitṛyāṇa* path, though productive of heaven, is, yet, not productive of Release, will, of course, choose that path out of the two, which is truly beneficial to him; and will not ignorantly follow the path, which is of a lower order; and it is to convey this idea that the words, "one who (essentially) understands these two *sṛtī*-s, that is, paths" have been used in the former stanza. These stanzas mean that the Karma-Yogin understands which path, out of the *devayāna* and the *pitṛyāṇa* leads where; and that he, therefore, naturally goes along that path, which is the better one, and acquires Release, avoiding the trips to and from heaven; and in the 27th stanza, the Blessed Lord has advised Arjuna to act accordingly.]

इति श्रीमद्भगवद्गीतासु उपनिषत्सु ब्रह्मविद्यायां योगशास्त्रे
श्रीकृष्णार्जुनसंवादे अक्षरब्रह्मयोगो नाम
अष्टमोऽध्यायः ॥ ८ ॥

Thus ends the eighth chapter entitled AKSHARA-BRAHMA YOGA in the dialogue between Śrī Kṛṣṇa and Arjuna on the Yoga included in the Science of the Brahman, (that is, on the Karma-Yoga) in the Upaniṣad sung (that is, told) by the Blessed Lord.

नवमोऽध्यायः ।

श्रीभगवानुवाच ।

§§ इदं तु ते गुह्यतमं प्रवक्ष्याम्यनसूयवे ।
ज्ञानं विज्ञानसहितं यज्ज्ञात्वा मोक्ष्यसेऽशुभात् ॥ १ ॥

CHAPTER IX.

[In order to show how a man, by practising the Karma-Yoga, acquires peace of mind or Release as a result of his acquiring full Knowledge of the Parameśvara, an exposition of Jñāna (Spiritual Knowledge) and Vijñāna (empirical Knowledge) has been started in Chapter VII; and the form of the immutable and imperceptible Spirit has been described; and the Blessed Lord has explained in the last chapter how the worship of the OM-kāra (*omkāropāsanā*) should be performed at the moment of the close of life, after entering into mental absorption according to the Pātañjala-Yoga, in order that that form of the Parameśvara should remain fixed in the mind even at the moment of death. But, acquiring the Knowledge of the immutable Brahman is in itself difficult; and if, in addition to that, mental absorption is prescribed as an essential, this path of life will have to be given up by ordinary people! Bearing this difficulty in mind, the Blessed Lord now explains a royal road, by following which the Knowledge of the Parameśvara will become easy for everybody. This path is called the Path of Devotion (*bhaktimārga*); and I have fully discussed that path in Chapter XIII of the Gītā-Rahasya. In this path, the form of the Parameśvara can be realised by means of love, and is *vyakta*, that is, actually perceptible; and the 9th, 10th, 11th, and 12th chapters contain an exhaustive description of that perceptible form. Nevertheless, it must not be forgotten that this Path of Devotion is not something independent, but a part of the Jñāna and Vijñāna necessary for acquiring the Karma-Yoga, of which a description was started in Chapter VII; and this chapter has been opened as being a part of the previous exposition of Jñāna and Vijñāna].

The Blessed Lord said:—(1) Now, as you are not a

राजविद्या राजगुह्यं पवित्रमिदमुत्तमम् ।
प्रत्यक्षावगमं धर्म्यं सुसुखं कर्तुमव्ययम् ॥ २ ॥

अश्रद्दधानाः पुरुषा धर्मस्यास्य परन्तप ।
अप्राप्य मां निवर्तन्ते मृत्युसंसारवर्त्मनि ॥ ३ ॥

fault-finder, I will expound to you the most mysterious Spiritual Knowledge, coupled with empirical Knowledge, by knowing which, you will become free from sin (to which, listen). (2) This (Knowledge) is the king, (that is, the most superior) of all mysteries, it is a *rājavidyā* [that is, the most superior science (*vidyā*) of all], it is holy, excellent, actually realisable, easy to observe, consistent with religion, and inexhaustible. (3) Those persons, O Parantapa! who do not put faith in this religion, return to the path of worldly life, circumscribed by death, instead of coming to Me (that is, they do not attain Release).

[The meanings of the words '*rājavidyā*', '*rājaguhya*' and '*pratyakṣāvagama*' in the second stanza, have been fully considered in Chapter XIII of the Gītā-Rahasya, at pp. 574 to 582, to which the reader is referred. The means of attaining to the Parameśvara are referred to as '*vidyā*' in the Upaniṣads; and it was usual to keep these Vidyās clothed in mystery. It is said here that the *bhaktimārga* (that is, the Path of Devotion, or the worship of the Perceptible) is a Vidyā, which is the king or the most superior of these mysterious Vidyās, and also that this religion, being something which is actually visible to the eyes, is easy to follow. Nevertheless, as this Yoga has come into vogue by the tradition of Ikṣvāku and the other kings (Gī. 4. 2), it may also be said to be the path followed by Rajas or eminent persons, and to be a '*rājavidyā*' also in that sense. Whichever meaning is taken, it is quite clear that this stanza does not refer to the Knowledge of the immutable or the imperceptible Brahman; and that the word '*rājavidyā*' indicates in this place the Path of Devotion. Having in this way praised this path of life, to start with, the Blessed Lord now describes it at length—]

§§ मया ततमिदं सर्वं जगदव्यक्तमूर्तिना ।
मत्स्थानि सर्वभूतानि न चाहं तेष्ववस्थितः ॥ ४ ॥

न च मत्स्थानि भूतानि पश्य मे योगमैश्वरम् ।
भूतभृन्न च भूतस्थो ममाऽऽत्मा भूतभावनः ॥ ५ ॥

यथाऽऽकाशस्थितो नित्यं वायुः सर्वत्रगो महान् ।
तथा सर्वाणि भूतानि मत्स्थानीत्युपधारय ॥ ६ ॥

(4) I have occupied or pervaded this universe by My imperceptible form. All created beings are in Me, I am not in them; (5) and at the same time, all created beings are not in Me! See this My divine Action or power of Yoga! My Ātman, which created (these) created things, although it is embodied in the created things, (yet,) is not in them; (6) just as, the great *vāyu* (atmosphere), which reaches everywhere, is perpetually in space, so are all created things in Me, this believe.

[This apparent contradiction in terms results from the Parameśvara being qualityless as also qualityful (see my commentary on stanza 12 of Chapter VII of the Gītā, as also Gītā-Rahasya, Chapter IX, pp. 281, 285, 286, and 287). Having in this way excited the curiosity of Arjuna, by giving him a surprising description of His own form, the Blessed Lord now again describes here how the universe is created from Him, and which His perceptible forms are, which (descriptions) are slightly different from those given above in Chapters VII and VIII of the Gītā (Gī. 7. 4-18; 8. 17-20). Although the word '*yoga*' is interpreted as meaning some supernatural power or device, yet, this Yoga or device for transforming the Imperceptible into the Perceptible is nothing but Māyā, as has been proved in my commentary on Gītā 7. 25, and in Chapter IX of the Gītā-Rahasya (pp. 325 to 330). As this Yoga is very easy for the Parameśvara, nay even His slave, He is referred to as the 'Lord of Yoga' (*yogeśvara*), (Gī. 18. 75). The Blessed Lord now explains how the transformations of the universe are carried on by the power of this Yoga—]

§§ सर्वभूतानि कौन्तेय प्रकृतिं यान्ति मामिकाम् ।
कल्पक्षये पुनस्तानि कल्पादौ विसृजाम्यहम् ॥ ७ ॥
प्रकृतिं स्वामवष्टभ्य विसृजामि पुनः पुनः ।
भूतग्राममिमं कृत्स्नमवशं प्रकृतेर्वशात् ॥ ८ ॥
न च मां तानि कर्माणि निबध्नन्ति धनञ्जय ।
उदासीनवदासीनमसक्तं तेषु कर्मसु ॥ ९ ॥
मयाऽध्यक्षेण प्रकृतिः सूयते सचराचरम् ।
हेतुनाऽनेन कौन्तेय जगद्विपरिवर्तते ॥ १० ॥

(7) At the end of a *kalpa*, O Kaunteya! all created beings are merged into My Prakṛti; and in the beginning of a *kalpa*, (that is, at the beginning of the day of Brahmadeva), I Myself create them again. (8) Taking in hand My own Prakṛti, I create again and again all this collection of created beings, which has become *avaśa* (that is, dependent, or, in other words, bound by its respective Karma) as a result of its having become subject to (that) Prakṛti. (9) (But) O Dhanañjaya! as I am not attached to this My Action (of creating the universe), and as I live like an '*udāsin*' (that is, apathetically—Trans.), these Actions do not bind Me. (10) Becoming the *adhyakṣa* (that is, Superintendent—Trans.), I cause Prakṛti to give birth to the moveable and immoveable universe. By reason of this, O Kaunteya! the make and break of this world is going on.

[It has been stated in the previous chapter that the perceptible universe begins to come to birth out of the imperceptible Prakṛti, when the day of Brahmadeva (that is, the *kalpa*) starts (8. 18); but, as the Parameśvara gives to every one a good or bad birth according to his own Karma, the Blessed Lord has explained here that He Himself is untouched by (that is, is not responsible for) this Karma. In a scientific exposition, all these principles are stated in one and the same place; but as the catechismal system has been adopted in the Gītā, the same subject has been dealt with partly in one place and partly in another place, as occasion arose. Some commentators have raised a point

§§ अवजानन्ति मां मूढा मानुषीं तनुमाश्रितम् ।
परं भावमजानन्तो मम भूतमहेश्वरम् ॥ ११ ॥
मोघाशा मोघकर्माणो मोघज्ञाना विचेतसः ।
राक्षसीमासुरीं चैव प्रकृतिं मोहिनीं श्रिताः ॥ १२ ॥

§§ महात्मानस्तु मां पार्थ दैवीं प्रकृतिमाश्रिताः ।
भजन्त्यनन्यमनसो ज्ञात्वा भूतादिमव्ययम् ॥ १३ ॥
सततं कीर्तयन्तो मां यतन्तश्च दृढव्रताः ।
नमस्यन्तश्च मां भक्त्या नित्ययुक्ता उपासते ॥ १४ ॥

that the words "*jagad viparivartate*" used in the 10th stanza have reference to the Vivartavāda (See p. 331 in Chap. IX of the Gītā-Rahasya—Trans.). But I do not think that the word '*viparivartate*' means anything more than that "the make and break of this world is going on" or, that "the Perceptible is transformed into the Imperceptible, and the Imperceptible re-transformed into the Perceptible"; and even the Śāṁkarabhāṣya does not say that anything more is meant. How a man becomes '*avaśa*' (that is, dependent), as a result of Karma, has been explained in Chapter X of the Gītā-Rahasya, to which the reader is referred—]

(11) Those foolish people, who do not realise my *parama* (that is, super-excellent—Trans.) form, namely, that I am the Highest Īśvara of all created beings, do not pay respect to Me, Who have taken a human form, (considering Me to be human-formed). (12) Their hopes are futile; (their) Actions, useless; (their) Knowledge, barren; (their) Mind misguided; and they have given shelter to a devilish and ungodly temperament, based on Ignorance.

[This is the description of the ungodly person; now the Blessed Lord describes the godly (*daivī*) nature—]

(13) But, O Pārtha! those *mahātmā*-s (that is, noble souls—Trans.), who have taken shelter in a godly nature (*prakṛti*), realise and recognise (that) Me, Who am the supreme inexhaustible source of all created beings; and believing that there is no one else, worship Me; (14) and being industrious,

ज्ञानयज्ञेन चाप्यन्ये यजन्तो मामुपासते ।
एकत्वेन पृथक्त्वेन बहुधा विश्वतोमुखम् ॥ १५ ॥

§§ अहं क्रतुरहं यज्ञः स्वधाऽहमहमौषधम् ।
मन्त्रोऽहमहमेवाऽऽज्यमहमग्निरहं हुतम् ॥ १६ ॥

fixed of purpose, and continually steeped in Yoga, they continually praise Me and bow to Me, and worship Me with devotion. (15) Similarly, others worship Me, Who am *sarvatomukha* (that is, all-facing—Trans.), looking at Me on the basis of '*ekatva*' (that is, synthetically), or, on the basis of '*pṛthaktva*' (that is, analytically), or in many other ways, by means of a Jñāna-yajña (that is, sacrifice by Knowledge—Trans.)

[The brief description given here of people of godly and ungodly natures has been amplified in Chapter XVI. As has been explained before, a Jñāna-yajña means, 'comprehending the form of the Parameśvara by Jñāna (Knowledge), and thereby acquiring Release'. (See my commentary of Gī. 4. 33). But, this Knowledge of the Parameśvara can also be of different kinds, such as dualistic, non-dualistic, etc.; and therefore, the Jñāna-yajña, may also be of many kinds; and stanza 15 says that, although the Jñāna-yajña may thus be of many kinds, yet, in as much as the Parameśvara is All-facing (*viśvatomukha*), He becomes the recipient of all these Yajñas. It is clear from the words "on the basis of *ekatva*", and "on the basis of *pṛthaktva*", that these ideas were ancient, though the *dvaita* (Dualistic), *advaita* (non-dualistic), and *viśiṣṭādvaita* (qualified monistic) systems are modern. The Blessed Lord now further exhaustively deals with the one-ness and diversity of the Parameśvara referred to in this stanza, and also explains how the one-ness exists in the diversity—]

(16) *kratu* (that is, the Yajña according to the Śrutis) is Myself; Yajña (that is, the Yajña according to the Smṛtis) is Myself; *svadhā* (that is, the food offered to one's ancestors

पिताऽहमस्य जगतो माता धाता पितामहः।
वेद्यं पवित्रमोङ्कार ऋक्साम यजुरेव च ॥ १७ ॥

गतिर्भर्ता प्रभुः साक्षी निवासः शरणं सुहृत्।
प्रभवः प्रलयः स्थानं निधानं बीजमव्ययम् ॥ १८ ॥

in the death-anniversary ceremony) is Myself; *auṣadha* (that is, the food prepared from vegetables for the purposes of a Yajña) is Myself; the hymns (chanted while offering sacrifice into the Yajña) are Myself; I (am) the clarified butter, I (am) the Fire; and, the offering, which is thrown into the Fire, is also Myself.

[The words '*kratu*' and '*yajña*' were originally synonymous; but, though the word '*yajña*' acquired later on a wider significance, by being applied to the worship of the household deities, the worship of the household Fire, the feeding of guests, breath-control, reciting prayers, and performing other ritual, the meaning of the word '*kratu*' has not been extended. The Yajñas, such as the *aśvamedha*, etc., to which this word had been applied according to the Śruti religion, were the only Yajñas, which were even later on signified by it. It is, therefore, stated in the Śāṁkarabhāṣya that the word '*kratu*' in this place should be taken to mean the Yajña according to the Śrutis, and that the word 'Yajña' should be taken to mean the Yajñas according to the Smrtis; and the same meaning has been given by me above; because, if this distinction is not made, the words '*kratu*' and '*yajña*' will become synonymous, and the stanza will become liable to the fault of containing a meaningless repetition of the two words.]

(17) I (am) the father, mother, supporter (support), grandfather of this world; I am also all that which is holy, or which is knowable; and I am the OM-kāra, the Ṛg-Veda, the Sāma-Veda and the Yajur-Veda; (18) I (am) the Ultimate State (of all), the Maintainer (of all), the Overlord, the Witness, the Rest, the Refuge, the Friend, the Origin, the Destruction, the Existence, the Repository, and the Imperishable Seed.

तपाम्यहमहं वर्षं निगृह्णाम्युत्सृजामि च ।
अमृतं चैव मृत्युश्च सदसच्चाहमर्जुन ॥ १९ ॥

(19) I cause the Sun to shine, I restrain and let loose the rain; (and) O Arjuna ! I am Immortality as also Death; and the Imperishable as also the Perishable.

[A description of the form of the Parameśvara similar to this description has again appeared in detail in Chapters X, XI, and XII. But the difference between the two descriptions is, that in this place instead of merely mentioning the manifestations of the Parameśvara, there is a specific statement, that the relationship of the Parameśvara to all created beings in the world is like that of a father, a mother, a friend, etc. It must be borne in mind that though causing the rain to fall or preventing the rain from falling, is either profitable or unprofitable from the human point of view, yet, scientifically speaking and essentially, both the acts are the acts of the Parameśvara. With this idea in mind, the Blessed Lord has said before (Gī. 7. 12) that He Himself creates all the things which are *sāttvika*, *rājasa* or *tāmasa*; and later on in Chapter XIV, there is an exhaustive description of how diversity is created in this world as a result of the difference between the three constituents of Prakṛti. Looking at the matter from this point of view, the words '*sat*' and '*asat*' in the 19th stanza can also be translated as meaning 'good' or 'bad'; and later on in the Gītā (Gī. 17. 26-28), such a meaning has once been given to those words. But the ordinary meaning of those words namely, '*sat*' meaning 'imperishable' and '*asat*' meaning 'perishable' (Gī. 2. 16) must have been meant here; and it would appear that this pair of opposites, namely, '*sat*' and '*asat*' must have been inspired by the Nāsadīya-Sūkta in the same manner as the words '*mṛtyu*' and '*amṛta*'. Nevertheless, whereas in the Nāsadīya-Sūkta, the word '*sat*' has been applied to the visible world, the Gītā applies the word '*sat*' to the Parabrahman, and the word '*asat*' to the visible world; this is the difference (See Gī. Ra. Ch. IX, pp. 336-339). But although there may be this terminological difference, yet,

§§ त्रैविद्या मां सोमपाः पूतपापा यज्ञैरिष्ट्वा स्वर्गतिं प्रार्थयन्ते ।
ते पुण्यमासाद्य सुरेन्द्रलोकमश्नन्ति दिव्यान्दिवि देवभोगान् ॥ २० ॥
ते तं भुक्त्वा स्वर्गलोकं विशालं क्षीणे पुण्ये मर्त्यलोकं विशन्ति ।
एवं त्रयीधर्ममनुप्रपन्ना गतागतं कामकामा लभन्ते ॥ २१ ॥

when the two words '*sat*' and '*asat*' are used together, they clearly include both the visible world and the Parabrahman. Therefore, in order to show that both the *sat* and the *asat* are the forms of the Parameśvara, although people might call this '*sat*' and that '*asat*', as a result of terminological difference, one may interpret this description by saying that a vague definition has been given of the words '*sat*' and '*asat*' in the expression 'I am both the *sat* and the *asat*', instead of defining those words (Gī. 11. 37 and 13. 12). The Blessed Lord now shows the difference between worshipping the forms of the Parameśvara, looking upon Him as One, and worshipping such forms looking upon Him as Diverse, though the forms of the Parameśvara may thus be numerous—]

(20) The sinless (persons) and the *somapī*-s (that is, performers of the Soma-yajña), who are *traividya* (that is, who perform the ritual prescribed in the three Vedas, namely, the Ṛg, Yajuh, and Sāma); who, worshipping Me by means of a Yajña, entertain a desire to obtain heaven, reach the holy sphere of Indra, and enjoy the numerous divine enjoyments of the gods, in heaven. (21) And when they have exhausted their merit, by enjoying that expansive heaven, they take birth again and come to the mortal world. In this way, those people, who observe the *trayī-dharma* (that is, the Śruti religion, consisting of Yajñas aad Yāgas prescribed in the three Vedas), and who entertain a desire for desirable enjoyments, have to go backwards and forwards (from heaven).

[The proposition that, although residence in heaven for some time becomes possible by worshipping various deities, and by performing such religious observances as Yajñas and Yāgas, one has to take birth again and come back to

अनन्याश्चिन्तयन्तो मां ये जनाः पर्युपासते ।
तेषां नित्याभियुक्तानां योगक्षेमं वहाम्यहम् ॥ २२ ॥

the mortal world when the acquired merit is over, has been mentioned several times before (Gī. 2. 42-44; 4.34; 6. 41; 7. 23; 8. 16 and 25). Release is not like that, but is permanent; that is to say, when once a person has reached the Parameśvara, the cycle of birth and death does not any more exist for him. The description of the happiness of heaven given in the Mahābhārata (Vana. 260) is similar. But a doubt may arise as to how the '*yoga-kṣema*' (that is, security and prosperity in life—Trans.), in the world will go on, if Yajñas and Yāgas are given up, seeing that the Yajñas and Yāgas are responsible for rain, etc., (see my commentary on Gī. 2. 45 and Gī. Ra. pp. 404-405). Therefore, the Blessed Lord gives a reply to that doubt, immediately after the above stanza—]

(22) Those none-other-worshipping persons, who, meditating (only) on Me, worship Me, of those perpetually steeped-in-Yoga persons, I carry on the *yoga-kṣema* (that is, security and prosperity—Trans.).

[Even the Śāśvatakoṣa defines '*yoga-kṣema*' by saying that 'getting the things one has not got' is '*yoga*'; and 'protection of the things one has got' is '*kṣema*' (see stanzas 100 and 292); the sum and substance of the expression is 'daily maintenance in worldly life'. The reader is referred to the explanation of what this means in the path of Karma-Yoga, given in Chapter XII of the Gītā-Rahasya (see pp. 535 to 537). It has been similarly stated in the Nārāyaṇīya doctrine that:—

manīṣino hi ye kecit yatayo mokṣadharmiṇaḥ ।
teṣāṁ vicchinnatṛṣṇānāṁ yogakṣemavaho hariḥ ॥

(Ma. Bhā. Śān. 348. 72).

And it is also stated there that such persons, though they may be '*ekānta-bhakta*-s', (that is, worshippers in solitude—Trans.) belong, nevertheless, to the Path of Action, that is, they perform Action with a desireless frame of mind. The Blessed Lord now explains what happens to those persons

§§ येऽप्यन्यदेवताभक्ता यजन्ते श्रद्धयाऽन्विताः।
तेऽपि मामेव कौन्तेय यजन्त्यविधिपूर्वकम् ॥ २३ ॥
अहं हि सर्वयज्ञानां भोक्ता च प्रभुरेव च।
न तु मामभिजानन्ति तत्त्वेनातश्च्यवन्ति ते ॥ २४ ॥

who worship the Parameśvara, looking upon Him as diverse (that is, analytically—Trans.)

(23) Even those, who, becoming faith-filled, and (becoming) devotees of other deities, perform sacrifice, they too, O Kaunteya! (indirectly) sacrifice to Me, though not in the prescribed way; (24) because, I am the recipient and the Lord of all Yajñas; but, as they do not understand Me essentially, they slip.

[See the explanation given by me in Chapter XIII of the Gītā-Rahasya (pp. 586 to 591) of the importance of the proposition laid down in these two stanzas. The principle that, whatever deity is taken, it is a kind of form of the Parameśvara, has been in vogue from very ancient times in the Vedic religion. For instance, it has been stated in the Ṛg-Veda that "*ekaṁ sadviprā bahudhā vadanty agniṁ yamaṁ mātariśvānamāhuḥ*" (Ṛg. 1. 164, 46), that is, "though the Parameśvara is only One, sages give Him such different names as, Agni, Yama, Matariśvā (Wind)". And consistently with that doctrine, there is a description of the various manifestations of the Parameśvara in the next chapter though He is only One. So also in the Nārāyaṇīyopākhyāna of the Mahābhārata, after stating that the devotee, who performs Actions in solitude, is the most excellent one out of the four kinds of devotees (see my commentary on Gī. 7. 19), it is stated as follows:—

brahmāṇaṁ kśitikaṇṭhaṁ ca yāścānyā devatāḥ smṛtāḥ ।
prabhuddhacaryāḥ sevanto māmevaiṣyanti yat param ॥
(Ma. Bhā. Śān. 347. 35.)

that is, "even those saints, who worship Brahmadeva or Śiva or the other deities, also ultimately come and reach Me"; and the ideas in the above stanzas in the Gītā have also been adopted in the Bhāgavata-Purāṇa (Bhāg. 10,

यान्ति देवव्रता देवान् पितॄन्यान्ति पितृव्रताः ।
भूतानि यान्ति भूतेज्या यान्ति मद्याजिनोऽपि माम् ॥ २५ ॥

pp. 408–10). In the same way, it is again stated later on in the Nārāyaṇīyopākhyāna, that:—

ye yajanti pitṛūn devān gurūnś caivātithīṁs tathā ।
gāś caiva dvijamukhyāṁś ca pṛthivīṁ mātaraṁ tathā ॥
karmaṇā manasā vācā viṣṇum eva yajanti te ।

(Ma. Bhā. Śān. 345, 26, 27).

that is, "those who worship deities, ancestors, preceptors, guests, Brahmins, cows, etc., indirectly worship only Viṣṇu." It is surprising that even the followers of the Bhāgavata religion should quarrel with the followers of Śaivism, though the Bhāgavata religion itself thus clearly states that Devotion should be taken as the principle factor, and that the symbol in the form of a deity is a matter of minor importance, or that though there may be a difference in the form of worship, yet, the worship is only of the One Parameśvara. To proceed: the Blessed Lord now explains how though the proposition, that whatever deity is worshipped, the worship is ultimately received by the Bhagavanta, is true, worshippers miss the Path of Release, as they do not realise that the deity is one and the same; and the Blessed Lord Himself gives different Fruits of Action to different persons according to their respective faith—]

(25) Those, who worship deities go to and are merged in the deities; those, who worship ancestors, in the ancestors; those, who worship (different) past beings, in (those respective) past beings; and those who worship Me, in Me.

[In short, although one Parameśvara alone pervades everything, yet, the fruit of the worship is of a higher or lower grade to every one according to his respective faith. Nevertheless, it must not be forgotten, that the act of giving the reward is not performed by the deity, but by the Parameśvara, as has been stated above (Gī. 7. 20–23). The statement made above by the Blessed Lord, in the 24th stanza that, "I am the recipient of all Yajñas" means the

§§ पत्रं पुष्पं फलं तोयं यो मे भक्त्या प्रयच्छति ।
तदहं भक्त्युपहृतमश्नामि प्रयतात्मनः ॥ २६ ॥

same thing. Even in the Mahābhārata, it is stated as follows:—

yasmin yasmins ca visaye yo yo yāti viniścayam ।
sa tam evābhijānāti nānyaṁ bharatasattama ॥
(Śān. 352. 3);

that is, "on whatever form (*bhāva*) any man is fixed, he gets a fruit, which is conformable to that form"; and there is a Śruti text that "*yaṁ yathā yathopāsate tad eva bhavati*" (see my commentary on Gī. 8. 6). After having described the state obtained by those, who worship the Parameśvara analytically, in the first part of the stanza, the second part states that those, who worship the Blessed Lord with the faith that there is none other, are really merged in the Blessed Lord. The Blessed Lord now enunciates the important principle in the Path of Devotion, that He does not pay any attention to what His Devotee offers to Him, but merely takes into account his faith or devotion—]

(26) Whoever with devotion offers Me a leaf, or a flower, or a fruit, or (according to his means) even a little water, that devotional offering of that '*prayatātmā*' (that is, person with a regulated Mind), I accept (gladly).

[The above stanza enunciates the devotional transformation of the principle of Karma-Yoga, that "the Reason is superior to the Action" (See Gī. Ra. Chap. XV, pp. 668 to 672). In this connection, the tradition of the boiled rice offered by Sudāmā to Śrī Kṛṣṇa is well-known; and in the Bhāgavata-Purāṇa, this stanza has appeared in the Sudāmācaritopākhyāna itself (Bhāg. 10. U. 81. 4). Having a large or a small quantity of the material for worship, is not subject to the control of a person, under all circumstances, and at all times. It is, therefore, said in the Śāstras, that the Blessed Lord is satisfied, not only with whatever little material for worship may be available according to one's means, but even by the mental material of worship offered with a pure mind. The Blessed Lord

§§ यत्करोषि यदश्नासि यज्जुहोषि ददासि यत् ।
यत्तपस्यसि कौन्तेय तत्कुरुष्व मदर्पणम् ॥ २७ ॥
शुभाशुभफलैरेवं मोक्ष्यसे कर्मबन्धनैः ।
संन्यासयोगयुक्तात्मा विमुक्तो मामुपैष्यसि ॥ २८ ॥

does not crave for materials of worship, but is concerned only with Devotion. This is the most important difference between the Mīmāṁsā Path and the Path of Devotion. For performing Yajñas and Yāgas, it is necessary to spend a lot of money, and also many other things have got to be done; but the devotional sacrifice can be performed even with a single leaf of the *tulsi* plant. There is an incident described in the Mahābhārata of Draupadī having performed this kind of Yajña when Durvāsa had come as a guest to her place, and having thereby pleased the Blessed Lord. To proceed: the Blessed Lord now advises Arjuna to perform various Actions in the way, in which the devotee of the Blessed Lord performs them; and explains to him what is obtained by doing so—]

(27) O Kaunteya! whatever you do, whatever you eat, whatever you offer as sacrifice, whatever you give, whatever austerity you perform, dedicate all that to Me. (28) Acting thus, (even performing Actions), you will be free from the bonds of Action, in the shape of a good or evil result; and, becoming a '*yuktātmā*' (that is, pure-hearted), and (becoming) Released, by means of this Yoga of Renunciation (of the Fruit of Action), you will come and reach Me.

[From this it becomes quite clear, that even the Devotee of the Blessed Lord (the *bhagavadbhakta*) has to perform all Actions with the idea of dedicating them to Śrī Kṛṣna, and that he cannot give up Action; and from this point of view, these two stanzas are important. The principle of the Jñāna-Yajña namely, "*brahmārpaṇaṁ brahma haviḥ*" (Gī. 4. 24), has now been enunciated in the 27th stanza in the terminology of Devotion. (See Gī. Ra. Ch. XIII, pp. 602 to 604). The Blessed Lord has advised Arjuna already in Chapter III that: "*mayi sarvāṇi karmāṇi*

§§ समोऽहं सर्वभूतेषु न मे द्वेष्योऽस्ति न प्रियः ।
ये भजन्ति तु मां भक्त्या मयि ते तेषु चाप्यहम् ॥ २९ ॥
अपि चेत्सुदुराचारो भजते मामनन्यभाक् ।
साधुरेव स मन्तव्यः सम्यग्व्यवसितो हि सः ॥ ३० ॥

saṁnyasya" (Gī. 3. 30), that is, "making a Renunciation of all Action in Me—fight"; and in Chapter V, the Blessed Lord has again said, that the person, who performs Actions unattachedly, dedicating them to the Brahman, is not affected by the Action (5. 10). This is true Renunciation according to the Gītā (Gī. 18. 2); and, one who performs all Actions, in this way, giving up (*saṁnyasya*) the Hope for Fruit of Action, is a '*nitya-saṁnyāsin*' (perpetual ascetic), (Gī. 5. 3). The Gītā does not approve of Renunciation in shape of the Abandonment of Action. It has been stated in various places before, that performing Actions in this way, is not obstructive of Release (Gī. 2. 64; 3. 19; 4. 23; 5. 12; 6. 1; 8. 7); and, the same thing has been repeated here in the 28th stanza. In the Bhāgavata-Purāṇa, the Nṛsiṁha-formed Lord has advised Prahlāda as follows namely, "*mayyāveśya manastāt kuru karmāṇi matparaḥ*", that is, "perform all Actions, fixing your mind on Me" (Bhāg. 7. 10. 23); and later on, in the 11th *skandha*, the principle of Yoga by Devotion has been enunciated by saying, that the Devotee of the Blessed Lord should dedicate all Actions to Nārāyaṇa (See Bhāg. 11. 2. 36 and 11. 11. 24). To proceed: it has been stated in the beginning of this chapter that the Path of Devotion is pleasant and easy. The Blessed Lord now describes the other great special quality of that Path, namely, Equability, as follows:—]

(29) I am the same towards all created beings; to Me (there) is not (some one, who is) *dveṣya* (that is, un-liked), nor (some one, who is) *priya* (that is, dear). But, those who worship Me with devotion, I am embodied in them, and they are embodied in Me. (30) Be he a great evil-doer, yet, if he worships Me with the faith that there is no one else, then he must be considered a saint; because, the determination of

क्षिप्रं भवति धर्मात्मा शश्वच्छान्तिं निगच्छति ।
कौन्तेय प्रतिजानीहि न मे भक्तः प्रणश्यति ॥ ३१ ॥
मां हि पार्थ व्यपाश्रित्य येऽपि स्युः पापयोनयः ।
स्त्रियो वैश्यास्तथा शूद्रास्तेऽपि यान्ति परां गतिम् ॥ ३२ ॥
किं पुनर्ब्राह्मणाः पुण्या भक्ता राजर्षयस्तथा ।
अनित्यमसुखं लोकमिमं प्राप्य भजस्व माम् ॥ ३३ ॥

his Reason is proper. (31) He soon becomes a '*dharmātmā*' (that is, 'a pious soul'—Trans.); and attains eternal tranquility. O Kaunteya! know this to be certain, that no devotee of mine is (ever) destroyed.

[The third stanza is not to be understood as meaning that the Blessed Lord loves his devotee, even if he is an evil-doer. All that the Blessed Lord says is that, even if a man is an evil-doer in the beginning, yet, when his mind has become definitely directed towards the Paramesvara, he cannot afterwards perform any evil Action; and, that he gradually becomes a pious soul (*dharmātmā*), and attains Perfection; and by such Perfection, his sin is ultimately fully destroyed. In short, the proposition stated in Chapter VI, that even if a man is merely inspired by the desire to know what Karma-Yoga is, he becomes helpless, as if he was put into a grinding-mill, and gradually goes beyond the fruit-promising ritualism (*śabda-brahma*), is now made applicable to the Path of Devotion. The Blessed Lord now explains more clearly how He is equable towards all created beings—]

(32) Because, O Pārtha! taking shelter in Me, women, Vaiśyas, Śūdras, and others born in a sinful class (such as the lowest classes, etc.) obtain the highest state; (33) then, all the more so, those, who are holy Brahmins and also King-Sages (i. e., '*rājarṣi*–s'—Trans.), (Kṣatriyas), who are My devotees. As you are living in this transient and unhappy (that is, painful) mortal world, do you be devoted to Me.

[Some commentators have said that the word '*pāpayoni*' in the 32nd stanza is not independent, but applies equally to women, Vaiśyas, and Śūdras, because no one is born as a woman, or a Vaiśya, or a Śūdra, unless he has committed some sin in previous births. According to them, the word '*pāpayoni*' is a common word, and women, Vaiśyas, and Śūdras, are specific divisions of such *pāpayoni*, given by way of illustration. But this interpretation is not correct according to me. The word '*pāpayoni*' indicates such tribes as are referred to as 'criminal tribes' in present legislation; and, the doctrine laid down in these stanzas is, that people belonging to even these classes obtain Perfection by means of Devotion to the Blessed Lord. Women, Vaiśyas, and Śūdras do not come under these tribes, and their difficulty in obtaining Release, is that they are not authorised to hear the Vedas; and it is, therefore, stated in the Bhāgavata-Purāṇa that:—

strī śūdra dvija-bandhūnāṁ trayī na śrutigocarā ।
karmaśreyasi mūḍhānāṁ śreya evaṁ bhaved iha ।
iti bhāratam ākhyānaṁ kṛpayā muninā kṛtam ॥
(Bhāg. 1. 4. 25)

that is, "in order that women, Sūdras, and the nominal Brahmins of the Kali-Yuga (i. e., the present age), who do not get a chance of hearing the Vedas, should not remain ignorant, the sage Vyāsa has benevolently and intentionally written the Mahābhārata,—and necessarily also the Gītā—for their benefit". The above stanzas from the Bhagavadgītā have, with minor alterations of reading, also appeared in the Anugītā (Ma. Bhā. Aśva. 19. 61, 62). The true worth of this royal road of Devotion to the Blessed Lord, which gives a good final state to all, without considering the difference between castes, or between classes, or between women and men, or between persons of black or white colour, will become fully intelligible to any one who considers the history of the Mahārāṣṭra saints. A fuller explanation of the above stanza has been given in Chapter XIII of the Gītā-Rahasya at pp. 613 to 618, to which the reader is referred. The advice given to Arjuna in the latter part of the 33rd stanza, to follow this religion of Devotion, is continued in the 34th stanza.]

§§ मन्मना भव मद्भक्तो मद्याजी मां नमस्कुरु ।
मामेवैष्यसि युक्त्वैवमात्मानं मत्परायणः ॥ ३४ ॥
इति श्रीमद्भगवद्गीतासु उपनिषत्सु ब्रह्मविद्यायां योगशास्त्रे श्रीकृष्णार्जुन-
संवादे राजविद्याराजगुह्ययोगो नाम नवमोऽध्यायः ॥ ९ ॥

(34) Keep your mind fixed on Me, become My devotee, worship Me, offer sacrifice to Me, and bow down before Me. When, becoming thus devoted to Me, you perform your Yoga, you will come and reach Me.

[Strictly speaking, this advice has been started in the 33rd stanza. The word '*anitya*', in the 33rd stanza, has been used consistently with the Metaphysical doctrine, that the expansion of Prakṛti, or the Name-d and Form-ed visible world, is non-permanent; and, that the Ātman, or the Paramātman alone is permanent; and the word '*asukha*' echoes the proposition, that there is more of unhappiness than of happiness in this life. Yet, this description does not pertain to the Philosophy of the Absolute Self, but to the Path of Devotion; and, that is why, instead of using the words '*parabrahman*' or '*paramātman*', the Blessed Lord has used words indicative of the first person, with reference to His perceptible form, and said "Worship Me, keep your Mind concentrated on Me, and bow down before Me"; and advised Arjuna, that, if he thus performed this Yoga or Karma-Yoga, with Devotion, and becoming attached to Him, (Gī. 7. 1), he would be free from the bonds of Action, and ultimately come and be merged in Him; and that is the final admonition of the Blessed Lord. And the same advice has been repeated later on at the end of Chapter XI. This is, indeed, the mystic import of the whole of the Gītā. The only difference is, that it has once been expressed from the Metaphysical point of view, and at another time, from the Devotional point of view.]

Thus ends the ninth chapter named RAJVIDYA-RAJA-GUHYA YOGA in the dialogue between Śrī Kṛṣṇa and Arjuna, on the Yoga included in the Science of the Brahman, (that is, the Karma-Yoga) in the Upaniṣad sung (that is, told) by the Blessed Lord.

दशमोऽध्यायः

श्रीभगवानुवाच ।

§§ भूय एव महाबाहो शृणु मे परमं वचः ।
यत्तेऽहं प्रीयमाणाय वक्ष्यामि हितकाम्यया ॥ १ ॥
न मे विदुः सुरगणाः प्रभवं न महर्षयः ।
अहमादिर्हि देवानां महर्षीणां च सर्वशः ॥ २ ॥
यो मामजमनादिं च वेत्ति लोकमहेश्वरम् ।
असंमूढः स मर्त्येषु सर्वपापैः प्रमुच्यते ॥ ३ ॥

CHAPTER X.

[The description of the royal road in the shape of the worship of the Perceptible, prescribed by the Blessed Lord for acquiring Karma-Yoga in the last chapter, is continued in this chapter; and in reply to the question of Arjuna, He gives in the end a description of the various perceptible forms or manifestations (*vibhūti*) of the Parameśvara; and hearing this description, Arjuna is filled with the desire of seeing the Form of the Parameśvara with his own eyes; therefore, in the next, that is, the eleventh chapter, the Blessed Lord has shown him His Cosmic Form, and satisfied his ambition.]

The Blessed Lord said :—(1) O Mahābāho ! to you, who are gratified (by My speech), I am once more describing (one) excellent thing, for your benefit, to which listen. (2) My origin is not understood even by the multitude of gods, or by great Ṛṣis; because, I am, indeed, in every way, the Fundamental cause of the gods and the great Ṛṣis. (3) He, who realises that I am the Great Īśvara of all spheres, (such as, the earth, etc.), and that there is no birth or origin for Me, he alone, among all men, becoming free from Ignorance, becomes free from all sins.

[The idea that the Parabrahman, or the Blessed Lord, was in existence even before the gods, and that the gods came afterwards, is to be found in the Nāsadīya-Sūkta in the Ṛg-Veda (See Gī. Ra. Ch. IX, p. 351). To proceed : this

§§ बुद्धिर्ज्ञानमसंमोहः क्षमा सत्यं दमः शमः ।
सुखं दुःखं भवोऽभावो भयं चाभयमेव च ॥ ४ ॥
अहिंसा समता तुष्टिस्तपो दानं यशोऽयशः ।
भवन्ति भावा भूतानां मत्त एव पृथग्विधाः ॥ ५ ॥

is, so far, the introduction; the Blessed Lord now explains how He is the Great Īśvara of all—]

(4) Reason, Knowledge, Non-delusion, forgiveness, Truth, sensual restraint, tranquility, happiness, unhappiness, '*bhāva*' (that is, coming to life), '*abhāva*' (that is, death), as also fear and fearlessness, (5) harmlessness, equability, '*tuṣṭi*' (satisfaction), austerity, charity, '*yaśa*' (that is, glory—Trans.), '*ayaśa*' (that is, disgrace—Trans.), and other similar '*bhāva*'-s (that is, temperaments) of all living beings, are born from Me alone.

[The word '*bhāva*' means 'condition', 'state', or temperament'; and Sāṁkhya philosophy makes a distinction between the *bhāva*-s of Reason, and the *bhāva*-s of the Body. As the Spirit is non-active, and Reason is an evolute of Prakṛti according to the Sāṁkhyas, they say that the various conditions or *bhāva*-s of the Reason, existing in the Subtle Body (*liṅga-śarīra*) are responsible for the various births, as a bird or a beast, which the Subtle Body assumes (see Gī. Ra. Ch. VIII. p. 261, and Sāṁ. Kā. 40 to 55); and most probably, these are the *bhāva*-s which have been referred to in the above two stanzas. But, as Vedānta says that there is only One Permanent Principle, in the shape of the Paramātman, Which is beyond both Matter and Spirit, and that the entire visible universe comes to birth as a result of the desire to create the universe, which arises in the mind of that Paramātman, as described in the Nāsadīya-Sūkta, even Vedāntists say, that all the created things in the world, which are embodied in in Māyā, are the Mental *bhāva*-s of the Parabrahman (see the next stanza). The words 'austerity', 'charity

महर्षयः सप्त पूर्वे चत्वारो मनवस्तथा।
मद्भावा मानसा जाता येषां लोक इमाः प्रजाः॥ ६॥

'Yajña'* etc. are to be understood as the frames of mind indicating faith in those things. To proceed: the Blessed Lord now says that—]

(6) The seven Great Ṛṣis, the former Four, as also the Manu-s from whom this generation was created in this '*loka*' (that is, world-Trans.), are My mental (that is, 'created by the Mind') '*bhāva*'-s (that is, 'states'-Trans.).

[Although the words used in this stanza are easy, yet, there is great difference of opinion between the commentators about the legendary personages to whom this stanza refers. Especially the explanation as to the terms to which the words "the former" and the word "Four" are to be applied, has been given by different commentators in different ways. The seven Maharṣis (i. e., "Great Ṛṣis") are well-known; but one *kalpa* of Brahmadeva consists of 14 Manvantaras (See Gī. Ra. p. 264); and for each of these Manvantaras, the Manu, the deity, and the seven Ṛṣis were different (See Harivaṁśa 1. 7; Viṣṇu. 3. 1, and Matsya. 9). Therefore, some commentators have taken the words "the former" as an adjective qualifying the 'Seven Maharṣis"; and have explained the stanza by saying that the seven Maharṣis of the Cākṣuṣa Manvantara, that is, of the Manvantara previous to the present Vaivasvata Manvantara, are indicated here. These seven Ṛṣis were Bhṛgu and others, namely, Bhṛgu, Nabha, Vivasvān, Sudhāmā, Virajā, Atināmā, and Sahiṣṇu. But according to me, this interpretation is not correct; because, there seems no reason to say anything in this context about the seven Great Ṛsis in the Manvantara, previous to the present one, that is, Vaivasvata Manvantara, in which the Gītā was told. Therefore, one must take the seven Ṛṣis to be those of the present Manvantara. Their names have been mentioned in

* The word 'Yajña' appears in the author's text; but I think '*yaśa*' is meant, as that is the word used in this stanza of the Gītā—Trans

the Nārāyaṇīyopākhyāna of the Śāntiparva of the Mahābhārata as: Marīci, Aṅgirasa, Atri, Pulastya, Pulaha, Kratu, and Vasiṣṭha (Ma. Bhā. Śān. 335. 28, 29; 340. 64 and 65); and in my opinion those are the seven Ṛṣis who are indicated here; because, it is the Nārāyaṇīya or Bhāgavata religion, with its relative ritual, which has been supported in the Gītā (See Gī. Ra. pp. 12 and 13). However, it must be mentioned here that the names of the seven Ṛṣis mentioned above, namely, Marīci, etc., are sometimes found started from Bhṛgu instead of from Aṅgirasa; and in some places, there is even a description that the seven Ṛṣis of the present Yuga are Kaśyapa, Atri, Bharadvāja, Viśvāmitra, Gautama, Jamadagni, and Vasiṣṭha (Viṣṇu. 3. 1. 32 and 33; Matsya. 9. 27 and 28; Ma. Bhā. Anu. 93. 21). In the Visnu-Purāna, Bhrgu and Daksa have been added to these seven Ṛṣis, namely, Marīci and the others, so as to make out nine (Visnu, 1. 7. 5. 6); and one more, namely, Nārada has again been added to those nine in the Manu-Smrti in describing the ten Mind-born sons (*mānasa-putra*) of Brahmadeva (Manu. 1. 34, 35); and the etymology of the words Marīci, etc., has been given in Bhārata (Ma. Bhā. Anu. 85). But, as we have to see for the present only which these seven Great Ṛṣis were, it is not necessary to consider here those nine or ten Mind-born sons or the etymological significance of their names. It is quite clear that the words "the Former" cannot be interpreted as meaning the seven Ṛṣis of the previous Manvantara. Let us now see to what extent the interpretation of some commentators, who have taken the words "the former Four" as referring to the word 'Manu-'s is correct. There are in all fourteen Manvantaras, of which there are fourteen Manus; and these are sub-divided into two classes of seven each. The first seven are called Svāyaṁbhuva, Svārociṣa, Auttamī, Tāmasa, Raivata, Cākṣuṣa, and Vaivasvata; and they are referred to as 'Svāyaṁbhuva and others' (Manu. 1. 62 and 63). Of these, the first six Manus are over; and the seventh, that is to say, the Vaivasvata Manu, is now going on, When this Manu is over, the seven subsequent Manus (Bhāg. 8. 13. 7) are called the Sāvarṇi Manus. Their names are, Sāvarṇi, Dakṣa-Sāvarṇi, Brahma-Sāvarṇi, Dharma-Sāvarṇi, Rudra-Sāvarṇi, Deva-Sāvarṇi, and Indra-Sāvarṇi (Viṣṇu. 3. 2; Bhāgavata. 8. 13; Harivaṁśa, 1. 7). Considering that there are seven Manus in each class, it cannot be explained why the Gītā should have referred only to "the former Four", that is to say, the "first four" only from either class. On account of the tradition in the Brahmāṇḍa-Purāṇa, that out of the Sāvarṇi Manus, the four after the first one, namely, the Dakṣa–, Brahma–, Dharma–, and Rudra–Sāvarṇi Manus, were all created at the same time, some commentators say that the Gītā refers to these four Sāvarṇi Manus. But to this suggestion, an objection is taken by others that as the Sāvarṇi Manus are all to come in the future, the words "from whom this generation was created in this world", which are indicative of the past tense, cannot be applied to the Sāvarṇi Manus, which are to come in the future. In short, the words "the former Four" cannot be taken to refer to the word "Manus". Therefore, the words "the former Four" must be taken to have independent reference to some former four Ṛṣis, or four personages; and if you say so, the question who these "former Four" were, naturally arises. Those commentators, who have interpreted this stanza in that way, say that these "former Four" were the four Ṛṣis named Sanaka, Sananda, Sanātana, and Sanatkumāra (Bhāg. 3. 12, 4). But, to this interpretation, there is the objection that although these four Ṛṣis were the Mind-born sons of Brahmadeva, yet, as they were Saṁnyāsins from birth, they refused to raise progeny; and, on that account, Brahmadeva had got angry with them (Bhāg. 3. 12; Viṣṇu. 1. 7); and, therefore, the sentence "from whom this generation was created in this world—"*yeṣāṁ loka imāḥ prajāḥ*"—cannot under any circumstances be applied to the Ṛṣis. Besides, although it is stated in the Purāṇas, that these Ṛṣis were four, yet, in the Bhārata, in the Nārāyaniya, that is, the Bhāgavata doctrine, Sana, Kapila, and Sanatsujāta have been added to these four, and these seven Ṛṣis are said to be the Mind-born sons of Brahmadeva; and it is stated that they followed the Path of Renunciation from birth (Ma. Bhā. 340. 67. 68). Besides, even if the Ṛṣis are thus taken to be seven, that is, Sanaka and others, yet, there seems to be no reason why only four of these should have been referred to here. Then, who are these "former Four"? In my opinion, the answer to this question must be given from the legendary stories pertaining to the Nārāyaṇīya, or, the Bhāgavata religion; because, in my opinion, it is unquestionable that the Bhāgavata doctrine alone is supported in the Gītā. Now, if one considers the Bhāgavata conception of the creation of the universe, the four entities Vāsudeva (Ātman), Saṁkarṣaṇa (Jīva), Pradyumna (Mind), and Aniruddha (Individuation) had come into existence before the seven Ṛṣis; and, it is there stated that, from the last of them, namely, from Aniruddha, that is, from Brahmadeva, the Mind-born sons Marīci, etc., came to be born (Ma. Bhā. Śān. 339. 34 to 40 and 60 to 72; 340. 27 to 31). The four entities, Vāsudeva, Saṁkarṣaṇa, Pradyumna, and Aniruddha, are collectively known as the 'Caturvyūha'; and whereas one sect of the Bhāgavata doctrine says that these four entities were all independent of each other, other sects look upon two or three, out of these four, as the more important ones. But, these conceptions are not acceptable to the Bhagavadgītā, which pertains to the 'Ekavyūha' school, that is, which is of the opinion that the four Vyūhas and everything else was created from '*eka*' or One, Parameśvara, as has been shown by me in the Gītā-Rahasya (Gī. Ra. p. 266 and 756). It is, therefore, stated in this stanza, that the four entities, Vāsudeva, etc., forming the 'Caturvyūha' are not independent of each other, and that all these four Vyūhas are the *bhāva*-s or 'states' of One Parameśvara, that is, of the All-pervading Vāsudeva (Gī. 7. 19). Looking at the matter from this point of view, it will be seen that the words "the former Four" have reference to the Caturvyūha of Vāsudeva and the others, who had come into existence before the Seven Ṛṣis according to the Bhāgavata religion. It has been stated in the Bhārata itself, that the distinction between the four Vyūhas according to the Bhāgavata religion was

§§ एतां विभूतिं योगं च मम यो वेत्ति तत्त्वतः ।
सोऽविकम्पेन योगेन युज्यते नात्र संशयः ॥ ७ ॥
अहं सर्वस्य प्रभवो मत्तः सर्वं प्रवर्तते ।
इति मत्वा भजन्ते मां बुधा भावसमन्विताः ॥ ८ ॥
मच्चित्ता मद्गतप्राणा बोधयन्तः परस्परम् ।
कथयन्तश्च मां नित्यं तुष्यन्ति च रमन्ति च ॥ ९ ॥
तेषां सततयुक्तानां भजतां प्रीतिपूर्वकम् ।
ददामि बुद्धियोगं तं येन मामुपयान्ति ते ॥ १० ॥

in vogue from former times (Ma. Bhā. Śān. 348. 57); this idea is not something new invented by me. In short, on the authority of the Nārāyaṇīyopākhyāna of the Bhārata, I interpret "the seven Maharṣis", to mean, Marīci and others; "the former Four", to mean, Vāsudeva and others forming the Caturvyūha; and 'Manu-s', to mean, the six previous Manus, and the seventh Manu then current, making up the Svāyaṁbhuva group of Manus. The idea of looking upon the four entities, namely, Aniruddha, (that is, Individuation), and the others, as the sons of the Parameśvara is also to be found in another place in the Bhārata (Ma. Bhā. Śān. 311. 7, 8). The *bhāva*-s or mental states of the Parameśvara have thus been mentioned. The Blessed Lord now explains the result of worshipping Him, after one has realised this fact—]

(7) He, who understands the principle of this my '*vibhūti*' (that is, manifestation) and this my Yoga (that is, device or power by which I cause this manifestation), undoubtedly attains the permanent (Karma-) Yoga. (8) Wise men, realising that I am the Origin of everything, and that all things spring from Me, become imbued with My *bhāva*-s (that is, states —Trans.) and thus worship Me. (9) Concentrating their minds on Me, fixing their life on Me, giving counsel to each other and telling each other legends about Me, they are always happy and engrossed (in doing that). (10) To those, who thus always remaining '*yukta*' (that is, content), worship Me, I give the Yoga of the (Equable) Reason,

तेषामेवानुकम्पार्थमहमज्ञानजं तमः ।
नाशयाम्यात्मभावस्थो ज्ञानदीपेन भास्वता ॥ ११ ॥

अर्जुन उवाच ।

§§ परं ब्रह्म परं धाम पवित्रं परमं भवान् ।
पुरुषं शाश्वतं दिव्यमादिदेवमजं विभुम् ॥ १२ ॥
आहुस्त्वामृषयः सर्वे देवर्षिर्नारदस्तथा ।
असितो देवलो व्यासः स्वयं चैव ब्रवीषि मे ॥ १३ ॥

which enables them to come and reach Me. (11) And in order to bestow favour on them, I enter their '*ātmabhāva*' (that is, their Inner Sense); and by the brilliant Lamp of Knowledge, destroy the darkness born of Ignorance (in their Minds).

[It has been stated above in Chapter VII that it is the Parameśvara Himself, Who creates the faith towards various deities (7. 21); in the same way, it is now stated in the 10th stanza that the act of increasing Equability of Reason in persons, who have taken to the Path of Devotion, is performed by the Parameśvara Himself; and this proposition in the Path of Devotion is similar in meaning to the statement made above (Gī. 6. 44) that once a man is inspired by a desire for Karma-Yoga, he is dragged towards complete perfection, as if he had been put into a grinding-mill. It is said that this capacity arises from Free Will according to the doctrine of Causality. But, even the Ātman is the Parameśvara; therefore, it is stated in the Doctrine of Devotion, that this Fruit or this Frame of Mind is given by the Parameśvara to each one according to his actions in previous births (Gī. 7. 20 and Gī. Ra. Ch. XIII, p. 596). After the Blessed Lord has in this way explained the principle underlying the Path of Devotion—]

Arjuna said :—(12) That You (are) the Highest Brahman, the most Exalted State, the most Sacred Thing, the Brilliant and the Permanent Spirit, the Highest Deity, the Unborn, the *sarva-vibhu* (that is, the All-pervading), (13) is said with reference to You by all Ṛṣis, as also by the Devarṣi

सर्वमेतदृतं मन्ये यन्मां वदसि केशव ।
न हि ते भगवन् व्यक्तिं विदुर्देवा न दानवाः ॥ १४ ॥
स्वयमेवात्मनाऽऽत्मानं वेत्थ त्वं पुरुषोत्तम ।
भूतभावन भूतेश देवदेव जगत्पते ॥ १५ ॥
वक्तुमर्हस्यशेषेण दिव्या ह्यात्मविभूतयः ।
याभिर्विभूतिभिर्लोकानिमांस्त्वं व्याप्य तिष्ठसि ॥ १६ ॥
कथं विद्यामहं योगिंस्त्वां सदा परिचिन्तयन् ।
केषु केषु च भावेषु चिन्त्योऽसि भगवन्मया ॥ १७ ॥
विस्तरेणात्मनो योगं विभूतिं च जनार्दन ।
भूयः कथय तृप्तिर्हि शृण्वतो नास्ति मेऽमृतम् ॥ १८ ॥

Nārada, by Asita, Devala, and even by Vyāsa; and You also tell me the same thing. (14) O Keśava! all this which You tell me, I look upon as true. O Blessed Lord! Your '*vyakti*' (that is, Your origin) is known neither to the gods nor to the demons. (15) O Bhūteśa, Who have created all these created beings! O God of gods, and Lord of the Universe! You alone are the one, O Puruṣottama! Who know Yourself! (16) Therefore, those your divine manifestations, by which You have pervaded all these spheres, (please) describe all those in detail to me. (17) O Yogin! how shall I Realise You, by continually meditating on You? and O Blessed Lord! in what different objects should I meditate on You? (Tell me that). (18) O Janārdana! tell me again in full detail Your *vibhūti*-s (that is, manifestations) and Your Yoga, because, I cannot hear enough of this (Your) nectar-like (conversation).

[The words '*vibhūti*' and '*yoga*' have appeared in the 7th stanza of this chapter, and Arjuna has repeated them here. See the meaning of the word 'Yoga' which has been given before (Gī. 7. 25). It must be borne in mind, as has been stated in the 17th stanza, that Arjuna's reason for asking about the different manifestations of the Blessed Lord was not in order to meditate on those different manifestations as deities, but in order to look upon all those different manifestations as being the All-Pervasive

श्रीभगवानुवाच ।

हन्त ते कथयिष्यामि दिव्या ह्यात्मविभूतयः ।
प्राधान्यतः कुरुश्रेष्ठ नास्त्यन्तो विस्तरस्य मे ॥ १९ ॥
अहमात्मा गुडाकेश सर्वभूताशयस्थितः ।
अहमादिश्च मध्यं च भूतानामन्त एव च ॥ २० ॥
आदित्यानामहं विष्णुर्ज्योतिषां रविरंशुमान् ।
मरीचिर्मरुतामस्मि नक्षत्राणामहं शशी ॥ २१ ॥

Parameśvara. Because, the Blessed Lord has already explained before that there is a world of difference, from the point of view of the Path of Devotion, between believing that there is only one Parameśvara in all places, and looking upon the different manifestations of the Parameśvara as different deities (Gī. 7. 20 to 25, 9–22 to 28).]

The Blessed Lord said:—(19) Very well! O Kuruśreṣṭha! I shall now describe to you the most important of My divine manifestations, because, there is no end to My expansion.

[There are descriptions of the form of the Parameśvara in the Anuśāsanaparva (14, 311–321) and in the Anu-gītā (Aśva. 43–44), which are similar to the description of manifestations given here. But, as the description in the Gītā is sweeter than those given elsewhere, it seems to have been copied in the other places. For instance, a similar description of manifestations has been made in the 15th chapter of the eleventh *skandha* of the Bhāgavata-Purāṇa by the Blessed Lord to Uddhava; and it has been stated there (Bhāg. 11. 16. 6–8), that the description is similar to the description given in this chapter.]

(20) O Guḍākeśa! I am the '*ātmā*' (that is, Self—Trans.), which exists in the heart of all created beings; and I am also the origin, the middle, and the end of (all) created beings. (21) I am the Viṣṇu among the (twelve) *āditya*-s (that is, Suns—Trans.); I am the radiating Sun, among the brilliant bodies; I am Marīci out of the (seven or forty-nine*)

* In the 1915 edition of the text, these are stated to be thirty-nine—Trans.

वेदानां सामवेदोऽस्मि देवानामस्मि वासवः।
इन्द्रियाणां मनश्चास्मि भूतानामस्मि चेतना ॥ २२ ॥

Maruta-s; I (am) the Moon, among the lunar asterisms. (22) I am the Sāma-veda, among the Vedas; (I) am Indra, among the gods; (I) am the Mind, among the senses; (I) am the *cetanā,* (that is, the movement of vitality) in created beings.

[Just as it is stated here, that "I am the Sāma-Veda among the Vedas" that is to say, that the Sāma-Veda is the principal Veda, so also is it stated in the Anuśāsanaparva of the Mahābhārata (14. 317) that "*sāmavedaś ca vedānāṁ yajuṣāṁ śatarudriyam*". But in the Anu-gītā, supreme importance among the Vedas is given to the Om-kāra by the words "*Om-kāraḥ sarva-vedānāṁ,* etc." (Aśva. 44. 6); and it has been stated in the Gītā itself, in a previous chapter (Gī. 7. 8), that "*praṇavaḥ sarvavedeṣu*" (that is, "I am the *praṇava* (Om-kāra) in all the Vedas—Trans.). So also in the Gītā (9. 17) a higher place has been given to the Ṛg-Veda than to the Sāma-Veda by the words "*ṛk-sāma-yajur eva ca*"; and the ordinary belief is the same. As these statements have been looked upon as mutually contradictory, several persons have come out with different explanations about them. In the Chāndogyopaniṣad, the Om-kāra is given the name '*udgītha*': and it is stated there, that this '*udgītha*' is the summary of the Sāma-Veda, and that the Sāma-Veda is the summary of the Ṛg-Veda (Chān. 1. 1. 2). This statement in the Chāndogya harmonises the various statements regarding which is the most superior among the Vedas; because, even in the Sāma-Veda, the hymns have been taken from the Ṛg-Veda. But, some persons are not satisfied with that; and say that there must be some deep reason for giving prominence to the Sāma-Veda in the Gītā in this place. Although the Sāma-Veda has been given prominence in the Chāndogyopaniṣad, yet, Manu has said "the voice of the Sāma-Veda is impure" (Manu. 4. 124). From this fact, one critic has drawn the inference that the Gītā, which gives prominence to the Sāma-Veda, must be anterior in point of time to

रुद्राणां शंकरश्चास्मि वित्तेशो यक्षरक्षसाम् ।
वसूनां पावकश्चास्मि मेरुः शिखरिणामहम् ॥ २३ ॥
पुरोधसां च मुख्यं मां विद्धि पार्थ बृहस्पतिम् ।
सेनानीनामहं स्कन्दः सरसामस्मि सागरः ॥ २४ ॥
महर्षीणां भृगुरहं गिरामस्म्येकमक्षरम् ।
यज्ञानां जपयज्ञोऽस्मि स्थावराणां हिमालयः ॥ २५ ॥

Manu; and another critic says that the writer of the Gītā was possibly a Sāma-Vedī; and that he has, on that account, given prominence to the Sāma-Veda. But, in my opinion, it is not necessary to go so far for giving a satisfactory explanation of the words "I am the Sāma-Veda among the Vedas". The worship or praise of the Parameśvara in the form of a song is always given prominence in the Path of Devotion. For instance, in the Nārāyaṇīya-dharma, Nārada has described the Blessed Lord as "*vedeṣu sa purāṇeṣu sāṅgopāṅgeṣu gīyase*" (Ma. Bhā. Śān. 334. 23); Vasurāja has been described as 'singing' the '*japya*': cf., "*japyaṁ jagau*" (Śān. 337. 27; and 342. 70 and 81), by making use of the root '*gai*' (to sing). There is, therefore, nothing to be surprised at in prominence being given in a devotional religion to the musical Sāma-Veda over the ritualistic Veda consisting of Yajñas and Yāgas; and in my opinion, this is the simple reason for saying "I am the Sāma-Veda among the Vedas".]

(23) And, among the (eleven) Rudras, I am Śaṁkara; Kubera, among the Yakṣa-rākṣasa-s; I am the Pāvaka, among the (eight) Vasū-s; I, the Meru among the (seven) mountains; (24) O Pārtha! and understand that among the preceptors, I am the principal one, namely, Bṛhaspati; I (am) Skanda (Kārtikeya) among the commanders of armies; I am the Samudra (the ocean), among collections of water. (25) I, Bhṛgu, among the great Ṛṣis; I am the one-syllabled sound '*oṁ-kāra*' in speech; I am the *japa-yajña*, among Yajñas; and from among the immoveable (that is, steady) things, I am the Himālaya;

अश्वत्थः सर्ववृक्षाणां देवर्षीणां च नारदः ।
गन्धर्वाणां चित्ररथः सिद्धानां कपिलो मुनिः ॥ २६ ॥
उच्चैःश्रवसमश्वानां विद्धि माममृतोद्भवम् ।
ऐरावतं गजेन्द्राणां नराणां च नराधिपम् ॥ २७ ॥
आयुधानामहं वज्रं धेनूनामस्मि कामधुक् ।
प्रजनश्चास्मि कन्दर्पः सर्पाणामस्मि वासुकिः ॥ २८ ॥
अनन्तश्चास्मि नागानां वरुणो यादसामहम् ।
पितॄणामर्यमा चास्मि यमः संयमतामहम् ॥ २९ ॥

[The sentence "I am the *japa-yajña* among the Yajñas" is of importance. In the Anu-gītā, it is stated that "*yajñānāṁ hutam uttamam*" that is, "out of the Yajñas, that Yajña, which consists of offering '*havi*' (into the fire) is the most important" (Ma. Bhā. Aśva. 44. 8); and the same is the opinion of Vedic ritualists; but, as the *nāma-yajña* or the *japa-yajña* is of greater importance than the *havir-yajña* in the Path of Devotion, the words "*yajñānāṁ japa-yajñosmi*" have appeared in the Gītā. Manu has stated in one place (2.87) that :—" whatever else the Brahmin may do or not do, he attains Release by *japa* (silent meditation) alone. The reading in the Bhāgavata is "*yajñānāṁ brahmayajñ'ohaṁ*"—]

(26) among the trees, the *aśvattha* (that is, the pippal) tree; Nārada, among the god-Ṛṣis; Citraratha, among the Gandharvas; Kapila Muni, among the Siddhas; (27) and the Uccaiśravas horse, which came into existence at the time of the churning for nectar, among horses; know that I am all these; the *airāvata*, among the excellent elephants; and the king, among men. (28) I, the sword, among instruments of war-fare; I am the *kāma-dhenu* among cows; and I am Kāma, which is responsible for the creation of progeny; I am Vāsuki among the serpents; (29) I am Ananta among the *nāga*-s; I, Varuṇa, among the *yādas*, (that is, the aquatic creatures); and I am the *aryamā* among the ancestors; I am Yama, among those, who regulate.

[The meanings of Vāsuki as the 'king of serpents' and of Ananta as 'Śeṣa' are to be found in the Amarakośa,

प्रह्लादश्चास्मि दैत्यानां कालः कलयतामहम् ।
मृगाणां च मृगेन्द्रोऽहं वैनतेयश्च पक्षिणाम् ॥ ३० ॥
पवनः पवतामस्मि रामः शस्त्रभृतामहम् ।
झषाणां मकरश्चास्मि स्रोतसामस्मि जाह्नवी ॥ ३१ ॥
सर्गाणामादिरन्तश्च मध्यं चैवाहमर्जुन ।
अध्यात्मविद्या विद्यानां वादः प्रवदतामहम् ॥ ३२ ॥

as also in the Mahābhārata (Ma. Bhā. Ādi. 35-39). But one cannot definitely say what the difference between *nāga*-s and serpents, is. In the Āstikopākhyāna of the Mahābhārata, these words have been used as synonymous; but the use of the words '*sarpa*' and '*nāga*' in this place, shows that two different kinds of the common class of serpents are intended. It is stated in Śrīdhara's commentary that the 'serpent' is poisonous, and the '*nāga*', non-poisonous; and in the Rāmānujabhāṣya, the distinction is made by saying that serpents have only one head, and *nāga*-s have many heads; but, both these distinctions do not seem to me correct; because, in some places, in mentioning the important families among the *nāga*-s, Ananta and Vāsuki are both mentioned in the beginning; and both are described as being many-headed and poisonous, but Ananta is described as fire-coloured and Vāsuki as yellow-coloured. The reading in the Bhāgavata is the same as in the Gītā.]

(30) And I am Prahlāda, among the demons; I, Kāla, among the swallowers-up; and I, the '*mṛgendra*' (that is, the lion) among the animals; and the eagle, among birds. (31) I am the wind, among the speeders. I (am) Rāma, among arms-bearers; I am the alligator, among fishes; and the Bhāgīrathī, among the rivers. (32) O Arjuna! I am the origin, the middle and the end of the entire creation; Metaphysics, among all sciences; I, the logic of all controversialists.

[It has been stated in the 20th stanza above, that the Blessed Lord is the origin of all activated (*sacetana*) things; and He now says, that He is the beginning, middle, and

अक्षराणामकारोऽस्मि द्वन्द्वः सामासिकस्य च ।
अहमेवाक्षयः कालो धाताऽहं विश्वतोमुखः ॥ ३३ ॥
मृत्युः सर्वहरश्चाहमुद्भवश्च भविष्यताम् ।
कीर्तिः श्रीर्वाक् च नारीणां स्मृतिर्मेधा धृतिः क्षमा ॥ ३४ ॥
बृहत्साम तथा साम्नां गायत्री छन्दसामहम् ।
मासानां मार्गशीर्षोऽहमृतूनां कुसुमाकरः ॥ ३५ ॥

end of the entire moveable and immoveable creation; this is the distinction.]

(33) I am the *akāra* (the letter '*a*'), among the letters; and among compounds, I am the (*ubhaya-pada-pradhāna*), (that is, copulative—Trans.) '*dvaṁdva*'; I am the inexhaustible Time (such as, *nimeṣa-muhūrta* etc.); I am the '*sarvatomukha*' (that is, having mouths or faces on all the four sides) '*dhātā*' (creator—Trans.) or Brahmadeva. (34) I am death, the destroyer of all; and I am the origin of all to be born in the future; among females, I am fame, fortune, speech, '*smṛti*' (that is, memory—Trans.), '*medhā*' (that is, intellect—Trans.), '*dhṛti*' (that is, courage—Trans.) and '*kṣamā*' (that is, forgiveness—Trans.).

[The words '*kīrti*', '*śrī*', '*vāk*', etc., indicate the several respective deities. The five out of these, excepting speech and forgiveness, and the other five (*puṣṭi*, *śraddhā*, *kriyā*, *lajjā*, and *mati*, (that is, sound-bodiedness, faith, action, shame, and understanding), these ten are the daughters of Dakṣa; and, as they had been given in marriage to Dharma, they are all described as "*dharma-patnī*-s" in the Mahābhārata (Ādi. 66. 13, 14).]

(35) Similarly, among the Sāma, (that is, those Vedic hymns, which are to be sung) I am the Bṛhatsāma; and among the metres, I am the Gāyatrī-metre; I am Mārgaśīrṣa among the months, and the Spring, among the six seasons.

[The first place has been given to the month of Mārgaśīrṣa among the months, because, it was usual in those days to start with the month of Mārgaśīrṣa in counting the months (Ma. Bhā. Anu. 106 and 109; Vālmīki Rāmāyaṇa

द्यूतं छलयतामस्मि तेजस्तेजस्विनामहम् ।
जयोऽस्मि व्यवसायोऽस्मि सत्त्वं सत्त्ववतामहम् ॥ ३६ ॥
वृष्णीनां वासुदेवोऽस्मि पाण्डवानां धनंजयः ।
मुनीनामप्यहं व्यासः कवीनामुशना कविः ॥ ३७ ॥
दण्डो दमयतामस्मि नीतिरस्मि जिगीषताम् ।
मौनं चैवास्मि गुह्यानां ज्ञानं ज्ञानवतामहम् ॥ ३८ ॥
यच्चापि सर्वभूतानां बीजं तदहमर्जुन ।
न तदस्ति विना यत्स्यान्मया भूतं चराचरम् ॥ ३९ ॥
नान्तोऽस्ति मम दिव्यानां विभूतीनां परंतप ।
एष तूद्देशतः प्रोक्तो विभूतेर्विस्तरो मया ॥ ४० ॥

3. 16). There is a similar reference in the Bhāgavata (11. 16. 27). I have pointed out in my book called 'Orion' that the Mṛgaśīrṣa constellation is called the *agrahāyaṇi*, or, 'the constellation at the commencement of the year'; that, the Mṛga constellation must have got the first place, when the computation starting with the Mṛga constellation was in vogue, and that the Mārgaśīrṣa month must also have acquired importance later on, on that account; and I have to refer the reader to that book. I am not going into the matter here for fear of taking up space.]

(36) I am the gambling, of those, who deceive; I, the brilliance of the brilliant; I am the victory (of the victorious); and I, the determination (of those who are determined); and I, the faithfulness of the faithful. (37) Among the Yādavas, I am Vāsudeva; among the Pāṇḍavas, Dhanañjaya; among the sages too, I am Vyāsa; and among the learned, I am Śukrācārya. (38) I am the rod (of authority) of those, who punish; I am the *nīti* (that is, the diplomacy) of those, who desire success; and among (all) mysteries, I am silence. I am the knowledge of the knowers. (39) Similarly, O Arjuna! I am the seed of all created beings; and there is not a single moveable or immoveable being, which can exist without Me. (40) O Parantapa! there is no end to My divine manifestations; I have mentioned this expanse of My emanations merely directionally.

§§ यद्यद्विभूतिमत्सत्त्वं श्रीमदूर्जितमेव वा ।
तत्तदेवावगच्छ त्वं मम तेजोंऽशसंभवम् ॥ ४१ ॥
अथवा बहुनैतेन किं ज्ञातेन तवार्जुन ।
विष्टभ्याहमिदं कृत्स्नमेकांशेन स्थितो जगत् ॥ ४२ ॥

इति श्रीमद्भगवद्गीतासु उपनिषत्सु ब्रह्मविद्यायां योगशास्त्रे
श्रीकृष्णार्जुनसंवादे विभूतीयोगो नाम
दशमोऽध्यायः ॥ १० ॥

[Having thus mentioned His principal emanations, the Blessed Lord now summarises the chapter—]

(41) Anything whatever, which is invested with power, glory, or splendour, has come into existence out of a portion of My brilliance. (42) Or, O Arjuna! what use have you for knowing all this emanation? (To tell you the whole, in short) by (only) one portion of Myself, have I pervaded the whole of this Cosmos.

[The last stanza is based on the *ṛcā* "*pādosya viśvā bhūtāni tripādasyā 'mṛtaṁ divi*" (Ṛg. 10. 90. 3) from the Puruṣa-Sūkta; and this hymn has also appeared in the Chāndogyopaniṣad (Chān. 3. 12. 6). The meaning of the word '*aṁśa*' has been explained at the end of Chapter IX of the Gītā-Rahasya (see pp. 338 to 343), to which the reader is referred. If the Blessed Lord has pervaded the whole of this universe with only a portion of Himself, it is quite clear that the entire emanation of the Blessed Lord must be still greater; and this last stanza has been added only to make that clear. In the Puruṣa-Sūkta, it is stated that "*etāvān asya mahimā 'to jyāyāṁś ca pūruṣaḥ*", that is, "this is only a description of His greatness, the Puruṣa Himself is much greater than this".]

Thus ends the tenth chapter entitled VIBHUTI-YOGA in the dialogue between Śrī Kṛṣṇa and Arjuna on the Yoga included in the Science of the Brahman, (that is, the Karma-Yoga) in the Upaniṣad sung (that is, told) by the Blessed Lord.

एकादशोऽध्यायः

अर्जुन उवाच ।

§§ मदनुग्रहाय परमं गुह्यमध्यात्मसंज्ञितम् ।
यत्त्वयोक्तं वचस्तेन मोहोऽयं विगतो मम ॥ १ ॥
भवाप्ययौ हि भूतानां श्रुतौ विस्तरशो मया ।
त्वत्तः कमलपत्राक्ष माहात्म्यमपि चाव्ययम् ॥ २ ॥
एवमेतद्यथात्थ त्वमात्मानं परमेश्वर ।
द्रष्टुमिच्छामि ते रूपमैश्वरं पुरुषोत्तम ॥ ३ ॥
मन्यसे यदि तच्छक्यं मया द्रष्टुमिति प्रभो ।
योगेश्वर ततो मे त्वं दर्शयात्मानमव्ययम् ॥ ४ ॥

CHAPTER XI.

[After the Blessed Lord had described His own manifestations in the last chapter, Arjuna was filled with the desire of seeing this Cosmic Form (*viśvarūpa*); and the description given in this chapter of the Cosmic Form shown by the Blessed Lord to Arjuna, at his request, is so entrancing that it is looked upon as an excellent part of the Gītā; and those who have written the other Gītās, have copied it. To begin with, Arjuna asks as follows—]

Arjuna said:—(1) That greatest mysticism known as 'Adhyātma' (that is, Metaphysics—Trans.), which You explained to me in order to show favour to me, has destroyed my ignorance. (2) In the same way, O Thou with eyes like lotus-leaves! I have heard from You in detail about the origin and the end of all created beings and about (Your) inexhaustible greatness. (3) (Now) O Parameśvara! as You have thus described Yourself, in that way, O Puruṣottama! I wish to see (actually) Your divine form. (4) O Lord! if you think that it is possible for me to see such a form, then, O Yogeśvara! show me Your imperishable form.

[Arjuna has, in the first stanza, signified by the word '*adhyātma*', the Knowledge of the imperishable or the imperceptible form of the Parameśvara, which was described by the Blessed Lord in Chapters VII and VIII

श्रीभगवानुवाच ।

§§ पश्य मे पार्थ रूपाणि शतशोऽथ सहस्रशः ।
नानाविधानि दिव्यानि नानावर्णाकृतीनि च ॥ ५ ॥
पश्यादित्यान्वसून्रुद्रानश्विनौ मरुतस्तथा ।
बहून्यदृष्टपूर्वाणि पश्याश्चर्याणि भारत ॥ ६ ॥

and the Knowledge of the various perceptible forms mentioned in Chap. IX and X, after He had started explaining Jñāna and Vijñāna in Chap. VII; and the words "the origin and the end of all created beings" in stanza 2, refer to the description of how numerous perceptible objects come out of one Imperceptible, which has been given in Chap. VII (7. 4–15), Chap. VIII (8. 16-21) and Chap. IX (9. 4–8). Some commentators consider the two halves of the third stanza as two independent sentences and interpret them as follows: "O Parameśvara! that description of Yourself, which You have given (of Your form) is true (that is, I have understood it). Now, O Puruṣottama, I desire to see Your divine form" (see Gī. 10. 14). But, it is better to consider the two halves as making up one sentence; and that has been done in the Paramārthaprapā commentary. The word "*yogeśvara*" in the 4th stanza means "the Īśvara or Lord of Yoga, (not of Yogins), (Gī. 18. 75). The interpretation of the word 'Yoga' as the power or device of creating the perceptible universe from the Imperceptible has appeared before (Gī. 7. 25 and 9. 5); and as the Blessed Lord is now going to show His Cosmic Form by the use of that power, the appellation 'Yogeśvara' seems to have been used here intentionally.]

The Blessed Lord said:—(5) O Pārtha! look at these thousands and thousands of My forms, of various kinds, of various colours, and of various sizes. (6) See these (twelve) Suns, (eight) Vasus, (eleven) Rudras, (two) Aśvinīkumāras, as also (forty-nine) Marudgaṇas. O Bhārata! see these wonders which you have never before seen.

इहैकस्थं जगत्कृत्स्नं पश्याद्य सचराचरम् ।
मम देहे गुडाकेश यच्चान्यद्द्रष्टुमिच्छसि ॥ ७ ॥
न तु मां शक्यसे द्रष्टुमनेनैव स्वचक्षुषा ।
दिव्यं ददामि ते चक्षुः पश्य मे योगमैश्वरम् ॥ ८ ॥

संजय उवाच ।

§§ एवमुक्त्वा ततो राजन्महायोगेश्वरो हरिः ।
दर्शयामास पार्थाय परमं रूपमैश्वरम् ॥ ९ ॥
अनेकवक्त्रनयनमनेकाद्भुतदर्शनम् ।
अनेकदिव्याभरणं दिव्यानेकोद्यतायुधम् ॥ १० ॥

[The description of the Cosmic Form (*viśvarūpa*) shown to Nārada in the Nārāyaṇīya doctrine is more specific; and says that the twelve Suns were on the left side; the eight Vasus, in the front; the eleven Rudras, on the right side; and the Asvinīkumāras, at the back (Śān. 339. 50–52). But this description does not seem to have been accepted everywhere (See Ma. Bhā. U. 130). The Ādityas, Vasus, Rudras, Aśvinīkumāras, and Marudgaṇas are Vedic deities, and a division into four classes among them has been made in the Mahābhārata by saying that the Ādityas were Kṣatriyas; the Marudgaṇas, Vaiśyas; and the Aśvinīkumāras, Śūdras (Śān. 208. 23, 24). See also Śatapatha-brāhmaṇa, 14. 4. 2. 23.]

(7) O Guḍākeśa! the entire moveable and immoveable universe, which has been collected here to-day, and whatever else you may desire to see, see that in (this) My Form! (8) But, with this vision of yours, you will not be able to see Me. Therefore, I am giving to you a supernatural vision; (by it) see this My divine Yoga (that is, Yogic Power).

Sañjaya said:—(9) Having spoken thus, O Dhṛtarāṣṭra! the great Lord of Yoga, namely, Hari, showed to Arjuna (His) excellent divine form (that is, the Cosmic Form or *viśvarūpa*). (10) To that (that is, to that Cosmic Form), there were innumerable mouths and eyes, and many wonderful sights were to be seen in it; (and) on it there

दिव्यमाल्याम्बरधरं दिव्यगन्धानुलेपनम् ।
सर्वाश्चर्यमयं देवमनन्तं विश्वतोमुखम् ॥ ११ ॥
दिवि सूर्यसहस्रस्य भवेद्युगपदुत्थिता ।
यदि भाः सदृशी सा स्याद्भासस्तस्य महात्मनः ॥ १२ ॥
तत्रैकस्थं जगत्कृत्स्नं प्रविभक्तमनेकधा ।
अपश्यद्देवदेवस्य शरीरे पाण्डवस्तदा ॥ १३ ॥
ततः स विस्मयाविष्टो हृष्टरोमा धनंजयः ।
प्रणम्य शिरसा देवं कृताञ्जलिरभाषत ॥ १४ ॥

अर्जुन उवाच ।

§§ पश्यामि देवांस्तव देव देहे सर्वांस्तथा भूतविशेषसङ्घान् ।
ब्रह्माणमीशं कमलासनस्थमृषींश्च सर्वानुरगांश्च दिव्यान् ॥ १५ ॥
अनेकबाहूदरवक्त्रनेत्रं पश्यामि त्वां सर्वतोऽनन्तरूपम् ।
नान्तं न मध्यं न पुनस्तवादिं पश्यामि विश्वेश्वर विश्वरूप ॥ १६ ॥

were shining ornaments of numerous kinds and there were erected (shining) in it numerous instruments of warfare. (11) To that, endless, all-facing and wonderful deity was applied an unguent of celestial smell, and it wore celestial flowers and clothes. (12) If the effulgence of a thousand suns arose at once in the firmament, it would be somewhat like the brilliance of this great Ātman. (13) Arjuna then saw that in this Body of the God of gods, the world, divided into numerous divisions, was to be seen synthesised. (14) Then, being filled with surprise, the hairs on his body rose; and joining his hands and lifting them to his forehead, Arjuna said to the God—]

Arjuna said:—(15) O Lord! in this Your body, I can see all the gods, and collections of various kinds of created beings, as also Brahmadeva, the lord (of all gods) seated on a lotus-seat, all Ṛṣis, and also all brilliant serpents (including Vāsuki and others). (16) I see, on all sides, You of endless form, Who have innumerable arms, innumerable stomachs, innumerable mouths, and innumerable eyes.

किरीटिनं गदिनं चक्रिणं च तेजोराशिं सर्वतो दीप्तिमन्तम् ।
पश्यामि त्वां दुर्निरीक्ष्यं समन्ताद् दीप्तानलार्कद्युतिमप्रमेयम् ॥ १७ ॥
त्वमक्षरं परमं वेदितव्यं त्वमस्य विश्वस्य परं निधानम् ।
त्वमव्ययः शाश्वतधर्मगोप्ता सनातनस्त्वं पुरुषो मतो मे ॥ १८ ॥
अनादिमध्यान्तमनन्तवीर्यमनन्तबाहुं शशिसूर्यनेत्रम् ।
पश्यामि त्वां दीप्तहुताशवक्त्रं स्वतेजसा विश्वमिदं तपन्तम् ॥ १९ ॥
द्यावापृथिव्योरिदमन्तरं हि व्याप्तं त्वयैकेन दिशश्च सर्वाः ।
दृष्ट्वाद्भुतं रूपमुग्रं तवेदं लोकत्रयं प्रव्यथितं महात्मन् ॥ २० ॥
अमी हि त्वां सुरसङ्घा विशन्ति केचिद्भीताः प्राञ्जलयो गृणन्ति ।
स्वस्तीत्युक्त्वा महर्षिसिद्धसङ्घाः स्तुवन्ति त्वां स्तुतिभिः
पुष्कलाभिः ॥ २१ ॥

O Lord of the Cosmos! O Cosmic-formed! I do not see (anywhere) either Your end, or Your middle, or Your beginning. (17) I see everywhere, You, Who are wearing a diadem, and holding a mace, and a discus, Whose effulgence is spread out in all directions, Who are a mountain of brilliance, unbearably hot, effulgent like Fire and the Sun, impossible to look at by the eyes, and boundless (-ly pervading). (18) I think that You are the ultimate Knowable, the imperishable Brahman, the ultimate support of this Cosmos; that You are imperishable, and the protector of the permanent religion, and the eternal Spirit. (19) I see that You, Who have no beginning, middle, or end, Who have innumerable arms, Whose eyes are the Sun and the Moon, Whose mouth is burning Fire, and Who possess inexhaustible strength, are giving warmth to this world by Your own shine. (20) Because, the (entire) distance between the earth and the firmament, as also all the cardinal points, have been pervaded by You alone; and, seeing this Your wonderful and terrible Form, O Great Ātman! the three spheres are confused (by terror). (21) See! these multitudes of gods are entering Your body; (and) some, being frightened, are praying to You with folded arms; and multitudes of great Ṛṣis and Perfect beings are praising

रुद्रादित्या वसवो ये च साध्या विश्वेऽश्विनौ मरुतश्चोष्मपाश्च ।
गन्धर्वयक्षासुरसिद्धसङ्घा वीक्षन्ते त्वां विस्मिताश्चैव सर्वे ॥ २२ ॥
रूपं महत्ते बहुवक्त्रनेत्रं महाबाहो बहुबाहूरुपादम् ।
बहूदरं बहुदंष्ट्राकरालं दृष्ट्वा लोकाः प्रव्यथितास्तथाऽहम् ॥ २३ ॥
नभःस्पृशं दीप्तमनेकवर्णं व्यात्ताननं दीप्तविशालनेत्रम् ।
दृष्ट्वा हि त्वां प्रव्यथितान्तरात्मा धृतिं न विन्दामि शमं च विष्णो ॥२४॥
दंष्ट्राकरालानि च ते मुखानि दृष्ट्वैव कालानलसंनिभानि ।
दिशो न जाने न लभे च शर्म प्रसीद देवेश जगन्निवास ॥ २५ ॥

You, uttering such words as '*svasti*' '*svasti*'! (22) Similarly, the Rudras, the Ādityas, and the Vasus, as also the Sādhya-gaṇas, the Viśvedeva-s, (both) the Aśvinīkumāras, the Marud-gaṇas, and the Uṣmapā-s (that is, the ancestors) and groups of Gandharvas, Yakṣas, Rākṣasas, and Siddhas, being astonished, are everywhere, looking at you.

[The food offered to the ancestors in the performance of the death-anniversary ceremony is accepted by them only while it is hot; that is why they are called "*uṣmapā*-s" (Manu. 3. 237); and the Manu-Smṛti enumerates seven groups of ancestors, such as, *somasad*, *agniṣvātta*, *barhiṣad*, *somapā*, *haviṣmān*, *ājyapā*, and *sukālin* (3. 194-200). Āditya-s and others are Vedic deities. See stanza 6 above. It is stated in the Bṛhadāraṇyakopaniṣad that the eight Vasus, eleven Rudras, twelve Ādityas, Indra, and Prajāpati make in all thirty-three gods; and their names and etymology have been stated in the Mahābhārata, Ādi-parva, Ch. 65 and 66 and Śānti-parva Ch. 208.]

(23) O Mahābāho! by seeing this Your immense, many-mouthed, many-eyed, many-armed, many-thighed, many-footed, many-stomached, and many-teethed—and consequently terrible—Form, everybody and I myself are frightened. (24) Seeing You, heaven-reaching, brilliant, many-hued, open-mouthed, and with tremendous and shining eyes, my heart has become restless; and, on that account, O Viṣṇu! I have lost both courage and peace. (25) And seeing these mouths of Yours, which are terrible on account of rows of teeth, and are like the Destructional Fire, I cannot

अमी च त्वां धृतराष्ट्रस्य पुत्राः सर्वे सहैवावनिपालसङ्घैः ।
भीष्मो द्रोणः सूतपुत्रस्तथाऽसौ सहास्मदीयैरपि योधमुख्यैः ॥ २६ ॥
वक्त्राणि ते त्वरमाणा विशन्ति दंष्ट्राकरालानि भयानकानि ।
केचिद्विलग्ना दशनान्तरेषु संदृश्यन्ते चूर्णितैरुत्तमाङ्गैः ॥ २७ ॥
यथा नदीनां बहवोऽम्बुवेगाः समुद्रमेवाभिमुखा द्रवन्ति ।
तथा तवामी नरलोकवीरा विशन्ति वक्त्राण्यभिविज्वलन्ति ॥ २८ ॥
यथा प्रदीप्तं ज्वलनं पतङ्गा विशन्ति नाशाय समृद्धवेगाः ।
तथैव नाशाय विशन्ति लोकास्तवापि वक्त्राणि समृद्धवेगाः ॥ २९ ॥
लेलिह्यसे ग्रसमानः समन्ताल्लोकान्समग्रान्वदनैर्ज्वलद्भिः ।
तेजोभिरापूर्य जगत्समग्रं भासस्तवोग्राः प्रतपन्ति विष्णो ॥ ३० ॥
आख्याहि मे को भवानुग्ररूपो नमोऽस्तु ते देववर प्रसीद ।
विज्ञातुमिच्छामि भवन्तमाद्यं न हि प्रजानामि तव प्रवृत्तिम् ॥ ३१ ॥

make out the cardinal directions, and I have become discomposed. O God of gods! O Cosmos-Pervader! be appeased! (26) See how all these sons of Dhṛtarāṣṭra, with multitudes of kings, this Bhīṣma, Droṇa, and also this Sūtaputra (Karṇa), together also with the most prominent warriors on our side, (27) are rapidly entering into these many terrible mouths of Yours, with frightful rows of teeth; and the heads of some of them are seen being crushed, as a result of having come between Your teeth. (28) Just as the many waves of the waters of a river rush towards the sea, so are these warriors from the world of humans entering Your several burning mouths. (29) Just as butterflies jump with great speed into the ignited fire, only to be killed, so also are all (these) people entering Your numerous mouths, with great velocity, only to be killed. (30) O Viṣṇu! You are licking Your tongues, while swallowing all persons around You, through Your flame-filled mouths! and, pervading the entire universe, Your fiery effulgence is shining (in all directions). (31) Tell me Who You are, Who have assumed this frightful form! O Super-excellent God of gods! I bow down to You! be appeased! I am desirous of knowing what Fundamental Spirit You are, because I do not (at all) understand this doing of Yours!

श्रीभगवानुवाच ।

§§ कालोऽस्मि लोकक्षयकृत्प्रवृद्धो लोकान्समाहर्तुमिह प्रवृत्तः ।
ऋतेऽपि त्वां न भविष्यन्ति सर्वे येऽवस्थिताः प्रत्यनीकेषु योधाः ॥३२॥

तस्मात्त्वमुत्तिष्ठ यशो लभस्व जित्वा शत्रून्भुङ्क्ष्व राज्यं समृद्धम् ।
मयैवैते निहताः पूर्वमेव निमित्तमात्रं भव सव्यसाचिन् ॥ ३३ ॥

द्रोणं च भीष्मं च जयद्रथं च कर्णं तथाऽन्यानपि योधवीरान् ।
मया हतांस्त्वं जहि मा व्यथिष्ठा युध्यस्व जेतासि रणे सपत्नान् ॥३४॥

The Blessed Lord said:—(32) I am the destroyer of all peoples; I am immensified "*kāla*" (that is, 'death'—Trans.); and I have come here for destroying everyone. Even if you are not there, (that is, even if you do not do anything), all these different warriors, standing in the various armies, are all going to be no more (going to die). (33) '*tasmāt*' (that is, 'therefore'—Trans.), arise! win success! and conquering your enemies enjoy opulent kingdoms! I have already killed these in advance. (Therefore) O Savyasācin (Arjuna)! do you (come forward to) become the nominal cause. (34) Droṇa and Bhīṣma and Jayadratha and Karṇa, and also other warriors have been killed by Me (long ago); kill them! do not be afraid! fight! you are going to conquer your enemies in the fight!

[In short, Śrī Kṛṣṇa has actually shown to Arjuna, the vision of what Bhīṣma had said merely by words to Him, in the Udyoga-parva, when He had gone to the Kauravas to bring about a compromise, and Duryodhana would not listen to any talk of compromise, namely, "*kālapakvam idaṁ manye sarvaṁ kṣatraṁ janārdana*" (Ma. Bhā. U. 127. 32), that is, "O Janārdana! all these Kṣatriyas have already become ripe for death (*kālapakva*)". (See stanzas 26 to 31 above). The 33rd stanza enunciates the doctrine of Causality that, all wicked persons die as a result of their own acts; that, the one, who kills them, is only a nominal cause; and that, therefore, the one who kills is not to blame.]

संजय उवाच ।

§§ एतच्छ्रुत्वा वचनं केशवस्य कृताञ्जलिर्वेपमानः किरीटी ।
नमस्कृत्वा भूय एवाह कृष्णं सगद्गदं भीतभीतः प्रणम्य ॥ ३५ ॥

अर्जुन उवाच ।

स्थाने हृषीकेश तव प्रकीर्त्या जगत्प्रहृष्यत्यनुरज्यते च ।
रक्षांसि भीतानि दिशो द्रवन्ति सर्वे नमस्यन्ति च सिद्धसङ्घाः ॥ ३६ ॥
कस्माच्च ते न नमेरन्महात्मन् गरीयसे ब्रह्मणोऽप्यादिकर्त्रे ।
अनन्त देवेश जगन्निवास त्वमक्षरं सदसत्तत्परं यत् ॥ ३७ ॥

Sañjaya said:—(35) Hearing this speech of Keśava, Arjuna, getting extremely frightened, having a choking sensation in his throat, and trembling, and folding his hands, bowed down low again, and said to Śrī Kṛṣṇa. Arjuna said:—(36) O Hṛṣīkeśa! the (whole) world is engladdened by singing (Your qualities), and is happy (in that); demons becoming frightened of You, run away in the (ten) cardinal directions, and concerts of Perfect beings are bowing down before you. (All) This is only proper. (37) O Noble Soul! You are the origin even of Brahmadeva, are even superior to him; why will they not worship You? O Ananta! O God of gods! O Pervader of the Cosmos! You are the *sat* (that is, 'immutable'—Trans.) and *asat* (that is, 'mutable'—Trans.); You are also the '*akṣara*' (that is, immutable—Trans.), Which is beyond both.

[It will appear from Gītā 7. 24; 8. 20; or 15. 16 that the words '*sat*' and '*asat*' in this place mean respectively perceptible and imperceptible, (*vyakta* and *avyakta*), or mutable and immutable (*kṣara* and *akṣara*); that Principle, which is beyond both *sat* and *asat*, has been described in the Gītā, as the Immutable Brahman (*akṣara-brahma*) in the words "I am neither *sat* nor *asat*" (Gītā 13. 12). The word '*akṣara*' is applied in the Gītā sometimes to Prakṛti and sometimes to the Parabrahman. See my commentary on Gītā 9. 19; 13. 12; and 15. 16.]

त्वमादिदेवः पुरुषः पुराणस्त्वमस्य विश्वस्य परं निधानम्।
वेत्तासि वेद्यं च परं च धाम त्वया ततं विश्वमनन्तरूप ॥ ३८ ॥
वायुर्यमोऽग्निर्वरुणः शशाङ्कः प्रजापतिस्त्वं प्रपितामहश्च।
नमो नमस्तेऽस्तु सहस्रकृत्वः पुनश्च भूयोऽपि नमो नमस्ते ॥ ३९ ॥
नमः पुरस्तादथ पृष्ठतस्ते नमोऽस्तु ते सर्वत एव सर्व।
अनन्तवीर्यामितविक्रमस्त्वं सर्वं समाप्नोषि ततोऽसि सर्वः ॥ ४० ॥

(38) You are the Fundamental God; (You are) the primordial Spirit; You are the supreme Support of this universe; You are the Knower and the Knowable; You are the Exalted State; and You, O Endless-formed! have entirely pervaded or occupied (this) Cosmos. (39) You are Vāyu, Yama, Agni, Varuṇa, Prajāpati (that is, Brahmadeva), and also the Great-grand-father! I bow down before You a thousand times! and once more again do I bow down before You!

[Seven mind-born sons, named Marīci and others, were born from Brahmadeva; from Marīci, was born Kaśyapa; and from Kaśyapa, all other progeny. (Ma. Bhā. Ādi. 65. 11); and therefore these Marīci and others, are known as 'Prajāpatis' (the lords of progeny), (Śān. 340. 65). Therefore, the word 'Prajāpati' is interpreted by some as 'Kaśyapa and other Prajāpatis'. But, as the word 'Prajāpati' has been used here in the singular number, the interpretation of 'Prajāpati' as 'Brahmadeva' seems more acceptable. Besides, as Brahmadeva is the father of Marīci and others, that is, the grand-father (*pitāmaha*) of all, the subsequent expression 'great-grand-father' (*prapitāmaha*) follows as a matter of course; and its propriety becomes clear.]

(40) I prostrate myself before You; and behind You; and on all sides, O Soul of everything! do I prostrate myself to You. Your procreativeness is inexhaustible. Your prowess is incomparable, and as You overcome everyone, You are '*sarva*' (that is, 'all-in-all'—Trans.).

[The words "I prostrate myself before you, and behind you" show the all-pervasiveness of the Parameśvara. This

सखेति मत्वा प्रसभं यदुक्तं हे कृष्ण हे यादव हे सखेति ।
अजानता महिमानं तवेदं मया प्रमादात्प्रणयेन वाऽपि ॥ ४१ ॥
यच्चाऽवहासार्थमसत्कृतोऽसि विहारशय्यासनभोजनेषु ।
एकोऽथवाप्यच्युत तत्समक्षं तत्क्षामये त्वामहमप्रमेयम् ॥ ४२ ॥
पिताऽसि लोकस्य चराचरस्य त्वमस्य पूज्यश्च गुरुर्गरीयान् ।
न त्वत्समोऽस्त्यभ्यधिकः कुतोऽन्यो लोकत्रयेऽप्यप्रतिमप्रभावः ॥ ४३ ॥
तस्मात्प्रणम्य प्रणिधाय कायं प्रसादये त्वामहमीशमीड्यम् ।
पितेव पुत्रस्य सखेव सख्युः प्रियः प्रियायार्हसि देव सोढुम् ॥ ४४ ॥

praise in the form of prostrations in the Path of Devotion is consistent with the descriptions of the Brahman given in the Upaniṣads ; *e. g.*, "*brahmaivedaṁ amṛtaṁ purastāt brahma paścāt brahma dakṣiṇataś cottareṇa* । *adhaś cordhvaṁ ca prasṛtaṁ brahmaivedaṁ viśvam idaṁ variṣṭham* ॥" (Muṇ 2. 2. 11 ; Chān. 7. 25).]

(41) Whatever I may have said disrespectfully to You, by mistake or by familiarity, considering you as my friend, not recognising this Your greatness, in addressing you as 'O Kṛṣṇa !' 'O Yādava !' or 'O Friend !'. (42) and whatever insult I may have offered to You in joke, when alone with You, or in the presence of others, while eating or sporting, or while sleeping or sitting, O Acyuta, for that forgive me, such is my prayer to You, O Immeasurable ! (43) You, being the father of this moveable and immoveable world, are worshippable, and the Preceptor of preceptors. In the three spheres, there is none, who is Your equal ; then, O One of immeasurable prowess ! how can there be any one greater ? (44) Therefore, to You, Who are praiseworthy, and powerful, I pray : "Be appeased", bending my body and bowing down to You. As a father (forgives the faults) of his son, or a friend (forgives the faults) of his friend, in the same way O God ! the '*priyaḥ*' (that is, Yourself) should forgive '*priyāya*' (that is, to me or on account of me, who am *priya* or beloved of You), (all my) faults.

[Some persons interpret the words "*priyaḥ priyāyārhasi*" as "as the lover, in the case of a woman, beloved by him".

But according to me that interpretation is not correct; because, the words '*priyāyārhasi*' cannot grammatically be broken up into *priyāyāḥ* + *arhasi* or *priyāyai* + *arhasi*; and the word '*iva*', which is indicative of a comparison, has appeared only twice in this stanza. Therefore, it is more proper to consider '*priyaḥ priyāyārhasi*' as the subject-matter of comparison (*upameya*) instead of looking upon it as a third comparison. It would have been much better if there had been a word in the possessive case, such as, '*priyasya*' (of the '*priya*') in the subject-matter of comparison (*upameya*), like the two comparisonal (*upamānātmaka*) words 'of the son' (*putrasya*), 'of the friend' (*sakhyuḥ*), which are in the possessive case. But we must here follow the rule "*sthitasya gatiś cintanīyā*". Imagining an ungrammatical feminine possessive case word like '*priyāyāḥ*', because the masculine-gender-sixth-cased word '*priyasya*' is not to be found in the text, and imagining the word '*iva*' as implied, because that description does not apply to Arjuna, and inventing a third comparison as, "*priyaḥ priyāyāḥ*", that is, 'as the lover in the case of a woman beloved by him' —which moreover is amorous, and totally out of place—is, according to me, not proper. Besides, if all the three words '*putrasya*', '*sakhyuḥ*' and '*priyāyāḥ*' go into the class of the standards of comparison (*upamāna*), then there remains no word in the possessive case in the subject-matter of comparison (*upameya*); and we have again to take '*me*' or '*mama*' (that is, 'to me') as implied; and if, with all this trouble, one brings about a similarity of inflections or case-terminations between the subject-matter of comparison and the standard of comparison, a new mistake of difference of gender between the two again arises. On the other hand, if one breaks up the sentence, plainly and grammatically, as *priyāya* + *arhasi*, the only objection which remains, is that, instead of having the possessive case '*priyasya*', we have the dative case '*priyāya*' in the subject-matter of comparison; and that too is not a very serious fault. Because, in this place the dative case conveys the same meaning as the possessive case, and such use is to be seen in other places also. This stanza has been

अदृष्टपूर्वं हृषितोऽस्मि दृष्ट्वा भयेन च प्रव्यथितं मनो मे ।
तदेव मे दर्शय देव रूपं प्रसीद देवेश जगन्निवास ॥ ४५ ॥
किरीटिनं गदिनं चक्रहस्तमिच्छामि त्वां द्रष्टुमहं तथैव ।
तेनैव रूपेण चतुर्भुजेन सहस्रबाहो भव विश्वमूर्ते ॥ ४६ ॥

श्रीभगवानुवाच ।

§§ मया प्रसन्नेन तवार्जुनेदं रूपं परं दर्शितमात्मयोगात् ।
तेजोमयं विश्वमनन्तमाद्यं यन्मे त्वदन्येन न दृष्टपूर्वम् ॥ ४७ ॥
न वेदयज्ञाध्ययनैर्न दानैर्न च क्रियाभिर्न तपोभिरुग्रैः ।
एवंरूपः शक्य अहं नृलोके द्रष्टुं त्वदन्येन कुरुप्रवीर ॥ ४८ ॥
मा ते व्यथा मा च विमूढभावो दृष्ट्वा रूपं घोरमीदृङ्ममेदम् ।
व्यपेतभीः प्रीतमनाः पुनस्त्वं तदेव मे रूपमिदं प्रपश्य ॥ ४९ ॥

interpreted in the Paramārthaprapā commentary in the same way as I have done.]

(45) Having seen that which no one has ever seen, I am glad; and my mind is strained by fear. O Pervader of the Cosmos! O God of gods! be appeased! and O God! show me Your previous form. (46) I desire to see You wearing the '*kirīṭa*' (that is, diadem—Trans.) and the mace, with a discus in Your hand, as before; and therefore, O Cosmic-Formed, thousand-armed Lord, appear again in that Your four-armed form.

The Blessed Lord said:—(47) O Arjuna! having become pleased (with you), exercising my power of Yoga, I have shown you this brilliant, beginning-less, endless, primeval, and super-excellent Cosmic Form, which no one else before you has seen. (48) O highest among the Kuru warriors! no other than you can have a chance of seeing, whether by the Vedas, or by Yajñas, or by silent meditation, or by charity, or by ritual, or by severe austerity, this such My Form, in this human world. (49) Do not allow your mind to suffer pain by seeing this My terrible form! and do not also become confused by fear. Giving up fear, and with a pleased frame of mind, see again that same form of Mine.

संजय उवाच ।

इत्यर्जुनं वासुदेवस्तथोक्त्वा स्वकं रूपं दर्शयामास भूयः ।
आश्वासयामास च भीतमेनं भूत्वा पुनः सौम्यवपुर्महात्मा ॥ ५० ॥

अर्जुन उवाच ।

दृष्ट्वेदं मानुषं रूपं तव सौम्यं जनार्दन ।
इदानीमस्मि संवृत्तः सचेताः प्रकृतिं गतः ॥ ५१ ॥

श्रीभगवानुवाच ।

§§ सुदुर्दर्शमिदं रूपं दृष्टवानसि यन्मम ।
देवा अप्यस्य रूपस्य नित्यं दर्शनकाङ्क्षिणः ॥ ५२ ॥

Sañjaya said :—(50) Speaking thus, Vāsudeva again showed to Arjuna His (former) form; and assuming again His peaceful form, that Noble Soul gave encouragement to the frightened Arjuna.

[The metre of these 36 stanzas, is the same as that of stanzas 5 to 8, 20, 22, 29, and 70 of Chapter II, stanzas 9,10,11 and 28 of Chapter VIII, stanzas 20 and 21 of Chapter IX, and stanzas 2 to 5 and 15 of Chapter XV, namely, of eleven letters in each quarter (*caraṇa*). But, as they are not governed by one and the same rule about the feet (*gaṇa*), these stanzas cannot be recited in the same way as can stanzas in the *indra-vajrā*, *upendra-vajrā* *upajāti*, *dodhaka*, *śālinī* and other metres used in the poetical compositions of Kālidāsa and others. Needless to say, this metrical arrangement is archaic (*ārṣa*), that is, on the basis of the '*triṣṭup*' metre used in the Veda-Saṁhitās. This fortifies the proposition that the Gītā must be very ancient indeed (see p. 726 of the Appendix to the Gītā-Rahasya.]

Arjuna said :—(51) O Janārdana! seeing this Your mild and human-bodied form, my mind is again in its proper place, and I have become conscious, as before.

The Blessed Lord said :—(52) This My form, which you have seen, is very difficult to see. Even the gods always

नाहं वेदैर्न तपसा न दानेन न चेज्यया ।
शक्य एवंविधो द्रष्टुं दृष्टवानसि मां यथा ॥ ५३ ॥
भक्त्या त्वनन्यया शक्य अहमेवंविधोऽर्जुन ।
ज्ञातुं द्रष्टुं च तत्त्वेन प्रवेष्टुं च परंतप ॥ ५४ ॥
§§ मत्कर्मकृन्मत्परमो मद्भक्तः सङ्गवर्जितः ।
निर्वैरः सर्वभूतेषु यः स मामेति पाण्डव ॥ ५५ ॥

desire to see this form. (53) It is not possible for any one to see Me, as you have seen Me, whether by Vedas, or by austerity, or by charity, or by Yajñas. (54) O Arjuna ! only by exclusive devotion, is it possible to thus acquire knowledge of Me, and O Parantapa ! to enter Me essentially.

[The proposition that by Devotion one first acquires the Knowledge of the Parameśvara, and ultimately the devotee is merged into the Parameśvara has appeared before in Gītā 4. 9 and later on in 18. 55 ; and the reader is referred to the explanation given by me in Chapter XIII of the Gītā-Rahasya at pp. 595 to 599. Now, the Blessed Lord briefly explains to Arjuna the summary of the entire Gītā—]

(55) Who performs Action with the conviction that all Actions are Mine (that is, of the Parameśvara), who is devoted to Me ; who is attachment-less , non-inimical towards all beings, such My devotee, O Pāṇḍava, comes and reaches Me !

[The above stanza means that (i) the devotee of the Blessed Lord should perform all worldly Actions with the idea of dedicating them to the Parameśvara, that is to say, with a prideless frame of mind, thinking that, the entire activity in the world is of the Parameśvara, who is the true Doer, and the One, Who truly causes to be done ; but that, He gets these actions done through us, by making us the nominal causes ; and that, (ii) thereby, all acts, which are done, do not obstruct tranquillity or Release (see stanza 33) ; and it is stated even in the Śāṁkarabhāṣya that this stanza contains the summary of the entire philosophy of the Gītā. This clearly shows that the Path of Devotion prescribed in the

इति श्रीमद्भगवद्गीतासु उपनिषत्सु ब्रह्मविद्यायां योगशास्त्रे श्रीकृष्णार्जुनसंवादे विश्वरूपदर्शनयोगो नाम एकादशोऽध्यायः ॥ ११ ॥

Gītā does not advise one to sit down doing nothing, and only saying 'Hari' 'Hari' (taking the name of God); but directs one to do all acts desirelessly, and enthusiastically, side by side with possessing an ardent devotion. In order to make it clear that the word '*nirvaira*' (non-inimical), does not here mean '*niṣkriya*' (actionless) as interpreted by those who follow the Path of Renunciation, the adjective '*mat-karmakṛt*' (that is, doing all acts with the idea of dedicating them to the Parameśvara, and believing that the acts are of the Parameśvara, and not one's own) has been added; but as this matter has been extensively considered by me in Chap. XII of the Gītā-Rahasya (pp. 545 to 556), I am not going to discuss it further here.

Thus ends the eleventh chapter entitled VIS'VARUPA-DARS'ANA YOGA in the dialogue between Śrī Kṛṣṇa and Arjuna on the Yoga, included in the Science of the Brahman (that is, on the Karma-Yoga) in the Upaniṣad sung (that is, told) by the Blessed Lord.

———

द्वादशोऽध्यायः

CHAPTER XII.

[In Chap. VII, the Blessed Lord has started an explanation of the Empirical and Spiritual Knowledge required for acquiring Perfection in Karma-Yoga; and in Chap. VIII, He has explained the form of the Immutable, Unshowable, and Imperceptible Brahman; and thereafter, He has started an explanation of the visible royal road in the shape of the Path of Devotion; and after having finished the Description of Manifestations (*vibhūti-varṇana*) and the showing of the Cosmic Form (*viśvarūpa-darśana*), incidental to that path, in Chapters X and XI, He has, at the end of Chapter XI, advised Arjuna to perform all Actions with Devotion and unattachedly, as the ultimate summary of everything. Now Arjuna says: "After proving to me in Chapters VII and VIII that the Imperceptible form of the Parameśvara is the most superior one to be worshipped, from the point of view of the Mutable and the Immutable, for success in Karma-Yoga, You have prescribed to me the worship of the Imperceptible or the Immutable (7. 19 and 24; 8. 21); and You have advised me to fight (8. 7) with a mind steeped in Yoga (*yukta-citta*); and afterwards in Chap. IX, after explaining to me the visible path of the worship of the Perceptible, You have asked me to perform all Actions with the idea of dedicating them to the Parameśvara (9. 27 and 34; and 11.55). Now which of these two paths is the better one?" In this question the 'worship of the Perceptible' means 'Devotion'. But, what is meant here is not Devotion to different objects of worship; and it is explained that the true worship of the Perceptible is the Devotion, according to which, there is only one All-Pervasive Parameśvara in all symbols or objects of worship, whatever symbol or object is taken for worship; and that is the kind of Devotion advocated in this chapter.]

अर्जुन उवाच ।

§§ एवं सततयुक्ता ये भक्तास्त्वां पर्युपासते ।
ये चाप्यक्षरमव्यक्तं तेषां के योगवित्तमाः ॥ १ ॥

श्रीभगवानुवाच ।

§§ मय्यावेश्य मनो ये मां नित्ययुक्ता उपासते ।
श्रद्धया परयोपेतास्ते मे युक्ततमा मताः ॥ २ ॥
ये त्वक्षरमनिर्देश्यमव्यक्तं पर्युपासते ।
सर्वत्रगमचिन्त्यं च कूटस्थमचलं ध्रुवम् ॥ ३ ॥
संनियम्येन्द्रियग्रामं सर्वत्र समबुद्धयः ।
ते प्राप्नुवन्ति मामेव सर्वभूतहिते रताः ॥ ४ ॥
क्लेशोऽधिकतरस्तेषामव्यक्तासक्तचेतसाम् ।
अव्यक्ता हि गतिर्दुःखं देहवद्भिरवाप्यते ॥ ५ ॥
ये तु सर्वाणि कर्माणि मयि संन्यस्य मत्पराः ।
अनन्येनैव योगेन मां ध्यायन्त उपासते ॥ ६ ॥

Arjuna said:—(1) Who are the better knowers of (Karma-) Yoga, those devotees who, always becoming *yukta* (that is, Yoga-*yukta*) worship You, or those, who worship the *akṣara* (that is, Brahman)?

The Blessed Lord said:—(2) In My opinion, those who, keeping their minds on Me, and becoming *yukta-citta* (that is, mind-united—Trans.) worship Me, with the highest Devotion, are the best '*yukta*' (that is, Yogins). (3) But those, who worship the *akṣara* (that is, the Brahman), Which is '*anirdeśya*' (that is, Which cannot be actually shown), Imperceptible, All-pervading, Unimaginable, '*kūṭastha*' (that is, Which is at the root of everything), Unmoving and Non-transient, (4) after having controlled their senses and become equable-minded towards everything, such (persons too), who are engrossed in the welfare of all beings, also come and reach Me. (5) Nevertheless, as their mind is attached to the Imperceptible, their task is more arduous; because (to men, who dwell in a perceptible body) the path of worship of the Imperceptible becomes successful with difficulty. (6) But those, who worship Me, making a

तेषामहं समुद्धर्ता मृत्युसंसारसागरात् ।
भवामि न चिरात्पार्थ मय्यावेशितचेतसाम् ॥ ७ ॥
मय्येव मन आधत्स्व मयि बुद्धिं निवेशय ।
निवसिष्यसि मय्येव अत ऊर्ध्वं न संशयः ॥ ८ ॥

saṁnyāsa (that is, dedication) of all Actions to Me, becoming devoted to Me, and meditating on Me with a Yoga (that is, union—Trans.) with no one else, (7) such persons who have become '*maccitta*' (that is, mind-united with Me—Trans.), O Pārtha ! I redeem, from this death-bound ocean of worldly life without delay. (8) (Therefore) keep your mind fixed on Me, concentrate your Reason on Me, so that, afterwards you will undoubtedly dwell in Me.

[The superiority of the Path of Devotion has been expounded in this paragraph. After first stating the proposition, in stanza 2, that the devotees of the Blessed Lord are the best Yogins, the conjunction "*tu*", which shows an alternative aspect, has been used in stanza 3; and in that and in the 4th stanza, it is stated that those, who worship the Imperceptible also come and are merged in Him. It is stated in stanza 5, that though this may be true, the path of those who worship the Imperceptible, is more difficult; and after explaining in the 6th and 7th stanzas the comparative facility of the worship of the Perceptible, the advice has been given to Arjuna ultimately in the 8th stanza to act accordingly. In short, the advice given at the end of Chap. XI (11. 55) has further been emphasised here in reply to the question of Arjuna. As the facility of the Path of Devotion has been considered by me in full detail in Chapter XIII of the Gītā-Rahasya, I shall not repeat the same subject-matter here. I shall only say here that though the worship of the Imperceptible may be difficult, yet, it is productive of Release; that, even in the Path of Devotion, one cannot give up Actions, but has necessarily to perform them, dedicating them to the Parameśvara; and that, the followers of the Path of Devotion should bear this in mind. And that is why the words "making a *saṁnyāsa* (that is, dedication) of all Actions to

§§ अथ चित्तं समाधातुं न शक्नोषि मयि स्थिरम् ।
अभ्यासयोगेन ततो मामिच्छाप्तुं धनंजय ॥ ९ ॥

अभ्यासेऽप्यसमर्थोऽसि मत्कर्मपरमो भव ।
मदर्थमपि कर्माणि कुर्वन् सिद्धिमवाप्स्यसि ॥ १० ॥

अथैतदप्यशक्तोऽसि कर्तुं मद्योगमाश्रितः ।
सर्वकर्मफलत्यागं ततः कुरु यतात्मवान् ॥ ११ ॥

Me" have been used in the sixth stanza. These words clearly mean that in the Path of Devotion, Actions have not to be literally given up, but one has to dedicate them, that is, their fruit, to the Parameśvara. And, this also makes it perfectly clear that the Devotee, whom the Blessed Lord has referred to at the end of this Chapter as being dear to Him, is to be understood as one, who follows this path, that is, the Path of the Desireless Karma-Yoga, and not one, who makes a literal *saṁnyāsa* or Abandonment of Action. To proceed: having in this way shown the facility and the superiority of the Path of Devotion, the Blessed Lord now explains the means or devices to be used for acquiring such Devotion to the Parameśvara, and ultimately gives the differential characteristics of these various means—]

(9) Now, if it is not possible for you to concentrate your mind well on Me (in this way), then, O Dhanañjaya! keep hope of attaining to Me, with the help of austere practice, by trying again and again. (10) If it is not possible for you even to perform practice, then perform (the) Actions (such as, Spiritual Knowledge, Meditation, Hymn-singing, Worship etc., which have been mentioned in the Śāstras) for Me, (that is, for attaining to Me); by performing (these) Actions for Me, you will also have success. (11) But, if it is impossible for You even to perform this ritual, then, take shelter in '*madyoga*' (that is, in the Yoga of dedicating everything to Me, namely, the Karma-Yoga); and becoming a '*yatātmā*' (that is, gradually controlling your mind), thereafter (ultimately) abandon the Fruit of all Actions;

श्रेयो हि ज्ञानमभ्यासाज्ज्ञानाद्ध्यानं विशिष्यते।
ध्यानात्कर्मफलत्यागस्त्यागाच्छान्तिरनन्तरम्॥१२॥

(12) because, Knowledge is superior to Practice; Meditation is superior to Knowledge; and Abandoning the Fruit of Action (is superior) to Meditation; and by (this) Abandonment (of the Fruit of Action), there is (acquired) tranquillity immediately afterwards.

[These stanzas are very important from the point of view of Karma-Yoga; and in them, after mentioning austere practice, Knowledge, prayer, and other ritual as means for successfully acquiring the Devotional Karma-Yoga, a differential consideration of the worth of the various means has been made; and in stanza 12, the superiority of the Abandonment of the Fruit of Action, that is to say, of the Desireless Karma-Yoga has been established. It is not that this superiority of the Desireless Karma-Yoga has been mentioned only in this place; but, the same doctrine has been clearly repeated previously in the third (3. 8), fifth (5. 2) and sixth (6. 46) chapters; and Arjuna has been advised in various places to practise Karma-Yoga in the shape of Abandonment of the Fruit of Action (See Gītā-Rahasya pp. 425 to 427). But those, who support a doctrine different from the Gītā-religion, find this theory inconsistent with themselves; and they have, therefore, attempted to twist the meaning of the above stanzas, and especially of the words in the 12th stanza. Those commentators, who support the pure Path of Knowledge, that is to say, the Sāṁkhya commentators, do not like that Abandonment of the Fruit of Action should be given a higher place than Spiritual Knowledge. They have, therefore, said that either the word '*jñāna*' must be interpreted as meaning 'mere bookish knowledge', or, that this praise of Abandonment of the Fruit of Action is merely an '*arthavāda*' (See Vol. I p. 31—Trans.), that is, 'fallow praise'. In the same way, those who support the Path of Pātañjala-Yoga, do not like that Abandonment of the Fruit of Action should be given a higher place than continued austere practice (*abhyāsa*). And those, who support solely the Path of Devotion, that is, those, who say that no Karma or Action other than Devotion should be performed, cannot tolerate Abandonment of the Fruit of Action being considered superior to Meditation, that is, Devotion. The practice of Karma-Yoga, which includes Devotion, which (path) is advocated by the Gītā, and which is different from the Pātañjala-Yoga, the Jñāna-Yoga, and the Path of Devotion, is at present practically non-existent; and therefore, there is no more any commentator available supporting that doctrine. Therefore, in the now extant commentaries on the Gītā, the praise of Abandonment of the Fruit of Action has been stated to be mere "fallow praise". But, in my opinion, that is wrong. If one accedes that the Gītā advocates the Desireless Karma-Yoga, no difficulty remains about the meaning of this stanza. When once it is admitted that one cannot give up Action, and that Desireless Action must be performed, the Path of Knowledge (*jñāna-mārga*), which advocates the 'literal' Abandonment of Action, the Pātañjala-Yoga, which advocates only the acrobatics of the organs, and the Path of Devotion, which gives the go-bye to all Actions, all naturally become inferior to Karma-Yoga. When the Desireless Karma-Yoga has thus been proved to be superior, the only question which remains is: what are the means for acquiring the Equability which is necessary in that path. These means are three in number, namely, continued practice (*abhyāsa*), Spiritual Knowledge (*jñāna*) and Meditation (*dhyāna*). Out of these, if some one cannot perform continued practice, he should adopt either of the two other means, namely, *jñāna* and *dhyāna* (Knowledge, and Meditation). The Gītā says that these means are easy of acquiring in the order in which they have been mentioned. But, if the man cannot do even this, then stanza 12 says that he should begin the practice of Karma-Yoga at once. Now, here a question arises, namely, how can a man, who cannot either perform continued practice or acquire Spiritual Knowledge or Meditation, carry on the Karma-Yoga? Therefore, some commentators have considered calling Karma-Yoga the easiest path as meaningless. But, if one considers the matter a little, it will be seen that there is no sense in this objection. Stanza 12 does not preach that the Abandonment of the Fruit of Action should be carried out 'at a stroke'. But, one has first to adopt the Karma-Yoga preached by the Blessed Lord; and, '*tataḥ*', that is, 'thereafter', that practice has to be gradually made successful. And when this interpretation is accepted, no inconsistency remains. It has been stated in the previous chapters that not only a little practice (Gī. 2. 40) of the Fruit of Action* (this is a mistake for ' Karma-Yoga'—Trans.), but even the desire to perform it (See Gī. 6. 44 and my commentary on it), drags a man towards ultimate perfection, as if he had been put into a grinding-mill. Therefore, taking shelter in the Karma-Yoga, that is, getting into one's mind the desire to follow that path, is the first means or step towards acquiring success in that path; and who will say that this means is not easier than continued practice, or Spiritual Knowledge, or Meditation? And the same is the import of stanza 12. Not only in the Bhagavadgītā, but even in the Sūryagītā, it is stated that :—

jñānād upāstir utkṛṣṭā karmotkṛṣṭam upāsanāt ।
iti yo veda vedāntaiḥ sa eva puruṣottamaḥ ॥
(Sūrya-Gī. 4. 77)

that is, "'*upāsanā*' i. e., Meditation or Devotion is better than Spiritual Knowledge, and Karma, that is, necessarily Desireless Action, is better than '*upāsanā*'; one who realises this principle of Vedānta should be looked upon as the best man (*puruṣottama*)". In short, it is the firm doctrine of the Bhagavadgītā that the Yoga in the form of Abandonment of the Fruit of Action, that is to say, the Desireless Karma-Yoga, which includes both Spiritual Knowledge and Devotion, is the most superior path of all; and the argument in stanza 12 is not only consistent with that opinion, but is in support of it. If persons belonging to a particular school of thought do not find this conclusion palatable or acceptable, they should give it up; but, they

* The word used here in all editions of the author's text is '*karma-phala*', (that is, Fruit of Action); but evidently 'Karma-Yoga' or '*karma-phala-tyāga*' and not '*karma-phala*' is meant—Trans.

§§ अद्वेष्टा सर्वभूतानां मैत्रः करुण एव च।
निर्ममो निरहंकारः समदुःखसुखः क्षमी ॥ १३ ॥
संतुष्टः सततं योगी यतात्मा दृढनिश्चयः।
मय्यर्पितमनोबुद्धिर्यो मे भक्तः स मे प्रियः ॥ १४ ॥
यस्मान्नोद्विजते लोको लोकान्नोद्विजते च यः।
हर्षामर्षभयोद्वेगैर्मुक्तो यः स च मे प्रियः ॥ १५ ॥
अनपेक्षः शुचिर्दक्ष उदासीनो गतव्यथः।
सर्वारम्भपरित्यागी यो मद्भक्तः स मे प्रियः ॥ १६ ॥
यो न हृष्यति न द्वेष्टि न शोचति न काङ्क्षति।
शुभाशुभपरित्यागी भक्तिमान् यः स मे प्रियः ॥१७॥

should not indulge in a useless stretching of meanings. To proceed: the Blessed Lord, having thus proved Abandonment of the Fruit of Action to be superior, now proceeds to describe the equable and peaceable frame of mind, which is obtained by one who practises it (and not by one, who 'literally' gives up Action); and He ultimately says that a devotee of this kind is exceedingly dear to Him—]

(13) One, who hates no one; who behaves in a friendly way towards all created beings; similarly, who is kind, and from whom possessiveness and Individuation have departed; to whom pain and happiness are the same; and who is forgiving, (14) always contented, controlled, determined, and who has dedicated his Mind and his Reason to Me, such a (Karma-) Yogin devotee of Mine, is beloved of Me. (15) One, of (or with) whom others are not tired (or disgusted), and who is not tired of others; similarly, who is untouched by joy, anger, fear, and discomfiture, is beloved of Me. (16) One, who is unexpecting, pure, industrious (that is, who performs any Action, giving up idleness), indifferent (about the Fruit of Action); whom no emotion can upset; and who has given up all commencements (that is, activity for desirable fruit), such My devotee is very dear to Me. (17) One, who experiences no joy (about anything), does not hate (anything—Trans.), does not regret, and does not even entertain any desire; who has

समः शत्रौ च मित्रे च तथा मानापमानयोः ।
शीतोष्णसुखदुःखेषु समः सङ्गविवर्जितः ॥ १८ ॥
तुल्यनिन्दास्तुतिर्मौनी संतुष्टो येन केनचित् ।
अनिकेतः स्थिरमतिर्भक्तिमान्मे प्रियो नरः ॥ १९ ॥

abandoned the good or bad (Fruit of Action), such a devoted man is dear to Me. (18) One, to whom enemies and friends, also honour and dishonour, heat and cold, pain and happiness, are the same; and who is not attached (to anything), (19) to whom praise and disparagement are both the same, who speaks little, and is contented with whatever he can get, whose mind is steady, and who is '*aniketa*' (that is, who has no abode in the form of a Desire for the Fruit of Action), such a devoted person is dear to Me.

[The word '*aniketa*' is also very often used in describing ascetics, who give up the state of a householder, renounce the world, and roam about begging in forests (Manu. 6. 25); and its root meaning is 'one who has no abode'. Therefore, commentators, who belong to the School of Renunciation say that, the words '*nirmama*', '*sarvārambha-parityāgī*' and '*aniketa*' used in this chapter, and other such words as '*tyakta-sarvaparigrahaḥ*', (4. 21), or '*viviktasevī*' (18. 52), prove that the doctrine preached by the Gītā is, 'giving up home, and spending the rest of one's life desirelessly in a forest', which is, indeed, the highest ideal of the Path of Renunciation; and in support of this they point to many stanzas from the chapters on Renunciation in Smṛti texts. But, although these renunciatory interpretations of these words from the Gītā may be important from the point of view of the Path of Renunciation, yet, they are not correct. Because, as has been stated by me several times before, becoming '*niragni*' (i. e., not performing Fire-ritual), or '*niṣkriya*' (i. e., Actionless), does not amount to true Renunciation according to the Gītā; and the firm doctrine of the Gītā is, that one must renounce only the Desire for Fruit, and never Action (See Gī. 5. 2 and 6. 1, 2). Therefore, the word '*aniketa*' cannot be interpreted as meaning "giving up home"; and, it must be given a meaning, which is consistent with the Karma-Yoga of the Gītā. In Gī. 4. 20, the adjective '*nirāśraya*' has been applied to the man, who does not entertain the hope for the Fruit of Action; and in Gī. 6. 1, the words "*anāśritaḥ karmaphalaṁ*" have been used in the same sense. The words '*āśraya*' and '*niketa*' are synonymous. Therefore, '*aniketa*' should not be interpreted as meaning 'one, who gives up his home and family', but as 'one, whose mind is not engrossed with his home and family'. Similarly, the word '*sarvārambha-parityāgī*' in stanza 16 is not to be interpreted as meaning 'one, who gives up all Action or activity', but as meaning 'one, who gives up desireful commencements of Actions', consistently with the stanza: "He, whose *samārambha*-s (that is, Actions) are devoid of Desire for Fruit, his actions are reduced to ashes by Knowledge" (Gī. 4. 19), as is apparent from Gī. 18. 2 and 18. 48 and 49. In short, all that the Gītā says is that, one, whose Mind is engrossed with household affairs, or with his wife and children, or with the other affairs of the world, experiences pain on that account later on; and that therefore, one should not allow one's Mind to be engrossed in these things; and the words '*aniketa*' and '*sarvārambha-parityāgī*', etc., have been used in the Gītā in the descriptions of the Steady-in-Reason (*sthitaprajña*) for describing the renounced state of his Reason. It is true that these very words have been used in the Smṛti texts in the descriptions given there of Yatins, that is, of ascetics who abandon Action; but, on that account it cannot be said that the Gītā supports Renunciation in the shape of the Abandonment of Action; because, there is, side by side, another definite proposition of the Gītā, that even the Jñānin, whose mind is saturated with this Renunciation, should, with this renunciatory frame of mind, give up the Fruit of Action, and perform all Actions, which befall him according to the Śāstras; and it would not be correct to assert that the Gītā supports the Path of Renunciation of Action, relying on words like '*aniketa*', etc., suggesting Renunciation, which one comes across in some places in the Gītā, without taking into account the posterior and anterior contexts.]

§§ ये तु धर्म्यामृतमिदं यथोक्तं पर्युपासते ।
श्रद्दधाना मत्परमा भक्तास्तेऽतीव मे प्रियाः ॥ २० ॥

इति श्रीमद्भगवद्गीतासु उपनिषत्सु ब्रह्मविद्यायां योगशास्त्रे
श्रीकृष्णार्जुनसंवादे भक्तियोगो नाम द्वादशोऽध्यायः ॥ १२ ॥

(20) Those devotees of mine, who follow this nectar-like doctrine mentioned above, becoming engrossed in Me, are extremely beloved of Me.

[The Blessed Lord has in this stanza given a description of that devotee of His, who is most beloved of Him, that is, of the excellent devotee of the Blessed Lord, who is a Karma-Yogin, consistently with His previous statement that the Devotee, who is also a Jñānin, is the most excellent of all. (Gī. 6. 47; 7. 18). But, in Gītā 9. 29, the Blessed Lord has Himself said that: "all are the same to Me; such a one is not dear, and such a one is not hateful". Apparently, this would seem to be a contradiction-in-terms. But, when one remembers that the one statement has been made with reference to the worship of the Perceptible, or relates to the Path of Devotion, whereas the other statement is from the point of view of Metaphysics or from the point of view of the Doctrine of Causality, this seeming inconsistency disappears. The reader is referred to the exposition of this matter made at the end (pp. 598 to 601) of Chapter XIII of the Gītā-Rahasya.]

Thus ends the twelfth Chapter entitled BHAKTI–YOGA in the dialogue between Śrī Kṛṣṇa and Arjuna, on the Yoga included in the Science of the Brahman (that is, on the Karma–Yoga) in the Upaniṣad sung (that is, told) by the Blessed Lord.

त्रयोदशोऽध्यायः

CHAPTER XIII.

[It has been proved in the last chapter that though it is true that Release can be achieved by meditating on the Unshowable (*anirdeśya*) and Imperceptible (*avyakta*) Parameśvara, yet the same Release can be obtained in an easier way by devoting oneself to the visible and perceptible form of the Parameśvara with religious faith, and by performing all Actions with the intention of dedicating them to Him. But, the explanation about Spiritual and Empirical Knowledge, which was started in Chapter VII is not finished with that. In order to acquire complete Knowledge of the Parameśvara, it is necessary to consider the Body and the Ātman of man, (that is, the '*kṣetra*' and the '*kṣetrajña*') at the same time as considering the mutable and immutable external universe. Similarly, although one may, in a general way, know that all perceptible objects are created from Gross Matter, yet the subject-matter of Spiritual and Empirical Knowledge is not exhausted unless one has explained by what quality of Nature this extensive development takes place and what the order of that development is. Therefore, the subject-matter of the Body and the Ātman has first been considered in Chap. XIII; and after describing the division of the three constituents in the next four chapters, the whole subject-matter has been summed up in Chapter XVIII. In short, the third '*ṣaḍādhyāyī*' (group of six chapters) is not independent; and the description of Spiritual and Empirical Knowledge, requisite for successfully acquiring the Karma-Yoga, which was started in Chap. VII has been completed in this group of six chapters. (See Gītā-Rahasya Ch. XIV pp. 457 to 459). In every edition of the Gītā, the following stanza is to be found in the beginning of Chapter XIII, namely, :—

Arjuna *uvāca*:

prakṛtiṁ puruṣaṁ caiva kṣetraṁ kṣetrajñam eva ca ।
etad veditum icchāmi jñānaṁ jñeyaṁ ca keśava ॥

श्रीभगवानुवाच ।

§§ इदं शरीरं कौन्तेय क्षेत्रमित्यभिधीयते ।
एतद्यो वेत्ति तं प्राहुः क्षेत्रज्ञ इति तद्विदः ॥ १ ॥

क्षेत्रज्ञं चापि मां विद्धि सर्वक्षेत्रेषु भारत ।
क्षेत्रक्षेत्रज्ञयोर्ज्ञानं यत्तज्ज्ञानं मतं मम ॥ २ ॥

which means:—"Arjuna said: I wish to know what *prakṛti, puruṣa, kṣetra, kṣetrajña, jñāna* and *jñeya* are. Therefore, tell me that". But, it is quite clear that some one, who has not understood how the Consideration of the Body and the Ātman has found a place in the Gītā, has subsequently interpolated this stanza into the Gītā. Commentators look upon this stanza as an interpolation; and if that is not done, the number of stanzas in the Gītā also exceeds seven hundred. Therefore, I too have looked upon this stanza as an interpolation and started this chapter as in the Śāṁkarabhāṣya.]

The Blessed Lord said:—(1) O Kaunteya! this Body itself is called the '*kṣetra*'. He, who understands this (Body), is called the '*kṣetrajña*' by the '*tadvida*-s' (that is, by those persons who understand this science). (2) O Bhārata! know that in all Bodies, I am the *kṣetrajña* (that is, the Self or the Ātman—Trans.). The Knowledge of the '*kṣetra*' and the '*kṣetrajña*' has been considered the Knowledge of Me (the Parameśvara).

[In the first stanza, the meanings of the two words *kṣetra* and *kṣetrajña* have been defined; and in the second stanza, the *kṣetrajña* has been defined by saying that "the *kṣetrajña* means Myself, i. e., the Parameśvara"; or that, "that which is in the Body, the same thing is in the Cosmos". The word '*cāpi*="also" in the second stanza indicates that He is not only the Ātman (*kṣetrajña*), but also the Body (*kṣetra*); because, it has been stated already in Chapters VII and VIII that the *kṣetra*, or the Body, originates from the five primordial elements, which in turn

§§ तत्क्षेत्रं यच्च यादृक् च यद्विकारि यतश्च यत् ।
स च यो यत्प्रभावश्च तत्समासेन मे शृणु ॥ ३ ॥

have come out of Prakṛti (Matter); and that, Prakṛti is only a minor manifestation of the Parameśvara (7. 4; 8. 4; 9. 8). As the *kṣetra* or the Body has thus been made up of the five primordial elements, it is included in what is known as the Mutable (*kṣara*), in the Consideration of the Mutable (*kṣara*) and the Immutable (*akṣara*); and the *kṣetrajña* is nothing but the Parameśvara. Therefore, the Consideration of the Body and the Ātman becomes a part of the Knowledge of the Parameśvara in the same way as the Consideration of the Mutable and the Immutable (See Gī. Ra. pp. 193 to 201); and that is why it is stated at the end of stanza 2, that "the Knowledge of the Body and the Ātman is the Knowledge of Myself or of the Paramesvara". Those, who do not accept the Non-dualistic Vedānta, have got to stretch the meaning of the words "I am also the Kṣetrajña"; and they have to maintain that these words do not prove the absence of difference between the "*kṣetrajña*" and "I, the Parameśvara"; and others take the word 'my' (*mama*) as relating to '*mataṁ*', that is, 'has been understood', instead of referring it to "*jñāna*"; and interpret the sentence as meaning, "I look upon the knowledge of these as Jñāna"; but these interpretations are not straightforward. It has been clearly stated in the beginning of Chapter VIII that "the Ātman (*adhideva*)*, which resides in the Body, is Myself"; or that whatever is in the Body, the same thing is in the Cosmos": and it has also been stated in Chapter VII (7. 5) that "the Jīva (the Personal Self) is my inferior Prakṛti"; and there are statements to the same effect further on in this Chapter in stanzas 22 and 31. The Blessed Lord now explains where and by whom the Consideration of the Body and the Ātman has been made—]

(3) What the *kṣetra* is, what its nature is, what its modifications are, and withal what comes out of what; as also Who the *kṣetrajña* is and what His prowess is, I shall

* The Author possibly means '*adhideha*'; see p. 1031 *supra*—Trans.

ऋषिभिर्बहुधा गीतं छन्दोभिर्विविधैः पृथक् ।
ब्रह्मसूत्रपदैश्चैव हेतुमद्भिर्विनिश्चितैः ॥ ४ ॥

explain all this in brief, to which listen. (4) In many ways, in different metres, by (many) Ṛṣis individually, as also by the words in the Brahma-Sūtras, which have been made perfectly definite by showing the motive (in the shape of cause and effect) has this (that is, this subject-matter) been sung.

[The word 'Brahma-Sūtra' in this stanza refers to the present Vedānta-Sūtras, as has been explained by me in detail in the Appendices to the Gītā-Rahasya (See Gī. Ra. pp. 748 to 758). The Upaniṣads are not one treatise written by one Ṛṣi; and the various metaphysical ideas, which inspired the minds of various Ṛṣis at different times or at different places, have been described in the various Upaniṣads, without considering their mutual inter-relation. Therefore, the Upaniṣads seem miscellaneous, and in several places mutually contradictory. The words '*vividha*' and '*pṛthak*' which appear in the first part of this stanza have been used with reference to this miscellaneous nature of the Upaniṣads. As these Upaniṣads are miscellaneous and mutually contradictory, Bādarāyaṇācārya wrote the Brahma-Sūtras or the Vedānta-Sūtras, in order to make them mutually consistent; and considering all the subjects in the Upaniṣads, he has conclusively proved in these Sūtras, by showing the why and wherefore, how it is possible to evolve one single doctrine from the various Upaniṣads. It is clear that a study of the Vedānta-Sūtras is always essential in order to understand the esoteric import of the Upaniṣads; and therefore, both have been referred to in this stanza. The *kṣetra* has been considered in the first sixteen Sūtras of the 3rd division (*pāda*) of the 2nd Chapter (*adhyāya*) of the Brahma-Sūtras; and thereafter the '*kṣetrajña*' has been considered upto the end of the division. As this consideration has been made in the Brahma-Sūtras, they are also called "the Śārīraka-Sūtras", that is to say, the canons (*sūtras*), which deal with the '*śarīra*' (kṣetra). To proceed: the Blessed Lord has thus

§§ महाभूतान्यहंकारो बुद्धिरव्यक्तमेव च ।
इन्द्रियाणि दशैकं च पञ्च चेन्द्रियगोचराः ॥ ५ ॥
इच्छा द्वेषः सुखं दुःखं संघातश्चेतना धृतिः ।
एतत् क्षेत्रं समासेन सविकारमुदाहृतम् ॥ ६ ॥

explained where and by whom the subject-matter of the Body and the Ātman has been considered; He now explains what the Body (*kṣetra*) is—]

(5) The (five gross) primordial elements (such as, the earth etc.), Individuality (*aham̐kāra*), Reason (*mahān*), and the Imperceptible (Prakṛti), as also the ten (subtle) senses and one (Mind); and the five (subtle) objects (such as, sound, touch, colour, taste and smell) of the five senses, (6) Desire, Hate, Happiness, Unhappiness, '*sam̐ghāta*' (that is, the group—Trans.), '*cetanā*', (that is, the visible activity of the Vital airs etc.), and '*dhṛti*' (that is, courage); this collection (of 31 elements) is known as the organised (*savikāra*) Body.

This is a definition of the *kṣetra* and of its *vikāra*-s. In Stanza 5 have been mentioned 24 out of the 25 elements of the Sām̐khyas except the Spirit (*puruṣa*). As the Mind is included in these 24 elements, it was not necessary to enumerate separately the qualities of the Mind, such as, Desire, Hate etc. These are the qualities of the Ātman according to the Kāṇādas; and if this idea is accepted, a doubt arises as to whether or not these qualities are included in the *kṣetra*. Therefore, in order to make the the definition of the word *kṣetra* perfectly unambiguous, the pairs of Opposites such as, Desire, Hate etc., have been clearly included here in the definition of the *kṣetra* itself; and these pairs include the other pairs such as, fear and fearlessness, etc., by implication. In order to show that the *sam̐ghāta* or the 'collection', of all these, is not an agent, independent of the Body, it has been included in the definition of the Body itself. The word '*cetanā*' is sometimes understood as Consciousness (*caitanya*); but in the present context, the word '*cetanā*' means only the 'activity of the Vital airs etc., to be seen in the Gross Body'; or 'the activity

§§ अमानित्वमदम्भित्वमहिंसा क्षान्तिरार्जवम् ।
आचार्योपासनं शौचं स्थैर्यमात्मविनिग्रहः ॥ ७ ॥

इन्द्रियार्थेषु वैराग्यमनहंकार एव च ।
जन्ममृत्युजराव्याधिदुःखदोषानुदर्शनम् ॥ ८ ॥

resulting from being alive'; and it has been stated in stanza 2 above, that the *cicchakti* (power of consciousness) or *caitanya*, which is responsible for the existence of this activity in gross bodies, is in the form of the *kṣetrajña*, which is different from the *kṣetra*. The word '*dhṛti*' has been defined later on in the Gītā itself (18. 33), to which the reader is referred. The word '*samāsena*' in the sixth stanza means "group made up of all these". A further explanation has been given at the end of Chapter VI of the Gītā-Rahasya (pp. 193 to 195), to which the reader is referred. After first stating that the *kṣetrajña* is the Parameśvara, the Blessed Lord has given an explanation of what the *kṣetra* is. Now an explanation is given of what Jñāna is, by stating what influence this Jñāna (Knowledge) has on the temperament of a man; and later on the nature of the Knowable (*jñeya*) has been explained. These two subjects seem to be different from each other; but practically speaking, these are the two divisions of the Consideration of the Body and the Ātman; because, it has been stated already in the beginning that the *kṣetrajña* is the Parameśvara. Therefore, the Knowledge of the *kṣetrajña* is the Knowledge of the Parameśvara; and the nature of this Knowledge has been described in the following stanzas. It is not that some totally different subject-matter has been pushed in here in the middle.]

(7) Not having vanity, not having hypocrisy; harmlessness, forgiveness, straightforwardness, service of preceptors, purity, steadiness, concentration of the Mind; (8) indifference towards the objects of the senses; also, absence of Individuation; and the feeling that life, death, old age, illness, and unhappiness are evils (which pursue one);

असक्तिरनभिष्वङ्गः पुत्रदारगृहादिषु ।
नित्यं च समचित्तत्वमिष्टानिष्टोपपत्तिषु ॥ ९ ॥
मयि चानन्ययोगेन भक्तिरव्यभिचारिणी ।
विविक्तदेशसेवित्वमरतिर्जनसंसदि ॥ १० ॥
अध्यात्मज्ञाननित्यत्वं तत्त्वज्ञानार्थदर्शनम् ।
एतज्ज्ञानमिति प्रोक्तमज्ञानं यदतोऽन्यथा ॥ ११ ॥

(9) non-attachment (towards Action); not being engrossed with one's wife and children, and one's home etc., having an equable frame of Mind, whether something good or something evil happens; (10) having an unswerving mono-focussed Devotion to Me; and remaining in a '*vivikta*' (that is, a chosen, or a solitary place); not liking the meeting-place of ordinary people; (11) beginning to realise that Metaphysical Knowledge is permanent; and meditation on propositions of philosophy, all this has been called '*jñāna*' (Knowledge), and all rest is '*ajñāna*' (Ignorance).

[According to Sāṁkhya philosophy, the Knowledge of the Body and the Ātman is the knowledge of the distinction between Spirit and Matter; and that has been explained later on in this chapter (13. 19-23; 14.19); similarly an exhaustive definition of the nature of Knowledge has been given in Chapter XVIII (18. 20) in the words "*avibhaktaṁ vibhakteṣu*". But, according to the science of Release, Knowledge of the *kṣetra* and *kṣetrajña* does not only mean, understanding by the Mind that a particular thing is of a particular kind. It is a proposition of Metaphysics that, Knowledge must create an effect on the mental temperament in the shape of Equability of Reason; and that otherwise, that Knowledge is incomplete or immature. Therefore, 'Jñāna' has been described in the above stanzas by saying that a man may be said to have 'Jñāna' when absence of vanity, hypocrisy, non-violence, non-attachment, equability etc. and the other twenty qualities mentioned in the above five stanzas are seen in him, instead of defining Jñāna as the understanding by the mind of particular things (see Gī. Ra. Chap. IX pp. 341 to 344). The description of one feature of Jñāna contained in the words, "remaining in a solitary

§§ ज्ञेयं यत्तत्प्रवक्ष्यामि यज्ज्ञात्वामृतमश्नुते ।
अनादिमत्परं ब्रह्म न सत्तन्नासदुच्यते ॥ १२ ॥
सर्वतः पाणिपादं तत्सर्वतोऽक्षिशिरोमुखम् ।
सर्वतः श्रुतिमल्लोके सर्वमावृत्य तिष्ठति ॥ १३ ॥

place and not liking a common meeting place", appearing in stanza 10, has been taken hold of by some commentators for proving that the Path of Renunciation is supported by the Gītā; but I have already stated before that such an interpretation is not correct, and that it is not even proper to put such an interpretation on these words (See note on Gī. 12. 19, and Gī. Ra. p. 391). The only thing which has been considered in this place is what Jñāna is; and there is no dispute about the fact that Jñāna means 'absence of Attachment for one's wife and children, for one's home, and for the common meeting-place of people'. Whether after the acquisition of this Jñāna, a man should remain in the world or among his wife and children with this Desireless Mind, and perform worldly Action for the benefit of the world, is the next question; and it is not proper to decide that question by merely considering the definition of the word 'Jñāna'. Because, the Blessed Lord has stated in many places in the Gītā itself that a Jñānin must continue to perform all Actions with an unattached frame of mind, without becoming engrossed in the Actions, and for universal welfare; and He has, in support of that proposition, mentioned the illustrations of the life of Janaka and of Himself (Gī. 3. 19–25; 4. 14). The life of Śrī Samartha Rāmadāsa clearly shows how it is possible for a man to take part in the affairs in the world as a duty, without having a desire to live in the town (See Dāsa-bodha 19. 6. 29 and 19. 9. 11). So far a description has been given of the nature of Jñāna. The Blessed Lord now gives a description of the Knowable—]

(12) (Now) I will tell (you) That, by knowing which, one attains to *amṛta* (that is, Release). (It is) eternal, (It is) the Brahman, Which is beyond (everything); It is not called '*sat*'; nor is It called '*asat*'; (13) It has arms

सर्वेन्द्रियगुणाभासं सर्वेन्द्रियविवर्जितम् ।
असक्तं सर्वभृच्चैव निर्गुणं गुणभोक्तृ च ॥ १४ ॥

बहिरन्तश्च भूतानामचरं चरमेव च ।
सूक्ष्मत्वात्तदविज्ञेयं दूरस्थं चान्तिके च तत् ॥ १५ ॥

अविभक्तं च भूतेषु विभक्तमिव च स्थितम् ।
भूतभर्तृ च तज्ज्ञेयं ग्रसिष्णु प्रभविष्णु च ॥ १६ ॥

ज्योतिषामपि तज्ज्योतिस्तमसः परमुच्यते ।
ज्ञानं ज्ञेयं ज्ञानगम्यं हृदि सर्वस्य धिष्ठितम् ॥ १७ ॥

and feet on all sides; eyes, heads, and mouths on all sides; and It pervades everything in this world; (14) It creates an impression that It has the qualities of all the senses; and It has no senses at all; though It is *asakta* (that is, untouched by anything), It, at the same time, supports everything; and being qualityless, It yet enjoys all the qualities, (15) (It) is in all things and outside all things; (It) is immoveable and at the same time moveable; being subtle, It is incapable of being known; and being far away, It is yet near. (16) (Though) It is (essentially) '*avibhakta*' (that is, unbroken), It is, so to say, divided among all beings (by diversity); and It must be looked upon as That Which supports, swallows up, and also creates (all) beings; (17) It is called the Brilliance of all brilliance, and Something beyond darkness; It is 'Jñāna'; It is the 'Jñeya' (that is, that which is to be known) and 'Jñāna-gamya' (that is, capable of being understood only by Jñāna) ; and It is installed in the heart of everybody.

[The above description of the Inconceivable and Imperishable Parabrahman, which is also known as the *kṣetrajña* or the Paramātman (Gī. 13. 22), has been made on the authority of the Upaniṣads, in the same way as that of the Imperishable Brahman in Chapter VIII (Gī. 8. 9-11). The whole of stanza 13 (Śve. 3. 16) and the subsequent demi-stanza: "It creates an impression that it possesses the senses, and it has no senses at all" have been taken literally from the Śvetāśvataropanisad (Śve. 3. 17); and the words "being far away, It is yet near" are to be found in the Īśāvāsya (5), and the Muṇḍaka (13. 1. 7) Upaniṣads. Similarly, the words "the Brilliance of all brilliance" are from the Bṛhadāraṇyaka (Bṛ. 4. 4. 16); and "something beyond darkness" are from the Śvetāśvatara (3. 8). The description "It is not called *sat*, nor is It called *asat*" is according to the well-known Sūtra on the Brahman, namely, *nāsadāsīt no sadāsīt*" from the Ṛg-Veda. The meaning of the two words '*sat*' and '*asat*' has been exhaustively considered in Chapter IX of the Gītā-Rahasya (Ch. IX pp. 336 to 338), as also in the commentary on Gītā 9. 19, to which the reader is referred. In Gītā 9. 19, it was stated that He is the '*sat*' as also the '*asat*'; and it is now stated that the true Brahman is neither '*sat*' nor '*asat*', which would seem to be a contradiction-in-terms: but this contradiction is not real; because, the proposition that, "though the *vyakta* (kṣara) and *avyakta* (akṣara) universe are both forms of the Parameśvara, yet, the true Parameśvara-Element is beyond both these, that is, totally incognisable", has been clearly enunciated before in the Gītā in the stanza "*bhūtabhṛn na ca bhūtastho*" (Gī. 9. 5), and also again where the description of the Puruṣottama has been given (Gī. 15. 16, 17). As the questions, 'what is called the *nirguṇa* Brahman', 'how that *nirguṇa* Brahman is outside the world, while being in the world', and 'how, though It might appear diverse or divided (*vibhakta*), It is fundamentally undivided (*avibhakta*), or only One' have already been considered in Chapter IX of fhe Gītā-Rahasya (p. 285 et seq.), I shall not repeat the same subject-matter here. The words "It is so to say divided among all beings" in stanza 16, are a translation of the words "*vibhaktam iva*"; and this word '*iva*' has been used several times in the Upaniṣads in this sense, that is to say, in the sense that the diversity in the world is illusory and that unity is the only truth. For example, see "*dvaitam iva bhavati*", "*yatha nāneva paśyati*" etc., (Bṛ. 2. 4. 14; 4. 4. 19; 4. 3. 7). It is, therefore, quite clear that the Gītā supports the Non-Dualistic proposition that Māyā, embodied in various Names and Forms is illusory, and that the Brahman which

इति क्षेत्रं तथा ज्ञानं ज्ञेयं चोक्तं समासतः ।
मद्भक्त एतद्विज्ञाय मद्भावायोपपद्यते ॥ १८ ॥

indivisibly permeates that Illusion is alone Real. In Gītā 18. 20, later on, it is again stated that, "*avibhaktaṁ vibhakteṣu*", that is to say, 'seeing Unity in Diversity', is a sign of *sāttvika* Knowledge. That this *sāttvika* Knowledge is the Brahman, and other similar topics have been discussed by me in the chapter of the Gītā-Rahasya, which deals with the Absolute Self (See Gī. Ra. Ch. IX, pp. 293 to 295 and Ch. VI. pp. 178 to 180).]

(18) I have thus briefly explained to you what the '*kṣetra*', '*jñāna*' and the '*jñeya*' are. Knowing this, My devotee is merged into My form.

[The *kṣetra*, *jñāna*, and the *jñeya* have so far been considered with the help of the Science of the Absolute Self or of the Vedānta-Śāstra. As the *jñeya* out of these is the *kṣetrajña* or the Parabrahman, and Jñāna is the Knowledge of the Body (*kṣetra*) and the Ātman (*kṣetrajña*), mentioned in stanza 2, this becomes a short description of all Knowledge of the Parameśvara; and since the Knowledge of the *kṣetra* and the *kṣetrajña* is the Knowledge of the Parameśvara, it follows, as a matter of course, that the fruit of it must be Release; and that proposition has been laid down in stanza 18. The Consideration of the Body and the Ātman according to the Vedānta-Śāstra ends here. But, since the organised *(savikāra)* Body, composed of the primordial elements, has sprung out of Prakṛti, and since what the Sāṁkhyas call '*puruṣa*' (Spirit) is the Ātman according to Vedānta, the Consideration of the Body and the Ātman becomes the Consideration of Prakṛti and Purusa according to the Sāṁkhyas. The Gītā does not look upon Prakṛti and Purusa as two independent elements, as is done by the Sāṁkhyas; and it has been stated in Chapter VII of the Gītā that they are respectively the inferior and superior forms of one and the same Parameśvara (7. 4, 5). But when once one accepts this Non-Dualism or Monism, instead of the Dualism of the Sāṁkhyas, then what the Sāṁkhyas say about the mutual relation between Prakṛti and Purusa is not un-

§§ प्रकृतिं पुरुषं चैव विद्ध्यनादी उभावपि ।
विकारांश्च गुणांश्चैव विद्धि प्रकृतिसंभवान् ॥ १९ ॥
कार्यकरणकर्तृत्वे हेतुः प्रकृतिरुच्यते ।
पुरुषः सुखदुःखानां भोक्तृत्वे हेतुरुच्यते ॥ २० ॥

acceptable to the Gītā. Nay, the Consideration of Prakṛti and Puruṣa is nothing but the Consideration of the Body and the Ātman in another form. (See Gī. Ra. Ch VII). Therefore, the Blessed Lord, having expounded the Knowledge of the Body and the Ātman on the authority of the Upaniṣads, now again explains the same Knowledge in the terminology of Sāṁkhya philosophy, but without accepting the Dualism of the Sāṁkhyas, in the shape of a discrimination between the Prakṛti and Puruṣa—]

(19) Know that both Prakṛti and Puruṣa are eternal. Know that the evolutes (*vikāra*) and the constituents (*guṇa*), all spring out of Prakṛti.

[According to Sāṁkhya philosophy, Prakṛti and Puruṣa are not only eternal but also independent of each other and self-created. According to Vedānta philosophy, Prakṛti originates from the Parameśvara and is, therefore, neither self-created nor independent (Gī. 4. 5, 6). But, as it cannot be said when Prakṛti originated from the Parameśvara, and as the Puruṣa (Jīva) is a part of the Parameśvara (Gī. 15. 7), Vedāntists admit that both are eternal. A further elucidation of this subject-matter has been made in Chap. VII of the Gītā-Rahasya, specially at pp. 219 to 226 and in Chapter X at pp. 362 to 366, to which the reader is referred.]

(20) Prakṛti is said to be the cause for the activity of the *kārya* (that is, the Body) and of the *karaṇa* (that is, the senses); and (without being a Doer) the Puruṣa (Kṣetrajña) is said to be the cause for experiencing pain or pleasure.

[In this stanza, the reading '*kāryakāraṇa*' is found in some texts instead of the reading '*kāryakaraṇa*'; with that reading the stanza means, that the 23 elements of Sāṁkhya philosophy, namely, Mahat and the others, spring one out of the other, the one being the cause for

पुरुषः प्रकृतिस्थो हि भुङ्क्ते प्रकृतिजान्गुणान् ।
कारणं गुणसङ्गोऽस्य सदसद्योनिजन्मसु ॥ २१ ॥
§§ उपद्रष्टाऽनुमन्ता च भर्ता भोक्ता महेश्वरः ।
परमात्मेति चाप्युक्तो देहेऽस्मिन् पुरुषः परः ॥ २२ ॥
य एवं वेत्ति पुरुषं प्रकृतिं च गुणैः सह ।
सर्वथा वर्तमानोऽपि न स भूयोऽभिजायते ॥ २३ ॥

the one which follows, and that the entire perceptible universe comes into existence out of Prakṛti. Such an interpretation would not be improper. But in the Consideration of the Body and the Ātman, a Consideration of the origin of the Body, is out of place. How the world has sprung out of Prakṛti has been explained before in Chapters VII and IX. Therefore, the reading '*kāryakaraṇa*' seems more appropriate in this place. The Śāṁkarabhāṣya adopts the reading '*kāryakaraṇa*'.]

(21) Because, when Prakṛti is superintended over by Puruṣa, It enjoys the constituents born of Prakṛti; and this union with the constituents (of Prakṛti) becomes the cause for the Puruṣa to take birth in a good or bad species.

[This description of the difference and the mutual relation between Prakṛti and Puruṣa is from Sāṁkhya philosophy (see Gī. Ra. pp. 219 to 221). The Blessed Lord now explains that the 'Puruṣa' of Sāṁkhya philosophy is called the 'Paramātman' by Vedāntists; He thus links the Sāṁkhya with the Vedānta philosophy; and when that is done, the Consideration of the Prakṛti and Puruṣa is harmonised with the Consideration of the Body and the Ātman.]

(22) This '*upadraṣṭā*', (that is, One, Who sits near and sees the constituents of Prakṛti), Who gives the consent, Who is the '*bhartā*' (that is, One, Who adds to the constituents of Prakṛti), and the Enjoyer, is known as the *parapuruṣa* (that is, the Highest Puruṣa—Trans.), the *maheśvara* (that is, the Highest Īśvara—Trans.) and the Paramātman, Who resides in the Body. (23) Who thus knows the Purusa (as qualityless) and (that) Prakṛti (alone

§§ ध्यानेनात्मनि पश्यन्ति केचिदात्मानमात्मना ।
अन्ये सांख्येन योगेन कर्मयोगेन चापरे ॥ २४ ॥
अन्ये त्वेवमजानन्तः श्रुत्वाऽन्येभ्य उपासते ।
तेऽपि चातितरन्त्येव मृत्युं श्रुतिपरायणाः ॥ २५ ॥

is) full of qualities, however he may be acting, does not get re-birth.

[When it has been proved in stanza 22, that the Puruṣa is the Paramātman within the Body, the inactivity and apathy, which are the qualities of the Puruṣa according to Sāṁkhya philosophy now become the inactivity of the Ātman; and a harmony is established between the arguments of the Sāṁkhyas and Vedānta. Some writers on Vedānta imagine that Sāṁkhya philosophy is inimical to Vedānta philosophy; and many Vedāntists look upon the Sāṁkhya arguments as entirely negligible. But instead of doing so, the Gītā has expounded the question of the Body and the Ātman, once from the point of view of Vedānta, and again from the point of view of Sāṁkhya philosophy (without, however, abandoning the Non-Dualism of Vedānta). This shows the equability of the Gītā-science. Nay, this may be said to be an important difference between the expositions in the Upaniṣads and in the Gītā respectively (See Gī. Ra. App. pp. 756 to 757). This clearly shows that though the Gītā does not accept the Dualism of Sāṁkhya philosophy, it does not fail to accept as much as is acceptable out of Sāṁkhya philosophy. It has been stated in stanza 2, that the Knowledge of the Body and the Ātman is nothing but the Knowledge of the Parameśvara. The Blessed Lord now incidentally explains in short the various means of acquiring Release, by acquiring this Knowledge of the Body (*piṇḍa*) and of the Parameśvara within the Body—]

(24) Some persons of their own accord see the Ātman within themselves by means of meditation; some by the Sāṁkhya-Yoga and some by the Karma-Yoga; (25) but those, who do not thus acquire the Knowledge (by themselves), many such worship (the Parameśvara, with religious faith) by hearing the advice of others. These persons, who act,

§§ यावत्संजायते किंचित्सत्त्वं स्थावरजङ्गमम् ।
क्षेत्रक्षेत्रज्ञसंयोगात्तद्विद्धि भरतर्षभ ॥ २६ ॥

समं सर्वेषु भूतेषु तिष्ठन्तं परमेश्वरम् ।
विनश्यत्स्वविनश्यन्तं यः पश्यति स पश्यति ॥ २७ ॥

समं पश्यन् हि सर्वत्र समवस्थितमीश्वरम् ।
न हिनस्त्यात्मनाऽऽत्मानं ततो याति परां गतिम् ॥ २८ ॥

accepting as correct what they have heard, also overcome death and go beyond.

[These two stanzas mention the various paths of Self-Realisation, namely, (i) Meditation, according to the Pātañjala-Yoga; (ii) Abandonment of Action after the acquisition of Knowledge, according to the Sāṁkhyas; (iii) (*a*) performing all Actions desirelessly and with the intention of dedicating them to the Parameśvara, and (*b*) placing confidence with faith in the statements of trust-worthy persons and becoming devoted to the Parameśvara, (Gi. 4. 39), according to Karma-Yoga. Whichever path one follows, one ultimately gains the Knowledge of the Parameśvara and attains Release. Therefore, the proposition laid down in the earlier chapters, that the Path of Karma-Yoga is the best, from the point of view of Universal Welfare, is not thereby affected in the least. Having in this way stated the various means of Self-Realisation, the entire subject has been summarised in the next stanzas in a general way; and even in doing that, a unanimity has been established between the Kāpila Sāṁkhya philosophy and Vedānta.]

(26) O Bharataśreṣṭha! remember that whatever moveable or imoveable thing is created, comes into existence as a result of the union between the Body and the Ātman. (27) He, who has seen the Parameśvara, Who is equally in all created things, and Who is not destroyed, even when all beings are destroyed, he may be said to have understood (the real principle). (28) Realising that the Parameśvara equally pervades everywhere, that man, who, by such Knowledge

§§ प्रकृत्यैव च कर्माणि क्रियमाणानि सर्वशः ।
यः पश्यति तथाऽऽत्मानमकर्तारं स पश्यति ॥ २९ ॥
यदा भूतपृथग्भावमेकस्थमनुपश्यति ।
तत एव च विस्तारं ब्रह्म संपद्यते तदा ॥ ३० ॥
§§ अनादित्वान्निर्गुणत्वात् परमात्माऽयमव्ययः ।
शरीरस्थोऽपि कौन्तेय न करोति न लिप्यते ॥ ३१ ॥
यथा सर्वगतं सौक्ष्म्यादाकाशं नोपलिप्यते ।
सर्वत्रावस्थितो देहे तथाऽऽत्मा नोपलिप्यते ॥ ३२ ॥

escapes self-destruction (that is, who, of his own accord, takes to the path of virtue) attains thereby an excellent state.

[The description of the Parameśvara given in stanza 27 has appeared before in Gī. 8. 20; and this subject has been explained in Chapter IX of the Gītā-Rahasya (See Gī. Ra. pp. 299 and 353). In the same way, the statement made before, that the Ātman is everybody's friend as also his enemy (Gī. 6. 5-7) has been repeated again in stanza 28. Having given a description of the feeling of equability towards all beings in stanzas 26, 27, and 28, the Blessed Lord now explains what happens as a result of this Knowledge—]

(29) He, who has understood that (all) Actions are in every way got performed by means of Prakṛti, and that the Ātman is Itself inactive (that is, One, who does nothing), may be said to have understood (the true principle). (30) When the diversity (that is, manifoldness) in various beings is seen as a unity; and when (all this) extension is seen (to have taken place) from this (unity), the Brahman is attained to.

[The Blessed Lord now explains how the Ātman is qualityless, untouched, and inactive—]

(31) Being eternal and qualityless, this inexhaustible Paramātman, O Kaunteya! does not perform anything, though remaining within the Body; and to Him, the contact (that is, bondage) of no Action attaches itself. (32) As ether, pervading everything, is not affected (by anything), being subtle, so the Ātman, pervading the Body everywhere, is not

यथा प्रकाशयत्येकः कृत्स्नं लोकमिमं रविः ।
क्षेत्रं क्षेत्री तथा कृत्स्नं प्रकाशयति भारत ॥ ३३ ॥
§§ क्षेत्रक्षेत्रज्ञयोरेवमन्तरं ज्ञानचक्षुषा ।
भूतप्रकृतिमोक्षं च ये विदुर्यान्ति ते परम् ॥ ३४ ॥

affected (by anything). (33) As the Sun alone illuminates this entire Cosmos, so also, O Bhārata! the Ātman illuminates the entire Body.

(34) Those, who thus, by spiritual eyes (that is, by eyes in the shape of Knowledge), understand the difference between the Body and the Ātman, and the Release of the (fundamental) Prakṛti of all beings, reach the Parabrahman.

[This is the summary of the entire chapter. I have interpreted the word "*bhūtaprakṛtimokṣa*" according to the Sāṁkhya doctrine. According to this doctrine, getting Release or not, are not states of the Ātman; because, It is always a Non-doer and unattached; but as It arrogates Activity to Itself, as a result of Its union with Prakṛti, the Prakṛti with which It is united, is liberated when this ignorance is destroyed; that is to say, the Prakṛti is Released; and then it gives up its dance in front of the Puruṣa. Therefore, the Sāṁkhyas maintain that the two states of being bound and being released are essentially states of Prakṛti (See Sāṁkhya-Kārikā 62, and Gī. Ra. Ch. VII p. 223). I think that the words "the Release of the Prakṛti" have been used in this stanza with reference to this Sāṁkhya doctrine. But some interpret this expression as meaning "*bhūtebhyaḥ prakṛteś ca mokṣaḥ*", that is, "the Ātman is Released from the five primordial elements and Prakṛti", that is to say, from Illusory Action. To proceed: this discrimination between the Body and the Ātman is made by means of the sight of Knowledge (Gī. 13. 34), whereas the king of Vidyās (*rāja-vidyā*) mentioned in Chapter IX is to be realised by the physical eyes (Gī. 9. 2); and the vision of the Cosmic Form is to be had, even by the highest devotee of the Blessed Lord, by divine eyes (Gī. 11. 8). This distinction between the

इति श्रीमद्भगवद्गीतासु उपनिषत्सु ब्रह्मविद्यायां योगशास्त्रे श्रीकृष्णार्जुनसंवादे क्षेत्रक्षेत्रज्ञविभागयोगो नाम त्रयोदशोऽध्यायः ॥ १३ ॥

explanations of Jñāna and Vijñāna given in the 9th, 11th, and 13th chapters should be bōrne in mind.]

Thus ends the thirteenth chapter entitled KSETRA-KSETRAJNA-VIBHAGA Yoga in the dialogue between Śrī Kṛṣṇa and Arjuna on the Yoga included in the Science of the Brahman (that is, on the Karma-Yoga) in the Upanisad sung (that is, told) by the Blessed Lord.

चतुर्दशोऽध्यायः

श्रीभगवानुवाच ।

§§ परं भूयः प्रवक्ष्यामि ज्ञानानां ज्ञानमुत्तमम् ।
यज्ज्ञात्वा मुनयः सर्वे परां सिद्धिमितो गताः ॥ १ ॥

CHAPTER XIV.

[In Chapter XIII, the doctrine of the Body and the Ātman has been expounded, once from the point of view of Vedānta and again from the point of view of Sāṁkhya philosophy; and it has been stated there that the entire activity is of the Prakṛti, and that the Puruṣa, that is, the *kṣetrajña* is apathetic. But, it has not been explained in what way this activity of Prakṛti continues going. Therefore, the Blessed Lord explains in this chapter how diverse forms of creation, and especially of the living creation, are created from one and the same Prakṛti. If one considers only the human creation, then, as this subject deals with the *kṣetra*, that is to say, with the Body, it can be easily included in the Consideration of the Body and the Ātman. But, as the immoveable world is also an expansion of the three-constituented Prakṛti, the exposition of the difference in the constituents of Prakṛti can also form part of the Consideration of the Mutable and the Immutable. The Blessed Lord has, therefore, given up a restricted description as 'Consideration of the Body and the Ātman', and started this chapter saying that He would explain to Arjuna in further detail the Jñāna (Spiritual Knowledge) and Vijñāna (Empirical Knowledge) which He had commenced to explain in Chapter VII. The reader is referred to the exhaustive explanation of this subject-matter, which has been given in Chapter VIII of the Gītā-Rahasya. This description of the diffusion or spreading-out of the three constituents of Prakṛti has also been given in the Anugītā and in Chapter XII of the Manu-Smṛti.]

The Blessed Lord said:—(1) Once more am I going to tell you the best knowledge of all Knowledge, by knowing which all sages have reached the highest state from this

इदं ज्ञानमुपाश्रित्य मम साधर्म्यमागताः ।
सर्गेऽपि नोपजायन्ते प्रलये न व्यथन्ति च ॥ २ ॥
§§ मम योनिर्महद्ब्रह्म तस्मिन्गर्भं दधाम्यहम् ।
संभवः सर्वभूतानां ततो भवति भारत ॥ ३ ॥
सर्वयोनिषु कौन्तेय मूर्तयः संभवन्ति याः ।
तासां ब्रह्म महद्योनिरहं बीजप्रदः पिता ॥ ४ ॥
§§ सत्त्वं रजस्तम इति गुणाः प्रकृतिसंभवाः ।
निबध्नन्ति महाबाहो देहे देहिनमव्ययम् ॥ ५ ॥
तत्र सत्त्वं निर्मलत्वात्प्रकाशकमनामयम् ।
सुखसङ्गेन बध्नाति ज्ञानसङ्गेन चानघ ॥ ६ ॥

world. (2) Those who, taking shelter in this Knowledge, have become merged in Me, do not come to birth when the Cosmos is created, nor do they die when the Cosmos is destroyed; (that is to say, they become entirely free from the cycle of birth and death).

[This is an introduction. Now the Blessed Lord says in the first instance that Prakṛti is only one form of Himself; and having thereby got rid of the Sāṁkhya Dualism, He now explains—without clashing with Vedānta—how the various perceptible objects come into existence in the world as a result of the three constituents of Prakṛti.]

(3) O Bhārata! the *mahadbrahma* (that is, Prakṛti) is My womb, and I lay in it the embryo of life; then all beings begin to come to life therefrom. (4) All beings, which come to birth in the various species (such as beasts or birds etc.), of them, O Kaunteya! the *mahadbrahma* is the place of generation, and I am the Father, Who impregnates it with the seed.

(5) O Mahābāho! the *sattva*, *rajas* and *tamas* constituents, which spring from Prakṛti, keep tied within the Body, the '*avyaya*' [that is, the unmodifiable (*nirvikāra*) Ātman], which resides in the Body. (6) Out of these, the *sattva* constituent, which illumines because it is pure, and which is faultless, O sinless Arjuna! keeps (beings) in bondage by the Attachment for happiness and Knowledge.

रजो रागात्मकं विद्धि तृष्णासङ्गसमुद्भवम् ।
तन्निबध्नाति कौन्तेय कर्मसङ्गेन देहिनम् ॥ ७ ॥
तमस्त्वज्ञानजं विद्धि मोहनं सर्वदेहिनाम् ।
प्रमादालस्यनिद्राभिस्तन्निबध्नाति भारत ॥ ८ ॥
सत्त्वं सुखे संजयति रजः कर्मणि भारत ।
ज्ञानमावृत्य तु तमः प्रमादे संजयत्युत ॥ ९ ॥

(7) The characteristic of the *rajas* constituent is to keep one engrossed; and know, that Desire and Attachment arise from this constituent. O Kaunteya! it keeps beings in bondage by the (Energistic) Attachment for performing Actions. (8) But the *tamas* constituent springs from Ignorance; and know, that it confuses all beings. O Bhārata! it keeps (them) in bondage by ignorance of duty, idleness, and sleep. (9) The *sattva* constituent creates an Attachment for happiness, and the *rajas* constituent, for Action; but O Bhārata! the *tamas* constituent throws a cloak on Knowledge, and creates an Attachment for '*pramāda*' (that is, ignorance of duty or forgetfulness of duty.)

[The individual natures of the three constituents have thus been explained. But these three constituents never exist individually, independent of each other; and they are always together. For example, although it is the nature of the *sattva* constituent to make a man do any good action, yet, as the inclination to do the good action results from the *rajas* constituent, there must also be some mixture of the *rajas* constituent with the *sāttvika* temperament. That is why the *sattva* constituent is mentioned as the pair of the *tamas* constituent, and the *rajas* constituent as the pair of the *sattva* constituent in the Anugītā, which gives a pairing description of these constituents (Ma. Bhā. Aśva. 36); and it is stated there, that all things in the world are created by the mutual support or mutual interrelations of these constituents. (See Sāṁ. Kā. 12 and Gī. Ra. pp. 213 to 215). This very principle is now first enunciated, and then the characteristics of the *sattva*, *rajas* and *tamas* constituents are described.]

§§ रजस्तमश्चाभिभूय सत्त्वं भवति भारत ।
रजः सत्त्वं तमश्चैव तमः सत्त्वं रजस्तथा ॥ १० ॥
सर्वद्वारेषु देहेऽस्मिन् प्रकाश उपजायते ।
ज्ञानं यदा तदा विद्याद्विवृद्धं सत्त्वमित्युत ॥ ११ ॥
लोभः प्रवृत्तिरारम्भः कर्मणामशमः स्पृहा ।
रजस्येतानि जायन्ते विवृद्धे भरतर्षभ ॥ १२ ॥
अप्रकाशोऽप्रवृत्तिश्च प्रमादो मोह एव च ।
तमस्येतानि जायन्ते विवृद्धे कुरुनन्दन ॥ १३ ॥
§§ यदा सत्त्वे प्रवृद्धे तु प्रलयं याति देहभृत् ।
तदोत्तमविदां लोकानमलान् प्रतिपद्यते ॥ १४ ॥
रजसि प्रलयं गत्वा कर्मसङ्गिषु जायते ।
तथा प्रलीनस्तमसि मूढयोनिषु जायते ॥ १५ ॥

(10) Defeating the *rajas* and *tamas* constituents, the *sattva* becomes (preponderant); (then, he is said to be *sāttvika*); and by defeating the *sattva* and *tamas* constituents, the *rajas* constituent becomes (preponderant); and by defeating the *sattva* and *rajas* constituents, the *tamas* becomes (preponderant). (11) When in this body, in all its apertures (senses), light (that is, spotless Knowledge) comes into existence, the *sattva* constituent may be understood to have grown. (12) O Bharataśreṣṭha ! when the *rajas* constituent increases, avarice, inclination towards Action, and the commencement of Actions, dissatisfaction, and Desire come into existence; (13) and O Kurunandana ! when the *tamas* constituent increases, darkness, a desire not to do anything, and *pramāda* (that is, forgetfulness of one's duties) and confusion, even these, come into existence.

[The Blessed Lord has explained what differences take place in the nature of a man, while he is alive, as a result of the three constituents. HE now explains what goal is reached by these three kinds of persons—]

(14) If a being dies when there is a preponderance of the *sattva* constituent, it goes to the pure spheres (such as, heaven, etc.) of those, who understand the exalted principles (that is, of gods, etc.). (15) If it dies when the *rajas*

कर्मणः सुकृतस्याहुः सात्त्विकं निर्मलं फलम् ।
रजसस्तु फलं दुःखमज्ञानं तमसः फलम् ॥ १६ ॥

सत्त्वात्संजायते ज्ञानं रजसो लोभ एव च ।
प्रमादमोहौ तमसो भवतोऽज्ञानमेव च ॥ १७ ॥

ऊर्ध्वं गच्छन्ति सत्त्वस्था मध्ये तिष्ठन्ति राजसाः ।
जघन्यगुणवृत्तिस्था अधो गच्छन्ति तामसाः ॥ १८ ॥

constituent is preponderant, it takes birth among those, who are engrossed in Action; and dying when there is preponderance of the *tamas* constituent, it takes birth in ignorant species, (such as, birds, beasts, etc.). (16) It is said that the result of virtuous Action is sinless and *sāttvika*; but the result of *rājasa* Action is pain, and the result of *tāmasa* Action is ignorance. (17) Whereas Knowledge arises from the *sattva* constituent, avarice springs from the *rajas* constituent, and not only forgetfulness of duty and confusion, but even Ignorance arises from the *tamas* constituent. (18) The *sāttvika* beings reach superior spheres, (that is, heaven, etc.), the *rājasa* beings remain in the middle (that is, human spheres), and the *tāmasa*, who have inferior qualities and inclinations, go to lower spheres.

[It has been stated even in the Sāṁkhya Kārikā, that the person actuated by the *sattva* constituent obtains heaven, because he is religious-minded and performs good actions; and that the one actuated by the *tamas* constituent goes to lower spheres, because he performs unrighteous actions. (Sāṁ. Kā. 44). Similarly, the 18th stanza appears literally in the Anugītā in the description of the three constituents (Ma. Bhā. Aśva. 39, 10; and Manu. 12. 40). But, even if a man may attain heaven by *sāttvika* Action, yet, he does not thereby attain the highest goal of manhood, since heaven is not permanent. In order to obtain this highest goal of manhood, or Release, the man must, according to the Sāṁkhya doctrine, not only have a completely *sāttvika* nature, but also acquire the Knowledge that Prakṛti is a different thing from the Puruṣa. This is what the

§§ नान्यं गुणेभ्यः कर्तारं यदा द्रष्टानुपश्यति ।
गुणेभ्यश्च परं वेत्ति मद्भावं सोऽधिगच्छति ॥ १९ ॥
गुणानेतानतीत्य त्रीन् देही देहसमुद्भवान् ।
जन्ममृत्युजरादुःखैर्विमुक्तोऽमृतमश्नुते ॥ २० ॥

Sāṁkhyas call the "*triguṇātītāvasthā*", that is, 'the state of being beyond and untouched by the three constituents'; and although this state is beyond the *sattva*, *rajas*, and *tamas* constituents, yet, in as much as it is the highest peak of the *sāttvika* state, it is ordinarily included in the *sāttvika* class; and it is not looked upon as a fourth class, as has been stated by me at the end of Chapter VII at pp. 227-8 of the Gītā-Rahasya. Yet, as the Gītā does not accept the Sāṁkhya Dualism of Prakṛti and Puruṣa, it alters the form of the above Sāṁkhya doctrine by saying that he who realises the one Ātman-formed Parameśvara or Parabrahman, Who is beyond both Prakṛti and Puruṣa, to be the Qualityless Brahman, is to be called the '*triguṇātīta*' (one beyond the three constituents); and that is what is described in the next stanza—]

(19) When the '*draṣṭā*' (that is, the apathetic looker-on Puruṣa) realises that there is no other active agent except the constituents (of Prakṛti), and realises (the Principle) beyond (all) the (three) constituents, then he reaches My form. (20) The embodied man, transcending these three constituents, which are the cause of the birth of the Body, and becoming free from the pain of birth, death, and old age experiences immortality (that is, Release).

[In as much as that which is 'Māyā', according to Vedānta, is '*triguṇātmaka prakṛti*' (three-constituented Prakṛti) according to Sāṁkhya philosophy, becoming '*triguṇātīta*' means 'casting off Māyā or Illusion, and recognising the Parabrahman' (Gī. 2. 45); and this is what is known as 'the Brāhmī state' (Gī. 2. 72; 18. 53). Hearing these characteristics of the '*triguṇātīta*' according to the philosophy of the Absolute Self, Arjuna becomes inspired with the desire of learning more about it; and as

अर्जुन उवाच ।

§§ कैर्लिङ्गैस्त्रीन् गुणानेतानतीतो भवति प्रभो ।
किमाचारः कथं चैतांस्त्रीन् गुणानतिवर्तते ॥ २१ ॥

श्रीभगवानुवाच ।

प्रकाशं च प्रवृत्तिं च मोहमेव च पाण्डव ।
न द्वेष्टि संप्रवृत्तानि न निवृत्तानि काङ्क्षति ॥ २२ ॥

उदासीनवदासीनो गुणैर्यो न विचाल्यते ।
गुणा वर्तन्त इत्येव योऽवतिष्ठति नेङ्गते ॥ २३ ॥

समदुःखसुखः स्वस्थः समलोष्टाश्मकाञ्चनः ।
तुल्यप्रियाप्रियो धीरस्तुल्यनिन्दात्मसंस्तुतिः ॥ २४ ॥

he has in Chapter II asked a question about the Steady-in-Reason (*stithaprajña*), (2. 54), so also he now asks—]

Arjuna said:—(21) O Lord! by what characteristic may a man (be said to) go beyond the three constituents? What is the behaviour of that (*triguṇātīta*) person? and how does he go beyond these three constituents? (tell me that). The Blessed Lord said:—(22) O Pāṇḍava! that man, who, when Enlightenment, Progression, and Ignorance (that is, respectively the products or the effects of the *sattva*, *rajas* and *tamas* constituents) overcome him, does not hate them; and, who does not desire to possess them, if he does not obtain them; (23) who remains like an Apathetic towards the Fruit of Action; whom the (*sattva*, *rajas*, and *tamas*) constituents cannot unsettle; who remains steady, only realising that the constituents are performing (their respective) functions, and does not move (that is, does not experience any emotion); (24) to whom pain and happiness are the same; who has become '*svasthaḥ*' (that is, steady in his own place); to whom earth, stone, and gold are just the same; to whom what is beloved and what is disliked, disaparagement and praise, are just the same; who is always

मानापमानयोस्तुल्यस्तुल्यो मित्रारिपक्षयोः ।
सर्वारम्भपरित्यागी गुणातीतः स उच्यते ॥ २५ ॥

courageful ; (25) to whom, honour and dishonour are '*tulya*' (that is, alike), and a friend's party, or an enemy's side are both alike ; whose (desireful) activities have come to an end, (because he has realised that it is Prakṛti, which is doing everything), such a man is known as a '*triguṇātīta*' (that is, one who has transcended the three constituents—Trans.).

[This is the reply to the two questions : (i) what are the characteristics and (ii) the conduct of the person, who is a '*triguṇātīta*' (that is, who has transcended the three constituents) ? These characteristics are the same as those of the Steady-in-Reason (*sthitaprajña*) described in Chapter II, and of the Devotee (*bhaktimān*) described in Chapter XII. Nay, some of the adjectives (namely, "*sarvāraṁbha-parityāgī*", "*tulya-nindā-stutiḥ*", "*udāsinaḥ*" etc.) are the same in two of the three or even in all the three places. From this it becomes clear, that whichever path, out of the four paths mentioned in the last chapter (13. 24, 25), is followed, the characteristics and the conduct of the man, who has reached Perfection (*siddhi*), are the same in all paths. Nevertheless, as the doctrine firmly established in the 3rd, 4th, 5th and other chapters, namely, that 'no one can escape the performance of Desireless Action', remains unaffected throughout, one must remember that all these persons, whether called '*sthitaprajña*' or '*bhagavad-bhakta*' or '*triguṇātīta*', all belong to the Path of Karma-Yoga. The reader is referred to the explanation of the word '*sarvāraṁbha-parityāgī*' given in the commentary on Gī. 12. 19. Commentators subscribing to the Path of Renunciation imagine that these descriptions of the person, who has reached the State of Perfection (*siddhāvasthā*) are independent of each other; and maintain that the Gītā supports their own doctrine. But, I have explained at great length in Chapters XI and XII of the Gītā-Rahasya, that such an interpretation is inconsistent with the anterior and posterior contexts, and not the correct interpretation (See

§§ मां च योऽव्यभिचारेण भक्तियोगेन सेवते ।
स गुणान् समतीत्यैतान् ब्रह्मभूयाय कल्पते ॥ २६ ॥
ब्रह्मणो हि प्रतिष्ठाऽहममृतस्याव्ययस्य च ।
शाश्वतस्य च धर्मस्य सुखस्यैकान्तिकस्य च ॥ २७ ॥

p. 450 and pp. 519–520). To proceed: the Blessed Lord has thus answered the two questions of Arjuna. He now gives the answer to the question, how such persons transcend the three constituents—]

(26) And he, who serves Me with the *avyabhicāra* (that is, single-aimed) Yoga of Devotion, dedicating all Actions solely to Me, goes beyond these three constituents, and becomes capable of attaining the *brahmabhūtāvasthā* (that is, the state of being '*brahmabhūta*', or 'merged in the Brahman'—Trans.);

[A doubt is likely to arise about this stanza, namely, how the state of being a *triguṇātīta* (that is, of transcending the three constituents), which pertains to the Sāṁkhya path, can be obtained by the Bhakti-Yoga, which includes Action. So the Blessed Lord now says—]

(27) because, I am the ultimate seat of the immortal and inexhaustible Brahman, of the Perpetual Religion, and of the '*ekāntika*' (that is, the highest) intense bliss.

[This stanza means, that as soon as one has given up the Sāṁkhya Dualism, there remains only one Parameśvara; and the state of being a '*triguṇātīta*' is reached by worshipping that one Parameśvara. Nevertheless, when once it is admitted that there is only one Parameśvara, the Gītā does not have any dogmatic insistence about the means of attaining to Him (see Gī. 13. 24 and 25). It is true that the Gītā has stated that the Path of Devotion is the easiest path, and therefore, most acceptable to everybody. But, it has nowhere stated that the other paths ought not to be followed, That the Gītā supports only the Path of Devotion, or only the Path of Knowledge, or only the Path of Yoga are opinions, which are fathered on the Gītā by the supporters of those respective doctrines.

इति श्रीमद्भगवद्गीतासु उपनिषत्सु ब्रह्मविद्यायां योगशास्त्रे
श्रीकृष्णार्जुनसंवादे गुणत्रयविभागयोगो नाम
चतुर्दशोऽध्यायः ॥ १४ ॥

The doctrine really established by the Gītā is something quite different. Whether, after a person has acquired the Knowledge of the Parameśvara—whatever the means he may have employed for the purpose—he should or should not continue to perform the various Actions of worldly life, for universal welfare, is the chief question in the Gītā; and the reply to that question has already been given before in clear and unmistakable terms to the effect that the Karma-Yoga is the most superior.]

Thus ends the fourteenth Chapter entitled GUNATRAYA-VIBHAGA YOGA in the dialogue between Śrī Kṛṣṇa and Arjuna on the Yoga included in the Science of the Brahman (that is, on the Karma-Yoga) in the Upaniṣad sung (that is, told) by the Blessed Lord.

पञ्चदशोऽध्यायः

श्रीभगवानुवाच ।

§§ ऊर्ध्वमूलमधःशाखमश्वत्थं प्राहुरव्ययम् ।
छन्दांसि यस्य पर्णानि यस्तं वेद स वेदवित् ॥ १ ॥

CHAPTER XV.

[In Chapter XIII, the Blessed Lord has considered the philosophy of the Body and the Ātman together with the similar Sāṁkhya discrimination between Prakṛti and Puruṣa; and in Chapter XIV, after explaining the differences which arise between the natures of different persons, as a result of the three constituents, and how on that account different final states are obtained by the *sāttvika* and other persons, He has explained what is meant by being a *triguṇātīta*, what is the Brahmī state according to Vedānta philosophy, and in what way that state can be reached. It is true that all this exposition has been made in Sāṁkhya terminology; yet, it has been made without accepting the Sāṁkhya Dualism; and, as being the Spiritual and Empirical Knowledge of that one Parameśvara, of whom Prakṛti and Puruṣa are both manifestations. In addition to this description of the form of the Parameśvara, the Blessed Lord has shown in Chapter VIII the differences between the *adhiyajña*, the *adhyātma*, the *adhidaivata* etc.; and He has also stated, that there is only one Parameśvara, Who pervades everything, and that He is also the Ātman (*kṣetrajña*) within the Body (*kṣetra*). The Blessed Lord now explains why the expansion of the Universe created by the Parameśvara, or the Name-d and Form-ed diffusion-out of the Parameśvara, is sometimes described by comparing it to a tree or a forest; and He then describes the Puruṣottama-svarūpa, which is the most excellent of the forms of the Parameśvara.]

The Blessed Lord said:—(1) Having its root (one) above and branches (manifold) below, and (which is) *avyaya* (that is, which will never perish); of which the '*chandāṁsi*' (that is, the Vedas) are the leaves, that man, who has understood the *aśvattha*-tree, which is described thus, is the (true) *veda-vettā* (that is, one who has understood the Vedas—Trans.).

[The above description is of the 'Brahma-vṛkṣa' (the Brahmic-Tree), or of the *saṁsāra-vṛkṣa* (the tree of the Cosmos). The word '*saṁsāra*' is understood in the Marāthī vernacular as meaning 'remaining in the midst of one's wife and children, and performing one's daily duties.' But, this narrow meaning is not intended in the present context; and *saṁsāra* means "the entire world, which can be seen by the eyes, or the visible Cosmos", which is known in Sāṁkhya philosophy as "the diffusion of Prakṛti", and in Vedānta philosophy as "the spreading-out of the Māyā (Illusion) of the Blessed Lord"; and the same thing has been described in the Anugītā as the "Brahma-vṛkṣa and the Brahma-vana" (*brahmāraṇya*), (See Ma. Bhā. Aśva. 35 and 47). The idea or the simile that the colossal visible universe has sprung from the One and Imperceptible Parameśvara, just as a sky-high tree springs from a minute seed, is to be found not only in the Vedic religion, but also in other ancient religions; and in modern European languages, it is described as the Cosmic-Tree (*jagat-vṛkṣa*). There is a description in the Ṛg-Veda (1. 24. 7) of a tree in the sphere of Varuṇa, the root of the rays of which is uppermost, the rays themselves extending downwards (*nicīnāḥ*); and in the Viṣṇu-Sahasranāma (thousand names of Viṣṇu), '*varuṇovṛkṣaḥ*' (the Tree of Varuṇa) is mentioned as one of the thousand names of the Parameśvara. It would seem that the '*supalāśa-vṛkṣa*', sitting under which Yama and the ancestors eat and drink together (Ṛg. 10. 135. 1); or at the "top of which is a sweet *pippala*, on which two *suparṇa* birds live" (Ṛg. 1. 164. 22); or "that *pippala* tree, which is shaken by the *āyu* deities (the Marudgaṇas)", (Ṛg. 5. 54. 12), is the same as this tree; and the description in the Atharva-Veda, namely, "the *aśvattha* tree, being the home of the gods, is in the third *svarga* sphere (in the Varuṇa-loka)", (Atharva. 5. 4. 3 and 19. 39. 6), would also seem to be with reference to this tree. The etymology of the word '*aśvattha*' has been given in the Taittirīya

Brāhmaṇa (3. 8. 12. 2) as follows, namely:—"This tree is called '*aśvattha*', because Agni or Yajña-Prajāpati fell from the sphere of gods (*deva-loka*) during the *pitṛyāṇa*,* and taking the form of a horse (*aśva*), remained invisible in it for a year" (See Ma. Bhā. Anu. 85). And many etymologists are of opinion that this tree is called '*aśvattha*', (i. e., horse-stable), because the horses of the Sun take rest under it in the Yama-loka (sphere of Yama), during the night of the *pitṛyāṇa*. The etymology of that word, given in Vedānta philosophy as:—'*a*' means 'not'; '*śva*', means 'to-morrow'; and '*ttha*' means 'remaining' (*aśvattha* = not remaining to-morrow), has been imagined afterwards. It is true that the form of Māyā can be described as "not remaining to-morrow", since the form of Name-d and Form-ed Māyā is perishable, mutable, and changing every moment; but, it is clear from the adjective '*avyaya*' (that is, "that which never suffers '*vyaya*' or is imperishable"), which is used here, that that meaning is not intended. The *pippala* tree was originally known as the *aśvattha* tree; and the Brāhmic immortal *aśvattha* tree, which has been described in the Kaṭhopaniṣad in the following words, namely,

ūrdhvamūlo' vākśākha ete 'śvatthaḥ sanātanaḥ ।
tad eva śukraṁ tad brahma tad evāmṛtam ucyate ॥

is the same '*aśvattha*' tree; and the description in the Bhagavadgītā must have been adopted from the description in the Kaṭhopaniṣad, as will become quite clear from the similarity of the words "*ūrdhvamūlam adhaḥśākhaṁ*". As the Parameśvara is in heaven above and the *jagad-vṛkṣa* (the Cosmic-Tree), which has grown out of Him, has come down to the human sphere, that tree has been described as having its root, that is, the Parameśvara above, and having its innumerable branches in the shape of the diffused Cosmos spread downwards. But, as the descending shoots of the '*vaṭa*' tree (banian or fig-tree) also grow downwards from above, we come across another idea in ancient religious works that this Cosmic-Tree must be the '*vaṭa*' or

* For meaning of *pitṛyāṇa*, see Vol. I pp. 408–412—Trans.

the banian tree, and not the *pippala* tree. For instance, there is a description that the *aśvattha* (pippala) tree is the tree of the Sun, and that, "*nyagrodho varuṇo vṛkṣaḥ*", that is, "the '*nyagrodha*' (*nyag*=downwards; and *rodha*= growing) *vaṭa* tree is the tree of Varuṇa" (See Gobhilagṛhya 4. 7. 24). There is a description in the Mahābhārata (Ma. Bhā. Vana. 188–91), that Mārkaṇḍeya Ṛṣi saw the Parameśvara in the form of an infant on the branch of an *avyaya* (that is, imperishable, even at the time of general destruction), '*nyagrodha*' (that is, downwards-growing) *vaṭa-vṛkṣa* (fig-tree) at the time of the *pralaya* (Cosmic destruction). Also, the illustration which has been given in the Chāndogyopaniṣad for showing how this tremendous visible Cosmos has been created from the Imperceptible Parameśvara is also of the seed of the '*nyagrodha*' (Chān. 6. 12. 1). The Cosmic-Tree (*viśva-vṛkṣa*) has also been described in the Śvetāśvataropaniṣad (Śve. 6. 6); but, what that tree is has not been clearly stated there; and there is a description in the Muṇḍakopaniṣad that on this tree there are seated two birds, namely, the Sentient or Personal Self (*jīvātman*) and the Highest Self (*paramātman*); and that one of them is eating the *pippala* tree, that is, the fruits of the *pippala* tree, which is a description borrowed from the Ṛg-Veda. The third idea about the form of the Cosmic-Tree in addition to the two ideas, namely, of the *pippala* and the *vaṭa* trees, is of the '*auduṁbara*' tree; and this tree has been ascribed to Dattatreya in the Purāṇas. In short, the three ideas of the world created by the Māyā (Illusion) of the Parameśvara being either a *pippala* or a *vaṭa* or an *auduṁbara* tree are to be come across in ancient treatises. And, on this account, the three names, in terms of a tree, namely, "*nyagrodho 'dumbaro 'śvatthaḥ*" (See Ma. Bhā. Anu. 149. 101), have been mentioned in the Viṣṇu-Sahasranāma; and these three trees have been considered deities and worshippable in common usage. Besides, the Viṣṇu-Sahasranāma and the Gītā are both parts of the Mahābhārata; and if the Sahasranāma mentions the three different names, '*auduṁbara*' '*vaṭa*' (*nyagrodha*), and

अधश्चोर्ध्वं प्रसृतास्तस्य शाखा गुणप्रवृद्धा विषयप्रवालाः।
अधश्च मूलान्यनुसन्ततानि कर्मानुबन्धीनि मनुष्यलोके ॥ २ ॥

'*aśvattha*', then the word '*aśvatha*' used in the Gītā must be taken as meaning the *pippala* (*aśvattha*), and not the *audumbara* or the *vaṭa* trees: and that too is the original meaning of that word. The word '*chandāṁsi*' in the sentence: "of which the leaves are the *chandāṁsi*, that is, the Vedas" is understood as being derived from the root '*chad*'=to cover (see, Chān. 1. 4. 2); and the similarity of the Vedas with the leaves which cover the tree has thus been described; and it has been stated at the end that, as all this description is according to the Vedic tradition, one who knows all this is a '*vedavettā*'. This is the description according to the Vedas. The same tree is now described in another way, that is, according to Sāṁkhya philosophy—]

(2) Its branches, which are fed by the (three) *sattva* and other constituents, and from which, shoots of objects of sense (in the shape of sound, touch, colour, taste, and smell) have sprung, have spread out downwards as also upwards; and ultimately, its root-lings, in the shape of Actions, are also grown downwards to a great distance in the human sphere.

[According to Sāṁkhya philosophy, there are only two fundamental elements, namely, Prakṛti and Puruṣa; and I have explained in great detail at p. 243 of Chap. VIII of the Gītā-Rahasya how the 23 elements, namely, *mahat* and others, come into existence, and how the Cosmic-Tree is formed, when the three-constituented Prakṛti (Nature) spreads out its diffusion before the Puruṣa (Spirit). But, as Prakṛti is not independent, but is only a part of the Parameśvara, according to Vedānta philosophy, the doctrine of that philosophy is, that this diffusion of the three-constituented Prakṛti cannot be looked upon as an independent tree, but should be taken merely as the branches of an '*ūrdhvamūla*' (upwards-rooted) pippala tree. Consistently with this doctrine, there is now a slightly different description to the effect that the branches, fed by the three constituents, of the Vedic *adhaḥ-śākha* (downwards-branched) tree, described in

§§ न रूपमस्येह तथोपलभ्यते नान्तो न चादिर्न च संप्रतिष्ठा।
अश्वत्थमेनं सुविरूढमूलमसङ्गशस्त्रेण दृढेन छित्त्वा ॥ ३ ॥
ततः पदं तत्परिमार्गितव्यं यस्मिन्गता न निवर्तन्ति भूयः।
तमेव चाद्यं पुरुषं प्रपद्ये यतः प्रवृत्तिः प्रसृता पुराणी ॥ ४ ॥

the first stanza, have speard out not only 'downwards' but also 'upwards': and thus the thread of the doctrine of Causality (*karma-vipāka-prakriyā*) has ultimately been interwoven into the texture. In the description of the Brāhmic-Tree (*brahma-vṛkṣa*) given in the Anugītā, no attempt has been made to harmonise the Vedic and the Sāṁkhya descriptions; and the *brahma-vṛkṣa* described there is of only the 24 Elements of Sāṁkhya philosophy (See Ma. Bhā. Aśva. 35. 22, 23; and Gī. Ra. Ch. VIII, p. 243). But that has not been done in the Gita; and an attempt has been made in these two stanzas to harmonise the Vedic description of the Parameśvara, as a tree in the form of this visible world, with the Sāṁkhya description of the Cosmic Tree (*brahmāṇḍa-vṛkṣa*) or the diffusion-out of Prakṛti. In order to obtain Release, one must be get rid of this development of the three-constituented upwards-rooted tree; but this tree is so tremendous, that it is impossible to find out its origin. Therefore, the Blessed Lord now shows the way how this universe-comprehending tree can be destroyed, and how the Immortal Principle at the root of it can be Realised—]

(3) But, in this world, one cannot ascertain the form of it (as has been described above); nor does one find its end, or commencement or support; cutting this *aśvattha* (tree), of which the roots have gone incalculably deep, with a powerful sword in the shape of Non-Attachment, (4) one should, thereafter, (saying) "I am now going to that primordial Puruṣa (Spirit—Trans.) from Which (this) ancient (creative) Pravṛtti (Activity—Trans.) arose", find out that seat, having gone where, there is no return.

[The '*saṁsāra*' (extensive development) of the universe is the Name-d and Form-ed Karma (Action), and this

Karma is eternal; destroying this Karma means giving up the feeling of Attachment to it: it is not possible to destroy it in any other way; because, by its very nature, it is eternal and inexhaustible. All this subject-matter has been discussed in Chap. X of the Gītā-Rahasya at pp. 394 to 401, to which the reader is referred. The doctrine that Karma is eternal has been expressed in the words, "one cannot ascertain the true form of it; nor does one find its end, or commencement", in stanza 2; and it has been stated later on that Non-Attachment is the only means for destroying the Tree of Karma. Besides, a man gets results according to the conviction of his mind at the time of worshipping (Gī. 8. 6). Therefore, stanza 4 describes the conviction (*bhāvanā*) one should have in one's mind while this process of cutting this Karma-Tree is going on. This interpretation has to be put on this stanza, because, in the reading adopted in the Śāṁkarabhāṣya, namely, "*tam eva cādyaṁ puruśaṁ prapadye*", the verb "*prapadge*" in the first person singular present tense has been used; and some such word as '*iti*' has to be taken as implied. If one accepts the reading mentioned in the Rāmānuja-bhāṣya, namely, "*tam eva cādyaṁ puruṣaṁ prapadyed yataḥ pravṛttiḥ* etc.", in order to get over this difficulty, it is possible to translate the stanza as: "one should find out the Seat, having gone where, there is no return; (and) one should go and reach That, from which this Cosmos was created". But, as the root '*prapad*' is an *ātmanepada* root, it cannot get the *vidhyarthi* third person form '*prapadyet*'. '*prapadyet*' is a *parasmaipada* form, which is grammatically incorrect; and that is why this reading has not been adopted in the Śāṁkarabhāṣya; and that was the right thing to do. The word '*prapadye*' has been used in some hymns in the Chāndogyopaniṣad in this way, implying '*iti*' (See Chān. 8. 14. 1). I need not point out that though the verb '*prapadye*' is in the first person, it cannot be taken to refer to the speaker, namely, to Śrī Kṛṣṇa, Who is giving the advice. The Blessed Lord now explains what beneficial result is to be obtained by acting in this manner—]

निर्मानमोहा जितसङ्गदोषा अध्यात्मनित्या विनिवृत्तकामाः ।
द्वन्द्वैर्विमुक्ताः सुखदुःखसंज्ञैर्गच्छन्त्यमूढा पदमव्ययं तत् ॥ ५ ॥
न तद्भासयते सूर्यो न शशाङ्को न पावकः ।
यद्गत्वा न निवर्तन्ते तद्धाम परमं मम ॥ ६ ॥
§§ ममैवांशो जीवलोके जीवभूतः सनातनः ।
मनःषष्ठानीन्द्रियाणि प्रकृतिस्थानि कर्षति ॥ ७ ॥

(5) Who are free from vanity and ignorance, who have conquered the fault of being attached; who are steadily engrossed in Metaphysical Knowledge; who are desireless, and liberated from the pairs of Opposites like pain and happiness etc., such Scients go and reach this inexhaustible Seat. (6) That is my super-excellent Seat, having gone where, there is no return. It is not illuminated, whether by the Sun, or by the Moon, or by Fire.

[Out of these, the sixth stanza has appeared in the Śvetāśvatara (6. 14), the Muṇḍaka (2. 2. 10), and the Kaṭha (5. 15) Upaniṣads. The Sun, the Moon, and the stars all fall into the class of Name-d and Form-ed things; and, as the Parabrahman is beyond Name and Form, it is quite clear that the Sun, the Moon etc., all derive their light from the Parabrahman, and that nothing else is needed for illuminating the Parabrahman. The word "*parama-sthāna*" (super-excellent Seat) in the above stanza means the Parabrahman; and being merged in this Brahman is the state of Release known as the 'Brahma-nirvāṇa'. The exposition of the Metaphysical Knowledge of the Parabrahman, taking the simile of a tree, is now over. It now remains to describe the form of the Puruṣottama (*puruṣottama-svarūpa*); but the Blessed Lord first explains the evolution of the Jīva, and the appurtenant description of the form of the Jīva, which is suggested by His last words, "having gone where, there is no return".]

(7) My primordial *aṁśa* (particle—Trans.) takes the form of Jīva in the Jīva-world (in the land of Karma), and draws (to itself), the 'six' including the Mind, (that is to say, the Mind and the five (subtle) senses; this is known as

शरीरं यदवाप्नोति यच्चाप्युत्क्रामतीश्वरः ।
गृहीत्वैतानि संयाति वायुर्गन्धानिवाशयात् ॥ ८ ॥
श्रोत्रं चक्षुः स्पर्शनं च रसनं घ्राणमेव च ।
अधिष्ठाय मनश्चायं विषयानुपसेवते ॥ ९ ॥

the '*liṅga-śarīra*'). (8) When (this) Īśvara (that is, Jīva) acquires a (gross) Body, and when it leaves the (gross) Body, then, just as the wind takes away the smell from the shelter (of the smell, such as, the flowers etc.), so also does this (Jīva) take away with itself the above-mentioned (Mind and five subtle senses). (9) Making its abode in the ears, the eyes, the skin, the tongue, and the nose, as also in the Mind, this (Jīva) thereby enjoys the objects of sense.

[In the first of these three stanzas has been described the Subtle or *liṅga*-Body; and then there is a description of how this Subtle Body (*liṅga-śarīra*) enters the Gross Body, how it leaves the Gross Body, and how remaining in the Gross Body, it enjoys the objects of sense. According to Sāṁkhya philosophy, this Subtle Body is made up of the 18 elements starting from Mahān upto the five subtle *tanmātra*-s; and it is stated in the Vedānta-Sūtras (3. 1. 1), that the five subtle elements and *prāṇa* (life) are also included in it (see Ch. VIII of the Gītā-Rahasya, pp. 255 to 262). Similarly, it is stated in the Maitryūpaniṣad (9. 10), that the Subtle Body is made up of 18 elements. Therefore, one has to conclude that the words "Mind and five organs" point to the collection of the other elements, which are in the Subtle Body. The doctrine that the Jīvātman does not come into existence over and over again each time from the Parameśvara, but that it is an 'eternal *aṁśa*' or particle of the Parameśvara (Gī. 2. 24) has also been enunciated in the Vedānta-Sūtras by using the two words '*nitya*' and '*aṁśa*' (Ve. Sū. 2. 3. 17 and 43); and this fact fortifies the statement in Chap. XIII (13. 4), that the consideration of the Body and the Ātman has been adopted into the Gītā from the Brahma-Sūtras. (See Gi. Ra. App. pp. 756 to 758). The word '*aṁśa*' has to be taken as meaning "just as space

उत्क्रामन्तं स्थितं वापि भुञ्जानं वा गुणान्वितम् ।
विमूढा नानुपश्यन्ति पश्यन्ति ज्ञानचक्षुषः ॥ १० ॥
यतन्तो योगिनश्चैनं पश्यन्त्यात्मन्यवस्थितम् ।
यतन्तोऽप्यकृतात्मानो नैनं पश्यन्त्यचेतसः ॥ ११ ॥
§§ यदादित्यगतं तेजो जगद्भासयतेऽखिलम् ।
यच्चन्द्रमसि यच्चाग्नौ तत्तेजो विद्धि मामकम् ॥ १२ ॥
गामाविश्य च भूतानि धारयाम्यहमोजसा ।
पुष्णामि चौषधीः सर्वाः सोमो भूत्वा रसात्मकः ॥ १३ ॥

(*ākāśa*) is part of the receptacle (*ghaṭa*), which contains it" (i. e., *ghaṭākaśādivat aṁśa*); and not as an '*aṁśa*' (particle), which has been cut out, as has been shown in Chapter IX of the Gītā-Rahasya (pp. 338–339). When in this way, the Actions of taking birth in a Body, leaving the Body, and enjoying the objects of sense are going on—]

(10) Fools do not realise That, Which leaves the body, or remains, or enjoys (not by Itself, but) as a result of being united with the constituents. People, who see with the *jñāna-cakṣu* (that is, eyes of Knowledge—Trans.) realise (It). (11) Similarly, those Yogins who strive, realise this Ātman installed in themselves; but, those, whose Ātman (that is, Reason) is not evolved, such ignorant people cannot realise It even by striving.

[After stating in the 10th and 11th stanzas, that Self-Realisation results by following the path of Karma-Yoga, by means of the "eyes of Knowledge", the description of the evolution of the Jīva (the Personal Self) has been completed. Now, some further description is given here of the all-pervasiveness of the Ātman, by way of introduction, as had been done previously in Chapter VII (see, 7. 8–19); and then from stanza 16 onwards, a description of the form of the Purusottama is given.]

(12) That brilliance, which being in the Sun, illumines the whole world; that brilliance, which is in the Moon and in Fire, know that that brilliance is Mine. (13) Similarly, entering the earth, I maintain (all) created beings by My

अहं वैश्वानरो भूत्वा प्राणिनां देहमाश्रितः ।
प्राणापानसमायुक्तः पचाम्यन्नं चतुर्विधम् ॥ १४ ॥
सर्वस्य चाहं हृदि संनिविष्टो मत्तः स्मृतिर्ज्ञानमपोहनं च ।
वेदैश्च सर्वैरहमेव वेद्यो वेदान्तकृद्वेदविदेव चाहम् ॥ १५ ॥

brilliance; and, becoming the fluid Soma (Moon), I maintain all *auṣadhī* (that is, all vegetable life).

[The word '*soma*' has the double meaning '*soma-valli*', and also 'Moon'; and as the Moon is fluid, radiant (*aṁśumān*), and white, so also is the *soma-valli*, according to the Vedas; and both have been called "the Lord of Vegetables". But, having regard to the anterior and posterior contexts, the Moon is clearly meant here. After having stated in this stanza, that He is the brilliance in the Moon, it is stated in this very stanza that He is also the property of the Moon to maintain vegetation. There are descriptions elsewhere also, that, as the Moon is fluid, it contains this quality, which causes the growth of vegetation.]

(14) Becoming the Vaiśvānara-formed Fire, I inhabit the the bodies of created beings; and being united with the *prāṇa* and the *apāna* * breaths, I digest the four kinds of food (namely, that which is to be eaten, to be sucked, to be licked, and to be drunk). (15) Similarly, I am installed in the heart of everybody; and Memory, Knowledge and their *apohanaṁ* † (that is, destruction) are My doing; and I am also That, Which is to be known by means of all the Vedas; I am the author of Vedānta; and I am also the Knower of the Vedas.

[The 2nd part of this stanza has appeared in the Kaivalyopaniṣad (Kai. 2. 3); and the only difference of reading there is "*vedair anekaiḥ*" instead of "*vedaiś ca sarvaiḥ*". Therefore, the inferences drawn by some critics,

---

* For meaning of *prāṇa* and *apāna*, see p. 959 *supra*—Trans.

† "*apohanaṁ*" is also translated as "Reasoning faculty" (See Apte, *Practical Sanskrit-English Dictionary*, 1924, p. 109—Trans)

§§ द्वाविमौ पुरुषौ लोके क्षरश्चाक्षर एव च ।
क्षरः सर्वाणि भूतानि कूटस्थोऽक्षर उच्यते ॥ १६ ॥
उत्तमः पुरुषस्त्वन्यः परमात्मेत्युदाहृतः ।
यो लोकत्रयमाविश्य बिभर्त्यव्यय ईश्वरः ॥ १७ ॥
यस्मात्क्षरमतीतोऽहमक्षरादपि चोत्तमः ।
अतोऽस्मि लोके वेदे च प्रथितः पुरुषोत्तमः ॥ १८ ॥

on the assumption that the word 'Vedānta' was not in existence at the time of the Gītā, that either this stanza must be looked upon as an interpolation, or the word 'Vedānta' must be taken as meaning something else, are wrong. The word 'Vedānta' has appeared in the Muṇḍaka (3. 2. 6), and in the Śvetāśvatara (6. 22) Upaniṣads; and some of the hymns from the Śvetāśvatara are to be found literally in the Gītā. Now, the Blessed Lord gives a description of the characteristics of the Puruṣottama, based on the etymology of that word—]

(16) In this sphere, there are two Puruṣa-s (that is, entities—Trans.), namely, the '*kṣara*' and the '*akṣara*'. The '*kṣara*' means all (perishable) beings, and That (Imperceptible Principle in the form of Prakṛti), Which is '*kuṭastha*' (that is, at the root (*kuṭa*) of all these beings)-is called the '*akṣara*'. (17) But that super-excellent *puruṣa* (*puruṣottama*) is different (from both these). It is known as the 'Paramātman'. That inexhaustible Īśvara pervades the three spheres and maintains (the three spheres). (18) As I am beyond the '*kṣara*', and am (a Purusa), even more excellent (*uttama*) than the '*akṣara*', therefore, in ordinary parlance and also in Vedānta, I am known as the 'Purusottama' (*puruṣa* + *uttama*).

[The words '*kṣara*' (Mutable) and '*akṣara*' (Immutable) used in stanza 16 are respectively synonymous with the words '*vyakta*' (Perceptible) and '*avyakta*' (Imperceptible)—or the perceptible universe and the imperceptible Prakṛti—used in Sāṁkhya philosophy. Out of these, the meaning of '*kṣara*' as "a perceptible perishable substance made up of the five primordial Elements" is patent. But, as the adjective '*akṣara*' has several times before been also applied to the Parabrahman (See Gī. 8. 3; 8. 21; 11. 37 and 12. 3), one must bear in mind that the word '*akṣara*' used in defining the 'Puruṣottama' does not mean the '*akṣara* Parabrahman' but means the '*akṣara* Prakṛti' of Sāṁkhya philosophy. And in order that such a confusion should not arise, the word '*akṣara*' has been intentionally defined in stanza 16 as meaning the "*kūṭastha* Prakṛti" (See Gī. Ra. Chap. IX pp. 275 to 280). In short, the AKSARA BRAHMAN, which is beyond both the perceptible Cosmos and the imperceptible Prakṛti (see my commentary on Gī. 8. 20-22) is essentially the same as the PURUSOTTAMA, Who is beyond the '*kṣara*' (visible Cosmos) and the '*akṣara*' (Prakṛti). Both these are known as the PARAMATMAN; and it has been stated in Chapter XIII that this Paramātman resides in the Body in the form of the *kṣetrajña* (Gī. 13. 31). From this it follows, that the Original Principle arrived at by the Consideration of the Mutable and the Immutable, namely, the '*akṣara* Brahman' is also the ultimate resultant arrived at by the Consideration of the Body and the Ātman: or, in other words, that there is only one Puruṣottama both in the Body (*piṇḍa*) and in the Cosmos (*brahmāṇḍa*). It has also been stated that the same Principle is to be found in the Adhibhūta, the Adhiyajña, etc., or in the (symbolical) ancient *pippala* tree. That man, who has Realised this Unity in the Cosmos, and continues to Realise till death that "there is only one Ātman in all beings", attains the Parameśvara, while he is practising the Karma-Yoga: such is the ultimate summary of this exposition of Spiritual and Empirical Knowledge. It is not that one cannot attain Release solely by Devotion to the Parameśvara, and without performing Actions. But, that is not the import of the exposition of Spiritual and Empirical Knowledge in the Gītā; for it has been stated already in the beginning of Chap. VII of the Gītā, that the exposition of Spiritual and Empirical Knowledge in the Gītā has been made solely (i) for showing that one

§§ यो मामेवमसंमूढो जानाति पुरुषोत्तमम् ।
स सर्वविद्भजति मां सर्वभावेन भारत ॥ १९ ॥

इति गुह्यतमं शास्त्रमिदमुक्तं मयानघ ।
एतद्बुद्ध्वा बुद्धिमान्स्यात् कृतकृत्यश्च भारत ॥ २० ॥

इतिश्रीमद्भगवद्गीतासु उपनिषत्सु ब्रह्मविद्यायां योगशास्त्रे
श्रीकृष्णार्जुनसंवादे पुरुषोत्तमयोगोनाम
पंचदशोऽध्यायः ॥ १५ ॥

should perform all worldly affairs with a Desireless Mind, which has been purified, whether by Knowledge or by Devotion; and (ii) for showing how Release can thereby be obtained. To proceed: the Blessed Lord now explains what beneficial result is obtained by knowing this—]

(19) Who thus Realises, without being engrossed by Ignorance, that I am the Puruṣottama, he, O Bhārata! becomes omniscient, and worships Me in all ways. (20) O sinless Bhārata! I have thus explained this science, which is a mystery of mysteries; by understanding this, (a man) will become '*buddhimān*' (that is, *buddha* or a Knower) and '*kṛtakṛtya*' (that is, 'one who has done all that ought to be done'—Trans.)

[The word '*buddhimān*' here means '*buddha*' or a Jñāta (Scient, Knower); because, the words '*buddha*' and '*kṛtakṛtya*' have been used in the same sense in the Bhārata (Śān. 248. 11). The ordinary meaning of the word '*buddha*' namely, 'the Buddha incarnation' has not appeared anywhere in the Mahābhārata (See Gī. Ra. App. pp. 788-789)].

Thus ends the fifteenth chapter entitled PURUSOTTAMA-YOGA in the dialogue between Śrī Kṛṣṇa and Arjuna on the Yoga included in the Science of the Brahman (that is, on the Karma-Yoga) in the Upaniṣad sung (that is, told) by the Blessed Lord.

षोडशोऽध्यायः

श्रीभगवानुवाच

§§ अभयं सत्त्वसंशुद्धिर्ज्ञानयोगव्यवस्थितिः ।
दानं दमश्च यज्ञश्च स्वाध्यायस्तप आर्जवम् ॥ १ ॥

अहिंसा सत्यमक्रोधस्त्यागः शान्तिरपैशुनम् ।
दया भूतेष्वलोलुप्त्वं मार्दवं ह्रीरचापलम् ॥ २ ॥

CHAPTER XVI.

[The Puruṣottama-Yoga is the climax of the Knowledge of the Mutable and the Immutable; and really speaking, the exposition of Jñāna and Vijñāna, which was started in Chapter VII, for showing how a man can attain Release by Realising the Parameśvara, while he is following the Path of Karma-Yoga, should have been finished here, and the summary started. But in Chapter IX (9. 12), the Blessed Lord has merely briefly stated that the ungodly person does not realise His imperceptible and excellent form; and He, therefore, now commences this chapter for describing the character of such an ungodly person; and after explaining in the next chapter why such differences arise between men and men, the entire Gītā has been summarised in Chapter XVIII.]

The Blessed Lord said:—(1) Fearlessness, a pure and *sāttvika* temperament, '*jñāna-yoga-vyavasthiti*' [that is, the well-calculated proportionment of *jñāna (-mārga)* and (Karma-) Yoga], generosity, endurance, sacrifice, '*svādhyāya*' (that is, following the religion prescribed for one's status-in-life), performing austerities, straight-forwardness, (2) harmlessness, veracity, not getting angry, '*tyāga*' (that is, Renunciation of the Fruit of Action), tranquility, '*apaiśūnya*', (that is, overgrowing one's narrow-mindedness, and acquiring a generous frame of mind), kindness towards all beings, absence of avarice, mildness, feeling ashamed (of evil action), '*acāpala*' (that is, giving up useless activity),

तेजः क्षमा धृतिः शौचमद्रोहो नातिमानिता ।
भवन्ति सम्पदं दैवीमभिजातस्य भारत ॥ ३ ॥

(3) brilliance, forgiveness, steadiness, purity, non-hatred, not being over-dignified, these (qualities), O Bhārata! are acquired by persons, who are born to godlike endowments.

[These 26 qualities of godlike endowment are practically the same as the characteristics of '*jñāna*' given in Chapter XIII (Gī. 13. 7-11); and that is why '*ajñāna*' has been included in the ungodlike characteristics in the next stanza. It is not possible to define the meaning of each word in the list of these 26 qualities in such a way that it will be different from the definitions of the other words; and such was not even the intention of the Blessed Lord. For instance, Harmlessness (*ahiṁsā*) is divided by some persons into '*kāyika*' (bodily), '*vācika*' (vocal), and '*mānasika*' (mental); and, they look upon angrily hurting the mind of another person as a kind of harmfulness (*hiṁsā*). If one, similarly, considers the three aspects of 'purity', not being angry, not hating any one, and other qualities can be included in 'mental purity'. There is a detailed description of self-restraint, austerities, veracity, and avarice in Chapters 160 to 163 of the Śāntiparva of the Mahābhārata. Out of these, the word '*dama*' (self-restraint) has there been taken in an extensive meaning, so as to include forgiveness, steadiness, harmlessness, truth, pleading, and other several 25 or 30 qualities (Śān. 160); and in exposition of '*satya*', (veracity), that quality is said to include by itself the following thirteen qualities, namely, truthfulness, equability, self-restraint, absence of jealousy, forgiveness, shame, patience, want of envy, sacrifice (*yāga*), meditation (*dhyāna*), '*āryatā*' (desire to benefit others), endurance, and kindness; and these various words have also been defined in the same place. Grouping together many qualities in this way under one heading is a matter of learning: and if each quality is considered in this way, it will be necessary to write a treatise on every one quality. All these qualities have been enumerated in the above stanza with the sole intention that one should thereby get a complete

दम्भो दर्पोऽभिमानश्च क्रोधः पारुष्यमेव च ।
अज्ञानं चाभिजातस्य पार्थ सम्पदमासुरीम् ॥ ४ ॥
दैवी सम्पद्विमोक्षाय निबन्धायासुरी मता ।
मा शुचः सम्पदं दैवीमभिजातोऽसि पाण्डव ॥ ५ ॥

idea of the *sāttvika* form of godlike endowment; and that, if some meaning is not conveyed by any one word, it should be included in another word. I have interpreted the word "*jñānayoga-vyavasthiti*" in the above list, in accordance with Gī. 4. 41 and 42, so as to support the Karma-Yoga. The words *tyāga* and *dhṛti* have been defined by the Blessed Lord Himself in Chapter XVIII, to which the reader is reterred (18. 4 and 29). Having thus mentioned the qualities included in godlike endowment, the Blessed Lord now describes the opposite, namely, the ungodlike endowment—]

(4) Hypocrisy, pride, over-dignity, and also, O Pārtha! anger, '*pāruṣya*' (that is, cruelty), and ignorance are (acquired) by those who are born in the ungodlike endowment.

[In the 164th and 165th chapters of the Śāntiparva of the Mahābhārata, some of these qualities have been described; and in the end, it is also stated who is to be called a '*nṛśaṁsa*'. As '*ajñāna*' (Ignorance) has been described in this stanza as one of the characteristics of the ungodlike endowment, it is clear that '*jñāna*' (Knowledge) is a characteristic of the godlike endowment. Having in this way described the two kinds of natures one comes accross in the world—]

(5) (Out of these) The godlike endowment is considered (ultimately) productive of Release; and the ungodlike (endowment), productive of bondage. O Pāṇḍava! you are born in the godlike endowment! Do not lament!

[The Blessed Lord has thus shortly explained the fate of persons possessing these two kinds of nature. He now describes in detail the ungodlike (*āsuri*) person—]

द्वौ भूतसर्गौ लोकेऽस्मिन्दैव आसुर एव च ।
दैवो विस्तरशः प्रोक्त आसुरं पार्थ मे शृणु ॥ ६ ॥
प्रवृत्तिं च निवृत्तिं च जना न विदुरासुराः ।
न शौचं नापि चाचारो न सत्यं तेषु विद्यते ॥ ७ ॥
असत्यमप्रतिष्ठं ते जगदाहुरनीश्वरम् ।
अपरस्परसंभूतं किमन्यत्कामहैतुकम् ॥ ८ ॥

(6) In this world, two kinds of beings come into existence, (one) godlike, and (the other) ungodlike. (Out of these) I have described to you in detail the godlike (variety); (now) O Pārtha! I am describing to you the ungodlike (variety), to which listen.

[As the description given by the Blessed Lord in the previous chapters of how a Karma-Yogin should behave, what the Brāhmī state is, who is to be called a '*stithaprajña*' or a '*bhagavadbhakta*' or a '*triguṇātīta*', and what Jñāna is etc., as also the description of the godlike endowment given in the first three stanzas is the same as the description of a person having a '*daiva*' (godlike) nature, the Blessed Lord has here said that the '*daiva*' variety has been described by Him in detail before. There is some reference in Chapter IX to the ungodlike endowment (9. 11 and 12); but as that description is incomplete, it is completed in this chapter.]

(7) Ungodlike persons do not understand what *pravṛtti* is, (that is, what should be done), nor what *nivṛtti* is, (that is, what should not be done); and, purity, good behaviour, or veracity have no place in them. (8) These (ungodlike persons) say: "the whole world is unreal, '*apratiṣṭha*' (that is, without any support), '*anīśvara*' (that is, existing without a Parmeśvara) and '*a-paraspara-sambhūta*' (that is, not created one from the other); (in short) what can be the object of it, if not enjoying the objects of sense by human beings?"

[Although the meaning of this stanza is clear, there is a great deal of difference of opinion about the interpretation of the words used in it. In my opinion, this is a description of the opinions of atheists like Cārvāka and others, who disputed both the Vedānta and Sāṁkhya doctrines relating to the construction of the world; and therefore, the words used in these stanzas refer to a doctrine contrary to both the Sāṁkhya and the Vedānta doctrines. The Vedāntist looks upon this world as perishable, and looks for the Imperishable Reality—"*satyasya satyam*" (Bṛ. 2. 3. 6)—in it; and looks upon that Real Element as the fundamental support or '*pratiṣṭhā*'—"*brahmapuccaṁ pratiṣṭhā*" (Tai. 2. 5.)-of it. But the demoniac persons believe that this world is '*a-satyam*', that is, not containing '*satya*' (Reality); and that it is, therefore, '*a-pratiṣṭham*', that is, not having a *pratiṣṭhā* or support. But, a doubt may be raised that although the Imperceptible Parabrahman of the Vedāntists may in this way be not acceptable to demoniac persons, they may be accepting the Perceptible Iśvara, Who is worshipped in the Path of Devotion. Therefore, the third word '*anīśvara*' (*ana* + *Īśvara*) has been used in this stanza, in order to make it perfectly clear that such demoniac persons do not even accept the existence of an Īśvara in the world. When once the fundamental foundation of the world has thus been denied, one is also compelled to deny the explanation of the order of creation of the world contained (i) in the Upaniṣadic words: "*ātman ākāśaḥ saṁbhūtaḥ* ı *ākāśad vāyuḥ* ı *vāyor agniḥ* ı *agner āpaḥ* ı *adbhyaḥ pṛthivi* ı *pṛthivyā oṣadhayaḥ* ı *oṣadhibhyaḥ annam* ı *annāt puruṣaḥ* ı" * (Tai. 2. 1), as also (ii) in the Sāṁkhya doctrine, which looks upon Prakṛti and Puruṣa as two independent Fundamental Elements, and looks upon all perceptible objects as being the result of the mutual support (*annyonyāśraya*), that is, of the intermixture, of the *sattva*, *rajas*, and *tamas* constituents. Because, if this chain or order of succession is accepted, then, going backwards from all the objects in the visible world, one will have to admit

* This quotation, which has not been translated into Marathi by the author, means: "Ether (or space), is born from the Self; the air, from Ether (or space); Fire, from the Air; Water, from Fire; Earth, from Water; vegetables, from the Earth; food, from the vegetables; and man from food"—Trans.

that there is some origin for the world. Therefore, the demoniac people do not admit that the various objects in the world are *parasparasaṁbhūta*, that is, created one from the other in a particular order. When once such a belief about the creation of the world is fixed in the mind of any person, the human being itself becomes the most important object; and it necessarily follows, as a natural conclusion, that all the things in the world have been created only for satisfying the Desire (*kāma-vāsanā*) of that human being, and have no other purpose; and this meaning is conveyed by the words "*kimanyat kāmahaitukaṁ*" that is "what other object can it have except to satisfy Desire?", used at the end of the stanza, and also by the subsequent stanzas. Some commentators refer the words "*aparaspara-saṁbhūtaṁ*" to the words '*kimanyaṁ*'; and interpret the stanza in the following way, namely, "does one see anything, which is not created by the '*paraspara*' that is, the union between the male and the female? No; and if no such thing is to be found, then this world is certainly '*kāmahetuka*' that is, come into existence as a result of the Desire (*kāmecchā*) of the male for the female": and some others break up '*aparaspara*' in a very strange way as "*aparaś ca paraś ca* =*aparasparau*"; and they interpret the stanza as meaning:—"*aparaspara* itself means 'male and female'; and the whole world being created from these two, the mutual desire of the male for the female is the only object for it; and there is no other object". But, this interpretation is not straight-forward. '*aparaś ca paraś ca*' will give rise to the compound "*apara-para*"; and there will not be the consonant '*s*', (the *sakāra*), in the middle, as is to be found in '*aparaspara*'. Besides, if one considers the previous words '*a-satya*', '*a-pratiṣṭha*' etc., it is clear that '*a-paraspara-saṁbhūta*' must be a *nañ*-compound; and then one has to admit that the word '*paraspara-saṁbhūta*' means "the mutual creation (*anyonya-janana*) of *guṇa*-s (constituents) out of *guṇa*-s" described in Sāṁkhya philosophy (Gī. Ra. p. 213 to 215). The two words '*anyonya*' and '*paraspara*' are synonymous with each other; and both these words are used in Sāṁkhya philosophy in describing the mutual

एतां दृष्टिमवष्टभ्य नष्टात्मानोऽल्पबुद्धयः ।
प्रभवन्त्युग्रकर्माणः क्षयाय जगतोऽहिताः ॥ ९ ॥
काममाश्रित्य दुष्पूरं दम्भमानमदान्विताः ।
मोहाद् गृहीत्वाऽसद्ग्राहान् प्रवर्तन्तेऽशुचिव्रताः ॥ १० ॥
चिन्तामपरिमेयां च प्रलयान्तामुपाश्रिताः ।
कामोपभोगपरमा एतावदिति निश्चिताः ॥ ११ ॥

effects of the constituents on each other (see Ma. Bhā. Śān. 305; and Sāṁ. Kā. 12. 13). The Mādhvabhāṣya on the Gītā accepts this meaning; and in explaining how the various things in the world spring one out of the other, it gives the same stanza as in the Gītā, namely, "*annād bhavanti bhūtāni*" etc., that is, "rain-showers spring out of the sacrifice (because, the oblations thrown into the fire reach the Sun), food springs from rain-showers, and living beings spring from food" (Gī. 3. 14; Manu. 3–79). But, as the statement in the Taittirīya Upaniṣad is more ancient and more exhaustive than this, I have quoted it above as an authority. Nevertheless, the words '*a-paraspara-saṁbhūta*' in the Gītā are, in my opinion, indicative of the Sāṁkhya theory, rather than the Upaniṣadic theory, of the creation of the universe. The Blessed Lord now explains what effect this opinion of these demoniac persons, regarding the creation of the universe, has on their behaviour. The expression '*kāmahaituka*' used at the end of the above stanza is now made further clear.]

(9) Accepting this view, these feeble-minded, soul-less, and malevolent persons perform cruel Actions, and come into existence only to destroy the world; (10) and sheltering themselves behind '*kāma*' (that is, the desire to enjoy the objects of sense), which can never be fully satisfied, these (demonic persons), saturated with hypocrisy, false dignity, and pride, entertain (in their mind) false conclusions, (that is, unreasonable ideas), and engage in dirty Actions. (11) Similarly, being engrossed lifelong with immeasurable anxiety (to enjoy happiness), being steeped in enjoying the objects of sense, and firmly believing

आशापाशशतैर्बद्धाः कामक्रोधपरायणाः ।
ईहन्ते कामभोगार्थमन्यायेनार्थसंचयान् ॥ १२ ॥

इदमद्य मया लब्धमिमं प्राप्स्ये मनोरथम् ।
इदमस्तीदमपि मे भविष्यति पुनर्धनम् ॥ १३ ॥

असौ मया हतः शत्रुर्हनिष्ये चापरानपि ।
ईश्वरोऽहमहं भोगी सिद्धोऽहं बलवान् सुखी ॥ १४ ॥

आढ्योऽभिजनवानस्मि कोऽन्योऽस्ति सदृशो मया ।
यक्ष्ये दास्यामि मोदिष्य इत्यज्ञानविमोहिताः ॥ १५ ॥

अनेकचित्तविभ्रान्ता मोहजालसमावृताः ।
प्रसक्ताः कामभोगेषु पतन्ति नरकेऽशुचौ ॥ १६ ॥

आत्मसंभाविताः स्तब्धा धनमानमदान्विताः ।
यजन्ते नामयज्ञैस्ते दम्भेनाविधिपूर्वकम् ॥ १७ ॥

that that is everything; (12) being bound by hundreds of bonds of hope, and being subject to Desire and Anger, (these demoniac persons) entertain the ambition of amassing huge wealth, by injustice, in order to enjoy pleasure. (13) (They say:) "To-day I have acquired this; (to-morrow) I shall get that desire satisfied; this wealth is (with me); and again that (wealth) also will become mine; (14) I have killed this enemy; and I shall also destroy others; I am the Īśvara, I (alone) am the enjoyer; I am perfect, powerful and happy; (15) I am wealthy, born in a good family; who other is there like me? I will perform sacrifices; I will give in charity, I will enjoy myself". Being misguided, as a result of Ignorance, as described in these words; (16) being mis-directed by all sorts of ideas, being entangled in the cob-webs of mental confusion, and steeped in the enjoyment of the objects of sense, these (demoniac persons) fall into a filthy hell! (17) (Who are) Self-praisers, who behave over-bearingly, and who are full of the pride of wealth and dignity, these (demoniac persons), abandon Śāstric admonitions, and hypocritically perform only nominal

अहंकारं बलं दर्पं कामं क्रोधं च संश्रिताः ।
मामात्मपरदेहेषु प्रद्विषन्तोऽभ्यसूयकाः ॥ १८ ॥
तानहं द्विषतः क्रूरान् संसारेषु नराधमान् ।
क्षिपाम्यजस्रमशुभानासुरीष्वेव योनिषु ॥ १९ ॥
आसुरीं योनिमापन्ना मूढा जन्मनि जन्मनि ।
मामप्राप्यैव कौन्तेय ततो यान्त्यधमां गतिम् ॥ २० ॥
त्रिविधं नरकस्येदं द्वारं नाशनमात्मनः ।
कामः क्रोधस्तथा लोभस्तस्मादेतत्त्रयं त्यजेत् ॥ २१ ॥
एतैर्विमुक्तः कौन्तेय तमोद्वारैस्त्रिभिर्नरः ।
आचरत्यात्मनः श्रेयस्ततो याति परां गतिम् ॥ २२ ॥

sacrifices. (18) Who, being bloated up by egoism, power pride, desire, and anger, hate Me (the Parameśvara), Who am in their body as also in the bodies of others; (and who are) maligners, (19) (these) haters, who commit unholy Actions and (these) cruel, and lowest of men, are always thrown by Me into demoniac (that is, sinful) births in this worldly life. (20) O Kaunteya! these foolish persons, thus taking birth in demoniac wombs, never come to me, and ultimately reach the lowest of low conditions.

[The Blessed Lord has so far described demoniac persons and the state they reach. HE now explains how one can escape from it—]

(21) The gate-way of hell is of three folds, namely, Desire, Anger and Avarice; and it is destructive of one's Self; therefore, these three should be given up. (22) O Kaunteya! when a man has escaped from these *tamodvāra*-s (that is, doors of darkness—Trans.), he begins to act in a way which is beneficial to himself, and ultimately reaches the highest state.

[It is clear that when the three gates of hell are escaped from, a good state must be obtained. But, it has not so far been stated by what kind of conduct this can be done Therefore, the Blessed Lord now explains what that path is—]

यः शास्त्रविधिमुत्सृज्य वर्तते कामकारतः ।
न स सिद्धिमवाप्नोति न सुखं न परां गतिम् ॥ २३ ॥

तस्माच्छास्त्रं प्रमाणं ते कार्याकार्यव्यवस्थितौ ।
ज्ञात्वा शास्त्रविधानोक्तं कर्म कर्तुमिहार्हसि ॥ २४ ॥

इतिश्रीमद्भगवद्गीतासु उपनिषत्सु ब्रह्मविद्यायां योगशास्त्रे श्रीकृष्णार्जुनसंवादे दैवासुरसंपद्विभागयोगोनाम षोडशोऽध्यायः ॥ १६ ॥

(23) (He) who has given up Śāstric directions, and begun to do what he likes, does not attain Perfection; nor does he reach an excellent state. (24) '*tasmāt*' (that is, therefore—Trans.), in order to decide the "*kāryākārya-vyavasthitī*", (that is, what ought to be done and what ought not to be done), you must accept the Scriptures (Śāstras) as authoritative; and after finding out what has been directed by the Scriptures, it is proper that you should act accordingly.

[The word '*kāryakārya-vyavasthitī*' used in this stanza clearly shows that the Gītā has been told, keeping before the mind the idea of Ethics; and it has been shown clearly in the Gītā-Rahasya (pp. 66 to 69) that this is known as the Karma-Yoga-Śāstra.]

Thus ends the sixteenth chapter entitled DAIVASURA-SAMPAD-VIBHAGA YOGA, in the dialogue between Śrī Kṛṣṇa and Arjuna, on the Yoga included in the Science of the Brahman (that is on the Karma-Yoga) in the Upaniṣad sung (that is, told) by the Blessed Lord.

सप्तदशोऽध्यायः

अर्जुन उवाच

ये शास्त्रविधिमुत्सृज्य यजन्ते श्रद्धयान्विताः ।
तेषां निष्ठा तु का कृष्ण सत्त्वमाहो रजस्तमः ॥ १ ॥

CHAPTER XVII.

[When a description has thus been made of persons, who maintain and protect the world by following the Karma-Yoga-Śāstra, as also of those, who, on the other hand, destroy the world, the question why these differences arise between men and men, naturally springs up. The ordinary answer to that question, namely, "*prakṛtyā niyatāḥ svayā*" that is, "that is according to everybody's nature", has been given in Chapter VII above (7.20). But, as a full exposition about the three constituents namely, *sattva*, *rajas*, and *tamas*, has not been made in that chapter, it was not possible to give there a detailed explanation of these differences, which arise from Prakṛti. Therefore, these three constituents have been described in Chapter XIV; and after explaining in this Chapter how diverse kinds of faith etc., arise on account of these constituents, the entire subject-matter of Jñāna and Vijñāna has been concluded in this chapter. In the same way, the reason for the differences in the Path of Devotion, mentioned in the Chapter IX (see 9.23 and 24), becomes clear by the explanation given in this chapter. Arjuna first asks—]

Arjuna said :—(1) O Kṛṣṇa! those who, notwithstanding that they are filled with Faith, yet perform sacrifice without observing the Scriptural methods, what should their '*niṣṭhā*' (that is, mental condition) be supposed to be? Is it *sāttvika*, or *rājasa*, or *tāmasa*?

[This is the doubt raised by Arjuna on the admonition given at the end of the last chapter that Scriptural methods should be followed. It sometimes happens that even having faith in the Scriptures, a man commits mistakes as a result of ignorance. For instance, instead of

श्रीभगवानुवाच
त्रिविधा भवति श्रद्धा देहिनां सा स्वभावजा।
सात्त्विकी राजसी चैव तामसी चेति तां शृणु ॥ २ ॥
सत्त्वानुरूपा सर्वस्य श्रद्धा भवति भारत।
श्रद्धामयोऽयं पुरुषो यो यच्छ्रद्धः स एव सः ॥ ३ ॥

worshipping the All-pervading Parameśvara, as has been enjoined by the Śāstras, he may run after deities (Gī. 9. 23). And the question of Arjuna is, what is the '*niṣṭhā*' or state, or mental condition of such a person. This question does not relate to persons, who despise the Śāstras and religion for want of faith in them, that is, to demoniac persons. Nevertheless, wherever there is occasion, the Actions of these people also have been described in this Chapter.]

The Blessed Lord said:—(2) This faith of living beings is naturally of three kinds, *sāttvika*, *rājasa*, and *tāmasa*. Hear (how) that (is so). (3) The faith of every person, O Bhārata! conforms to his '*sattva*' (that is, to his inherent nature). Man is imbued with faith. In whatever matter (he puts) his faith, so is he (formed).

[The word '*sattva*' in stanza 2* means 'natural temperament', 'Reason' or 'conscience'. This word '*sattva*' has been used in that sense in the Kaṭhopaniṣad (Katha. 6. 7); and in the Śāṁkarabhāṣya on the Vedānta-Sūtras also, the term '*sattva-kṣetrajña*' has been used in stead of *kṣetra-kṣetrajña*' (Ve.-Sū. Śāṁ. Bhā. 1. 2. 12). In short, the word '*svabhāva*' in stanza 2, and the word '*sattva*' in stanza 3 are synonymous; because, the doctrine that nature is nothing but Prakṛti, and that Reason, and later on, Conscience, spring from Prakṛti, is accepted both in Vedānta and in Sāṁkhya philosophy. The principle, "in whatever matter (he puts) his faith, so is he (formed)" is only a repetition of of the theories, "those who worship deiti s, go to the deities" etc., which have appeared before (Gī. 7. 20, 23; 9. 25); and I have discussed this subject in Chapter XIII of the Gītā-Rahasya (see Gītā. Ra. pp. 589 to 598). When it is

* This ought to be stanza 3 and not stanza 2—Trans.

यजन्ते सात्त्विका देवान् यक्षरक्षांसि राजसाः ।
प्रेतान्भूतगणांश्चान्ये यजन्ते तामसा जनाः ॥ ४ ॥

admitted that every person reaps a reward according to his desires, and that having or not having a particular inclination or desire depends on his Prakṛti (that is, nature), the question, how this nature should be improved, naturally arises. The answer to this question is: as the Ātman (Self) is independent, this bodily temperament can gradually be changed by practice and by renunciation; and this subject has been discussed in Chapter X of the Gītā-Rahasya, to which the reader is referred. (see pp. 382 to 390). All that has to be considered for the moment is why and how these differences in faith arise. Therefore, after having stated that the faith changes according to a man's nature, the Blessed Lord now explains (i) what three kinds of faith are to be found in different men as a result of Prakṛti itself being composed of the three constituents *sattva*, *rajas* and *tamas*, and (ii) what the results of this difference are.]

(4) Persons, who are '*sāttvika*', that is, in whom the *sattva* (benevolent) constituent predominates, sacrifice to the deities; the *rājasa* (passionate), to gnomes (*yakṣa*-s) and to demons (*rākṣasa*-s); and other remaining *tāmasa* (ignorant persons) offer sacrifice to dead bodies and ghosts (*bhūta*-s).

[The Blessed Lord has now explained the three classes into which men having faith in the Śāstras fall as a result of the difference of their Prakṛti, and He has also explained their characteristics. HE now describes the class of the lustful and hypocritical persons, who are such, as a result of not having faith in the Śāstras. It is clear that these persons are not *sāttvika*; but one cannot on that account simply call them '*tāmasa*'; because, although their actions are contrary to the Śāstras, yet they have a tendency to perform these Actions; and, tendency to Action is a feature of the *rajas* constituent. In short, the adjectives *sāttvika*, *rājasa*, or *tāmasa* cannot be simply applied to such people. That is why men are divided into the two classes '*daivī*'

अशास्त्रविहितं घोरं तप्यन्ते ये तपो जनाः ।
दम्भाहंकारसंयुक्ताः कामरागबलान्विताः ॥ ५ ॥
कर्षयन्तः शरीरस्थं भूतग्राममचेतसः ।
मां चैवान्तःशरीरस्थं तान्विद्ध्यासुरनिश्चयान् ॥ ६ ॥
आहारस्त्वपि सर्वस्य त्रिविधो भवति प्रियः ।
यज्ञस्तपस्तथा दानं तेषां भेदमिमं शृणु ॥ ७ ॥

(godlike) and '*āsurī*' (demoniac); and these evil-minded persons are put into the '*āsurī*' class; the same idea has been conveyed in the two following stanzas.]

(5) But, those persons who, being imbued with hypocrisy and egoism, perform intense austerities contrary to the Śāstras, on the strength of Desire and Attachment, (6) and oppress not only the group of the five primordial elements etc., in their body, but also Me, Who saturate that body, such undiscriminating (persons) may be understood to possess a demoniac temperament.

[All the questions of Arjuna have now been answered. The faith of different persons may be *sāttvika*, *rājasa* or *tāmasa* according to their nature; and there being a consequent difference in their Actions, they will attain various goals according to their respective Actions; but, from that alone it cannot be said that a particular person will fall into the demoniac class. It is the duty of everybody to gradually improve his nature by making use of Freedom of Will (*ātmasvātaṁtrya*) and acting according to the Scriptures (*śāstra*-s). These stanzas mean that those, who, instead of doing so, pride themselves on their own evil inherent nature, and flout the Śāstras are to be called '*āsurī*' (demoniac). The Blessed Lord now explains the different kinds of food (*āhāra*), sacrifice (*yajña*), religious austerity (*tapas*) and charitable gifts (*dāna*), which are the result of the *sattva*, *rajas* and *tamas* constituents of Prakṛti, just as there are different kinds of Faith; and He also explains how in consequence of diversity in nature, there is also diversity in Actions—]

(7) Now, the food which each person likes is also divided into three classes; and the same is the case with Sacrifice,

आयुःसत्त्वबलारोग्यसुखप्रीतिविवर्धनाः ।
रस्याः स्निग्धाः स्थिरा हृद्या आहाराः सात्त्विकप्रियाः ॥ ८ ॥
कट्वम्ललवणात्युष्णतीक्ष्णरूक्षविदाहिनः ।
आहारा राजसस्येष्टा दुःखशोकामयप्रदाः ॥ ९ ॥
यातयामं गतरसं पूति पर्युषितं च यत् ।
उच्छिष्टमपि चामेध्यं भोजनं तामसप्रियम् ॥ १० ॥

Austerity and Knowledge. I will explain to you this difference, to which listen. (8) The food liked by a *sāttvika* person is such as increases life, the *sāttvika* temperament, strength, health, happiness, and love; it is savoury, viscous, and such as will be absorbed into the body, and will remain in it for a long time, and is enjoyable to the mind. (9) The food liked by the *rājasa* persons is '*kaṭu*' (that is, hot), pungent, saltish, very warm, irritating, dry, exciting, and such as creates pain, lamentation, and disease.

[In Sanskrit '*kaṭu*' means 'burning'; and '*tikta*' means 'bitter'; and accordingly, in Sanskrit medical treatises, mustard is described as '*kaṭu*', and lemon or lime as *tikta* (See Vāgbhaṭa-Sūtra, Ch. 10). The words '*kaḍu*' and '*tikhaṭ*' in the Marathi language are corruptions of the words '*kaṭu*' and '*tikta*' in Sanskrit; but the meanings of those two words in the Marathi language have got interchanged. The Sanskrit and Marathi meanings of the word '*aparokṣa*' are similarly interchanged; and this thing is important from the point of view of etymology.]

(10) A *tāmasa* person likes food, which has remained standing, (that is, which has become cold), is tasteless, bad-smelling, which has become stale (for one day), has been tasted (by other people), and is also impure.

[Not only does the *sāttvika* person like *sāttvika* food; the *rājasa* person, *rājasa* food; and the *tāmasa* person, *tāmasa* food; but conversely, by eating *sāttvika* food, the inherent nature of a person also gradually becomes pure or *sāttvika*, as has been stated in the Upaniṣads: cf. "*āhāraśuddhau sattva śuddhiḥ*" (Chān. 7. 26. 2). Because, as the Mind and

§§ अफलाकाङ्क्षिभिर्यज्ञो विधिदृष्टो य इज्यते ।
यष्टव्यमेवेति मनः समाधाय स सात्त्विकः ॥ ११ ॥
अभिसंधाय तु फलं दम्भार्थमपि चैव यत् ।
इज्यते भरतश्रेष्ठ तं यज्ञं विद्धि राजसम् ॥ १२ ॥
विधिहीनमसृष्टान्नं मन्त्रहीनमदक्षिणम् ।
श्रद्धाविरहितं यज्ञं तामसं परिचक्षते ॥ १३ ॥

the Reason are only evolutes of Prakṛti, if the food is *sāttvika*, the inherent nature also becomes *sāttvika* in consequence. These are the different kinds of food. The Blessed Lord now explains how there are three different kinds of sacrifices.]

(11) The Sacrifice performed without entertaining any desire for the fruit, and looking upon the performance of Sacrifice as a duty, and with a peaceful mind, and according to the Sāstric rites, is *sāttvika*; (12) but the Sacrifice performed with a desire for fruit, or only hypocritically (that is, for making an exhibition of one's riches), know that, such a sacrifice, O Bharata-śreṣṭha! is a *rājasa* sacrifice; (13) and, the Sacrifice performed without Scriptural ceremony, without the sacrifice of food, without the recitation of hymns without giving charitable gifts, and without faith, such a sacrifice is *tāmasa*.

[Just as there are three kinds of food and sacrifice, so also are there three kinds of austerities. But austerities have first been divided into '*kāyika*' (bodily), '*vācika*' (vocal), and '*mānasika*' (mental); and then the three sub-divisions of each of these as a result of the *sattva, rajas* and *tamas* constituents have been explained. The word '*tapa*' in this place is not to be taken in the narrow meaning of 'going into a forest and mortifying the body according to the Pātañjala-Yoga', but means 'Yajña, Yāga, study of the Vedas, or whatever anybody's duty may be according to that one of the four classes to which he belongs; *e. g.* fighting for the Ksatriya, trade for the Vaiṣya, etc., which is the austerity (*tapa*) or penance for that particular person'. This comprehensive meaning of the word '*tapa*' (religious austerities

§§ देवद्विजगुरुप्राज्ञपूजनं शौचमार्जवम् ।
ब्रह्मचर्यमहिंसा च शारीरं तप उच्यते ॥ १४ ॥

अनुद्वेगकरं वाक्यं सत्यं प्रियहितं च यत् ।
स्वाध्यायाभ्यसनं चैव वाङ्मयं तप उच्यते ॥ १५ ॥

मनःप्रसादः सौम्यत्वं मौनमात्मविनिग्रहः ।
भावसंशुद्धिरित्येतत्तपो मानसमुच्यते ॥ १६ ॥

or Penance), given by Manu (Manu. 11. 236) is intended in the following stanzas of the Gītā.]

(14) Worshipping deities and Brahmins, as also those who are learned; cleanliness, straight-forwardness, celibacy, and harmlessness is called '*śārīra*' (that is, *kāyika* or bodily) penance. (15) Speech, which does not cause pain (to the mind), which is true, likeable, and beneficial and also, the practice of '*svādhyāya*' (that is, one's own duties) is called '*vāṅgmaya*' (*vācika* or vocal) penance. (16) Keeping one's mind pleased, gentleness, and maintaining '*mauna*' (that is, silence, like a *muni*), mental control, and pure feelings is called '*mānasa*' (mental) penance.

[The words, *satya*, *priya*, and *hita* used in stanza 15 seem to refer to the dictum of Manu: "*satyaṁ brūyāt priyaṁ brūyān na brūyāt satyam apriyaṁ । priyaṁ ca nānṛtaṁ brūyād eṣa dharmaḥ sanātanaḥ* ॥" (Manu. 4. 138), that is, "one should speak what is true; one should speak what is sweet; one should not speak what is true, if it is not sweet; * this is the ancient religion". But Vidura has told Duryodhana in the Mahābhārata itself (Sabhā. 63. 17) that "*apriyasya ca pathyasya vaktā śrota hi durlabhaḥ*" (that is, "of what is disagreeable and beneficial, the speaker as also the hearer are hard to find"—Trans.). Each of the

* The words "*priyaṁ ca nānṛtaṁ brūyāt*" in the above quotation, which mean: "nor what is sweet, if it is false" are not included in the author's Marathi translation of the Sanskrit quotation—Trans.

§§ श्रद्धया परया तप्तं तपस्तत्त्रिविधं नरैः ।
अफलाकाङ्क्षिभिर्युक्तैः सात्त्विकं परिचक्षते ॥ १७ ॥
सत्कारमानपूजार्थं तपो दम्भेन चैव यत् ।
क्रियते तदिह प्रोक्तं राजसं चलमध्रुवम् ॥ १८ ॥
मूढग्राहेणात्मनो यत् पीडया क्रियते तपः ।
परस्योत्सादनार्थं वा तत्तामसमुदाहृतम् ॥ १९ ॥
§§ दातव्यमिति यद्दानं दीयतेऽनुपकारिणे ।
देशे काले च पात्रे च तद्दानं सात्त्विकं स्मृतम् ॥ २० ॥
यत्तु प्रत्युपकारार्थं फलमुद्दिश्य वा पुनः ।
दीयते च परिक्लिष्टं तद्दानं राजसं स्मृतम् ॥ २१ ॥

three divisions of Penance, namely, *kāyika*, *vācika* and *mānasika* falls into the following sub-divisions—]

(17) If each of these three kinds of religious austerities (or penance) is performed without entertaining the Desire for Fruit, and with excellent Devotion, and with a mind steeped in Yoga, it is called *sāttvika*; (18) and when the austerities are performed with the intention that one should be appreciated, or held in dignity, or worshipped, or hypocritically, then those unsteady and fleeting austerities are here (that is, in the Scriptures) known as *rājasa*; (19) those austerities, which, being self-injurious, are performed out of a foolish persistence, or with the idea of harming others [by incantations for propitiation (*jāraṇa*), or causing death (*māraṇa*) etc.], are called *tāmasa*.

[Having thus described the divisions of Penance, the Blessed Lord now explains the three divisions of charitable gifts (*dāna*).]

(20) That gift, which is made with the conviction that it is one's duty to make the gift, after considering (the propriety of) the place, the time, and the (receiving) person, and to a person, who has not obliged the giver, is called *sāttvika*; (21) but the gift, which is made unwillingly, as a return for some obligation (received), or with the idea of getting

अदेशकाले यद्दानमपात्रेभ्यश्च दीयते ।
असत्कृतमवज्ञातं तत्तामसमुदाहृतम् ॥ २२ ॥

some reward for it in future, is called '*rājasa*'; (22) and that gift, which is made at an improper place, or at an improper time, or to an improper person, unappreciatingly, or disrespectfully is called *tāmasa*.

[The three divisions into which Knowledge, Action, Doers, Reason, Perseverance, and Happiness fall, similar to the divisions of food, sacrifice, penance, and gifts, are explained in the next chapter (Gī. 18.20–39). The differentiation between the constituents given in this chapter is here over. The Blessed Lord now refers to the definition of the Brahman (the *brahma-nirdeśa*); and proves the superiority and adoptability of *sāttvika* Action mentioned above. Because, a doubt is likely to be raised to the exposition made above, that, whether an Action is *sāttvika*, *rājasa*, or *tāmasa*, it is still faulty and pain-causing; that, therefore, it is not possible to attain to the Brahman, unless all these Actions are given up; and that, if this is true, there is no sense in pointing out the difference, that a particular act is *sāttvika*, and a particular act *rājasa*. The answer of the Gītā to this objection is that these divisions of Action into *sāttvika*, *rājasa*, and *tāmasa* are not inconsistent with the Parabrahman. The canon (*saṁkalpa*), which defines the Brahman, includes *sāttvika* Actions or good Actions; and therefore, it is proved beyond doubt that these Actions are not metaphysically eschewable (see Gī. Ra. p. 338). All the Knowledge acquired by man regarding the nature of the Parabrahman is concentrated in the definition composed of the three words "Om, Tat, Sat". Out of these 'Om' is the *akṣara-brahman*, and that has been described in different ways in different Upaniṣads (Praśna. 5; Kaṭha. 2. 15–17; Tai. 1. 8; Chān. 1. 1; Maitryu. 6. 3, 4; Māṇḍukya. 1. 12). And as this Brahman in the form of a consonant (*varṇākṣara-rūpī*) was the only thing in existence at the commencement of the universe, all Action (or ritual) commences with that letter. 'Tat' = 'that'

§§ ॐ तत्सदिति निर्देशो ब्रह्मणस्त्रिविधः स्मृतः ।
ब्राह्मणास्तेन वेदाश्च यज्ञाश्च विहिताः पुरा ॥ २३ ॥

means 'something beyond the ordinary Action', that is to say, the *sāttvika* Action performed desirelessly, and having given up the Hope of Fruit; and 'Sat' means pure Actions, performed according to Scriptural directions, notwithstanding that they may have been performed with a Hope for Fruit. Such is the meaning of this canon; and if this meaning is accepted, not only *sāttvika* Actions, performed with a desireless frame of mind, but also good Actions performed according to Scriptural directions are included in the ordinary and commonly accepted definition of the Parabrahman. Therefore, it is wrong to say that these Actions are eschewable. Besides the '*tat*' and '*sat*' Actions, there remain the '*asat*' Actions, that is, evil Actions. But, as such Actions are harmful both in this life and the next, they are not included in the definition, as has been stated in the last stanza. The Blessed Lord says—]

(23) The Parabrahman is defined (in the Scriptures) in three ways, as "Om-Tat-Sat". By this (very) definition* were the Brahmins, the Vedas, and the Sacrifices created formerly.

[It has been stated before that in the beginning of the world, the first Brahmin in the form of Brahmadeva, the gods, and Yajnas were first created (Gī. 3. 10). But, the form of that Parabrahman, from which all this has been created, is contained in the three words 'Om', 'Tat' and 'Sat'. Therefore, this stanza means that the canon 'Om-Tat-Sat' is the root of the entire universe. The Blessed Lord now gives the respective connotations of the three words 'Om', 'Tat', and 'Sat' in this canon, from the Karma-Yogic point of view—]

---

* It is difficult to understand how anything can be created by a definition (*nirdeśa*). Śrīdhara explains the word 'this' as meaning 'Parabrahman'.—Trans.

§§ तस्मादोमित्युदाहृत्य यज्ञदानतपःक्रियाः ।
प्रवर्तन्ते विधानोक्ताः सततं ब्रह्मवादिनाम् ॥ २४ ॥

तदित्यनभिसंधाय फलं यज्ञतपःक्रियाः ।
दानक्रियाश्च विविधाः क्रियन्ते मोक्षकाङ्क्षिभिः ॥ २५ ॥

सद्भावे साधुभावे च सदित्येतत्प्रयुज्यते ।
प्रशस्ते कर्मणि तथा सच्छब्दः पार्थ युज्यते ॥ २६ ॥

यज्ञे तपसि दाने च स्थितिः सदिति चोच्यते ।
कर्म चैव तदर्थीयं सदित्येवाभिधीयते ॥ २७ ॥

(24) "*tasmāt*" (that is, 'since the world starts with this canon'), Brahmists* (*brahma-vādinaḥ*) start their Sacrifice, Charity, Penance, and all other Scriptural Actions first uttering the word 'OM'. (25) By using the word 'TAT', people perform Actions, such as, Sacrifice, Penance, Charity etc., without entertaining the Hope of Fruit, in order to obtain Release. (26) Reality (*astitva*) and saintliness (*sādhutva*) are signified by the use of the word 'SAT'; and O Pārtha! the word 'SAT' is also applied to proper (that is, good) Actions. (27) Fixity (that is, having an unswerving faith in Sacrifices, Austerities, and Charity) is also known as 'SAT'; and the Action performed for that purpose is also known as 'SAT'.

[Sacrifices, Austerities, and Charity are the important religious Actions; and the Actions performed for this purpose have been given the generic name '*yājñārtha-karma*' (Action for the purpose of a Sacrifice) by the Mīmāmsakas. Though a man may entertain the Hope for Fruit in performing these Actions, yet, as that Hope is consistent with Morality, these Actions fall into the category of 'Sat'; and all Desireless Action falls into the class of 'Tat'='that', that is to say, 'that which is beyond this'. As both these kinds of Actions are thus included

* This word 'Brahmist' has been coined by me on the analogy of 'theist', 'atheist' etc.,—Trans.

§§ अश्रद्धया हुतं दत्तं तपस्तप्तं कृतं च यत् ।
असदित्युच्यते पार्थ न च तत्प्रेत्य नो इह ॥ २८ ॥

in the Brahma-saṁkalpa "Om-Tat-Sat", which is uttered at the commencement of every ritualistic Action, both of them must be said to be consistent with the attainment to the Brahman (see Gī. Ra. p. 338). Now there remains only the '*asat*'. The Blessed now explains what the result of that Action is—]

(28) That oblation, which is thrown into the fire, or that (gift), which is given, or that penance, which is performed, or any whatsoever (Action), which is done, without faith is called '*asat*'. O Pārtha! that (Action) is not beneficial whether after death (in the next life), or in this life.

[In short, the commonly accepted canon, indicative of the form of the Brahman, includes all Actions performed with a desireless frame of mind, and merely as duties, and which are either *sāttvika* or are proper Actions, or good Actions, performed with a pure intention, and according to Scriptural directions. All other Actions are futile. This proves that it is not proper to ask any one to give up Action, which is included in the definition of the Brahman, which came into existence with Brahmadeva (Gī. 3. 10), and which no body can escape from. And that is why the above Karma-Yogic interpretation of the canon 'Om-Tat-Sat' has been given in this chapter immediately after the disquisition on Karma. Because, a mere description of the form of the Brahman has been given before in Chap. XIII, as also before that chapter. What the words 'Om', 'Tat', and 'Sat' must have originally meant has been explained at the end of Chapter IX of the Gītā-Rahasya (p. 338). The description of the Brahman as "Saccidānanda" is now in vogue. But, as the definition of Brahman as 'Om-Tat-Sat' has been taken here, instead of the definition 'Saccidānanda', it is possible to draw an inference that the definition of the Brahman as "Saccidānanda", as a generally accepted definition, must have come into vogue after the date of the Gītā.]

इति श्रीमद्भगवद्गीतासु उपनिषत्सु ब्रह्मविद्यायां योगशास्त्रे श्रीकृष्णार्जुनसंवादे श्रद्धात्रयविभागयोगोनाम सप्तदशोऽध्यायः ॥ १७ ॥

Thus ends the seventeenth chapter entitled ŚRADDHA-TRAYA-VIBHAGA YOGA in the dialogue between Śrī Kṛṣṇa and Arjuna on the Yoga included in the Science of the Brahman (that is, on the Karma-Yoga) in the Upaniṣad sung, (that is, told) by the Blessed Lord.

अष्टादशोऽध्यायः

CHAPTER XVIII.

[The eighteenth chapter is the summary of the entire Gītā-science. I shall, therefore, make a review (literally, 'cast a lion-glance') of all that has been stated so far (for greater details, see Chapter XIV of the Gītā-Rahasya). It is clear from Chapter ONE that the Gītā has been told in order to induce Arjuna to do his own duty, when he was on the point of giving up the warfare, which was his lot according to his own-status (*svadharma*), and of starting to beg. Arjuna was filled with the doubt that if he performed such evil actions as killing his own preceptors etc., his Self would not be benefitted. Therefore, in the beginning of Chapter TWO are mentioned the two ways of living one's life, which are accepted by Jñānins (i. e., Sages); namely, Sāṁkhya (*saṁnyāsa* or Renunciation), and Karma-Yoga (Yoga); and the ultimate conclusion has been arrived at, that though both these paths are equally productive of Release, yet the path of Karma-Yoga is the superior of the two (Gī. 5. 2). According to the Path of Karma-Yoga, out of these two, the Reason is supposed to be superior; if the Reason is steady and equable, Karma (Action) does not prejudicially affect anybody; no one has escaped Karma, and no one should give up Karma; it is quite enough if one gives up the Hope of Fruit; it is necessary to perform Karma at any rate for universal welfare, if not, for one's self; if one's Reason is pure, Jñāna does not conflict with Karma; and if one considers tradition, then Janaka and others behaved in the same way. These and other logical arguments have been advanced from Chapter THREE to Chapter FIVE. The next subject-matter is how to acquire this Equability of Reason, which is necessary for making Karma-Yoga successful, and how one ultimately attains Release, while following the Path of Karma-Yoga. In order to acquire this Equability of Reason, one must acquire sense-control (*indriya-nigraha*), and thereby fully realise that there is only one Parameśvara pervading the entire creation; there is no other way. Out of these, sense-control has been dealt with in Chapter SIX; and from Chapter VII to Chapter XVII, is given the explanation of (i) how the Knowledge of the Parameśvara is acquired while practising the Karma-Yoga, and (ii) what that Knowledge is. Out of these, Chapter SEVEN and Chapter EIGHT deal with the Spiritual and the Empirical Knowledge (*jñāna-vijñāna*) of (i) the Mutable and the Immutable and (ii) the Perceptible and the Imperceptible; and Chapters NINE to TWELVE deal with the doctrine that though the Imperceptible form of the Parameśvara is superior to the Perceptible form, yet, worshipping the Perceptible, without losing sight of the fact that there is only one Parameśvara, is a path which is easy for everybody, because it is a matter which is capable of practical realisation. Then in Chapter THIRTEEN, the theory of the Body and the Ātman (*kṣetra-kṣetrajña-vicāra*) has been explained by saying that, that which is known as the '*avyakta*' (Imperceptible) in the Consideration of the Mutable and the Immutable, is, indeed, the Ātman within the body of a man; and thereafter, there has been a detailed consideration from Chapter FOURTEEN to Chapter SEVENTEEN of the way in which persons of diverse natures in the world, as also the other diversified expansion of the world, came into existence, as a result of the constituents of Prakṛti—which subject-matter, is really an off-shoot of the Consideration of the Mutable and the Immutable; and in this way, the exposition of Spiritual and Empirical Knowledge has been completed. But everywhere, the only advice given to Arjuna is that he should perform Action; and the definite doctrine has been enunciated, that the Karma-Yogic way of living one's life, namely, the path of "worshipping the Parameśvara, and doing all Actions with a pure mind, according to one's status, till death, and with the idea of dedicating everything to the Parameśvara" is, indeed the best path of life. When, in this way, the Karma-Yoga, based on Knowledge, and in which Devotion is the supreme factor, has been explained in all its bearings, that very religion has

अर्जुन उवाच ।

§§ संन्यासस्य महाबाहो तत्त्वमिच्छामि वेदितुम् ।
त्यागस्य च हृषीकेश पृथक्केशिनिषूदन ॥ १ ॥

been summarised in Chapter EIGHTEEN; and Arjuna has been induced to fight of his own free will. In this path, which has been pronounced to be the best of all by the Gītā, Arjuna has not been advised to take up the fourth state of life or Renunciation; but, it has been stated that the man, who lives according to this path of life is a '*nitya-saṁnyāsin*' (perpetual ascetic), (Gī. 5. 3). Therefore, the next question of Arjuna is whether the principle of (i) taking sometime or other to the fourth state of life, namely, the state of an ascetic, and (ii) literally abandoning all kinds of Action, is or is not included in the Path of Karma-Yoga; and if not, then, what the meaning of the two words '*saṁnyāsa*' and '*tyāga*' is (see Gītā-Rahasya pp. 481 to 487.]

Arjuna said:—(1) O Mighty-armed Ṛhṣīkeśa! the principle of Renunciation (*saṁnyāsa*), and O Keśidaityaniṣūdana! the principle of Abandonment (*tyāga*), I wish to know these severally.

[This question has not been asked with the intention of merely knowing the dictionary meanings of the words '*saṁnyāsa*' and '*tyāga*', or the difference between them. The root-meaning of both is "to give up"; and it is not that Arjuna did not know this. But, the Blessed Lord has nowhere advised the giving up of Action; and wherever Renunciation has been dealt with in the 4th, 5th, or 6th chapters (4. 41; 5. 13; 6. 1), or in other places, He has directed that one should only make a '*tyāga*' (abandonment) of the Hope of Fruit (Gī. 12. 11), and should make the '*saṁnyāsa*' of, that is, 'dedicate', all Actions to the Parameśvara, (3. 30; 12. 6); whereas, if one considers the Upaniṣads, one comes across statements describing the Path of Renunciation, which are indicative of the Abandonment of Action, such as, "*na karmaṇā na prajayā*

श्रीभगवानुवाच ।

काम्यानां कर्मणां न्यासं संन्यासं कवयो विदुः ।
सर्वकर्मफलत्यागं प्राहुस्त्यागं विचक्षणाः ॥ २ ॥

dhanena tyāgen aike amṛtatvam ānaśuḥ", that is, "many persons have obtained Release by abandoning, or making a literal '*tyāga*' of all Actions" (Kai. 1. 2; Nārāyaṇa 12. 3); or, "*vedānta-vijñāna suniścitārthaḥ* । *saṁnyāsayogād yatayaḥ śuddhatatvāḥ* ॥", that is, "*yatin*s (ascetics), who have become pure by the Yoga of '*saṁnyāsa*', in the shape of the Abandonment of all Actions" (Muṇḍaka. 3. 3. 6); or, '*kim prajayā kariṣyāmaḥ*" that is, "what have we got to do with sons, grandsons, or other progeny" (Bṛ. 4. 4. 22). It is quite clear that Arjuna had seen that the Blessed Lord was using the two words '*saṁnyāsa*' and '*tyāga*' in some other meaning, instead of applying them to the state of Renunciation, in the shape of the Abandonment of Action, out of the four states of human life, prescribed by the Smṛti texts, and he has asked this question in order to clear up that point. See the detailed elucidation of this subject-matter, which has been made by me in Chapter XI (pp. 481 to 487) of the Gītā-Rahasya.]

The Blessed Lord said :—(2) Making a '*nyāsa*' (that is, giving up) of (all whatsoever) Desire-prompted Actions, is known by wise people as 'Saṁnyāsa'; (and) making an Abandonment of the Fruit of all Actions is known by the learned as 'Tyāga'.

[This verse clearly explains what is meant by the words '*saṁnyāsa*' and '*tyāga*' according to the Path of Karma-Yoga. But, as this opinion was not acceptable to the commentators, who belonged to the Path of Renunciation, they have stretched the meaning of this stanza to a considerable extent. In this stanza, the word '*kāmya*' appears in the very beginning. Therefore, these commentators say, that the divisions of Actions into *nitya*,*

* For definitions of '*nitya*', etc., see Vol. I, p. 74, *et seq.*—Translator.

naimittika, *kāmya*, and *niṣiddha*, according to the Mīmāṁsā school are indicated here; and that according to the advice of the Blessed Lord, only '*kāmya*' (desire-prompted) "Actions should be given up". But, the followers of the Path of Renunciation have to declare that the '*nitya*' and '*naimittika*' Actions have also been included in the '*kāmya*' Actions. Even doing so, the statement in the second half of the stanza that the Hope of Fruit should be given up, and that Actions should not be given up, (see stanza 6, later on) does not become consistent with their mode of life. Therefore, these commentators have satisfied themselves by passing a remark, on their own authority, that the Blessed Lord has here only showered empty praise on the Path of Karma-Yoga; and that His real intention was that all Actions should be given up. It is quite clear that this stanza cannot be satisfactorily explained from the doctrinal point of view of the School of Renunciation or other schools. It can be rightly interpreted only so as to support the Karma-Yoga, that is to say, so as to support the principle enunciated on numerous occasions in the Gītā, that one must continue to perform Actions, till death, giving up the Hope of Fruit; and such a meaning indeed, is the straight and plain meaning. One must bear in mind, in the first place, that the word '*kāmya*' does not indicate the division of Actions into *nitya*, *naimittika*, *kāmya* and *niṣiddha*, made by the Mīmāṁsā school. According to the doctrine of Karma-Yoga, all Actions fall into only two divisions, namely, '*kāmya*' that is, 'performed with Hope of Fruit' and '*niṣkāma*', that is, 'performed giving up the Hope of Fruit'; and these two are respectively called "*pravṛtta* Karma", and "*nivṛtta* Karma" in the Manu-Smṛti (See Manu. 12. 88 and 89). Whether the Actions are Daily (*nitya*), or Occasional (*naimittika*) or Bodily (*kāyika*), or Vocal (*vācika*), or Mental (*mānasika*) or any other kind, according to the division into *sāttvika*, etc., they must fall into one of the two divisions, '*kāmya*' (Desire-prompted) and '*niṣkāma*' (Desireless); because, besides the two divisions, (i) 'having *kāma*', that is, Hope of Fruit, and (ii) 'not having *kāma*', no third division is possible from the point of view of *kāma* ('Hope of Fruit'). If a particular Action is done for a particular purpose, having regard to the purpose for which it is prescribed by the Śāstras, e.g., the '*putreṣṭi*' sacrifice for obtaining a son, then it becomes '*kāmya*'; and if the same thing is done merely as a matter of duty, that is to say, without entertaining the Hope of Fruit, it becomes '*niṣkāma*'. When all Actions are thus divided into '*kāmya*' and '*niṣkāma*' (or '*pravṛtta*' and '*nivṛtta*' according to the terminology of Manu), the Karma-Yogin gives up all Actions which are '*kāmya*' or inspired by Desire. It, therefore, follows that even in the Karma-Yoga, it is necessary to perform a '*saṁnyāsa*' (Renunciation) of all '*kāmya*' (desired-prompted) Actions. Now, let us turn to the second out of the two divisions of Karma, namely, the division of '*niṣkāma*' (desireless) Actions. It is true that the Gītā definitely enjoins the performance of these *niṣkāma* Actions on the Karma-Yogin; but even in them, one has to perform the total '*tyāga*' (abandonment) of the Hope of Fruit (Gī. 6. 2). Therefore, even the principle of '*tyāga*' remains constant in the Gītā-religion. In short, in order to impress on the mind of Arjuna that the principles of '*saṁnyāsa*' and of '*tyāga*' both remain constant in Karma-Yoga, the Blessed Lord has in this stanza given these two definitions, namely, "'*saṁnyāsa*' means the total *saṁnyāsa* (Renunciation) of *kāmya* (desire-prompted) Action"; and "'*tyāga*' means the *tyāga*, or the Abandonment, of Hope of Fruit, in all Desireless Actions which are to be performed". In an earlier chapter, in showing that Saṁnyāsa (or Sāṁkhya) and Yoga are essentially the same, the word '*saṁnyāsin*' (Gī. 5. 3–6 and 6. 1, 2), and later on in this chapter, the word '*tyāgin*', have been defined in the same way; and the same is the proper meaning in the present stanza. The doctrine of the Smṛtis that, unless one follows the order of the *brahmacāri*, *gṛhastha*, *vānaprastha* and *saṁnyāsa* states, and "ultimately takes up the *saṁnyāsa* state or the fourth state of life, in the shape of Renunciation of all Actions, Release is not possible", is not meant here. This clearly proves that even though the

§§ त्याज्यं दोषवदित्येके कर्म प्राहुर्मनीषिणः ।
यज्ञदानतपःकर्म न त्याज्यमिति चापरे ॥ ३ ॥
निश्चयं शृणु मे तत्र त्यागे भरतसत्तम ।
त्यागो हि पुरुषव्याघ्र त्रिविधः संप्रकीर्तितः ॥ ४ ॥
यज्ञदानतपःकर्म न त्याज्यं कार्यमेव तत् ।
यज्ञो दानं तपश्चैव पावनानि मनीषिणाम् ॥ ५ ॥
एतान्यपि तु कर्माणि सङ्गं त्यक्त्वा फलानि च ।
कर्तव्यानीति मे पार्थ निश्चितं मतमुत्तमम् ॥ ६ ॥

Karma-Yogin may not take up the saffron-coloured robes of an ascetic and abandon all Actions, yet, since he is essentially following the same principles as a *saṁnyāsin*, there is no conflict between Karma-Yoga and the Smṛti texts. The Blessed Lord now summarises the dispute about Karma between the supporters of the Saṁnyāsa School and the supporters of the Mīmāṁsā school, and gives the ultimate decision of the Karma-Yoga-Science in the matter—]

(3) Some learned men say that as Karma is faulty, it must be given up (altogether); and others say that Sacrifice, Charity, Austerities, and Karma should never be abandoned. (4) Therefore, O Bharataśreṣṭha ! listen to My decision on the question of *'tyāga'*. O Puruṣaśreṣṭha ! *'tyāga'* is said to be of three kinds. (5) Sacrifice, Charity, Austerities, and Karma should not be abandoned under any circumstances. Those (Actions) must be performed. Sacrifice, Charity and Austerities are *'pāvana'* (that is, mind-purifiers), for (even) the wise. (6) Therefore, even these Actions (such as, Sacrifice, Charity etc.) must be performed, without Attachment, and having abandoned the Fruit (like other desireless Actions, and for universal welfare). This, O Pārtha, is My definite (and correct) opinion.

This is a summary of the doctrine of Karma-Yoga enunciated before on numerous occasions, that the fault or the defect of Karma is not in the Karma itself, but is in the Hope of Fruit; and that all Actions should, therefore, be performed desirelessly, and having given up the Hope of Fruit. The Gītā does not countenance the doctrine of the Saṁnyāsa school, that all Action is faulty and, therefore, such as ought not to be performed (See Gītā. 18. 48 and 49). The Gītā advocates the *saṁnyāsa* (Renunciation) of only *kāmya* (desire-prompted) Actions. But, from this it would follow that since all the ritual and, rites laid down by the Scriptures are '*kāmya*' or 'based on desire' (Gī. 2. 42-44), one must necessarily renounce them: and if that is done, the Cycle of Yajñas (*yajñacakra*) will come to an end (Gī. 13. 16), and the world will run the risk of being devastated. Then, what is to be done? The Gītā answers this question by saying that although the Scriptures have prescribed the performance of Yajñas, Charity etc. for obtaining heaven, it is not that these very Actions cannot be performed desirelessly, and for universal welfare, with the idea, that performing sacrifices, or giving gifts, or performing austerities is one's duty in this life. (See Gī. 17. 11, 17, and 20). Therefore, just as other Desireless Actions are to be performed according to one's status in life, so also should Sacrifices, Charity and other Actions be performed, giving up the Hope of Fruit, and without Attachment; because, such actions are always "*pāvana*", that is, purifiers of the mind, and increase one's generosity. The words "*etāny-api*"=" even these", used in the original text mean:—"*yajña*, *dāna*, and other acts also, in the same way as other desireless actions". When, in this way, these Actions are performed, giving up the Hope of Fruit—or from the devotional point of view, only with the idea of dedicating them to the Parameśvara—the wheel of the world continues to roll; and, as there is no more any Hope of Fruit in the mind of the doer, these Actions do not obstruct Release; and all matters are properly settled. And this is, indeed, the final and definite doctrine of the Karma-Yoga-Science with reference to Actions. (see my commentary on Gītā. 2. 45). As this difference between the Path of Karma of the Mīmāṁsā school and the Path of Karma-Yoga of the Gītā has been clearly expounded by me in the

§§ नियतस्य तु संन्यासः कर्मणो नोपपद्यते ।
मोहात्तस्य परित्यागस्तामसः परिकीर्तितः ॥ ७ ॥
दुःखमित्येव यत्कर्म कायक्लेशभयात् त्यजेत् ।
स कृत्वा राजसं त्यागं नैव त्यागफलं लभेत् ॥ ८ ॥
कार्यमित्येव यत्कर्म नियतं क्रियतेऽर्जुन ।
संङ्ग त्यक्त्वा फलं चैव स त्यागः सात्त्विको मतः ॥ ९ ॥

Gītā-Rahasya (see pp. 403 to 409 and pp. 478 to 482), I shall not further labour the point here. To proceed: after the Blessed Lord has thus defined the meanings of the words '*saṁnyāsa*' and '*tyāga*' according to the Karma-Yoga-Science, in reply to the question of Arjuna, He further emphasises what He has said by showing the different ways of performing Karma, e. g., *sāttvika* etc.—]

(7) That Action which is '*niyata*' (that is, 'prescribed' according to one's religion) must not be abandoned. The Abandonment (*tyāga*) of such Actions, as a result of Ignorance, is called '*tāmasa*'. (8) If Action is abandoned, fearing that it will produce bodily hardship, (that is, for the sole reason that it is painful), such Abandonment becomes *rājasa*; and he will not obtain (that which is) the result of *tyāga*. (9) O Arjuna! when Action, which is '*niyata*' (that is, 'prescribed') is performed as a '*kārya*' (that is, only 'as a duty'), and having abandoned the Attachment as also the Fruit, such Abandonment is looked upon as a *sāttvika* abandonment.

[The interpretation by some commentators of the word '*niyata*' as the '*nitya*' variety of Actions, out of the '*nitya*', '*naimiṭtika*' etc., is not correct. The word '*niyata*' must be taken here in the same sense as in the sentence '*niyataṁ kuru karma tvam*' (Gī. 3. 8). As has been already stated above, the Mīmāṁsā terminology is not intended here. In Gī. 3. 19, the word '*kārya*' has been used instead of '*niyata*'; and in stanza 9 above, the words '*kārya*' and '*niyata*' have both appeared in one and the same stanza. This stanza is a justification of the statement in stanza 2 at the commencement of the Chapter, that performing the

§§ न द्वेष्ट्यकुशलं कर्म कुशले नानुषज्जते।
त्यागी सत्त्वसमाविष्टो मेधावी छिन्नसंशयः ॥ १० ॥
न हि देहभृता शक्यं त्यक्तुं कर्माण्यशेषतः।
यस्तु कर्मफलत्यागी स त्यागीत्यभिधीयते ॥ ११ ॥
§§ अनिष्टमिष्टं मिश्रं च त्रिविधं कर्मणः फलम्।
भवत्यत्यागिनां प्रेत्य न तु संन्यासिनां क्वचित् ॥ १२ ॥

Actions, which have fallen to one's lot according to the Śāstras, looking upon such Actions as a 'duty' (see Gī. 3 19), is known as a *sāttvika* Abandonment; and that this is, indeed, what is known as '*saṁnyāsa*' (Renunciation) or '*tyāga*' (abandonment) in the Karma-Yoga-Science. The words '*tyāga*' and '*saṁnyāsa*' have thus been explained. Now, the Blessed Lord explains who the true '*tyāgin*' or '*saṁnyāsin*' is, according to this principle—]

(10) Who does not dislike a particular Action, because it is '*akuśala*' (that is, not beneficial), and who is not attached to another Action, because it is profitable or beneficial, he is to be called a *tyāgin* or *saṁnyāsin*, endowed with the *sattva*-quality, intelligent, and free from doubt; (11) because, whosoever is embodied, for him it is not possible to totally give up Action. Therefore, that man, who (without abandoning Action) has abandoned only the Fruit of Action, he alone is said to be a (real) *tyāgin* (that is, *sāṁnyāsin*).

[The Blessed Lord now says that a person, who has become a *tyāgin* in this way, that is, by giving up merely the Hope of Fruit of Action, without giving up Action itself, is not affected by the bondage of any Action whatsoever—]

(12) The '*a-tyāgin*', (that is, one, who does not abandon the Hope of Fruit), obtains after his death three kinds of Fruit of Action, namely, evil (*aniṣṭa*), good (*iṣṭa*) and mixed (*miśra*), (that is, partly good and partly evil); but the *saṁnyāsin* (that is, one who performs all Actions, having given up the Hope of Fruit) never gets (this Fruit), (that is, Actions can never bind him).

§§ पञ्चैतानि महाबाहो कारणानि निबोध मे ।
सांख्ये कृतान्ते प्रोक्तानि सिद्धये सर्वकर्मणाम् ॥ १३ ॥

अधिष्ठानं तथा कर्ता करणं च पृथग्विधम् ।
विविधाश्च पृथक्चेष्टा दैवं चैवात्र पञ्चमम् ॥ १४ ॥

शरीरवाङ्मनोभिर्यत्कर्म प्रारभते नरः ।
न्याय्यं वा विपरीतं वा पञ्चैते तस्य हेतवः ॥ १५ ॥

§§ तत्रैवं सति कर्तारमात्मानं केवलं तु यः ।
पश्यत्यकृतबुद्धित्वान्न स पश्यति दुर्मतिः ॥ १६ ॥

[These ideas about '*tyāga*', '*tyāgin*', and '*saṁnyāsin*' have appeared before in the Gītā in many places (Gī. 3. 4–7; 5. 2–10; 6. 1); and they have been summarised here. The literal Abandonment (*saṁnyāsa*) of all kind of Action has never been accepted by the Gītā. According to the Gītā, the true or the *nitya* (perpetual) *saṁnyāsin*, is the person who abandons only the Fruit of Action (Gī. 5. 3). The real *tyāga* (Abandonment) is the Abandonment of the Hope of Fruit, which (Hope) is imbued with selfishness, that is to say, the Abandonment of Egoism. In order to further emphasise this proposition, further reasons are now given—]

(13) O Mighty-armed! I will mention (to you) the five essentials, which have been mentioned in Sāṁkhya philosophy, as causes for anything to happen, to which listen. (14) These are '*adhiṣṭhāna*' (place), as also a doer, various kinds of '*karaṇa*' (that is, *sādhana*, implements), various kinds of diverse '*ceṣṭā*' (that is, Actions on the part of the doer), and along with these, the fifth, namely, Destiny. (15) Whatever Action is commenced by man, whether by his body, or speech, or mind, whether that Action is '*nyāyya*' (that is, justifiable) or '*viparīta*' (that is, unjustifiable), these are the five causes of it.

(16) When this is the (true) state of things, that '*durmati*' (evil-minded person—Trans.) who, as a result of an undeveloped Reason, thinks that he alone is the Doer,

यस्य नाहंकृतो भावो बुद्धिर्यस्य न लिप्यते।
हत्वाऽपि स इमाँल्लोकान्न हन्ति न निबद्ध्यते ॥ १७ ॥

does not (it must be said) understand anything. (17) Who does not possess the belief that "I am the doer", and whose Reason is unattached, such a person, even destroying other persons, cannot be said to have killed them; and that (Action) does not bind him.

[The word '*sāṁkhya*' in stanza 13 has been interpreted by some commentators as meaning the Vedānta-Śāstra; but as the next, that is, the fourteenth stanza, has appeared literally in the Nārāyaṇīya doctrine, and as there is a previous reference in that treatise to the two Kāpila Sāṁkhya elements, namely, Prakṛti and Puruṣa, the word '*sāṁkhya*', in my opinion, must be taken in this place to mean the 'Kāpila Sāṁkhya philosophy'. The proposition that a man should not entertain the Hope for the Fruit of Action, nor the egotistical idea that he will do any particular thing, has often before appeared in the Gītā (Gī. 2. 19; 2. 47; 3. 27; 5. 8–11; 13. 29); and that very proposition has been further emphasised here by saying, that "man is not the only reason for the effect of any Action coming into existence (see Gī. Ra. Ch. XI). Stanza 14 means, that whether human beings exist in this world or not, the uninterrupted activity of the world will go on according to the natural course of Prakṛti; and that, things, which a man believes to have been done by him, are not the result merely of his efforts, but have been brought about by his efforts combined with the other activities in the world. For instance, agriculture does not depend merely on the efforts of a man, but the natural qualities or the activities of other things like land, seed, rain, manure, oxen etc. are necessary, in order that agriculture should be successful. Some of the various activities in the world which are thus necessary to make human efforts successful, are partly known to us; and man makes an effort after considering the favourableness or otherwise of these factors. But, there are also several other activities in the world, of which men are not aware, and which are either favourable or unfavourable to the efforts he makes; and these are known as DESTINY; and this is said to be the fifth reason for any particular result coming about. If all these things are necessary in order that human effort should be successful; and if many of these things are not within one's control or even not known, then, (i) proudly saying that one will do a particular thing or (ii) entertaining a Hope of Fruit that a particular result should follow the particular Action which one does, is clearly a sign of folly (Gī. Ra. pp. 452 to 455). But, stanza 17 is not to be understood as authorising that one, who has conquered the Hope of Fruit, may do any evil Action he likes. As that which ordinary persons do, is done by them with the idea of satisfying selfish purposes, they perform wrong actions. But, the man, whose selfishness, avarice, or Hope of Fruit, have been fully annihilated, and to whom all created beings are the same, is not capable of injury to another; because, the sin is in the Reason and not in the Action. It, therefore, necessarily follows, that, even if a man, (whose Reason has first been proved to be pure and clean), does something, which may appear improper from the worldly point of view, yet, the seed of that Action must be pure; and stanza 17 says that such a pure-minded person cannot be held responsible for such Action. The principle of the sinlessness of the Stithaprajña, that is, of the person, whose Reason has become pure, has also been enunciated in the Upaniṣads (See Kauṣī. 3. 1 and Pañca-daśī, 14. 16 and 17). But, as this subject-matter has been fully thrashed out by me in Chapter XII of the Gītā-Rahasya, I will not further labour the point here. As the Blessed Lord has, in this way, fully analysed the meaning of the words '*saṁnyāsa*' and '*tyāga*', which (analysis) was made necessary by the question of Arjuna; and proved that (i) true or *sāttvika* Abandonment (*tyāga*) consists of performing all Actions, which befall a person on account of Scriptural directions proper for his status in life, after he has given up egoism and the Hope of Fruit; and that (ii) giving up Action is not true Abandonment, He now completes,

§§ ज्ञानं ज्ञेयं परिज्ञाता त्रिविधा कर्मचोदना ।
करणं कर्म कर्तेति त्रिविधः कर्मसंग्रहः ॥ १८ ॥
ज्ञानं कर्म च कर्ता च त्रिधैव गुणभेदतः ।
प्रोच्यते गुणसंख्याने यथावच्छृणु तान्यपि ॥ १९ ॥

from the Karma-Yogic point of view, the consideration of the divisions of Karma into *sāttvika*, etc., started in Chap. XVII.]

(18) *jñāna, jñeya,* and *jñātā* is the three-fold division of '*karma-codanā*; and *karaṇa, karma* and *kartā* is the three-fold division of *karma-saṁgraha*. (19) *jñāna, karma,* and *kartā* each falls into three sub-divisions by reason of the difference in the three (*sattva, rajas,* and *tamas*) constituents, as has been stated in the *guṇasaṁkhyāna-śāstra* (that is, in the Kāpila-Sāṁkhya-Śāstra). Hear those (sub-divisions) just as they have been mentioned (which I am describing to you).

[The words '*karma-codanā*' and '*karma-saṁgraha*' are technical expressions. Before any act is performed by the organs, that Action has to be decided upon by the Mind. Therefore, this mental operation is called '*karma-codanā*', that is 'the first inspiration to do the act'; and that has naturally three aspects, namely, the '*jñāna*', the '*jñeya*' and the '*jñātā*'. For instance, before actually manufacturing an earthen pot, the potter (*jñātā*) says in his own mind: "I have to do this particular thing (*jñeya*), and it can be done in a particular way (*jñāna*)". This is the '*karma-codanā*'. When in this way, a decision has been arrived at in the Mind, the potter (*kartā*) gets together implements (*karaṇa*) like earth, wheel etc., and actually manufactures the earthen pot (*karma*). This is the *karma-saṁgraha*. Though the earthen pot is the '*karma*' (Action) of the potter, it is also referred to as the '*kārya*' of the earth. To proceed: it will be seen that the word '*karma-codanā*' indicates the Action which takes place in the Mind or in the 'internal sense'; and the word '*karma-saṁgraha*' indicates the external Actions, which correspond with that mental Action. In order to fully

§§ सर्वभूतेषु येनैकं भावमव्ययमीक्षते ।
अविभक्तं विभक्तेषु तज्ज्ञानं विद्धि सात्त्विकम् ॥ २० ॥
पृथक्त्वेन तु यज्ज्ञानं नानाभावान् पृथग्विधान् ।
वेत्ति सर्वेषु भूतेषु तज्ज्ञानं विद्धि राजसम् ॥ २१ ॥
यत्तु कृत्स्नवदेकस्मिन्कार्ये सक्तमहैतुकम् ।
अतत्त्वार्थवदल्पं च तत्तामसमुदाहृतम् ॥ २२ ॥

consider any Action, one must take into account both the '*codanā*' as well as the '*saṁgraha*'. Out of these, the characteristics of *jñāna*, *jñeya*, and *jñātā* (*kṣetrajña*) from the Metaphysical point of view have been considered before in Chapter XIII of the Gītā (13. 18). Yet, as the characteristics of *jñāna* in the shape of Action are somewhat different, the word '*jñāna*' out of the former triad, and the words '*karma*' and '*kartā*' out of the latter triad are now defined by the Blessed Lord—]

(20) That *jñāna*, by which one realises that in all '*vibhakta*' (that is, diverse beings) there is only One '*avibhakta*' (that is, undivided—Trans.) and Inexhaustible '*bhāva*' (that is, Principle), is called *sāttvika* Knowledge; (21) that *jñāna* (Knowledge), which creates an impression that there are diverse *bhāva*-s (Principles) in the various created things, is *rājasa jñāna*; (22) but that insignificant Knowledge, which unreasonably and without understanding elementary principles, confines itself to only one thing, looking upon it as the all-in-all, is *tāmasa jñāna*.

[These characteristics of the various kinds of *jñāna* are very comprehensive. The idea that one's wife and children is the entire '*saṁsāra*' is *tāmasa* Knowledge. When one rises a little above this frame of mind, one's vision becomes more comprehensive; and a man begins to look upon a fellow-townsman or a fellow-countryman as his own. Nevertheless, the idea that men from different places or different countries are different from each other is still there. This Knowledge is *rājasa*; but, when one rises even above this stage and realises that there is only one Ātman in all created beings, that Knowledge is complete and *sāttvika*. In short, seeing

§§ नियतं सङ्गरहितमरागद्वेषतः कृतम्।
अफलप्रेप्सुना कर्म यत्तत्सात्त्विकमुच्यते ॥ २३ ॥

the Indivisible (*avibhakta*) in that which seems divided (*vibhakta*), or seeing unity in diversity, is the true characteristic of Knowlege; and he who has thus understood that "*neha nānāsti kiṁcana*", that is, "there is no manifoldness in this universe", is really Released; and, "*mṛtyoḥ sa mṛtyum āpnoti ya iha nāneva paśyati*" (Bṛ. 4. 4. 10), that is, "one who sees diversity in this world, falls into the cycle of birth and death", as has been stated in the Bṛhadāraṇyaka and in the Kaṭhopaniṣad (see Kaṭha. 4. 11). This is all that is to be Realised in the world (Gī. 13. 16); and this is the climax of Knowledge; because, when all things are looked upon as one, the mental process of synthesis has no further field to operate (Gī. Ra. pp. 320-1). How this synthesising mental process goes on, has been described in Chapter IX of the Gītā-Rahasya (pp. 295 to 297), to which the reader is referred. The effect of this *sāttvika* Knowledge on one's bodily nature, when it is indelibly impressed on the mind, has been described under the name of 'the qualities of godlike endowment' in the beginning of Chapter XVI; and in Chapter XIII, this kind of bodily nature has been called '*jñāna*' (13. 7-11). This clearly shows that (1) the perfection of the synthesising mental process and (2) the change in one's bodily nature as a result of such perfection, are both included by the Gītā in the connotation of the term '*jñāna*' (Knowledge). Therefore, although the characteristics of Knowledge, as mentioned in stanza 20, may appear to be the description of a mental process, yet, that description includes the description of its effect on the bodily nature, as has been made clear at the end of Chap. IX of the Gītā-Rahasya. To proceed: the Blessed Lord having thus described the various kinds of Jñāna, now describes the various kinds of Karma—]

(23) That Action, which is performed by a man, without entertaining the desire for obtaining the Fruit, without entertaining love or hate (in the mind), without being attached,

यत्तु कामेप्सुना कर्म साहंकारेण वा पुनः।
क्रियते बहुलायासं तद्राजसमुदाहृतम् ॥ २४ ॥

अनुबन्धं क्षयं हिंसामनपेक्ष्य च पौरुषम्।
मोहादारभ्यते कर्म यत्तत्तामसमुच्यते ॥ २५ ॥

and as being '*niyata*' (that is, prescribed) for him, according to his own *dharma* (religion), is called *sāttvika* Action; (24) but that Action, which is performed with much labour (by a man), entertaining '*kāma*' (that is, the desire for reward), or having an egotistical feeling, is called *rājasa*; (25) and that Action, which is ignorantly commenced, without considering the '*anubandha*' (that is, 'what its result will be'), or one's '*pauruṣa*' (that is, what one's strength is), and whether (from it) there will or will not result destruction or '*hiṁsā*' (that is, 'harm'—Trans.), is called *tāmasa*.

[These three kinds of Action embrace all Action. Why Desireless Action has been called the *sāttvika*, or the best Action has been explained in Chapter XI of the Gītā-Rahasya, to which the reader is referred. This is also the true '*akarma*' or Non-Action (see my commentary on Gī. 4. 16). As the doctrine of the Gītā is, that the Reason (*buddhi*) is superior to the Action (*karma*), the Reason (frame of mind) of the Doer has each time been mentioned in giving the above characteristics of Karma. It must be borne in mind that whether an Action is *sāttvika* or *tāmasa* has not been determined by reference to the external effects of the Action (see Gī. Ra. Ch. XII, pp. 530-531). Similarly, one is not to understand the Gītā as preaching that when one has abandoned the Hope of Fruit, one may do what one likes, without considering the pros and cons, and indiscriminately, as will appear from stanza 25; because, stanza 25 emphatically says that, Action performed without seeing the '*anubandha*' or considering the Fruit, is *tāmasa* and not *sāttvika* (see Gī. Ra. pp. 530-531). The Blessed Lord now explains the divisions into which all Doers fall, according to the same principle—]

§§ मुक्तसङ्गोऽनहंवादी धृत्युत्साहसमन्वितः ।
सिद्ध्यसिद्ध्योर्निर्विकारः कर्ता सात्त्विक उच्यते ॥ २६ ॥
रागी कर्मफलप्रेप्सुर्लुब्धो हिंसात्मकोऽशुचिः ।
हर्षशोकान्वितः कर्ता राजसः परिकीर्तितः ॥ २७ ॥
अयुक्तः प्राकृतः स्तब्धः शठो नैष्कृतिकोऽलसः ।
विषादी दीर्घसूत्री च कर्ता तामस उच्यते ॥ २८ ॥

(26) Who is not Attached; who does not say: 'I' or "mine"; who is not (mentally) moved, (both) when the work is successful and when it is not successful; (and) who (nevertheless) performs Action, being embued with enthusiasm and perseverence, he is called (a) *sāttvika* (Doer); (27) who is attached to objects of sense, (and) avaricious; who is filled with joy or sorrow (on the success or failure respectively of Action); who entertains the desire for obtaining the Fruit of Action; who is harmful and impure, such a Doer is called *rājasa*; (28) who is *'ayukta'* (that is, with an unsteady Reason), ignorant, proud, a cheater, *'naiṣkṛtika'* (that is, one who deprives others of their goods); who is idle, *'dīrgha-sūtrī'* (that is, difficult to get rid of; or, who takes a month to do what is ordinarily done in an hour), such a Doer is called *tāmasa*.

[The word '*naiṣkṛtika* (*nis*+*kṛt*=to cut) in stanza 28 means "one who cuts the work of others, or ruins it". But some commentators accept instead the reading '*naikṛtika*'. '*nikṛta*' has been defined as a 'cheat' in the Amarakośa: but, as the adjective 'cheat' has once appeared above, I have accepted the reading '*naiṣkṛtika*'. Out of these three kinds of Doers, the *sāttvika* Doer is the true non-doer (*akartā*), the untouched-doer (*alipta-kartā*), or the Karma-Yogin. This stanza clearly shows that though he has given up the Hope of Fruit, his enthusiasm, ambition and discrimination do not cease to exist. The Blessed Lord now applies this description of the three-fold development of the universe to Reason (*buddhi*), Steadfastness (*dhṛti*), and Happiness (*sukha*). The word '*buddhi*' in these stanzas has to be taken to mean

§§ बुद्धेर्भेदं धृतेश्चैव गुणतस्त्रिविधं शृणु ।
प्रोच्यमानमशेषेण पृथक्त्वेन धनंजय ॥ २९ ॥
प्रवृत्तिं च निवृत्तिं च कार्याकार्ये भयाभये ।
बन्धं मोक्षं च या वेत्ति बुद्धिः सा पार्थ सात्त्विकी ॥ ३० ॥
यया धर्ममधर्मं च कार्यं चाकार्यमेव च ।
अयथावत्प्रजानाति बुद्धिः सा पार्थ राजसी ॥ ३१ ॥
अधर्मं धर्ममिति या मन्यते तमसाऽऽवृता ।
सर्वार्थान्विपरीतांश्च बुद्धिः सा पार्थ तामसी ॥ ३२ ॥

the '*vyavasāyātmikā buddhiḥ*' or the 'deciding mental organ' described in Chapter II (2. 41); and this subject has been fully explained in Chapter VI of the Gītā-Rahasya, pp. 187 to 192, to which the reader is referred.]

(29) O Dhanañjaya! I am mentioning to you in their entirety the three divisions, arising as a result of the three constituents, into which Reason and Steadfastness fall, which hear. (30) *pravṛtti* (that is, commencing to perform any particular Action), *nivṛtti* (that is, not commencing any particular Action), *kārya* (that is, what should be done), and *akārya* (that is, what should not be done), what should be feared, and what should not be feared, what leads to bondage and what to Release, that Reason, which understands all this, is called *sāttvika*; (31) that Reason by which a proper discrimination is not arrived at between the righteous and the unrighteous, between the doable and the not-doable, such a Reason, O Pārtha! is *rājasa*; (32) that Reason, which being steeped in ignorance, looks upon unrighteousness, as righteousness, and causes a *viparīta* (that is, wrong) view to be taken about everything, such a Reason, O Pārtha! is *tāmasa*.

[When Reason has been divided in this way, Conscience (*sadasadviveka-buddhi*) no more remains an independent thing, but has to be included in the *sāttvikā buddhiḥ*, as has been explained in the Gītā-Rahasya (pp. 191, 192), to which the reader is referred.]

§§ धृत्या यया धारयते मनःप्राणेन्द्रियक्रियाः ।
योगेनाव्यभिचारिण्या धृतिः सा पार्थ सात्त्विकी ॥ ३३ ॥
यया तु धर्मकामार्थान् धृत्या धारयतेऽर्जुन ।
प्रसङ्गेन फलाकाङ्क्षी धृतिः सा पार्थ राजसी ॥ ३४ ॥
यया स्वप्नं भयं शोकं विषादं मदमेव च ।
न विमुञ्चति दुर्मेधा धृतिः सा पार्थ तामसी ॥ ३५ ॥

(33) That '*a-vyabhicāri*' (that is, not swerving this side or that side) Steadfastness, with which the various activities of the Mind, life, and of the various senses are carried on by Yoga (in the shape of the Abandonment of the Fruit of Action) is *sāttvika.* (34) O Arjuna! that Steadfastness by which *dharma*, *kāma* and *artha* (these *puruṣārtha*-s) are carried on, and which entertains the desire for the fruit (of that *dharma*, *artha* or *kāma*) as occasion arises, that Steadfastness, O Pārtha! is *rājasa*; (35) that Steadfastness, by which a person becoming evil-minded, does not abandon sleep, fear, lamentation, dislike, and pride, such a Steadfastness or perseverance, O Pārtha! is *tāmasa.*

[The word '*dhṛti*' literally means 'courage'; but, what is meant here is not physical courage, but mental determination. Coming to a decision is something to be done by the Reason. But, even if the Reason has come to a proper decision, such decision must remain steady. Giving, in this way, strength to the determination, is a quality of the Mind. It is, therefore, said that Steadfastness or moral courage is a quality, which arises by the co-operation of Mind and Reason. But, the description of *sāttvika* Steadfastness is not complete by merely saying that a man must carry on the activities of the Mind, life, and the organs by a 'courage', which is '*a-vyabhicāri*', that is, which does not run here and there. One must also be told with reference to what these activities are to be performed, or what the Karma of this activity is; and that Karma has been described by the word 'Yoga'. Needless to say, it is not enough to define the word 'Yoga' as meaning merely 'concentrated Mind'. Therefore, I have

§§ सुखं त्विदानीं त्रिविधं शृणु मे भरतर्षभ ।
अभ्यासाद्रमते यत्र दुःखान्तं च निगच्छति ॥ ३६ ॥

यत्तदग्रे विषमिव परिणामेऽमृतोपमम् ।
तत्सुखं सात्त्विकं प्रोक्तमात्मबुद्धिप्रसादजम् ॥ ३७ ॥

interpreted it as meaning, 'Yoga in the shape of Abandonment of the Fruit of Action', having regard to the anterior and the posterior contexts. Just as in describing the characteristics of the *sāttvika* Karma or the *sāttvika* Doer, the quality of 'giving up the Attachment to the Fruit' has been considered important, so in considering the characteristics of *sāttvika* Steadfastness, the same quality must also be considered important. Besides, it is stated in the next stanza that *rājasa* Steadfastness desires the Fruit of Action. It, therefore, follows even from the next stanza, that *sāttvika* Steadfastness must be the opposite, that is to say, must be indifferent to the Fruit of Action. In short, strength of determination is only a mental process; and in order to decide whether that determination is good or bad, one must take into account the Action to which that mental process is applied. If the Steadfastness is only in the matter of sleep, idleness, etc., then it is *tāmasa*; if it is in the matter of performing the ordinary daily Actions with the Hope of Fruit, it is *rājasa*; and if it is in the Yoga, in the shape of the Abandonment of Fruit of Action, then it is *sāttvika*. These are the sub-divisions of Steadfastness. Now, the Blessed Lord explains how happiness is sub-divided into three kinds as a result of the difference in the three constituents—]

(36) Now, O Bharata-śreṣṭha! I will also explain the three kinds of happiness, which hear. That, in which a man is engrossed by *abhyāsa* (that is, by constantly having it), and in which, unhappiness comes to an end; (37) that, which is like poison in the beginning, but nectar-like in its effects; that happiness, arising from the satisfaction of the Self-engrossed Reason, (that is to say, Metaphysical happi-

विषयेन्द्रियसंयोगाद्यत्तदग्रेऽमृतोपमम् ।
परिणामे विषमिव तत्सुखं राजसं स्मृतम् ॥ ३८ ॥
यदग्रे चानुबन्धे च सुखं मोहनमात्मनः ।
निद्रालस्यप्रमादोत्थं तत्तामसमुदाहृतम् ॥ ३९ ॥

ness) is *sāttvika*. (38) That, which arises from the contact of the senses with the objects of sense (that is to say, Material happiness), which is nectar-like in the beginning, but poisonous in its effects, that happiness is said to be *rājasa*. (39) And that, which in the beginning as also in its *anubandha*, (that is, in the result) causes Ignorance, and which springs from sleep, idleness, or '*pramāda*' (that is, forgetfulness of one's duties), that happiness is called *tāmasa*.

[I have interpreted the word '*ātma-buddhi*' in the 37th stanza, as '*ātma-niṣṭha-buddhi* (i. e., Self-engrossed Reason); but, taking the word '*ātma*' to mean 'one's self', the word '*ātma-buddhi*' can also be explained to mean "one's own Reason"; because, it has been stated above (6. 21) that 'intense happiness' is only '*buddhi-grāhya* (Mind-Realised) and '*atīndriya*' (imperceptible to the senses). But, whichever meaning is taken, the result is the same. Even if it is said that real or permanent happiness does not lie in the enjoyment of the objects of sense, but is '*buddhi-grāhya*' (Mind-Realised), yet, when one considers what is necessary to be done, in order that one's Mind should acquire this true and intense happiness, it becomes quite clear from Chapter VI, that this intense happiness cannot be acquired, unless one's Reason has become Self-engrossed (Gī. 6. 21, 22). '*buddhi*' is such an organ, that, on the one hand, it casts a glance towards the diffusion-out of the three-qualitied Prakṛti, and on the other hand, it can also realise the Parabrahman in the shape of the Ātman, Which is at the root of that diffusion. Therefore, when by controlling the senses, one removes the Reason from the diffusion of Prakṛti embodied in the three constituents, and makes it introspective and self-engrossed—and that is all which can be acquired by the

§§ न तदस्ति पृथिव्यां वा दिवि देवेषु वा पुनः ।
सत्त्वं प्रकृतिजैर्मुक्तं यदेभिः स्यात्त्रिभिर्गुणैः ॥ ४० ॥

Pātañjala-Yoga—it (the Reason) becomes happy (*prasanna*); and man experiences true and intense happiness. For an explanation about the superiority of Metaphysical happiness, the reader is referred to the end of Chapter V of the Gītā-Rahasya (pp. 155 to 160). The Blessed Lord now explains in a general way that this three-fold difference is to be found everywhere in the world—]

(40) There is nothing on this earth or in the firmament, or in the gods (that is, in the abode of the gods), which is '*mukta*' (that is, free) from these three constituents of Prakṛti.

[From stanza 18 upto here, the Blessed Lord has explained the different kinds of *jñāna*, *karma*, *kartā*, *buddhi*, *dhṛti*, and *sukha*; and placed before the eyes of Arjuna, a picture of how diversity arises in the entire world as a result of the difference between the three constituents of Prakṛti; and He has thereby proved, that in the case of each of these various things, the *sāttvika* variety is the best and the most acceptable. The highest stage in even these *sāttvika* varieties, is known as the '*triguṇātītāvasthā*' (the state of being beyond the three constituents). That, '*triguṇātīta*' or '*nirguṇa*' is not a fourth and independent division according to the Gītā, has been explained by me in Chapter VII of the Gītā-Rahasya (pp. 227, 228); and following the same argument, the *sāttvika* condition is also sub-divided in the Manu-Smṛti into *uttama* (best), *madhyama* (medium) and *kaniṣṭha* (inferior); and '*uttama sāttvika*', is said to be productive of Release, and '*madhyama sāttvika*' is said to be productive of heaven (Manu. 12. 48–50 and 89–91). To proceed: this finishes the description of the diversity of Prakṛti in the world. The Blessed Lord now explains how the arrangement of the four classes has been made on the basis of this division of constituents. It has been stated over and over again, that it is the duty of every one in this world to perform all the

§§ ब्राह्मणक्षत्रियविशां शूद्राणां च परंतप ।
कर्माणि प्रविभक्तानि स्वभावप्रभवैर्गुणैः ॥ ४१ ॥

शमो दमस्तपः शौचं क्षान्तिरार्जवमेव च ।
ज्ञानं विज्ञानमास्तिक्यं ब्रह्मकर्म स्वभावजम् ॥ ४२ ॥

'*niyata*' Action, that is, all Action which is prescribed for him, according to his own-status (*svadharma*), having given up the Hope of Fruit, and maintaining his steadiness, enthusiasm, and determination (Gī. 18. 7–9, 23 and 3. 8); but, the essential factor by which that particular Action becomes '*niyata*' (ordained) in each case, has not so far been explained anywhere. A succinct reference to the arrangement of the four classes has appeared before (4. 13); and it has been stated there that the discrimination between the Doable and the Not-doable should be made by reference to the Śāstras (Gī. 16. 24). But, the Scriptural arrangement of the four classes, which has been arrived at on the basis of the division of Action according to the constituents, in order that the various activities of the world should go on in an orderly way, has not been explained in that place (see, Gī. Ra. pp. 463–464; 555–556 and 697–698). For this reason, the Blessed Lord now explains the institution by means of which the duty of everybody in society becomes '*niyata*', that is, 'ordained', namely, the four-class-arrangement, on the basis of the divisions of Prakṛti into three constituents; and He, at the same time, also explains what duties have been '*niyata*' (ordained) for each of the four classes.]

(41) O Parantapa! the respective duties of Brahmins (priests), Kṣatriyas (warriors), Vaiśyas (tradesman) and Śūdras (menials) have been individually fixed with reference to the qualities arising from their inherent natures, that is, from Prakṛti. (42) The inherently natural duties of a Brahmin are peace, self-restraint, religious austerities, cleanliness, quietness, straight-forwardness (humility), Knowledge (that is, Spiritual Knowledge), Vijñāna (that is, Emperial Knowledge), and *āstikya-buddhi* (that is, belief in

शौर्यं तेजो धृतिर्दाक्ष्यं युद्धे चाप्यपलायनम् ।
दानमीश्वरभावश्च क्षात्रं कर्म स्वभावजम् ॥ ४३ ॥
कृषिगोरक्ष्यवाणिज्यं वैश्यकर्म स्वभावजम् ।
परिचर्यात्मकं कर्म शूद्रस्यापि स्वभावजम् ॥ ४४ ॥

a future world—Trans.). (43) The inherently natural duty (Karma) of the Kṣatriya is bravery, brilliance, courage, intentness, not running away from the battle, generosity, and exercising authority (over subject people). (44) '*kṛṣi*' (that is, agriculture) '*gorakṣya*' (that is, the business of of keeping cattle), and *vāṇijya* (that is, trade) is the inherently natural duty of the Vaiśya; and in the same way, service is the inherently natural duty of the Śūdra.

[The arrangement of the four classes has come into existence as a result of the difference between the inherently natural qualities; but, it is not that this explanation has for the first time been given in the Gītā. This explanation about the difference between the qualities has, with nominal differences, appeared (i) in the conversation between Nahuṣa and Yudhiṣṭhira, and in the conversation between the Brahmin and the Hunter in the Vanaparva of the Mahābhārata (Vana. 180 and 211); (ii) in the conversation between Bhṛgu and Bhāradvāja in the Śānti-parva (Śān. 188); and (iii) in the conversation between Umā and Maheśvara in the Anuśāsanaparva (Aśva. 39. 11). It has been stated before that the various activities of the world result from the differences in the constituents of Prakṛti; and it has been proved that the four-class-arrangement, which determines what each of these classes has to do, is itself the result of the difference in the constituents of Prakṛti. The Blessed Lord now says, that (i) all these Actions must be carried on by everybody with a desireless frame of mind, that is, with the idea of dedicating them to the Parameśvara, as otherwise, the world will not go on; that (ii) a man acquires Perfection when he conducts himself in this way; and that (iii) it is not necessary to perform any other austerity for obtaining Perfection—]

§§ स्वे स्वे कर्मण्यभिरतः संसिद्धिं लभते नरः।
स्वकर्मनिरतः सिद्धिं यथा विन्दति तच्छृणु ॥ ४५ ॥
यतः प्रवृत्तिर्भूतानां येन सर्वमिदं ततम्।
स्वकर्मणा तमभ्यर्च्य सिद्धिं विन्दति मानवः ॥ ४६ ॥
§§ श्रेयान् स्वधर्मो विगुणः परधर्मात् स्वनुष्ठितात्।
स्वभावनियतं कर्म कुर्वन्नाप्नोति किल्बिषम् ॥ ४७ ॥

(45) That man, who is engrossed in the performance of his own duties (which have befallen him as a result of inherently natural qualities) acquires (by that alone) ultimate highest Perfection. Hear, how a man acquires Perfection by adhering to his own duties. (46) When a man, (not merely by speech or flowers, but) by performing the Actions which befall him (according to his own religion), worships That, from Which all created beings have sprung, and Which has pervaded or occupied the whole of this Cosmos, he (merely thereby) attains Perfection.

[The Blessed Lord has explained that performing desirelessly, and with the idea of dedicating to the Parameśvara, the various duties, which befall one as a result of the four-class-arrangement, is a kind of worship of the Virāṭa-formed Parameśvara, and leads to Perfection (Gī. Ra. pp. 611-612). But this duty, which has befallen one as a result of the division of Action according to divergent qualities, may appear faulty, undesirable, difficult, or unlikeable from another point of view. For instance, in the present case, the religion of Kṣatriyas may appear faulty, because it entails killing. Therefore, the reply to the questions, (i) whether, in these circumstances, a man should give up his own religion and accept another religion (Gī. 3. 35); or (ii) should perform his own duties under any circumstances; and (iii) if so, how he should perform them, is now given by using the same argument as was used in the beginning of this Chapter in dealing with Actions likes Yajñas and Yāgas—]

(47) Though another religion may be easy of observance, and one's own Action according to the four-class-arrangement

सहजं कर्म कौन्तेय सदोषमपि न त्यजेत् ।
सर्वारम्भा हि दोषेण धूमेनाग्निरिवावृताः ॥ ४८ ॥
असक्तबुद्धिः सर्वत्र जितात्मा विगतस्पृहः ।
नैष्कर्म्यसिद्धिं परमां संन्यासेनाधिगच्छति ॥ ४९ ॥

may be '*viguṇa*' (that is, faulty), yet, it is more proper; when a person is performing his own inherently natural duty (that is, the duty which has been ordained for him according to the four-class-arrangement, based on natural inherent qualities), he does not thereby incur (any) sin. (48) O Son of Kunti ! that Action, which is naturally (that is, by result of birth) '*niyata*' (that is, ordained—Trans.), according to the division of the qualities, such Action, even if improper, should not (ever) be given up; because, all *āraṁbha* (that is, activities) are enveloped in (some) fault (or other), as fire in smoke. (49) (Therefore), when a man behaves, without being attached to anything, and having controlled his mind, and with a desireless heart, then, by Renunciation (of the Fruit of Action), the highest Perfection by Non-Action (*naiṣkarmya-siddhi*) is obtained.

[The ideas that "one's own religion is better than the religion of another" (Gī. 3. 35), and that "in order to obtain the *naiṣkarmya-siddhi*, it is not necessary to abandon Action" (Gī. 3. 4), which had been mentioned before, have again been made clear in this summarising Chapter. The meaning of '*naiṣkarmya*', and what true '*naiṣkarmya-siddhi*' is, have been made clear by me in my commentary on Gī. 3. 4, to which the reader is referred. When one remembers that persons following the Path of Renunciation aim only at Release, whereas, the Blessed Lord aims equally at Release and at Universal Welfare, the importance of this principle becomes easily clear. Universal Welfare, that is, 'the maintenance and sustenance of society', needs the man endowed with Spiritual and Empirical Knowledge, as much as the brave warrior, who wins success on the battle-field by his sword, the agriculturist, the merchant, the labourer, the carpenter, the ironsmith, the potter, or even the butcher, who sells flesh. And, if it is said that Release cannot be obtained unless Action is abandoned, then, all these people will have to give up their respective business, and become ascetics! People, who adhere to the Path of Abandonment of Action (*karma-saṁnyāsa*) do not attach much importance to this; but, the vision of the Gītā is not narrow like that. Therefore, the Gītā says that, it is not proper for a person to give up the profession which has befallen him as a result of his status-in-life (*adhikāra*), and take up the profession of somebody else, on the ground that it is better. Whatever profession is taken, there is bound to be some weak point or other in it. For instance, that '*kṣānti*' (forgiveness), which is considered to be specially proper for a Brahmin (18. 42), has attached to it the great fault that "a person, who is forgiving, is looked upon as weak" (Ma. Bhā. Śān. 160. 34); and it is a misfortune that one has to sell flesh, if he follows the business of a butcher (Ma. Bhā. Vana. 206); but it is not proper, on that account, to give up these Actions. When once one has accepted a particular Action as one's own, for whatever reason one may have done so*, one must perform it, unattachedly, however difficult or undesirable it might be; because, the greatness or smallness of a man does not depend on the profession he follows; and his worth, from the spiritual point of view, depends on the frame of mind with which he follows that profession or performs that Action (Gī. 2. 49). Though a man, having a peaceful mind and having realised the Unity, which underlies the entire creation, may be a merchant or a butcher, whether by caste or by profession, yet, if he follows his profession with a desireless frame of mind, he is as much entitled to Release, and is as great as the Brahmin, who is engaged in ablutions and religious duties, or the brave warrior. Not only is this so, but it is clearly stated in stanza 49, that the Release

* This is difficult to understand. There can be only one reason for accepting the Action, namely, that it is 'Śāstra-ordained' (*niyata*)—Translator.

§§ सिद्धिं प्राप्तो यथा ब्रह्म तथाऽऽप्नोति निबोध मे ।
समासेनैव कौन्तेय निष्ठा ज्ञानस्य या परा ॥ ५० ॥

बुद्ध्या विशुद्धया युक्तो धृत्याऽऽत्मानं नियम्य च ।
शब्दादीन्विषयांस्त्यक्त्वा रागद्वेषौ व्युदस्य च ॥ ५१ ॥

विविक्तसेवी लघ्वाशी यतवाक्कायमानसः ।
ध्यानयोगपरो नित्यं वैराग्यं समुपाश्रितः ॥ ५२ ॥

अहंकारं बलं दर्पं कामं क्रोधं परिग्रहम् ।
विमुच्य निर्ममः शान्तो ब्रह्मभूयाय कल्पते ॥ ५३ ॥

ब्रह्मभूतः प्रसन्नात्मा न शोचति न काङ्क्षति ।
समः सर्वेषु भूतेषु मद्भक्तिं लभते पराम् ॥ ५४ ॥

to be obtained by abandoning Action is equally well obtained by persons, who perform their various duties with a desireless frame of mind. This is, indeed, the deep principle which underlies the Bhāgavata religion; and it is clear from the history of Mahārāṣṭrīya saints, that it is not impossible to carry into effect this principle of modelling one's conduct accordingly (see Gī. Ra. Ch. XIII, pp. 614 and 615). The Blessed Lord now explains how a man ultimately obtains Release by restricting himself to his own Actions—]

(50) I will briefly explain to you, O Son of Kunti! how, when Perfection is thus obtained, the Brahman, which is the highest state of Jnāna, is gained (by that man); to which, listen. (51) That man who, being inspired with a pure Reason and courageously controlling himself, gives up the objects (of the senses) such as, sound etc., and eschews love or hate; (52) and stays in a '*vivikta*' (that is, a chosen, or a solitary) place; who eats little, and whose body, speech, and mind are under his control, and who is continually meditative and apathetic; (53) who (similarly), having given up egoism, power, pride, desire, and anger and all '*parigraha*' (that is, bonds), has become peaceful, or self-less, such a man is fit to become Merged-in-Brahman (*brahma-bhūta*). (54) When he is merged in the Brahman, he becomes happy in mind, and does not entertain a desire for

भक्त्या मामभिजानाति यावान्यश्चास्मि तत्त्वतः ।
ततो मां तत्त्वतो ज्ञात्वा विशते तदनन्तरम् ॥ ५५ ॥

सर्वकर्माण्यपि सदा कुर्वाणो मद्व्यपाश्रयः ।
मत्प्रसादादवाप्नोति शाश्वतं पदमव्ययम् ॥ ५६ ॥

anything, and does not hate anything; and, becoming equal towards all beings, acquires intense Devotion towards Me. (55) By Devotion, he acquires the essential knowledge of how much I am, and Who I am; and when he has thus essentially recognised Me, he becomes merged in Me. (56) Even while he is performing all actions, having taken shelter in Me, he, by My favour, obtains a permanent and inexhaustible state.

[It must be borne in mind that the above description of the *siddhāvasthā* is of a Karma-Yogin and not of a Karma-Saṁnyāsin. It has been stated already in the beginning, in stanzas 45 and 49, that this description is of the person, who performs all actions without Attachment; and at the end, in stanza 56, we find the words "even while he is performing all Actions". This description is similiar to the description of a Devotee or of a *triguṇātīta*. Nay ! some words have even been taken from that description. For instance, the word '*parigraha*' in stanza 53 has appeared in the description of the Yogin in Chapter VI (6. 10); the words "*na śocati na kāṅkṣati*" in stanza 54, are to be found in the description of the Path of Devotion in Chapter XII (12. 17); and the words "remaining in a '*vivikta*', that is, a chosen (solitary) place", have appeared before in Gī. 13. 10. As this final state, attained by the Karma-Yogin, is the same as the final state reached by the Karma-Saṁnyāsin, from the purely mental point of view, commentators, subscribing to the Path of Renunciation, have got a chance of imagining that these descriptions support their school. But, I have stated any number of times before, that this procedure is not correct. To proceed: the Blessed Lord has, in the beginning of this Chapter, (i) defined 'Saṁnyāsa' by stating, that Saṁnyāsa does not

चेतसा सर्वकर्माणि मयि संन्यस्य मत्परः
बुद्धियोगमुपाश्रित्य मच्चित्तः सततं भव ॥ ५७ ॥

mean 'Abandonment of Action'; but means 'Abandonment of the Hope of Fruit'; and (ii) maintained that Actions, such as giving up of food etc., whether they are *kāmya*, *nitya*, or *naimittika*, must be performed like other Actions, without the Hope of Fruit, enthusiastically, and with an equable frame of mind; and thereafter, He has explained the doctrine laid down by the Gītā by saying that (i) although the various matters in the world, such as, *karma*, *kartā*, *buddhi* etc., may be diverse as a result of the difference of qualities, yet, the *sāttvika* quality is the best of all; that (ii) in performing, unattachedly, all the Actions, which have befallen anybody on account of his own-status, according to the four-class-arrangement, one thereby sacrifices to, and performs the worship of, the Parameśvara and thereby gradually acquires the Parabrahman or Release; that (iii) no other practice nor Sāṁnyāsa in the form of Abandonment of Action is necessary for obtaining Release; and that (iv) by Karma-Yoga alone, all states of Perfection including Release are to be had. Now the Blessed Lord again and finally advises Arjuna to accept this path of Karma-Yoga—]

(57) '*saṁnyasya*' (that is, having dedicated) all Actions to Me, mentally, and having become devoted to Me, keep your mind always fixed on Me, taking shelter in the Yoga of (equable) Reason.

[The word '*buddhi-yoga*' (Yoga of Reason) has appeared before already in Chapter II (2. 49); and there it has been interpreted to mean 'the device of performing Actions without allowing one's mind to be fixed on the Hope of Fruit', or, 'the equable Reason'. The same meaning is intended in this place; and this is only a repetition of the statement in Chapter II, that Reason is better than or superior to Action. 'Karma-saṁnyāsa' is also defined here as meaning, 'mentally (that is, not by the actual Abandonment of Action, but merely by the Mind) dedicating all Actions to Me'; and the same idea has been

मच्चित्तः सर्वदुर्गाणि मत्प्रसादात्तरिष्यसि ।
अथ चेत्त्वमहंकारान्न श्रोष्यसि विनङ्क्ष्यसि ॥ ५८ ॥
§§ यदहंकारमाश्रित्य न योत्स्य इति मन्यसे ।
मिथ्यैष व्यवसायस्ते प्रकृतिस्त्वां नियोक्ष्यति ॥ ५९ ॥
स्वभावजेन कौन्तेय निबद्धः स्वेन कर्मणा ।
कर्तुं नेच्छसि यन्मोहात्करिष्यस्यवशोऽपि तत् ॥ ६० ॥
ईश्वरः सर्वभूतानां हृद्देशेऽर्जुन तिष्ठति ।
भ्रामयन्सर्वभूतानि यन्त्रारूढानि मायया ॥ ६१ ॥
तमेव शरणं गच्छ सर्वभावेन भारत ।
तत्प्रसादात्परां शान्तिं स्थानं प्राप्स्यसि शाश्वतम् ॥ ६२ ॥
इति ते ज्ञानमाख्यातं गुह्याद्गुह्यतरं मया ।
विमृश्यैतदशेषेण यथेच्छसि तथा कुरु ॥ ६३ ॥

expressed before in Chap. III (3. 20), and in Chap. V (5. 13)]

(58) Fixing your mind on Me, you will, by My favour, conquer all difficulties in the shape of the beneficent or evil results of Actions. But, if you egotistically do not listen to Me, then (indeed) you will be lost.

[The effect of Egoism, mentioned at the end of stanza 58, is now further explained.]

(59) Your egotistical belief that: "I will not fight", is futile. Prakṛti (that is, inherent nature) will compel you to do so. (60) O Son of Kunti! being bound by the Action inherently natural to you, you will have to perform that, which, by Ignorance you do not wish to perform, you having become subject to another (that is, to your own Prakṛti or inherent nature). (61) O Arjuna! the Īśvara, remaining in the hearts of all beings, agitates all beings by (His) Illusion, as though they were put into a machine. (62) Therefore, O Bhārata! surrender yourself to Him whole-mindedly! By His favour, you will attain the highest tranquility and a permanent place. (63) Thus have I explained to you this Knowledge, which is a mystery of mysteries. Think over all this fully, and do what you think best.

[The dependence or subjectivity in the matter of Action, of which the mysterious principle has been explained in the above stanzas, has been fully dealt with in Chapter X of the Gītā-Rahasya, to which the reader is referred. Although the Ātman is independent by itself, yet, if one considers the ordinary affairs of the world, that is, of Prakṛti, it will be seen, that the Ātman has no control over the Wheel of Action, which has been moving from times immemorial. Even if we may not wish them, nay, even if we may wish otherwise, hundreds and thousands of things are going on in the world; and either the results of their activity are felt by us, or we ourselves have to perform some part of that activity, and cannot say no. In these circumstances, the wise man performs these Actions, keeping his mind pure, and looking upon pain and happiness as alike: whereas, the fool gets entangled in the bonds of those Actions: this is the important difference between the behaviour of the two. The Blessed Lord has mentioned already in Chap. III, that "all created beings conform to their inherent nature, no amount of determination is of any avail" (Gī. 3. 33). In these circumstances, all that the Science of Release, or Ethics, can say is that one should not become attached to Action. Thus far, I have considered the matter from the Metaphysical point of view. But, even from the point of view of Devotion, Prakṛti or Nature, is only a part of the Īśvara. And, therefore, the same proposition has been repeated in stanzas 61 and 62, by giving credit for all Action to the Īśvara. All the activities, which go on in the world, are got done by the Parameśvara, just as He wants them to be done. It is, therefore, proper that a wise man should abandon Egoism and surrender himself entirely to the Parameśvara. It is true that in stanza 63, the Blessed Lord has said, "do what you think best"; but, the meaning of that is very deep. Since no evil desire remains when the mind reaches a state of complete equability, whether by Knowledge or by Devotion, the 'Freedom of Will' of such a scient can never prejudicially affect either him or the world. Therefore, the true meaning of those words is: "when you have Realised

§§ सर्वगुह्यतमं भूयः शृणु मे परमं वचः ।
इष्टोऽसि मे दृढमिति ततो वक्ष्यामि ते हितम् ॥ ६४ ॥
मन्मना भव मद्भक्तो मद्याजी मां नमस्कुरु ।
मामेवैष्यसि सत्यं ते प्रतिजाने प्रियोऽसि मे ॥ ६५ ॥
सर्वधर्मान्परित्यज्य मामेकं शरणं व्रज ।
अहं त्वा सर्वपापेभ्यो मोक्षयिष्यामि मा शुचः ॥ ६६ ॥

this Knowledge (*vimṛśya*), you will be self-enlightened; and thereafter (not before), whatever Action may be voluntarily performed by you, will be consistent with morality, and correct; and when you have thus reached the state of a Sthitaprajña, it will no more be necessary for you to control your Desire". To proceed: I have shown at the end of Chap. XIV of the Gītā-Rahasya that Devotion has been given a higher place than Knowledge in the Gītā. Consistently with this proposition, the Blessed Lord now summarises the entire doctrine of the Gītā in terms of Devotion—]

(64) I shall once more give you a final admonition, which is the mystery of all mysteries, to which listen. You are extremely beloved of Me; and therefore, I am going to tell you something, which is to your advantage. (65) Keep your mind fixed on Me, become My devotee, offer sacrifice or worship to Me, and offer reverence to Me; (thereby) you will come and be merged in Me; this truth I am imparting to you as an absolute certainty, (because), you are my beloved (devotee). (66) Give up all other religions, and surrender yourself to Me alone; I will redeem you from all sin; do not be afraid!

[Those commentators, who subscribe only to the Path of Knowledge, do not appreciate this summing up, which is in favour of Devotion. They, therefore, include '*adharma*' (immorality) in '*dharma*' (morality), and say (i) that this stanza conveys the same advice as that given in the Kaṭhopanisad in the words: "give up morality and immorality, that which is done and that which is not yet done, the past and the future, and Realise the Supreme

Brahman beyond all that" (Kaṭha. 2. 14); and (ii) that it advises one to surrender oneself to the Qualityless Brahman. The stanza from the Kaṭhopaniṣad is also to be found in the description of the Qualityless Brahman in the Mahābhārata (Śān. 329. 40; 331. 44). But in both these places the two words 'morality' and 'immorality' have been distinctly mentioned, which is not the case in the Gītā. It is true that the Gītā accepts the Qualityless Brahman, and also propounds the doctrine that the Qualityless Brahman is the super-excellent form of the Parameśvara (Gī. 7. 24). Yet, as the Gītā also maintains that the worship of the Perceptible is easy and excellent (12. 5), and as the Blessed Lord is here referring to His own perceptible form, I am firmly of opinion that this summing up supports the Path of Devotion. Needless to say, the Qualityless Brahman is not intended here; and the word '*dharma*' used here must be understood to mean, the religion of Harmlessness, the religion of Truth, the religion of Service of one's parents, the religion of Service of one's preceptors, the religion of performing sacrificial ritual, the religion of Charity, the religion of Renunciation, and other ways of reaching the Parameśvara, which have been mentioned in the Scriptures. And, where the subject-matter has been discussed in the Śāntiparva (Śān. 344), and in the Anu-Gītā (Aśva. 49), in the Mahābhārata, these ways of obtaining Release have been referred to by the word '*dharma*'. But, the Blessed Lord definitely says in this place, with reference to the religion enunciated by the Gītā, that Arjuna should not concern himself with these various religions, but should "surrender yourself to Me alone, I will redeem you, do not be afraid" (see Gī. Ra. Ch. XIII, pp. 616–618). In short, the Blessed Lord, giving the advice nominally to Arjuna, but really to everybody, says that one should be deeply devoted to Him, and becoming engrossed in Him, perform all Actions, which become one's duties, according to one's own status, with a Reason devoted to Him; and that, thereby, one will acquire benefit not only in this life, but also in the next. This is what is known as KARMA–YOGA; and this is the

§§ इदं ते नातपस्काय नाभक्ताय कदाचन ।
न चाशुश्रूषवे वाच्यं न च मां योऽभ्यसूयति ॥ ६७ ॥
य इदं परमं गुह्यं मद्भक्तेष्वभिधास्यति ।
भक्तिं मयि परां कृत्वा मामेवैष्यत्यसंशयः ॥ ६८ ॥
न च तस्मान्मनुष्येषु कश्चिन्मे प्रियकृत्तमः ।
भविता न च मे तस्मादन्यः प्रियतरो भुवि ॥ ६९ ॥
§§ अध्येष्यते च य इमं धर्म्यं संवादमावयोः ।
ज्ञानयज्ञेन तेनाहमिष्टः स्यामिति मे मतिः ॥ ७० ॥
श्रद्धावाननसूयश्च शृणुयादपि यो नरः ।
सोऽपि मुक्तः शुभाँल्लोकान् प्राप्नुयात्पुण्यकर्मणाम् ॥ ७१ ॥

sum and substance of the Gītā-religion. The Blessed Lord now explains how to maintain and keep alive the tradition of this Gītā-religion, that is, of the Karma-Yoga based on Knowledge, and in which Devotion is the most important factor—]

(67) Do you never mention this (mystery) to anybody, who does not perform austerities, who has no devotion, nor a desire to hear it, nor to one who vilifies Me. (68) He, who expounds this highest mystery to My devotees, will be filled with intense devotion towards Me, and will come and reach Me; about this, there is no doubt. (69) And no one can be found among all men, who does something more dear to Me, than such a man; and no one will be more beloved of Me than him in this universe.

[In continuation of this advice, given with the intention of maintaining the tradition of the Gītā, the Blessed Lord now explains the beneficent effects of following the Gītā-religion—]

(70) Whoever meditates on this conversation of us two on religion, will be considered by Me as having worshipped Me by a Sacrifice of Knowledge. (71) In the same way, he who follows this religion without carping, and with Faith, he also will be redeemed from all sin, and reach the happiest spheres, which are in store for saintly people.

§§ कच्चिदेतच्छ्रुतं पार्थ त्वयैकाग्रेण चेतसा ।
कच्चिदज्ञानसंमोहः प्रणष्टस्ते धनंजय ॥ ७२ ॥
अर्जुन उवाच ।
नष्टो मोहः स्मृतिर्लब्धा त्वत्प्रसादान्मयाऽच्युत ।
स्थितोऽस्मि गतसन्देहः करिष्ये वचनं तव ॥ ७३ ॥
संजय उवाच ।
§§ इत्यहं वासुदेवस्य पार्थस्य च महात्मनः ।
संवादमिममश्रौषमद्भुतं रोमहर्षणम् ॥ ७४ ॥

[In this way, the advice is over. Now, in order to find out whether or not Arjuna has properly understood this religion, the Blessed Lord asks him—]

(72) O Pārtha! have you listened to all this, with a concentrated mind? (and) O Dhanañjaya! has your confusion, in the shape of Ignorance, now been totally destroyed? Arjuna said:—(73) O Unfallen One! by Your favour has my ignorance been destroyed; and I have regained memory (of my duties); I am (now) free from doubt; I shall now do (fight) as told by You!

[Those, who have got the traditional idea that the Gītā-religion advises the Abandonment of family life, have, without the slightest justification, stretched the meaning of the last, that is, of the 73rd stanza. If we consider of what Arjuna had lost memory, we see that in Chapter II, he has said: "my mind does not understand what my '*dharma*' or my duty is" (cf. "*dharma sammūḍha cetāḥ*"); and the plain meaning of the above stanza is, that he has now remembered that duty. As the Gītā has been told in order to induce Arjuna to fight, and the Blessed Lord has, in various places, said: "Do you, therefore, fight!" (Gī. 2. 18; 2. 37; 3. 30; 8. 7; 11. 34), the words "I shall now do as told by You", can only mean, "I shall fight". To proceed: the conversation between Śrī Kṛṣṇa and Arjuna is now over; now, with reference to the narration in the Mahābhārata, Sañjaya, having narrated this story to Dhṛtarāṣṭra, summarises his own narration—]

Sañjaya said:—(74) In this way, I heard this wonderful and

व्यासप्रसादाच्छ्रुतवानेतद्गुह्यमहं परम् ।
योगं योगेश्वरात्कृष्णात्साक्षात् कथयतः स्वयम् ॥ ७५ ॥

hair-raising conversation between Vāsudeva and the noble-souled Arjuna. (75) By the favour of Vyāsa, I was enabled to hear this mystery of mysteries, that is, Yoga,—(of course, the Karma-Yoga),—when Śrī Kṛṣṇa, the Lord of all Yoga Himself was personally expounding it.

[It has been stated in the beginning of the Gītā, that as Vyāsa had given super-natural vision to Sañjaya, he could, sitting in his own place, see in reality whatever was happening in the battle-field; and that he used to repeat everything he saw to Dhṛtarāṣṭra. The Yoga, expounded by Śrī Kṛṣna was nothing but the Karma-Yoga (Gī. 4. 1-3); and Arjuna himself has referred to it before (Gī. 6. 33), as 'Yoga' (the Yoga of Equability); and now, Sañjaya also refers to the conversation between Śrī Kṛṣṇa and Arjuna in this stanza as 'Yoga'. From this, it becomes clear that Karma-Yoga is the subject-matter of exposition in the Gītā, according to the opinions of Śrī Kṛṣṇa and Arjuna, as also of Sañjaya; and the expression (*saṁkalpa*) used to denote the end of the chapter at the end of every chapter also contains the word "*yoga-śāstra*". But the word 'Yoga', in the phrase 'Yogeśvara' is more comprehensive. The ordinary meaning of the word 'Yoga' is 'the device of, or the skill or proficiency in, performing any Action'; and in this sense, the *bahurūpi* (one who shows many appearances) is said to perform his personifications by Yoga, that is, by skill. But, if one considers what is the best way in which Action can be performed, one has to say, that the way by which the Parameśvara, Who is essentially Imperceptible and Qualityless, gives Himself a perceptible appearance is the best 'Yoga' or device. This is referred to in the Gītā as the 'Īśvarī-Yoga' (Gī. 9. 5; 11. 8); and this is what is known as 'Māyā' or 'Illusion' in Vedānta (Gī. 7. 25). For that man, who has successfully acquired this wonderful and unequalled Yoga, all other Yogas or devices are mere child's play. The Parameśvara is the Over-Lord of all these Yogas, or

राजन्संस्मृत्य संस्मृत्य संवादमिममद्भुतम् ।
केशवार्जुनयोः पुण्यं हृष्यामि च मुहुर्मुहुः ॥ ७६ ॥
तच्च संस्मृत्य संस्मृत्य रूपमत्यद्भुतं हरेः ।
विस्मयो मे महान् राजन् हृष्यामि च पुनः पुनः ॥ ७७ ॥
यत्र योगेश्वरः कृष्णो यत्र पार्थो धनुर्धरः ।
तत्र श्रीर्विजयो भूतिर्ध्रुवा नीतिर्मतिर्मम ॥ ७८ ॥

devices: that is why He has been referred to as the 'Yogeśvara', or the 'Lord of Yogas'. The word 'Yoga' in the phrase 'Yogeśvara' does not indicate the Pātañjala-Yoga.]

(76) O King Dhṛtarāṣṭra! remembering this unprecedented and holy conversation between Keśava and Arjuna, I experience joy over and over again. (77) And O King! thinking of that most wonderful Cosmic-Form of the Blessed Lord, I am filled with astonishment, and again with joy. (78) And, in my opinion, wherever there is Śrī Kṛṣṇa, the Lord of all Yoga, and the bow-holder Arjuna, there also will be found Wealth, Victory, Eternal Prosperity, and Morality.

[In short, the doctrine enunciated here is, that wherever skill is combined with power, there do both *ṛddhī* (prosperity) and *siddhī* (success) take up their permanent abode; and that, mere skill, or mere power is not enough. When the ways and means of killing Jarāsaṁdha were being considered, Yudhiṣṭhira said to Śrī Kṛṣṇa: "*andhaṁ balaṁ jaḍaṁ prāhuḥ praṇetavyaṁ vicakṣaṇaiḥ*" (Sabhā. 20. 16), that is, "power is blind, and material; the wise must show it the way". Thereupon, the Blessed Lord, saying: "*mayi nītir balaṁ bhīme*", (Sabhā. 20. 3), that is, "I am the store of diplomacy and Bhīma, that of strength", has taken Bhīma-sena with Himself, and skilfully brought about the death of Jarāsaṁdha by his (Bhīma's) hands. The one, who merely gives the diplomatic advice, may be looked upon as only half-wise*. Therefore, the word '*yogeśvara*' means the 'Lord of Yoga, or skill', and the word '*dhanurdhara*' means 'the fighter', and both these adjectives have been used here intentionally.]

* This will be construed as a depreciatory reference to the Blessed Lord Śrī Kṛṣṇa, which is, indeed, unfortunate.—Trans.

इति श्रीमद्भगवद्गीतासु उपनिषत्सु ब्रह्मविद्यायां योगशास्त्रे
श्रीकृष्णार्जुनसंवादे मोक्षसंन्यासयोगो नाम
अष्टादशोऽध्यायः ॥ १८ ॥

Thus ends the eighteenth chapter named MOKSA-SAMNYASA YOGA in the dialogue between Śrī Kṛṣṇa and Arjuna on the Yoga included in the Science of the Brahman (that is, on the Karma-Yoga) in the Upaniṣad sung (that is, told) by the Blessed Lord.

[It must be borne in mind that the word '*saṁnyāsa*' in the phrase '*mokṣa-saṁnyāsa-yoga*', means the '*saṁnyasa* or Renunciation of Desire-prompted Action'; and not 'the state of an ascetic', which is the fourth stage of life. As it has been propounded in this chapter that Release is obtained by mentally making a Saṁnyāsa or Renunciation of one's prescribed Actions, in favour of the Parameśvara, instead of by abandoning them, this chapter has been named 'Moksa-Saṁnyāsa-Yoga'.]

IN THIS WAY
THE
RAHASYA-SAÑJĪVANA

being the translation, into the Marāṭhī vernacular, of the Śrīmad Bhagavadgītā, together with the commentary on it, written by Bal Gangadhar Tilak, comes to an end.

In the Mahārāṣṭra, in the town of Poona, there lives one, who was born in a Brahmin family, and is devoted to the Śrutis, whose name is BĀL, and who is the son of GAṄGĀDHARA, and whose surname is ṬILAK; and he has, by publishing the RAHASYA of the GĪTĀ in the year 1837, of the Śaka era, dedicated it to the LORD of ŚRĪ.*

OM TAT SAT BRAHMĀRPAṆAM ASTU
ŚĀNTIH PUṢṬIŚ TUṢṬIŚ CĀSTU.

ŚRĪ INDIRĀ'RPAṆAM ASTU †

* The above dedication is in Marāṭhī verse in the original—Trans.

† This is my dedication (see Vol. I p. xxxvii). —Translator.

An index of the stanzas of the

GĪTĀ

showing the first quarter of each stanza, by reference to the chapter and the stanza.

An index of the words occurring in the

GĪTĀ

by reference to the chapter and the stanza.

(This index has been incorporated in this book as it is from the edition of the Bhagavadgītā by Dr. Annie Besant and Babu Bhagavandas, published by the Theosophical Publishing House, Adyar, Madras, India, 1926, for which incorporation, both Babu Bhagavandas, and the Theosophical Publishing House have very kindly granted permission to the Translator).

मा

INDEX to PERSONAGES referred to.

(Not being Indian or Foreign Authors).

(*Note*:—The original text of the author was not indexed at all. The first index above (of stanza-beginnings), and this and the three following indexes were first added to the fourth Marathi edition of the text, published in 1923, after the death of the author, as stated in the Publisher's foreword to that edition. The references to the pages in this 1923 Marathi edition, in this and the three following indices, have been replaced by the corresponding references to the pages of the present English edition, except such as I have not been able to trace. Also, the words in the original indexes, which had been arranged according to the Marathi alphabet, have been re-arranged by me according to the English Alphabet, letters with diacritical signs, being indexed as if there were no such signs. (ii) in front of a figure, or row of figures, means Vol. II—Translator.)

INDEX to FOREIGN AUTHORS.

AN INDEX of AUTHORS (not foreign) and of their WORKS, referred to in the Gītā-Rahasya.

Note:—Even if this index is merely glanced at, readers will get an idea of its arrangement. The names of authors and of their works have been given according to the Marathi alphabet, and works of the same nature have been grouped together, as will be realised by the readers on the face of the index. Those personages, who have been referred to in the course of the expositions of the various subject-matters, for expounding the true import of the Gītā, have already been indexed separately (see p. 77 to 79 above—Trans.); and the last. Index of Definitions includes technical words. (see p. 89 *et. seq.*—Trans.).

(*The above is the heading of the Index added to the 1923 Marathī edition of the text, which was published after the death of the author. The words in this index had been arranged according to the Marathi alphabet, as stated above, and I have re-arranged them according to the English alphabet, except such references as I have been unable to trace in spite of due and diligent search. Letters with diacritical signs have been indexed as if there were no such signs; and the figure* (ii) *before a figure or row of figures means Volume II.*—Translator.)

* The words "see list", used in this index, mean : "see this index". 'Brāhmaṇas' is the name of a class of treatises, just as 'Purāṇas,' or 'Gītās'; and the various Brāhmaṇas are not indexed under 'Brāhmaṇas' but in their respective alphabetical order, as 'Ārṣeya-Brāhmaṇa', 'Aitareya-Brāhmaṇa', etc.; or, in the case of the Gītās, as: Brahma-Gītā, Śiva-Gītā etc.—Trans.

INDEX OF DEFINITIONS of Terminological Expressions given in the Gita-Rahasya.

This Index was first added to the 1923 Marathi edition of the text published after the death of the author. The index, which is of Sanskrit expressions, had been arranged in the original, according to the Sanskrit alphabet, and has been re-arranged by me according to the English alphabet, letters with diacritical signs being indexed, as if there were no such signs. After each Sanskrit word, I have, wherever necessary, added its English translation in brackets, as appearing in the translation of the text. I have named this as Part I of the Index of Definitions. In Part II, I have indexed the English translation of the same words, according to alphabetical arrangement, and placed within brackets after the English word its Sanskrit equivalent as appearing in Part I of the Index. Part II has been specially prepared by me for the convenience of readers, who are unacquainted with the Sanskrit language. The figure (ii) before a figure or row of figures means Vol II.—Translator.

(N. B. This Index covers only pages 1 to 831 of the translation.)

PART I—SANSKRIT.

PART II—ENGLISH.

SOME GENERAL INFORMATION ABOUT HINDU RELIGIOUS TREATISES.

(*N B.:*—This note was not written by the author, but was first included in the 1923 edition of the Marathi text, which was published after the death of the author in 1920.—Trans.).

Among the treatises, on which the Hindu Religion is based, the Vedas are the most superior and the most ancient, from the point of view of importance and chronology; and the Saṁhitās, the Brāhmaṇas, and the Upaniṣads are included in them. The Karma-Kāṇḍa, consisting of Yajñas and Yāgas (religious sacrifices), and the Jñāna-Kāṇḍa, consisting of Metaphysical conceptions, both spring from this triad. Nevertheless, the Upaniṣadic treatises form the basis of the Jñāna-Kāṇḍa. The social relations, included in the Hindu religion, are regulated according to the Smṛti texts; but these are based on the Gṛhya-Sūtras. There are many Sūtra-treatises besides the Gṛhya-Sūtras; but they have nothing to do with Ethics; and deal only with the various Metaphysical speculations started in order to solve the Riddle of the Universe. These Metaphysical speculations, are called tha Ṣaḍ-Darśanas. The Nyāya-Sūtras of Gautama, the Vaiṣeśika-Sūtras, the Pūrva-Mīmāṁsā-Sūtras of Jaimini, the Vedānta-Sūtras or the Brahma-Sūtras of Bādarāyaṇa, the Yoga-Sūtras of Pātañjali etc., are included in the Ṣaḍ-Darśanas. But there are many Sūtra-treatises, besides the Ṣaḍ-Darśanas; and the Pāṇini-Sūtras, the Śāṇḍilya-Sūtras, the Nārada-Sūtras etc., are included among them. The Purāṇas came into existence, when the ancient Vedic religion, which did not contain idol-worship, and which was purely Metaphysical in its aspect, was changed, and the worshipping of deities came into vogue. The Mahābhārata and the Rāmāyaṇa are not Purāṇas, but are historical treatises. The various Gītās are included in the Purāṇas. This subject-matter has been discussed in the Gītā-Rahasya as occasion arose; but this information has been given below in the form of a list, in order that readers should have complete information about them collected in one place:–

(1) THE VEDAS AND THE ŚRUTI TREATISES:—

The Saṁhitās (i. e., the collection of Ṛcās or Mantras)	Karma-Kāṇḍa or Yajña-Kāṇḍā
The Brāhmaṇas (Araṇyakas) ...	
The Upaniṣads	(Jñāna-Kāṇḍa).

(2) ŚĀSTRAS:—

(1) Scriptures: Gṛhya-Sūtras, Smṛti treatises (Manu, Yājñavalkya, and Hārīta.)

(2) Sūtras: (Ṣaḍ-Darśanas), Jaimini–, (Mīmāṁsā- or Pūrva-Mīmāṁsā); Brahma–, (Vedānta-, Śārīrika-, or Uttara-Mīmāṁsā); Nyāya–, (Gautama); Yoga–, (Pātañjala), Sāṁkhya-, Vaiṣeśika–, (Sāṁkhya-Kārika).

(3) OTHER SŪTRAS:—

Vyākaraṇa-Sūtras (Pāṇini); Treatises relating to the Path of Devotion (Nārada, Śāṇḍilya).

(4) HISTORY:—

Rāmāyaṇa, Mahābhārata, (Harivaṁśa).

(5) PURĀṆAS:—

Mahāpurāṇas, Upapurāṇas, and Gītās.

These include 18 Mahāpurāṇas, 18 Upapurāṇas, and and the various Gītās.

The different Vedā-,Smṛti–, and Purāṇa-treatises, referred to in the Gītā-Rahasya are mentioned in the following list:—

VEDAS:—

Atharva. Ṛg-Veda.

SAṀHITĀS:—

Taittiirīya. Vājasaneyī.
Manu. Sūta.

BRĀHMAṆAS:—

Ārṣeya. Kauṣika. Kauṣītakī.
Aitarīya. Taittirīya. Śatapatha.

UPANIṢADS:—

Amṛtabindu. Chāndogya. Mahānārāyaṇa.
Īśa (Īśāvāsya). Churikā. Māṇḍukya.
Aitareya. Jābāla-Saṁnyāsa. Muṇḍaka (Maṇḍa)
Kaṭha. Taittirīya. Maitrī (Maitrāyaṇī).
Kena. Dhyāna-bindu. Yogataa.
Kaivalya. Nārāyaṇīya. Rāmapūrva (lāpini)
Kauṣītakī (Kau. Brāhmaṇa). Nṛsiṁhottara-tāpanīya. Vajrasūcī.
Śvetāśvatara.
Garbha. Praśna. Sarva.
Gopālatāpanī. Bṛhadāraṇyaka.

SMṚTIS :—

Manu.
Yājñavalkya.
Hārīta.

SŪTRAS :—

Āpastamba.
Āśvalāyana.
Gṛhyaśeṣa.
Gautama-Nyāya.
Taittirīya.
Nārada.
Nārada-Pañcarātra.
Pāṇinī.
Pātañjala-Yoga.
Baudhāyana-Dharma.
Baudhayana-Gṛhya.
Brahma-(Vedānta-, Śārīrika-).
Mīmāṁsā.
Vedānta (Brahma-Śārīrika-).
Śārīrika (Brahma-, Vedānta-).
Śāṇḍilya.
Gobhilagṛhya.

KĀRIKĀS :—

Sāṁkhya-Kārikā.

VYĀKARAṆA :—

Pāṇinī.

HISTORIES :—

Rāmāyaṇa.
Mahābhārata (Harivaṁśa).

PURĀṆAS :—

Agni.
Kūrma.
Gaṇeśa.
Garuḍa.
Gauḍīya-Padmottara.
Devībhāgavata.
Nārada.
Nṛsiṁha.
Padma.
Brahmāṇḍa.
Bhāgavata.
Matsya.
Mārkaṇḍeya.
Liṅga.
Varāha.
Viṣṇu.
Skanda.
Harivaṁśa.

GĪTĀS :—

Avadhūta.
Aṣṭāvakra.
Īśvara.
Uttara.
Kapila.
Gaṇeśa.
Devī.
Parāśara.
Pāṇḍava.
Piṅgala.
Brahma.
Bodhya.
Bhikṣu.
Maṅki.
Yama.
Rāma.
Vicikhyu.
Vyāsa.
Vṛtra.
Śiva.
Śaṁpāka.
Sūta.
Sūrya.
Hari.
Haṁsa.
Hārīta.

PALI TEXTS :—

Amitāyusutta.
Udāna.
Cullavagga
Tārānātha.
Tevijja–sutta. (Traividya-Sūtra).
Theragāthā.
Daśaratha-jātaka.
Dīpavaṁsa.
Dhammapada.
Brahmajāla-sutta.
Brāhmaṇa-dhamikā.
Mahāparinibbāṇa-sutta.
Mahāvaṁsa.
Milinda-Praśna.
Vatthugāthā.
Saddharma-puṇḍarīka.
Suttanipāta.
Sela-sutta.
Sabbāsava-sutta.
Saundarānanda.

GLOSSARY.

OF

Important Terminological Expressions.

abhyāsa, repetition; continued practice.

ācāra, conduct.

ācāra-saṁgraha, code of conduct.

ādhibhautika, Material; Materialistic.

ādhidaivika, Intuitional.

adhikāra, authority; qualification according to inherent natural qualities.

adhyātma, Metaphysics; the Highest Atman.

ādhyātmika, Metaphysical; relating to the Absolute Self.

adhyavasāya, discriminating decision. (see, *vyavasāya*).

adṛṣṭa, Accumulated Action, which is invisible (also called, *apūrva*).

advaita, Non-Dual.

advaitavāda, Non-Dualism.

ahaṁkāra, Individuation; Egoism.

ahiṁsā, Harmlessness; Non-violence.

ajñāna, Ignorance.

amṛta, Release; sphere of deities; immortality; sacrifice-remnant food; Fundamental Substance; the Brahman;

amṛtatva, Immortality.

anādi, eternal.

ānanda, Beatitude,
 –maya, beatific.
 –maya kośa, beatific envelope.

ananta, endless; eternal.

anārabdha, Uncommenced (Action).

aniruddha, Individuation (same as, *ahaṁkāra*).

annamaya-kośa, food-envelope.

anubhavādvaita, combination of Knowledge and Action, based on Non-dualism: this is more or less the same as the Desireless Karma-Yoga doctrine (see p. 508).

anṛta, invisible, or imperceptible, (the opposite of, *satya*, Real).

āptavacana, advice of persons in whom one puts faith.

apūrva, (see, *adṛṣṭa* above).

ārabdha, Commenced (Action).

āraṁbha, Commencement.

āraṁbhavāda, Theory of Commencement, (see, pp. 204, 205, 331).

arhat, Perfect being (Buddhistic), (same as, *siddha*).

ārtam, perishable (same as, *vināśī*).

arthavāda, statements, which are in the nature of *obiter dicta* (see pp. 31–32.)

asaṁbhūti, ignorance, (same as, *vināśa*, *avidyā*).

asat, unreal, (same as, *anṛta*).
asi, art (thou), (see, *tat-tvam-asi*).
asteya, non-stealing.
āsurī, ungodly.
āsurī-saṁpat, ungodly endowment.
ātman, the Self.
ātma-svātaṁtrya, Freedom of Will.
avidyā, Illusion, (same as, Māyā).
avyakta, Imperceptible.

bhakti, devotion.
bhaktimārga, the Path of Devotion.
bhakti-yoga, the Yoga of Devotion.
bhāṣya, Commentary, (see, *ṭīkā*: see, p. 16.).
Brahman, the ultimate Essential Principle, which is the Root-Cause of the Cosmos.
brahmārpaṇa, dedication to the Brahman.
brahma-vṛkṣa, the Brahman-Tree.
buddha, sage; wise man.
buddhi, Reason; the Mind; Desire.
buddhibheda, destroying the conviction of a person.
buddhi-yoga, the Yoga of the Equable Reason.

caturvyūha, the four-fold scheme of the genesis of the world. from Vāsudeva

caturvyūhv—(contd.)
(Īśvara) to Saṁkarṣaṇa (*jīva*), to Pradyumna (*manas*), to Aniruddha (Individuation). (see, pp. 756-758.
cetanā, vital activity seen in living beings (see p. 194).
cit, or *citta*, consciousness.
caitanya, that thought-power. which is responsible for activity in gross bodies (see, p. 194).
codanā, inspiration.

dātavya, that which it is a duty to give.
daiva, Destiny.
daivī, Godly (opposite of *āsuri*, ungodly).
daivī-saṁpat, godly endowment,
dayā, kindness; pity.
devatā, deity.
devayāna, the path along which the subtle body of a deceased person passes, if the man has died at a particular time, being what is known as the 'lighted path' (*śukla-mārga*), (see pp. 408-410).
dharma, a deity; morality; right; duty; religion, (see references given under '*dharma*' in Index of Definitions, part I).
dharmādharma, right and wrong.
dhṛti, that principle of co-hesion by which all the various elements of the Body remain steady (see p. 195).

duḥkha, pain ; unhappiness.
dvaita, Duality.
dvaitādvaita, Dual-non-dualism
daitavāda, Dualism.

ekāntika, solitudinal.
eṣaṇā, desire, (same as, *icchā*, *vāsanā*, *saṁga*, and *kāma*).

gati, goal ; path (same as, *sṛti*).
gītā, song.
guṇa, constituent ; strand ; quality.
guṇapariṇāma, the unfolding of the constituents of Prakṛti.
guṇotkarṣa, (same as *guṇa-pariṇāma*).

hinayāna, (Buddhistic), the inferior path.

icchā, Desire, (same as *eṣaṇā*, *kāma*, *vāsanā*, *saṁga*).
icchāsvātaṁtrya, freedom of desire or will (same as *ātma-svātaṁtrya* above).
indriya, senses, or organs.

jaḍa, gross.
jaḍādvaita, gross, or materialistic non-dualism (see p. 219).
jīva, the Personal Self ; (same as the embodied Self, or the *śarira-ātman*).
jīvātman, (same as, *jīva*).
jīvanmukta, Released-in-life ; birth-released.
jīvamuktāvasthā, the state of being Released-in-life.
jña, the Knower.
jñāna, Knowledge ; wisdom ; Realisation.
jñāna-kāṇḍa, treatises which maintain that the Knowledge of the Brahman is superior to sacrificial ritual.
jñāna-niṣṭhā, the Path of Knowledge.
jñāna-mārga, (same as, *jñāna-niṣṭhā*).
jñānin, Knowledgeful ; sage ; wise.
jñātā, Knower.
jñeya, the Knowable.

kaivalya, Isolation.
kāla, Time ; death.
kāma, Desire (same as *icchā*, *eṣaṇā*, or *vāsanā*).
kāmya, Desire-prompted.
karma, Action.
karma-bhoga, the suffering for Action.
karma-jijñāsā, the desire to know Right Action.
karma-kāṇḍa, ritualistic treatises.
karma-mukti, Release from the effects of Action.
karma-niṣṭhā, the Path of Knowledge.
karma-phala, the Fruit of Action.
karmaphala-tyāga, abandonment of the Fruit of Action.
karma-pravāha, the course of Action.
karma-saṁnyāsa, Abandonment of Action.

karma-tyāga, Abandonment of Action.

karma-vipāka, Causality.

karma-yoga, Union by Right Action.

karma-yogīn, one who follows the Path of Karma-Yoga.

karma-yogin-sthitaprajña, the Steady-in-Reason, following the Path of Karma-Yoga.

kārya, duty; product; effect; doable.

kāryākārya, the doable and the not-doable.

kośa, envelope.

karma-mukti, gradual release.

krīyamāṇa, (Action) to-be-performed.

kṛṣṇa, dark; Śrī Kṛṣṇa.

kṛṣṇa-mārga, the dark path (same as *pitṛyāna*, and opp. of *śukla-mārga)*.

kṛṣṇārpaṇa, dedication to Kṛṣṇa.

kṣamā, forgiveness.

liṅga, subtle.

liṅga śarīra, subtle-body.

loka, world, sphere.

lokasaṁgraha, cosmic, or universal welfare.

mahāyāna, the superior path (Buddhistic), (the opp. of *hīnayāna*).

manas, the Mind.

manaḥpūta, mind-, or consciencesanctioned.

mānavadharma, the religion of humanity.

manodevatā, the mental deity, of Conscience.

manomaya-kośa, the mental envelope.

mātrā, the external world.

mātrā-sparśa, contact with the external world.

māyā, Illusion.

mithyā, unreal (same as *asat*).

moha, delusion; confusion.

mokṣa, Release.

mṛtyu, death; mortal sphere.

mukta, Released.

mukti, Release, (same as *mokṣa*).

naimittika, occasional (Action).

naiṣkarmya, abstinence from Action; desireless Action.

naiṣkarmya-siddhi, Release by abstinence from Action, or by Desireless Action.

nāma-rūpa, Name and Form.

nāmarūpātmaka, Name-d and Form-ed.

nānātva, diversity; manifoldness.

niragni, one who does not maintain a sacrificial fire.

nirāśa, freedom from hope; despair.

nirāśāvādi, Pessimist. (opp. of *āśāvadi*).

nirguṇa, qualityless.

nirguṇa-bhakti, worship of the Qualityless.

nirvaira, non-inimical.

nirvāṇa, final emancipation; Release.

niṣkāma, desireless.

nissaṁga, unattached

niṣṭhā. the ultimate state.
nitya, daily (Action or ritual).
nitya-saṁnyāsin, perpetual ascetic.

pañca-mahābhūta, five Primordial Elements.
pañcikaraṇa, union of five primeval elements.
paramāṇuvāda, theory of atoms; atomic theory.
paramārtha, the highest interest.
paramātman, the Highest Self (same as the *adhyātman*).
parārtha, other's-interest.
pātañjala-yoga, the system of Yoga enunciated by Patanjali.
phala, Fruit.
phalāśa, Hope for Fruit (of Action).
phalāśa-tyāga, abandonment of Hope for Fruit (of Action).
piṇḍa, the Body.
pitṛyāṇa, the dark path, (see p. 408 etc.)
poṣaṇa, Divine dispensation, or pleasure.
prākṛta, vernacular; with Prakṛti.
prakṛti, Nature; Matter; inherent quality or temperament.
pralaya, Cosmic destruction.
pramāda, forgetfulness of duty, or heedlessness.
pramāṇa, measure.
prameya, measurable,
prāṇa, life.
prāraṁbha, commencement.
prārabdha, Commenced (Action).
prasthāna-trayī, the three fundamental treatises of the Vedic religion, dealing with the paths of Action and of Inaction, namely the Upaniṣads, the Vedānta-Sūtras, and the Bhagavadgītā.
pratijñā, a vow.
pratijñā-pālana, observance of a vow.
pratīka, a symbol.
pravṛtti, Activity; inclination.
pravṛtti-mārga, Path of Action.
pravṛtti-svātaṁtrya, freedom of activity (or Will), (same as, *ātma-svātaṁtrya)*.
pṛthaktva, individuality;
puruṣa, Spirit.
puruṣārtha, ideals of manhood.
puruṣottama, the Highest Spirit.
puṣṭi, divine pleasure (same as *poṣaṇa*).
puṣṭi-mārga, the Path of Divine Pleasure.

rāga, liking; love; pleasure.
rāja, king.
rajas, the passionate or active constituent, out of the three constituents of Prakṛti.
rājasa, passionate; active; progressive.
rāja-guhya, the King of Mysticisms.

rāja-vidyā, the King of Sciences.

sadsadviveka, discrimination between right and wrong.

sadasadviveka-buddhi, the Reason, which discriminates between the right and the wrong.

sadasadviveka-devatā, the deity which discriminates between the right and the wrong; Conscience.

samatā, equability.

samatva-buddhi, equable Reason.

samatva-buddhi-yoga, the Yoga of the equable Reason.

saṁbhūti, Knowledge, which is the fundamental cause of the world (see p. 501); (opp. of *asaṁbhūti,* above).

saṁcaya, accumulation.

saṁcita, Accumulated (Karma).

saṁga, Desire, (same as, *icchā, eṣaṇā,* or *vāsanā*); Attachment.

saṁghāta, collection; aggregate (same as, *samuccaya,* below).

saṁgraha, collection; protection; maintenance; regulation; welfare., (see *loka-saṁgraha* above).

saṁhāra, destruction.

saṁkalpa, the mental decision that a particular thing is of a particular kind.

sāṁkhya, counters; the followers of the Sāṁkhya philosophy.

saṁnyāsa, Renunciation; asceticism; the '*nyāsa*', or giving up of Desire-prompted Action (*cf.* Gī. 18. 2).

saṁnyāsin, an ascetic; a renouncer; one who follows the Path of Renunciation.

saṁpat, endowment (see *daivī saṁpat,* and *āsurī saṁpat*) above).

saṁsāra, worldly life; worldly activity.

samuccaya, collection (same as *saṁghāta*).

sāmya, (same as, *samatā*) equability.

śānti, tranquility.

śarīra, the Body (same as *piṇḍa*).

śārīra-ātman, the embodied Self.

sarvabhūtahita, universal welfare; (same as, *loka-saṁgraha*).

śāstra, science.

satkāryavāda, (see p. 210), the doctrine that something must come out of some other thing, and that the fundamental cause of an evolute must possess the qualities of the evolute in some form or other.

sattāsāmānya, pervasiveness; existing in a constant form in every thing.

sattāsāmānyatva, the theory of constant pervasiveness.

sattva, the placid, equable. and pure, out of the three constituents of Prakṛti.

sāttvika, possessing the *sattva* quality.

satya, reality; real; existence.

satyānṛta, Reality, and Unreality.

satyānṛtaviveka, the discrimination between what is eternally existent, and what is not.

siddha, perfect, released (same as, *mukta).*

siddhāvasthā, the state of perfection.

smārta, following the path laid dov n by the Smṛtis.

smārta-karma, ritual ordained by the Smṛtis.

smārta-yajña, sacrifice prescribed by the Smṛtis.

sneha, attachment (same as, *saṁga).*

sparśa, contact (see *mātrā-sparśa).*

sṛti, path, or goal (same as, *gati).*

śṛti, that which was heard.

sthitaprajña; Steady in-Reason.

sthūla, gross (opp. of *sūkṣma* below).

śuddha, pure.

śuddhādvaita, pure non-dualism.

śuddha vāsanā, pure desire.

sukha, happiness (opp. of *duḥkha).*

sukhavāda, the theory of happiness.

śukla-mārga, the lighted path (opp. of *kṛṣṇa-mārga).*

sūkṣma, subtle (opp. of *sthūla,* above).

sūkṣma śarīra, the subtle body.

svadharma, own-religion; own-duty.

svādhyāya, following the religion prescribed for one's status in life (cf. Gī. 16. 1).

svārtha, own-interest (opp. *parārtha).*

tamas, ignorance; darkness, the inert, out of the three constituents of Prakṛti.

tāmasī, inert; ignorant; dark.

tanmātra, fine element.

tapas, religious austerity.

tat, THAT.

tatva, element.

tat-tvam-asi, THOU ART THAT.

trayī-dharma. the religious sacrificial paths prescribed by the three Vedas.

trayī-vidyā, same as, *trayī-dharma,* above.

triguṇa, three constituents, or strands.

triguṇātmaka, three-constituented.

triguṇātīta, beyond the three constituents.

trivṛtkaraṇa, union of three elements.

tṛṣṇā, Desire (same as *kāmā, vāsanā).*

tuṣṭi, contentedness.

tyāga, abandonment; abandonment of the Fruit of Action (see Gī. 18. 2).

varṇāśrama-dharma, the Smṛti arrangement of four classes, and four stages of life.

vāsanā, Desire, (same as *icchā*, *tṛṣṇā*).

vāsanā-svātaṁtrya, freedom of desire, (same as *ātma-svātaṁtrya*).

vāsanatmaka, based on desire ; Practical (Reason).

vastutatva, the Fundamental Element, the Thing-in-itself ; *ding an sich.*

videha-mukti, the Release, after death, by reaching the sphere of the Brahman (see p. 412).

vidyā, science.

vighas, food remaining over after every body has eaten (see p. 403).

vikalpa, the mental decision that a particular thing is not of a particular kind.

vikṛti, evolute, (same as *vikāra*).

vināśa, ignorance (same as *avidyā* or *asaṁbhūti*, see p. 501).

viśeṣa, the five primeval elements.

viśiṣṭādvaita, Qualified Monism (see p. 21).

vyakta, perceptible.

vyavasāya, discrimination.

vyavasāyātmaka, discriminating, and deciding; Pure (Reason.).

yāga, sacrifice, minor than *yajña.*

yajña, sacrifice.

yoga, union ; merger ; assimilation ; the device of skilful performance of Action (see Gī. 2. 50).

yoga-bhraṣṭa, one fallen from Yoga.

yoga-śāstra, the science of Yoga.

yoga-sūtras, the canons dealing with Yoga.

ॐ तत्सत्.